Religion on the Rocks

RELIGION ON THE ROCKS

Hohokam Rock Art, Ritual Practice, and Social Transformation

AARON M. WRIGHT

THE UNIVERSITY OF UTAH PRESS
Salt Lake City

The Defiance House Man colophon is a registered trademark of the University of Utah Press. It is based on a four-foot-tall Ancient Puebloan pictograph (late PIII) near Glen Canyon, Utah.

LIBRARY OF CONGRESS CATALOGING-IN-PUBLICATION DATA

Wright, Aaron M. (Aaron Michael)
Religion on the rocks : Hohokam rock art, ritual practice, and social transformation / Aaron M. Wright.
pages cm
Includes bibliographical references and index.
ISBN 978-1-60781-364-4 (hardback) — ISBN 978-1-60781-365-1 (ebook)
1. Hohokam culture—Arizona—South Mountains. 2. Petroglyphs—Arizona—South Mountains. 3. Rock paintings—Arizona—South Mountains. 4. Sacred space—Arizona—South Mountains. 5. Religion, Prehistoric—Arizona—South Mountains. 6. Social change—Arizona—South Mountains—History—To 1500. 7. South Mountains (Ariz.)—Social life and customs. 8. South Mountains (Ariz.)—Antiquities. 9. Social archaeology—Arizona—South Mountains. I. Title.
E99.H68W74 2014
979.1'73—dc23

2014018329

Contents

Figures

Tables

Acknowledgments

Almost a decade ago a small coterie of anthropologists and land managers coalesced around a shared concern for recording and preserving the petroglyphs in South Mountain Park, a nearly 17,000-acre municipally managed nature preserve in Phoenix, Arizona, visited by an estimated four million recreationalists annually. This initiative, known as the South Mountain Rock Art Project (SMRAP), was supported by a grant from Arizona State Parks as well as private contributions from area residents. As a doctoral student in 2006, I was awarded an anonymously funded, four-year Preservation Fellowship from the Center for Desert Archaeology (now Archaeology Southwest) to develop and complete a dissertation project in collaboration with the SMRAP. Our combined goal was threefold: (1) to pioneer, test, evaluate, and revise rock art recording techniques and analyses for local applicability; (2) learn as much as possible about the park's archaeological landscape through low-impact, nondestructive procedures; and (3) to promote the preservation of the thousands of endangered petroglyphs scattered among the granitic boulders and outcrops. While the insights and interpretations in the following chapters are solely mine, and therefore any faults must fall squarely on my shoulders, this book owes a great deal to the team of researchers and volunteers who established and executed the SMRAP and the generous and prescient philanthropy of Archaeology Southwest. Thank you.

Little did I know at the onset of my involvement in the SMRAP how truly rewarding the experience would be or the extent of exposure to world-class scholarship I would receive. I first wish to thank Bill Doelle, president of Archaeology Southwest and Desert Archaeology, Inc., for developing the Preservation Fellowship program and ultimately taking a chance on me. Bill's vision for preservation archaeology in and beyond the American Southwest is an inspiration to all. I also want to acknowledge the close community of present and former Archaeology Southwest staff with whom I have shared many unforgettable experiences over the years: Jeff Clark, Matt Devitt, Doug Gann, Kate Sarther Gann, Deb Huntley, Andy Laurenzi, Debbie Lee, Anna Neuzil, and Matt Peeples. I am also immeasurably indebted to Linda Pierce for her encouragement and unyielding assistance in bringing this book to publication. Together this community of colleagues and friends made my relocation from the Columbia Plateau to the Sonoran Desert more accommodating and my transition from Ancestral Pueblo to Hohokam archaeology less confusing than it would otherwise have been.

Through the SMRAP I had the great pleasure of hashing out ideas, working through conceptual and theoretical hurdles, and devising analytical strategies with a talented and brilliant team of scholars. I am grateful to the project's staff for taking me under their wing and showing me the ropes of Hohokam archaeology and rock art research. I credit Michael Winkelman, the original grant applicant, as the impetus for the SMRAP, and I appreciate the oversight from the project's advisers and directors, including Glen Rice, Pete Welsh, and Dave Jacobs. Arleyn Simon, the acting principal investigator under whom I conducted fieldwork, was and continues to be a wonderful source of support and voice of reason. I owe much to Todd Bostwick, who as Phoenix's City Archaeologist authorized the SMRAP and set the standard through his own professional, high-quality research into Hohokam rock art. Conversations with both Arleyn and Todd helped me refine my perspective and keep the end goal in sight. My research is also obliged to Tina Carpenter, who piloted the SMRAP's recording techniques, and the project's field directors, Rex Weeks and Steve Swanson, who trained and led crew members, including myself.

A number of institutions sponsored the SMRAP, hosted lectures and meetings, and provided volunteers. I thank the Archaeological Research Institute (ARI) at Arizona State University (ASU), the Pueblo Grande Museum, the Deer Valley Rock Art Center, the Arizona Rock Art Coalition, Mesa Community College, and the Arizona Archaeological Society for their commitment to local professional and avocational archaeological research and preservation. Over the field seasons, I bonded with and learned valuable lessons from a wide array of volunteers. I thank Al Arpad, Albert Acken, Ryan Arp, Barry Bertani, Dave Burkett, Ryan Champagne, Joyce Clark, Michael Corder, Kyle Cramsey, Garrett Dauphars, Sharon and Dennis Dubose, Ellen Edwards, Ken Gometz, Frank Grinere, Caitlin Guthrie, Emma Harrison, Tom Kreuser, Mary Lawrence, Donna and Tim Manion, Gerald Mead, Sarah Niskanen, Chris Reed, John Rukkila, Jolanta and Kryzstof Sokol, and David Wood for generously offering their companionship and free time to assist in surveying and recording the South Mountains petroglyphs, often under rugged, hot, and semi-painful conditions. Two enjoyable classes on archaeological field methods through ASU also contributed eyes, hands, legs, and data to the SMRAP, for which I am thankful. I also wish to acknowledge the professional and technical assistance I received from Jim Heidke (ceramic typology), Andrew Lack (ceramic petrography), Mike Brack (GIS), Stacey Ryan (flaked stone), Lauren Falvey (groundstone), Steve Savage (database management), and Catherine Gilman (cartography). I was privileged to have had the aid of project interns Will Russell, Chris Whiting, and Elyssa Gutbrod and lab assistant Cherie Freeman, whose contributions to site recording, map production, artifact curation, and editing were essential to the SMRAP and the results presented in this book. I especially thank Will for his friendship, artistic acumen, and help in drafting many of the book's figures. I am also grateful for the camaraderie of Destiny Crider, Tatsuya Murakami, Alanna Ossa, Kim Savage, Steve Schmich, and Sara Stryker during my stay at ARI.

Since this book began in my doctoral research, I wish to recognize my professors at Washington State University (WSU), who guided me along a rigorous and rewarding path of academic research and scholarship. I am indebted to my dissertation committee: Andrew Duff, chair and champion of bringing this research to publication; John Jones; and Tim Kohler. A number of other WSU faculty, including Bill Lipe, Karen Lupo, Melissa Elgar-Goodman, Mary Collins, and John Bodley, helped steer my theoretical and methodological development. I appreciate the financial support received from departmental awards endowed by Richard and Phyllis Daugherty and Elaine Burgess. I am also fortunate to have studied under several other renowned professors at other universities, including archaeologists Geoff Clark, Bill Dancey, Jeff Dean, Michelle Hegmon, and Ron Towner; art historian Kate Duncan; and cultural geographer Chris Lukinbeal. Henry Wallace, my outside dissertation committee member, deserves special recognition for his advisory role throughout my research. For years, Henry has been the foremost scholar yet a lone voice on the difficult and neglected subject of Hohokam rock art, and his contributions will surely be recognized for years to come. I am grateful to have had his wisdom, calm demeanor, and knack for scientific rigor guide my own endeavors.

This research has also benefited greatly from discussions about the Hohokam and their rock art with numerous anthropologists, archaeologists, rock art researchers, and native informants. I acknowledge the useful insights and advice I received from Dave Abbott, Jenny Adams, Kurt Anschuetz, Beth Bagwell, Larry Benson, Peter Boyle, Nicole Cervany, Tiffany Clark, Jean Clottes, Elizabeth Culley, Andrew Darling, Ron Dorn, T. J. Ferguson, David Gregory, Gayle Hartmann, Kathy Henderson, Jenny Huang, Jim Keyser, Keith Kloor, Melissa Kruse-Peeples, Barnaby Lewis, Carolyn Merrill, Fred Nials, Adam Okun, Scott Ortman, Todd Pietzel, Bill Robinson, Greg Schachner, Sharon Urban, Mark Varien, Josh Watts, and Holly Young. Credit is also due to the groundwork laid by previous research into South Mountains rock art by Wes Holden, J. J. and Mike Golio, and Ernest Snyder, who first recorded many of the petroglyphs. My research would not have been possible without the private-sector archaeologists who helped me get my feet in the door and from whom I gained much valuable field experience over the years: Tim Baugh, Sharon Brown, Steve Dominguez, Dave and Dawn Greenwald, Ed Huber, Steve Mack, Dave Purcell, Cherie Scheick, Scott Sundermeyer, Carla Van West, and Jim Vint.

Finally, this book benefited immensely from formal, constructive reviews by Dave Wilcox and an anonymous reviewer and from the care and dedication of the behind-the-scenes staff at the University of Utah Press. This work owes much to copyeditor Kim Vivier's careful eyes, and I sincerely thank Acquisitions Editor Reba Rauch for her patience and guidance as this work moved through the publication process. I am also incredibly grateful to Don and Catherine Fowler, who believed in the contribution of this research to cultural and historical studies of the American West.

CHAPTER 1

Introduction

This book is an exercise in the social analysis of rock art, with a particularly close examination of a corpus of petroglyphs crafted by the Hohokam, desert farmers of the ancient North American Southwest. Insights from this case study lead to a conclusion that Hohokam rock art, as both symbol and practice, was an active, ritualized medium in the negotiation of religious knowledge. How such knowledge was acquired, distributed, and controlled reveals relationships of power—a power sanctified by other-than-human entities—that steered the historical trajectory of the Hohokam world. Ultimately, transformations in the control over, access to, and distribution of religious knowledge were catalysts for the usurpation of social power by a few select segments or lineages within Hohokam communities. To demonstrate this, I establish contexts of practice that unite Hohokam rock art with the actors, spectators, and social conditions responsible for its ritualized production. I emphasize social relevance, rather than the functional and symbolic dimensions of action, because I aim to mesh rock art with social and historical processes that, over centuries and in seemingly sudden bursts, reproduced and transformed the Hohokam world.

This introductory chapter briefly reviews and critically evaluates the major theoretical and methodological trends informing the current state of Americanist rock art inquiry. For nearly a century, rock art has occupied the periphery of archaeological research, often taken as an uninformative, passive reflection of daily life and the natural environment or a benign "aesthetic" of the past. In the past two decades, however, archaeology has witnessed a resurgence of rock art studies. Here I trace how the discipline has arrived at its current state regarding rock art, a point that I characterize as promising yet still highly challenging despite increased attention in recent years. I then present the basis for employing a practice-oriented framework that, for the time being, eschews the quest for symbolic meaning to focus instead on the importance of action and the reflexive nature of social relations. Such an approach ultimately entails asking different types of questions as well as looking at data about rock art in new, unconventional ways.

A Brief History of Theory in Americanist Rock Art Research

Rock art is a fascinating and popular topic because, as a corpus of vivid images representing scenes of life, relationships, and past realities, it provides a rare glimpse into immaterial worlds of historically distant and long-gone societies not available from other types of relics. In many cases, rock art is one of the few remaining tangible links to ancient communities, as natural forces all too often eradicate more perishable and ephemeral materials, so it has much to offer for anthropology. Rock art analysis is nonetheless daunting and challenging because ideation and symbolic meaning, immaterial aspects of society that seemingly lurk beyond the reach of archaeologists' trowels and shovels, are intrinsic to its manufacture and use. This conundrum is not the sole purview of archaeologists, since interest in rock art and its origins comes from a wide range of disciplines, such as art history, psychology, biology, linguistics, and geography, each bringing its own questions, methods, and theories.

The following discussion presents a summary of anthropological theory as applied to rock art with a focus on North America, and the Southwest in particular. I organize this review in a diachronic manner, conforming to trends in the major theoretical orientations of Americanist archaeology. Some may argue that rock art studies are largely atheoretical and concerned primarily with design classification and speculative interpretations of meaning. This review, however, shows that while these criticisms may hold for some studies, rock art research has generally adhered to an implicit theoretical orientation, and its greatest contributions to archaeology and anthropology are realized when rock art is approached with broader research objectives.

Colonialism

From a continental perspective, the earliest documentation of rock art occurred in the context of European exploration, settlement, and subsequent colonial expansion. In what is now the United States, rock art analysis and interpretation began with French explorers along the Mississippi River and its tributaries and with Spanish missionaries along the Gila River during the seventeenth and eighteenth centuries. In 1673 Jacques Marquette, a French Jesuit missionary explorer, recorded in his journal the presence of two large pictographs on a bluff near the confluence of the Mississippi and Missouri Rivers (Thwaites 1900:139–141).[1] Foreshadowing centuries of racism, Marquette denied their indigenous creation, commenting that they were "so well painted that we cannot believe that any savage is their author" (Thwaites 1900:141). These early explorers weren't entirely negligent, however; Henri Joutel, a member of La Salle's infamously ill-fated expedition a decade later, made an insightful ethnographic observation describing how offerings were devoted to these large pictographs by indigenous passersby (Parkman 1897:68n1).

Rock art in New England also drew the attention of seventeenth-century colonists, most notably Cotton Mather, who pondered the origin and significance of petroglyphs on Dighton Rock (Mather 1714). Aside from the debate over its cultural origin, Mather and subsequent philologists (e.g., Davis 1809; Kendall 1809; Rafn 1845) sought to decipher the inscriptions on Dighton Rock, believing the images represented a mode of ancient script. Philological concerns such as this remained commonplace well into the nineteenth century (e.g., Whittlesey 1878) and linger in contemporary popular studies (e.g., Martineau 1973; Patterson-Rudolph 1997).

The first recorded European sighting of Hohokam rock art in Arizona was by Father Jacob Sedelmayr, a German Jesuit missionary who, while exploring the Gila River in 1749, noted the existence of "painted" images on rocks (Dunne 1955:56–57). These images are likely part of the "Painted Rocks" district near Gila Bend (Wallace 1989). Additional accounts of petroglyphs at Painted Rocks were provided by military expeditions and travelers after the United States appropriated large portions of the Southwest from Mexico with the Treaty of Guadalupe Hidalgo in 1848 (e.g., Bartlett 1854; Emory 1848; Hammond and Howes 1950; Johnston 1848). Although most of these early accounts were largely descriptive, some revealed an awareness of rock art's sacred nature and ritual importance as well as its continued religious significance among contemporary Native American communities (e.g., Emory 1848:91), whereas others presciently speculated about rock art's more "functional" qualities (e.g., Rusling 1877:368).

Nineteenth-Century Unilinear Evolution

A scientific approach to social institutions and human behavior, which would mature into the disciplines of sociology and anthropology, came about during the nineteenth century as one facet of the broader Age of Enlightenment. A major inquiry in this fledgling field of social science was how to account for the differences between Western and non-Western societies, a question of increasing relevance as Europeans expanded their dominion over indigenous communities throughout the world. Social scientists were quick to draw on principles from the biological sciences, principally concepts from Darwinian evolutionary theory, to explain socio-cultural patterns and change. Seeing aspects of European society as culturally and aesthetically superior to those of indigenous peoples, sociologists came to conceptualize culture as an adaptational "progression" toward social complexity. The era of classical social evolutionism, or unilinear evolution, was thus born and rose to theoretical preeminence in the social sciences by the mid-nineteenth century.

A mainstay of unilinear evolution entailed ranking cultures into stages along a continuum of social complexity, as popularized in Lewis Henry Morgan's (1877) classification of savagery, barbarism, and civilization, for example. Morgan's scheme, which attributed formalized writing and alphabets to civilizations, came to prominence at a time when the forerunners of American anthropology, of whom Morgan was a leading voice, were debating the degree of evolutionary advancement attained by Native Americans. This sentiment was captured well in a passage by Abbé Emmanuel Domenech regarding Southwestern rock art:

> Among the archaeologists and the ethnographers of the two worlds who have noticed the Indian ideography and American antiquities, few have attempted to decipher the species of hieroglyphics by means of which the Red Skins have at all times endeavoured to make their thoughts understood; whether simply to recall a fact, an article of faith, or a custom, or to transmit to posterity the memory of some great event that marks with vital interest the life of a man or the history of a nation. The cause of this want of exactitude is less in the difficulty of the study and the want of materials to pursue it, than in that affectation of disdain generally professed for Indians, who are rather rashly denied all intellectual and artistic capacity. It is true that the variety of hieroglyphic signs and ideographic images, and their strange and ill-formed figures, may have discouraged some antiquarians, who would prefer seeing in these vagaries nothing but the productions of rude imaginations, tracing on rocks, trees, and animals' skins, fantastic figures and characters without any meaning whatever. (1860:407–408)

Whether or not petroglyphs and similar repertoires of symbols constituted forms of writing was thus a crux in the then-politically charged (and overtly racist) debate over the social attainment, indeed humanity, of native peoples. Consequently, in the mid-1880s the newly formed Bureau of Ethnology at the Smithsonian Institution commissioned Garrick Mallery (1886, 1893) to investigate the indigenous use of symbols in both modern and archaeological contexts and determine whether or not they in fact made up a written language. Mallery (1893:27–28) played it safe, concluding that some Native American iconography constituted a form of "proto-writing" because it conveyed information and expressed thought without reference to sound.[2] Mallery's interest in unraveling the meaning of unfamiliar and ancient symbols is an understandable natural impulse in the face of foreign iconography, and it remains a major theoretical issue in archaeology (e.g., Robb 1998). His functionalist bent and emphasis on information exchange, however, would not make its way to the forefront of North American rock art studies for another 70 years.

Culture History

The advent of anthropology as a coherent field of academic research in the late nineteenth century brought about a considerable degree of interest in rock art, not only by academics but also by governmental agencies whose purview concerned issues of land management and Native American interests. Many early rock art studies used ethnography and the "direct historical approach" to broach the meaning of imagery, a point I return to in Chapter 2. Mallery (1886, 1893), for example, relied to a great extent on ethnography in his study of Native American picture-writing. The scale and scope of his research was so colossal, however, that aside from the Northern Plains and around the Great Lakes, where Mallery had years of field experience, his insights were mostly cursory. Southwest-focused researchers, working mostly on the Colorado Plateau and in the northern Rio Grande valley, nevertheless soon followed Mallery's lead and relied on ethnographies to interpret Ancestral

Pueblo rock art (e.g., Colton and Colton 1931; Fewkes 1892a, 1897, 1898a; Reagan 1933, 1935; and Titiev 1937).

After Mallery, the next interregional, synthetic analysis of North American rock art was carried out by Julian Steward. Using only photographs and other records curated by the University of California at Berkeley, Steward mapped the distribution of various rock art motifs throughout the western states, looking for points of origin and paths of diffusion that he could compare with other culture traits (Steward 1929). Steward's pioneering efforts are noteworthy because he had a clear interest in the social contexts of rock art production, commenting for instance on its cross-cultural use in puberty rites. He also acknowledged the religious significance indigenous people attributed to rock art and encouraged further research in order to better understand its meaning.

Another influential culture-historical rock art study was Luther Cressman's (1937) survey in Oregon. Cressman, who approached rock art "style" as a culture-historical trait, followed the historical particularism espoused by the Boasian school of anthropology. Historical particularism took individual cultures, rather than broad cross-cultural comparisons, as worthwhile topics of research and contended that detailed historical reconstructions were an essential component of any archaeological research. Accordingly, historical particularists avoided using ethnographies from people not directly related to or descendant of the archaeological cultures of interest. As Steward (1942) noted, however, historical particularism and the direct historical approach were not necessarily opposed paradigms, and he advocated integrating the two schools, as Jesse Fewkes had done with Southwestern rock art. Steward's stance on the reliability of ethnography to provide reliable interpretations of rock art, though, wavered throughout his career; once a proponent, he later claimed that informants' responses were largely "speculative" (Steward 1937:405) and came to reject interpretations from indigenous communities altogether (Steward 1968). In retrospect, Steward seems to have adopted the position that, given certain cross-cultural regularities in rock art practice such as its use in puberty rituals, ethnographically gleaned social contexts of rock art production were useful for interpreting archaeological ones, but the symbolic meaning of imagery was largely unobtainable since that type of interpretation varied among descendant community members.

Functionalism and Structuralism

While Americanist archaeologists were largely preoccupied with culture-historical reconstructions, by the dawn of the twentieth century researchers on other continents were dabbling in more functionalist endeavors. With regard to rock art, European archaeologists came to rely heavily on Australian Aborigine ethnography to interpret aspects of Europe's archaeological past because, clearly inspired by sociology's prior scheme of unilinear evolution, they considered Australia's native peoples to be at a similar stage of cultural development as the early humans of the Upper Paleolithic. For example, an ethnographic account of the Arunta of central Australia described the aboriginal production of animalistic rock art during ceremonies to increase the abundance of game animals and aid hunters in their capture (Spencer and Gillen 1899). Once the antiquity of European cave paintings had been unequivocally shown (Cartailhac 1902), this magico-ritualized function for Australian Aborigine rock art provided an explanatory framework for Paleolithic rock art. With a quick draw, Solomon Reinach (1903) was first to pose hunting magic as an explanation for European cave paintings, a popular interpretation firmly entrenched by famed French archaeologists Count Henri Bégouën (e.g., 1929) and Abbé Henri Breuil (e.g., 1933). The hunting magic hypothesis cast a wide net over multiple forms of sympathetic magic but explained rock art mostly in terms of missives for hunting, fertility, and protection. This interpretation fit well with existing and emerging strains of functionalism and persisted largely unchallenged until the 1950s (Ucko and Rosenfeld 1967:128–129). By the 1960s, however, researchers had come to realize that most Paleolithic rock art was geometric and abstract—arguably not representative of animals—and that the ethnographic support for a hunting magic interpretation was very weak (Ucko and Rosenfeld 1967; see Keyser and Whitley [2006] for a North American critique).

During the 1950s a new theoretical movement, structuralism, was brewing among French anthropologists. As popularized by Claude Lévi-Strauss (e.g., 1958), structuralism posited a universal structure to human cognition, a sort of "unity" of mind. One of its key assumptions was that binary oppositions, such as night and day, structured the natural world and thus the infrastructure of the human mind. Structuralism held that dualisms were the foundation of cultural structures and were expressed in various cultural media such as myths. Structuralist leanings were soon brought to bear on Paleolithic rock art, where researchers investigated how the production and placement of different designs were guided or conditioned by mythology (e.g., Laming-Emperaire 1959, 1962; Leroi-Gourhan 1958, 1965). This contention that rock art has a "syntax" or "grammar," reminiscent of philology, encouraged innovation in rudimentary quantitative methods to reveal patterns taken as the structure and myth underlying rock art assemblages (e.g., Lewis-Williams 1972; Vinnicombe 1967, 1972). Explicit structural analyses of rock art were short-lived, however; they never gained prominence in North America, and they did not persist in French studies beyond the careers of Leroi-Gourhan and Laming-Emperaire.

Processualism

By the time North American culture historians all but relegated rock art to the archaeological dustbin, the discipline was focusing less on the *whats* and *hows* of history and more on the *whys* of cultural change. This desire for explanation ushered in a "New Archaeology" and its progeny, processualism, both concerned with nomotheticism and the adaptation of cultural systems to external stimuli, principally the environment. Lewis Binford, a pioneering figure of processualism, espoused a holistic systems approach to the past, arguing that the assemblage of artifacts moving through a culture's technological, social, and ideological subsystems and their intercontextual relationships "should and do present a systematic and understandable picture of *the total extinct* cultural system" (Binford 1962:219; emphasis in original). To show this, he classified artifacts with reference to the particular subsystems in which they participated: technomic, socio-technic, and ideo-technic. In this formulation, rock art would be considered an ideotechnic artifact, and according to Binford's logic, its "formal diversity and structural complexity... must generally be related to changes in the structure of the society" (1962:220).

The New Archaeology and processualism afforded a place for rock art in the archaeological analysis of cultural systems. With a few notable and influential exceptions (e.g., Heizer and Baumhoff 1962), this opportunity was not seized. This is, in my opinion, where the growing divergence between rock art research and mainstream Americanist archaeology came to a head, and the reason is twofold. First, at the doorstep of the New Archaeology, Christopher Hawkes (1954) offered his infamous "ladder of inference," which arranged aspects of cultural reconstruction into a hierarchy of induction. Hawkes suggested that archaeologists could approach past economies and investigate political and social systems with some degree of certainty, but the ancient mind (including religion and the meaning of symbols) posed too much of an inferential leap of faith for valid interpretations to be made. The second reason was methodological, as rock art research was still struggling with the building blocks of culture history—chronology and classification—which had been largely put to rest in other areas of archaeological study. In fact, these archaeological fundamentals remain methodological and theoretical hurdles for rock art research to this day.

Shamanism and Neuropsychology

David Lewis-Williams and Thomas Dowson (1988) mounted a much-needed revolution in rock art studies with their neuropsychological, or altered states of consciousness (ASC), model for Upper Paleolithic rock art. Drawn largely and explicitly from clinical and ethnographic studies, the ASC hypothesis explains a suite of geometric and abstract rock art designs found throughout the world as portrayals of simple shapes seen during hallucinatory visions induced by trance experiences. According to Lewis-Williams, "certain altered states of consciousness produce specific and definable visual percepts and other effects because they are wired into the universal human nervous system" (2001:336). According to the ASC hypothesis, in trance experiences, humans enter three different stages, or levels, of altered consciousness, wherein the visual percepts, or entoptic phenomena, change as the mind contorts them into recognizable forms. The first stage consists of basic geometric shapes, primarily grids, circles, and lines. During stage two the trancer attempts to attribute iconic meaning to the geometric designs. Between stages two and three the trancer experiences a vortex-like sensation (Lewis-Williams and Dowson 1993) and emerges into the third stage, a hallucinatory world of comprehensively formed and sometimes fantastical images alongside the original simple geometric visual percepts of earlier stages.

The neuropsychological model has been used to explain rock art in practically every corner of the globe. Reasons for its widespread popularity include the worldwide ubiquity of geometric rock art, the breadth of shamanistic religions among past and present peoples, and the universality of entoptic phenomena and trance experiences. There are considerable ethnographic data pertaining to shamanism, altered states of consciousness, and entoptic phenomena, but unequivocal associations between shamanic trance and rock art production in the ethnographic past and present are scant (Quinlan 2000a; Ross and Davidson 2006). This has not stopped shamanism from becoming a dominant paradigm in studies of western North American rock art (e.g., Bostwick and Krocek 2002; Boyd 2003; Hedges 1992; Patterson 1998; Turpin 1994; Whitley 2000a), even though the applicability of the ASC hypothesis remains a matter of lively and vigorous debate (e.g., Helvenston and Bahn 2003, 2005; Hodgson 2000; Lewis-Williams 2003, 2004; McCall 2007; Quinlan 2000a, 2000b; Riel-Salvatore 2005; Whitley 2000b).

Though the neuropsychological model is undoubtedly an apt explanation in some cases, an issue of concern is that, as a hypothesis, it has rarely been tested. Instead, it has been taken for granted all too often, and some of the model's proponents seem to fit their data to the assumption rather than test it as a hypothesis (Whitley 2011:142–144). Since visions experienced under altered states of consciousness may range from the basic geometric entoptic shapes to complex and representational images, interpretations based on imagery alone can be post hoc, teleological, and self-proving. Convincing interpretations necessitate a considerable degree of ethnographic support (e.g., Lewis-Williams 1977, 1980, 1981; Whitley 2000b), which becomes increasingly problematic as the antiquity of the imagery increases. The cross-cultural presence of the same elementary geometric designs in rock art may be due to the mere fact that they are the rudiments of all design structures (e.g., Dronfield 1996; Hodgson 2006).

Landscape Phenomenology

Paralleling the surge in neuropsychological interpretations, many rock art studies of the past 20 years have drawn on principles of phenomenology borrowed from landscape anthropology (e.g., Bradley 1991, 1997; Chippindale and Nash 2004; David and Wilson 2002; Nash 2000; Nash and Chippindale 2002). In archaeology the phenomenology of landscape pertains to the creation and transformation of meaningful social identities and collective memories through engagement with one's surroundings, where surroundings consist of the rules and resources with which people actively construct a lived experience (e.g., Anschuetz et al. 2001; Ashmore and Knapp 1999; Bender 1993; Latour 2005; Thomas 1993, 2001; Tilley 1994, 2004; Ucko and Layton 1999). Following a phenomenological paradigm, rock art is an experiential practice instigated in a reflexive network of subject-to-subject relationships between self and place, observer and observed.

Rock art, like landmarks, monuments, and other instruments of placemaking, embeds the landscape with experiences and perceptions that constitute social memory, and it thus has hermeneutic value for understanding how societies replicate themselves in relation to their social and physical environments. Landscape archaeology, however, has been criticized as a "fashionable umbrella, an empty shell containing everything yet nothing in particular...a junk drawer, a disorderly place where we store things that are sometimes needed and useful" (Kowalewski 2008:253). Stephen Kowalewski's lament is that phenomenological landscape archaeology, in theory, is appealing—because we know that practice is connected to place—but its want of methodological rigor, absence of a coherent and unifying ontology, and lack of explanatory power have led it astray.

Although fraught with subjectivity and ambiguity, phenomenological approaches lay down new theoretical horizons for rock art studies. At the core of a phenomenology of landscape is a relational ontology with an emphasis on subject-subject relationships between place and person. Rock art analysis has found a comfortable home in this frame of reference, as many will agree that much rock art is situated in visually prominent or unique aspects of the landscape—places that intuit significance. The rock art, though, tends to be given a rather inchoate and undefined agency in this "socialization of the landscape" (sensu Quinlan and Woody 2003). Why are such places marked, and how does the rock art inform on relations among humans, other-than-humans, and environments? Can it be that if you "walk across the field with the wind in your hair...you just *know*" (Johnson 2006:129; emphasis in original)?

While critical of the neuropsychological model and phenomenological approaches, I acknowledge their importance and welcome the turn toward greater theoretical sophistication. The neuropsychological model's value lies in its highlighting of the social situations in which rock art was made, engaged, and interpreted, whereas landscape approaches remind us to consider the importance of rock art's physical contexts and its influence on subsequent human actions, sometimes long after its production. This reorientation from "codebreaking" ancient symbols toward a consideration of context is significant because it establishes rock art as a meaningful practice, one performed by individuals in particular social situations and tied to time and place.

The Social Practice of Rock Art

Margaret Conkey once asked why principles of social theory have not been applied to rock art, and she seemingly answered this question by noting that rock art researchers, for the most part, had avoided archaeology's processual/postprocessual debate (Conkey 2001:291). By the time processualism took center stage in the 1960s and 1970s, archaeology had marginalized rock art to the point where almost any interpretation was welcomed with open arms (Dowson 2001). Archaeology's general dismissal of rock art's heuristic value and informative though untapped potential spawned generations of researchers who perpetuated this tradition of negligence, and in so doing relegated rock art research to avocational practice. On the other hand, rock art researchers, who became increasingly diverse with regard to academic background, professionalism, and interests, openly rejected many of processualism's adaptationist principles and scientific rigor, with some applauding the divergence as a liberation from what they perceived as the limitations of mainstream theoretical discourse (e.g., Dowson 2001).

For rock art research to advance and be given its due by the academic community, and for it to contribute to anthropology in general, it must be theorized. An agency- and structure-based approach, as advocated by Conkey (2001), has much to offer in terms of bringing rock art back into the anthropological fold. A focus on social process, which eschews symbolic interpretation for the time being, locates rock art as a meaningful and transformative cultural practice. By adopting a social perspective, we can temporarily sidestep the conceptual dilemmas and pitfalls the discipline has faced when seeking "meaning." It is not that meaning lacks importance, but that symbols are polysemous and their meanings embedded in layers of abstraction (Robb 1998). Before tackling meaning, then, we need to get at the cultural basis and social impetus for producing and using symbols. Here we can move beyond "studying ancient pictures as pictures" (Chippindale 2001) and ask how communities used rock art, what importance its producers and viewers attributed to it, and how its manufacture molded and mediated certain social relations, but to do so requires the necessary contextual data.

Context is essential for getting at the social basis of rock art, and this case study relies on five interdependent contextual elements to shed light on the practice of petroglyph production:

1. Physical context: As landscape phenomenologists contend, rock art holds an intimate relationship with its physical surroundings. Knowing "where" and "where not" is the contextual backbone of rock art analysis because spatial relationships among practices and places provide a more holistic understanding of rock art production than the imagery alone. Physical contexts include elements of the geological and ecological environments as well as rock art's location relative to places and other practices.
2. Behavioral context: Rock art was not an isolated social practice but instead part of a spectrum of meaningful social action. Knowing which practices were and were not associated with rock art informs on how people used rock art in various aspects of their lives.
3. Historical context: Rock art is bound up in the histories of those who made it and those who engage it, even when the original artisans are unknown or long gone. Understanding rock art as a social practice requires attention to the social conditions under which its producers and subsequent viewers and users lived and acted.
4. Temporal context: Establishing rock art's antiquity is fundamental to ascertaining its historical context. Understanding the tempo and rhythm of rock art production and change also enables us to study it as a dynamic social practice involved in processes of structuration and history making.
5. Social context: In visual arts and similar systems of communication, a message's sender (artisan) and receiver (audience) are as important as the content. The crafters and consumers of rock art held social identities reflexively established by and constituted through their actions, or lack thereof. Gleaning rock art's social relevance necessitates a sense of the social agents involved in its manufacture and use.

I draw on these five contexts in the following chapters to explore how the Hohokam implemented rock art in a process of social reproduction that bears ultimately on the historical trajectory of the ancient North American Southwest.

Hohokam Rock Art as Ritual Practice

In this book I argue that making rock art, specifically petroglyphs, was a ritual practice among the Hohokam, and relationships of power were established, manifested, and contested in its production. In Chapter 2 I make the case that social power is drawn and exerted through ritual practices because they showcase the control and distribution of a vital form of capital: religious knowledge. The authority to access and wield such knowledge is justified through social consensus and sanctified by other-than-human forces. To demonstrate this, I take a close look at rock art in the South Mountains, a landscape situated in the center of the Phoenix Basin in the North American Southwest and in the heart of the Hohokam world. In Chapter 3 I present a historic outline for the Hohokam, with an emphasis on ritual practice and religion, in order to enmesh rock art in a ritual system and orient it to a larger social body. In Chapter 4 I provide an overview of the South Mountains archaeological landscape to contextualize the rock art within a broader network of human-environment relations and to understand how the Hohokam integrated it with other social, economic, and religious practices.

Building on initial insights proffered by artifacts scattered throughout the mountains, in Chapter 5 I show how the production of rock art was not uniform throughout the Hohokam past. Rather, four lines of evidence suggest that a tradition of Hohokam petroglyph manufacture in the South Mountains did not persist into the

Classic period, signaling a change in mountain-oriented ritualism and the control of religious knowledge. However, we should not assume that all rock art was produced in ritualized settings. I instead use Chapter 6 to test a robust model of ritual practice through careful attention to the contexts of the rock art's production and use. This contextual analysis nevertheless reveals the ways the South Mountains petroglyphs conform to a generalized ritual structure and therefore constitute practices that communicated religious knowledge between performers and audience. As I show in Chapter 7, rock art production was thus a ritualized means of gaining and displaying one's access to religious knowledge and relationship with metaphysical, spiritual, other-than-human essences and entities. Eventually, a cessation in rock art ritualism coincided with a Classic period reorganization in the control of religious knowledge and ritual authority. In Chapter 8 I consider how this apparent usurpation of a widely shared body of religious knowledge and constriction in authority to engage in ritual performance were pivotal in the transformation of Hohokam society.

CHAPTER 2

Ritual Practice, Religious Knowledge, and Social Reproduction

The worlds in which humans live are not fully constituted by tectonic, meteorological, and organic processes. They are not only made of rocks and trees and oceans, but are also constructed out of symbolically conceived and performatively established cosmologies, institutions, rules, and values. (Rappaport 1999:8)

My goal for this book is to contextualize Hohokam rock art in a broader realm of ritual practice, yet a question remains: Can there be an archaeology of ritual? Within this admittedly vague question swirls a multitude of constituent methodological and interpretive questions, such as what is ritual, how can rituals be identified archaeologically, and what are the objectives of a ritual-oriented archaeology? Further still, why is ritual socially important and what is its heuristic value?

Perspectives on these questions are generally polarized between anthropology's symbolic and scientific faces or, more canonically, the thick descriptions of culture history and structuralism and the nomologic of structural-functionalism and processualism. I take an alternative perspective, one that views ritual *as* action, and by doing so situates rock art in a network of power relations.

Most of us develop implicit understandings of what ritual is through our unique life experiences. Due to common cultural upbringings, language, and epistemologies, our notions of ritual share certain themes, such as performance, spectatorship, repetition, and a connection to religion. A clear definition, however, remains elusive. Indeed, it seems easier to determine what is not ritual than to reach agreement on what is, let alone what it does in a sociological sense and how we can study it. In this chapter I weave through a sophisticated body of anthropological scholarship to gather insight from others who have devoted considerable time and effort to the ritual problem. While I do not solve the issue, I offer a framework in which ritual and religion are essential to social analysis and are not beyond the reach of archaeologists.

Ritual, like any mode of human action, has many dimensions, both material and immaterial; it may entail objects and thoughts, preparation and performance, scripts and symbols, knowledge and secrecy, and power and submission. Underlying these are the people who engage in ritual, their actions and intentions, and their place in the reproduction of their social worlds. Ritual is thus more than a descriptive label for the embodiment and performance of religious ideas.

Ritual's humanistic depth and connectedness to social, political, and religious institutions and systems ensure that analyses of it need not be limited to unraveling symbolic meaning, and any such meaning need not be the end product of ritual analysis. It has the potential to be studied instead as action operating in relation to the social conditions of its constitution. In this light, ritual can be operationalized to address issues of power acquisition, distribution, and exertion and the dynamics at work in these inherently social processes. Consequently, in this chapter I (1) explain the interplay among power, agency, and structure in processes of social reproduction; (2) define ritual as a field of social action; (3) establish religious and ritual knowledge as capital; and (4) implement ritual practice in the process of social transformation. I end by substantiating how ancient ritual and religion can be approached through archaeological practice.

Structure, Agency, and Power

I refer to social reproduction as a process by which people create the conditions of their own existence through the course of routinized daily life (Bourdieu 1977, 1990). Social transformation is social reproduction that results essentially in structural conditions altered from their previous configuration. In this (re)generative process the actions of people, whether intentional or not, alter the rules and resources and the organizational schemes (structural principles) that constitute a community's social structure (Giddens 1979, 1984).

In the past 25 years archaeologists have been applying nuanced takes on agency and structure to the social analysis of past communities through the lens of material culture (e.g., Barrett 2001; Dobres 2000; Dobres and Robb 2000; Gell 1998; Hodder 1988; Johnson 1989; Pauketat 2001; Shanks and Tilley 1987; Varien and Potter 2009). Such studies, however, have met varying degrees of criticism (e.g., Arnold 2001; Berggren 2000; Johnson 2006; Joyce and Lopiparo 2005; Knapp and van Dommelen 2008; Layton 2003; Ortner 2001). One of archaeology's struggles with applying principles of a dialectic sociology has been an inconsistent use of concepts and terminology (Joyce and Lopiparo 2005). In an effort to avert this, below I briefly outline this book's take on social structure, agency, and power. I later bring these concepts to bear on an understanding of the social relevance of ritual and the more nebulous subject of religion.

Social Structure

As used here, *social structure* is analogous to Anthony Giddens's (1979) "structural conditions," which John Barrett (2001) cogently defines as the accumulated mass of history within which people act. Structure encompasses both the physical and social worlds, the collective memory of these worlds, and the organizational principles on which they are founded. This accounts for the rules and resources (both material and ideational) as well as the relationships among these and people (Giddens 1984:17–25). It is historical in that existing structures derive from the structural conditions and transformations of previous social configurations within which people were enmeshed. Social structure consists of the more concrete dimensions of economy, religion, politics, and so on, as well as the pathways between people and the rules and resources that constitute these dimensions. Social structure is thus the situation in which people find themselves in relation to other persons, human and nonhuman alike, and resources. These relationships elicit issues of power and the capacity to act in both conformance and contestation to social rules and norms, or what is often conceived of as agency.

Agency

Agency has become a divisive and problematic concept in terms of its applicability and appropriateness in archaeological practice. For example, some consider agency a possession of certain actors, where those that "have" agency tend to be elites, or the Big Men in history. This is characteristic of an individualist approach (Pauketat 2001) and is common in studies of political economy (e.g., Blanton et al. 1996) and the emergence of social inequality (e.g., Hayden 1995). In this sense, agency is attached to certain people; it is consequently static and most apparent in and best approached by focusing on elites. Evidence of "human-possession-of-agency" is thus often identified analogically through the association of types and quantities of costly material goods with particular persons, such as in mortuary assemblages (where material "wealth" can be equated with economic power, and thus agency). Alternatively, according to structuration theory, agency is not a possession; rather, it is the situational and fluid capacity to act, and it is dependent on one's negotiated position within potentially malleable social relations (Giddens 1984:83–92). A stance such as this necessitates a nuanced and flexible investigation of agency in the past (Barrett 2001).

Recent reconsiderations of agency have questioned its applicability in archaeology because it reduces intentionality to the scale of the individual. For example, critical theory challenges the ontology of "in" of individual, arguing that notions of "self" and "free will" may simply be signatures of Modernism and perhaps irrelevant to the past (Fowler 2004; Knapp and van Dommelen 2008; Thomas 2004). Inasmuch as individualism and personal agency may be chimeras, there is a growing consensus that interests and intentions can also manifest at the scale of social groups and be realized through a collective agency. In this way, individual intentions are downplayed and social groups are vested with the faculty to exert their influence to meet communal interests.

Collective agency enables us to sidestep the trouble with finding material traces of individual agency in archaeology and diverts attention from the problem of individual intentionality as conceived in structuration theory. However, Giddens specifically addresses the role of collectives in structuration, arguing that they do not have the capacity for agency (Giddens 1979). Collective action is instead brought about through consensus, and it is membership in the collective—as a social relationship—that creates the situation in which individuals are afforded the capacity to express agency in a social strategy to achieve personal interests.

This book adopts the position that agency is the contextual and impermanent ability for people, not groups, to act at any point in space and time in ways that reproduce or transform a community's social structure, whether intentional or not. Agency is thus not necessarily action (as is often implicitly suggested), nor is it always materialized by acting differently—the perpetuation of existing structural conditions is a form of agency if the actors could have conducted themselves differently. Given agency's relationship to (or dependence on) structure and vice versa, power is an essential concept in social theory because it is the means by which actors *can* act differently.

Power

Power, according to Michel Foucault (1978:93), "is not an institution, and not a structure; neither is it a certain strength we are endowed with; it is the name that one attributes to a complex strategical situation in a particular society." Contrary to Sherry Ortner's (2006) contention, power is a major theme in structuration theory (see Giddens 1984:14–16, 256–262). In fact, Giddens asserts that "there is no more elemental concept than power," since it is the *capability* "to get things done" (1984:283). Power is intrinsic to agency, in that to act differently, or to successfully resist the transformative action of others, necessitates power. Power, however, is manifest through the reproduction of what Giddens describes as "structures of domination" (1984:258), and these are constituted through allocative and authoritative resources. Allocative resources are those tangible items generally considered essential to corporeal existence (i.e., goods, foods, technology). Due to their material nature, allocative resources leave palpable and visible traces in the archaeological record. Authoritative resources, on the other hand, are more abstract principles of organization and "command over persons and actors" (Giddens 1984:33), including opportunities and authorities to access, store, and distribute allocative resources. Authoritative resources include rules, laws, cultural mores, and bodies of knowledge.

Power is often conceptualized in relation to various spheres of social life. Here we commonly distinguish among economic, military, and political sources and forms of power (e.g., Mann 1986; Russell 1938). Moreover, as Angus Stewart (2001:6–7) outlines, conceptions of power tend to fall into dichotomous notions of power's relationship to social process. In regard to social analysis, this division can be likened to the debate over structure or agency as the principal force in social reproduction. Stewart (2001:6) suggests that power analyses traditionally equate power *as* domination, a stance of "power over," or one that can be characterized as "structure-centric." In such analyses social institutions tend to be seen as the loci of power. In contrast, a "power to" perspective emphasizes power *as* action and expression, a more agency-oriented approach. Stewart (2001:7) refers to this as "empowerment," recognizing the fluid and situational nature of power. When empowerment and domination are distinguished, the creation, perpetuation, and transformation of those structures of domination are understood as arising through processes of empowerment; nevertheless, structures of domination and empowered persons operate simultaneously. According to Foucault, "power is exercised from innumerable points in a set of unequal, shifting relations" (Sheridan 1980:184). It is when these nodes in the network of power relations become contrasted that we see "sites of struggle" (Stewart 2001:7) or "crises" (Giddens 1984) conducive to the transformation of social institutions and structures of domination.

Even though distinction between empowerment and domination facilitates social analysis, power is fluid and transcendent, and it should not be restricted to a particular dimension of social structure. Instead, power is best "regarded as continually passing from any one of its forms into any other" (Russell 1938:13–14). Foucault too sees power as "something that circulates" (1980: 98), and he conceptualizes power relations as a "network" that "ends by forming a dense web that passes through apparatuses and institutions, without being exactly localized in them" (1978:96). Accordingly, power resides in the organizational qualities of structures, it flows between dimensions of social life (i.e., political and economic), and it manifests through one's relation to allocative and authoritative resources. This dimensionless quality of power conforms to Pierre Bourdieu's (1977:171–183; 1986) notion of symbolic capital, not that power is capital but that power can be garnered through access to the symbolic capital of authoritative resources. This power can therefore be drawn on later in the course of actions and interactions within other dimensions of the social body.

The foregoing discussion buttresses an analytical framework in which actors as well as the social and material conditions within which they conduct themselves are implicated in processes of social reproduction. The fluidity and contextuality of agency and power bring about several key points. Power, and the corollary agency, are not possessions but are rather temporally and socially situational, embedded in webs and "fields" (Bourdieu 1985) of social relations. In turn, the capacity to act differently—agency—depends on one's relation to various forms of capital, that is, allocative and authoritative resources. The breadth of resources among the various dimensions of social structure ensures that there are innumerable and diverse means by which people can act differently, and thus social reproduction cannot be limited to one dimension of social life. There are instead multiple "pathways" to power (sensu Hayden 1995), and social transformation can occur within and ripple through any mechanism of the social apparatus along what Foucault (1978:96) describes as "cleavages in a society." In this scheme, ritual cannot be readily dismissed from the social formula; rather, when paired with religion, ritual becomes a potent realm for power and a major arena for transformation of structural conditions and social hegemonies (Aldenderfer 1993).

Ritual and Religion in Social Reproduction

It is far too easy to conflate ritual with religion or dichotomize them. By doing so, however, we miss their nuanced connections and fall short of effectively operationalizing the strategic interplay between ritual and religion and their counterpoised yet equipollent roles in processes of social reproduction. When we do recognize this interplay, though, ritual is often taken as an avenue by which structures of domination and hegemonies are perpetuated by allusions to the numinous and supernatural and legitimated by the temporary empowerment of ritual performers. Ritual empowerment can reinforce structures of domination because other imbalanced relationships of power are obfuscated through co-participation. This reversal of structure, what Victor Turner (1966) calls *communitas*, temporarily neutralizes social differences, but in so doing, the preexisting network of power relationships is strengthened by the ruse of temporary empowerment afforded by ritual participation and religious engagement. However, rituals are also catalysts for social transformation because they provide arenas for reinterpreting religious dogma, challenging the hegemonies inherent in the liturgy, and altering structures of domination within the social body. Ritual is thus both regenerative and transformative, depending on the intentions of the performers. To understand this important dialectic between action and structure, we need to address both religion and ritual together but not as the same affair.

Like power, the religion/ritual dichotomy can easily be subsumed within a broader discourse on social structure and agency, the reflexive and dialectical dynamics between them, and the primacy of one over the other as instruments of social reproduction. This is somewhat atypical because, as I've alluded to above, the history of the anthropology of ritual and religion has been structure-centric. While I pull from a cadre of structuralist scholars renowned for their contributions to the study of religion and ritual, such as Victor Turner, Maurice Bloch, and Clifford Geertz, I infuse their foundational insights with those of practice theorists such as Catherine Bell in an effort to level the scales of the structure-and-agency debate. This balancing act acknowledges the structural rigidity and immense weight and girth of some social bodies while accommodating the very real potential for individuals to tip the scale ever so slightly and alter the course of history through their actions. In the following I therefore define ritual not as a symbol or an event but as a realm of action that ushers forth issues of agency, structure, and power. In a complementary fashion I then argue that religion is a structuring principle and establish religious knowledge as an authoritative resource of symbolic capital, which by its very nature educes relations of power.

Ritual

Ritual's sociological importance has long been recognized by many prominent anthropologists, and since ritual performance is a cultural universal, much of the inquiry has aimed to explain ritual's pervasive nature in functional terms. These functional explanations range from social integration (e.g., Durkheim 1961) to the communication of social norms and structures (e.g., Douglas 1973; Leach 1976); from relieving anxiety of the unknown (e.g., Malinowski 1925; cf. Homans 1941) to reducing societal tension and conflict (e.g., Gluckman 1963, 1965; Turner 1968, 1974); and from establishing identities amid disruptive social change (e.g., van Gennep 1960) to equilibrating populations with resource availability (e.g., Rappaport 1979). A focus on power, agency, and social action, however, shifts the discussion from ritual's functions to how ritual is an integral domain of social life and can be a potent catalyst in social reproduction and transformation.

The ritual concept, as forwarded in this book, should be specified so that we may understand its place in social reproduction. Defining ritual has proven problematic, however, in that there is no consensus among anthropologists and ritual theorists as to what ritual actually is and how it is distinct from other modes of action (Bell 1992:69–74, 1997:93–137; Rappaport 1999: 23–68). Bell (1992, 1997) suggests that attempts to define ritual trend toward theoretical circularity and generalization, and they distract attention from operationalizing the ritual concept. It may be that "precise definitions are neither possible nor are they necessary" (Aune and DeMarinis 1996:7), but a basic idea of what ritual is (and is not) is necessary if we are to effectively implement it in social analysis, especially since we are dealing with relics from an unseen past and cannot witness the acts outright. I therefore adopt Roy Rappaport's definition of ritual as "the performance of more or less invariant sequences of formal acts and utterances not entirely encoded by the performers" (1999:24). Yet since this conception is somewhat terse and vague, and encompasses much more than religious behavior, I concentrate on what Lars Fogelin (2007) specifies as "religious ritual." Religious ritual is a field of action where performance showcases the repetitive embodiment of religious knowledge. This definition not only serves to distinguish ritual from other realms of action that share an emphasis on formality, rules, and performance (i.e., games and theatre; Rappaport 1999:38–46), but also specifies its relation to a structuring principle, that of religion.

Religion

Structuralists conceptualize religion as a system of symbols that imbue people with particular "moods and motivations" (Geertz 1973:90) which are authenticated by metaphysical principles or dogma (Rappaport 1999) and intrinsically resistant to social change (Bloch 1977, 1986). This is a concise and adequate formulation, but I add that religion is an indispensable part of a structural totality (Giddens 1984:185–186). Accordingly, religion is a structural principle that organizes people in relation to one another via social roles, legitimates distributions of power, provides a shared epistemology, and defines society and the self in relation to the natural and not-so-natural worlds. This perspective adds breadth to the classic though antiquated notion of religion as simply belief in supernatural things, powers, and beings.

Religion entails a body of knowledge and actions that together serve as a distinct set of authoritative rules and resources girding the web of power relationships brought to bear in processes of social reproduction. Religion actually compels action through ritual, since authoritative resources are continuously reproduced through engagement with them. As Timothy Pauketat (2009:12) articulates, "religion is not simply a set of abstract beliefs, but the regular ritual engagement of people with these various forces."

Religion's influence on human action has typically been placed at two extremes. One of these is analogous to Emile Durkheim's (1961) polarization between the sacred and profane: since the sacred realm is considered distinct, doctrine and actions infused with religious purpose can be segregated from other (or profane) aspects of life. The other extreme considers religion to be omni-pervasive, or the structuring element of *all* human thought and action (e.g., Eliade 1964). Since religious ritual can aptly be taken as the embodiment and performance of religious tenets and currents (Bell 1992:94–101), sometimes its relevance to the structural totality falls into camps of similar opposition; either ritual comprises a set of activities distinguished from other practices or it is the symbolic dimension of all actions (Douglas 1973:19–20; Lewis 1980:6). These extremes are captured in Fiona Bowie's (2000) distinction between "world" and "traditional" religions. In this schema the world's major religious structures (i.e., those characteristic of state- and nation-levels of social organization) tend to secularize ritual actions and religious thought, whereas among more traditional ones (i.e., those characteristic of societies with less institutionalized hegemonies) social and spiritual/religious life are indistinguishable. In truth, however, most religious traditions arguably fall somewhere along a continuum of secularization, and this is due in part to the extent that religious knowledge is distributed and access to it is bound up in institutions and social positions. A key way of demonstrating one's access to religious knowledge and acceptance of religious dogma is through participation in ritual performance. Since ritual performance is the embodiment of religious knowledge, ritual participation serves to legitimate the knowledge and reproduce existing structures of domination.

Religious Knowledge as Symbolic Capital

Ritual entails an array of interdependent material and ethereal "things," including knowledge, paraphernalia, and performance. As considered here, religious knowledge encompasses both the knowledge of the intricacies of a ritual performance—the correct procedures, statements, and symbols—and the religious principles and understandings embodied during ritual actions. Like ritual paraphernalia, religious knowledge can be understood as a possession, but as a form of symbolic rather than physical capital that, when brought forth in social interactions, becomes a form of "intellectual" (Harrison 1992) and "incorporeal" (Lowie 1921:224) property. This view of knowledge is in line with Giddens's (1984) formulation of intangible, authoritative resources. As capital and resource, knowledge of any type is socially distributed (Simpson 1997). Forms of property, however, are not relationships between people and things. They are instead relationships between people about things; they are social relationships (e.g., Bloch 1975; Carter 1989) and thus evocative of power. Knowledge always presupposes and constitutes power relations (Foucault 1980). Accordingly, ritual knowledge can be asymmetrically distributed, controlled, and withheld from individuals or different factions within society (Barth 1975, 1987; Dirks 1992).

The distribution of knowledge is both the result and the constitution of power relationships. This is exemplified by Foucault: "Relations of power are not in a position of exteriority with respect to other types of relationships (economic processes, *knowledge relationships*, sexual relations), but are immanent in the latter; they are the immediate effects of the divisions, inequalities, and disequilibriums which occur in the latter, and conversely they are the internal conditions of these differentiations" (1978:94; emphasis added). There is therefore no room for an assumption "that all individuals share a synchronic blueprint of meanings and understandings rather than participate in a partial and inchoate project in which knowledge and access to knowledge are variably distributed and expressed" (Simpson 1997:44). We should instead expect religious knowledge to be differentially distributed among individuals, and anticipate the importance and value of this knowledge to also vary. As a resource, religious knowledge is a medium "through which power is exercised, as a routine element of the instantiation of conduct in social reproduction" (Giddens 1984:16). Possession of religious knowledge, either permanent or temporary, is thus generative of power that may be drawn on to exert one's interests in other dimensions of social life, that is, it affords the fluid power and situational agency involved in social reproduction.

Ritual performance is the demonstration that one "has" not only religious knowledge but also the authority to access and use it, display it, or conceal it. Ritual action is thus a highly effective way to broadcast one's power in various structural dimensions, as it connects performers to the forces that define their and their community's relation to the natural world and the explanation of reality—religion—or what Fernando Granero (1986:657) terms "the mystical means of reproduction." When religious knowledge becomes increasingly scarce as it is bound up and crystallized in institutions and positions of authority, those who possess it become increasingly empowered as others are disenfranchised. Indeed, ritual's effectiveness as a tool of social control can be correlated with the degree of hierarchy and lack of social cohesion within a society (Douglas 1973). In turn, a monopoly on religious knowledge is available when those who already have it put restrictions on the means of its acquisition; this can be accomplished by controlling who can access it, where it can be stored, and how it can be wielded. It can also be restricted by requiring reciprocity for learning it. In this way, ritual becomes a strategic situation in which performers demonstrate, negotiate, and legitimate to themselves and others their connection to religious dogma and supernatural, other-than-human agents.

Ritual as Strategic Action

The oft-cited works of Catherine Bell (e.g., 1992, 1997) have been highly instrumental for moving ritual beyond functionalist and structuralist paradigms and into ones focused on action and performance. Her notion of "ritual practice" borrows from Bourdieu's (1977) sociological elements of practice, habitus, and doxa, and it has shifted ritual away from a domain of symbolic expression and into one of action, intentionality, and struggle (see also Stortz 1996). Bell's emphasis has been "to look at how human activities establish and manipulate their own differentiation and purposes—in the very doing of the act within the context of other ways of acting" (Bell 1992:74). Accordingly, she construes ritual as a *strategy* to distinguish specific practices from others by imbuing them with properties that we identify as ritualistic, such as formality, fixity, and repetition. Bell's interest revolves around the process by which people manipulate contexts to distinguish certain practices as ritual as opposed to others—a process she refers to as "ritualization" (Bell 1992:88–93)—and the effect this has on agents of ritualization and others to which this distinction is legitimated.

Although this book is concerned with how ritual is implicated in social transformation rather than how ancient rituals came to be, Bell's notion of ritualization implies a number of important concepts on which I draw. That ritual involves strategy serves to activate ritual performers and underlies the consciousness of their performances. Ritual performers knowingly follow established modes of action, and this conformance generates a form of power as it demonstrates one's relation to religious resources and one's social position vis-à-vis others'. Even when performers disagree with the dogma embodied through ritual performance, their conscious conformance is a strategic means of empowerment through associations with religious resources (Rappaport 1999). "Ritual is the thing to do when one is negotiating for authority, and when the power that one needs to tap must have an extra-communal source" (Bell 2007:286).

The ritualization of social agents is another powerful social process to consider. "Ritualization endows these agents with some degree of ritual mastery. This mastery is an internalization of schemes with which they are capable of reinterpreting reality in such a way as to afford perceptions and experiences of a redemptive hegemonic order. Ritualization always aligns one within a series of relationship[s] linked to the ultimate sources of power" (Bell 1992:141). Here Bell reiterates that ritual actively delineates one's access to religious knowledge as well as the structures of domination that administer and ordain such knowledge. Mastery, as an element of ritualization, refers to a network of power relations between subordinate and insubordinate, master and minion. In this way, "ritual mastery" (Bell 1992:107–108), adapted from Bourdieu's "practical mastery" (1977:87–95), is a strategy by which performers vie for possession of religious knowledge. "Ritual mastery is the ability—*not equally shared, desired, or recognized*—to (1) take and remake schemes from the shared culture that can strategically nuance, privilege, or transform, (2) deploy them in the formulation of a privileged ritual experience, which in turn (3) impresses them in a new form upon agents able to deploy them in a variety of circumstances beyond the circumference of the rite itself" (Bell 1992:116; emphasis added).

The third aspect of ritualization on which I draw is the suite of features Bell argues to be intrinsic to systems of ritual specialists (1992:134–135). For one, the specialist's authority rests on ritual's importance in mediating between human and other-than-human agents, whereas a ritual's correct performance is critical to its efficacy. The capability to perform the ritual correctly lies within the specialist's socially recognized status and not necessarily in his or her personality. Ergo, specialists are empowered and restrained by virtue of their status, which is socially constituted and legitimated; thus, judgment of the specialist's performance or the ritual's efficacy ultimately lies with the audience. In religious rituals where there is no physical audience of "others," judgment resides within the performer and a spiritual or ethereal audience (Rappaport 1999:51).

Second, the ranking of various rituals seemingly substantiates the variable authority of specialists. Even though different ritual practices constitute a larger ritual system (see below), their importance is not always equal, and those rituals overseen by specialists tend to be more integral to, and thus powerful for, the whole society. Lastly, the end product of ritualization is the "evocation of a consensus on values, symbols, and behavior" (Bell 1992:110) through ritual mastery. This underscores the importance of the legitimation of the ritual performance in order for it to be effective and to reproduce the authority of ritual specialists. However, "it is through dialogues in the context of performance, as well as in the transmission of knowledge, that the legitimacy, authenticity and authority of ritual practitioners are challenged and tested" (Simpson 1997:53).

One means of ensuring consensus and legitimating authority is to wield secrecy, ambiguity, and even subterfuge in the symbols employed and messages transmitted through ritual performance. The ambiguity of symbols and symbolic actions suggests that some rituals fail to communicate shared experiences and understandings, yet such ambiguity may actually be integral to a ritual's efficacy (Bell 1992:183–184). It is difficult to contest hegemonic social institutions and structures of domination when the knowledge on which they are based and justified is obfuscated. In fact, Bell (1992:109) contends that the potential for misrecognition is key to ritual's efficacy (see also Bourdieu 1977:22).

Along the lines I have developed through this scrutiny of action-centric ritual studies, ritual practice can be understood as a corporeal materialization of religion, where cosmological understandings and structural principles are embodied in the performers and, to a certain degree, an audience. And although a ritual performance may be situational and finite, or limited to a particular duration and/or place, the materialization of religion embodied by performers and attendants to ritual performances may not end in concert with the ritual performance. People involved in rituals may, as Rappaport suggests, "leave the ritual performance with their statuses in some way formally transformed" (1999:39–40). Indeed, such is the intended outcome of rites of passage, for example, in which performers move from one social position to another by virtue of participation in certain rituals (van Gennep 1960).

Ritual practice is a theater where people put their "religion in motion" (sensu Pauketat 2012: 226) and are empowered by their possession of religious knowledge and connection to the consensual legitimation of religiously important and ritually efficacious symbols, values, and behaviors. This empowerment can temporarily or permanently alter one's social status beyond the ritual's duration, and it situationally offers actors an opportunity (i.e., agency) that can both reproduce and transform social structure. Since power is fluid, however, the empowerment afforded by ritual practice can be transferred to other realms of social life. For example, political power is all too often legitimated through religious symbolism (Kertzer 1988). As Bowie (2000) has furthermore pointed out, in pre-Modern, non-Western societies with relatively minimal degrees of social differentiation—the types of societies many archaeologists usually study—there may be little distinction between the religious and nonreligious spheres of life (see also Harvey 2000). This facilitates the transference of power among social domains in small(er)-scale societies. Accordingly, archaeologists can gain holistic insight into the social dynamics of past societies through analyses of ritual practice and religion, the topic to which I now turn.

Ritual and Religion in Archaeology

The foregoing returns us to the introductory question: Can there be an archaeology of ritual or religion? Undoubtedly so, as Marxist archaeologists who took an early lead on the matter showed (e.g., Hodder 1988; Hodder, ed. 1982; Miller and Tilley 1984; see also McGuire 1992a), but as Timothy Insoll (2004:52) points out, ritual and religion remained largely undefined and were subsumed under a broader concept of "ideology." The recent burgeoning of archaeological literature on the subject suggests that straightforward investigations of ancient ritual and religion are now more common and in greater alignment with other fields of inquiry (e.g., Bradley 2005; Fogelin 2007, 2008; Garwood et al. 1991; Glowacki and Van Keuren 2012; Hall 1997; Howey and O'Shea 2006; Insoll 2004; Kyriakidis, ed. 2007; Lewis-Williams 2002; Pauketat 2013; Rakita 2009; Rakita and Buikstra 2008; Renfrew 1985, 1994; Steadman 2009; C. VanPool et al. 2006; Verhoeven 2002; Whitley and Hays-Gilpin 2008; Whitley and Keyser 2003). This heightened interest, however, centers largely on the reconstruction of ritual performance; the decipherment of meaning from ritual forms evidenced through arrangements of artifacts, symbols, and architecture; and the advantages and adaptive qualities of ritual (e.g., Hayden 1987; Mithen 1997). Although such contributions yield "substantial knowledge about past ritual activities" (Whitley and Keyser 2003:391) and showcase ritual's "social significance" (Whitley 2009:184), they seemingly still fall short of activating ritual and religion in the social dynamics of the past. Many investigations serve instead to craft ethnographies of ritual and religion by identifying, describing, and interpreting the material remains of diaphanous ritual practices. These need not be the sole products of an archaeology of ritual. More appropriately, such contributions and emphases provide much-needed historical contexts on which further analyses should be directed. I therefore swap the introductory question with another: What can an archaeology of ritual accomplish?

Structuralists emphasize the ways social norms and cultural values are expressed and reinforced through ritual (e.g., Turner 1966). As discussed above, these passive and domineering aspects of ritual studies have been increasingly criticized by archaeologists (e.g., Emerson and Pauketat 2008; Fogelin 2007, 2008) and scholars of religion (e.g., Bell 1992, 1997) who apply a more action-oriented framework to ritual. As Howey and O'Shea argue, "archaeology should contribute to the investigation of long-term processes of ritual practice and change" (2006:279).[1] Practice theorists conceptualize ritual as the enactment of religious structure, or the embodiment of religious knowledge, and through performance actors are capable of manipulating the structural principle of religion (Bell 1992, 1997; Humphrey and Laidlaw 1994). Even though rituals may be enduring, their symbolic meanings and religious connotations are constantly recontextualized to meet the current agendas of an evolving cast of participants. In turn, it behooves us to distinguish between ritual and religion if we are to get at the nuances of ritual practice in relation to religious structures. Studying one without the other, however, provides a one-sided perspective on the issue. "Given the dialectic nature of religion and ritual and the fragmentary evidence of ancient ritual, blended approaches are both necessary and successful" (Fogelin 2007:66).

One means of operationalizing both ritual and religion in the past is to embed these concepts into the voids of existing models of social reproduction. As the first half of this chapter established, this is the objective of the following chapters, because "if we preserve the study of ritual as a thing in itself with its own logic and its own history, then it is difficult to satisfactorily explain how social agents operate between political and ritual domains" (Barrett 1991:5). This kind of explanation, however, necessitates lower-order theoretical and methodological refinements regarding our ability to identify bygone ritual actions through relics of performance and to engender past peoples with a religious system.

Ritual in the Past

Without the aid of ethnohistorical records, archaeologists tend to be more comfortable with the concept of ritual than religion. This is because rituals may leave physical traces that are amenable to objective analysis (weighing, sorting, counting, etc.) and do not require a priori knowledge of the religious structures that guided such practice (Howey and O'Shea 2006:279). Palpable vestiges of ritual practice are highly varied and can include—among many things—tangible items such as masks and censers; natural places such as caves and groves; public architecture such as mounds, temples, and plazas; and symbols depicted in rock art or on ritual paraphernalia. We should thus expect the archaeological record to be replete with indicia of ritual action, and indeed it is. Yet we face two interrelated problems: (1) what sets ritual apart from other realms of action, a question discussed at length in ritual studies (e.g., Bell 1992, 1997; Aune and DeMarinis, ed. 1996); and (2) how can we establish that the objects and data we purport as signatures to ancient ritual are, in fact, evidence thereof as opposed to artifacts of nonritualized activities?

Archaeologists are inclined to conceptualize rituals as solitary events that are constrained to a certain place, occur within a specified timeframe, and are performed by a particular individual or group of people. In this way, ritual is again separated from the larger domain of human action, and it is compartmentalized into a structuralist dichotomy of sacred and profane. This opposition implies that an action either is or is not a ritual, a far too simplistic categorization. By placing actions and artifacts into distinct behavioral and systemic categories, we can choose to study those we feel are the most important to our research and relegate the more nebulous and fuzzy observations (i.e., ritual artifacts) to the sideline. Indeed, the ritual label has all too often been evoked as a "dustbin" (Hulkrantz 1978:27) or "trash-bin category" (Verhoeven 2002:234) for those items or actions that to archaeologists seem to have no apparent practical or utilitarian value (see Brück 1999; Hodder 1982:194; Howey and O'Shea 2006:261–262; Insoll 2004:1–2; Renfrew 1994; Whitehouse 1996).[2] The problem lies in the fact that many actions meld aspects of what we would ordinarily consider the domestic and religious spheres of life. This blurring should not be surprising, since the dilemma in determining if an action is ritual or not stems from our empiricist epistemology and not necessarily from how the original performers conceptualized their society and practices.

Just as ritual cannot be segregated from the larger social body, ritual practices can breach the spatial and temporal edges of performance because they are often constituents of larger systems of ritual action (Bell 1997:173–177; Kyriakidis 2007; van Gennep 1973). For example, seasonal rituals are calibrated and integrated through the annual solar cycle, thus making up a network of rituals in which each is integral to the system's operation. Pilgrimages provide another example of an interwoven system of ritual actions. In these, devotees shift their ritual performance through both space—moving from one ritually important place to another and performing various other ritualized acts along the way—and time as the journey unfolds. In cases such as these, the ritual practices at the heart of the ritual system transcend the loci and timeframes of the constituent ritual performances. As a result, the complexities of ritual systems can be difficult to discern archaeologically. Rarely are we afforded the evidence to tie spatially and temporally finite rituals together into a coherent ritual system. Teasing apart respective rituals may require acute attention to detail and pattern, especially when they shared the same stage of performance. These intricacies demonstrate that recognizing characteristics of and diversity among ritual practices and larger ritual systems as well as the contexts of performance is neither simple nor straightforward.

The identification of ritual items and places, and their distinction from the residues of other social actions, requires attention to repetitive patterns in material culture (Marcus 2007) and contexts of artifact use and deposition (e.g., Walker 1996, 1999, 2002, 2008)—something archaeologists are clearly adept at—as well as attention to significant deviations from patterns, or the "oddities" that do not mesh well with functional perspectives (Boivin 2009).

When locating ritual in the past, we should move beyond the static logic of objects and stages and realize the dynamic logic of relations (Salmon 1973). There are unequivocal ritual objects, but they are not inherently ritualized. We intuitively deduce such classification through perceived relations among observations. For example, we might consider a quartz crystal interred with other unusual objects in a burial a likely item of ritual esoterica because of (1) its spatial and contextual relationship with the burial and other assumed grave goods and (2) its physical likeness to crystals used in shamanic rituals among ethnographically descendant communities. A quartz crystal in a Swiss watch, however, leads to an utterly different connotation. Along these lines, it is important to remember that typically mundane or "profane" things can move in and out of ritualized contexts throughout their histories of production, use, and discard (e.g., Walker 1995, 1999). The same goes for ritual paraphernalia; just think of the broken effigies strewn around refuse piles. In an archaeology of ritual, context is everything. It might also do us some good to step away from our Cartesian typologies and rethink how ritual operates and generates material culture within non-Western epistemologies. Ethnographic approaches, as discussed later in this chapter, can provide some insights.

One way to identify ritual in the archaeological record is to develop a "checklist" (Insoll 2004:60) or model of agreed-on characteristics of ritual action for the observations under analysis (e.g., Renfrew 1985; Verhoeven 2002). While generalizing and beset with problems inherent to classification systems (Dunnell 2008), a checklist approach is nevertheless useful be-

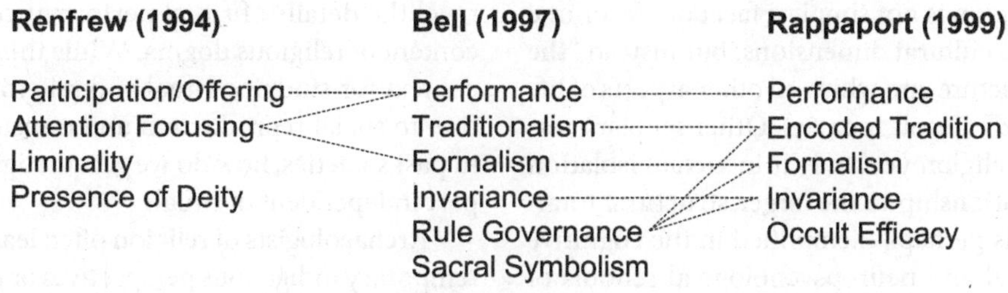

FIGURE 2.1. Three models of ritual's defining features.

cause it specifies the criteria by which material culture evidences ritual action. Insoll (2004:60), however, criticizes such approaches as devoid of theory. This is not exactly true; the checklist approach is a methodology ontologically grounded in Cartesian objectivity. Theory resides in the defining qualities of ritual specified by the checklist. To its credit, a checklist opens the definition and application of ritual to debate, critique, and refinement as opposed to impressionistic takes on what is and is not ritual. Checklists also facilitate analysis of the many nuances among different forms of ritual action.

What one considers evidence of ritual, as discerned through relics, ruins, and ancient symbols, depends largely on how one defines ritual. As discussed above, defining ritual has proven problematic whereas overarching definitions are tragically generalizing. Alternatively, ritual theorists prefer to isolate the qualities they consider common to all rituals and rely on them as the suite of variables for identifying and distinguishing ritual practices. Three examples of just such an approach have been forwarded by Renfrew (1994), Bell (1997), and Rappaport (1999) (Figure 2.1).[3] These checklists differ, however, not only with regard to the defining qualities of ritual but also in the degree to which a ritual needs to adhere to those qualities. Rappaport argues that the combination of these qualities is definitive of ritual, whereas those in Bell's model are only suggestive and serve as an "initial lexicon for analyzing how cultures ritualize or deritualize social activities" (Bell 1997:138). I take Rappaport's model as a sort of ritual archetype, yet Bell's more flexible model is probably more appropriate for archaeology, considering some of the inherent limitations of archaeological data to evidence each and every characteristic of ritual action. Either way, checklist-like models of this sort are effective at delineating rituals in the past and contextualizing those rituals as strategic social actions. An effective analysis of the dialectic between ritual and religion nevertheless requires archaeologists to approach religion to some degree.

Establishing Religion in the Past

The anthropological study of ancient religion is commonly approached from two perspectives, one viewing religion as fundamental to all action and the other seeing religion as a quasi-independent "subsystem" within a social whole (Tambiah 1990). Most archaeological practice to date has unfortunately taken the second perspective because, since details of "false consciousness," or religion, are "infinite, the archaeologist has no hope of being able to infer the specific content of these beliefs in the absence of written records or oral traditions" (Trigger 1989:262). If religion and ritual occupy merely a peripheral, inessential segment of the social structure, or make up at most a subsystem, then its understanding is not necessary for us to study more accessible cultural domains such as subsistence and social organization (e.g., Hawkes 1954).

Alternatively, archaeologists of religion sometimes emphasize the religious dimension *over* the economic and political spheres. This is because the archaeology of religion, whether particularistic or generalizing, is inherently embedded in structuralist frameworks. Insoll (2004), for example, takes this perspective to the extreme, arguing that religion should be regarded as the potential source for all behavior and organizational principles. According to this view, religion is not simply a facet of life, or one of several cultural dimensions, but instead "the superstructure into which all other aspects of life are placed" (Insoll 2004:85). Other scholars emphasize religion yet study it in virtual isolation of its relationship to the larger structural totality. This is perhaps exemplified in the cognitive processual and neuropsychological schools of archaeological practice (Lewis-Williams 2001; Renfrew 1994; see also Whitley, ed. 1998), where identification of cognitive universals is a sufficient explanation for some religiously inspired phenomena. The relevance of these essentializing universals to society, however, often remains obscure or underemphasized.

A structuralist take on ancient religion is not an issue of debate here. In fact, I argue above that religion is productively understood as a structuring principle of society. My qualm is not with theory but rather with application, in that symbolic and structuralist interpretations of religion, while informative and worthwhile scholarship, tend to do little more than construct culture histories. Aside from substantiating religion as an important and meaningful sphere of social life, researchers need to take a further step and implement it along with ritual in analyses of social reproduction.

The content or specificities of religious knowledge, such as details of myths, beliefs, or symbolic meanings, are understandably much more difficult than ritual to ascertain from objects or architecture alone. Few would nevertheless deny the inherent, mutually dependent relationship between ritual and religion, and as Fogelin contends, "most [archaeologists] recognize that a dialectic exists between [them]; aspects of one are naturally related to the other. Ritual elements can be used to infer belief systems, just as knowledge of the mythology of a particular society can be used to investigate its rituals" (2007:56). Fogelin's proposal, albeit encouraging, exposes the circular reasoning on which some investigations of past ritual and religion rely when evidence of ritual is used to "infer belief systems." And we are left with that uneasy impression that the objective of an archaeology of ritual and religion is to simply unravel the details of ritual performance and the content of religious dogma. While this provides context for studying ritual and religion in relation to social reproduction and transformation in past societies, how do we get at religion in the past independent of ritual?

Archaeologists of religion often lean on contemporary indigenous perspectives or ethnohistoric records to inform on the immaterial past, whether that is to identify ritual practices, uncover symbolic meanings of artifacts and symbols, or ascertain aspects of religious thought. Without written records, ethnographic analogy between the present or recent past with the historically distant is one of the few ways to get at religion in the past. The well-known case of the Magician's burial at Ridge Ruin in northern Arizona (McGregor 1943) attests to the occasional veracity of ethnographic analogy, in this case the Hopi, especially when the analogy is drawn by a descendant community (see Mason 2000). Ethnographic analogy, however, does not always imply a one-to-one correlation between the present and the past. In fact, various strains of analogical reasoning have been used to interpret past religions. Whitley (2009:184) recently discussed three of these: (1) classical ethnographic analogy, (2) the direct historical approach, and (3) direct ethnographic interpretation.

Anthropologists and other social inquirers have long employed ethnographic analogy to interpret past religions, and the approach's underlying logic, though faulty and simplistic, is fairly straightforward. Its assumptions are rooted in the unilinear cultural evolutionist theories of the nineteenth century (see Chapter 1). As conceived, since all societies "progress" from one stage to another, those that share the same stage of development are sociologically comparable, that is, Australian Aborigine religion can be applied to Upper Paleolithic cave art because of shared "child-like" mental faculties (e.g., Reinach 1903). This mode of cultural comparison later gave way to cross-ecological assumptions that societies living under similar environmental conditions and pressures would eventually evolve similar cultural customs. Though not explicitly addressed in this early style of cultural ecology, religion, as a cultural subsystem, was implied to be an adaptation to environmental stimuli (e.g., hunting magic for hunter-gatherer cultures). Hulkrantz (1966, 1979, 1986) later formulated a "comparative religio-ecological approach" that explicitly theorized religion through a cross-ecological perspective. Historians of religion eventually realized the weaknesses (and racist undertones?) of classical ethnographic and cross-ecological analogies (see Lewis-Williams 1991).

Aware of earlier flaws in unilinear evolutionism and its mode of unrestrained classical ethnographic analogy, proponents of the historical particularist school of anthropology of the early twentieth century began to explore the past through the direct historical approach (Steward 1942; cf. Hulkrantz 1967). Instead of looking cross-culturally, or drawing "horizontal" analogies, the direct historical approach takes the deliberate "approach to the unknown through the known, the prehistoric through the historic" (Strong 1935:6). In this way, analogies are still employed, but the comparisons and interpretations are "vertically" aligned and historically contingent. This interpretive methodology and its assumptions are still commonplace in archaeological practice. The theoretical dilemma revolves around how far through space and time historical information can be applied. The greater the degree of separation in space, time, or social custom between the archaeological societies and their modern and historic descendant communities, the more speculative and less reliable are the interpretations of the past.

As described by Whitley (2009:184), direct ethnographic comparison, a third and presumably more reliable style of analogy, entails interpreting aspects of late prehistoric societies from "relevant records" of known descendant communities. Hypothetically, a direct ethnographic comparison would rely on ethnographically derived accounts, such as oral histories collected from Apache communities in the late nineteenth century, to interpret Apachean archaeological materials from, perhaps, the seventeenth century. This may seem logical and straightforward, but how late is "late prehistoric" and who makes this decision? Inasmuch as this is a more specific version of the direct historical approach, it differs only in that history is limited to a short time span—yet still unspecified—and to situations where there is good correlative evidence that the communities providing the ethnographic accounts are descendant from the past societies of inquiry and that little to no cultural change has occurred. It is this latter assumption that poses the greatest challenges.

I draw on the protohistoric Akimel O'odham as an illustration of some of the potential challenges a direct ethnographic comparison faces. In the late nineteenth and early twentieth centuries ethnographers wrote compendious records of both the O'odham and Pee Posh peoples living along the middle Gila River valley in present-day south-central Arizona (e.g., Russell 1908; Spier 1933). It is well known that at some time between the seventeenth and nineteenth centuries the Pee Posh left their prior homeland on the lower Colorado River and migrated eastward into the vicinity of O'odham villages. Once the Pee Posh were allied with the O'odham, these two cultural entities created a single community while maintaining distinct social identities, mytho-religious traditions, and languages. Their material culture and settlement structures, however, were practically identical. Given this, which body of ethnography would be most appropriate for interpreting religion from an ambiguous archaeological assemblage of ritual esoterica found at an eighteenth-century hamlet on the middle Gila River? From another angle, would we not also be making considerable interpretive miscalculations if we directly applied historic O'odham religion onto their sixteenth- and seventeenth-century ancestors since systems of Spanish, Mexican, and finally American colonialism made impressions on O'odham mythology (Bahr 1971; Bahr et al. 1994)? As this historical scenario shows, without an awareness of potential though materially imperceptible cultural hiatuses and a means to account for them, direct ethnographic interpretations of religion position archaeologists as metaphorical "ventriloquists" (sensu Quinlan 2000a) for others' pasts. Indeed, by "assuming that certain legends or myths were transmitted unchanged over centuries... we create structural regularity and (re)invent religious tenets, principles, and orthodoxies where none may have existed" (Pauketat 2012:223).

With regard to addressing religion in the past, additional fashions of ethnographic analogy permeate the literature. The first may be regarded as an ethnographic-structuralist approach, since it involves identifying cross-cultural universals among known religions (e.g., Eliade 1964). These shared features are explained as either survivals of a primordial religion (i.e., shamanism) to which people clung but molded to new situations and environments as they migrated across the globe (e.g., Hulkrantz 1981; Whitley 2008) or indicative of neuropsychological processes hardwired into the brain and thus shared by all (e.g., Lewis-Williams and Dowson 1988). Regardless of the underlying causes for such broadly shared features, ethnographic-structuralist approaches demonstrate that certain socio-religious qualities are ubiquitous and that these can be explained through deep and distant historical connections. These broad, cross-cultural commonalities, though generalizing, offer a basic albeit crude interpretation of religion for the extremely remote and the completely unknown, such as the posthumously famous cave painters of Paleolithic Europe.

A middle ground exists, however, between direct historical and ethnographic-structuralist approaches, where a degree of particularity is offset by one of generalization, and what could be considered particularistic structuralism. Along these lines, characteristics and themes of past religions can be extrapolated by comparing religions among contemporary and historic indigenous communities with known historical connections and drawing out the commonalities. Caroline Boyd (1996, 2003) has recently applied just such a style of analysis to the religion of archaic hunter-gatherers along the lower Pecos River in western Texas, where she relied on shared features among Huichol, Aztec, Yaqui, and Pueblo religions to interpret local rock art as ritual practice embedded in a shamanistic epistemology. Even though the rock art predates the ethnographic information by thousands of years, and was crafted by communities practicing different subsistence economies and modes of social organization than the ethnographic counterparts, Boyd's religious interpretations, and those of a growing body of similar approaches to ancient Southwestern religions (e.g., Coulam and Schroedl 2004; Crown 1994; Hays-Gilpin and Hill 1999; Mills and Ferguson 2008; Wilcox 1987a), are fairly convincing because the regionally proximate informant communities share history. The shared religious features and themes among historically entwined communities show how aspects of an earlier, and perhaps quite old, religious structure were refashioned to meet contemporary needs and interests.

The blending and balancing of particularistic and structural approaches is not novel; it is often implicit in many of our interpretations of the archaeological past. For example, some ritualized features are recurrent among contemporary Pueblo communities in the northern Southwest, such as plazas, kivas, and kachina iconography, and their archaeological predecessors extend many centuries back into the precontact past. Based on shared practices, linguistic connections, consanguinity, and similarities in social organization among diverse Pueblo communities, few Southwestern archaeologists deny that ancient kivas and plazas were loci of ritual performance, that sipapus were symbolic openings to the underworld, or that kachina depictions in rock art and on pottery were, in fact, depictions of such mytho-religious personae. What supports these inferences about past religion and ritual is not necessarily a direct historical analogy (as we are not sure which ritual dances were performed in the plaza, for example), but that these contemporary communities share history. This is a shared history of place and ancestry, reciprocity and conflict, and meaning and memory. We should also cede that in all likelihood they share a history of religion. This serves as perhaps the most reliable means of extrapolating elements of ancient religion when major demographic shifts and social transformations have transpired, and when the nature and character of ancestral relations between past and present communities, while not in question, remain obscure. This is the widely held, though perhaps a slightly *ben trovato*, portrayal of the social landscape of the late precontact Greater Southwest (Adams and Duff 2004; Hill et al. 2010).

Anthropologists working in the Greater Southwest are fortunate to have at their fingertips a considerable breadth of past and present ethnographic sources on religion and ritual among Pueblo, O'odham, and other indigenous Southwestern communities. In fact, some broad commonalities have already been compiled and synthesized (e.g., Underhill 1948). In the remainder of this book I employ a particularistic-structural approach to address Hohokam religion, not to decipher meaning per se but to show how certain places, times, and things held religious significance. As Whitley and Keyser have forwarded:

> The goal [of an archaeology of religion] then should not be to create one-to-one analogues between prehistoric and recent non-western religions, nor to base our studies on simplistic formal ethnographic analogies. Instead it is to develop a range of intellectual possibilities within which models and evidence can be placed and their plausibility evaluated. Ethnography, then, continues to be critical to archaeological interpretation because it provides a ballpark within which the specifics of prehistoric religions can be assumed to lie. (2003:390–391)

This particularistic structuralism sets parameters around the themes and principles of ancient religious structures even though the content of religious knowledge remains elusive. The next chapter reviews our current knowledge of Hohokam social transformations, existing evidence of ritual practices, and prior conceptions and portrayals of Hohokam religion. Once rock art is addressed as ritual action in Chapter 6, I integrate Hohokam religion with ritual action and actuate these powerful and transformative social forces in the historical trajectory of the Hohokam, ancestors of the O'odham, who continue to create history in the low desert of the American Southwest.

CHAPTER 3

Ritual, Religion, and Society among the Hohokam

I have said that we might consider the history of any special culture as beginning with the conception or,—perhaps better—the adoption *of a general idea. It remains for me to add that it would also seem, while these general ideas,* after *their adoption, have had more to do with the special development of a culture, as such, than environment, yet their original conception or adoption has been unmistakably due to environment.* (Cushing 1890:152; emphasis in original)

I use this chapter to provide a culture-historical framework for this book, with the goal of highlighting those crises (sensu Giddens 1984) in which the Hohokam transformed their communities, institutions, and society in profound ways. Existing models have long posited aspiring political actors as the principal agents of social change in the Hohokam world (e.g., Doyel 1981, 1991a; Grebinger 1976; Howard 1993; Nichols and Feinman 1989; Rice 1987a, 1990, 1992; Teague 1985; Upham and Rice 1980). In Chapter 2, however, I brought forth ritual practice and the control of religious knowledge as crucial components in the reproduction of societies, especially when the various spheres of social life—politics, economics, religion, and so on—are blurred. Political actors may draw on ritual practices and religious symbols to usher forth structural transformations in the relations of power within societies (Kertzer 1988), and they often justify their actions and the outcomes by allusion to other-than-human (i.e., supernatural, mythical, celestial, etc.) agents and essences (e.g., Aldenderfer 1993; Bloch 1986; DeMarrais et al. 1996; Granero 1986; Jarman 1992; Joyce and Winter 1996; Lucero 2003; McGuire 1992b; Miller and Tilley 1984; Rogers 2008; Schachner 2001; Stockett 2007; Stone 1992). The idea that the manipulation of religious symbols and principles by leaders and aspiring elites had a hand in some profound social changes among the Hohokam has gained traction in recent years (e.g., Abbott 2000; Elson 2007; Elson and Abbott 2000; Howard 2006; Wallace 2014; Wallace and Lindeman 2012, 2013), and this book continues that trend but from a unique perspective.

I structure this chapter in four parts. At first I outline a general culture-historical sequence and emphasize the major social transformations that rippled through Hohokam society. In the second part I review previous interpretations of Hohokam religion to draw together a structural basis for understanding how the Hohokam organized themselves in relation to the metaphysical principles that defined their world. I then spotlight the architecture and paraphernalia that evidence Hohokam religious ritual practice and what these reveal about the ways in which religious knowledge was accessed and distributed among community members. I end with an examination of how symbolism changed in concordance with significant social transformations.

The Hohokam Concept

"Hohokam" is an O'odham term adopted by early-twentieth-century archaeologists to classify a distinctive and widely shared suite of ancient architectural forms and artifacts found throughout south-central Arizona (Figure 3.1).[1]

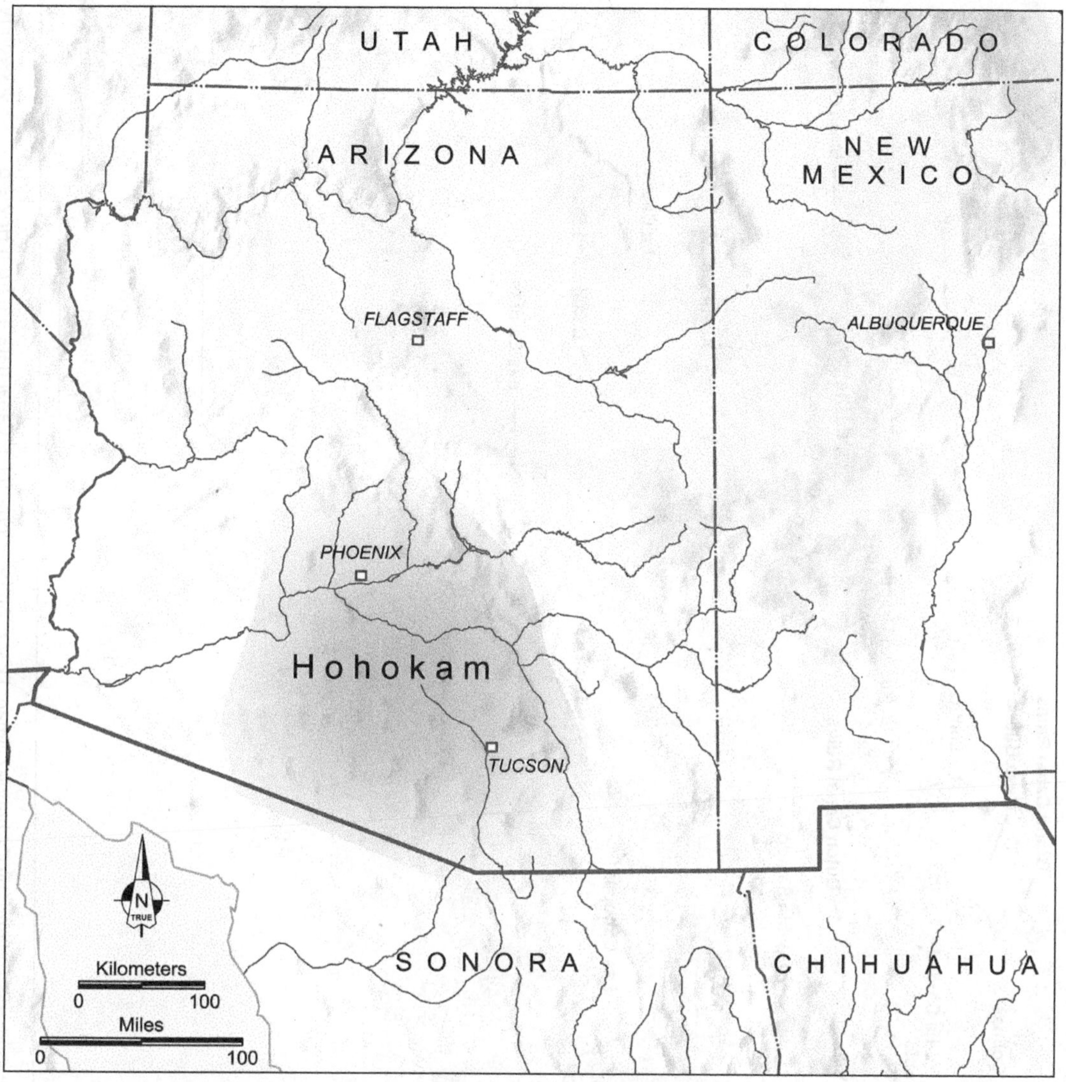

FIGURE 3.1. Reach of the Hohokam world, circa AD 1100 (figure by Catherine Gilman, Desert Archaeology, Inc.).

The Hohokam are particularly renowned for their extensive canal irrigation systems, a well-developed craft goods economy, monumental public architecture, and densely inhabited villages. Over the past several decades archaeologists have turned away from a homogeneous concept of Hohokam culture in favor of a view of distinct regional "systems" centered on particular river basins or watersheds, such as the Santa Cruz, San Pedro, middle Gila, lower Salt, and Verde Rivers; the Tonto Basin; and the Paguería. These more localized social entities are evidenced by regional nuances in material culture (e.g., Doelle and Wallace 1991; McGuire 1991), unique developmental histories (e.g., Lerner 1984), different ecological adaptations (e.g., Crown 1984; Doyel 1984; Weaver 1972), and possibly distinct languages and identities (e.g., Hoffman 1997; Shaul and Andresen 1989; Shaul and Hill 1998). Though historically, ecologically, and socially varied, these regional systems were united under shared social and religious structures and integrated through an exchange network that circulated goods and vital social

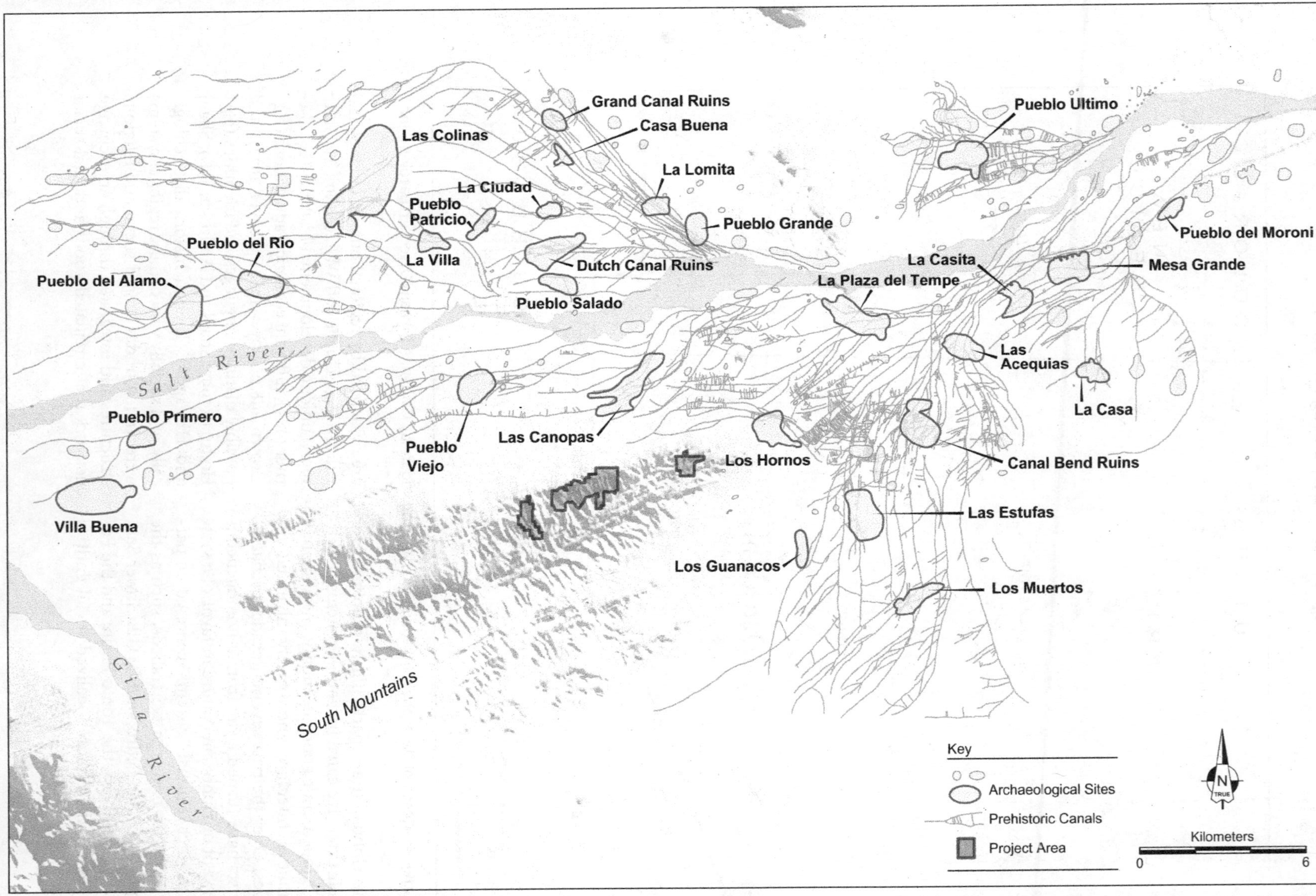

FIGURE 3.2. Hohokam canals and villages in the lower Salt River valley (figure by Catherine Gilman, Desert Archaeology, Inc.). Canal data are from Howard and Huckleberry (1991).

information across social, environmental, and geographical boundaries (Wilcox 1979).

The Hohokam concept has undergone a series of theoretical permutations over the past century (Whittlesey 1997). In the late nineteenth century, when the first archaeological expeditions to the Southwest rolled into southern Arizona, the dominant paradigm held that the vacated Hohokam settlements in the Phoenix Basin were ancestral villages of Pueblo peoples (e.g., Bandelier 1884, 1892; Cushing 1890; Fewkes 1912; Moorehead 1906). As the city of Phoenix grew, and development began to encroach on and level many of the nearby ruins, several concerned local citizens of influence took it on themselves to map the distribution of villages and canals before they were plowed down and paved over. Early maps by Herbert Patrick (1903) and Omar Turney (1924, 1929) laid bare for the first time the vast canal systems and the checkered pattern of architectural mounds and ovals of the ancient "canal builders" throughout the Salt River valley (Figure 3.2). After a considerable investment in regional survey, a budding cadre of regional archaeologists observed that the large, bermed ovals (ballcourts; variably interpreted as reservoirs, corrals, mud quarries, dance plazas, and temples) and a red-painted, mica-tempered, and buff-colored pottery type were, in fact, unique features of a bygone "Red-on-Buff culture" spread across southern Arizona (Gladwin and Gladwin 1929a, 1929b, 1930, 1935). Excavations at the quintessential villages of Casa Grande (Gladwin 1928) and Snaketown (Gladwin et al. 1937) along the middle Gila River allowed Harold Gladwin, founder of the privately funded research center at Gila Pueblo, and a batch of young, up-and-coming archaeologists to formulate an incipient culture history whose refinement would be the main area of Hohokam research for the next 30 years.

Gladwin (1928; Gladwin et al. 1937) originally proposed that Hohokam culture developed out of a local Archaic base, and he relied on rare Mesoamerican imports and the piecemeal adoption of Central and West Mexican–inspired artifact and architectural forms (i.e., cultural diffusion) as chronological anchors for a fledgling Hohokam culture history (Figure 3.3). However, the Mesoamerican connection was too complicated to explain with simple diffusionist models, so Gladwin (Gladwin and Gladwin 1948) eventually reversed course and adopted the position that the rise of Hohokam culture was instead due to a migration of Mesoamerican farmers into the desert Southwest. A Mesoamerican migration explanation gained favor with many of the leading Southwest researchers at the time, including Jesse Jennings, Carl Sauer, Charles DiPeso, and Albert Schroeder (Haury 1976:352); and Emil Haury, who had once preferred the Archaic-base argument (e.g., Haury et al. 1950), ultimately came to "reject [that view] in favor of the migration hypothesis, putting [himself] in the Gladwin-DiPeso camp" (Haury 1976:352).

With the flush of new data generated through salvage archaeology and a general refutation of migration/diffusion models in Americanist archaeology in the 1960s and 1970s, the Mesoamerican migration hypothesis was soon countered by more evolutionary models that recast Hohokam as a cultural adaptation to the Sonoran Desert (e.g., Doyel 1980; Doyel and Haury 1976; Weaver 1972). This perspective gained popularity because it accounted for the broadly shared subsistence regime concerned with irrigation agriculture as well as localized nuances that seemed bound to certain ecological niches and geographic terrains. However, since this adaptationist paradigm was based primarily on subsistence and settlement patterns, it offered little explanation for the hard-to-ignore widespread sharing of more social and ritual ingredients in the Hohokam recipe.

Dissatisfied with both the migration and adaptation perspectives, Wilcox (1979, 1980) found common ground through a regional systems model. This reformulation offered a means to explain how and why shared adaptive technologies (irrigation and architecture), goods (shell, obsidian, and pottery), and information (social organization and religion) could flow between communities near and far. This system united villagers in the Phoenix Basin core, long considered the center of the Hohokam world, with communities in peripheral regions. Wilcox

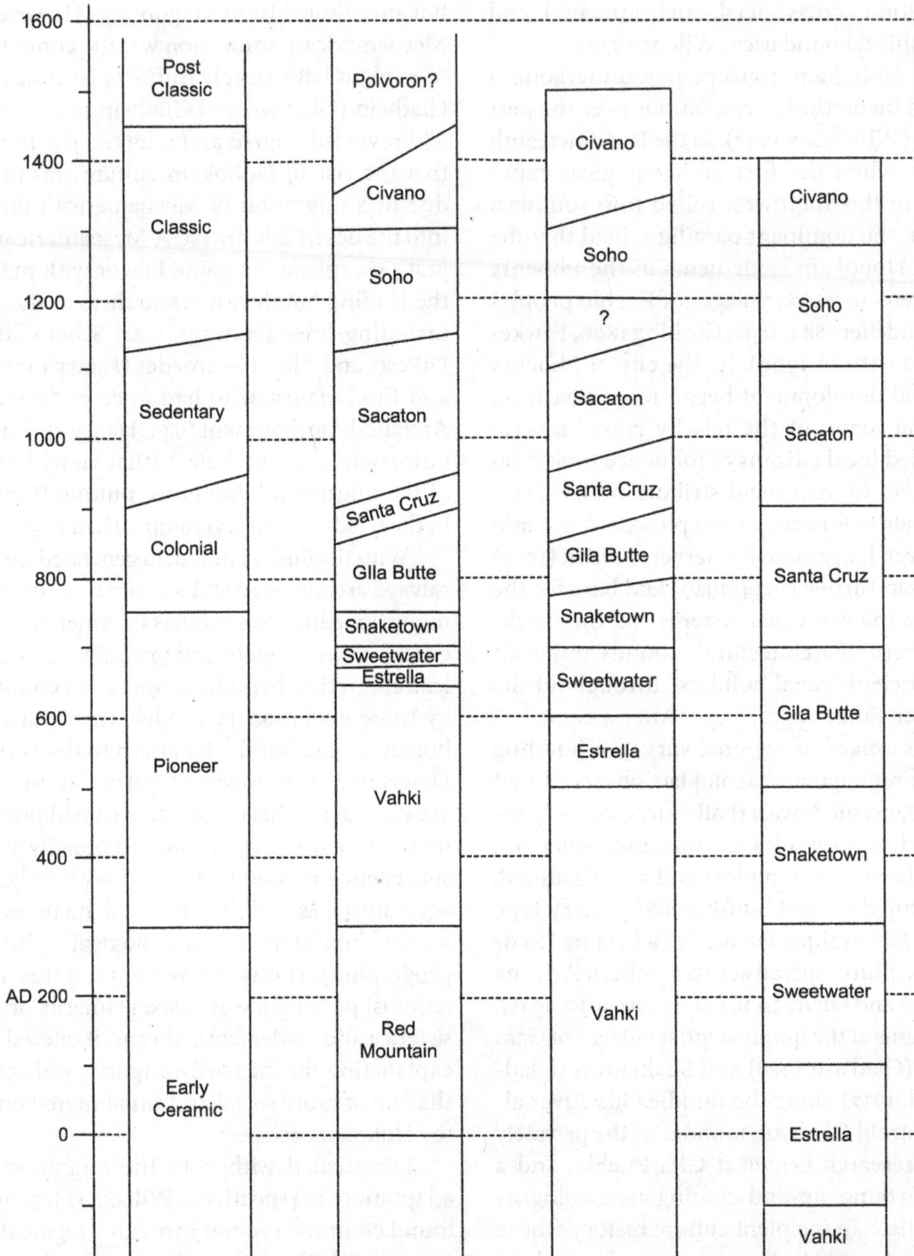

FIGURE 3.3. Archaeological period and phase sequences for the Phoenix Basin. The starting point of Hohokam cultural history is usually assigned to the Vahki phase of the Pioneer period. The three different sequences shown here reflect the difficulty of dating the Hohokam's "origins." This book follows Wallace et al.'s (1995) chronology.

invested considerable effort to show how ballcourts mapped onto different ecological zones, which he argued functioned as a ritually regulated network designed to distribute diversified subsistence resources. This process of interregional redistribution acted as a buffer against agricultural shortfalls within any region, or subsystem, of the larger Hohokam world. The sharing of more symbolic features proxied the exchange of information critical to the agricultural base.

The Hohokam regional system was tied together by a network of periodic social congregations during, for example, ritual ballgames. Noting that some villages did not have ballcourts while others had two, and that courts tended to be variably oriented to cardinal directions and regularly spaced along canals and drainages, Wilcox (1988, 1991a) argued that the ritual ballcourt network integrated Hohokam communities and mirrored a dyadic mode of social organization within villages (i.e., a moiety). In Wilcox's regional system model a religion with Mesoamerican roots provided the mental and symbolic glue to unite socially and spatially distant Hohokam communities through a common identity and shared sense of purpose (Wilcox 1987a, 1991a, 1991b; Wilcox et al. 1981; Wilcox and Sternberg 1983). I return to the topics of Hohokam ritual and religion later in this chapter.

Hohokam Social Transformations

One of the most enduring features of Gladwin's early research is its chronological framework, which Phoenix Basin Hohokam archaeologists still follow (Figure 3.3). This period-and-phase historical sequence was based on stratigraphic excavations and ceramic cross-dating with intrusive pottery types found first at Casa Grande (Gladwin 1928) and later at Snaketown (Gladwin et al. 1937; see also Schmidt 1928). The ceramic cross-dating established a series of anchors in the middle of the sequence that bracketed the Sacaton phase to a 200-year epoch around AD 1000. Accordingly, each of the other phases was given a tentative span of 200 years, establishing a "long count" of 1,700 years and placing Hohokam beginnings around 300 BC. Gladwin (1942) later adopted a "short count" starting around AD 600 that cut the sequence to approximately 800 years.

While the sequence and terminology remained generally unchanged, the duration of and beginning and end dates for each period and phase in the Gladwinian model became matters of debate (Haury 1976:325–326). These disagreements inspired Haury to revisit Snaketown and undertake further stratigraphic investigations and ceramic cross-dating analyses as well as perform other chronometric tests unused or unavailable in the 1930s (Haury 1976:326–340). Nonetheless, the final results encouraged Haury to uphold the original long count basically unmodified. Since Haury's reexcavation of Snaketown, abundant new chronological sampling from cultural resource management projects throughout the Hohokam region has fostered continued reevaluation, and despite Haury's masterful work, there is now general agreement on a short count beginning in the first millennium AD (see Dean [1991] for a thorough review).

The discussion below outlines the major transitions that define the turning points in the Hohokam cultural sequence. I place emphasis on the Phoenix Basin, following Wallace's (2001, 2004; Wallace et al. 1995) refined chronology. I draw my inferences of the Preclassic era (Pioneer, Colonial, and Sedentary periods) largely from excavations at the villages of Snaketown and Grewe in the middle Gila River valley (Craig 2001; Gladwin et al. 1937; Haury 1976; Wilcox et al. 1981) and Valencia Vieja in the Tucson Basin (Wallace 2003), whereas for the Classic period I rely predominantly on insights from Pueblo Grande (Abbott, ed. 2003) and Las Colinas (Teague and Deaver 1989) along the lower Salt River. Since I take a somewhat synthetic, bird's-eye view, the historical portrait I paint here may not accord fully with that of other Southwestern archaeologists. Indeed, there is a healthy bit of disharmony within Hohokam research, and for good reason, because (1) perspectives are often formed from personal experiences and local research within certain areas of the larger Hohokam world (see the regional system model above); (2) chronology remains a naggingly unresolved issue; and (3) although broader trends are how we have come to map out the Hohokam world, structural patterns and historical trajectories were not synchronic or identical across this vast area. So there is ample room for disagreement and plenty of opportunity for further clarification and revision. For comparison, additional reviews and slightly different takes can be found in Bayman (2001), Crown (1990, 1991a), and Doyel (1991a), whereas Lekson (2008) offers a somewhat roguish and grandiose Hohokam history as it unfolded in lockstep with events throughout the Greater Southwest, Mesoamerica, and North America.

Pre-Hohokam

Several of the cultural traits once believed diagnostic of the Hohokam actually had Archaic antecedents during the Early Agricultural period, an aeon (2,000+ years) of small-scale residence by formative farmers along rivers and creeks in what is now southern Arizona. These early manifestations include incipient canal-irrigation agriculture, quasi-sedentary pithouse villages, pottery for storage, and anthromorphic figurines, all seemingly localized in the Tucson Basin and surrounding areas (e.g., Gregory 2001; Gregory et al. 2007; Heidke 1999; Mabry 1998, 2002, 2008; Mabry et al. 1997). Due to these recent discoveries, most archaeologists have come to agree with Gladwin's (1928) and Haury and colleagues' (1950) first impression that Hohokam culture arose out of an Archaic (i.e., Cochise) base (see also Rogers 1966). However, life in this region of the northern Sonoran Desert at that time was unusual since this early agricultural style of living was largely absent from other regions of the Southwest (Huckell 1996).

In contrast to our expanding knowledge of early agricultural life literally under Hohokam villages in and around the Tucson Basin, the Archaic prehistory of the Phoenix Basin remains virtually unknown. Legacy of a Paleoindian presence is limited to a handful of isolated projectile points along the basin's upland margins (North et al. 2005), and there is only scant evidence for Archaic and Early Agricultural occupation or land use in the basin's interior (e.g., Hackbarth 1999; Stubing and Mitchell 1999; Wright 1999). It is unclear whether mobile hunter-gatherers would have found the Salt and Gila floodplains useful (Wilcox 1979). Alternatively, oddments of early villages may exist in locations where little to no land development has occurred and thus remain unexplored and underreported (Henderson and Hackbarth 1995:14). It is also quite possible that such sites remain deeply buried under alluvium on the floodplain, have been lost to erosion as the river channels shifted, or are obfuscated by overlying Hohokam villages (Doyel 1991a:241–242). Of course, it is equally plausible, if not more so, that the "origins" of Hohokam culture and its founding villages lie outside the Phoenix Basin (Bayman 2001:266; Wallace et al. 1995).

The pivotal Red Mountain phase (~AD 1–300) was added to the Gladwinian model to account for cultural traits transitional between the Early Agricultural period and the Vahki phase at the beginning of the Hohokam sequence in the Phoenix Basin (Cable and Doyel 1987; Mabry 2000; Morris 1969). This phase likely encapsulates the advent of canal-irrigation agriculture in the Phoenix Basin (Henderson and Clark 2004), as the earliest known canals have been dated to the Red Mountain at La Cuenca del Sedimento (Henderson 1989). Red Mountain–phase contexts and materials were also found at Pueblo Patricio (Cable et al. 1985) and La Escuela Cuba (Hackbarth 1992). Life in the Phoenix Basin during the Red Mountain was probably quite similar to Early Agricultural lifeways in and around the Tucson Basin: semi-sedentary groups living in true pithouses (as opposed to earlier house-in-pit architecture), inhabiting optimal resource zones along drainage systems, using brown plainware pottery for storage, and subsisting on a medley of cultigens and wild plants (Gregory 2001; Wallace 2003). Red Mountain farmers grew a mix of local domesticates and Mesoamerican transplants such as maize (Mabry 2005). Maize was doubtless a staple food item, but it may have been stored and eaten in unground and possibly green forms since groundstone technology appears minimally changed from earlier periods and whole fragments have been found in some contexts (Mabry 2005; see also Adams 2003). Villages were small, usually having fewer than 15 houses at any one time (Gregory 2001), but seemingly organized around conspicuously larger structures, or Big Houses. This is suggestive of a level of supra-household socio-political organization, perhaps tied to the management of the new canal infrastructure. Because of their low population, these fledgling farming communities probably participated in broad regional systems of economic exchange and mating (Wallace and Lindeman 2003; see also McBrinn 2005).

Pioneer Period

The Pioneer period demarcates the arrival into the northern Sonoran Desert of some Mesoamerican-inspired traits long considered emblematic of the Hohokam. As touched on above, however, some of the traits once considered unique to Hohokam culture had antecedents in an Early Agricultural lifestyle. The defining features of the Pioneer period are thus the introduction of cooking vessels and red-painted pottery types, new crops and shell jewelry, a well-developed figurine complex, larger and more expansive canal networks, public earthworks, increased settlement size and organizational complexity, and the development of more sophisticated groundstone technologies. The following phases define the chronological sequence of these changes in the Phoenix Basin.

Vahki (AD 300–650)

The first appearance of ceramic cooking vessels and trough-style grinding technologies typical of maize-based economies occurred in the Vahki phase (Wallace and Lindeman 2003). These new modes of production accompanied a new maize cultivar, Maize de Ocho, which is conducive to fine grinding. Very thin, small, red-slipped pottery vessels as well as cotton were also introduced during this time. There is little doubt that communities were fully sedentary and highly invested in irrigation agriculture. Villages grew in size and presumably population, and they exhibit a greater degree of organized layout around plazas, possibly evidencing incipient courtyard groups. Courtyard groups, intravillage organizational units characteristic of later periods, contain two to four pithouses oriented toward a shared open-air space with communal cooking facilities (Howard 1985; Wilcox et al. 1981).

The continued presence of Big Houses, abodes of small-scale leaders or forms of communal architecture, suggests a degree of corporate social organization and identity above the courtyard groups. This was also the time when cemeteries became central to community structure and identity, as some possible cremations were interred in the plazas at Valencia Vieja and Snaketown (Wallace and Lindeman 2003:387). This pattern signals a heightened emphasis on ancestor veneration, perhaps a religious strategy to show village membership or lay claim to fields in response to increased territoriality in the face of growing populations and heightened demand for agricultural lands. The communal practice of ancestor veneration may have also fostered the fruition of an elaborate complex of hand-molded ceramic figurines (Stinson 2004). The bulk of this complex consisted of human forms, but quadruped casts were also made on occasion (Haury 1976:267). The ritualized figurine complex, notably the human-form emphasis, may evidence a revival or refashioning of an Early Agricultural ritual practice in which the figurines stressed the human form and portrayed themes of fertility (Stinson 2005).

Estrella and Sweetwater (AD 650–700)

In addition to increased village size, Hohokam life during the Estrella and Sweetwater phases saw a decreased use of red-slipped pottery and the adoption or invention of red-on-grey pottery types, including animal and human effigy vessels that carried through the remaining Hohokam sequence. It is debatable whether these two brief phases should be considered distinct because, for instance, they are differentiated largely by slight ceramic design shifts that probably persisted for little more than a generation each (Wallace 2001). During the Estrella, potters began grooving the exteriors of some red-on-grey vessels, providing a visual allusion to coil-and-scrape technologies employed by contemporaneous

Pueblo and Mogollon peoples to the north and east. Lifeform designs in a negative layout were a notable innovation in symbolism during the subsequent Sweetwater. In addition to these technological and stylistic changes in pottery, Doyel (1991a:243) observed that in the course of this "red-on-grey horizon" the ratio of Big Houses to regular pithouses increased, yet the size of the average Big House decreased. He suggested that this may proxy increasing community segmentation and socio-political factioning within villages.

Snaketown (AD 700–750)

The Snaketown phase may best be considered a period of "firsts" (Doyel 1991a). It was an era when the first trash mounds, low rises that would come to serve as ritual stages in later times, were raised at Snaketown. The decorated pottery assemblage included a new red-on-buff type alongside the red-on-greys, while Vahki Redware became all but obsolete. Some Snaketown Red-on-buff pottery continued to be grooved but in increasingly inconsistent and haphazard ways. Largely abstract and geometric pottery designs of the prior centuries persisted, but rare instances of lifeforms painted in a *positive* layout began to adorn pots. At Snaketown, villagers excavated large roasting pits along the periphery of the central plaza. This may evidence a new mode of communal ceremonial feasting, or perhaps the addition of a sahuaro wine festival akin to those among the O'odham (Lumholtz 1912; Mason 1920) to the Hohokam ritual cycle. On the whole, the Snaketown phase was a sprightly time of social experimentation and ritual innovation that laid the foundation for a subsequent religious reorganization and the formalization of a network of intervillage relationships tied to and substantiated by a ritual ballgame.

Colonial Period

The onset of the Colonial period marks one of the cardinal transitions in Hohokam society. This period saw many of the distinctive symbols of Hohokamness that arose in the Pioneer become commonplace in peripheral regions. A broadly shared social identity across a large swath of what is now central and southern Arizona seems to have coalesced, perhaps signaled through micaceous buffware pottery and *Glycymeris* shell jewelry. New villages were founded as existing ones grew in size, and such demographic growth in the Phoenix Basin was spurred and sustained by an expansion of the irrigation system (e.g., Howard and Huckleberry 1991). Fieldhouses became a ubiquitous feature in the irrigated landscape (Henderson and Clark 2004) and likely attest to an organizational change in land allocation and tenure practices within or among villages. The focus of communal architecture broadened from plazas and the large, square Big Houses of prior centuries to include the highly visible circular earthworks of ballcourts and caliche-capped trash mounds.

Although they were diminished in size, the persistence of Big Houses into the Colonial suggests that the segmented nature of village leadership continued to organize communities. At Grewe much of the new Colonial flair was concentrated in and around Big Houses (Craig 2000), a further indication that these structures housed a low-order network of economic, political, and possibly religious authority or governance. There was also an upsurge in the consumption of shell jewelry procured from the West Mexican coast, and some of the more exquisite pieces may have been insignia for new political or religious associations or offices (Bayman 2002). Altogether, Hohokam communities of the Colonial witnessed rapid population growth across multiple ecological zones and concomitant innovations and transformations in the ritual system, socio-political organization, and social identity. It was the beginning of what many consider "Hohokam," and this time it sprang from the Phoenix Basin.

Gila Butte (AD 750–900)

During the Gila Butte phase the Hohokam elaborated some aspects of their material culture and accepted a number of significant additions. Potters infused ceramic iconography with an assortment of new lifeforms, now in both negative and positive relief, and a new suite of geometric elements, many with clear similarities to pottery designs from northwestern Mexico. Direct importation of exotic and esoteric goods from West Mexico, such as pyrite mirrors, reinforces notions of a Mesoamerican connection. Discrete cemeteries in plazas for cremation burials, which had come to involve secondary interment in urns, indicate that the mortuary ritual had become increasingly formalized and theatrical. Communities also commenced erecting a network of large, bermed ballcourts of a Mesoamerican inspiration. An incipient market system, which helped move buffware pottery, shell jewelry, and other tokens of Hohokamness, likely followed on the coattails of this ballcourt network as it spread throughout southern Arizona (Abbott et al. 2007; see also Wilcox and Sternberg 1983:213). To complement ballcourts, at some point in the Gila Butte phase villagers started capping trash mounds with caliche, thus cementing their position as central pillars of the Hohokam village.

Even though some of the material hallmarks of the Gila Butte had antecedents in the Pioneer period, it was during this early portion of the Colonial that they "assume[d] a much more cohesive character" (Wallace et al. 1995:606). It was not one artifact type or architectural form alone, but the suite of new concepts and organizational schemes with Mesoamerican and West Mexican qualities that defines the Gila Butte. That these major social and religious innovations caught fire and rapidly spread throughout communities far and wide shows that Hohokam villagers not only accepted what had developed in the Pioneer but in fact welcomed the entirely new worldview, identity, economy, and organizational structure that soon followed (Wallace 2014; Wallace and Lindeman 2003, 2012, 2013).

Santa Cruz (AD 850–950)

Changes in ritual practice under way during the Gila Butte continued and perhaps intensified in the Santa Cruz phase. At Snaketown a crematory floor was built over an existing communal cooking area, perhaps uniting feasting, fire, death, and the ancestors in the memories of the villagers through richly sensual mortuary rituals. The cremation ritual seemingly grew in complexity as well, as the quantity and diversity of grave goods magnified. By the end of the Santa Cruz, Big Houses had become relics of the past. Nevertheless, greater separation in material wealth among both households and cremations (Craig 2000) reveals that village leadership probably remained segmented, but social checks and balances kept potential aggrandizers from amassing substantial and conspicuous sums of valuables.

Sedentary Period

The Sedentary period, made up solely of the Sacaton phase (~AD 900–1150), is now considered by many to have been the florescence of Hohokam life (Abbott 2003b:202; see also Gladwin et al. 1937:260). During this gilded age the Phoenix Basin Hohokam reconfigured their irrigation system (Howard 1991), and many canals reached their maximum extent (Nichols and Neitzel 1984). At its height in the Sacaton the canal network in the Salt River valley spanned several hundred kilometers; some of the main distribution canals measured up to 20 m wide and 6 m deep (Masse 1991). The ritual ballgame also reached its pinnacle, and extensive networks of production and exchange had developed to usher prestige goods and commodities such as pottery, shell jewelry, obsidian, and groundstone tools across physical and social boundaries and between ecological zones (Crown 1991b). The Sedentary period, however, was not one of gradual growth, development, and maturation of a regional system but rather a turning point in the lifeways and memories of Hohokam villagers. Indeed, the Sedentary encompasses both the height of its cultural florescence and the beginning of the end for the Hohokam world.

At some early Sacaton villages small ballcourts were raised alongside earlier and larger ones, typically at opposed orientations, suggesting an increase in the complexity of the ritual cycle as well as inter- and intravillage competition and cooperation. By the middle Sacaton, the ballcourt network had expanded to its greatest breadth, with at least 238 courts among 194 villages (Fish and Fish 2007:Map 3; Marshall 2001:120). Household investment in residential facilities varied (Craig 2000), and distinct social segments within villages, above the level of the courtyard group, began to bury their dead together in cemeteries (Henderson 1987). These spatial distinctions in death likely corresponded with social differences during life, perhaps tied to social status or corporate association delineated through consanguine and fictive kinships such as clans, phratries, or sodalities. Whereas members of these communities appear to have continued a process of segmentation in identity and wealth that had been stewing for several centuries—as witnessed by increased variability in high-valued items among households and burials and the splintering of the central communal cemeteries into ones spatially associated with village segments—crematory death rituals continued to symbolically erase those differences on death (McGuire 1992b).

The capped mounds of prior times continued to be built and recapped in the Sacaton, and the suite of public architecture at Snaketown had by then been arranged along cardinal directions and fully encircled the central plaza. Also at Snaketown, villagers erected a palisade around Mound 16, a precursor to Classic period public architecture (see below). As for pottery, red-slipped vessels, absent since the early Pioneer, were resurrected to complement a fairly standardized set of household buffware vessels (Abbott et al. 2001). Throughout the Sacaton, lifeforms and other figurative designs depicted on pottery declined until they virtually disappeared from the lexicon by AD 1150. They were gradually replaced with abstract and complex rectilinear patterns reminiscent of woven basketry (Wallace 2004). Even though the vast majority of red-on-buff pottery in earlier times was crafted at villages along the middle Gila River and exchanged outward (Kelly 2013), in the first half of the Sacaton production of this key token of Hohokam identity increased substantially and its reach expanded considerably (Abbott 2000; Wilcox 1999).

The latter half of the Sacaton, circa AD 1050–1150, witnessed a series of notable social transformations that would cascade through the following centuries. This era of abrupt changes in regional demography, public architecture, social organization, ritual objects, and religious iconography had once been singled out as a unique phase, the Santan, in the cultural sequence (Doyel 2000a).[2] Around AD 1070, communities in small regions (e.g., the New River and lower Verde River drainages) disassociated themselves from events (or people) in the core area, and several major villages (e.g., Snaketown and Grewe), once persistent places in the Hohokam world, reorganized or withered while significant population growth occurred elsewhere (e.g., Gila Bend, Grand Canal, Adamsville) (Doyel 1993, 2000a). This signals that considerable demographic restructuring was under way, yet continued residence near some long-established villages (e.g., Las Colinas and Casa Grande near Grewe) reveals that village history and ancestral ties to land were still vital parts of community life and identity. Indeed, though the irrigation network was reengineered (Howard 2006; Woodson 2010), daily life in the Phoenix Basin continued to flow along the same canals built hundreds of years before.

During the mercurial late Sacaton, platform mounds—a new form of public architecture that would come to dominate the Classic period domestic landscape—were raised alongside ballcourts (Gregory 1987). Abbott and colleagues (2007:471) find little evidence that traditional use of ballcourts continued past AD 1070. Nonetheless, ballcourts remained prominent features on the domestic landscape, and although the ballgame may have ceased to be a central communal ritual, it persisted in the villagers' social memories.[3] Along with demographic and architectural tumults, the distribution of red-on-buff pottery diminished and the production of plainware—once undertaken by specialists at select villages who traded or sold their wares to other communities along common social ties—became highly localized (Abbott 2000, 2009). This shift reveals that the market-like system that shuffled vital goods and information throughout the Hohokam world, and perhaps even farther, languished and waned, quite possibly in response to the demise of the ballcourt network. These reconfigurations in social organization, village structure, and economic relations mark a turning point from the past and transformation into a very different social world.

Classic Period

The Hohokam Classic period denotes one of the most notable social transformations in the Greater Southwest, as villagers turned their backs on many of the long-held traditions of the previous 500 years and even several extending back to the ancestral communities of the Red Mountain phase (or earlier?) in the Phoenix Basin and elsewhere. To fill the void, many looked to and found answers in late Sedentary innovations (e.g., palisaded mounds) or entirely new phenomena (e.g., polychrome pottery). Nonetheless, the demographic trends of the Sacaton continued as residents of long-established villages packed their wares and moved up-canal, yet entirely new but short-lived communities sprouted up elsewhere too, such as at Marana (Fish et al. 1992). Over several centuries a cataclysm of deleterious events and compounding stressors—floods, warfare, malnutrition, and poor leadership—ultimately won out and closed this chapter in the Hohokam historical trajectory.

Abbott and colleagues (2003) succinctly characterize these "centuries of decline" as follows: (1) a movement from pithouse courtyard groups to aboveground contiguous masonry and adobe roomblocks and compounds; (2) a shift from ballcourts to platform mounds as the focus of public architecture and village life; (3) declines in intervillage migration and increased aggregation at certain villages coincident with an overall population reduction throughout the region (see also Hill et al. 2004); (4) the replacement of red-on-buff pottery with red-slipped wares and later imported polychrome vessels; (5) the addition of inhumations (or rejection of cremations) into the mortuary ritualism; and (6) the jettison of a suite of ritual paraphernalia in use since the Colonial period. Communities of the Classic period social world also experienced an overall decrement in health (Sheridan 2003; Smith and Rice 2009), a shift in socially recognized gender roles (Crown and Fish 1996), and perhaps endemic warfare (Wilcox 2005; Wilcox and Holmlund 2007; Wilcox et al. 2001a, 2001b). These changes, however, were not coeval, and the Classic period has thus been divided into the following two phases.

Soho (AD 1125–1300)

During the Soho, typical Hohokam domiciles underwent a sequence of transitions from pithouses to narrow-walled adobe pithouses, then to aboveground adobe and masonry structures arranged in rectangular patterns, and finally to compounds surrounded by precinct walls (Abbott et al. 1994; Abbott and Foster 2003). The number of inhumation burials surpassed that of cremations, and there was a continued pattern of disproportionate amounts of grave goods between burials and among cemeteries within villages (e.g., Mitchell 2003; Watkins and Rice 2009). Red-slipped pottery, often burnished, became the dominant decorated pottery type at the expense of red-on-buffs, although the latter persisted in low frequencies (i.e., Casa Grande Red-on-buff). Like decorated buffwares of earlier eras, this new redware was used for interring the ashes of those few villagers who held onto the tradition of ritual cremation.

Rectangular platform mounds, some enclosed by palisades, became the normative form of public architecture in the Soho (e.g., Gregory 1991; Gregory et al. 1988); at that time in the Phoenix Basin the mounds had little to no architecture on them aside from an occasional oversized pithouse (Downum and Bostwick 2003). These large pitstructures may have been communal features, elite residences, or something else entirely. Not much is known about these early platform mounds since few have been excavated and later remodeling events of the moundtops obliterated or obfuscated the Soho contexts. At new villages platform mounds were raised anew, but at previously established villages some, if not all, were built over and enclosed older and smaller late Sedentary mounds (Downum and Bostwick 2003; Gregory 1987, 1988). Soho-era platform mounds, as revealed at Las Colinas in the Salt River valley, for example, were part of distinct precincts within villages with a patterned arrangement of structures around them (e.g., Gregory 1988).

By the Soho, many villages and settlement clusters in the northern periphery of the Phoenix Basin, from west of the Salt-Gila confluence to the lower Agua Fria and Verde Rivers, had emptied out and a defensive network of hilltop forts, lookouts, and fortified pueblos had risen in their wake (Wilcox et al. 2001a, 2007, 2008). Social conflict was reaching new heights across much of the Southwest (LeBlanc 1999; Rice and LeBlanc 2001), and in the Hohokam world northern friends may have turned into enemies, a break in social relations that would continue to escalate.

Civano (AD 1300–1425)

One of the defining features of the Civano is the importation of Salado polychrome vessels (Abbott 2000:78–79) linked with religious and social transformations originating in the Mogollon Highlands to the north, the Tonto Basin to the east, and the upper Gila River region to the southeast of the Phoenix Basin (Crown 1994; Dean 2000). By this time platform mounds had radiated outward but were refashioned to meet local needs in peripheral regions (Doelle et al. 1995). There are 125 platform mounds known from 95 villages in the Phoenix, Tonto, and Tucson Basins; the San Pedro Valley; and the Papaguería (Elson 2007:52; Fish and Fish 2007: Map 4). Instead of large pithouses, walled-in compounds were built on Civano phase platform mounds (Gregory 1991), possibly as a product of continued social stratification between individuals, groups, and lineages. Likewise, at Las Colinas and probably elsewhere, large compound walls were built around the platform mounds (Gregory 1987, 1988), thus quarantining the central precinct from the larger community.

There is general agreement that these moundtop compounds housed something special, but what that was remains controversial. Some researchers see them as stages for communal events such as public rituals, feasts, or other large social gatherings, whereas others interpret them as residences for an elite class (priesthoods, clans, ruling families? see Elson and Abbott 2000). Both camps largely agree, however, that the moundtops had become the central stage for village ritualism and the seats of religious authority. The expansion in moundtop architecture culminated with a handful of engineering marvels, including the erection of the Casa Grande (Wilcox and Shenk 1977), another multistoried structure at Pueblo Grande, and a few others elsewhere in the Phoenix Basin during the final years (Doelle et al. 1995; Wallace 2009). To the north the hilltop defensive network along the middle and upper Agua Fria River of the prior century fell out of use around AD 1250. Concerns over warfare, however, escalated as people massed into larger villages on and around Perry Mesa and in the lower Verde River watershed. Wilcox (2005; Wilcox and Holmlund 2007; Wilcox et al. 2001a, 2001b, 2007, 2008) believes these northern villages made up a "Verde Confederacy" that was "organized for war" against late Classic communities in the Phoenix Basin. Population massing and continued aggregation at the largest villages in the Phoenix Basin created a wide buffer zone between the northern uplands and southern river valleys. The northern villagers buffered themselves from the Phoenix Basin communities as well as from their past social identities as they shed long-held ritual practices and tokens of cultural identity, including a prior sense of Hohokamness, in favor of a blank cultural slate (Russell 2014; Russell et al. 2011).

The Post-Classic

The fifteenth century witnessed the end of the Hohokam world as it previously existed. A chain of massive floods followed by a decade-long drought in the late 1300s (Graybill et al. 2006), continued environmental degradation (James 2003; Kwiatkowski 2003), chronic population decrease (Hill et al. 2004), and rancorous social conflict (Oliver 2001; Rice 2001; Wallace and Doelle 2001; Wilcox et al. 2001b) across the Hohokam world had taken their toll, and the final years must have been a time of suffering (Abbott 2003b; Anderies 2006; Hegmon et al. 2008). While O'odham oral histories offer epic accounts of these final years that map onto the archaeological picture quite well (Bahr et al. 1994; Teague 1993), details of the mysterious societal quietus that followed remain unclear. In some Classic period villages pithouses were built over the top of Civano phase compounds (Chenault 1996, 2000) and along village peripheries (Henderson and Hackbarth 2000), evidencing a continued visitation to, if not occupation of, these withering settlements. This phase, the Polvorón, remains controversial since there is little unambiguous chronological evidence for it, and what is available may be contemporaneous with Civano era contexts. The high frequency of Salado pottery in Polvorón pithouses further muddles the picture.

It is hard to conceive of once-vibrant river valleys, home to tens of thousands of people for over a thousand years, becoming completely bereft of life after the dissolution of the platform mound communities (however, consider the case in the northern Southwest [Kohler et al. 2010]). A significant yet incomplete depopulation could have entailed a considerable "downsizing" of the settlement system and its social organization, and the amounts, types, and distribution of artifacts and residences would thus be radically different from those of prior centuries. There very well may have been a post-Classic human presence or transience in the Phoenix Basin, but light and diffuse settlement patterns, high residential mobility, perhaps seasonal occupation, and insignificant impacts to the landscape limit our ability to see it (see Wells et al. 2004). Details of this archaeological hiatus between the fall of the Hohokam platform-mound villages and the O'odham rancherías described by sixteenth- and seventeenth-century Spanish entradas may remain murky for some time (e.g., Reff 1991; Wells 2006; see also Wilcox 2010:116–122).

Social transformations in Hohokam history were both gradual and rapid. The pace of change can be considered a slow transmutation from dispersed, small-scale villages practicing incipient farming strategies to complexly organized, large-scale villages invested in intensive canal-irrigation agriculture with overt social differences materialized in architecture and village layout. This long, accumulative history was punctuated by the rapid spread of revolutionary and novel concepts introduced during the early Gila Butte, the equally rapid desertion of long-held traditions during the late Sacaton, an overhaul of the ritual system and the rise of a new social order in the Soho, and eventually the rejection of the Hohokam lifeway and dissolution of once-flourishing communities at the tail end of the Civano. Ritual and religion clearly factored into this historical trajectory from the villages' rise to their demise, but the extent to which they were wielded as tools for social transformation remains in question. In the next section I review various interpretations of Hohokam religion in order to illuminate some of the religious principles and themes by which the Hohokam organized themselves in relation to the natural order. This sets the stage for understanding Hohokam ritual practice, a topic I address at the end of this chapter.

Hohokam Religion

Religion has been an underlying theme in Hohokam studies since the Hemenway expedition in 1887. Frank Cushing's (1890) excavations at Pueblo de los Muertos and Fewkes's (1912) at Casa Grande led them to interpret much about the Hohokam through ethnographic analogies to Pueblo religion and custom. Although never fully explicated, the Mesoamerican migration hypothesis that emerged in the mid-twentieth century implied that the Hohokam adhered to a watered-down Mesoamerican-like religion. As Haury (1976:348) professed, "the filtering system must have been a combination of lessening of cultural values and meanings and a function of distance" that left "faint echoes" of Mesoamerican religious and political systems among the Hohokam. Religion has since emerged as an explicit topic in Hohokam archaeology, and researchers have proposed a number of models, most of which either build on the underlying Mesoamerican themes materialized in Hohokam artifacts, architecture, and village structure (e.g., Doyel 2000a; Feinman 1991:465–470; Mills et al. 2013; Preucel 1996; Wallace 2014; Wallace and Lindeman 2003, 2013; Wallace et al. 1995; Wilcox 1987a, 1991a, 1991b; Wilcox and Shenk 1977; Wilcox et al. 1981; Wright and Russell 2011) or draw direct interpretive parallels to Mesoamerican religion (e.g., Bostwick et al. 2009; Whittlesey 2004, 2007). These are summarized below.

After intensive reexaminations of Snaketown and Casa Grande, David Wilcox (1987a; Wilcox et al. 1981; see also Wilcox 1991a, 1991b, Wilcox and Shenk 1977; Wilcox and Sternberg 1983) adapted Marvin Cohodas's (1975) concept of the Mesoamerican Cosmological Metastructure (MCM) to explain the Hohokam scenario. This religious structure emphasized agriculture and fertility, lauded celestial deities, centered the world along four cardinal directions, and divided the universe into a tiered cosmos. These vertical and horizontal divisions of the world were integrated via the annual solar cycle, which also set the tempo of the ritual system and scheduled important ritual activities, such as ballgames and feasts. Along these lines, certain places in the natural landscape—springs, mountains, cracks in rocks, caves, outcroppings, and trees—served as an *axis mundi*, or liminal place between the middle, lower, and upper worlds. Color symbolism, cremation ritual, and a quartered division of the world as materialized in pottery layouts and village arrangements were part and parcel of this metastructure. Wilcox (1987a) suggested that local nuances of the MCM were evident in the mythologies, ritual systems, and belief structures of historic indigenous Southwestern communities from northern New Mexico to the lower Colorado River valley, and that qualities of it are discernible in the artifacts, architecture, and village layouts of Ancestral Pueblo and Hohokam peoples. This religious framework was presumably in place by the end of the Pioneer period, when the Mesoamerican connection became most readily apparent. Robert Preucel (1996) has referred to a very similar pan-Southwest religious structure as a "Mesoamerican Worldview."

Subsequent models of Hohokam religion have touched on different aspects of the MCM. For example, Doyel (1992, 2000a) proposed a "Rainbow Way" cult for the Hohokam that expanded thematic interpretation through a close look at artifacts and iconography. Along with the currents of the MCM, Doyel recognized water as an important theme, given the ubiquitous presence of what he took as water symbolism in iconography and other realms of decorative material culture, including the prevalence of reflective materials in ritual objects—mica schist as a tempering agent in buffware and redware pottery, the use of schist and phyllite in items like palettes, and the presence of pyrite mosaic mirrors. According to Doyel's model, the Rainbow Way persisted into the Classic period, but the "cult" reorganized and augmented its iconography with mythical serpent symbolism depicted on Salado polychromes.

Wallace (2014; Wallace and Lindeman 2003, 2012, 2013; Wallace et al. 1995) offers a more particular and chronologically detailed rendition of the MCM. He suggests that the appearance of many Mesoamerican-inspired ritual practices was rather abrupt and likens it to a Hohokam Revitalization Movement (HRM; see also Lekson's [2008] "Hohokam Canon"). According to the HRM model, a religious revitalization in the Gila Butte phase was initiated by a few charismatic people who sought esoteric religious knowledge from Mesoamerica and brought new ideas, such as the ballgame, and possessions back to Hohokam villages. These sojourners to the south were probably existing religious leaders who endeavored to revitalize their weakened authority and waning power in the face of the severe floods, long droughts, and spectacular solar phenomena that transpired in the late 700s. Over a few generations, communities reconfigured this religious base to suit local needs, but as the demise of ballcourt ritualism attests, the revitalization wore off during the Sedentary period and was replaced with a new mode of platform mound ceremonialism.

The HRM is a powerful model of the Preclassic religious structure because it explains why some Hohokam ritual practices have roots extending to the Archaic while others seemingly burst onto and across the Colonial period social landscape, and why regional nuances in ritual paraphernalia and architecture took hold during the Sedentary period. It is a notable shift from earlier models because it positions people—aspiring religious leaders and their adherents—as the agents of social change rather than vague, external, population-dependent processes such as information flow and resource depletion. The transition to the Classic period, however, and what that entailed in terms of religion, ritual, and social organization, remains unexplained by a Colonial period religious revitalization.

The MCM model of Hohokam religion, and derivations of it, are examples of what I consider particularistic structuralism, as discussed in the previous chapter. This approach is both convincing and appealing because it establishes a rudimentary religious structure that contextualizes forms and patterns we see and read into material culture without providing direct interpretations of religious content and ritual performance. Unlike strictly interpretive methods and direct historical and ethnographic analogies, particularistic structural models provide nascent themes of ritual and religion rather than interpretations of symbols, reconstructions of myths, or identifications of deities. Other particularistic structural models have been proposed to explain religious commonalities between Mesoamerica and the Southwest, and thus bear on Hohokam religion to a degree.[4] These include the Flower World (Hays-Gilpin and Hill 1999, 2000; Hill 1992; see also Taube 2001), the Mesoamerican Rain Cult (Schaafsma and Taube 2006), and the Southwestern Cult (Crown 1994).

The Flower World links Uto-Aztecan speakers, the Maya, and Pueblo peoples through a shared lexicon of conceptual metaphors and verbal art with an Archaic linguistic base. Flowers, central to this model, are metaphors for religious concepts such as the soul, heart, and spirit world. The Flower World is materialized in flower, rainbow, bird, and butterfly symbolism in various media, including rock art and pottery designs. Like the Flower World, the Mesoamerican Rain Cult is argued to be an Archaic religious structure, but it is specifically concerned with weather control and associated with maize agriculture. Schaafsma and Taube (2006; see also Taube 2000) suggest that it accompanied the spread of agriculture and/or farmers as they moved out of the proto-Mesoamerican world and into the Greater Southwest. Rain Cult symbolism includes clouds, lightning, corn plants, and the sort. Though considered a much more recent religious movement, the Southwestern Cult too emphasized water, as evidenced by the florescence of feathered- and horned-serpent imagery and outlined crosses, designs reminiscent of symbols of the Mesoamerican rain and fertility deity Quetzalcoatl, on Salado and Ramos polychromes (Crown 1994:166; Schaafsma 2001; however, see Phillips et al. 2006). The Southwestern Cult could feasibly be understood as a blend of Pueblo, Mogollon, and Hohokam religious principles concerning water with a splash of exotic Mesoamerican symbolism. It should be pointed out that these proposed religious cults, movements, and worldviews, as well as others considered more Pueblo-specific (i.e., the Katsina Cult [Adams 1991] and the Kiva Cult [Kidder and Guernsey 1919]), were not necessarily bounded religious structures or institutions but could rather have been variations on the same religious themes at different scales (contra T. VanPool et al. 2006). In fact, Hayes-Gilpin and Hill (1999), for example, see elements of the Flower World in symbolism of both the Salado and Katsina Cults.

Symbolism serves as the primary archaeological indicia for participation in the Rain and Southwestern Cults or adherence to a Flower World epistemology. There is, however, little to no iconographic evidence of the Flower World epistemology in Hohokam symbolism (see also Mills et al. 2013). "Hohokam people do not appear to have represented this complex in their surviving visual arts until after AD 1300, if at all" (Hayes-Gilpin and Hill 1999:4). There is further very little crossover between key motifs in Rain Cult symbolism, such as stepped clouds, and elements in Hohokam iconography; and as discussed below, participation in a Southwestern Cult by the Phoenix Basin Hohokam, as would be attested to by the production and consumption of Salado polychromes, awaits clarification. It is premature to say that Phoenix Basin Hohokam communities did not play a role in these religious structures and movements, but as it stands now there is little *visual* evidence to suggest that they ever caught on to any great extent.

The Mesoamerican Cosmological Metastructure, and nuances of it such as the Rainbow Way and the Hohokam Revitalization Movement, currently provide the best formula for

Hohokam religion. The various themes recognized in this religious metastructure include an importance of animals, color symbolism, ancestor veneration, fertility, water, smoke, directional symbolism and a tiered cosmos, ballgames, intoxication, and fire as a mode of transformation. These themes allow us to contextualize the symbols and ritual practices that were the arenas in which religious knowledge was acquired and showcased. I outline the architectural and artifactual signatures of these ritual practices in the following section.

Hohokam Ritual Practice

Ritual practices may leave anomalous and patterned material traces, and while ritual and religion have only recently become serious research topics, Hohokam archaeologists have long acknowledged that an array of architectural forms and artifacts supported an elaborate and well-developed ritual system. In the next section I describe a range of public architectural features generally acknowledged as stages for ritual performances, and I then review a suite of artifacts that evidence those ritual practices. Accordingly, the spatio-temporal distribution of such items, and how and the extent to which access to these and the stages of their accompanying performances (i.e., ritual architecture) was controlled, proxy the organization of religious knowledge in Hohokam communities.

Ritual Architecture

The Hohokam built several types of edifices to host ritual performances, some with more revealing and compelling indications than others. This constellation of ritual architecture may include the large pithouses of the Pioneer period often referred to as either Big Houses or communal houses (Gladwin and Gladwin 1948; Wallace 2014; Wallace and Lindeman 2003, 2012, 2013; Wilcox et al. 1981). Likewise, some ritual performances were undertaken in the confines of domestic space (Aragon 2013; Stinson 2004, 2010; Thomas and King 1985). This review, however, outlines those conspicuous public works seemingly intended predominantly or specifically as stages for ritual performances.

Plazas

Plazas undoubtedly hosted an assortment of ritual performances, from communal dances to individual orations (Moore 1996; see also Chamberlin 2012). Ruscavage-Barz and Bagwell (2006) have made the case that Pueblo plazas were the loci of ritual performances as well as architectural metaphors of a middle world in the tiered cosmos of Amerind religions. Perhaps Hohokam plazas had similar symbolic importance; they were after all the center places of communities for hundreds of years and witnessed the gradual addition of large public earthworks and buildings around them. Plazas were surely stages for communal feasts, as evidenced by nearby large hornos and, at Snaketown, a row of roasting pits in a designated area of the plaza (Haury 1976; see also Wallace 2014). They were also the places prescribed for cremation rituals, which at Snaketown were enacted on large crematoria floors (Haury 1976:166–171) to an audience of community members. The cremated remains were also ritually interred in the plazas, a communal practice of ancestor veneration starting at least by the Pioneer period (Wallace and Lindeman 2003) and continuing throughout the Preclassic era. Indeed, Wallace (2014) suspects that plaza-oriented cemeteries and showy cremation rituals were common across much of the Preclassic Hohokam world.

Since they staged an array of highly sensual public and communal ritual practices, plazas were undoubtedly important places in the Hohokam social and ritual landscapes. Most research, however, has focused on monumental architectural forms—capped mounds, ballcourts, platform mounds, and multistory architecture—some of which required considerable investment of communal labor to construct, maintain, and remodel.

Capped Mounds

The first capped mounds date to the Colonial period, when trash mounds, some of which originated as trash pits but whose fill had breached their capacity (Haury 1976:Figure 6.6), were capped with layers of caliche. Haury (1976:82) originally reported that the capped Mound 40 at

Snaketown was built during the late Pioneer, but according to Craig (1988) and Wallace (2014:15n), Gila Butte sherds were found below the capping, indicating a Colonial period origin. Later, capped mounds were built with both refuse and sterile soil (e.g., Snaketown's Mound 39), and by the Sedentary period most appear to have been built entirely from clean desert sediments (e.g., Snaketown's Mound 16). Many mounds underwent multiple construction events in which they were expanded and heightened, each episode terminated, celebrated, and ritualized by a new cap of caliche.

Capped mounds were situated adjacent to plazas, and by the Sedentary period they evidence formal planning by virtue of the initial leveling of the moundtops. By the end of Snaketown's reign as an active civic center, sometime in the middle-to-late Sacaton, eight mounds, a combination of capped and other forms, encircled the plaza, perhaps bounding and centering it in relation to the four cardinal and four solar equinoctial directions (Wilcox et al. 1981). As elevated stages with formal surfaces, these mounds probably buttressed ritual performances on top of them and, like rostrums, they would have amplified the rituals' visual and auditory properties to accommodate groups of onlookers. Little evidence exists for what these performances might have entailed, but judging by comparable use of naturally elevated spaces among the O'odham, they may have staged ritual dancing (Haury 1976:93). Located in the village center, they would have been ideal settings for public addresses, including possibly ritual orations and singing, important ritual performances among the O'odham (Bahr 1986, 2001; Bahr and Haefer 1978; Bahr et al. 1973, 1979; Brown 1906; Darling 2006; Darling and Lewis 2007; Kozak and Lopez 1999; Russell 1908; Underhill 1938, 1946; Underhill et al. 1979).

Ballcourts

The ballcourt is one of the defining features, if not *the* defining feature, of Preclassic Hohokam village structure. Ballcourts were first raised at the beginning of the Colonial period, or perhaps slightly earlier in the final days of the Pioneer. These "ovals" of bermed sand and soil (and occasionally dry-laid masonry) have been known to Anglo-American explorers since at least the 1850s, when John Russell Bartlett (1854:275–276) likened one at Casa Grande to a corral. Adolf Bandelier noted their recurrence at several Hohokam villages during his early reconnaissance of the Southwest, but at the time he believed them to be large elliptical tanks for storing water (Bandelier 1884:69, 1892:404–469). Cushing later referred to those with openings at opposed ends as "reservoirs" and to fully enclosed versions as "Sun Temples" where the "Mythic Sun drama" and other theatrical "feats of Occult Medicine powers" were enacted or carried out (Cushing 1890:165–166). Haury (in Gladwin et al. 1937: 36–49; see also Haury 1937) later drew on commonalities to features in Mesoamerica to show that these large, open yet bounded places were in all likelihood ballcourts.[5] Five hundred people, a figure probably close to or more than the average Preclassic village population, could have stood along the rim of the large ballcourt at Snaketown (Doyel 1991a:249). However, while ballcourts could accommodate large audiences, perhaps even whole villages, they were equally exclusive because they would effectively block the view of people not on or within their embankments (Wilcox and Sternberg 1983).

As reviewed above, the ballcourt network was integral to the social and economic fabric of the Hohokam world. Ballcourts of the Colonial period tended to be oriented along an east-west axis; villagers began building smaller, north-south-aligned courts later during the Sacaton. Some of the smaller courts were built at villages that already had larger Colonial ones, but it is unclear if they were in operation at the same time. By the end of the Sacaton, the Hohokam rejected the ballcourt network as a means of community integration, ritual participation, and religious communion. The effects cascaded throughout the Hohokam world as the widespread exchange of goods across the region, facilitated by an incipient market economy tied to the ritual ballgame, also deteriorated and the outward signs of Hohokam identity retracted to the Phoenix Basin.

Platform Mounds

Platform mounds were a hallmark of Classic period communities across the Hohokam world (Doelle et al. 1995). These massively constructed, rectangular, leveled, and sheer-sided earthworks were the end product of a tradition of mound building that started in the Preclassic era (Gregory 1987, 1988).[6] Although several in the Phoenix Basin were built over earlier mounds (e.g., Downum and Bostwick 2003; Gregory 1987), platform mounds were not just capped mounds writ large; they differed in "*both* form and function" (Doelle et al. 1995:438, emphasis in original; see also Lekson 2008:169–171). Preclassic mounds were circular and probably used exclusively in ritual pursuits since they lack features atop them. Classic period platform mounds, on the other hand, were rectangular with architectural units atop them. Also, unlike earlier mounds, these platforms were slowly cordoned off from the rest of the village. For example, some early Classic platform mounds were encircled by palisades—like the Sedentary Mound 16 at Snaketown—and supported large pitstructures, perhaps the residences or workshops of privileged individuals, households, or social groups. By the end of the Soho, circa AD 1275, walled-in compounds were built atop platform mounds, and palisades gave way to full-on masonry and adobe compound walls around the mounds (e.g., Downum and Bostwick 2003; Gregory 1987, 1988; Hayden 1957; Wilcox 1987b).

There is no consensus on the use of mound-top compounds in the late Classic (Elson and Abbott 2000); some appear to have been elite residences whereas others may have been the periodic abodes of ritual specialists (e.g., Downum and Bostwick 2003; Gregory 1987; Lindauer 2000; Rice 1995, 2000). It is quite possible that platform mounds served different purposes at different times and places throughout the Hohokam world (Doelle et al. 1995:440), perhaps an architectural impression of the fractured nature of Hohokam social and economic organization that rippled through the landscape after the decline of the ballcourt network. What is evident is that starting in the late Sedentary, platform mounds took precedent over ballcourts as the primary ritual edifices within villages. These mounds lifted ritual performances and performers above the villages and, over time, the heads and grasps of the broader community. It started visually, as mound height blocked line of sight; then symbolically, as palisades and large pithouses delineated positions of ritual authority vis-à-vis relatively insubstantial and perhaps temporary blockades; and finally physically, as compounds and precinct walls barricaded the mounds. Platform mounds, then, were both symbols of and tools for the distancing of certain people, presumably ritual specialists and/or leading political actors, from the domestic landscape and average villagers.

Multistory Architecture

Multistory buildings, the latest and largest specimens of public architecture, are unique and perplexing monuments of the late Classic Hohokam world. They all date to the late 1300s, near the end of the Hohokam cultural sequence and long after the social, economic, and religious fervor surrounding the ballcourt network had soured. The best-known example is the Casa Grande, which still stands as a national monument along the middle Gila River (e.g., Fewkes 1892b, 1912; Mindeleff 1896, 1897; Wilcox and Shenk 1977; Wilcox and Sternberg 1981). The Casa Grande is four stories high, has walls several meters thick, and was raised in a single construction episode. Two other multistory edifices were built adjacent to the Casa Grande: the two-story Font's Room and the three-story Southwest Building. There is good evidence that three- or four-story structures were erected at other Classic period villages, including La Ciudad (Wilcox 1987b) and Pueblo Grande (Wilcox 1993); Cushing's (1890) description of Los Muertos, albeit rather romantic and fanciful, hints at the presence of another. Two-story versions are known from the Tonto Basin (Doelle et al. 1995) and probably once stood at Adamsville along the middle Gila River and at La Plaza del Tempe along the lower Salt River (Wallace 2009).

The immense size of some multistory buildings, their rarity and seemingly selective positioning in the Hohokam world, and their association with the largest late Classic villages suggest that they housed some sort of conspicuous and institutionalized authority, political and/or religious. Although little is known about them other than the Casa Grande, there is cause to believe they were centers for religious activities. For instance, Casa Grande's layout is reminiscent of directionally consecrated Hopi cornfields (Cushing 1892), and Wilcox (1987a:150) has speculated that the multiple stories and orientation may embed religious concepts of a tiered cosmos and cardinal-direction symbolism. There is scant evidence that the rooms were living quarters, and the upper "zenith" floor had architectural features designed for observing the sun and its annual cycle (Evans and Hillman 1981; Opperman 1979, 1980). In the eighteenth century O'odham villagers related the following account to the Jesuit friar Pedro Font: "To light the rooms there is nothing but the doors, and some round holes in the middle of the walls that face east and west—the Indians said that through these holes, which are fairly large, the prince, whom they call 'the bitter man,' used to watch the sun at its rising and setting in order to salute it" (Teggart 1913:23). There is also reasonable evidence that some late Classic, single-story compounds atop platform mounds too had architectural features engineered for astronomical observance (e.g., Downum and Bostwick 2003; Howard 1995; Jacobs 1992).

Experiencing Hohokam Ritual Architecture

Public architecture, and the rituals held upon and within it, underwent a series of changes throughout the Hohokam cultural sequence. In the earliest villages public ritual space was centered largely in the plazas and cemeteries. During the Colonial period villagers began constructing both elevated (capped mounds) and subterranean (ballcourts) stages for particular ritual performances, all the while continuing to use plazas for others, such as feasting and mortuary rites. This pattern persisted, and the corollary ritual system was enriched with the accretion of new mounds and ballcourts. The complexity and formality of the Preclassic village layout came to a head in the Sedentary period; by that time Snaketown's central plaza was encircled by eight mounds with nearby ballcourts to the west and east. This symbolically tiered quality of the ritual landscape—ballcourt as underworld, plaza as middleworld, and mound as upperworld—and the gradual enclosing of the plaza through the Colonial and Sedentary periods seem to indicate a religiously inspired organizational principle of Hohokam society (Wilcox 1987a; Wilcox et al. 1981). From our gaze the Preclassic ritual system, at least as seen through public architecture, was mostly open, visible, and participatory. Ritual performances often involved large numbers of performers or spectators, perhaps even whole communities at times, and the ritual system fully engaged the participants' and audiences' senses; many rituals were intended to be seen and heard (i.e., oration and the ballgame), others tasted (i.e., feasting and intoxication) or smelled (i.e., cremation), and some felt (i.e., dancing).

The Sedentary/Classic transition witnessed the rejection of ballcourts as the heart of community ritualism, followed by the centralization of ritual performance on top of platform mounds and behind compound walls. This was an overt move from relatively open and fluid to increasingly guarded and restricted access to religious symbolism and ritual performance (Howard 1992). Elements of this transition—although "schism" may be a more apt characterization—actually began during the Preclassic with, for example, the erection of a palisade around Snaketown's Mound 16, and peaked near the end of the Classic with the enclosing of platform-mound precincts with thick adobe walls and the raising of multistory buildings. These trends in monumental architectural form and village structure intimate that communities always concentrated ritual space within portions of the village, but over time access to religious knowledge through ritual participation or spectatorship became increasingly circumscribed, separated from the broader community. This organizational shift in ritual privilege and religious knowledge is readily acknowledged to have underscored fundamental differences in the Preclassic lifeways and style of socio-political organization from those of the

Classic period (e.g., Bayman 2001, 2002; Downum and Bostwick 2003; Doyel 1991a, 2000a, 2007; Gregory 1991; Howard 2006; Neitzel 1991; Preucel 1996; Wilcox 1987a, 1991b, 1991c).

Ritual Paraphernalia

This section reviews the myriad of tools wielded in Hohokam ritual practices, the array of exotic, unusual, and seemingly non-utilitarian objects we usually regard as symbolic or artistic in nature (see Chapter 2). A considerable amount of research has addressed the production, consumption, and distribution of exotic materials, such as shell, obsidian, turquoise, and steatite, across the Hohokam world (e.g., Bayman 1996; Bradley 1996; Doyel 1991b, 1996; Kisselburg 1987; McGuire and Howard 1987; Neitzel 1991; Nelson 1991; Stone 2003). Such exotic objects likely had a more than material significance to the Hohokam, perhaps functioning as costly displays of status (Bleige Bird and Smith 2005) within a prestige goods economy (Bayman 2002). These valued items may have had religious importance as well, or life histories that bridged domestic and ritual domains (Walker 1995). I nevertheless focus this review on those items with clear connections to ritual actions (see also Mills et al. 2013; Wallace 2014).

Anthropomorphic Figurines

Anthropomorphic figurines are one of the best-documented specimens of ritual paraphernalia in the Hohokam world (e.g., Aragon 2013; Chenault and Lindly 2006; Foster and James 2004; Haury 1976; Morss 1954; Stinson 2004, 2010; Thomas and King 1985; Wilcox and Sternberg 1983). These ceramic figurines effigize women, men, and children as well as flute players and ballgame players (Stinson 2004). Haury (1976) proposed an evolutionary design sequence for Hohokam figurines, but Susan Stinson (2004:85) points out that there was little change between the early Pioneer and late Colonial periods. Since figurines were most often disposed of on house floors or in domestic trash pits during the Pioneer, Haury (1976) suggested they were used symbolically within households for fertility and general well-being. With the onset of the Colonial, however, figurines started to complement the mortuary ritual, following people through the crematory fires. This prompted Haury to suggest they took on a symbolism of spirits that accompanied people into the afterlife. Similarly, Wilcox and Sternberg (1983) posited that anthropomorphic figurines after the Pioneer were part of a cultural practice of ritualized ancestor veneration. Thomas and King (1985) provided an alternative view, seeing the production process, not necessarily the final product, as central to figurine importance.

Stinson's (2004, 2010) reanalysis of the Grewe and Snaketown figurine assemblages found common ground among these earlier interpretations. According to her, anthropomorphic figurines were crafted by women and men within households during the Pioneer and Colonial periods as part of a regional cult focused on ancestor veneration. Small-scale production and consumption within the domicile unified households and kin groups through the memorialization of their ancestors and linked lineages to places and possessions. Over time, figurine use was increasingly concentrated within wealthier households, suggesting to Stinson (2004:197–198) that these higher-status families were more concerned with and invested more effort and resources into maintaining ties to land and possessions.

In the Colonial period, figurines took the shape of hollow-head molds lacking torsos and limbs, and their faces portray greater degrees of realism. Their primary mode of deposition also shifted from domestic refuse to cremation burials. Ancestor veneration was likely still a factor in their significance, since they were interred with the dead, but its relationship to the domicile and death was modified in some way. This new context of deposition implies that figurine use moved from the relative seclusion of domestic space in the Pioneer to public display during cremation ceremonies in later times.

At some time during the Sedentary, probably in the latter half, anthropomorphic figurines ceased to be produced or consumed altogether, signaling an outright dismissal of this tradition and underscoring a transformation in the religious lives of Hohokam communities. Nevertheless, ancestor veneration may very well have remained a key tenet of Hohokam religious structure into the Classic period. Drawing from cross-cultural ethnographic analogies, Mark Elson (1998) has made an interesting case for the rise of moundtop ritualism in the Classic as a form of ancestor veneration tied with claims to land and agricultural surpluses. If so, this suggests that the ritual practice of how ancestors were venerated metamorphosed from a communal ritual to one overseen, if not co-opted by, those privileged individuals or groups associated with platform mounds.

Zoomorphic Figurines

Ceramic zoomorphic figurines have been found at a number of Hohokam villages in contexts dating from the early Pioneer through the Classic period, but currently their limited distribution suggests that not all communities crafted or consumed them (Chenault and Lindly 2006:120). This may be a factor of sample size, or it could, in fact, imply that they held less religious significance in Hohokam social life than their anthropomorphic counterparts (Haury 1976:267). Animal forms include bighorn sheep and quail (Haury 1976:268; Stone and Foster 1994:250–252), but the vast majority are ambiguous quadrupedal shapes.[7] Cushing interpreted these as South American guanacos, and curiously provided the same interpretation for a series of quadruped petroglyphs in the South Mountains (Cushing 1890:178–179). It is more likely that they depict deer (Haury 1976:177), canids such as dogs or coyotes (Chenault and Lindly 2006; Foster and James 2004), or mountain sheep (Haury 1976:Figures 13.21 and 13.22), although the last-mentioned are incredibly rare. Haury (1976:267), who interpreted zoomorphic figurines as toys, described the Pioneer and Colonial versions as cruder and smaller than later forms.

During and after the Colonial period, zoomorphic figurines were crafted in the new buff-ware tradition, became larger and more detailed, and were sometimes painted (Haury 1976: 176–177, 267–268; Stone and Foster 1994). These changes in form and quality led Haury (1976) to posit that zoomorphic figurines took on a new, ritualized importance in the Colonial period. Their use seems to have been most prevalent during the Sedentary period (Chenault and Lindly 2006:Table 7.1), corresponding with the pinnacle in their craftsmanship. Zoomorphic figurines persisted into the Classic period but seemingly reverted to a pre-Sedentary state of quality (Haury 1976). Their rarity and occasional recovery from domestic refuse led Chenault and Lindly (2006) to suggest that they were symbols or insignia for a merchant class, but considering what we now know from Stinson's (2004) reanalysis of anthropomorphic figurines, deposition in domestic trash does not rule out ritual use or religious significance.

Palettes

The palette, one of the more transfixing elements of the Preclassic ritual toolkit, first came on the scene during the Pioneer period as a tabular stone and later as a rectangular tablet with raised borders (Haury 1976:286). Palettes were cut and ground from a number of raw stone materials, but reflective schist and phyllite were favored. During the Colonial some palettes were shaped into effigies of humans and animals and decorated with lifeform motifs (White 2004). Representational designs fell out of favor during the Sedentary, and palettes were no longer in use by the onset of the Classic. Palettes were most often disposed of in crematory contexts (Lowell 1990; White 2004), pointing toward an affinity with fire, death ritualism, and perhaps the afterlife or ancestor veneration.

Different perspectives on the use of palettes, prior to accompanying people through the crematory fires, have been offered. Florence Hawley (1937, 1942), having found traces of lead within chemical encrustations on a number of palettes, suggested that minerals were heated on them; this would have transformed the white lead into a strong orange/red-colored pigment in a bright and colorful display of light. Based on use-wear, Haury (1976:288–289) alluded to the grinding of pigments and incense burning as possibilities. Kari Kruger (1993) proposed that some palettes with holes were worn by people or hung from walls, and Edith Lowell (1990) found resemblances between Hohokam palettes and

South American *tabletas* used for snuffing hallucinogenic plants. A range of use-wear patterns appear on Hohokam palettes (White 2004:66–68), and since not all were burned and interred with cremations or had lead encrustations, they may have served multiple purposes that shifted between contexts and through time.

Censers

Stone and ceramic censers have also been found in both mortuary and domestic contexts, yet they had a clear depositional relationship with palettes, suggesting a joint and equally enigmatic ritual use (Haury 1976:288). Regarding ceramic censers, Haury (1976:226) quipped that the "most likely function was that of holding and burning incense"; yet, even as he contends, there is no evidence that anything was ever burned inside them, and their use may have been "symbolic" (Haury 1976:227). Their ornamentation parallels that of palettes, with linear grooves and hachuring during the Pioneer period and zoomorphic effigy forms thereafter. However, the serpent-eating-toad motif, likely a religiously charged mythological event or metaphor occasionally etched on shell, appears in censer symbolism but not on palettes (Wallace 2008:209–210). Of chronological relevance, Haury (1976:183–188) uncovered a group of stone censers from Cache 1:10G in a Sacaton phase pithouse at Snaketown, but there is little evidence for their continued use after the Sedentary.

Pyrite Mirrors

Pyrite plaques, or mirrors, most from a clear Mesoamerican source, have been noted from cache and mortuary contexts at several Preclassic villages (Gladwin et al. 1937; Haury 1976; Nelson 1981; Woodward 1941). Their initial appearance in Hohokam contexts corresponds with the arrival of the ballcourt network at the end of the Pioneer and onset of the Colonial period. These plaques consist of a sandstone or siltstone "frame" with either a slab or mosaic of pyrite pieces inlaid or affixed to it. Most examples have been burned, but the backing of some unburned fragments from Snaketown were painted red (Haury 1976:299). Their reflective quality was undoubtedly essential to their significance and central to their use. Similar mirrors made from minerals with reflective and luminous qualities were used throughout the Americas, a consistency that prompted Nicholas Saunders (1988) to suggest that they served divinatory purposes in Amerind religions. Like many other ritual implements, pyrite mirrors were dropped from the Hohokam ritual system by the end of the Sedentary period.

Medicine Stones

Along with censers, stone sculptures, and pyrite mirrors, Cache 1:10G at Snaketown contained two "medicine stones" (Haury 1976:188–189), also known as "plummets." These unusual cylindrical objects were carved and ground from scoria, and their association with other esoteric items implies that they too held ritualistic importance.[8] Haury included small effigies crafted from scoria and other vesicular volcanic stones in this catchall category of ritual paraphernalia (1976:292–293). Consistency in the choice of vesicular volcanic stone among effigies and medicine stones hints at a similar ritual significance, or perhaps medicine stones are unrecognizable effigies. Regardless, both forms first surfaced in late Pioneer settings and persisted into the Sedentary period. Cushing unearthed medicine stones from Los Muertos, Las Acequias, Los Hornos, Las Conopas, and Pueblo de las Piedras (Haury 1945:141, 169, 182, 185, 188). Some of these villages had large Classic period occupations; however, the data from Cushing's excavations are too vague to provide sound temporal contexts for these uncanny stones. Accordingly, Haury (1976:292) stated, rather conservatively, that they had only a "minimal survival into the Classic period."

Pipes and Tubes

Clay pipes and bone tubes have occasionally been found at Classic and Preclassic villages. Clay pipes seem to be associated almost exclusively with Classic period contexts (e.g., Haury 1945: Figure 112h; Morris and El-Najjar 1971:32; Stone and Foster 1994:261; Vivian 1965:139–140, Figure 8b), with the exception of one from a Sacaton context at Snaketown (Haury 1976:271). Bone and clay tubes, on the other hand, have turned up in both Preclassic and Classic period contexts (e.g., Gillespie 1995:714; Gladwin et al. 1937:155; Haury 1976:251, 304–305; Hunter 1995:244–245; James 1994a:295–297). During the Pioneer, crafters incised bone tubes with geometric patterns like those found on contemporaneous palettes, censers, and pottery. Such designs, however, did not persist past the Pioneer period since most later examples were left unadorned. Haury (1976: 271) likened pipes to cloud-blowers and, along with censers, implicated them in the ritualized creation of smoke. Punctated bone tubes were possibly whistles, but how others were used remains unknown. Lowell (1990:328) suggested that the Hohokam may have stored snuff in them; it is equally plausible that if they were used for snuffing they would have served as inhalation devices. Alternatively, Wilcox (1991b:49) postulated that they were sucking tubes used in shamanistic curing practices.

Geological Oddities

The Hohokam had a propensity to deposit unworked or unusually shaped stones in arguably ritualistic contexts. These have rarely been studied, and I suspect they are often overlooked and thus more prevalent than what has been reported. Cushing first commented on such stones in his report on Pueblo de los Muertos, where he found the repeated presence of water-worn stones along canal banks and suggested they were magical water tamers for conjuring and directing water onto fields (Cushing 1890:169). Cushing also compared unworked concretions found in residential areas to fetishes and amulets like those crafted and consumed at Zuni (Cushing 1890:179–180; see also Haury 1945:144–145, Plate 67). Weaver (1977:79) found a cache of 17 oddly shaped, water-worn pebbles in a room at the Classic period village of Pueblo del Monte.[9] Colors varied, but most were of a reddish hue, and one of these had red pigment adhering to a distal end, indicating that it was probably used to grind minerals (hematite?). He also found six other out-of-place alluvial pebbles scattered among other rooms.

Similar caches, stores, and miscellaneous occurrences of geological oddities are known from other Classic villages such as University Ruin, Pueblo Grande, and Casa Grande (Fewkes 1912; Hayden 1957:169–170, 172, 175). The ones from Casa Grande, which Fewkes called charm stones, ceremonial stones, and shrine stones, were found amid two shrine rooms inside Compound B with other ritual objects and colorful exotic minerals, such as stone effigies of humans and animals, green copper ore (chrysocolla?), white kaolin, and black shale (Fewkes 1912:98, 101). Other curious stones and concretions have been found inside Classic period burials and effigy vessels (Bostwick 2008a:82; Bostwick et al. 2009) and atop platform mounds (Downum and Bostwick 2003; Doyel 1974; Ferg 1988; Rice 1995). Similarly, one of the ballcourts at Snaketown had water-worn boulders buried at its entrances (Gladwin et al. 1937), perhaps as consecrations for the ritual ballgame. In addition to water-worn stones, Haury (1976:276–277) unearthed unworked quartz, amethyst, and chalcedony nodules and a fossil at Snaketown. The yellow mineral limonite, a naturally grooved pebble, a cache of chalcedony nodules, and fulgurites (lightning-fused sand) have also turned up at Los Morteros in the Tucson Basin (Dart 1995:516; Wallace 1995a:608–615; see also Wallace 2008:217).

Shell Trumpets

Trumpets crafted from conch shells show up at archaeological sites throughout the Americas (Hodge 1910, cited in Boekelman 1936:30). Among the Hohokam, their use was seemingly brief and limited primarily to the Sedentary and early Classic periods (Nelson 1981, 1991), suggesting they were somehow instrumental to the social transformations under way as the ballcourt system declined and moundtop ritualism came to dominance. They are found most often with Sacaton phase male burials and on platform mounds or in adjacent compounds in the Classic period (Bayman 2002:84). Some conch shells may have been used as adornments on staffs (Vokes, cited in Mills and Ferguson 2008: 355) like the one in the Magician's burial (McGregor 1943). Of course, they quite likely served

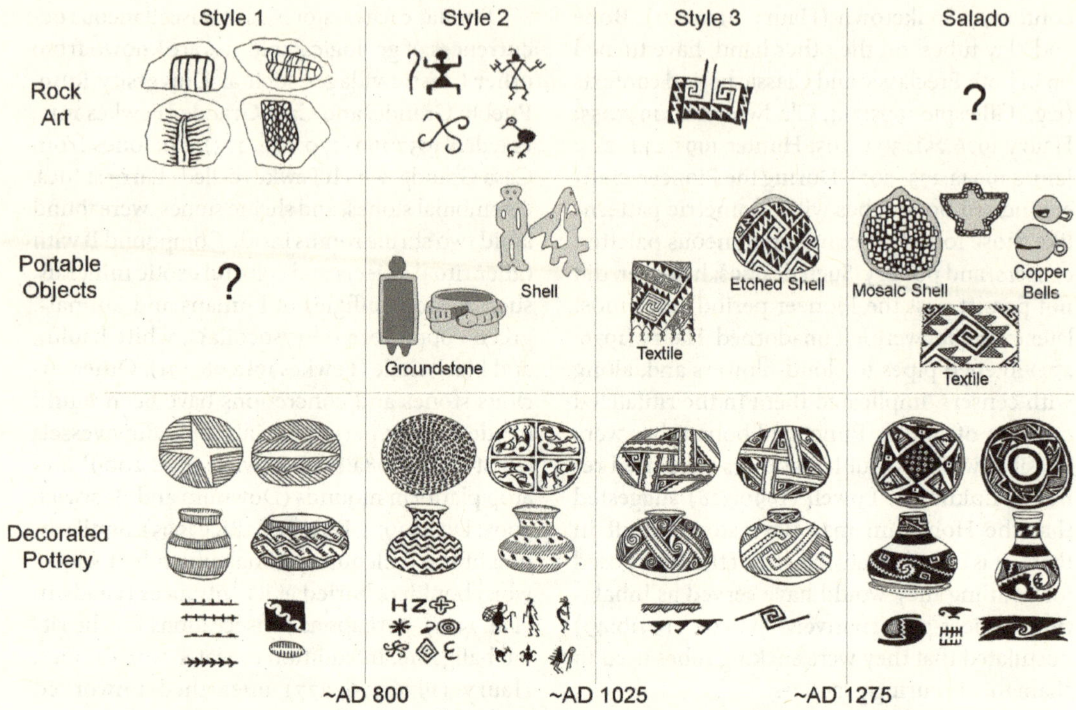

FIGURE 3.4. Styles in Hohokam visual arts (figure by Will Russell; adapted from Wallace 1995b:Figure 7.2).

as instruments as well, like the shell trumpets sounded during rituals tied to the Plumed Serpent among Pueblo peoples (Bayman 2002:84; Mills and Ferguson 2008:341–343; see also Brown 2005).

Copper Bells

Copper bells of West Mexican manufacture have been encountered at a number of Hohokam sites, most notably in caches of 28 at Snaketown, 35 at Gatlin, 25 at Romero Ruin (Vargas 1995), and a "mammoth"-sized one from a late Classic village in the San Pedro River valley (Haury 1947). Although rare, copper bells were traded across the Ancient Southwest (Sprague 1964; Sprague and Signori 1963) and are known from Preclassic and Classic villages throughout the Hohokam world (Vargas 1995, 2001). Vargas (1995, 2001) speculates that the Gatlin site, near Gila Bend, and Snaketown were northern hubs in a distribution network that shuffled copper bells northward through the Casas Grandes communities and into more distant reaches of western North America. While their role in Hohokam society remains elusive—they have been found in caches, graves, middens, pithouses, storerooms, and other settings (Vargas 1995)—their auditory properties were probably important in some ritual performances. Given their novelty and rarity, ownership of copper bells may have been restricted to particular ritual participants or politico-religious leaders or office holders, but clarification of their use and shifting importance through time awaits further research.

Other Suggestive Items

A number of other items found in Hohokam villages may have had ritual connotations, but intensive studies await. These include such things as pigments, animal bones, shell jewelry, unmodified schist slabs, carved hair ornaments, and effigy vessels. We also need to keep in mind that some common utilitarian items were used in ritual practices—evidenced, for example, by their accompaniment in mortuary assemblages and caches—alongside the more exotic and unusual items. Along these lines, there was surely a miscellany of other ritualized items that do not preserve well, such as wooden staffs and wands, clothing, foods, and beverages. For instance, a series of recent residue analyses has identified theobromine, a biomarker for cacao, on Classic redware vessels from elite contexts at Los Muertos (Washburn et al. 2011; see also Crown and Hurst 2009). Cacao, a tropical plant indigenous to Central America, was ritually consumed in beverages among Mesoamerican political and religious leaders. Its presence on similar vessels (i.e., cylinder jars, beakers, bowls, and pitchers) in the American Southwest suggests that it was traded vast distances northward and presumably brewed and served in ritualized settings among the upper echelon of Hohokam communities in the Classic period, if not earlier. Fortunately, methodological advances continue to shed new light on such ephemeral traces of ritual practice.

Controlling Ritual Objects

The types of Hohokam ritual objects and shifting patterns of use and discard through time convey a scenario of Hohokam social transformation compatible with that inferred from ritual architecture. In early villages, before the advent of the ritual ballgame, figurines crafted and consumed within households were individuals' principal tokens of ritual practice. A refreshingly new suite of ritual objects was part of the social transformation that accompanied the rise of the ballcourt network at the onset of the Colonial period. Like the ballgame, some of these items were clearly Mesoamerican (i.e., pyrite mirrors) and West Mexican (i.e., copper bells) imports, and others were Mesoamerica-inspired items that likely held similar symbolic meanings and served like purposes (i.e., censers). As with ritual space, items of the Pioneer period ritual toolkit, such as figurines, palettes, censers, and bone tubes, persisted into the Colonial period but took on new forms or were wielded in new ways. The broad distribution and depositional variability of ritual paraphernalia—in caches, cremations, and domestic middens, and on house floors—suggest that community members had relatively open access to religiously important items as well as free reign over the knowledge of their significance, symbolism, and ritual engagement during the Colonial period. This air of openness and aura of communalism persisted into the Sedentary; however, certain items eventually became concentrated in particular types of places, such as the zoomorphic figurines in burials (Chenault and Lindly 2006) and mountain sheep horn cores in buildings (Haury 1976:62). This intimates that although ballgames and cremation ritualism neutralized status differences and kept aggrandizers largely in check, by the middle Sedentary certain social segments or privileged individuals had come to exert control over or gain ownership of select ritual tools and religious symbols—and the associated religious knowledge—a practice that precipitated and intensified in the following centuries.

By the end of the Sacaton, Hohokam villagers no longer found much of the existing ritual paraphernalia useful—figurines, medicine stones, pyrite mirrors, censers, stone sculptures, and palettes evanesced from the ritual toolkit. Instead, relatively new ritual items, such as shell trumpets and clay pipes (cloud-blowers?), were concentrated on and near platform mounds and in opulent burials (e.g., Mitchell 2003). This spatial and social contraction in the possession of and privilege to use ritual paraphernalia parallels the general concentration of ritual and religious knowledge and authority within places and people evident in the form and arrangement of Classic period public architecture.

Iconography

Haury notes: "The complexity of materials on which art was lavished and the range of technological processes suggest that to explain it all as remarkable embellishments, as a cultural flamboyance without meaning, is not enough. Shifts in style, form, motif, the evolutionary trends, technological processes, the origins and derivations, and reasons for being deserve attention for they still have much to tell us" (1976:356). Iconography offers not only a window into Hohokam symbolism but also glimpses into the deeper social dynamics of Hohokam society. The Hohokam are renowned for the figurative designs that adorned their red-on-buff pottery; much of this figurative symbolism corresponds with contemporaneous or slightly earlier designs south of the Hohokam world, from present-day Chihuahua in northern Mexico to the Teotihuacan Valley in the Basin of Mexico (e.g., Carot 2001; Haury 1976:343–348; Johnson 1958; Nelson and Crider 2005). These similarities are impossible to ignore, and the urge to hark back to Gladwin's (Gladwin and Gladwin 1948) and Haury's (1976) models of Mesoamerican migration and colonization are hard to resist. However, Hohokam iconography drew inspiration from both the local and the distant, and the types of designs, their layouts, and the media on which they were depicted shifted through time. Indeed, major transitions in Hohokam iconography serve as chronological anchors for much of the period-and-phase culture history. Recently, Wallace (1995b, 2001, 2004; Wallace et al. 1995; see also Lack 2013) has defined three broad styles of Hohokam visual art—simply labeled Styles 1, 2, and 3—whose transitions correspond to significant Hohokam social transformations in the late Pioneer and late Sedentary periods (Figure 3.4).

Style 1

The earliest style of Hohokam iconography consists of mainly nonfigurative abstract patterns, some very intricate and complex. This style appears to be a generally unchanged continuation of a long-lasting and widespread decorative system found throughout the North American Desert West. Referred to variably as the Great Basin Abstract (e.g., Schaafsma 1980:36–47; Steward 1929:220) and Western Archaic Tradition (Wallace and Holmlund 1986:84; see also Hedges 1982), this style is most often found in rock art but was also depicted on portable stones (e.g., Thomas 1983), groundstone (e.g., Dixon 1965), projectile technology (e.g., Cosgrove 1947), and the earliest ceramics (e.g., Heidke 1999). In rock art, rare instances of figurative elements like anthropomorphic figures, zoomorphic footprints, and geometric designs interpreted as atlatls are known from certain regions (Wallace 2008:185–199). Style 1's abstract character is reminiscent of entoptic forms seen in altered states of consciousness (see Chapter 1). Consequently, such rock art designs are often interpreted as records of hallucinatory visions induced by trances and related shamanistic activities (e.g., Hedges 1976; Lewis-Williams and Dowson 1988; Wellman 1979).

Style 2

During the late Pioneer and early Colonial periods Hohokam artisans infused their design lexicon with a new repertoire of figurative and geometric motifs. While Style 1 iconography persisted, its design elements were used in different frequencies, layouts, and contexts. New motifs include a range of human, amphibian, avian, and mammalian lifeforms and a suite of patterned geometric elements (Haury 1976:228–251), whereas linear designs were typically fluid, curvilinear, and scroll-like. The lifeform motifs are visually striking and are understandably the most oft-cited innovation accompanying the spread of Style 2 iconography; however, figurative red-on-buff pottery designs are actually quite uncommon. Wallace (2004:Table 3.6) calculated a peak frequency of their occurrence on decorated sherds at just over 5 percent, with an overall frequency of about 1 percent. Clearly, lifeforms were never as common on Hohokam red-on-buff pottery as the many plates and illustrations in published reports would lead us to believe. This admixture of lively and naturalistic motifs and elements, many of a foreign inspiration, with a widely shared and very ancient design lexicon found in Style 1 iconography nevertheless evidences an abrupt change in symbolism related in some manner to the broader series of social and religious transformations sweeping across the Hohokam world at that time (Lack 2013; Wallace 2014; Wallace and Lindeman 2003, 2012, 2013; Wallace et al. 1995; Wilcox 1991b).

Besides pottery, Hohokam crafters etched and carved Style 2 imagery on shell jewelry and on a variety of ritual paraphernalia, such as palettes. The breadth of human and animal effigy forms—including vessels, figurines, sculptures, and censers—that became notably more common and diverse during the Colonial period should also be considered part of the general corpus of figurative visual art forms associated with Style 2 iconography. In rock art the body of Style 2 motifs has been termed the Gila (Schaafsma 1980:83) and Hohokam styles (Wallace and Holmlund 1986:82). The prevalence of certain Style 2 lifeforms (i.e., birds, toads, and lizards) on Hohokam artifacts inspired Wilcox (1991b; Wilcox et al. 2008) to postulate that these animals were deities of the Hohokam.

Style 2's genesis alongside those of the ritual ballcourt network, mound architecture, and an assortment of ritual objects—most either imported from or inspired by Mesoamerican and West Mexican communities far to the south—firmly couples this invitingly figurative iconography with the religious movement or revitalization that first trickled into the Hohokam world in the late Pioneer and then flooded throughout south-central Arizona's river valleys in the early Colonial period. Middle Gila buffware bearing Style 2 iconography was traded across south-central Arizona during the Colonial, and potters in communities just beyond the peripheries of the Hohokam world emulated Style 2 iconography on local wares (Wallace 2014). Given their far-reaching popularity, and since they adorned a variety of media, Style 2 designs and motifs were likely key symbols of both Hohokam identity and participation in a broader religious movement in the Colonial and Sedentary periods (Lack 2013; Wallace 2014; Wilcox 1991b).

Style 3

The shift from Style 2 to 3 is emblematic of the broader Preclassic-to-Classic transition. Most prevalent on pottery, this late mode of symbolism is dominated by rectilinear motifs arranged in complicated and intricate patterns reminiscent of basketry and textile weaves. Style 3 followed a long developmental sequence, with some common designs like the rectilinear scroll found on pottery as early as the Pioneer period. The full-on turn from Style 2 to 3 involved experimentation, gradual innovation, and piecemeal substitution of Style 2 motifs and layouts over the approximately 200-year span of the Sedentary period. By the Soho phase of the early Classic, Style 3 had supplanted most of the earlier curvilinear and figurative iconography. In this way, Style 3's tapered rise to Classic period decorative dominance mirrored the equally gradual rise of platform mounds that came to tower over Classic period villages. Indeed, these pivots from the past were tied to the same social, religious, and political transformations falling across the late Sedentary/early Classic period world. Both were symbols of a new social order, perhaps signs of a phoenix rising from the embers of a derelict religious movement of prior centuries. The widespread use of Style 3 on ceramics from the Tucson to the Phoenix Basin nonetheless suggests that historical threads of interregional connectivity and identity persevered through the tumultuous Sacaton and Soho phases in spite of apparent and presumably deep tears in the social fabric of the Hohokam world (Mills et al. 2013).

Though familiar from Sacaton and Casa Grande Red-on-buff and Tanque Verde Red-on-brown, Style 3's depiction in rock art remains unclear. Wallace (1995b:37) suggested that the Hohokam continued to portray lifeforms along with Style 3's nonfigurative rectilinear designs in rock art after the turn away from Style 2 in other media. In fact, the presence of rectilinear designs such as scrolls has long been considered diagnostic of late Sedentary and Classic period Hohokam rock art (Ferg 1979; Wallace and Holmlund 1986:104). Wallace's (2001) refinement of the buffware design chronology, however, showed that some rectilinear designs were in vogue at a much earlier date. While they dominated the iconography on late buffware vessels, adorning nearly 80 percent of late Sacaton and Casa Grande buffware pots, rectilinear designs were also painted on about one-third of the buffware vessels circulating during the Colonial and early decades of the Sedentary (Wallace 2001:Table 10.13). Rectilinear scrolls—one easily recognizable type of rectilinear motif found both in rock art and on decorated pots—were nevertheless rare as Preclassic pottery designs, but they became quite common during the late Sedentary and early Classic periods, showing up on over 50 percent of vessels (Wallace 2001:Table 10.13). They are thus somewhat reliable but not entirely foolproof indicators of Classic period iconography.

Although rectilinear scrolls occur as Hohokam rock art motifs, their presence alone is not necessarily a definitive a priori measure of Classic period production. As the situation in pottery warns, it is the rectilinear scroll's frequency compared with other seemingly contemporaneous designs that is important. For example, only one such scroll was recorded during a large survey of petroglyphs in the Picacho Mountains just north of the Tucson Basin (Wallace and Holmlund 1986:Table C-1). This single petroglyph accounts for less than one-tenth of 1 percent of the nearly 2,000 Hohokam petroglyphs Wallace recorded there, and this is the only rectilinear scroll among more than 7,500 petroglyphs known from the Tucson Basin and its surroundings at the time of his study (Wallace and Holmlund 1986:Table C-2). Likewise, there are only eight rectilinear scrolls among the sample of 831 Hohokam petroglyphs Wallace documented at Painted Rocks near Gila Bend, which is less than 1 percent of that petroglyph assemblage (Wallace 1989:Tables D-1 and D-2). Both of these rock art corpora indicate that the Hohokam rarely depicted rectilinear scrolls as petroglyphs, and the motif's frequency in Hohokam rock art is essentially equivalent to that on Preclassic red-on-buff pottery. So far there have been few concerted efforts to date Hohokam rock art (although see Wallace and Holmlund 1986), and most attempts have been intuitive claims based primarily on the co-presence, not frequency, of temporally diagnostic ceramic motifs in rock art. The occurrence of rectilinear motifs, principally scrolls, alongside and integrated with figurative designs in narrative scenes has led to the widely held but questionable post hoc conclusion that Hohokam artisans continued to craft rock art in the Classic period but decided to retain elements of Style 2 and mix them with those of Style 3.

Curiously, no one has seriously considered the possibility that rectilinear rock art designs were crafted in the Preclassic and are thus part of Style 2 iconography as materialized in parietal art. The occasional rectilinear scroll painted on Pioneer and Colonial period pots shows that this motif was not unknown or off-limits to Preclassic artisans, and since the rarity of this and other rectilinear motifs as petroglyphs uncannily matches the infrequency of such elements as Preclassic pottery designs, this is an equally if not more plausible explanation. This renders two scenarios: either Style 2 rock art persisted relatively unchanged into the Classic while Style 3 took hold in other media, or the Hohokam quit crafting rock art at some point during Style 3's slow rise to decorative dominance in the late Sacaton and Soho phases. Clearly, the portrait of Hohokam rock art begs a few new brushstrokes of chronological revision and calls for a fresh set of interpretive eyes. This book goes to great strides to clarify this fuzzy temporal picture.

Salado

A fourth and final style in Hohokam iconography is made up of the design repertoire and layouts found on Roosevelt Redware series vessels of the late Classic period. Commonly termed Salado, these polychrome bowls and jars seem to be the hybridization of Hohokam, Mogollon, and Ancestral Pueblo concepts, designs, and technologies (Clark 2001; Crown 1994; Lyons 2003; Lyons et al. 2005; see also Dean 2000). Design layouts and motif arrangements are quite distinct from those of the earlier Style 3 iconography on Casa Grande Buffware, but many of the geometric motifs on Salado pottery can be found in a horizon of simple geometric designs used by earlier Hohokam, Mogollon, and Pueblo potters, petroglyph makers, and similar artisans. Most unique to Salado iconography were new layouts and abstracted renditions of mythological agents such as the Plumed Serpent (Crown 1994; Searcy 2010).

Neuzil and Lyons (2006:26–30) have proposed Phoenix and Los Muertos polychromes as two new Salado ceramic types for the Phoenix Basin. They suggest these vessels were amassed in late Classic villages such as La Ciudad, Pueblo Salado, Escalante Ruin, Las Colinas, and Pueblo de los Muertos (see also Wasley and Doyel 1980), but it is debatable whether or not a Salado iconographic style should be attributed to the Phoenix Basin Hohokam since there is currently little petrographic evidence for local production of Roosevelt Redwares in the lower Salt River valley

(Abbott and Schaller 1992).[10] It is quite possible that Phoenix and Los Muertos polychromes were brought in from somewhere outside the Phoenix Basin; further petrographic studies should help clarify this issue. Salado-like iconography has not yet been identified in other realms of Hohokam visual art, making it questionable that the Phoenix Basin Hohokam painted Salado style iconography on their pottery and even more unlikely that they did so in other media such as rock art.

In summary, chronological changes in Hohokam iconography paralleled the tempo of metamorphoses in village layouts, architecture, and ritual paraphernalia, with significant symbolic reformulations occurring during the Pioneer Colonial and Sedentary Classic period transitions. When considered together, harmonious shifts in symbolism, monumental architecture, and ritual tools amounted to outright social transformations that transcended the material and immaterial domains of Hohokam life. Characteristics of the symbolism, the media on which it was conveyed, and the contexts of its use therefore provide unique insight into the historical and dynamic social processes that reproduced and at times transformed Hohokam lifestyles, social institutions, and relations of power.

Hohokam Rock Art, Ritual, and Religion

Along with a broad-brushed portrayal of the history of the Hohokam, this chapter described their religious structure, ritual system, and suite of symbols they used strategically on various media and in different contexts. After the Colonial period renewal of the Hohokam religious structure, brought about through its augmentation with Mesoamerica-inspired themes, architecture, and ritual objects and apparently accepted across the Hohokam world as part of a revitalization movement, Hohokam ritual practice, the religious knowledge embodied in its performance, the requisite ritual items, and the stages that simultaneously sheltered, supported, and aired those performances became increasingly flamboyant and formalized. This florescence culminated during the Sedentary period, when the reach and complexity of the ballcourt network and the distribution of red-on-buff pottery peaked. The Sedentary period, however, was also a turning point, as particular social groups and individuals within communities began to capitalize on certain ritual practices and paraphernalia. By the early Classic period, access to ritual space and paraphernalia had shifted toward the center of the communities and became elevated on platform mounds, above and out of reach of the rest of the community. Along the way, the design lexicon on pottery used in the domestic realm moved from a fluid arrangement of geometric and figurative symbols (Style 2), some shared across the Greater Southwest and others bearing affinities to symbols in West Mexico and Mesoamerica, to a complicated and nonfigurative decorative system (Style 3) restricted largely to late Sacaton and early Classic buffwares.

As I claimed in Chapter 2, rock art—as a peculiar mode of ritual practice—was much more than a symbolic reflection of dominating religious structures. Forms and patterns of ritual practices and symbolism reveal how religious knowledge was accessed, distributed, and controlled within and between Hohokam villagers and across communities. Rock art empowered people as instruments of social reproduction in the Hohokam world, and we can therefore implicate it as one of several performative fields where a struggle over the authority to gain, wield, and ultimately show off religious knowledge played out. Historicizing rock art in a network of power relations in such a way affords a lens on how religion and religious leaders, or ritual masters, factored into the transformation of Hohokam society. This lens frames a novel view of social and religious transformations because rock art was undertaken outside the villages, and the authority to access and broadcast religious knowledge through ritual practice on such occasions and in such solitary and removed settings may have differed from that of villages in two critical ways. For one, the types of activities pursued outside villages, including ritual practices, differed from those carried out under the gaze of other community members; in seclusion they may have adhered to a unique structure that only such settings can reveal. Second, practices undertaken beyond the village were less likely to be seen and governed. In this manner, people were temporarily free of public judgment and more empowered to act as they chose, which may have conflicted with social norms and community mores. In fact, such nonvillage settings may have been conducive to those interested in contesting the structural conditions, institutions, and orthodoxies imposed by village life.

Rock art offers a potential gauge for how community-wide and possibly leader-initiated reorganizations of religious knowledge were acknowledged, legitimized, or countered by individuals. I suspect that if the deep social transformations of the Hohokam world were partly founded on and justified through organizational shifts in the distribution, access, and control of religious knowledge—a scenario to which patterns in ritual artifacts and architecture strongly attest—then traces of these transformations should be evident in the ritual practices surrounding rock art production and use. Alternatively, since rock art was performed beyond the prying eyes of the larger community and auspices of religious leaders, its continued and unaltered production despite other well-known changes in the ritual network or social institutions responsible for organizing religious knowledge may evidence resistance to new religious rules and orthodoxies. To demonstrate this, however, I must contextualize rock art in relation to the Hohokam historical sequence reviewed in the first part of this chapter. This is my directive for the remainder of the book.

The following chapters present data and arguments derived from new research in the South Mountains, a series of sharp and darkly sheened ridges bearing thousands of Hohokam petroglyphs near the heart of the Phoenix Basin in south-central Arizona. In the following pages I establish an array of contextual factors that help illuminate the identities of the crafters and consumers of Hohokam rock art and pinpoint significant turns in rock art production and symbolism. My first objective is to embed Hohokam rock art into a larger experience of landscape engagement (Chapter 4). I then tackle chronology—perhaps the most difficult task in rock art studies—in order to compare the rock art with better-known and more securely dated aspects of Hohokam society (Chapter 5). Building from this temporal foundation, I use a model of ritual practice to tease out the ritualized qualities of Hohokam rock art (Chapter 6). I do not simply draw assumptions but rather compare the South Mountains petroglyphs with what many ritual scholars consider the defining characteristics of ritual practice. The co-occurrence of rock art with other cultural features and artifacts, as well as with particular topographic settings, provides insight regarding the social contexts surrounding the crafting, viewing, and use of rock art, the number of participants, audience sizes, and associated ancillary activities. I then revisit Hohokam religion and extrapolate from its Mesoamerican structural themes to demonstrate that rock art was more than a static lexicon of symbols—it was a strategic means of accessing and displaying religious knowledge to others, both human and other-than-human (Chapter 7). Finally, I implicate this religious knowledge as a form of capital and therefore a source of power and force in transforming the Hohokam world (Chapter 8). I show that Hohokam rock art can no longer be regarded as benign or whimsical caricatures, but instead represents a clutch of powerful tools integral to understanding Hohokam social transformations from a beyond-the-village, outside-looking-in point of view.

CHAPTER 4

The South Mountains Archaeological Landscape

This is not to say that Southwest landscape studies have entirely flipped from a scientific to a humanistic mode of inquiry, far from it. Analyses of settlement patterns, agricultural systems and the like continue to be regarded as critical. But there is now a widespread sense that questions of meaning are at least as important as questions of behavior and that a rigorous investigation of past landscapes must also seek to understand the way in which they were perceived and experienced on the ground by culturally situated people. (Fowles 2010:458–459)

To bring to light a beyond-the-village perspective on qualities of and transformations in Hohokam ritual practice, in this chapter I draw on a series of recent investigations into the South Mountains archaeological landscape. The South Mountains—known as Mahatuk to the Akimel O'odham (Turney 1929:124) and Vikwaxa's among the Pee Posh (Spier 1933:253)—are a prominent series of four southwest-to-northeast-trending ridges just south of the Salt River and east of its confluence with the Gila River near the center of the Phoenix Basin in south-central Arizona (Figure 4.1).[1] These steep though low-rising mountains are composed predominantly of granite, granodiorite, and gneiss (Reynolds 1985), whose great antiquity is attested to by a well-developed desert varnish characteristic of igneous landforms in the Desert West. This varnish lends a dark, reddish-brown, glassy complexion to the mountains, which was an alluring canvas for Hohokam rock art for hundreds of years. Indeed, the South Mountains offer one of the largest and most studied corpora of rock art in the Greater Southwest (e.g., Bostwick 1998, 1999; Bostwick and Krocek 2002; Carpenter 2007; Golio and Golio 2004, 2005; Golio and Snyder 1993; Golio et al. 1995; Holden 1980; Russell and Wright 2009; Russell et al. 2009; Snyder 1966, 1975; Wright 2011; Wright and Bostwick 2009).

Project History and Methodology

The research I report in this chapter derives from systematic archaeological surveys undertaken through the South Mountains Rock Art Project (SMRAP; see Bostwick 2008b; Wright et al. 2007). The SMRAP was a joint research, education, and preservation initiative by the City of Phoenix Parks and Recreation Department and Arizona State University with support from the Center for Desert Archaeology (now Archaeology Southwest) and the Arizona Archaeological Society. The City of Phoenix manages most of the South Mountains landscape as a nature preserve and recreational park, one of the largest municipal parks in the world. The mountains have long been known as a milieu for thousands of petroglyphs. Indeed, the earliest archaeological explorers of nearby ruins took brief forays into the mountains to inspect these curious symbols (e.g., Cushing 1890; Moorehead 1906). While there have been many casual investigations since, surprisingly few were systematic or looked much beyond the rock art. There was thus little

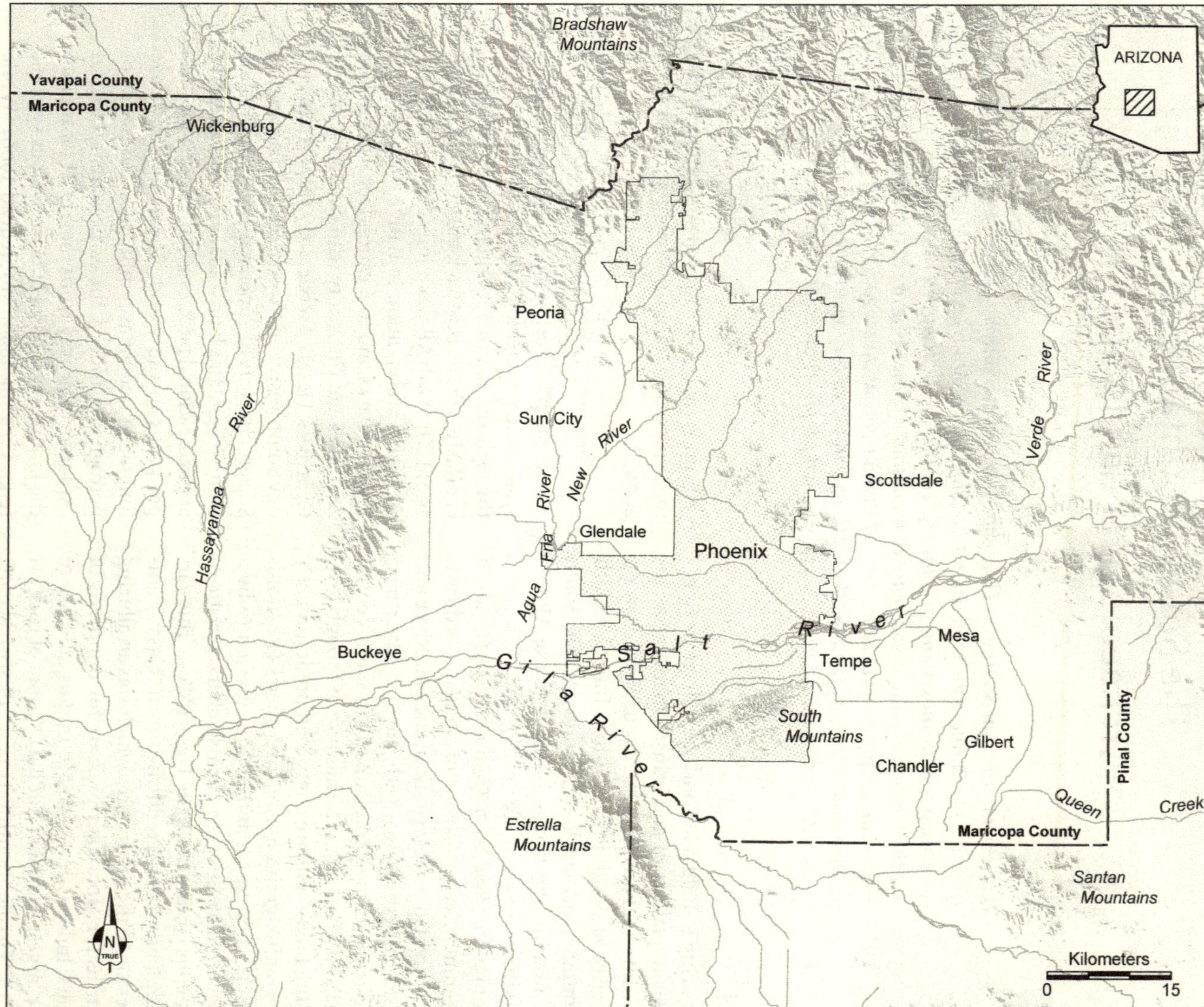

FIGURE 4.1. Overview of the Phoenix Basin (figure by Catherine Gilman, Desert Archaeology, Inc.).

information on the contexts and settings of the petroglyphs or the other types of archaeological manifestations found in and around the mountains. Very little of the rock art had ever been recorded to meet the basic standards of the state's cultural property site files. More troublesome, though, was that the rock art was disappearing at an alarming rate (Golio and Snyder 1993; see also Hedges 1994a).

As a major recreational park for one of the largest urban populations in North America, the South Mountains are visited by millions of people in any given year (Bostwick 2008b). This constant foot traffic, year after year, has taken a heavy toll on the park's rock art through increased erosion, neglect, and outright theft and vandalism. Much of this is due to an ignorance shared equally by vandals, who may not be aware of or care about the rock art's antiquity and cultural significance, and the city, which lacked a comprehensive management plan for the park's archaeological and historical properties. These shortcomings led to the SMRAP, which was therefore designed to (1) inventory and research the park's archaeological landscape to professional and state standards; (2) engage the public through educational opportunities, including volunteerism, university field schools, public lectures, and popular press and publications; and (3) assist in developing a management plan that would mitigate future impacts to the petrolgyphs and other historic properties.

Inspired by Swartz and Zancanella's (1991) call for hierarchical levels in rock art recording, the SMRAP developed a four-stage system of rock art site recording that necessitates repeated visits under different lighting conditions (Swanson and Bostwick 2007). The utility of a hierarchical approach is twofold. For one, it allows for the prioritization of fieldwork following initial observations of site context and condition and assessments of research potential and threat level. This is important when archaeological sites exhibit spatial, cultural, temporal, functional, and conservable variability, since areas of particular interest or concern can be targeted for more detailed investigation and preservation. Secondly, multiple site visits increase thoroughness of survey coverage due to seasonal shifts in vegetation density and daily fluctuations in lighting, both of which condition visibility. This is especially relevant for rock art because lighting affects petroglyph visibility at multiple scales (Huang 2005), and such light-and-shadow effects may have been an intended element of the site's or the rock art's narrative (e.g., Díaz-Andreu 2003). The SMRAP's hierarchical recording strategy ensured that we visited each archaeological feature and site in the South Mountains at least twice, and we returned to most, especially the more complex settings with dense concentrations of petroglyphs, far more times throughout the seasons.

The Survey

The SMRAP centered on three project areas in the northeastern reach of the South Mountains (Figures 3.2 and 4.2) because previous investigations revealed this stretch as one of the most dense in terms of rock art. It has also experienced a great amount of land disturbance and vandalism. Tina Carpenter's (2007) master's thesis, which surveyed Goodman Canyon in the central project area and 16th Street Canyon in the western project area (Figure 4.2), served as the SMRAP's pilot study. The SMRAP revisited sites in 16th Street Canyon and resurveyed the lower reaches of Goodman Canyon. Our survey efforts relied entirely on volunteers who walked parallel transects spaced at 10- and 15-m intervals. Data collection procedures followed a siteless survey strategy (Dunnell and Dancey 1983; see also Thomas 1974), in which each observation was documented individually and mapped with handheld geographic positioning system (GPS) devices (Tripcevich 2004). This facilitated distributional analyses by sidestepping the confines of site boundaries and spatial/associational biases inherent to in-field site recording. Siteless strategies are important for rock art because distributions may be meaningful at different spatial scales (Chippindale 2004; Troncoso Melendez 2008). We followed this technique for both archaeological features (including petroglyphs) and artifacts. For management purposes and site records, we generated site boundaries through

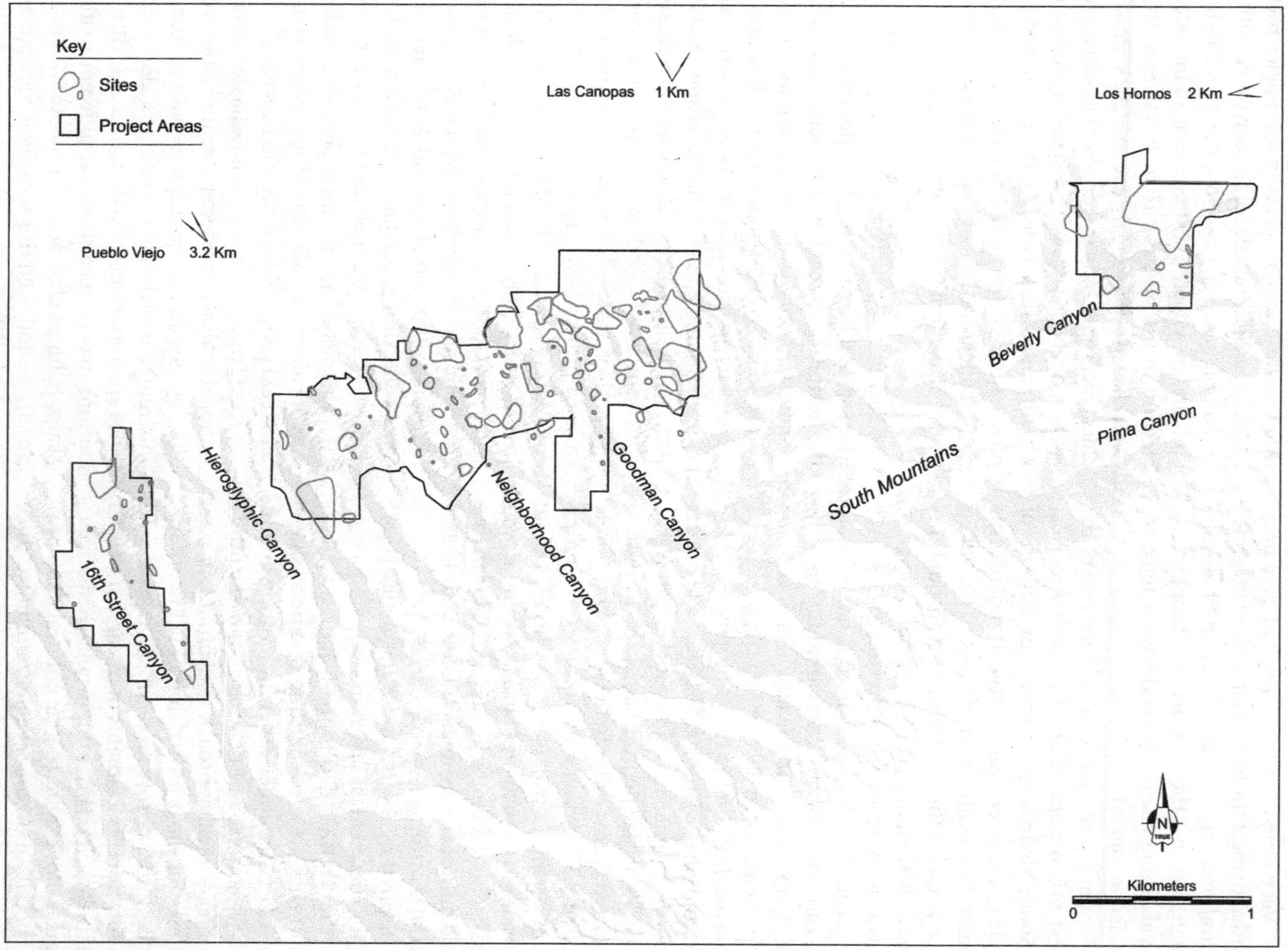

FIGURE 4.2. Archaeological sites recorded by the South Mountains Rock Art Project (figure by Catherine Gilman, Desert Archaeology, Inc.).

geographic information system (GIS) analysis long after fieldwork was completed.

Petroglyph Documentation

The SMRAP recorded petroglyphs at the feature, panel, and motif levels. Features are any contiguous rock exposure bearing petroglyphs, whereas panels are unbroken surfaces of the feature. Boulders and outcrops typically exhibit multiple "faces," or sides, each of which presents the petroglyph artisan and his or her audience with a potential "canvas." Many of these faces, however, can be further divided into panels by the presence of fractures, subtle curvatures, or veins of quartz within the rock face. Individual designs within the panels are the petroglyph motifs, the smallest units of in-field recordation. Our data consist of quantitative and qualitative measures of the petroglyph features, panels, and motifs. These include commonly recorded rock art variables, such as aspect, technique, lithology, orientation, size, and execution, which are familiar to many rock art researchers.[2] We also photographed each petrolgyph panel to scale with digital cameras on each visit to capture nuances of lighting and to document ongoing erosion and vandalism.

Regarding the motif typology, I borrow from Albert Spaulding's definition of an artifact type to describe a motif type as "a group of [petrolgyphs] exhibiting a consistent assemblage of attributes whose combined properties give a characteristic pattern" (1953:305). Contrary to Spaulding's stance, however, I do not consider typologies to be a priori patterns waiting to be discovered. A type is better considered a "working tool of the cultural student" (Ford 1954:52), or in J. O. Brew's words, they are "entities and realities only in the minds of students, they have no other existence" (1946:46). In this, I do not assume that the rock art artisans followed typologies (or grammars, lexicons, etc.). Our typologies are heuristic tools; they simply serve as categorical devices for our analyses, and I warn that by employing them we likely impose some structure where none may have existed.

The motif typology used by the SMRAP is provided in the appendix. It is a modified version of a long-used classification scheme for rock art designs in western North America with roots in early inventories (Cressman 1937; Steward 1929) and subsequently formalized by Heizer and Baumhoff (1962). Similar typologies have been used in previous studies of Hohokam rock art (e.g., Ferg 1979; Snyder 1966; Wallace 1983; White 1965). We modeled the SMRAP typology from one formulated by Henry Wallace (1989:83–89; 1997; 2000:Appendix D; 2008:Figure B.2; Wallace and Holmlund 1986:64–67, Figure D.3). It was imperative to follow Wallace's typology because it is thoroughly defined in the literature, and for comparative purposes, most recent Hohokam rock art studies have followed it.

Results

In all, the SMRAP's systematic, full-coverage, volunteer-supported survey recorded thousands of artifacts and, in addition to petroglyphs, hundreds of archaeological features in the three project areas. Regarding the rock art, our efforts turned up 3,333 petroglyphs on 1,050 panels scattered among 108 archaeological sites (Figure 4.2). Before delving directly into an analysis of South Mountains petroglyphs, however, I use this chapter to contextualize petroglyph production in relation to the broader suite of cultural practices carried out in this landscape.

Archaeological Features

Along with petroglyphs, the South Mountains harbor an array of other archaeological features and artifacts, most of which shed light on the various spheres of life in which rock art was produced and used. Here I provide a brief synopsis of the petroglyph assemblage and then expand it with an overview of the South Mountains archaeological landscape in which petroglyph crafting and viewing were embedded. Petroglyphs are elements of a mélange of agricultural and ritualized settings in this landscape, and as I show in Chapters 6 and 7, some of these contexts bear directly on understanding petroglyph production as a ritual practice. In the second half of this chapter I address the artifacts littered throughout the mountains; these add breadth to the contexts of landscape use and experience

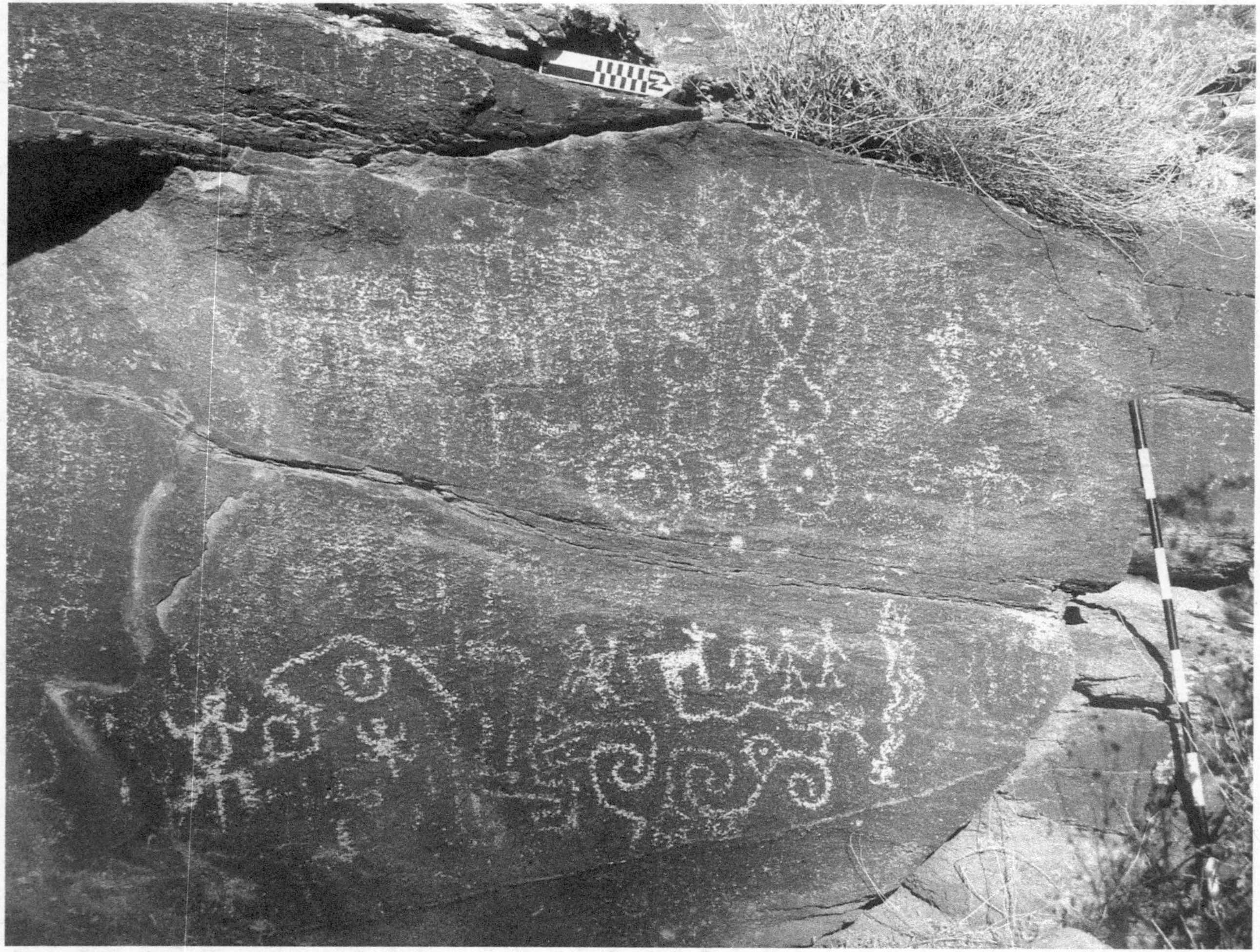

FIGURE 4.3. Panels with characteristic Gila-style petroglyphs in the South Mountains.

and, with regard to ceramics, help approximate the social identities of the mountains' ancient custodians as well as the historical periods of their sojourns into this multifaceted topography.

Petroglyphs

Most of the South Mountains petroglyphs conform to the Gila (Schaafsma 1980:83), or Hohokam, style (Wallace and Holmlund 1986:82), consisting predominantly of lifeforms and geometric designs (Figure 4.3). This suite of symbols and motifs corresponds with Style 2 iconography in Hohokam visual arts (Figure 3.4). None of the petroglyphs in SMRAP project areas can be clearly assigned to the Western Archaic Tradition (Hedges 1982), which accords with the earlier Style 1. A scratched "style" has also been attributed to the Hohokam (Ferg 1979), and examples have been located in the South Mountains and on nearby landforms in the lower Salt River valley (Bellavia et al. 2007; Wright and Bostwick 2009). Only 30 scratched or scratched-and-abraded petroglyphs were found in the project areas, an especially low frequency relative to the size of the entire assemblage. Our efforts also happened upon 63 purely abraded petroglyphs, a manufacturing technique not previously recognized for the Hohokam. I consider these nuances in petroglyph manufacturing technologies, and their implications, in greater detail in Chapter 6.

Density contours in Figures 4.4, 4.5, and 4.6 show how petroglyphs are spread and patterned across the landscape, and counts and percentages of the different petroglyphs, thematic class and motif are enumerated in Tables 4.1 and 4.2 respectively. This inventory reveals considerable diversity in petroglyph iconography, but it also shows how the majority of petroglyphs fall within relatively few motif types and how lifeforms and curvilinear designs dominate the glyph repertoire, a matter I address in the following chapter. Although Table 4.1 lists miscellaneous designs as the second-most common motif type, this category comprises frequent occurrences of indistinct and unrecognizable forms as well as miscellaneous and random pecking. This dominance of faint and loosely executed designs underscores the expedient nature of Hohokam petroglyphs. Indeed, Figure 4.7 shows that approximately half the petroglyphs were lightly and probably expediently pecked.[3] I return to these aspects of redundancy and pecking expediency later in Chapter 6. In the remainder of this chapter I detail the practices carried out in the South Mountains in addition to petroglyph production.

TABLE 4.1. Counts and Percentages of Petroglyph Design Classes.

Class	Count	Prehistoric %	Total %
Anthropomorphs	542	17.7	16.3
Miscellaneous Designs	514	16.8	15.4
Quadrupeds	445	14.6	13.4
Circle Designs	409	13.4	12.3
Linear Designs	248	8.1	7.4
Miscellaneous Curvilinear	197	6.4	5.9
Reptiles/Amphibians	169	5.5	5.1
Concentric Circles	108	3.5	3.2
Curvilinear Scrolls	100	3.3	3.0
Zig-Zags	80	2.6	2.4
Rectilinear Solids	70	2.3	2.1
Crosses	59	1.9	1.8
Miscellaneous Lifeforms	41	1.3	1.2
Miscellaneous Representational	20	0.7	0.6
Rectilinear Lines	20	0.7	0.6
Rectilinear Scrolls	20	0.7	0.6
Birds	13	0.4	0.4
Prehistoric Total	3,055	100.0	91.7
Historic Total	278	—	8.3
Project Total	3,333	100.0	100.0

Agricultural Facilities and Roasting Pits

The South Mountains' bajada provided Hohokam farmers an agricultural niche away from their better-known canal-irrigated fields. There were previous hints that the Hohokam took advantage of runoff rainwater to feed a vast system of agricultural terraces along the mountains' northeast bajada between the villages of Las Canopas and Los Hornos (Hayden 1941:178–179, cited in Schroeder 1953:186–187; Howard 1990:75; Midvale 1930s; Turney 1924:Map, 1929:34–35;

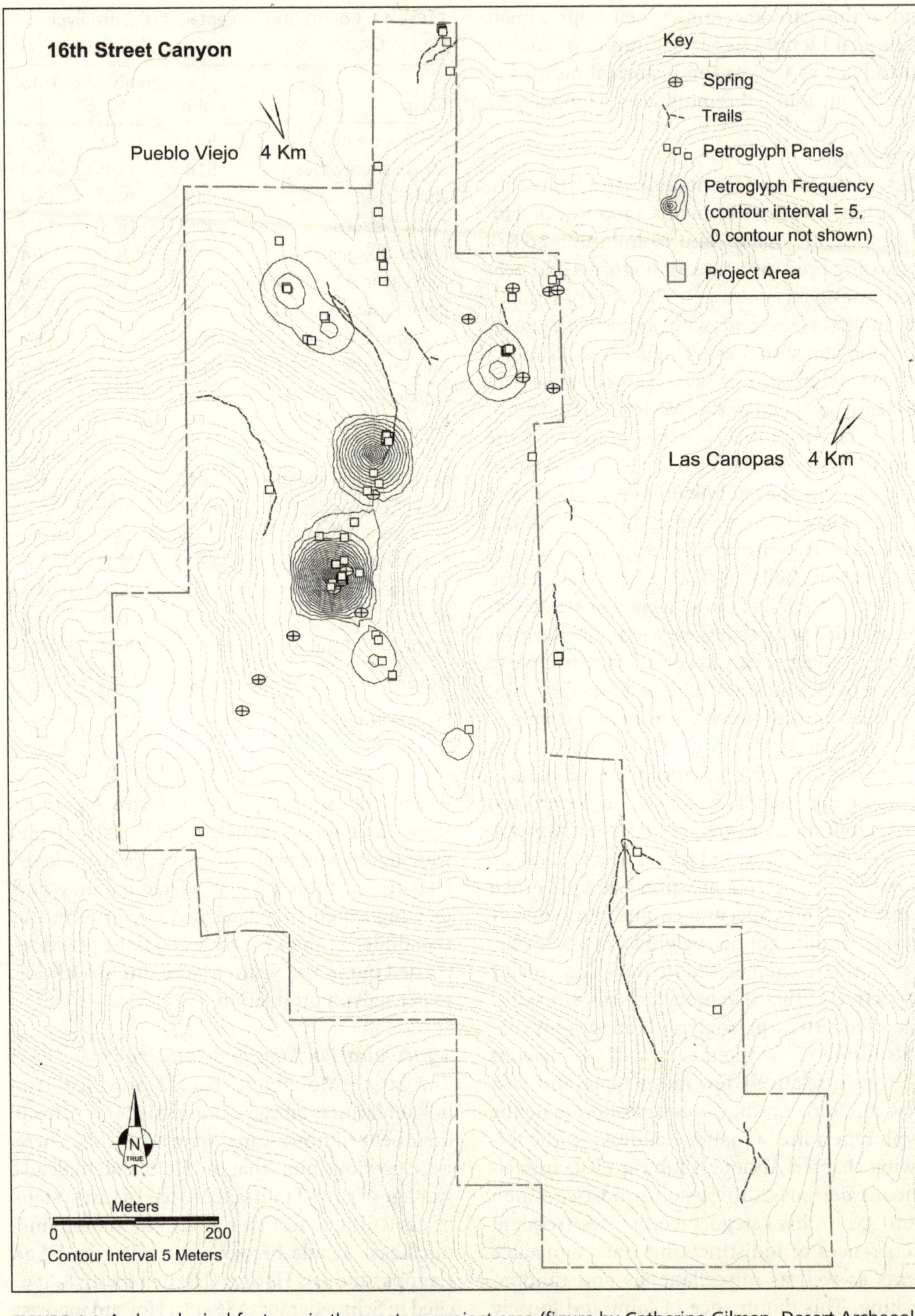

FIGURE 4.4. Archaeological features in the western project area (figure by Catherine Gilman, Desert Archaeology, Inc.).

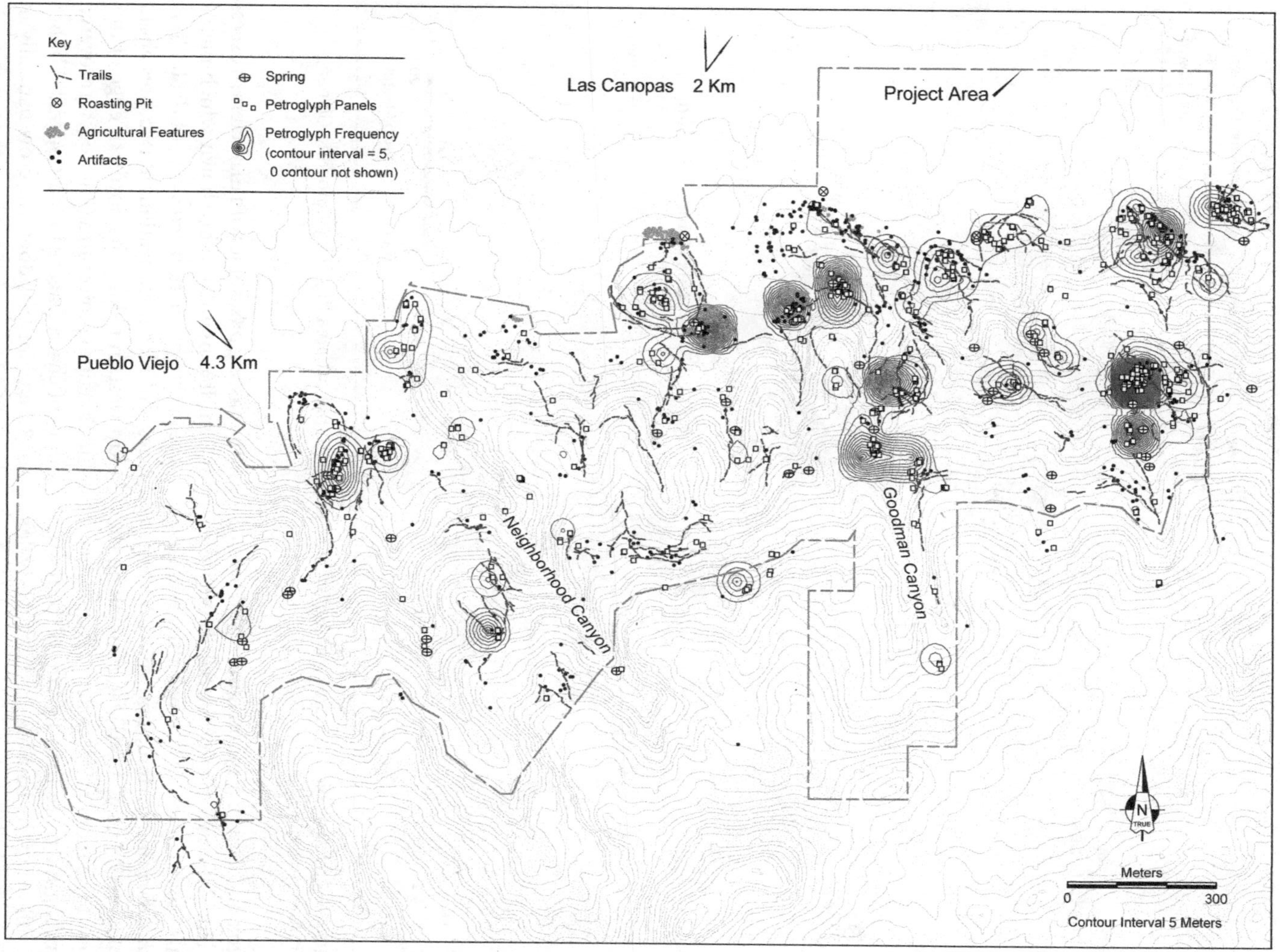

FIGURE 4.5. Archaeological features and artifacts in the central project area (figure by Catherine Gilman, Desert Archaeology, Inc.).

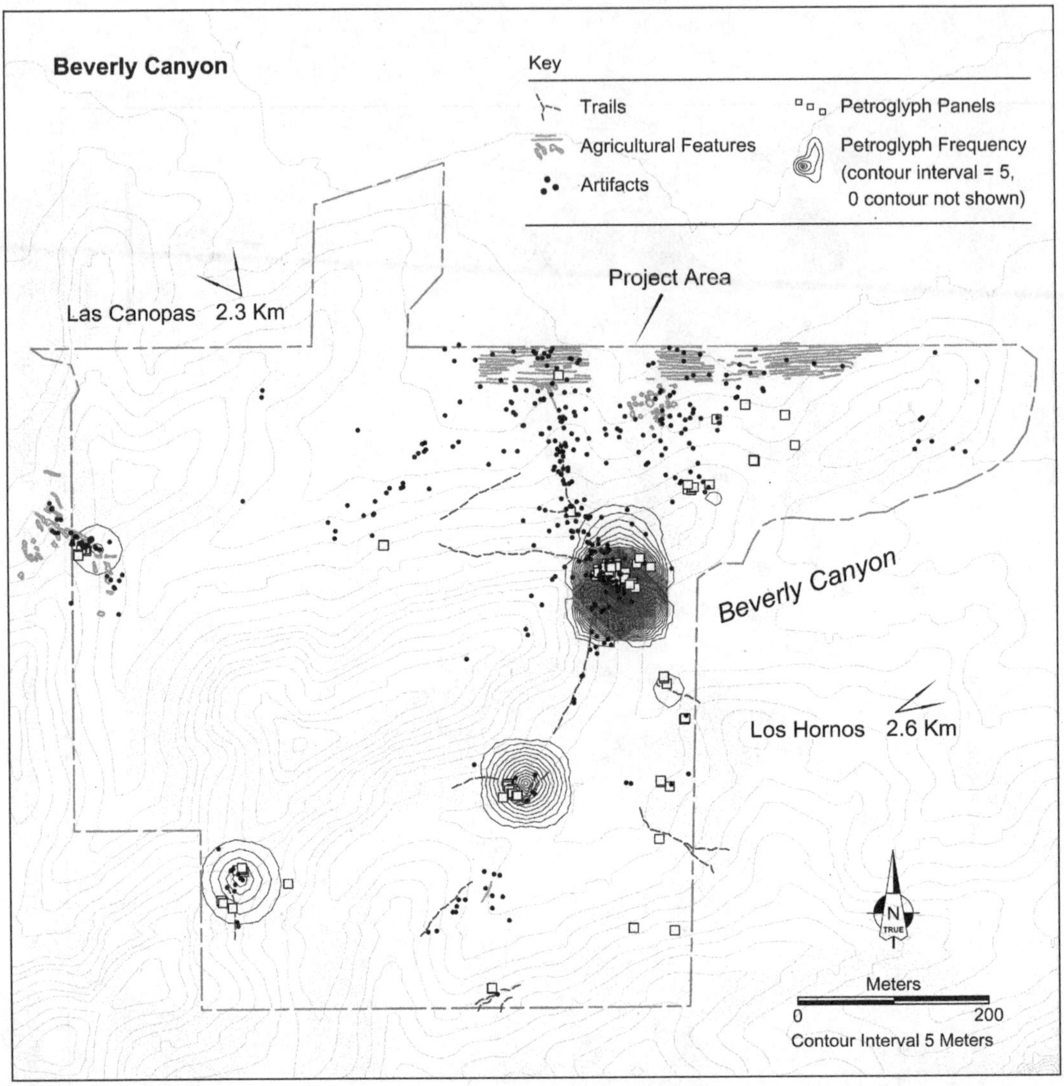

FIGURE 4.6. Archaeological features and artifacts in the eastern project area (figure by Catherine Gilman, Desert Archaeology, Inc.).

Wilcox and Howard 1990:Figure 10). Howard and Huckleberry's map of the Salt River valley canals (1991:Figure 1.1) shows this extensive *ak-chin* farming system, known as Midvale's Terraces (AZ U:9:9[ASM]), starting along the slopes at the mountains' eastern terminus and extending for more than 1.5 km to the northeast, following the bajada's gradient. Midvale's (1930s) unpublished sketch maps and photographs show what appear to be linear contour terraces constructed of cobbles and intermixed with roasting pits, some with diameters in excess of 8 m. It remained to be shown which plants were grown or encouraged along Midvale's Terraces, but recent excavations at two sites about 3 km west and along the northern edge of this study's central project area (Figure 4.5) recovered pieces of charred agave in roasting pits (Phillips 2008), a plant that does not grow naturally in the South Mountains or along the nearby valley floor and floodplain. Since those contract projects, we identified agricultural features

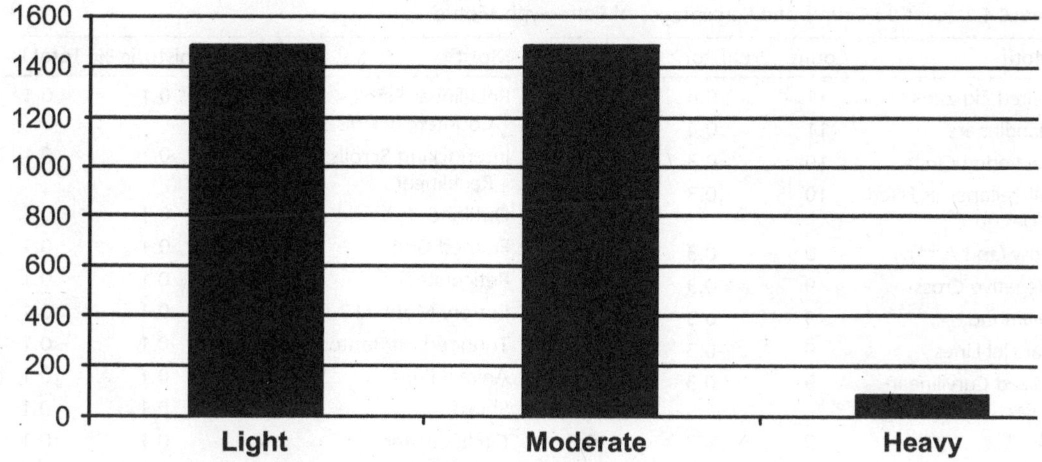

FIGURE 4.7. Counts of petroglyphs by execution intensity.

TABLE 4.2. Counts and Percentages of Petroglyph Motifs.

Motif	Count	Prehistoric %	Total %
Prehistoric			
Anthropomorph	453	14.8	13.6
Indeterminate Design	323	10.6	9.7
Indistinct Quadruped	263	8.6	7.9
Line; Straight, Curved, or Bent	194	6.4	5.8
Circle	180	5.9	5.4
Miscellaneous Pecking	175	5.7	5.3
Canid	149	4.9	4.5
Lizard	101	3.3	3.0
Unfinished Anthropomorph	89	2.9	2.7
Curvilinear Line; Meandering	78	2.6	2.3
Concentric Circles; 2 Rings	67	2.2	2.0
Bull's-Eye; 1 Ring	63	2.1	1.9
Arc/Semicircle	48	1.6	1.4
Wavy/Sinuous Line	47	1.5	1.4
Curvilinear Scroll, Counterclockwise	44	1.4	1.3
Extended Snake	40	1.3	1.2
Tailed Circle	33	1.1	1.0
Curvilinear Scroll, Clockwise	32	1.0	1.0
Paired Circles/ Figure 8	31	1.0	0.9
Miscellaneous Curvilinear Design	31	1.0	0.9
Miscellaneous Tailed Circle	30	1.0	0.9
Uncategorizable Lifeform	26	0.9	0.8
Deer/Elk/Antelope	25	0.8	0.8
Cross	24	0.8	0.7
Tortoise/Turtle	22	0.7	0.7
Zig-Zag	22	0.7	0.7
Bull's-Eye; 2 Rings	21	0.7	0.6
X	19	0.6	0.6
Curvilinear Line; Branching Meander	18	0.6	0.5
Miscellaneous Rectilinear Design	16	0.5	0.5
Connected Scrolls; Curvilinear	15	0.5	0.5
Pseudo-pipette	14	0.5	0.4
Sun Disk/Rayed Circle	13	0.4	0.4
Filled Circle	13	0.4	0.4
Double-Tailed Circle	12	0.4	0.4
Circle Chain	12	0.4	0.4
Concentric Circles; 3 Rings	11	0.4	0.3
Rectilinear Line; Meandering	11	0.4	0.3
Square	11	0.4	0.3

TABLE 4.2. (cont'd.) Counts and Percentages of Petroglyph Motifs.

Motif	Count	Prehistoric %	Total %
Paired Zig-Zags	11	0.4	0.3
Handlebars	11	0.4	0.3
Sectioned Circle	10	0.3	0.3
Miscellaneous Filled Design	10	0.3	0.3
Bow (and Arrow)	9	0.3	0.3
Negative Cross	9	0.3	0.3
Diamond	9	0.3	0.3
Parallel Lines	9	0.3	0.3
Mixed Curvilinear-Rectilinear Design	9	0.3	0.3
H	9	0.3	0.3
Sheep	8	0.3	0.2
Waterbird	8	0.3	0.2
Bull's-Eye; 3+ Rings	8	0.3	0.2
Asterisk	8	0.3	0.2
Horns	7	0.2	0.2
Trident	7	0.2	0.2
Coiled Snake	6	0.2	0.2
Pipette	6	0.2	0.2
Cloud	5	0.2	0.2
Running Connected Scrolls; Curvilinear	5	0.2	0.2
Rectilinear Maze or Pattern	5	0.2	0.2
Atlatl	4	0.1	0.1
Bird Track/Leg	4	0.1	0.1
Shell/Gridiron	4	0.1	0.1
Connected Circles	4	0.1	0.1
Dint Framing	4	0.1	0.1
Interlocking Scrolls; Curvilinear	4	0.1	0.1
Running Connected Scrolls; Rectilinear	4	0.1	0.1
Outlined Cross	4	0.1	0.1
Double Rake	4	0.1	0.1
Swastika	4	0.1	0.1
Terrace	4	0.1	0.1
Pinwheel/Whorl	4	0.1	0.1
Invertebrate/Insect	3	0.1	0.1
Miscellaneous Bird	3	0.1	0.1
Circle w/Concentric Arc	3	0.1	0.1
Rectilinear Scroll; Counterclockwise	3	0.1	0.1
Interlocking Scrolls; Rectilinear	3	0.1	0.1
Outlined X	3	0.1	0.1
Framed Grid	3	0.1	0.1
Reticulate	3	0.1	0.1
Pottery Motif 113	3	0.1	0.1
Thunderbird/Raptor	2	0.1	0.1
Animal Print	2	0.1	0.1
Shield	2	0.1	0.1
Circle Cluster	2	0.1	0.1
Barbell	2	0.1	0.1
Rectilinear Scroll; Clockwise	2	0.1	0.1
Connected Scrolls; Rectilinear	2	0.1	0.1
Butterfly	2	0.1	0.1
Rake	2	0.1	0.1
Triangle	2	0.1	0.1
Unique or Complex Design	2	0.1	0.1
Crenulation	2	0.1	0.1
Textile/Box	2	0.1	0.1
Basket Weave	1	0.1	< 0.1
Plant	1	< 0.1	< 0.1
Circle Pattern	1	< 0.1	< 0.1
Concentric Circles; 4 Rings	1	< 0.1	< 0.1
Ladder	1	< 0.1	< 0.1
Key	1	< 0.1	< 0.1
Opposed "L"s	1	< 0.1	< 0.1
Concentric Squares	1	< 0.1	< 0.1
Interlocked Hooks	1	< 0.1	< 0.1
Prehistoric Total	3,055	100.0	91.7
Historic			
Name/Initials	182	65.5	5.5
Designs	58	20.9	1.7
Writing	19	6.8	0.6
Name and Date	16	5.8	0.5
Date	3	1.1	0.1
Historic Total	278	100.0	8.3
Project Total	3,333	100.0	100.0

(C-shaped terraces discussed below) adjacent to those roasting pits, suggesting that agave was transplanted and husbanded there and probably in other portions of the bajada, including at Midvale's Terraces.

SMRAP representatives discerned five general varieties of agricultural facilities in the course of fieldwork. The first is an unusual form with a distinctive C shape designed to capture, channel, and retain runoff rainwater. From surface observations and limited testing, these C-shaped terraces appear to have been built by cutting into the gradient and lining the downslope portion with rocks. The dug-up talus was used for this retention lining, and excess rocks were piled adjacent to the terraces. These terraces are either anthropogenically or naturally infilled with cobble-free sediments, some in excess of 30 cm deep (Simon et al. 2013). Kruse-Peeples (2013:46) refers to very similar features on Perry Mesa, along the Phoenix Basin's northern rim, as U- or L-shaped terraces.

From the surface the C-shaped terraces look like half-moons of clean sediment encircled by scree, and in the SMRAP project areas they always occur in clusters, ranging from 6 to 40. These terrace clusters, sometimes accompanied by roasting pits, tend to form a network of interconnected terraces patterned like a honeycomb. In between the individual terraces are piles of dug-up talus, which may have been used to grow cultivars too or to encourage economically useful cacti. Upslope of the terrace clusters are shallow ditches, some containing rudimentary check dams, designed to channel and direct runoff onto the terraces. Upright slabs and large boulders positioned between the terraces were also designed to control runoff as it entered the terrace networks. We found these agricultural systems at five sites, with all but one situated at the base of the mountains, where talus boulders meet the sandy valley floor.

The South Mountains' C-shaped terrace networks resemble in form and presumably function the better-known "rock-bordered grids" (e.g., Doolittle and Neely 2004). Judging by these similarities and the known functions of such grids (Neely and Doolittle 2004:126–127), the South Mountains' systems likely served to (1) catch slope wash, retard its velocity, and direct it toward crops; (2) retain moisture and reduce its evaporation alongside and under the rock alignments and piles; and (3) increase levels of soil nutrients that promote plant growth (i.e., organic carbon, nitrogen, and phosphorus) along and under the rock features (see also Kruse-Peeples 2013).

There are nevertheless a few notable differences between rock-bordered grids and the C-shaped terrace systems in the South Mountains. First, and most obvious, is that the South Mountains' "grids" are composed of semicircular alignments in reticulated or honeycomb patterns instead of the rectangular checkered patterns of rock-bordered grids. Second, the C-shaped features are true terraces in that their rock linings also served to collect sediment, and constant infilling has leveled the features in a sort of stepwise fashion along the slopes. Thus it is possible that crops were grown in the rock piles, along the rock linings, and within the leveled terraces. The relatively small size of these clusters, and their opportunistic positioning in what seem to be optimal hydrological locations, suggests that they may have been built, operated, and cultivated by households or small task groups. Some if not all of the harvests were processed in adjacent roasting pits. Higher densities of palo verde trees within the terraces and cholla cacti along the rock linings and in the rock piles indicate that the terrace clusters still retain more moisture than the surrounding slopes.

Another form of agricultural facility we located consists of linear rock alignments, or terraces, along the northeastern flank of the South Mountains (Figure 4.6). Based on previous maps, these were probably part of the Midvale Terraces system discussed above; however, most of that system now lies under the paved streets of Tempe, Arizona. The portion documented during our endeavors may well be the highest upslope remnant of Midvale's Terraces. A few surface ceramics at this site date to the Pioneer period, and there are many early Colonial period sherds, particularly Gila Butte and Cañada del Oro varieties, scattered around the terraces.

Accordingly, Hohokam farmers were probably using this section of the terrace system by the early Colonial, coincidentally when the nearby villages of Los Hornos and Las Canopas hosted sizable populations. It is reasonable to assume that denizens of Los Hornos and Las Canopas were the tenders of this and other portions of the Midvale Terraces agricultural system, built sometime during the early Colonial period or earlier.

The linear terraces are similar to better-known contour terraces (e.g., Kruse-Peeples 2013:44–47; Masse 1991; Vivian 1974:96–97; see also Woodbury's [1961:12] "linear borders"). The South Mountains', though, do not contour slopes, but rather run several hundred meters along cardinal directions, passing through arroyos and cross-cutting slopes. They are spaced 2 to 3 m apart and are made up of loosely arranged residual cobbles. Test excavations yielded several insights regarding these linear terraces (Simon et al. 2013). From the surface it would appear that the leveled, skree-free terraces between the rock alignments would be the intended areas for cropping. Sediments in these portions of the system, however, are only 1 to 3 cm deep, whereas in locations adjacent to the rock alignments the depth is on the order of 8 to 10 cm. The rock alignments thus act to retain both moisture and soil, and they still function, given the greater amount of weedy taxa and cacti growing on them compared with surrounding soils. Microbotanical analyses of the soils from around the rock alignments yielded agave pollen, maize phytoliths, and high concentrations of microfossils from economically useful cholla cacti (Stuart 2013).

Our limited test excavations suggest that these linear terraces supported a medley of domesticated, transplanted, and encouraged plants, including agave. Agave does not naturally grow on the floor of the Salt River valley or along the South Mountains bajadas, but as Charles Miksicek (1982) discovered, it was an important transplanted cultivar for the Phoenix Basin Hohokam. Gasser and Kwiatkowski (1991:427) posited that agave was initially traded into the Salt River valley and that Hohokam villagers later developed the requisite facilities for local cultivation. Our research shows that the South Mountains linear terraces may have served as such a facility for the communities of Los Hornos and Las Canopas, at least by the Colonial period and perhaps as early as the Pioneer. Indeed, numerous flotation samples across the Salt River valley floodplain speak to the importance of agave to the Phoenix Basin Hohokam by at least the Colonial period (Gasser and Kwiatkowski 1991).

Even though we did not find any roasting pits near the linear terraces—which is a typical indicator of agave farming—their absence is likely due to the limited extent of the system still preserved. Indeed, our project areas' northern edges coincide with the property boundary of South Mountain Park (Figure 4.6)—the entire area to the north and east had long ago been leveled and paved over. Midvale's (1930s) photographs and sketches provide ample evidence that roasting pits were once present in the general vicinity. The enormity of the original system (the small portion in our project area alone has thousands of meters of terraces!), which once extended over a kilometer to the north and east, leads me to reason that its construction and maintenance were communally organized, although individuals or households may have had investments in or control over certain lengths.

A third type of agricultural facility we identified consists of long and narrow excavated "ditches" that run perpendicular to a landform's gradient (Figure 4.6, far left). These features have the appearance of arroyos that channel runoff downslope. The dearth of historic and modern disturbance, however, and the prevalence of other archaeological features and artifacts encircling them suggest they were anthropogenically created, and fully grown palo verde trees within the ditches evidence their antiquity. These ditches measure from 5 to 30 m long, from 1 to 3 m wide, and on average about 0.5 m deep, and each is bermed around its margins, presumably by the earth excavated from them. Their identification as agricultural facilities is not as evident as for terraces, but artifact associations and vegetation patterns betray that they constitute some sort of farming technology. Lithic artifacts common at the other farming localities, such as flake and core tools, flake knives, and hammerstones (discussed below), cluster among these features. Vegetation, principally palo verde trees and cholla, is also denser along the rimmed borders and within the ditches, indicating that they still promote plant growth.

Two more types of agricultural facilities, although evidenced by only one example each, warrant discussion. One is a low earth-and-cobble berm contouring the base of a slope just above an arroyo in the eastern project area (Figure 4.6, bottom center). The berm is less than 10 cm high and composed largely of sandy soil with a few residual cobbles. This contour terrace still encourages plant growth since it hosts a higher density of creosote bushes than surrounding areas. The other feature consists of a rectangular alignment of boulders, measuring approximately 2 × 3 m and one course high, positioned at the foot of a steep slope and on an alluvial terrace above the western mouth of Neighborhood Canyon (Figure 4.5). From this plot an approximately 30-m-long rock alignment extends up the slope of a conical hill. This alignment, ranging from 30 to 80 cm high, is formed by a single course of massive boulders that were repositioned and curved in a manner to capture and direct runoff onto the rock-bordered plot. Neither of these later two agricultural facilities have accompanying roasting pits, and their relatively small sizes indicate that they could have been built and managed by individuals or relatively small groups.

Quarries

A 500-m-long dike of fine-grained felsite passes through a ridge in the western edge of the central project area (Figure 4.5, bottom left). Surface exposures are patinated orange-white, but fresh heartrock ranges from a cream to gray color. We found one minimally exploited quarry of this material at the northern extent of this dike, along the base of the mountains.[4] We also found numerous stations of material testing and initial core reduction of felsite across the top of the ridge. Flaking stations are easily recognizable on level portions of this ridge, where cleared areas are encircled by sizable quantities of flaked felsite and usually accompanied by one or two hammerstones. Small amounts of plainware and buffware sherds in and around these flaking stations suggest that it was the Hohokam who sought this toolstone; however, earlier Archaic quarrying activities cannot be ruled out. Interestingly, flaked pieces of felsite are rarely found away from this dike, evidencing a logistical pattern of toolstone procurement; villagers may have ventured into the mountains solely to gather this stone for further processing outside the mountains, probably at nearby villages.

Strong associations between petroglyphs and quarries, including those of felsite, are known from areas south of the Phoenix Basin (Wallace 1983; Wallace and Holmlund 1986). This suggests that the two activities had some relation, perhaps being undertaken together during forays into these other landscapes, but that does not appear to have been the situation in the South Mountains. Petroglyphs are not positioned near the minor quarry, and only a handful are scattered around the larger quarry and dike atop the ridge. At the latter there is no clear relationship between the glyphs, the dike, or the flaking stations; instead, the petroglyphs correspond more with several trails that pass over and along the ridge. If Wallace's (Wallace and Holmlund 1986:138–140) suggestion that glyphs scattered about the Picacho Mountains quarries were signs of gratitude or esoteric requests to access the toolstone is accurate or close the point, such suppliant practices of tribute or orison apparently were not needed at the South Mountains quarries. Alternatively, had certain social groups sought to control access to the quarries, we might expect property concerns to be signaled by highly visible petroglyphs bounding the dike (e.g., Hartley 1991, 1992; Hartley and Vawser 1997, 1998), but this does not appear to have been the case in the Salt River valley either, at least in the South Mountains.

Quartz is abundant in the South Mountains, yet there is little to no evidence that it was ever quarried. With the exception of a single site with a few tested nodules, we found no evidence of mining, flaking, or other styles of working local quartz in any of the project areas. Much of the quartz occurs as small residual nodules, and if desired as toolstone it may have been picked up, carried off, and reduced at locations outside the mountains, or it may have been sought for purposes other than tool production. For example, as touched on in Chapter 3, unworked pieces of quartz have been found in ritual caches and some burials, arguably as esoteric offerings or status items (e.g., Mitchell 2003). While potentially ritually important and religiously symbolic, there is no indication that locally available quartz, nor pieces brought in to the mountains, were used for pecking petroglyphs, a ritualized technological practice David Whitley and his colleagues show was used to manufacture some petroglyphs in California's Coso Range (Whitley, Dorn et al. 1999; Whitley, Simon et al. 1999).

Rockshelters

The South Mountains' rugged and eroded slopes offer many nooks and crevices that could, in theory, provide shelter or a secluded space. We found 37 such rockshelters with some relic of a Hohokam presence, that is, associated stone or ceramic artifacts, internal or nearby features, or petroglyphs. Petroglyph-bearing rockshelters are also known from the Picacho Mountains, where they have been interpreted as locales for solitary Hohokam ritual activities (Wallace and Holmlund 1986:131–138). Most of the utilized rockshelters in the South Mountains lack petroglyphs, and the only indication they were ever used is often just a handful of artifacts in or around them. Instead of ritualized places, these may have been ad hoc shades and shelters for when the need arose: (1) most are quite small and can accommodate only a few individuals at a time, probably no more than two; (2) their topographic settings do not afford expansive views of the horizon or nearby portions of the mountains; and (3) they are not hidden and secluded but rather are noticeable and easy to reach and enter. These factors suggest that the uses for these shelters concerned the immediate surroundings and were probably ancillary to vicinal activities geared toward farming or gathering other resources from the local environment.

Other rockshelters, however, drew a greater degree of investment and hosted different activities or a wider range of them than the small unmodified overhangs. For example, a few small overhangs bear petroglyphs over or adjacent to their entrances (Figures 4.8 and 4.9). While their general shape, size, and viewsheds conform to the expedient rockshelters discussed above, associated petroglyphs intimate that they served different purposes or that there was a desire to visually mark and distinguish these from similar locations. Diagnostic ceramics found in or just outside these decorated shelters are consistently Hohokam buffware; a lack of redware or polychrome sherds suggests they were visited most frequently, if not exclusively, during the Preclassic era.

In contrast to the 30 Hohokam petroglyph panels found inside rockshelters at the Shelter Gap site in the Picacho Mountains (Wallace and Holmlund 1986:131–134), only four of the small shelters in the South Mountains sample have interior petroglyphs, accounting for just five panels bearing 15 petroglyphs. Of these, only one panel, bearing just one petroglyph, can be considered "hidden" (see Chapter 6), while the other four are visible at some distance from outside the rockshelters or overhangs. It seems that seclusion and privacy for petroglyph production and associated activities in and around rockshelters were not as much of a concern in the South Mountains as they were at certain places in the Picachos.

There is one more class of anthropogenically used rockshelters in the South Mountains, a group that should be considered a tier above the others. These rockshelters, however, are quite rare, as we found only three examples in the project areas. Each is idiosyncratic in various aspects, but they share attributes that likely relate to practical uses and symbolic significance. For one thing, unlike the other, minimally visited and ephemerally used shelters, these three are much larger and can accommodate actual groups of people, perhaps up to six at a time, but each is nevertheless extremely squat, with ceilings less than 1 m high. As a result, any activities carried out inside them would have mandated crawling,

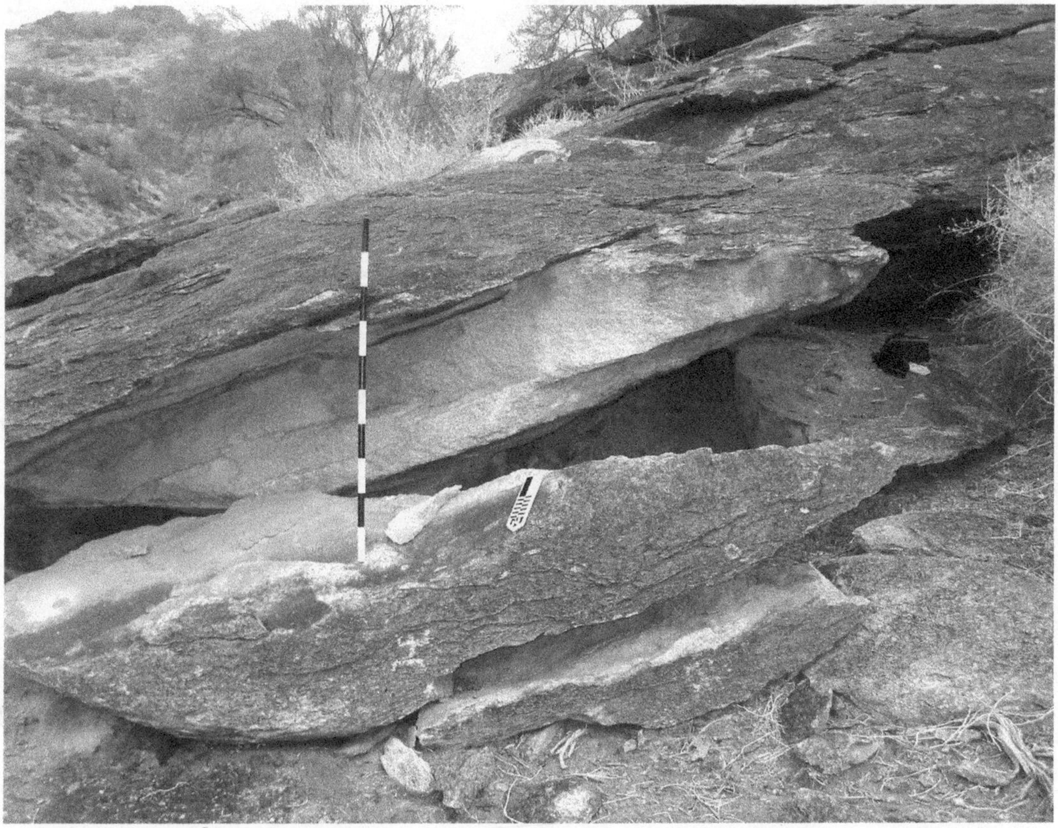

FIGURE 4.8. Small petroglyph-adorned rockshelter with a collapsed roof. Motifs consist of two anthropomorphs and a circle. This rockshelter had Preclassic buffware pottery eroding out of it.

crouching, sitting, or lying. Another shared but unwonted characteristic is that these shelters are more than simple recesses in the bedrock. Each is formed by a large table rock boulder resting on prominent, towering bedrock exposures, and all three have north- and south-facing entrances that frame and direct expansive views over the Salt River valley to the north. In fact, these large shelters are situated in the choicest elevated portions of the immediate landscape for maximizing viewsheds, suggesting that observing the horizon and the valley below was integral to the shelters' significance. Indeed, the shelters emphasize unbroken vistas that extend from the White Tank Mountains on the western skyline to the Superstition Mountains in the east and include commanding views of the smaller landforms, canals, and villages that once dotted the Salt River valley.

In addition to their unique natural qualities and unlike the smaller overhangs, the three large shelters are in the midst of dense petroglyph concentrations. One has petroglyphs above each entrance, and another contains the only truly hidden petroglyph panel since it is found at the end of a dark recess. The imagery, consisting of a large and possibly pregnant bighorn sheep with some peripheral but mostly indiscernible glyphs, is also quite exceptional (Figure 4.10). This scene portrays the only possible example of a successfully hunted quadruped: the bighorn appears to have projectiles (either atlatl darts or arrows) protruding from its back. These hunting and fertility themes and the animal's notable boat-shaped body have uncanny similarities to scenes in the Coso Range, which have been interpreted as products of hunting magic (e.g., Grant et al. 1968; Heizer and Baumhoff 1962;

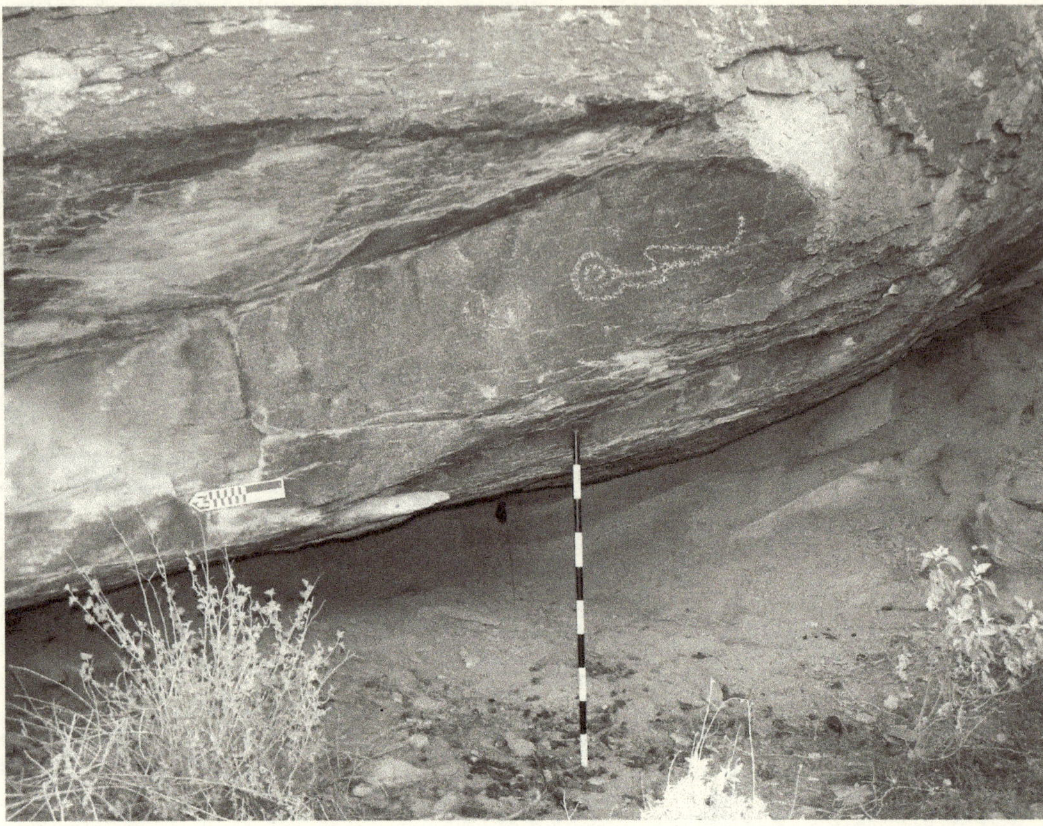

FIGURE 4.9. Small petroglyph-adorned rockshelter. This rockshelter had a Preclassic buffware sherd inside it. Motifs include a curvilinear scroll with an elaborate tail (*at right*) and a pair of wavy lines (*at left*).

Wellman 1979), emblems of a religious cult (e.g., Garfinkel 2006), or metaphors for shamanic control over rain (e.g., Whitley 1992, 1994, 1998, 2000a, 2008). Several unquestionable hunting narratives occur in the South Mountains petroglyphs (e.g., Figure 4.11; see also Golio and Golio 2005), but depictions of successfully shot animals are incredibly rare in Hohokam rock art in general; Weaver (1985) did not find any in the Superstition Mountains, and Wallace and Holmlund (1986) encountered just one, a petroglyph of an impaled deer, in the Picacho Mountains. The uniqueness of an impaled bighorn among the South Mountains petroglyphs, therefore, likely informs on the shelter's symbolic and probably ritual significance.

As for artifact associations, all three of the large rockshelters have plainware and buffware sherds in and around them to the complete exclusion of any redware or polychrome sherds, and two have small dry-laid masonry walls constructed along their drip lines. The wall-less shelter, the one enshrouding the impaled bighorn petroglyph, has a natural analogue where boulders have collapsed around the drip line, creating a makeshift wall. The constructed walls are single-coursed, and rather than impeding entry or offering seclusion, they seem simply to have been a means of visually and symbolically bounding the shelters' internal space. These shelters were probably not habitation quarters either, since artifact densities are low, internal features are mostly absent, and there is no evidence of thermal activity in the form of charcoal residue or smoke-blackened ceilings. Unlike the other, smaller shelters, various threads of evidence point to the three large, walled-in shelters as once having a predominantly and intensely ritualized

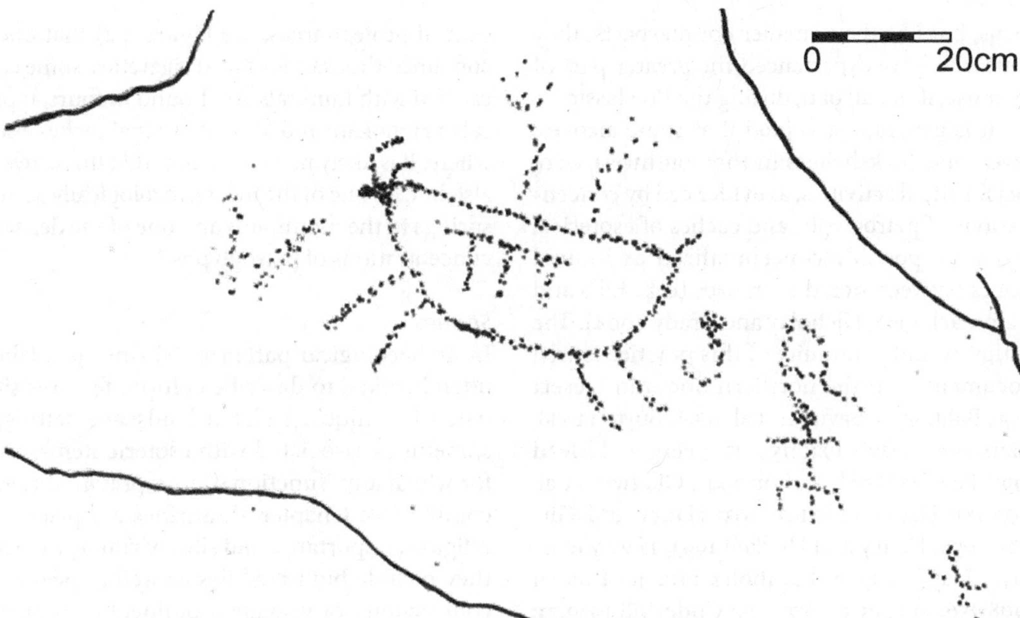

FIGURE 4.10. Panel with a bighorn sheep and associated petroglyphs hidden inside a rockshelter. The bighorn may be pregnant and impaled by arrows or darts. This rockshelter is above a spring and had plainware sherds inside it and Preclassic buffware sherds around its entrance.

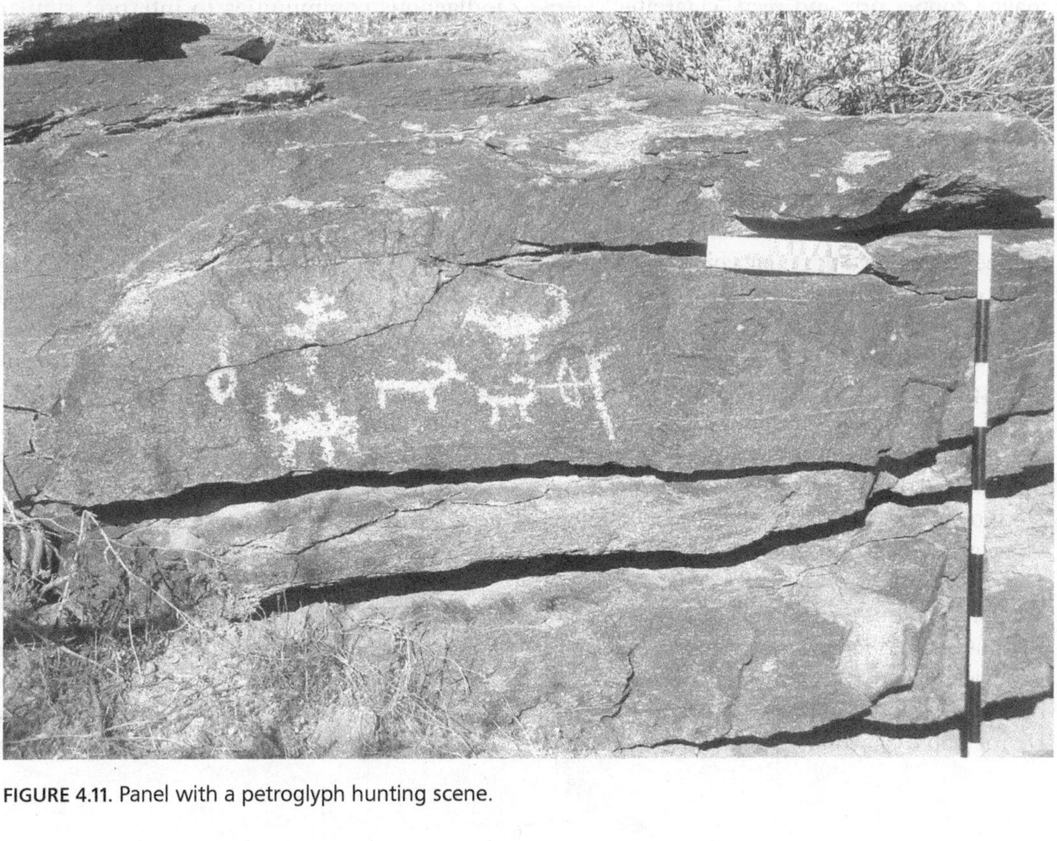

FIGURE 4.11. Panel with a petroglyph hunting scene.

focus, but like their smaller counterparts, they appear to have experienced the greater part of their use, if not all of it, during the Preclassic.

It is generally accepted that some alcoves, caves, and rockshelters in the Southwest were loci for ritual activities, as evidenced by concentrations of petroglyphs and caches of esoterica, and were possibly conceptualized as liminal places between tiered cosmoses (e.g., Ellis and Hammack 1968; Nicholay and Brady 2004). The antiquity and continuity of this practice is well documented in the northern Sonoran Desert (e.g., Bahti 1970; Bayman et al. 1996; Burton 1988; Clark 1967; Davis 1920:159–177; Ferg and Mead 1993; Fewkes 1898b; Fulton 1941; Gladwin et al. 1937:131; Haury 1945:193–203; Haury and Gifford 1959; Haury and Huckell 1993; Haury et al. 1950; Hayden 1977; Lumholtz 1912:42; Russell 1908:256; Turney 1929:73–75; Underhill 1939:71; Wasley 1962). The most convincing examples are the rockshelters or caves that Hohokam ritualists used as reliquaries. For instance, in the Phoenix Basin, pottery, textiles, gourds, arrows, and esoteric items including pahos (prayer sticks), maybe copper ore, and reed "cigarettes" were once cached in Double Butte cave (Haury 1945: 193–202). Turney (1929:79–80) reports further that this cave contained an iron pyrite mirror made partly of *Glycymeris* shell. The "Ceremonial Grotto" at Camelback Mountain (Turney 1929:Map), whose natural salt deposit has been mined for millennia, once contained shell beads, incised and painted fragments of cane, and hundreds of cane cigarettes (*Arizona Republic* 1959).

Although we did not turn up any large, luxuriant, or ostentatious ritual caches in rockshelters during the SMRAP, ritual oblations have been found in the South Mountains. For example, in the 1950s, a Siktyaki bowl, an example of a nonlocal, late-fourteenth-century, proto–Hopi Jeddito yellowware renowned for its religious imagery (Bernardini 2005; see also Munson 2011:87), was once ensconced in a crevice in the South Mountains and is now housed in the collections of the Smoki Museum in Prescott (Todd Bostwick, personal communication 2007). Turney (1929:74), too, described a rockshelter in Hieroglyphic Canyon (between the western and central project areas; see Figure 4.2) that once contained thousands of reed cigarettes, some encrusted with minerals and bound in fours, typical of Hohokam and Mogollon ritual caches elsewhere. It is likely no coincidence that this canyon also houses one of the most hydrologically active springs in the mountains and one of the densest concentrations of petroglyphs.[5]

Shrines

In archaeological parlance, "shrine" is a label often invoked to describe cultural features situated in unique, isolated landscape settings, sometimes associated with esoteric items, and for which any "functional" interpretation is recondite (see Chapter 2). Shrines are places of religious importance and sites of ritual practice; they include built facilities as well as peculiar, conspicuous, or visually prominent landforms, sources and bodies of water, caves, forests, and so on (e.g., Bradley 2000; Brown and Emery 2008; Chouin 2002; Insoll 2007; Ranger 2007). In the American Southwest, archaeologists commonly reference shrines of contemporary and historic indigenous communities to interpret similar archaeological manifestations as sites of ritual practice and religious observance in the past (e.g., Fewkes 1906; Zedeño 1997). Complementing ethnographic information, archaeological and natural landscape settings provide contextual factors that speak to the religious importance of certain cultural features and topographic settings for the area's indigenous residents. Along these lines, the walled-in rockshelters discussed above may constitute Hohokam shrines, given their proximity to springs, their elevated positions, and the sizable density of petroglyphs around them.

In addition to a few large rockshelters, a number of stone constructs in the South Mountains have affinities to shrines used by contemporary Southwestern indigenous communities. One class of these curious features consists of single-coursed rectangular, circular, and "U"-shaped rock alignments and enclosures built atop ridges and knolls with expansive views across the Salt River valley. Cultural, practical, and temporal attributes are difficult to discern

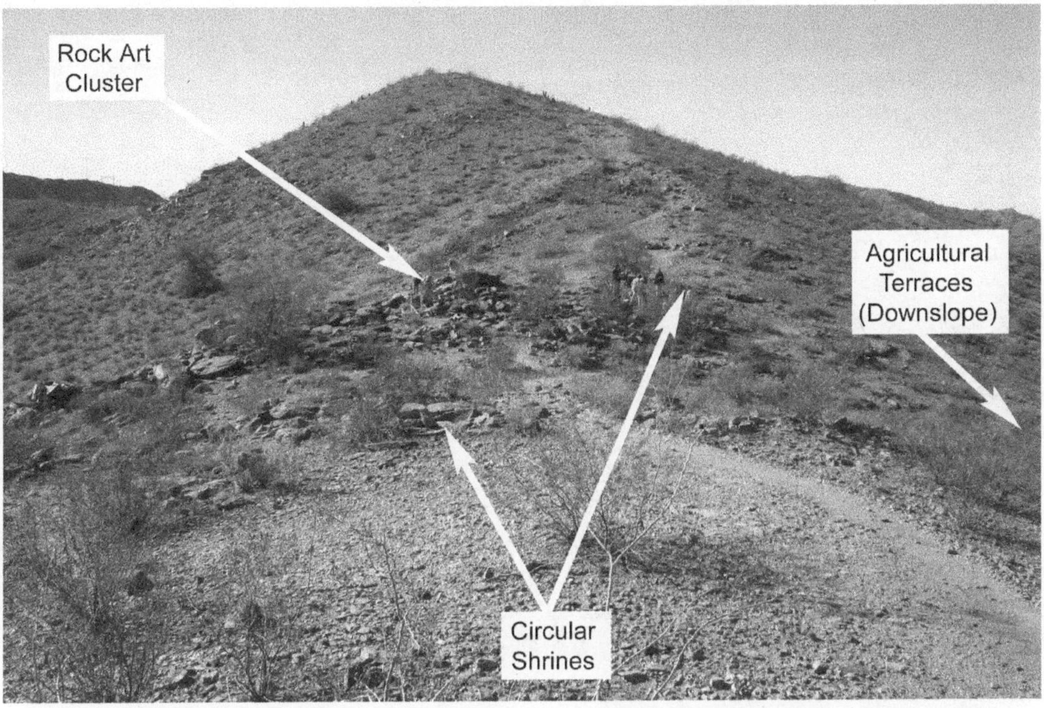

FIGURE 4.12. Overview of the saddle shrine (facing southwest). Circular shrines are single-coursed, dry-laid stone enclosures. The terraces downslope are probably part of an extensive farming system recorded by Frank Midvale in the 1930s.

because these small, dry-laid masonries tend to be found in remote and hard-to-reach settings away from other archaeological contexts, and artifacts, if present, are scant and not clearly associated with the alignments. Although they are conventionally interpreted as hunting blinds, lookouts, signaling stations, or brush-structure foundations, their occasional comingling with petroglyphs, relatively negligible wall heights that would not provide seclusion, and the fitful presence of shrine stones (discussed below) suggest that these stone enclosures may also or rather be shrines (see also Bostwick and Plum 2005).

Two circular rock enclosures, measuring 1 to 2 m in diameter, are nestled in the saddle of a low ridge, just upslope of the linear agricultural terrace system (Midvale's Terraces) at the eastern extremity of the mountains (Figure 4.6). These circular masonries were constructed adjacent to one of the densest concentrations of Hohokam petroglyphs in the South Mountains (Figure 4.12). Test excavations uncovered Colonial period red-on-buff pottery sherds on the floor of one (Simon et al. 2013), reinforcing its Hohokam affiliation. Elsewhere we found two rectangular stone enclosures, both in elevated settings affording expansive viewsheds. One of the rectangular masonries was fashioned by simply erecting two stone alignments between and perpendicular to two bedrock outcrops. The other was raised on the top of a prominent knoll amid a small cluster of petroglyph panels and other ritualized features. Four summit trails at this site (discussed below) converge at the knoll's summit, where this amalgamation of ritualized features is found.

Additional stone constructs suggestive of shrines include a set of upright slabs and a U-shaped rock alignment. At the former, two tabular pieces of granodiorite were positioned upright and chinked with smaller cobbles. These upright slabs create a right angle and are oriented to the cardinal directions. A nearby stone tool

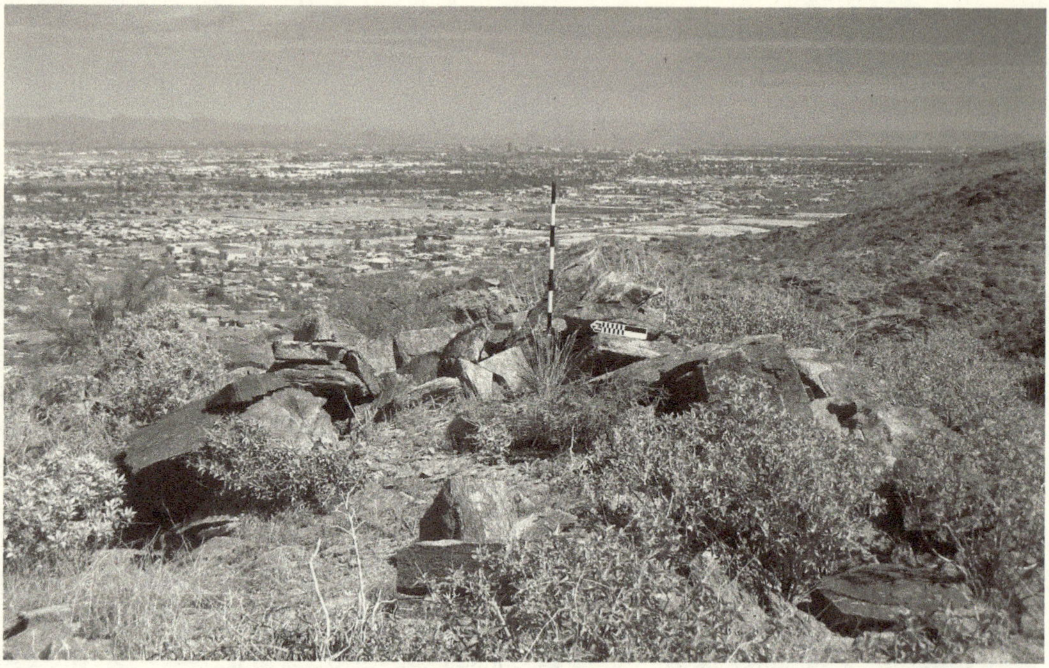

FIGURE 4.13. Overview of a U-shaped shrine (facing northeast). Perched atop a high rise, this dry-laid stone construct opens to the west and offers expansive views across the lower Salt River valley to the north.

and a seemingly old trail hint at a possible Hohokam origin for this feature. The other rock alignment, a U-shaped masonry enclosure on a prominent hill with an opening to the west (Figure 4.13), is reminiscent of Pueblo keyhole- and C-shaped shrines oriented to the cardinal directions and sited on hilltops around villages (e.g., Ortiz 1969; Ortman 2009). However, as in some Pueblo hilltop shrines (Ortman 2009:Table 7.1), we did not find any artifacts in or around the U-shaped alignment in the South Mountains, leaving any cultural and temporal affiliation ambiguous.

In addition to rock alignments, we located three rock piles atop low ridges or hills, and they are the most convincing examples of Hohokam shrines because they parallel known O'odham ones. Frank Russell (1908:254) described the O'odham shrine of Hâhâtesumiehĭn in the Santan Mountains, just southeast of the South Mountains, as a mound of cobbles brought from the villages and piled at the base of a large and prominent Hohokam petroglyph panel. As O'odham passersby and pilgrims visited the shrine, they would place a stone on the pile. Additional offerings included beads, cloth, twigs, shell, fulgurites, bullets, coins, and stone effigies (Russell 1908:254, Plate 60). Outside our project areas a very similar O'odham shrine is situated at the western edge of the South Mountains bajada, near the historic O'odham village of Komatke. This shrine, a large, low dome of cobbles with a diameter of about 8 m and a height of about 1 m, is positioned atop an earthen mound on a hillock with quartz and chrysocolla outcrops nearby. Like the Hâhâtesumiehĭn shrine, this cobble mound bridges the Hohokam-O'odham hiatus: on a recent visit, offerings included Hohokam red-on-buff sherds, historic Papago Red sherds, and one- and five-cent coins dated to the 1970s and 1980s.

The South Mountains cobble-pile shrines were amassed at the upslope termini of summit trails (discussed below), and Hohokam villagers pecked a number of petroglyphs on nearby boulders. These shrines are composed of locally available stones that were concentrated and mounded at the apices of a conical hill and ridge, perhaps

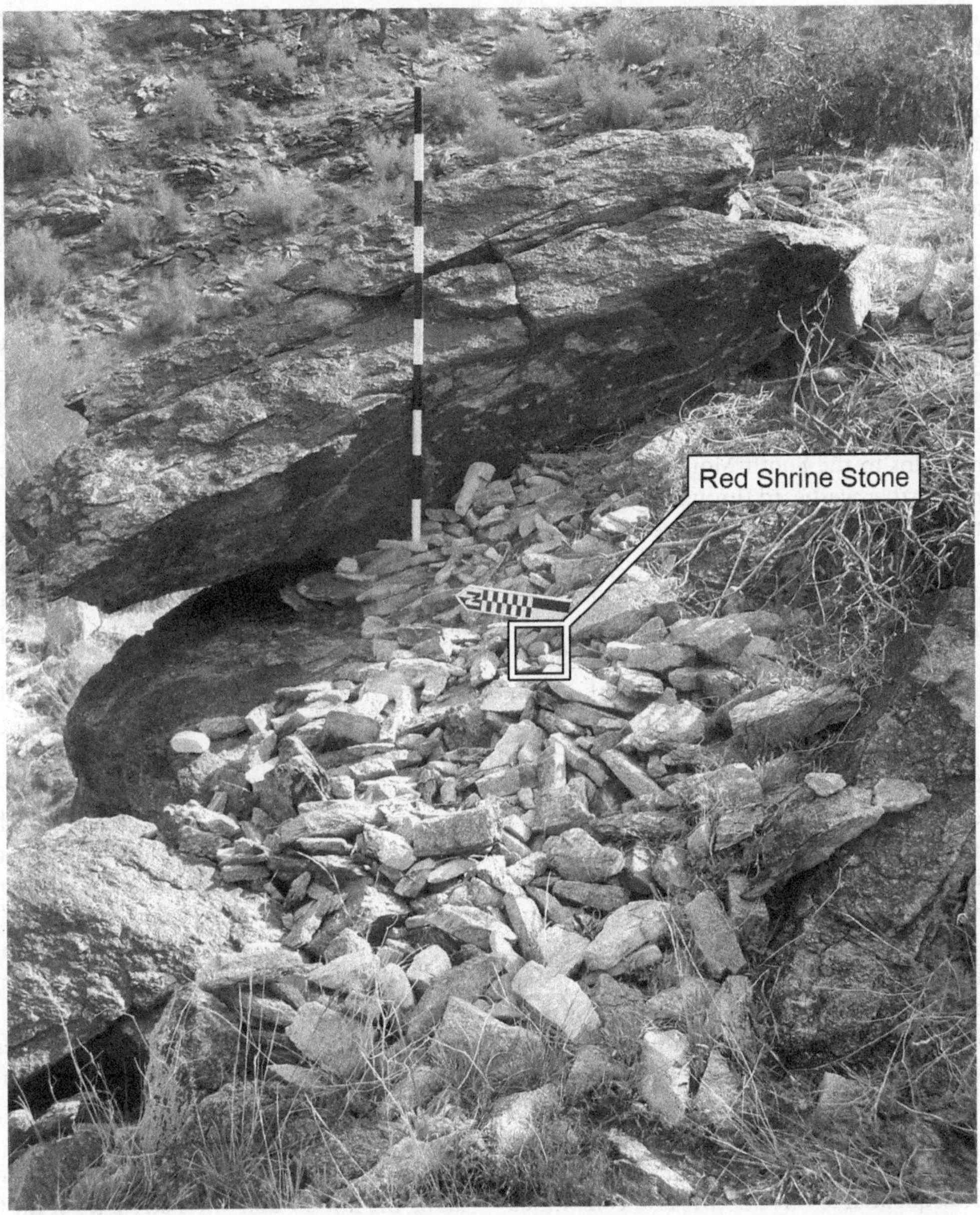

FIGURE 4.14. A rock-pile shrine. This feature, with a red shrine stone atop it, is located at the apex of the summit trail at Goodman Gardens (see Figures 4.15 and 4.17).

deposited as offerings during ritual processions up the summit trails. A lack of historic artifacts and offerings suggests they have not been used for several centuries. Nevertheless, we found several shrine stones—small, alluvially rounded, transported pebbles (see Chapter 3)—on or in close proximity to each of these cobble mounds, supporting their interpretation as Hohokam shrines (Figure 4.14).

Trails

Ancient paths, trails, and roads in the Southwest make up networked systems of transportation and conveyance whose webbed, sinuous, and maze-like structures model intercommunity relations and reveal how people moved through, engaged, conceptualized, and experienced landscapes (e.g., Darling 2006; Darling and Eiselt 2009; Snead 2008:113–132; Stein and Lekson 1992; Van Dyke 2007; White 2007; see also Fowles 2010; Tilley 1994). In the Sonoran Desert, remnant trails, some thousands of years old, connect distant communities, resources, and important places via long-established routes (Darling 2006; Darling and Eiselt 2009; Hayden 1967, 1972; Lumholtz 1912; Riley 1975; Rogers 1966; White 2007). One such long-trodden path, the Komatke-Oyadoibuic Trail, links the Santan Mountains to the South Mountains, then traverses farther westward through a saddle in the Estrella Mountains to villages near Gila Bend, and ultimately turns south and extends all the way to the Gulf of California (Darling 2006; Darling and Eiselt 2009:222–226).

Trails are a pervasive feature on the South Mountains landscape (Figures 4.4–4.6). Nearly all the South Mountains trails conform to Darling and Eiselt's (2009:222) Type II trails, footpaths that lead short distances from villages and are probably related to short-term forays in search of various natural biotic and abiotic resources in the immediate landscape. As Figures 4.4, 4.5, and 4.6 show, the South Mountains trails form an interlaced network linking places in the South Mountains to one another, and they most likely once led to the adjacent Hohokam villages.[6] This trail network blends petroglyph-adorned stages, farming facilities, quarries, and limited-use activity areas into a cohesive continuum of movement and experience. Such connectivity implies that many of these activities were sequential to one another and constituted a repetitive and integrative pattern and style of landscape engagement, with points along the bajadas as places of ingress and egress into the mountains, and those in the upper reaches as intermediate stations along this cycle of coming and going.

Five trails within the project areas are notably different from the Type II trails. These peculiar paths are short segments that start at the base of a relatively steep slope and extend straight, or nearly straight, to the summit of a knoll, hill, or ridge (Figure 4.15). These "summit trails," described elsewhere as "ascent trails" (Darling and Eiselt 2009:204) and "summit paths" (Wallace 2008), are one of the more enigmatic legacies the Hohokam etched into the South Mountains landscape. Summit trails are cleared, sometimes rock-lined, footpaths that ascend an elevated landform in an unbent fashion. On steep, rocky slopes, straight up is the least efficient and most cumbersome way of reaching a summit. This attests that linearity, directionality, and difficulty were intrinsic to the purpose and significance of these trails. Petroglyphs and shrine-like contraptions tend to be found at the trails' apices (Wallace 2008:214–219). More often than not, the hills on which these trails were engineered are conically shaped, and with their light, sandy brown complexion amid a dark backdrop of patinated igneous boulders the trails can be quite noticeable from a long distance away. As I discuss in greater detail in Chapters 7 and 8, these conical summits may be natural, nondomestic analogues for capped mounds in Preclassic villages, or vice versa.

Found only at two sites at the mouth of Goodman Canyon in the central project area (Figure 4.5), these trails are the only documented summit trails in the lower Salt River valley. This is probably not because they occur only in the South Mountains; most likely, researchers are not fully aware of them or their antiquity, and they are overlooked or misunderstood as a result. The small number of known summit trails, however, suggests they are rather uncommon, and this scarcity is perhaps quite telling of their significance. They are better known, albeit still rare, along the middle and lower stretches of the Gila River (e.g., Hedges and Hamann 1992; Landon 1979; Stein 1981:19–22; Wallace 2008:214–219).[7]

The function(s) and cultural affiliation(s) of summit trails are poorly understood. They may have been quick paths to reach hilltop forts or lookouts in times of war, or perhaps they are examples of landscape "art," like the intaglios on the lower Gila and Colorado Rivers (e.g., Stein 1981). Wallace (2008:214–219) has elsewhere surveyed the known distribution of summit trails

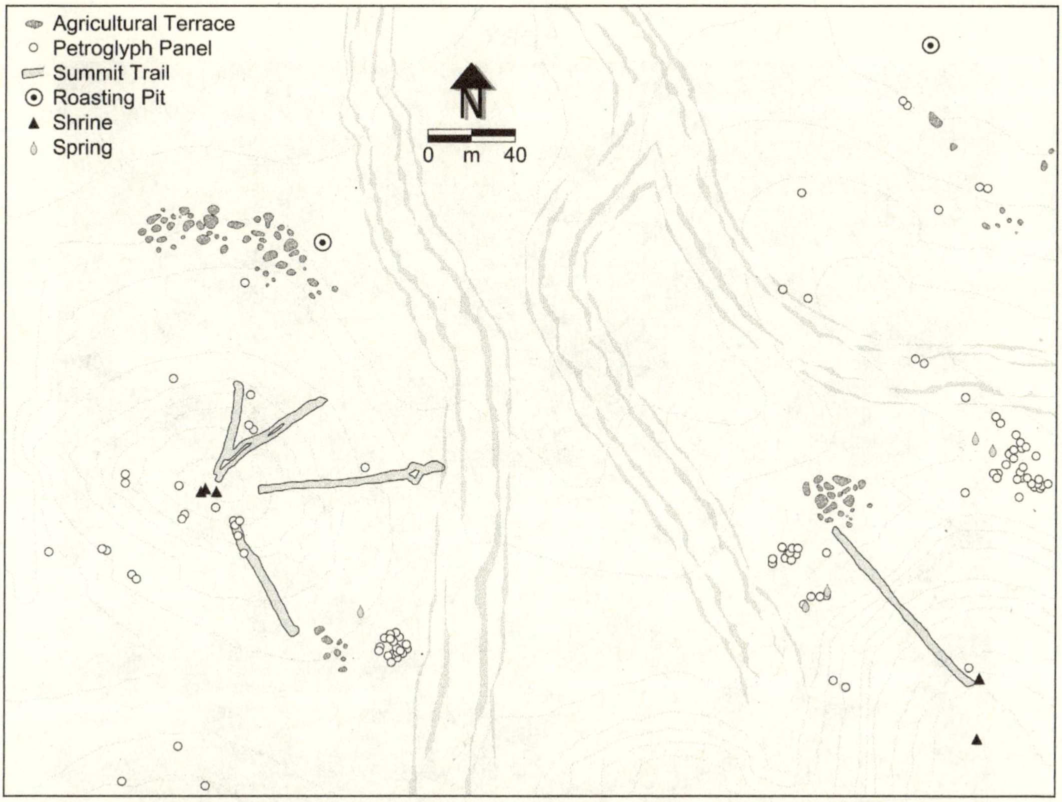

FIGURE 4.15. Summit trail complexes (figure by Will Russell, adapted from Wright 2011:Figure 36). Goodman Hilltop, with four summit trails, is in the western half while Goodman Gardens is to the east. Note the cluster of rock art and terraces at the bases of the summit trails and the shrines at their apices.

and made a sound case for their ritual importance. While the use(s) for these trails may have varied across space and time, as I describe below, those in the South Mountains were undoubtedly constructed by the Hohokam and ritually revered.

At Goodman Hilltop, four summit trails merge at the top and center of a naturally leveled conical hill (Figure 4.15, left). These four trails are confined to the hill's eastern half, and two have been dug into the slope and lined with boulders and cobbles. Much of its rock lining has since slumped, but the depth of the southeast/northwest-oriented trail, when the excavated and mounded portions are considered together, was somewhere in the range of 50 to 80 cm (Figure 4.16). This trail has petroglyphs pecked into it, one of a spiral on a loose boulder about mid-slope and a series of other panels on bedrock near the summit. The other dug-out and lined trail, the one oriented east/west, is not as deep, less than 40 cm at any point. At the basal ends of these lined trails are rectangular depressions, measuring approximately 2 to 2.5 m in length and width, from which the trails emanate. The other two summit trails are well-worn tracks, and one is partially rock-lined near its zenith, but neither was excavated into the slope nor has adorning petroglyphs.

On the summit of Goodman Hilltop is an assortment of features indicative of ritual performances. The four summit trails merge at the summit's center, where a rock pile and rectangular stone shrine were erected (see discussion above). A large dirt mound, approximately 4 m wide and 1 m high, is also found at the center of this hilltop. The dirt appears to have been brought to the summit, since the landform

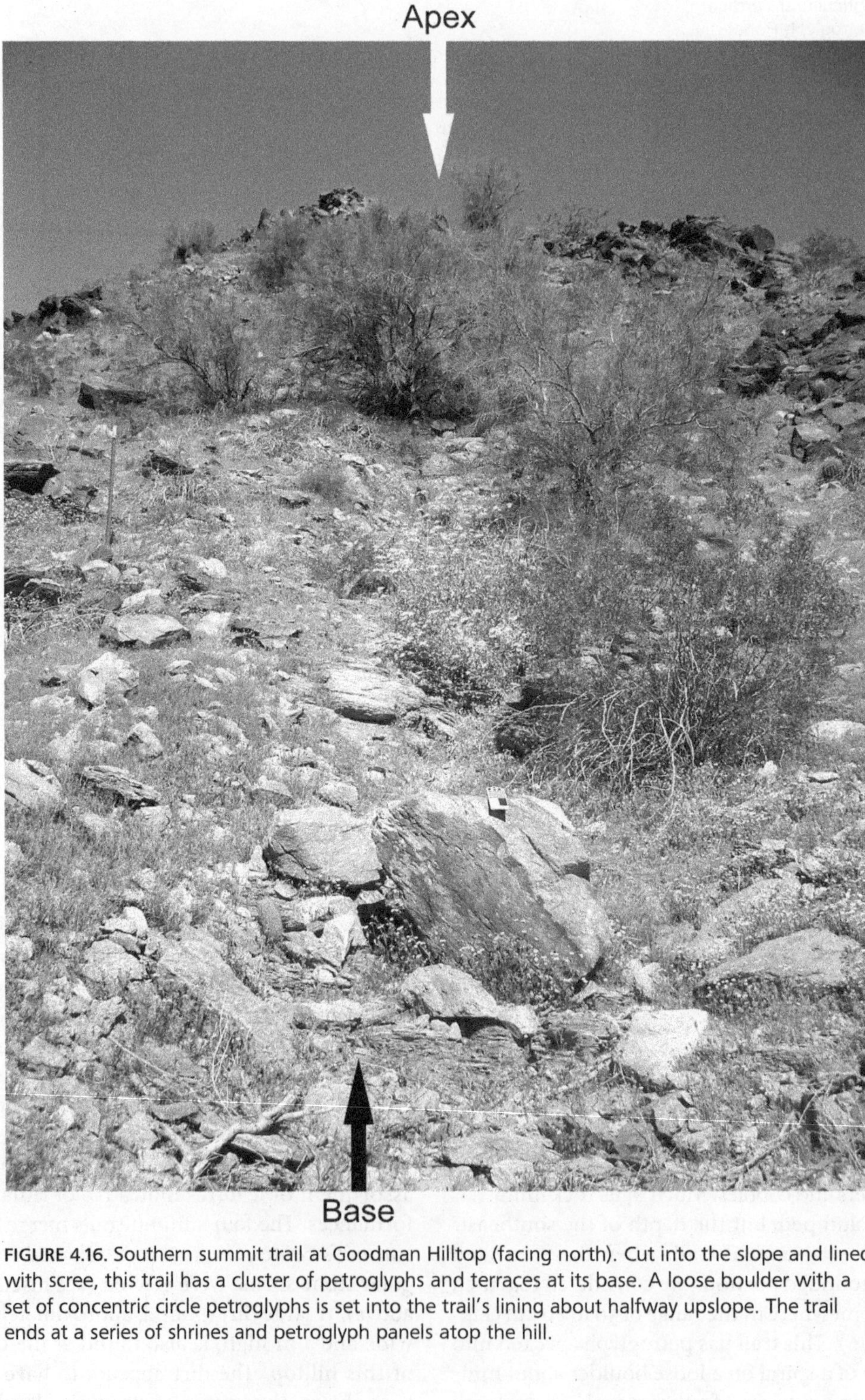

FIGURE 4.16. Southern summit trail at Goodman Hilltop (facing north). Cut into the slope and lined with scree, this trail has a cluster of petroglyphs and terraces at its base. A loose boulder with a set of concentric circle petroglyphs is set into the trail's lining about halfway upslope. The trail ends at a series of shrines and petroglyph panels atop the hill.

exhibits only a thin coat of residual and aeolian sands, and its moundedness is reminiscent of a melted adobe structure. There is also a trail that skirts the circumference of the ridgetop, with a cairn and three bedrock outcrops stationed at the four cardinal points. On the summit's far western edge is a large cleared area, and other, smaller clearings are scattered about. A modicum of petroglyphs also occur across the top of the hill, but they are concentrated along the summit's periphery, perhaps as a symbolic delineation of space (e.g., Swartz and Hurlbutt 1994).

The fifth summit trail ascends a low ridge at Goodman Gardens just across an arroyo from and well within sight of the four at Goodman Hilltop (Figure 4.15, right). Like the two at Goodman Hilltop, this summit trail was dug into the slope and lined along its sides, and it is estimated to have once been between 50 and 80 cm deep (Figure 4.17). A rectangular depression also forms the nadir portion of this trail. Atop the ridge the trail peters out at a rock-pile shrine (Figure 4.14) below and in front of a petroglyph panel bearing a single anthropomorphic figure (Figure 4.18). Another rock-pile shrine is sited about 10 m farther along the ridge. This single summit trail lacks adorning petroglyphs, and it ascends a ridge rather than a hill, but its formal similarities with and proximity to the others at Goodman Hilltop suggest it held comparable if not identical importance. Together they evidence a complex, spatially choreographed yet bifurcated set of stages for a ritual network in this pocket of the mountains.

The summit trails at Goodman Hilltop and Goodman Gardens share other qualities as well. For example, C-shaped agricultural terraces cluster at the bases of each trail (Figure 4.15). Moreover, one trail at each site, arguably the paramount trails, judging by their greater depth and rock lining (Figures 4.16 and 4.17), radiate upslope from nearby springs. These trails thus unite, both symbolically and corporeally, the springs and agricultural terraces at the landforms' feet with the zenith zone at their summits, both of which bear a series of probable shrines. Lastly, and perhaps most significantly, there are dense concentrations of petroglyphs around the base of each of these summit trails (Figures 4.19 and 4.20).[8] This cohesion of economically designed and religiously inspired places and activities constituted a collective body of performances and practices that bridged ritual and subsistence and transcended any divisions of sacred and profane. In this manner, petroglyphs are not solely ritualized features, and farming terraces are not simply a source of food.

The foregoing inventory of archaeological features casts a portrait of the predominant range of practices carried out by the Hohokam in the South Mountains. In this synthetic overview I omitted some details, and there are surely more, possibly different, types of archaeological features in other, uninvestigated areas of the mountains. The inventoried features, however, offer a general context for understanding petroglyphs in their broader cultural settings. For additional insight, below I incorporate into the picture the ceramic and stone artifacts people dropped, broke, lost, and left as they traveled into and out of this landscape while carrying out that array of economic and ritual practices.

Artifacts

Like the archaeological features, artifacts provide heuristic glimpses of the ways people engaged the South Mountains landscape, including the types of practices performed alongside or in conjunction with petroglyph manufacture, interaction, and viewing. In this section I report on the artifact assemblage at large in order to piece together a broad chronological, social, and behavioral framework for the South Mountains cultural landscape. I draw on these data in Chapters 5 and 6 to specifically address their connection with the South Mountains petroglyphs.

Ceramics

There have been three previous investigations of the types of ceramics scattered across the South Mountains. During his pioneering reconnaissance of the petroglyphs, Ernest Snyder (1966) relied on ceramic associations to help support his position that the South Mountains petroglyphs were crafted by the Hohokam. Although he did not publish any quantitative data, Snyder

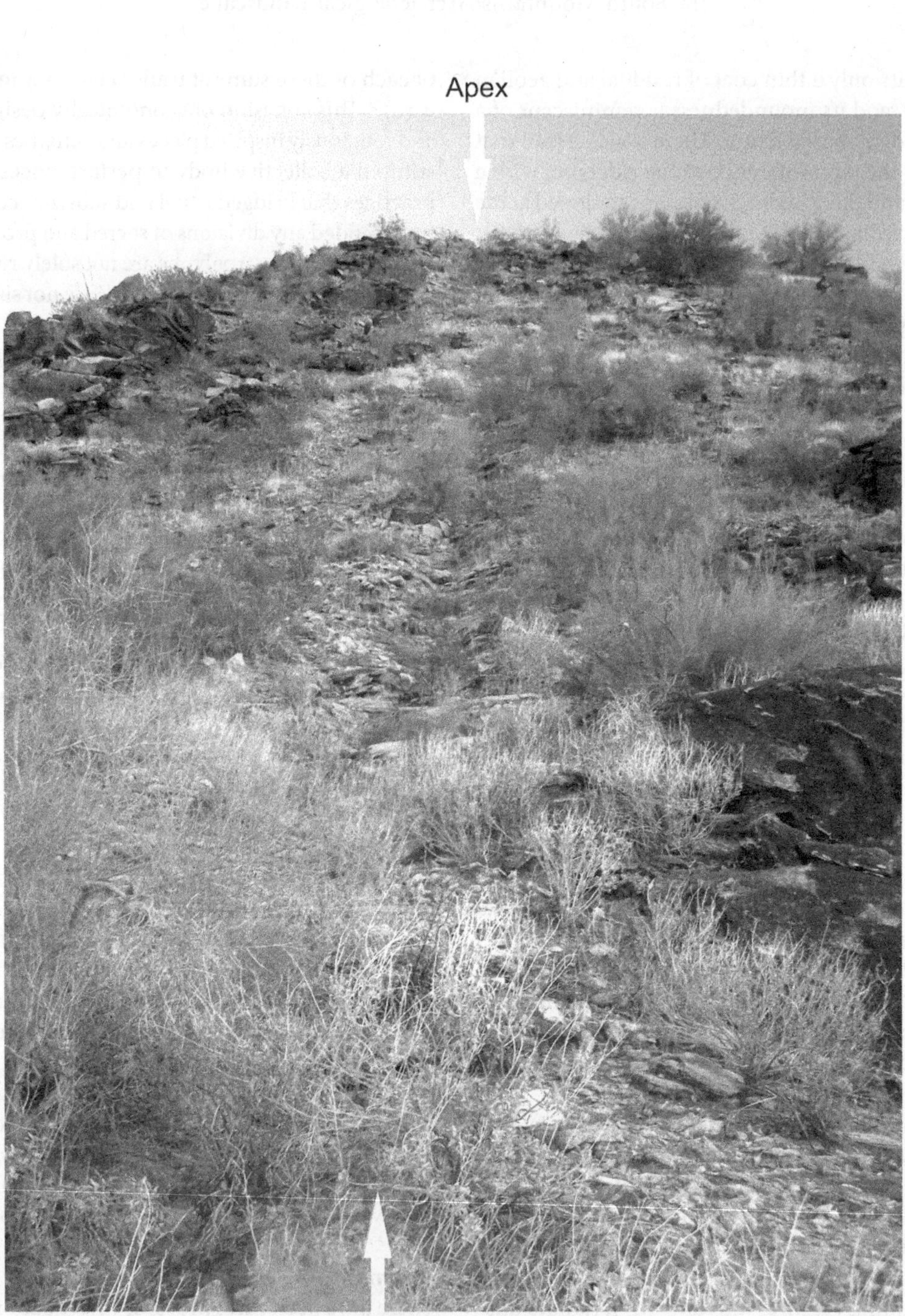

FIGURE 4.17. Summit trail at Goodman Gardens (facing southeast). Cut into the slope and lined with skree, this trail has a cluster of petroglyphs and terraces at its base. It ends at two rock-pile shrines (Figure 4.14) and an anthropomorph petroglyph (Figure 4.18).

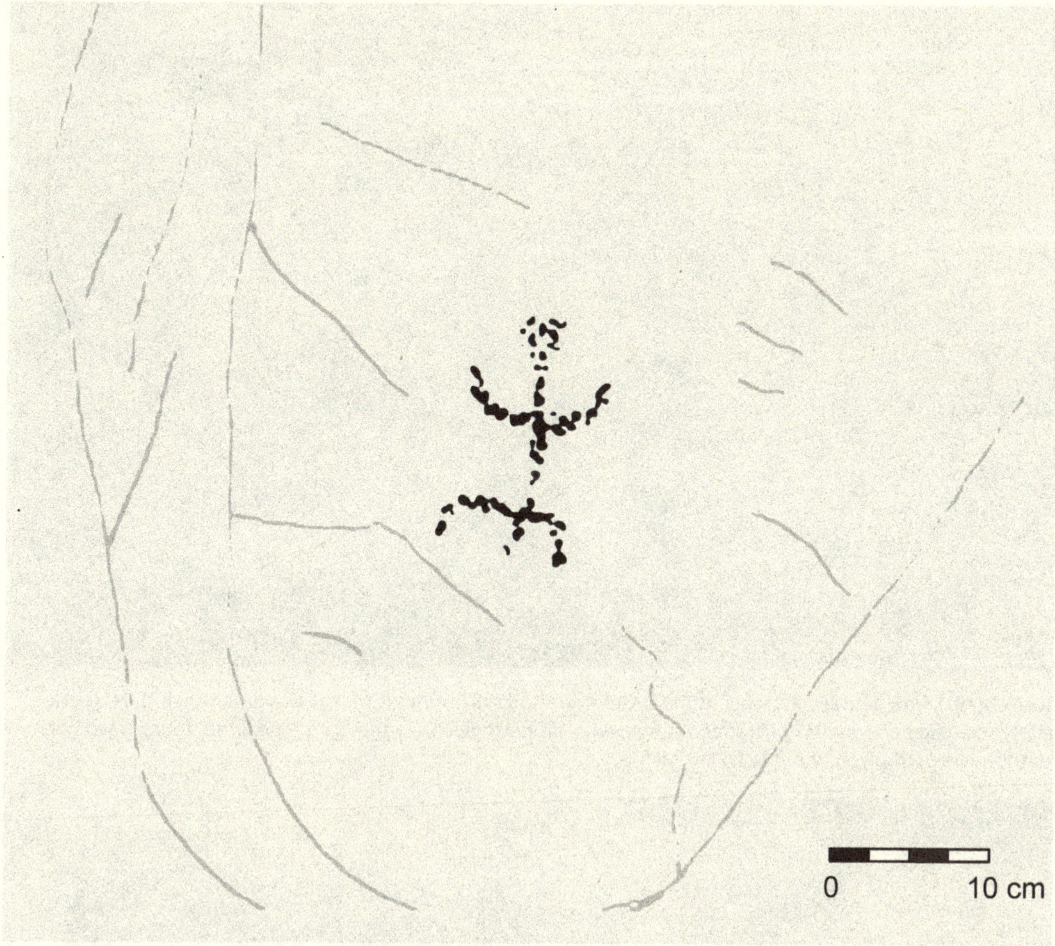

FIGURE 4.18. Panel with an anthropomorph petroglyph at the apex of the Goodman Gardens summit trail.

commented that the broken pottery found near petroglyphs "consisted primarily of red sherds with a very few red-on-buff" (1966:706). Results of the SMRAP suggest that Snyder's observation holds true for red-on-buff ceramics, though his assessment regarding a preponderance of red sherds is not mirrored in our data (Table 4.3). Our systematic survey analyzed more than 2,800 surface ceramics; buffware (including red-on-buff) makes up nearly 25 percent of the assemblage whereas redware is just shy of 7 percent. Snyder's point is technically accurate, however, since he did not specify whether the red sherds were actually slipped *redwares* characteristic of the Hohokam Classic period. Many, if not most, of the *plainware* sherds found in the South Mountains have a strong red-brown to brick-red hue that is due not to a red slip but rather to their long-term exposure to the elements while lying on the granitic sands. To be sure, on several occasions we found modern coins, all dating to the 1980s and 1990s, patinated to a near black and actually warped from continuous exposure to the intense heat of the desert sun. Surface ceramics were subject to this same intensity of solar heat for hundreds of years, and as they (plainware and buffware alike) slowly baked, year after year, they continued to oxidize, turning progressively redder over time.

The second concerted effort to address the types of archaeological ceramics in the South Mountains was carried out by Todd Bostwick

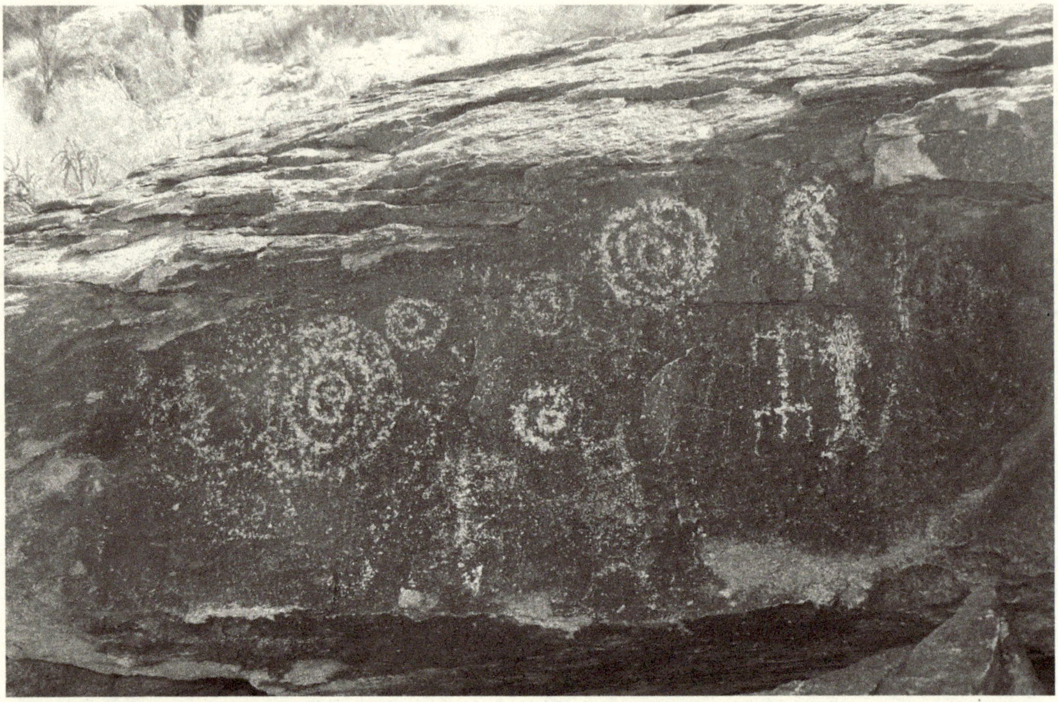

FIGURE 4.19. Large petroglyph panel at the base of the southern summit trail at Goodman Hilltop. Note the faintly scratched and partially abraded anthropomorph petroglyphs to the right. The large, four-ringed concentric circle petroglyph at left is 20 cm tall.

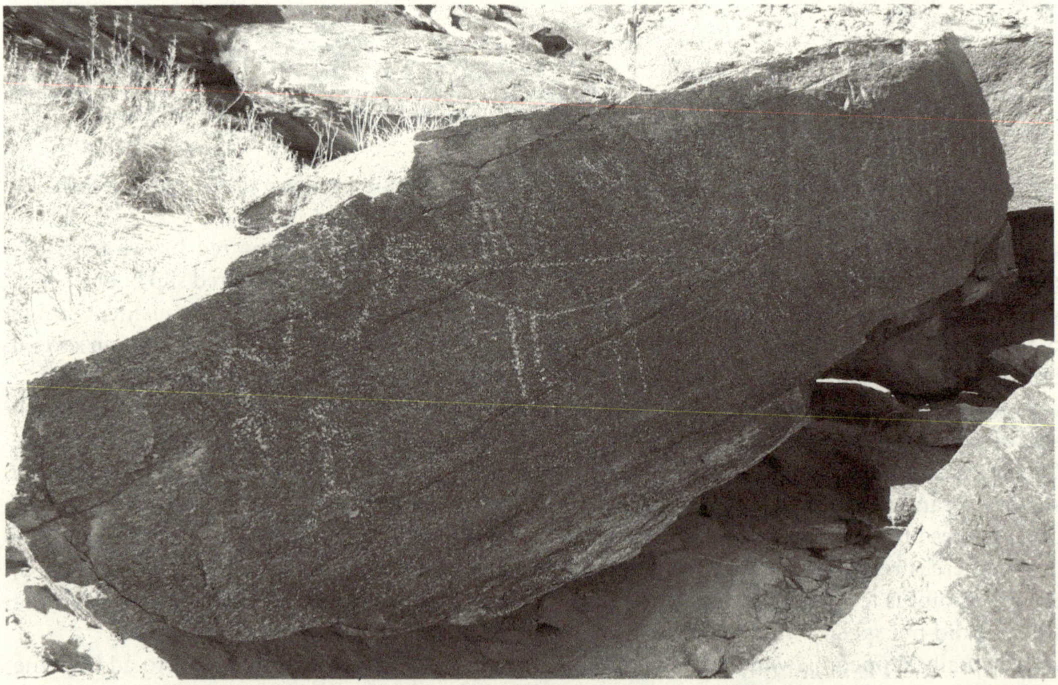

FIGURE 4.20. Large petroglyph panel at the base of the Goodman Gardens summit trail (facing west). With an integrated arrangement of anthropomorphs, a large bighorn sheep, and several long, wavy snakes, the panel may depict a narrative scene. The anthropomorph petroglyph at lower left is 21 cm tall.

TABLE 4.3. Counts and Percentages of Sherds and Minimum Number of Vessels (MNV) by Ware and Vessel Form.

	Bowls		Jars		Indeterminate		Other		Total	
Ware	Sherds	MNV	Sherds	MNV	Sherds	MNV	Sherds	MNV	Sherds	MNV
Plainware[a]	2	2	932	289	979	341	—	—	1,913	632
	0.1%	0.2%	33.0%	27.8%	34.7%	32.8%			67.8%	60.8%
Buffware[b]	107	59	307	116	286	170	1[d]	1[d]	701	346
	3.8%	5.7%	10.9%	11.2%	10.1%	16.4%	<0.1%	0.1%	24.8%	33.3%
Redware[c]	20	7	152	31	24	12	—	—	196	50
	0.7%	0.7%	5.4%	3.0%	0.9%	1.2%			6.9%	4.8%
Polychrome	2	2	—	—	—	—	—	—	2	2
	0.1%	0.2%							0.1%	0.2%
Indeterminate	—	—	—	—	10	9	—	—	10	9
					0.4%	0.9%			0.4%	0.9%
Total	131	70	1,391	436	1,299	532	1[d]	1[d]	2,822	1,039
	4.6%	6.6%	49.3%	42.1%	46.0%	51.2%	<0.1%	0.1%	100.0%	100.0%

[a] Plainwares include two sherds, representing two MNV, of likely Protohistoric origin.

[b] Buffwares include brown-paste variants and six Classic period Casa Grande Red-on-buff sherds representing one MNV (no lower Colorado buffware observed in this study).

[c] Redwares include 14 Sedentary period Sacaton Red sherds, representing five MNV.

[d] This specimen is the rim of either a double jar form (e.g., Haury 1976:Figure 12.26.i') or anthropomorphic vessel (Haury 1976:Figure 11.10).

during his petroglyph survey in the 1990s. Bostwick opportunistically collected 769 sherds and offered several interesting observations regarding the ceramic types and temper petrographies represented in his sample (Bostwick and Krocek 2002:32–34). Bostwick's data, which also exhibit a rather low redware frequency, suggested to him that the South Mountains evidence a predilection for Hohokam engagement during the Preclassic, but he noted that potential symbolic or functional differences between buffware and redware could account for the sparseness of redware in the mountains. Bostwick also found that the sherds are tempered predominantly with sands of South Mountains granodiorite and secondarily with Estrella gneiss. David Abbott's studies of Hohokam ceramic production and exchange in the Phoenix Basin have revealed that most plainwares were produced with locally available sands and were principally exchanged within irrigation communities along canals (Abbott 2000, 2003a, 2009; Abbott et al. 2006; Van Keuren et al. 1997). This has afforded strong spatial control over analyses of pottery manufacture and distribution because within the Salt River valley there are seven discrete geological sources, or petrofacies, on which the Hohokam relied for material for tempering their pots. Accordingly, aplastic tempering agents can reveal not only a vessel's location of manufacture but potentially also the village(s) from where the vessels originated before their discard in the South Mountains.

The South Mountains are actually the parent source for two of the Phoenix Basin sand petrofacies: South Mountains granodiorite along the north-central and eastern slopes and Estrella gneiss along the western extremities (Reynolds 1985). Since Hohokam potters probably gathered tempering materials from sources close to their domiciles and workshops (Arnold 1985), settlements atop the South Mountains granodiorite and Estrella gneiss petrofacies were the most likely sites of manufacture for vessels containing these distinctive sands. In fact, Las Canopas, at the northeastern edge of the mountains and within the South Mountains granodiorite petrofacie (Figure 3.2), is the only Hohokam village in the Phoenix Basin aside from Snaketown with unequivocal evidence for on-site pottery manufacture (Czarzasty and Bustoz 2012). The presence of South Mountains granodiorite sand in a vessel, however, may not be a reliable indicator of where the vessel originated immediately before it was brought into and left or disposed of in the South Mountains. This is because during the Sedentary period villagers living around the north-central and eastern edges of the South Mountains, such as at Las Canopas, started specializing in making large plainware ollas (with granodiorite temper) and traded their wares in great quantities across the valley (Abbott 2000:202–208; Rice and Peterson 2009; Van Keuren et al. 1997). In the early Classic they added polished redware bowls and jars to their craft assemblage, so such vessels tempered with South Mountains granodiorite and left in the South Mountains (or elsewhere) may have been brought there from any number of villages, not just those where the vessels were originally manufactured.

While the complexity of Hohokam ceramic specialization and distribution blurs the provenance picture, the types of temper in sherds nonetheless provide useful insights into who was using and visiting the South Mountains landscape at gross spatial and temporal scales. Intuitively, we should expect the South Mountains to have been visited most often by the people residing nearest to them, principally denizens of villages and hamlets along the canals to the immediate north (Canal 7) and east (Canal System 1) (Figure 3.2). Indeed, nonindustrial farmers tend to concentrate their daily productive endeavors within about 2 km of their homes (Chisholm 1979), and archaeologists generally consider a distance of about 7 km to be an appropriate threshold for an agricultural community's "catchment area" in the American Southwest (e.g., Varien 1999). These ethnographically derived thresholds imply that the South Mountains lie within the daily range of villagers from Villa Buena, within the Estrella gneiss petrofacie, and Pueblo Viejo, Las Canopas, Los Hornos, and Los Guanacos, all within the South Mountains granodiorite petrofacie. We can rely on the types of temper in sherds found in the South Mountains to test this assumption. Accordingly, if these local villagers were responsible for most of the activities carried out in the South Mountains, I expect (1) plainwares and redwares in the western half of the mountains to be tempered mostly with gneiss; (2) those in the eastern half to be tempered predominantly with granodiorite; and (3) a more mixed assemblage of gneiss and granodiorite temper types in sherds found in the central region of the mountains.

One of our aims in the SMRAP was to model village interaction with the South Mountains by considering the provenance of certain artifacts, principally ceramics through their aplastic additives. Our project areas, however, are not reflective of the entire South Mountains landscape because we concentrated our efforts on the northeastern slopes. Fortunately, Bostwick's earlier work spanned the entire mountain range, and his data (Bostwick and Krocek 2002:Table 1) provide a nice synopsis of how wares with different tempering agents are patterned across the larger landscape. Figure 4.21 portrays the east-to-west distribution of plainware sherds when grouped by the seven sand petrofacies used for temper, and even though many of the localities are plagued by small sample sizes, these data show a general trend of decreasing granodiorite and increasing gneiss as one moves west. A shift from a predominantly granodiorite-tempered assemblage to a gneiss-dominated one near the Central Avenue locality corresponds with the general geological divide between these parent bedrocks (Wright 2011:Figure 8). This gradation matches my expectations of the ceramic assemblage if the mountains were used and visited most often by the villagers residing nearest to them—from villages along the mountains' northern slopes, within the Estrella gneiss and South Mountains granodiorite petrofacies, and exploiting the western and eastern portions, respectively. It is thus reasonable to conclude that most of the activities carried out on the north face of this landscape, including petroglyph production, were undertaken by residents from the nearby villages of Villa Buena, Pueblo Viejo, Las Canopas, Los Hornos, and Los Guanacos (Figure 3.2).

Watts and Lack (2008) provided the third analysis of ceramics found within the South Mountains landscape. Instead of offering a re-

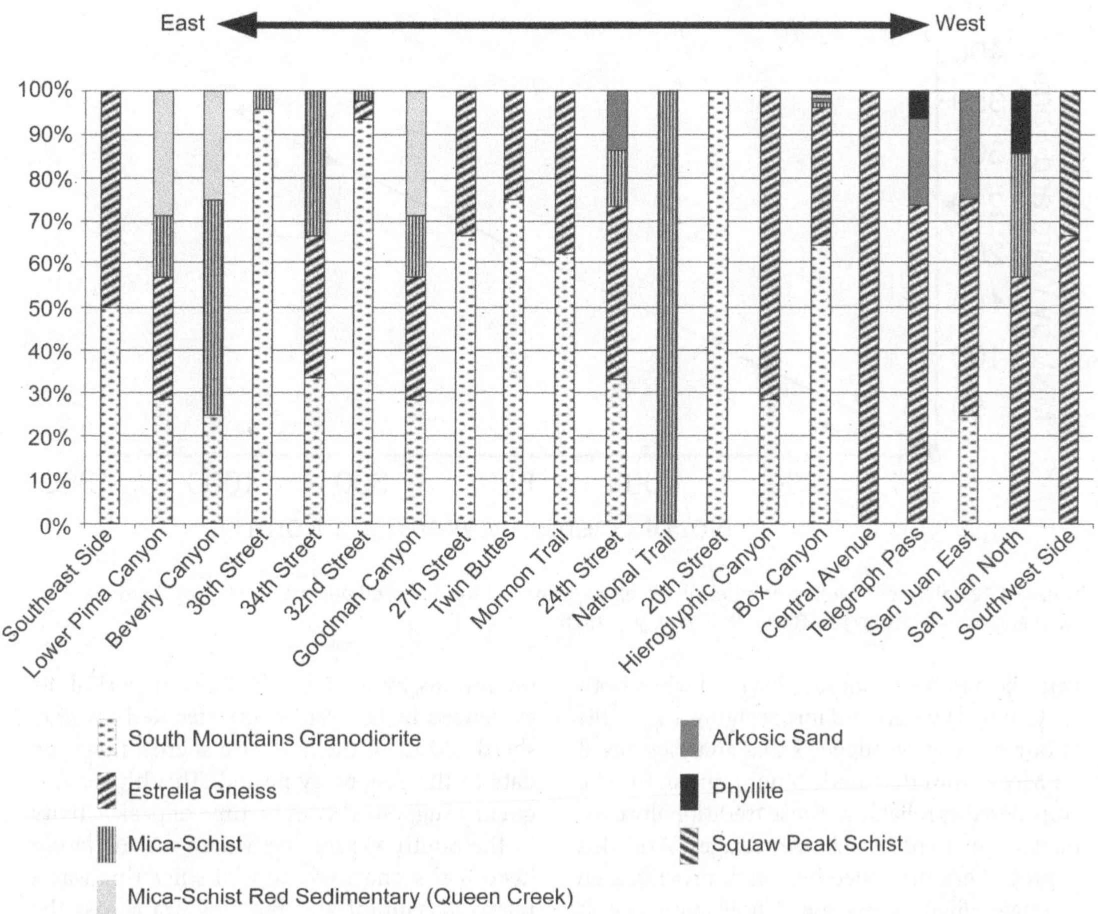

FIGURE 4.21. Temper types in Hohokam plainware sherds from the South Mountains. These data are from Bostwick's survey and are grouped according to his localities (see Bostwick and Krocek 2002:Table 1 and Figure 2). There is a spatial shift in plainware temper types, from a predominance of sherds with South Mountains granodiorite at the east end of the range to a preponderance of sherds with Estrella gneiss at the west end.

gional perspective, however, they focused on a small sample from surface and excavated contexts adjacent to a cluster of C-shaped agricultural terraces and roasting pits in the northeastern reaches of our central project area (Figure 4.5). These data also register a strong Preclassic signature, and most of the plainware sherds were tempered with variable amounts of South Mountains granodiorite. This led the authors to suggest that the pots were made in the general vicinity of the project area, probably at one of the adjacent villages, hamlets, or farmsteads, the closest of which was Las Canopas.

Although our recent surveys were not as spatially extensive as Bostwick's, the SMRAP's systematic collection offers a strong representation of the wares, forms, and temper types found within the mountain's north-central and northeastern reaches, and helps clarify how the broken pottery vessels are associated with other facets of the cultural landscape. The SMRAP survey turned up 2,822 ceramic sherds representing at least 1,039 vessels, a calculation I refer to as the minimum number of vessels (MNV) (Table 4.3).[9] Converting sherd counts to vessel estimates adds a level of abstraction to an already fuzzy archaeological dataset; however, the estimated 1,039 vessels are strongly and significantly correlated

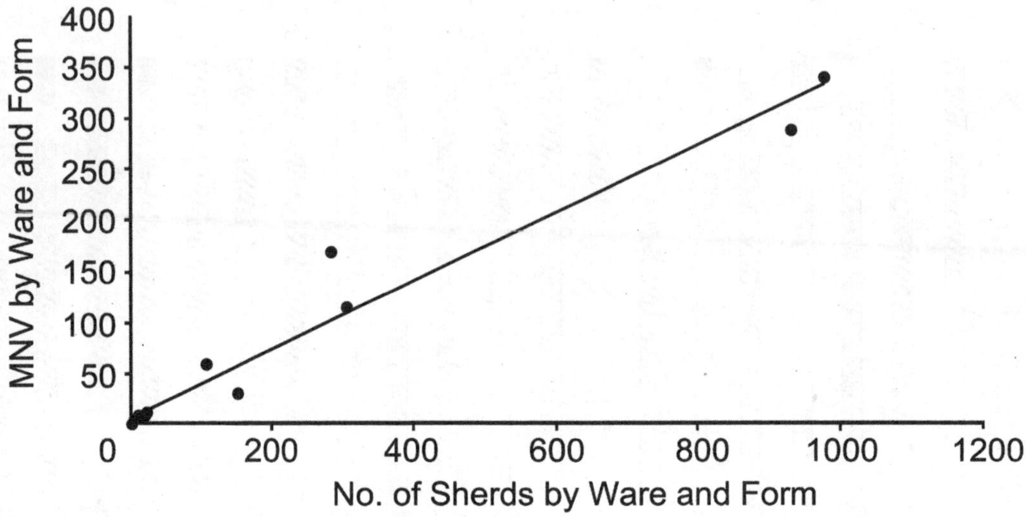

FIGURE 4.22. Inferred minimum number of vessels by ware and form plotted against number of sherds by ware and form ($y = 0.333x + 8.833$, $R^2 = .957$, $p < .001$).

with the number of sherds observed when both are grouped by ware and form (Figure 4.22). This strong correlation suggests that analyses based on MNV from the South Mountains should be considered as reliable as those traditionally conducted on sherd-based assemblages. And this approach has the added benefit of providing an estimate, albeit a gross one, of how many vessels were actually broken and discarded in the project areas.

Table 4.3 presents rough counts and percentages of ceramic wares and forms in the current sample. As expected, plainwares dominate the assemblage, followed by buffwares, then redwares, and finally a trace of polychromes.[10] As Bostwick pointed out (Bostwick and Krocek 2002:33–34), the small amounts of redware and polychrome sherds in the South Mountains point to a predominantly Preclassic overtone to the array of activities once carried out in this landscape. While most buffware sherds are fractured and heavily weathered, nearly 20 percent of the assemblage can be assigned to a cultural period, and in some cases a particular phase (Table 4.4), a fairly high success rate for a surface collection.

The South Mountains Buffware assemblage shows that the Hohokam were frequenting the mountains by at least the Pioneer period, as evidenced by several Sweetwater Red-on-gray sherds. Most of the buffware sherds, however, date to the Sedentary period. This higher frequency suggests this was a time of peak activity in the South Mountains, which fits the larger historical scenario quite well since this was a relatively vibrant and bustling era across the Hohokam world—ballcourt ritualism and the widespread exchange of craft goods were in full swing, the canal systems had reached their maximum extent, and village sizes and presumably populations had culminated (see Chapter 3). Nevertheless, a number of factors could be contributing to a possible overrepresentation of Sedentary buffware: (1) buffware frequency could simply be correlated with population growth during the Preclassic and not necessarily indicative of increased activity relative to population size; (2) more Sedentary period sherds can be typed based on factors that lead to better preservation, including, for example, greater tensile strength, which has been demonstrated between Sacaton and Casa Grande Buffwares (Beck 2002); (3) Sedentary period buffware sherds have more diagnostic attributes and are thus easier to type; (4) a reduction in the ratio of plainware

TABLE 4.4. Counts and Percentages of Buffware Sherds and Minimum Number of Vessels (MNV) by Period and Vessel Form.

	Bowls		Jars		Other		Indeterminate		Total	
Period	Sherds	MNV	Sherds	MNV	Sherds	MNV	Sherds	MNV	Sherds	MNV
Pioneer	6 0.9%	2 0.6%	—	—	—	—	1 0.1%	1 0.3%	7 1.0%	3 0.9%
Pioneer/Colonial	8 1.1%	5 1.4%	—	—	—	—	10 1.4%	5 1.4%	18 2.6%	10 2.9%
Colonial	16 2.3%	7 2.0%	10 1.4%	5 1.4%	—	—	7 1.0%	6 1.7%	33 4.7%	18 5.2%
Colonial/Sedentary	—	—	8 1.1%	4 1.2%	—	—	—	—	8 1.1%	4 1.2%
Sedentary	2 0.3%	1 0.3%	93 13.3%	21 6.1%	1[a] 0.1%	1[a] 0.3%	35 5.0%	3 0.9%	131 18.7%	26 7.5%
Sedentary/Classic	—	—	36 5.1%	1 0.3%	—	—	—	—	36 5.1%	1 0.3%
Classic										
Soho	—	—	6 0.9%	1 0.3%	—	—	—	—	6 0.9%	1 0.3%
Civano	—	—	—	—	—	—	—	—	—	—
Indeterminate	75 10.7%	44 12.7%	154 22.0%	84 24.3%	—	—	233 33.2%	155 44.8%	462 65.9%	283 81.8%
Total	107 15.3%	59 17.1%	307 43.8%	116 33.5%	1[a] 0.1%	1[a] 0.3%	286 40.8%	170 49.1%	701 100.0%	346 100.0%

Note: Sample includes red-on-gray and brown-paste variants (no lower Colorado buffware observed in this study).
[a] This specimen is the rim of either a double jar form (e.g., Haury 1976:Figure 12.26.i') or anthropomorphic vessel (Haury 1976:Figure 11.10).

to buffware vessels brought into the mountains took place between the Colonial and Sedentary periods; or (5) Sedentary period buffwares were more plentiful or better distributed among communities (Abbott et al. 2001) and were therefore used for a greater variety of tasks and in more diverse settings.

Potential representation biases aside, the ceramic data bolster previous suppositions that the South Mountains contain a considerable Preclassic component. To understand how this compares with village contexts, in Table 4.5 I compiled the counts of various ceramic wares recovered from some of the major Hohokam villages in the Phoenix Basin. While the samples from each village were not randomly selected, since most of the excavations were conducted as environmental mitigation projects and spatial representativeness was thus predetermined, the pooled data likely provide a fairly accurate approximation of the proportions of the different wares and forms as they occur in village contexts. It proved difficult to impossible to distinguish between purely Preclassic and Classic period contexts from the data tables in the original reports, so the temporal components in Table 4.5 should be considered rough approximates.

Figure 4.23 compares the South Mountains assemblage with those from the Phoenix Basin villages. The South Mountains assemblage, with high buffware and low redware proportions, compares more favorably with Preclassic village contexts than Classic ones. The obvious differences in proportions of plainware, redware, and buffware between the mountains and villages are statistically significant ($\chi^2 = 19{,}230.5$, df = 2, $p < .001$), but a low measure of association ($V^2 = 0.29$) cautions that such discrepancies may be due to different sample sizes. Curiously, the proportion of buffware in the South Mountains

TABLE 4.5. Pooled Counts of Ceramic Wares and Vessel Forms from Selected Hohokam Villages in the Phoenix Basin.

Village	Represented Temporal Component[a]	Wares[b,c]						Forms[b,c]		References
		Plainware	Buffware[d]	Redware[e]	Poly[f]	Other[g]	Total	Bowls	Jars	
Casa Grande Community	Predominantly Preclassic	4,145 67%	1,708 27%	321 5%	1 <.5%	36 1%	6,211	429 57%	325 43%	Abbott (2001:Table 4.3); Abbott and Henderson (2001); Smith (2001:Table 5.1)
Dutch Canal Ruins	Preclassic/Classic	10,222 75%	697 5%	2,081 15%	313 2%	299 2%	13,612	501 43%	659 57%	Henderson (2003:Tables 6.1 and 6.7); Motsinger (1994:Tables 12.3 and 12.8)
La Ciudad de los Hornos	Predominantly Preclassic	12,304 84%	2,342 16%	56 <.5%	—	22 <.5%	14,724	9 28%	23 72%	Howard and Effland (1990); Wilcox and Howard (1990:Table 6)
Las Acequias	Preclassic/Classic	12,562 80%	1,723 11%	1,194 8%	150 1%	13 <.5%	15,642	56 76%	18 24%	Hackbarth (1997a:Appendices B.1 and B.2)
Las Canopas	Preclassic	40,668 92%	3,415 8%	297 1%	1 <.5%	33 <.5%	44,414	50 38%	81 62%	Abbott (1997:98, Table 6.1); Hackbarth (1997b:Tables 3.2, 3.4, and 3.5)
Las Colinas	Sedentary/Classic	93,633 67%	15,981 12%	24,557 18%	1,492 1%	3,257 2%	138,920	—	—	Crown (1981:Table 7)
Los Guanacos	Sedentary/Classic	6,149 90%	167 2%	315 5%	166 2%	—	6,797	172 82%	39 18%	Ruscavage-Barz (1993:Table 5.1)
Los Muertos	Predominantly Classic	347 25%	86 6%	735 53%	110 8%	109 8%	1,387	700 57%	529 43%	Brunson (1990:Tables 25 and 29)
Moroccan Ruin	Classic	1,447 93%	18 1%	85 5%	5 <.5%	—	1,555	—	—	Lack (2007:Table 24)
Pueblo Blanco Community	Preclassic/Classic	5,101 75%	615 9%	921 13%	202 3%	1 <.5%	6,840	182 63%	107 37%	McDonnell et al. (1995:Tables 8.01, 8.08, 8.09, 8.18, and 8.44)
Pueblo del Monti	Classic	7,634 81%	71 1%	1,624 17%	33 <.5%	12 <.5%	9,374	—	—	Weaver (1977:Figure 7)
Pueblo Grande	Sedentary/Classic	269,310 81%	11,836 4%	45,760 14%	2,081 1%	3,584 1%	332,571	2,319 62%	1,422 38%	Abbott (1994a:Table 2.1, 1994b: Table 6.4, 1995a:Tables 4.1 and 4.4); Foster (1994:Table 4.1); Walsh-Anduze (1994:Table 5.1)
Pueblo Patricio	Preclassic/Classic	7,077 95%	152 2%	207 3%	48 1%	—	7,484	59 28%	152 72%	Cable and Allen (1982:Tables 14, 21, and 24); Henderson (1995:103, Tables 4.1 and 4.9)

Pueblo Poniente	Preclassic/Classic	8,936 84%	1,259 12%	416 4%	29 <.5%	—	10,640	—	—	Lack (2007:Table 20)
Pueblo Salado	Classic	41,817 76%	522 1%	8,425 15%	4,073 7%	248 <.5%	55,085	3,474 38%	5,768 62%	Greenwald, Greenwald et al. (1996:Table 3.1); Greenwald, Walsh-Anduze et al. (1996:Tables 2.1 and 2.2); Motsinger (1995: Tables 5.3 and 5.7); Walsh-Anduze (1996a:Table 11.8, 1996b:Tables 4.1 and 4.2, 1996c:Tables 5.1, 5.11, 5.15, 5.16, and 5.22)
Pueblo Viejo	Predominantly Classic	1,455 70%	72 3%	521 25%	24 1%	—	2,072	104 43%	139 57%	Abbott (1993:88, Tables 4.1, 4.5, and 4.6); Walsh-Anduze (1993:229, 231, and Table G.1)
Tres Pueblos	Classic	46,458 79%	1,776 3%	10,383 18%	361 1%	68 <.5%	59,046	191 44%	239 56%	Abbott (1995b:Tables 10.1 and 10.4, 1995c: Tables 13.3 and 13.35)
Total		574,568 79%	43,215 6%	98,354 14%	9,149 1%	7,697 1%	726,374	8,277 46%	9,552 54%	

[a] Periods of occupation or those represented in the sample.
[b] Including sherds as well as whole and reconstructible vessels; whole and reconstructible vessels tallied as one observation.
[c] Excluding Historic O'odham sherds.
[d] Including red-on-gray, brown-paste variants, and lower Colorado buffware.
[e] Including trace counts of Vahki and Sacaton Redware.
[f] Including polychromes and Roosevelt Redwares.
[g] Unidentifiable sherds, ambiguous sherds of redware/plainware, and sherds of regionally intrusive wares.

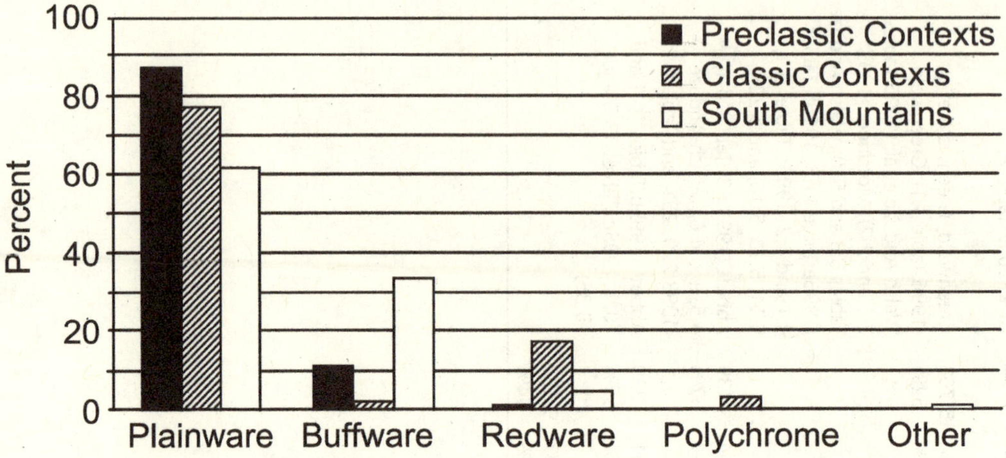

FIGURE 4.23. Comparison of ceramic wares between village contexts and the South Mountains.

exceeds that of most Preclassic villages, but this, too, may be a product of sample size or regional variation. In fact, the proportion of buffware in the mountains, measured by either sherds (25 percent) or MNV (33 percent), is close to that of the Preclassic Grewe/Casa Grande complex (27 percent), a similarity supported by a Fisher's Exact test ($p = .10$). This suggests the South Mountains assemblage is in the range of what should be expected for a predominantly Preclassic assemblage if village assemblages are appropriate standards for comparison.

We cannot rule out a unique social or religious value for redware vessels—after all, they were a preferred mortuary accompaniment and circulated among communities in ways different from plainwares—as a reason for their lower frequency in the mountains. Even so, redwares are found in fairly high proportions in domestic refuse (10–20 percent; Abbott et al. 2006), suggesting they also served utilitarian purposes, and their rareness in the South Mountains is thus probably not due solely to any greater social or religious value or significance. If redwares manifested religious value, we might in fact expect them to be found in higher frequencies around rock art (assuming rock art had a religious draw or purpose). As the next chapter shows, this is not the case, reaffirming a chronological explanation for the infrequency of redware. This lack of a Classic period signature to the corpus of decorated pottery sherds is mirrored in the plainware assemblage; the SMRAP sample contains only 12 sherds (5 MNV) of unequivocal Classic period plainware (Table 4.6), distinguished by a burnished surface treatment and/or grog temper.

While the ceramic assemblage signals a predominantly Preclassic utilization of the South Mountains landscape, from a social perspective most of this activity can be attributed to villagers from adjacent communities. The temper attributes of the plainwares and redwares indicate that most vessels were manufactured within the South Mountains granodiorite petrofacies (Table 4.6) and, correspondingly, were likely dropped by villagers from Pueblo Viejo, Las Canopas, Los Hornos, and hamlets in between. The SMRAP sample also contains a small percentage of vessels produced at other villages, within petrofacies to the northeast, east, south, and west. Bostwick's assemblage also contained low percentages of sherds made with these more distant tempering agents (Figure 4.21), which led him to suggest that villagers from these other areas of the valley also visited the South Mountains (Bostwick and Krocek 2002:35). Peregrine villagers likely visited the South Mountains at various times and places, and probably for a range of reasons, but low frequencies of these "foreign" vessels are not a priori evidence for this because small quantities of plainware were traded between irrigation communities (Abbott 2000). In fact, temper

TABLE 4.6. Counts and Percentages of Plainware and Redware Sherds and Minimum Number of Vessels (MNV) by Temper Type.

	Plainware		Redware		Total	
Temper	**Sherds**	**MNV**	**Sherds**	**MNV**	**Sherds**	**MNV**
South Mountains Granodiorite[a]	1,435 68.0%	503 73.8%	170 8.1%	37 5.4%	1,605 76.1%	540 79.2%
Estrella Gneiss/Coarse Schist[b]	126 6.0%	38 5.6%	16 0.8%	6 0.9%	142 6.7%	44 6.5%
Phyllite[c]	125 5.9%	36 5.3%	3 0.1%	2 0.3%	128 6.1%	38 5.6%
Arkosic Sand and Squaw Peak Schist	90 4.3%	16 2.3%	2 0.1%	1 0.1%	92 4.4%	17 2.5%
Mica Schist with Red Sediment (Queen Creek drainage)	23 1.1%	10 1.5%	3 0.1%	2 0.3%	26 1.2%	12 1.8%
Petrofacie N (near Snaketown)	1 <0.1%	1 0.1%	—	—	1 <0.1%	1 0.1%
Crushed Sherd/Grog[d]	12 0.6%	5 0.7%	2 0.1%	2 0.3%	14 0.7%	7 1.0%
Indeterminate	101 4.8%	23 3.4%	—	—	101 4.8%	23 3.4%
Total	1,913 90.7%	632 92.7%	196 9.3%	50 7.3%	2,109 100%	682 100%

[a] Includes samples with hornblende.
[b] Includes mixtures of South Mountains granodiorite with Estrella gneiss.
[c] Includes Phoenix Mountains phyllite.
[d] Counts include one protohistoric or historic plainware specimen.

variability in the South Mountains ceramics is nearly identical to that of pottery assemblages from the nearby villages of Pueblo Viejo and Las Canopas (Figure 4.24). This parallel further demonstrates that the residents of these nearby villages are those who had the most contact with the regions encompassed by the SMRAP project areas.

As for vessel form, the South Mountains assemblage is dominated by jars (Table 4.3). Bowls are uncommon, and scoops and other forms are very rare or nonexistent. In comparison to village contexts (Table 4.5), the ratio of bowls to jars in the South Mountains is significantly lower (Fisher's Exact, $p < .001$, $Q = 0.73$). This shows that the activities in the South Mountains involved jars far more often than bowls, due probably to the logistics of carrying items to and from the villages, such as water or harvested and gathered plants.

In all, the ceramic artifacts littered across the South Mountains provide a number of key social, temporal, and practical insights regarding the archaeological landscape. The majority of vessels likely served to transport items and water between the villages and the mountains; however, the infrequent presence of some bowl sherds shows that the range of activities was more inclusive. The assemblage also contains one sherd of either an anthropomorphic effigy vessel or double-jar form, both of which are incredibly rare vessel forms of probable ritualistic importance. This sherd was found near the top of the mountains and in close proximity to a petroglyph panel, tentatively suggesting a ritual association between them. Petrographic data from South Mountains sherds show that villagers residing along the south bank of the Salt River, along Canal 7 and Canal System 1, were likely responsible for much of the farming, quarrying, and petroglyph making in the South Mountains, and they probably undertook those activities in relatively close proximity to their home villages. Pueblo Viejo, Las Canopas, and possibly Los

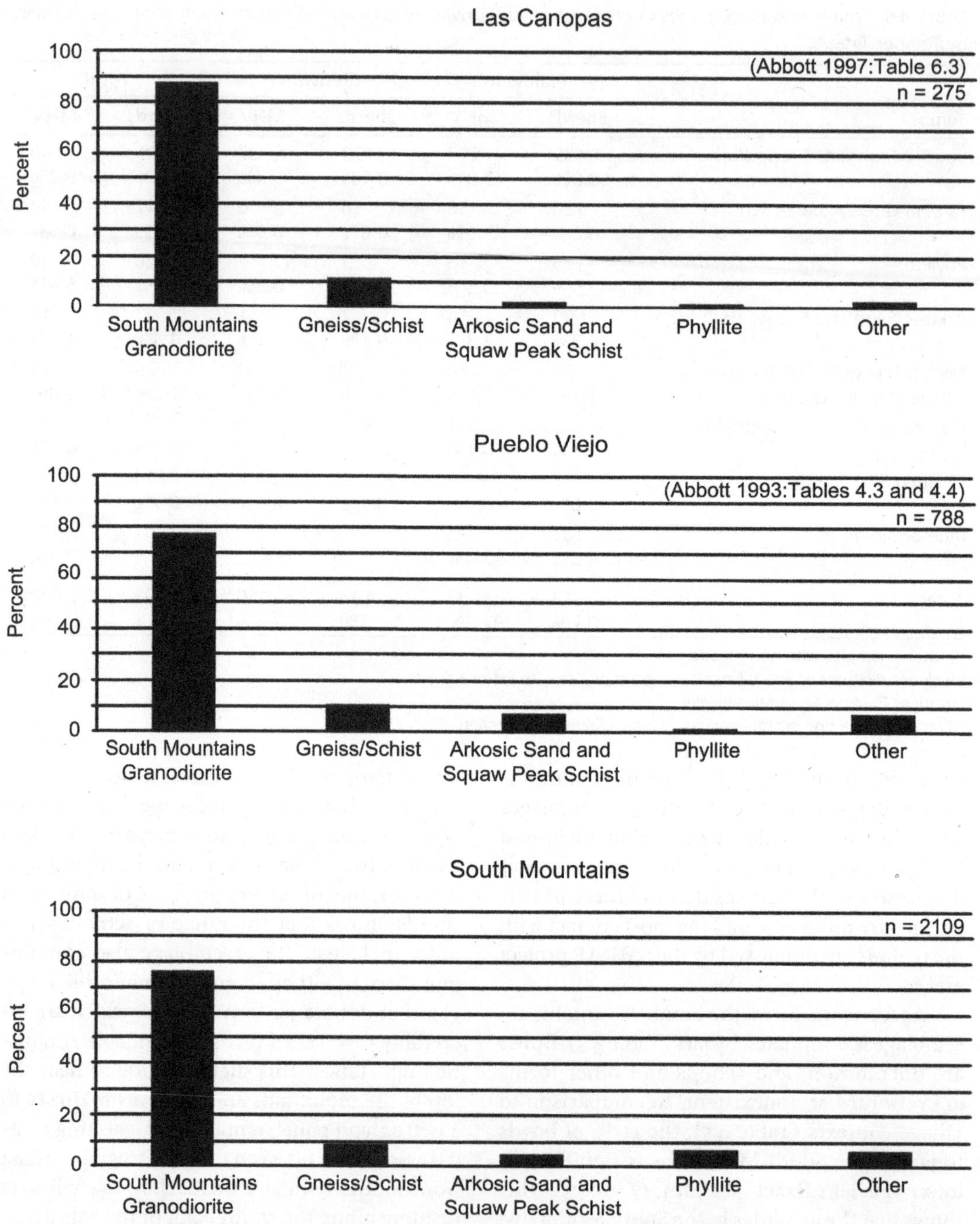

FIGURE 4.24. Comparison of temper types in plainware and redware sherds between assemblages from the South Mountains and nearby Las Canopas and Pueblo Viejo. The Las Canopas sample consists of plainwares only; the Estrella gneiss petrofacies is grouped with the gneiss/schist category.

Hornos are the most probable village candidates for the regions covered by our project areas (Figure 3.2). Las Canopas and Los Hornos were relatively large Preclassic villages, and all three had raised platform mounds and thus persisted as important villages or ritual centers into the Classic period. The South Mountains ceramic assemblage nevertheless contains a strong Preclassic component, pointing toward a shift in how neighboring Hohokam villagers engaged this landscape and/or how frequently they visited during the tumultuous social transformations we characterize as the transition from the Sedentary to Classic period. I expand on this important finding in the following chapters.

Lithics

In addition to ceramic artifacts, our recent efforts recorded 695 stone artifacts, 503 of which we subjected to more focused analysis. These data complement those of the ceramics and provide added detail to the fullness and complexion of the South Mountains archaeological landscape. The stone artifact assemblage in the South Mountains is unique when compared with those from village settings. One basic yet notable observation is that, outside quarry locations, debitage is extremely rare. The majority of stone artifacts are expedient tool forms, including multiple types and shapes of hammerstones, core tools, flake tools, and scrapers. Most of these tools were crafted from hard, darkly colored igneous materials, usually of felsic lithology, and probably quarried as alluvial cobbles from the gravel bars of the Salt River floodplain. Initially, this suggests that stone tools were employed in a variety of tasks in the South Mountains and that most were made in the villages before they were brought and discarded in the mountains. This pattern highlights the logistics by which Hohokam villagers engaged with the South Mountains.

Specialized and quantitative analyses of stone tools in the South Mountains, however, are hindered by the fact that most span tool classifications. Many of the tools exhibit two or three different kinds of use-wear, and it is impossible to discern which use-wear attributes are due solely to activities in the mountains because they may have served prior uses in the villages. It is nonetheless reasonable to consider that these versatile stones were more than just broken or exhausted tools recycled from the villages' refuse piles. The consistency of reuse and the redundancy in those tasks—chopping, cutting, pounding, and so on—across tool forms and settings indicate instead that these artifacts were designed to combine the functions of different tool types into a single stone.

Figures 4.5 and 4.6 show that stone artifacts are concentrated around agricultural features. As detailed in the first half of this chapter, the Hohokam used these farming terraces for growing agave, encouraging some economically useful cacti, and possibly husbanding corn. Harvesting agave, in particular the highly desirable edible parts and fibers for weaving, necessitates a series of processing techniques, including cutting thick leaves, stalks, and stems; removing troublesome spines; pulping meaty flesh; and scraping tough fibers. Many of the stone tools exhibit use-wear consistent with these activities, and some bear the full range of use-wear patterns indicative of processing hard, pulpy, and fibrous materials (see Irwin 1993; Osborne 1965; Rogers 1939). In fact, a fair number of tools, crafted from large cortical flakes detached bipolarly from alluvially rounded cobbles, bear serrated edges, steep step fractures, and polished "blades" (Figure 4.25). These are found most often near the C-shaped terraces, those agricultural facilities with the best indicators for agave husbandry.

The cortical flake tools in the SMRAP project areas have a consistent size and shape, and they fit nicely in the hand, with the platform edge serving as a suitable grip; such consistencies in size, shape, and attributes are indicative of a designed knife-like tool. These expedient flake "knives" were probably crafted for harvesting and processing agave in a manner very similar to better-known schist "agave knives" and "mescal knives"; the primary difference is that the South Mountains examples, while planar, are not made of tabular stone material. The discovery of charred agave remains in nearby roasting pits and agave pollen from adjacent terraces points

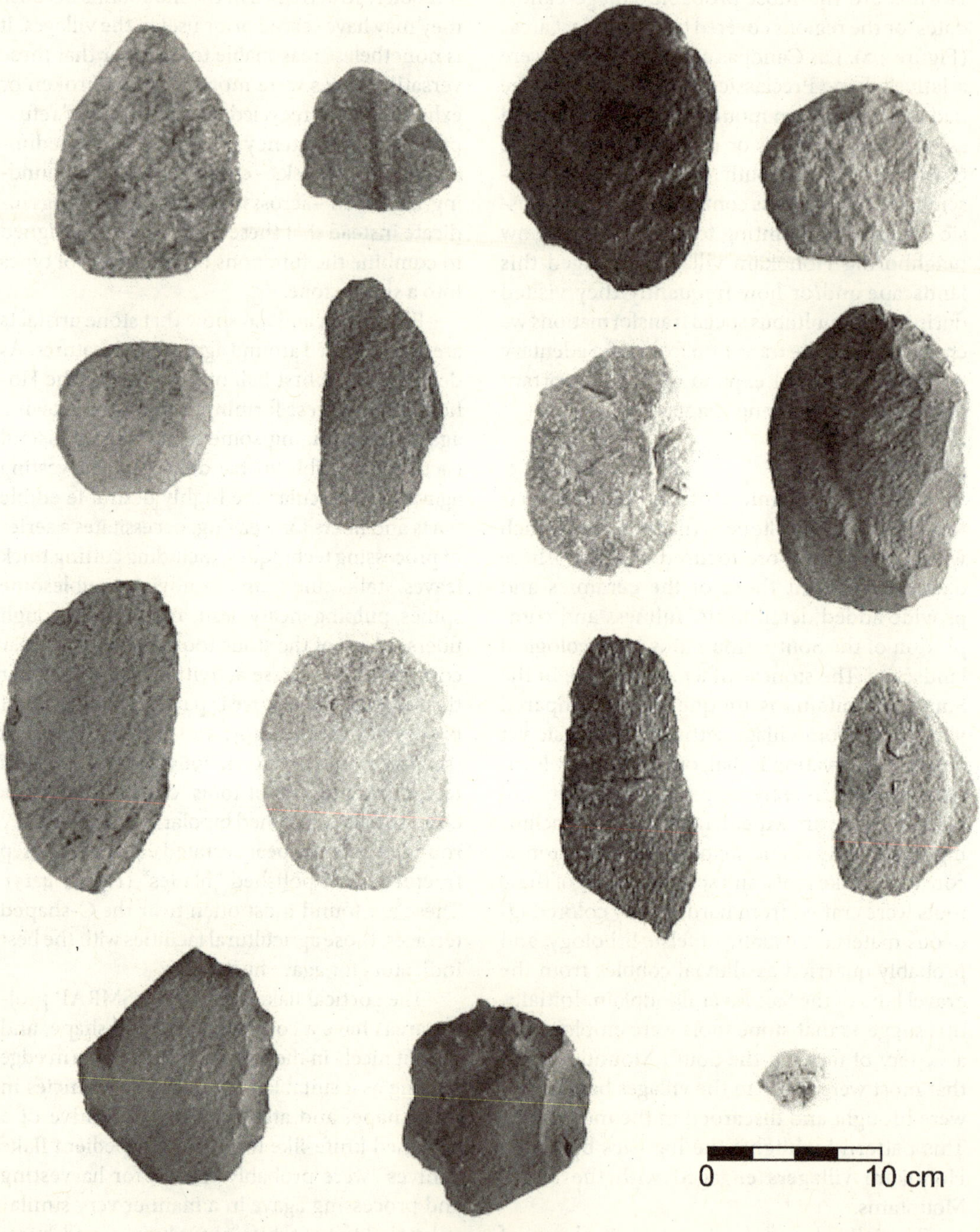

FIGURE 4.25. Examples of stone tools in the South Mountains. *Top three rows:* cortical flake "knives"; *bottom row:* steep-edged flake unifaces (two planer/scrapers and a "thumb scraper").

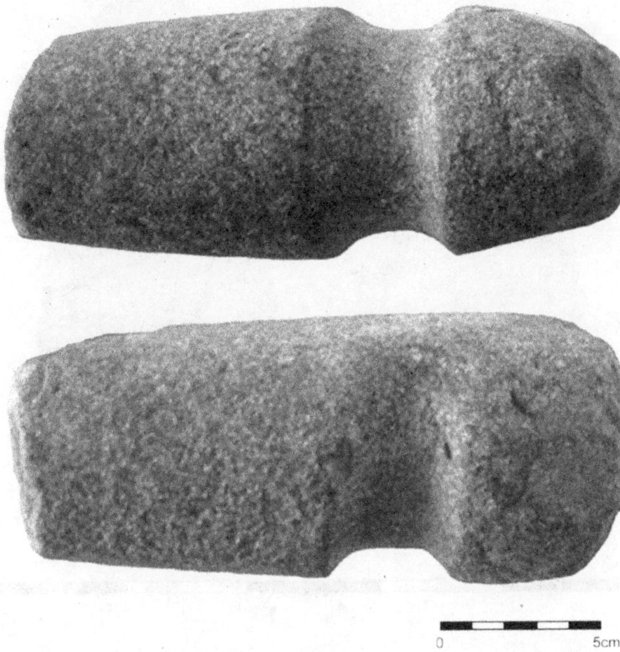

FIGURE 4.26. Example of a three-quarter-grooved ax or maul in the South Mountains. This tool has been recycled as a pestle.

toward these flake knives' employment in cultivating and processing locally grown agave.

While concentrated around farming localities, cortical flake knives and other stone tools with use-wear consistent with plant processing activities are found throughout the mountains, albeit less often and in lower frequencies. They were occasionally left on level and cleared areas along ridgetops and are sometimes found in association with a few sherds, but more often than not, these tools are found removed from other artifacts and features, hinting that plant collecting and processing in the mountains and away from farming terraces were carried out by individuals or relatively small task groups. It remains to be shown which plants were sought beyond those cultivated on and around the farming terraces, although a wide variety of useful seeds, fruits, roots, and leaves of a broad spectrum of cacti, trees, shrubs, forbs, and grasses were the likely culprits. More than 120 plant species, half of the known indigenous flora, in the South Mountains have documented ethnographic uses, and the remains of 59 of these have been recovered from domestic Hohokam contexts (Wright 2011:Appendix A). A scarcity of pestles and bedrock grinding facilities suggests, nonetheless, that if hard parts, such as the seeds of leguminous trees like mesquite and palo verde, were targeted, the pounding and grinding were chores left for the comfort of village courtyards.

The stone tool assemblage also contains several fragments of broken groundstone axes. All but one of these are small, distal spalls, and the type of use-wear, consisting of stippled battering on the ax heads' blunt ends opposite the blades, indicates that these ax head fragments did not spall off while felling trees in the South Mountains. In fact, the only "complete" ax we recovered had been recycled into a pestle (Figure 4.26), and it may well never have been an ax because the Hohokam also crafted hafted mauls. The hafting groove on this tool is typical of Haury's Type 2 axes (1976:291–292), which were the dominant form from the late Colonial through the Classic period. The other three ax fragments are too small for their form or use to be determined, but since they were found near

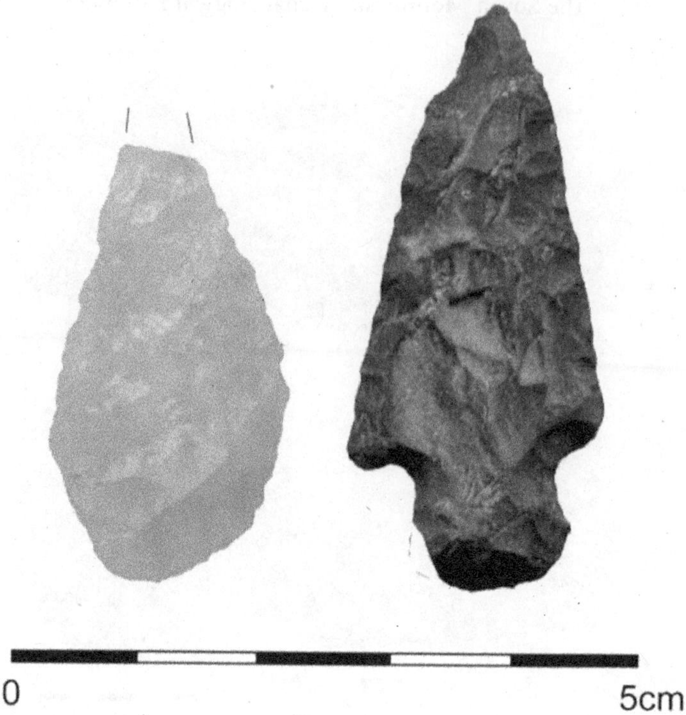

FIGURE 4.27. Examples of bifacially flaked stone tools in the South Mountains. *Left:* undiagnostic white quartz lanceolate point; *right:* basalt San Pedro projectile point with secondary drilling use-wear.

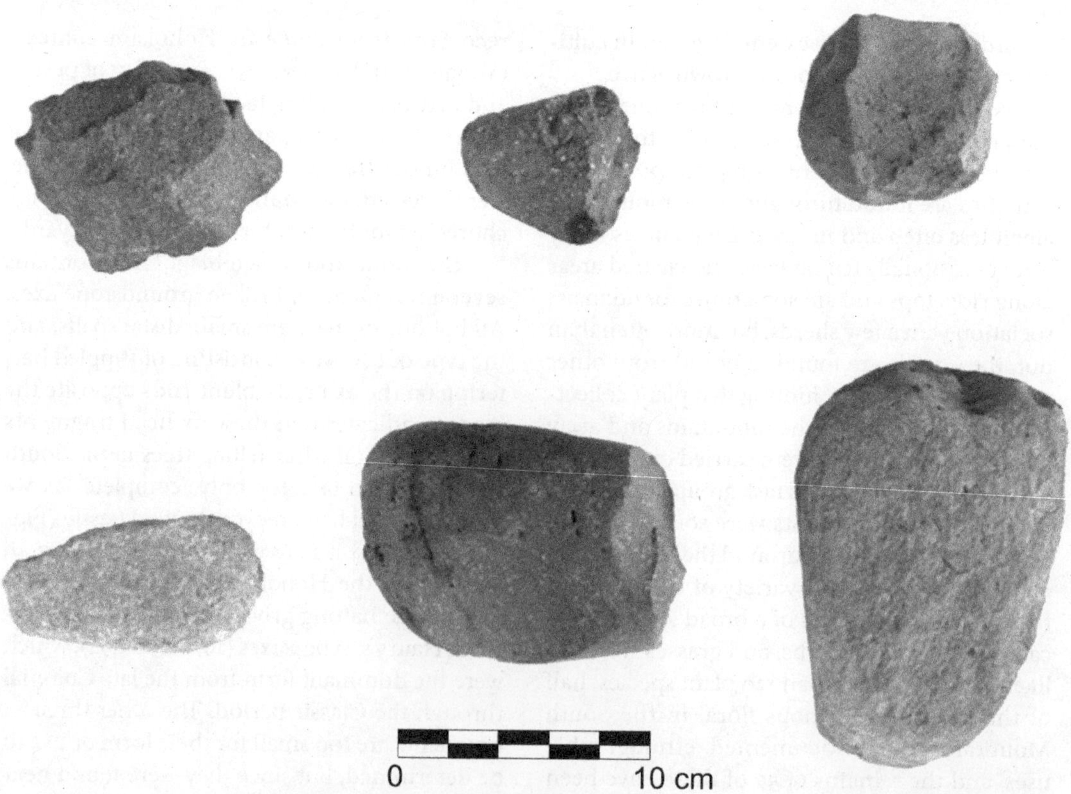

FIGURE 4.28. Examples of probable petroglyph hammerstones in the South Mountains. The Hohokam crafted most petroglyphs via a direct percussion technique using the pointed edges of cores, core tools, broken groundstone implements, and unworked cobbles.

rock art concentrations they were probably spalled from recycled axes or mauls used to peck out petroglyphs.

In addition to axes and farming tools, the South Mountains lithic assemblage recorded during the SMRAP includes two bifaces (Figure 4.27) and a uniface (Figure 4.25, bottom right). One biface is an undiagnostic quartz point whereas the other is a basalt San Pedro projectile point (1200–600 BC) with drill-like use-wear. Both of these and the chalcedony uniface were found amid Hohokam plainware and buffware sherds. The secondary use-wear and association with pottery suggest that the San Pedro point had been found at an Archaic site somewhere else and reused as a drill. Other Hohokam points may have been scavenged by park visitors and collectors over the years, but the plethora of decorated pottery still in the mountains, with some sherds larger than one's hand, shows that the paucity of projectile points cannot be attributed solely to recent arrowhead collecting. This sparseness of projectile points indicates that big-game hunting was not a common undertaking in the South Mountains.

Earlier in this chapter I alluded to the shrine stones consecrated at rock-pile shrines (Figure 4.14). These are alluvially rounded and smoothed pebbles, often red-hued, and found in arguably ritual contexts; in the South Mountains they were also placed in and around agricultural terraces and sometimes below petroglyph panels. Similar stones have been interpreted as water-related fetishes when found along canals and in shrine-room caches (see Chapter 3). If so, those located around farming terraces may have been symbols of fertility or supplications for rain.[11] Their association with agricultural terraces, petroglyph panels, and shrines, at the exclusion of other contexts, points toward a ritual purpose for their presence in the mountains.

A final class of stone artifacts in the South Mountains consists of the hammerstones wielded in the crafting of petroglyphs (Figure 4.28). While it is difficult to pinpoint a hammerstone's function, several factors inform on the South Mountains assemblage. First, away from quarries most hammerstones are found near petroglyph panels, establishing a relational consistency between them. The other line of evidence is the distinctive battering on the steep-edged corners and margins of the hammerstones. This is unlike the other hammerstones in the assemblage, where battering use-wear clusters along the stones' larger, wider, and more blunt facets, which is consistent with toolstone testing at quarries and plant processing elsewhere. Similar petroglyph hammerstones have been reported from Hohokam rock art sites in the Tucson Basin (Wallace 1983:205), the Picacho Mountains (Wallace and Holmlund 1986:33, 38), near Gila Bend (Wallace 1989:125), and along northern margins of the Phoenix Basin (Kearns 1975:325; Rodgers 1974:40, 1976:40, 55).

I have suggested elsewhere that pecked South Mountains petroglyphs were produced consistently via direct percussion with a hammerstone on a rock face (Wright and Bostwick 2009). This is because we have yet to find evidence for chisels or other means of indirect percussion (e.g., Weeks 2001; Whittaker et al. 2000) in the project areas, and only hammers and hammerstone spalls are found below petroglyph panels. Gila style glyphs have undulating edges, are composed of large peck marks, and exhibit line widths usually greater than 0.5 cm, all of which are characteristics consistent with direct percussion technology (e.g., Busby et al. 1978; Keyser 1992:70; Keyser and Rabiega 1999; Schaafsma 1980:29; Turner 1963; von Werlhof 1965). Replicative experiments of direct percussion using river cobbles on South Mountains granodiorite (Whiting 2008; Wright and Bostwick 2009), moreover, have successfully reproduced pecked Gila style glyphs as well as use-wear on the experimental hammers congruous with that on the hammers in the South Mountains (Figure 4.29).

There are far too few hammers to account for the large number of petroglyphs in the South Mountains. These tools may have been venerated by the petroglyph makers, and thus kept and reused on subsequent visits to the mountains. Some of the petroglyph hammers, however, are recycled core tools (see also Rodgers 1977:109), like those clustered around farming terraces, and do not seem to have been specialized tools for

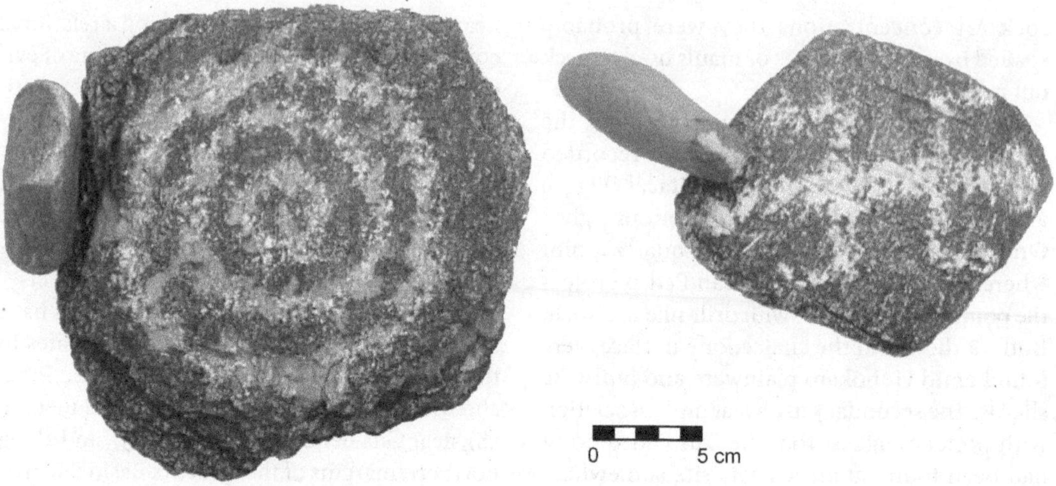

FIGURE 4.29. Replicated petroglyphs and corresponding use-wear on hammerstones. These average-sized petroglyphs each required approximately 15 minutes of steady, concentrated pecking (petroglyphs and photos by Al Arpad).

manufacturing petroglyphs. This is a further line of evidence that the two practices, one symbolic and the other economic, were sometimes intertwined in a network of performances.

Summary

The archaeological residues in the South Mountains evidence an ancient palimpsest of diverse deeds, doings, and practices carried out for centuries across this greasy-sheened, rock-strewn landscape. Petroglyphs are scattered widely about, but they are conspicuously concentrated in certain areas. Entrepreneurial Hohokam farmers practiced runoff agriculture along the bajadas, and stone artifacts and roasting pits indicate that they grew agave and other crops on these terraces starting in the Colonial period, or possibly earlier. Shrines, rockshelters, and summit trails were sited on hilltops offering unobstructed vistas and expansive panoramas of the lower Salt River valley, linking these places through line of sight with the bustling Hohokam villages that once dotted the valley floor and the numerous jagged landforms that rim the horizon. Broken pots implicate villagers from nearby communities as the farmers and petroglyph makers who employed these vessels in an array of activities. Most of these pots, however, were jars used for carrying and storing water and gathered plants. Significantly, decorated wares evidence further that these activities were most common during the Colonial and Sedentary periods, the era of cultural florescence in the Hohokam world.

The ceramic data intimate a chiefly Preclassic signature to the South Mountains landscape, but it remains equivocal whether or not the petroglyphs also date predominantly to this early era of ballcourt ritualism and before the rise of platform-mound ceremonialism. If so, this implies that a major shift in ritual practices performed in the mountains coincided with broader structural changes in ritual, religion, and social relations sweeping across the Hohokam world during the Preclassic/Classic transition. The chronological baseline afforded by the ceramics sets the stage for the next chapter, which deals specifically with dating the South Mountains petroglyphs. Then, in Chapter 6, I revisit much of the contextual information provided here to better understand rock art as a ritual practice. Combined, these studies provide a fuller picture of how religious knowledge was controlled, distributed, and embroiled in the transformation of Hohokam society.

CHAPTER 5

Chronicling Hohokam Rock Art

The greatest obstacle to the acceptance of rock art as useful archaeological evidence has been the problem of dating it. (Morwood 2002:146)

In archaeology, time is of the essence. Chronology is one of the discipline's strengths and surely its backbone, but dating rock art remains a considerable challenge. The pioneering work of White (1965), Snyder (1966), Ferg (1979), Schaafsma (1980), and Wallace (1983, 1989; Wallace and Holmlund 1986) clearly established the types of designs in Hohokam rock art, but we have yet to effectively, quantitatively, and objectively discern temporal shifts in the Hohokam petroglyph design repertoire or the contexts of its production. Addressing transformations in the production of South Mountains petroglyphs therefore calls for a more resolute temporal framework in order for us to fully comprehend its social relevance and historical importance. My goal in this chapter, then, is to provide a chronological refinement of Hohokam petroglyph iconography in the Phoenix Basin.

There is an amazingly diverse body of relative and chronometric dating techniques applicable to rock art (for reviews see Bednarik 1996, 2002; Dorn 2001; Keyser 2001; Rowe 2005). Relative methods include many old hats like superimpositioning, differential weathering, and cross-media design comparisons. Researchers use these techniques to develop relational sequences within the rock art iconography; their utility lies in the fact that they are generally inexpensive, nondestructive, and widely applicable and often rely on large sample sizes. Chronometric techniques (sensu Whitley 2011:83), such as cation-ratio and cosmogenic dating for petroglyphs and accelerator mass spectrometry and optically stimulated luminescence dating for pictographs, offer more exacting results, often with calibrated calendrical date estimates. Some of these more "absolute" techniques, developed mostly in the 1980s and 1990s, were once heralded as panaceas for rock art researchers, but after years of testing and application this horizon of high-tech techniques began waning as inconsistencies in results mounted and skepticism grew (Bednarik 2002). Fortunately, perseverance snatched the proverbial baby before we threw it out with the bathwater, and over time the troublesome techniques were largely abandoned in favor of ones that have withstood scrutiny and repeated testing (Whitley 2011:83–92).

Rock art dating techniques, like all chronometric methods, have their limitations. Relative methods are notoriously weak and yield only free-floating chronologies, in which turning points in the durations of "styles" are not grounded to a calendrical framework. Chronometric techniques, on the other hand, are often invasive and may permanently alter or damage the rock art, require specialized training and equipment, and are costly and time-consuming. They tend to be applied sparingly as a result, usually to too few samples for us to develop actual chronological sequences of design types or styles within a body of rock art. They are most useful for dating individual specimens of rock art. The general consensus, then, is to apply as many relative techniques as appropriate to the case at hand

and, if possible and applicable, ground the relative sequence to a calendrical chronology with a careful selection of chronometrically derived dates (Morwood 2002; Whitley 2011). This is what Sundstrom (1990:220) refers to as a "broad but integrated contextual approach" and what Chippindale and Taçon (1998:92–93), following Wylie's (1989) logic, consider "cabling." If several weak, relative dating techniques yield compatible sequences in rock art iconography or other elements of style, then the integrated results should be considered a highly reliable "cable." Due to the synergistic effect of intermethod compatibility, such a cable is perhaps more veracious than a "chain" of deduction based on results of a few chronometric techniques. Accordingly, in this chapter I cable qualitative and quantitative measures of relative ordering in petroglyph iconography to develop a more robust chronicle of rock art production in the South Mountains.

I rely on four relative dating techniques to refine the South Mountains petroglyph chronology. Even though each technique—proximity analysis, cross-media design correlation, repatination, and associated artifacts—is methodologically and inferentially limited, correspondence among the results frames a fuller picture of temporal change in Hohokam rock art than what was previously available. As I show, these results indicate that shifts in the Hohokam rock art lexicon mirrored those in pottery designs, but also that petroglyph production in the South Mountains practically ceased amid the many other social changes that ushered in the Classic period.

Relatively Dating South Mountains Petroglyphs

At the most basic chronological level, South Mountains petroglyphs date between AD 450 and 1450, when the Hohokam domesticated the Phoenix Basin. This is because there is little evidence that the O'odham, cultural descendants of the Hohokam, made petroglyphs (Russell 1908; however, see Bostwick and Krocek 2002:38; Martynec and Martynec 1995), and thus most of the rock art was manufactured before the early historic or protohistoric era. The best evidence for early historic rock art in the region is found to the south in the Picacho Mountains, yet production is a possible misnomer since it primarily involved the repecking of earlier Hohokam petroglyphs (Wallace and Holmlund 1986:153–161).

From the other end of the temporal spectrum, we can tentatively dismiss an Archaic origin for most and probably all of the South Mountains petroglyphs in this study. As reviewed in Chapter 3, there is little evidence to date for any significant pre-Hohokam presence along the floor of the lower Salt River valley. Bostwick and Krocek (2002:35–38), however, believe, based on the types of motifs, that a few of the South Mountains petroglyphs have an Archaic origin. Perhaps so, but we know that Archaic designs persisted into the Hohokam design lexicon (Wallace 1995b, 2001, 2004, 2008; Wallace et al. 1995), and thus motif type alone can be a weak line of evidence. Atlatl petroglyphs are generally considered diagnostic of Western Archaic rock art (e.g., Grant et al. 1968), but those illustrated by Bostwick and Krocek (2002:Figures 5–11) can be easily likened to Hohokam petroglyphs, especially the ones integrated in composite scenes involving lifeforms and other characteristic Hohokam motifs. One of the atlatl petroglyphs they illustrate is actually part of a Hohokam petroglyph arrangement and shows little to no difference in patination or execution compared with the other glyphs (Figure 5.1). Archaic petroglyphs—identifiable by a combination of design choice, the manner in which the panel surface was used, and deep executions in the rock face—may be found in the South Mountains, but I have yet to see any clear and convincing cases. The most compelling examples of Archaic rock art in the Phoenix Basin are located along the lower Salt River valley's northern rim (e.g., Bruder 1983; Huang 2010; Moreno 2003), which is more in line with known Archaic-era occupations and land-use patterns in the region (see Chapter 3).

The spatial arrangement and density of petroglyphs, like the larger South Mountains archaeological landscape, were conditioned to some extent by proximity to Hohokam villages and canals in the Salt River valley. Indeed, this geo-spatial correspondence reveals, albeit in a very broad sense, that the general corpus of

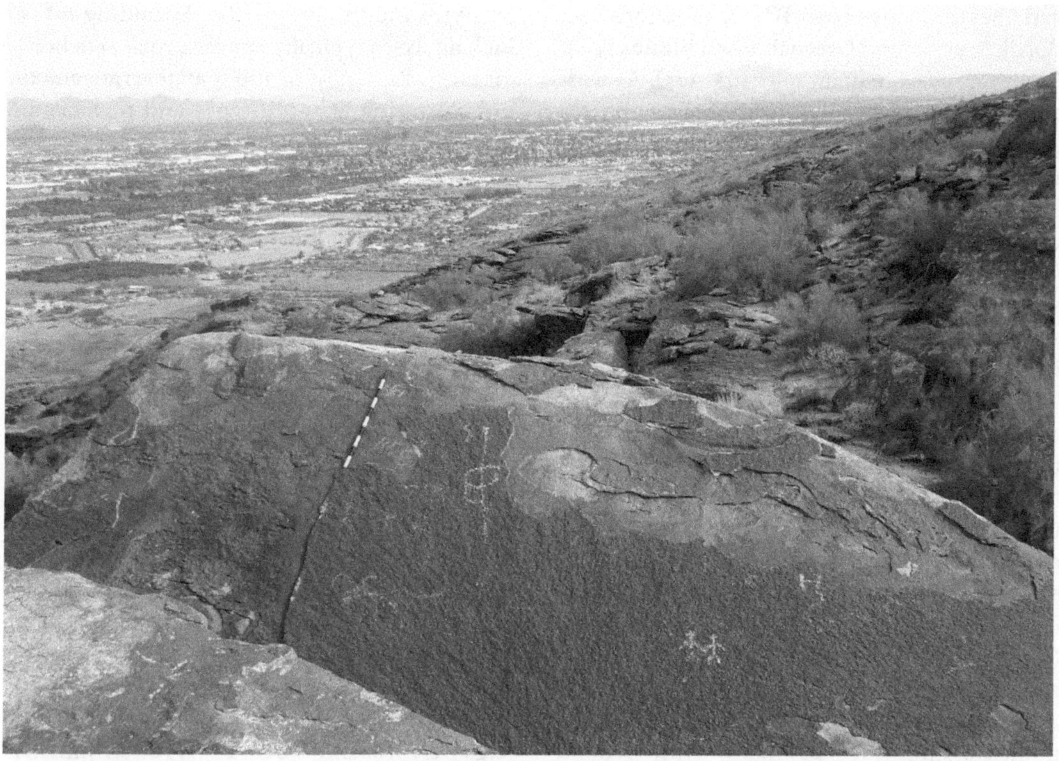

FIGURE 5.1. Overview of a panel with an atlatl motif (*center*) amid associated Hohokam petroglyphs (facing northeast).

South Mountains petroglyphs is attributable to the Hohokam. This was argued years ago by Snyder (1966), who drew on this association, along with the presence of numerous Hohokam pottery sherds scattered about, to establish that most of the petroglyphs are of Hohokam craftsmanship. The petroglyph motifs also bear strong affinities with a range of Style 2 designs painted on Hohokam buffware pottery (Figure 3.4). Since some petroglyph designs fall within this "Hohokam school of design" (sensu Hayden 1972:81; Kearns 1975:327), it is not a giant leap of faith to believe that at least the petroglyphs akin to pottery designs on buffware were pecked during the Hohokam millennium. This still presents an unclear picture of how the larger corpus of Hohokam rock art varied through time with regard to iconography, production rates, and contexts of practice. In the remainder of this chapter I address the chronological issues at hand.

First, I use correspondence analysis to explore how petroglyph motifs are associated with each other across the landscape. Then I address the types and frequencies of petroglyph motifs that were also painted on Hohokam buffware pottery; this cross-media comparison provides an inchoate assessment of when certain petroglyphs were produced. Combined, these two analyses hint that trends and shifts in Hohokam petroglyph iconography paralleled those in pottery designs and that most of the South Mountains petroglyphs have a Preclassic origin. I use the subsequent two sections, one concerning repatination and the other associated artifacts, to clarify the petroglyph chronology and ground it to the broader Hohokam culture history.

Correspondence Analysis

Correspondence analysis (CA) is a multivariate exploratory data technique that reduces a great amount of attribute variability into a simplified structure of correlations among nominal variables and cases (e.g., Baxter 1994:100–109; Bølviken et al. 1982; Greenacre and Blasius 1994; Ringrose 1992; Shennan 1997:308–345). As with other multivariate analyses (MVA) (e.g., Baxter 1994; Cowgill 1968; Doran and Hodson 1975: 187–213; Madsen 1988; Shennan 1997:265–307; Spaulding 1977), the procedure is geared toward ordination, or "the representation of relationships between items and between variables in a space of a small number of dimensions which still retains most of the information in the original descriptive variables" (Shennan 1997:265). One of MVA's chief applications is to transform cross-tabulated data into graphic displays, often scatter plots, in order to facilitate analysis (Greenacre 1994). Each of the various MVA techniques provides abstracted dimensions, also known as factors, of differing explanatory strength (measured in eigenvalues) as well as the correlations for each nominal variable and case (measured as both inertia and factor loadings) along each dimension.

Archaeological applications of MVA are numerous and varied, but many revolve around issues of seriation (e.g., Cowgill 1972; Duff 1996; Madsen 1989; Marquardt 1978; Shennan 1997: 341–345; Wallace 2001). When spatial correlations are reasonably due to contemporaneity of observations, such as with stratigraphic associations, MVA can serve as a relative dating procedure that chronologically orders cases and/or variables based on frequencies of co-occurrence. Some MVA techniques emphasize relations among cases (i.e., principal components analysis), or Q-mode analyses, whereas others emphasize relations among the nominal variables (i.e., principal coordinates analysis), or R-mode analyses. CA performs Q- and R-mode analyses simultaneously.

In rock art research, MVA is most often used to develop typologies and investigate structural patterns in regionally or culturally delineated petroglyph assemblages (e.g., Clouse 2004; McCall 2010; Morwood 1980; Munson 2002; Wallace and Holmlund 1986:113–125; Whitley 1982, 1987; Wilson 1998; see also Magne and Klassen [1991] for a nonordinational approach), or what are commonly conceptualized as rock art styles and motif types (cf. Spaulding 1977). Such analyses typically concern rock art's horizontal stratigraphy, or the spatial arrangement and clustering of motif types and nuances in stylistic attributes across the landscape. Given the emphasis on spatial correspondence, this mode of rock art research is sometimes referred to as either proximity analysis (Wallace and Holmlund 1986) or spatial analysis (Morwood 2002:123–124). As a tool for rock art seriation, any MVA hinges largely on a fundamental assumption that spatial structure within a rock art assemblage, witnessed through patterns of association, is partly due to time. Chronological interpretations drawn from MVA of rock art data alone should therefore serve as hypotheses in need of further evaluation because not only is the concept of style in rock art problematic (Francis 2001; Schaafsma 1985), but there is a growing corpus of studies showing that multiple styles were used at the same time by the same communities but under differing social environments or by people of sundry social identities (e.g., Berrocal and García 2007; Fairén-Jiménez 2007; Gallardo and De Souza 2008; Hays 1992; Sundstrom 2002; Whitley 1987). Chronological interpretations are warranted when there is independent yet supporting evidence (i.e., associated artifacts) or when the seriations correspond with extant chronological sequences derived through other means. This is because site function and an indefinable range of social reasons may also bear on the nature of correspondence among observations (Baxter 2003:107).

If the assumption that "spatial associations = temporal affiliations" is warranted, MVA can serve as a high-powered tool for revealing chronological changes in rock art. As a case in point, Whitley (1982:153–164) used factor analysis to seriate a corpus of more than 1,500 rock art designs in the Great Basin portion of southeastern California. In that study, he classified the petroglyphs into 29 different motif types and showed that some cluster together on panels, a subtle phenomenon he did not recognize during fieldwork. These horizontally seriated clusters correspond well with previously defined regional styles in southern California rock art. Whitley nevertheless interpreted his MVA results cautiously, making clear that the spatial structure he observed could be due to a range of possibilities other than or in concert with time, including regional, functional, and cultural variability. Marit Munson's (2002) doctoral research provides another exemplary case of the application of MVA to develop a rock art chronology. She used CA to seriate an assemblage of Ancestral Pueblo rock art on the Pajarito Plateau in northern New Mexico into several chronologically distinct styles. What makes her work unique, however, is that she included temporally diagnostic aspects of the rock art site areas (i.e., artifacts and architecture) in the CA to ground the styles to the area's culture history.

Rock art seriations developed through MVA are most convincing when there is reason to believe that habitation areas and patterns in land use, including practices apropos of the rock art, shifted through time, and that attributes of the rock art also changed. The least convincing cases would seem to concern sedentary societies residing in the same regions for centuries or millennia and whose design repertoires shifted at relatively slow rates, if at all. Unfortunately, this scenario aptly describes the Phoenix Basin Hohokam. I am not implying that the Hohokam design repertoire, as we know well from pottery designs, was static or resistant to change, but the individual motifs or icons depicted on pottery were in vogue for considerably long durations, on the order of centuries in most cases. Nevertheless, this is not entirely limiting for my purposes because any finer resolution in Hohokam rock art chronology than what currently exists would be a considerable leap forward. If designs or themes in the rock art were in some part contemporaneous with those painted on pottery, then we should expect some synchronous changes in the two media. Our ability to detect such transitions, however, is not so straightforward.

My goal at this stage of study is to determine whether there is spatial structure among the motifs that *could* indicate, among a range of potential causal factors, chronological trends in South Mountains petroglyph iconography or sites of production. This is a reasonable possibility, since even though the Hohokam lived out their lives in the nearby villages for centuries, there may have been temporal shifts in how communities engaged with the South Mountains or in the locations people chose to visit and revisit in the course of producing petroglyphs. I performed a series of CAs on the South Mountains petroglyph data to investigate this potentiality at two scales.

In the first spatial analysis I grouped the motifs into design classes at the site level—with "sites" as the bounded spaces displayed in Figure 4.2. I included only those sites (n = 83) containing more than one petroglyph (since correspondence necessitates that multiple cases be present), which cut the sample to 2,593 petroglyphs. The CA reduced the variability into 16 factors, none of which accounts for more than 15 percent of the variability. A bivariate plot of the first two factors, which capture a combined 25.5 percent of the variation, shows little distinction among most of the design classes (Figure 5.2). Birds, rectilinear solids, rectilinear lines, circle designs, and miscellaneous designs are differentiated from the other design classes, but this accounts for just a little more than 13 percent of the variability. Factor 2, however, hints at a possible distinction between mostly curvilinear designs, which load positively, and various lifeforms and rectilinear designs, which load negatively; yet these possible thematic distinctions are not finite since curvilinear scrolls load negatively and birds and anthropomorphs load positively. The relatively weak factors defined through this CA suggest that not much variability exists within the dataset, or that the variability is too great or complex to be easily captured in a few factors. This implies that there is either little difference in the types of petroglyph design classes among the various site settings or too much variability for us to draw clear and convincing conclusions.[1]

Before we cede that spatial correspondence among petroglyph designs does not exist or is too complex to be easily recognized, a subsequent CA on these same data when grouped by *panel* provenance yields more inspiring results (Figure 5.3). The first point of interest is that Factor 1 captures more than 70 percent of the

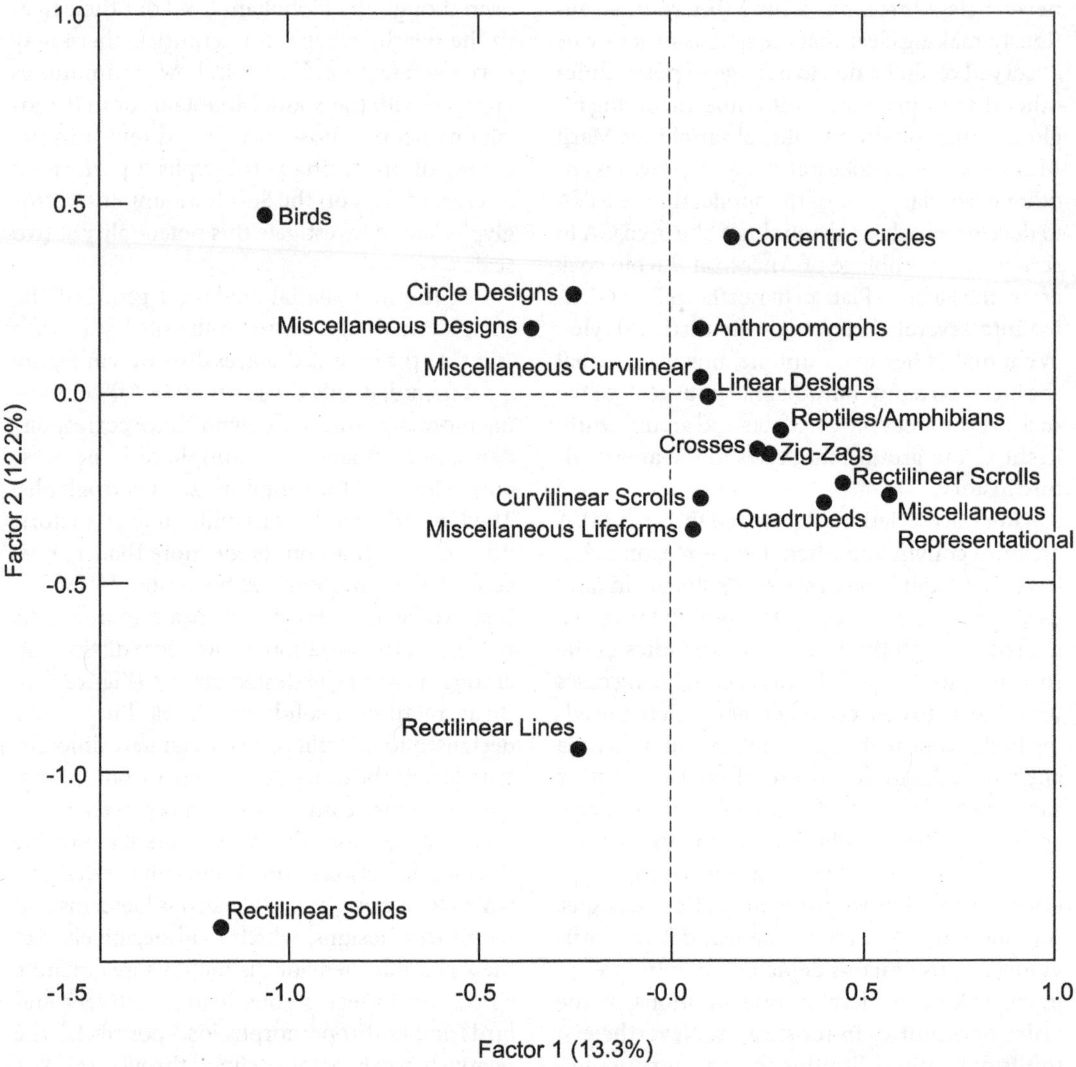

FIGURE 5.2. Correspondence analysis plot of petroglyph design classes at the site level (individual cases not shown).

variability in the dataset, while the next strongest dimension, Factor 2, accounts for a much smaller 6 percent. A monotone structure to the reduced variability, when present, is typically evident in the first dimension (Bølviken et al. 1982:57), and if time is a strong element of the variability it is usually apparent in the first two factors (Hill 1974).

Figure 5.3 shows how the petroglyph design classes tend to correlate with each other on panels. The first, and by far strongest, factor differentiates zig-zags and rectilinear designs, including scrolls, lines, and solids, as well as reptiles/amphibians and quadrupeds from curvilinear designs (scrolls, concentric circles, etc.), linear designs, and crosses (compare Figures 5.4 and 5.5). The CA suggests that this distinction, which is a more pronounced rendering of how the weak Factor 2 in the site-based CA (Figure 5.2) differentiated the designs, is the strongest relationship

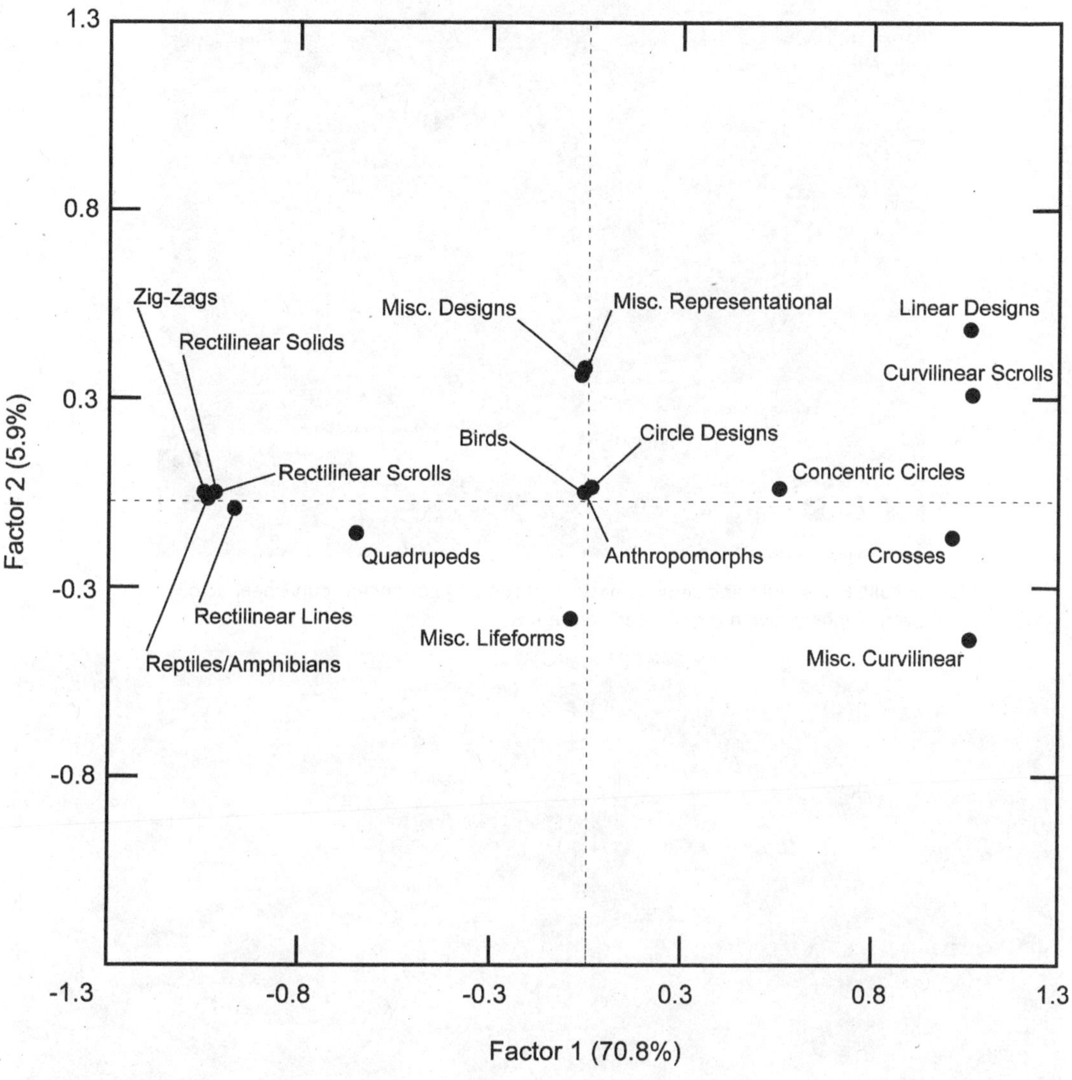

FIGURE 5.3. Correspondence analysis plot of petroglyph design classes at the panel level (individual cases not shown).

in the dataset. I believe Factor 1 is registering a temporal signal in the data because, to foreshadow the remainder of this chapter, this split on the horizontal axis is replicated in each of the following analyses.

Factor 2 in the panel-level CA accounts for only a small amount of variability, but it distinguishes the miscellaneous curvilinear, miscellaneous lifeform, and cross design classes from curvilinear scrolls, linear designs, miscellaneous representational, and other nonrepresentational designs. Noteworthy here is that aside from the curvilinear scrolls, the design classes registering mainly on Factor 2 are relatively uncommon and their constituent motifs difficult to classify, hence the classes' "miscellaneous" labels. Neither factor distinguishes among anthropomorphs, birds, and circle designs, nor differentiates these from the other design classes. This suggests that the relationships these designs have with the other

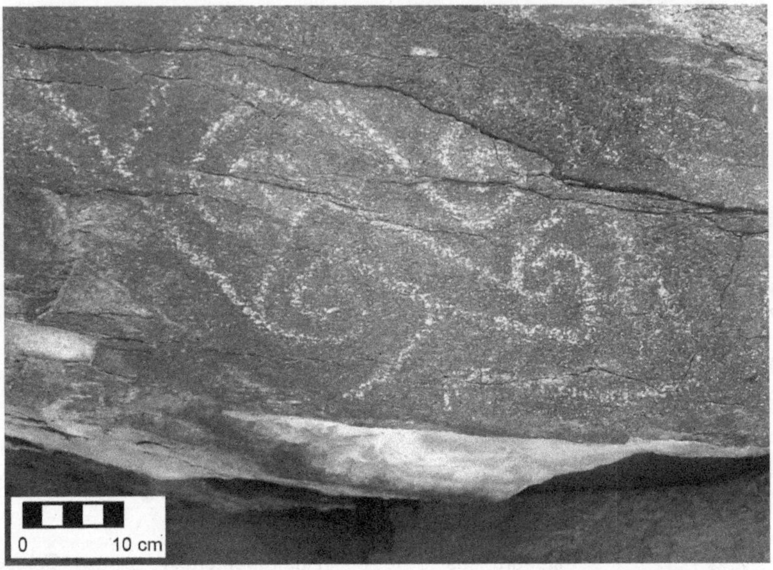

FIGURE 5.4. A fluid and sinuous pattern of running connected-curvilinear scroll petroglyphs above a rockshelter's entrance.

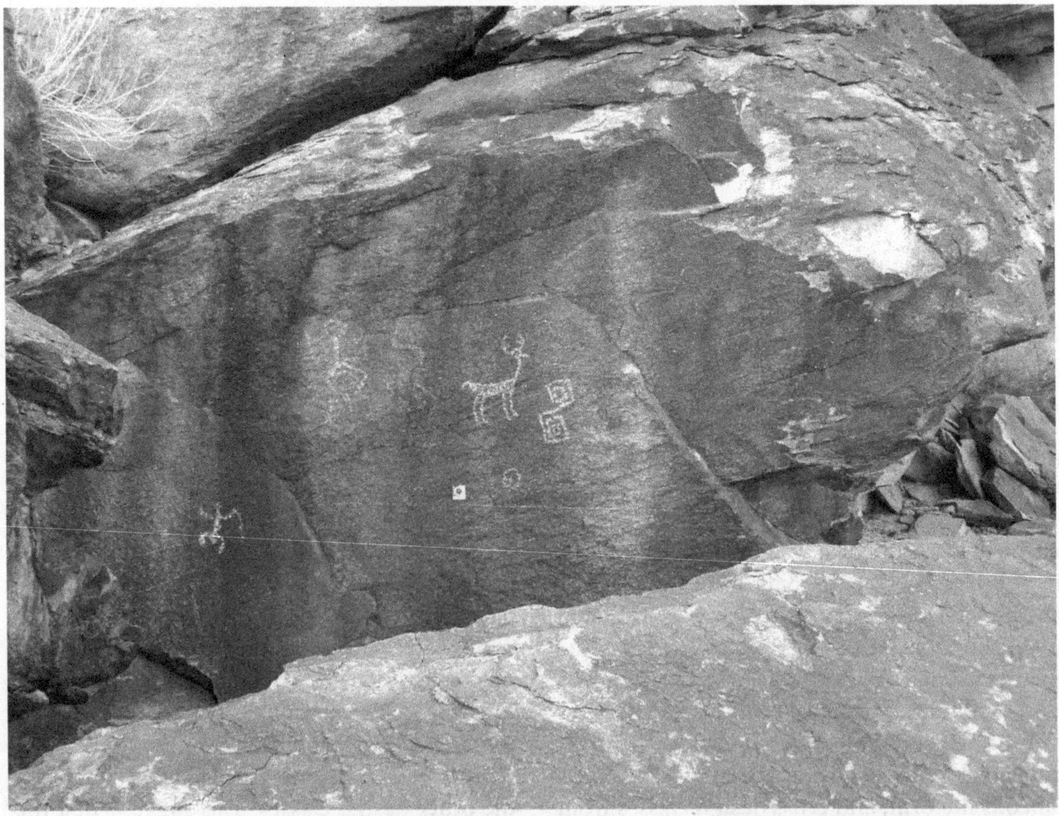

FIGURE 5.5. Panels with connected rectilinear scrolls and lifeform petroglyphs hidden near a spring (facing southeast). The connected scrolls are 24 cm tall.

classes are the weakest in the dataset. I suggest that Factor 2 is expressing either some of the latent error and ambiguity I introduced in the various miscellaneous design classifications or some minor spatial variation in where these less common and difficult-to-classify designs were placed.

Overall, the spatial analyses suggest that some petroglyph design classes, when considered at the panel level, tend to co-occur while others do not, but these relationships are weakly expressed at the larger site level. These correspondences and discrepancies among design classes on the same panels reveal structure in the South Mountains petroglyph assemblage, which controverts Snyder's (1966:706) position that "there is no convincingly positive correlation with regard to design or symbol associations." If we consider the chronological trend in Hohokam ceramic designs—a broad move from curvilinear to rectilinear designs with an infusion of lifeforms along the way (see Chapter 3)—as a rough proxy for that of petroglyphs, the CAs tentatively suggest that this transition also took place in the iconography of South Mountains petroglyphs. On Factor 1 in the panel-level CA (Figure 5.3), curvilinear designs cluster to the right whereas rectilinear designs cluster to the left, and lifeforms are spread amid these extremes. Factor 1 quite possibly registers older-to-younger design classes from right to left.

The CAs also hint that the places of petroglyph manufacture remained relatively stationary over time. Indeed, it seems that over the centuries the Hohokam tended to craft petroglyphs in the same general areas of the landscape, but over generations they opted for different yet nearby panels. Perhaps as the accretion of additional petroglyphs exhausted available panel space, the crafters pecked petroglyphs on new or less-covered panels. Regardless, it remains to be shown that the correspondences are due to time rather than any number of other functional or social reasons. The following analyses, starting with a cross-media design comparison, then an assessment of relative patination, and finally an analysis of artifact associations, help fill out the South Mountains petroglyph chronicle.

Ceramic Design Cross-Correlation

Correlations between rock art iconography and designs in other datable media provide perhaps one of the most basic and inductive approaches available for dating the rock art. Cross-media design correlations are a fundamental first step in assigning rock art cultural and temporal affinities. However, design correlations, or lack thereof, across media should not be taken as a priori indicators of cultural or temporal affiliation for the rock art because there may be underlying social, religious, and functional factors that influence choices in motifs and designs, compositions and layouts, frequencies, and stylistic forms among different media (Wallace and Holmlund 1986:103; see also Bunzel 1929:85). In fact, the extent of design correlation across media may approximate the fluidity of knowledge regarding emotionally and religiously charged symbolism, and the authority to access, possess, and display that knowledge, within the society in question (e.g., DeBoer 1991; Smith 1992). In the following, I briefly outline how the South Mountains petroglyph corpus compares with Hohokam pottery designs, providing a basic framework on which to build a relative chronology.

Omar Turney, well known for his thorough mapping of Hohokam canals in the lower Salt River valley, conducted the first and only quantitative cross-media design analysis between Hohokam decorated pottery and rock art (Turney 1928, 1929). He compared the designs on approximately 12,000 sherds from the Salt River ruins with 815 "rock pictures" around the Phoenix area, including the South Mountains (Turney 1929:123–126).[2] Turney's pioneering work on Hohokam iconography was rivaled only by Harold Gladwin's (1928) and Erich Schmidt's (1928) contemporaneous stratigraphic excavations at Casa Grande and Pueblo Grande, respectively, but these formally trained archaeologists focused solely on pottery. It was almost 40 years until another more than cursory account of designs shared between Hohokam pottery and petroglyph iconography was published by Ernest Snyder (1966). Snyder drew on the presence of spirals and scrolls in both media

TABLE 5.1. Frequencies of Chronologically Sensitive Motifs on Pottery and in Rock Art.

Pottery Designs			Corresponding Petroglyph Motifs[a]		
	Span[b] & Frequency	Peak[b]		Count	Frequency (%)[c]
Key	LSN – SC (0.8%)	LSN (4.3%)	Key	1	<0.1
Lifeforms[d]	EGB – MSAC (1.1%)	LGB (4.2%)	Thunderbird/Raptor	2	0.1
			Miscellaneous Bird	3	0.1
			Insects/Invertebrates	3	0.1
			Coiled Snake	6	0.2
			Sheep	8	0.3
			Waterbird	8	0.3
			Tortoise	22	0.7
			Deer/Elk/Antelope	25	0.8
			Extended Snake[e]	40	1.3
			Lizard	101	3.3
			Canid	149	4.9
			Indistinct Quadruped	263	8.6
			Unfinished Anthropomorph	323	10.6
			Anthropomorph	453	14.8
			Total	1,406	46.0
Small Geometric Element Group A[f]	LGB – MSAC (?%)	?	Pottery Motif 113	3	0.1
			Pinwheel/Whorl	4	0.1
			Diamond	9	0.3
			Square	11	0.4
			Paired Zig-Zag	11	0.4
			Total	38	1.2
Crenulation	ESAC – MSAC (2.0%)	MSAC (5.2%)	Crenulatione	2	0.1
Small Geometric Element Group E[f]	MSAC (?%)	MSAC (?%)	Opposed "L"s	1	<0.1
			Concentric Squares	1	<0.1
			Swastika	4	0.1
			Total	6	0.2
Small Geometric Element Group C[f]	MSAC – Soho (?%)	?	Interlocked Hooks	1	<0.1
Rectilinear Scrolls[g]	EGB – Soho (7.2%)	Soho (71.4%)	Rect. Scroll, Clockwise	2	0.1
			Rect. Connected Scrolls	2	0.1
			Rect. Scroll, Counterclockwise	3	0.1
			Rect. Interlocked Scrolls	3	0.1
			Rect. Running Connected Scrolls	4	0.1
			Total	14	0.5
Totals	LSN – Soho (11.9%+)[h]			1,468	48.1

Note: Ceramic data from Wallace (2004:Table 3.6) except for rectilinear scrolls, which are from Wallace (2001:Table 10.13).

[a] See appendix for examples.

[b] LSN = late Snaketown, EGB = early Gila Butte, LGB = late Gila Butte, SC = Santa Cruz, ESAC = early Sacaton, MSAC = middle Sacaton, LSAC = late Sacaton.

[c] As calculated out of entire sample of 3,055 prehistoric petroglyphs.

[d] Category does not include uncategorizable lifeforms, plants, horns, animal prints, or butterflies. Waterbirds and lizards appear in the Snaketown phase, and miscellaneous birds and thunderbird/raptor may appear in the Snaketown phase.

[e] Crenulated snakes are classified as extended snakes, not crenulations; such versions may be diagnostic of Sacaton phase snake motifs.

[f] See Wallace (2004:Table 3.7) for definitions and examples of Small Geometric Element Groups. Frequencies of these motifs were not reported by Wallace (2004).

[g] Includes some elements that Wallace (2004:Table 3.7) grouped in the Small Geometric Element Group C.

[h] Does not include the Small Geometric Elements Groups since these were not quantified in the ceramic data.

as a line of evidence to suggest that Hohokam hands crafted the South Mountains petroglyphs. Aside from Henry Wallace's work on Hohokam iconographic styles (see Chapter 3), which was concerned chiefly with chronological refinements to the Hohokam red-on-buff pottery sequence (Wallace 1995b, 2001, 2004; Wallace et al. 1995; see also Wallace and Holmlund 1986), few studies since Turney's have explicitly addressed either the connections or the gaps in iconography between rock art and other Hohokam visual media. (Bostwick and Krocek [2002] and Smith [2000], however, have offered several interesting yet cursory comparisons for a few selected motifs.)

In light of the above shortcomings, in the following section I present a basic comparison of motif frequencies between Hohokam rock art and painted buffware designs. I consider only those motifs that are chronologically sensitive in the pottery sequence, as shown by Wallace's (2001, 2004) work. It is important to note that there were other motifs depicted in both media, but unfortunately most are not temporally diagnostic, so measures of their frequencies as pottery designs remain to be published. In Table 5.1 I present the frequencies of 13 chronologically sensitive designs as they are found both in the sample of South Mountains petroglyphs and on the pottery sherds Wallace used to refine the buffware chronology (2001:Table 10.13, 2004:Table 3.6). This table also outlines the chronological phases in which these motifs were part of the design corpus painted on buffware vessels, the phases in which their popularity peaked, and their overall frequencies as buffware pottery designs throughout the Hohokam cultural sequence.

One compelling point brought out in Table 5.1 is that more than 48 percent of the petroglyphs are of motifs that fall within these chronologically sensitive ceramic design groups, and the vast majority (46 percent) are of lifeforms (e.g., Figure 5.6). With a few exceptions, lifeform designs, such as deer, canids, lizards, and birds, were painted on ceramic pots only during the Colonial and Sedentary periods with a peak popularity during the late Gila Butte. On the other hand, just 15 of the South Mountains petroglyphs, which make up less than one-half of one percent of the SMRAP sample of 3,055 petroglyphs, are of motifs that parallel rectilinear scroll designs and similar motifs in Wallace's Small Element Group C painted on pottery, both of which are design groups generally considered diagnostic of the late Sedentary and Classic periods (e.g., Figure 5.7). This very low rate of occurrence of Classic period ceramic iconography as petroglyph designs in the South Mountains seems to be a broadly shared aspect of Hohokam rock art, since similarly low frequencies of rectilinear scrolls have been reported from the Tucson Basin, Picacho Mountains, and Gila Bend region. In fact, nearly all the pottery motifs that also show up in rock art date largely to an era encapsulated between the Gila Butte and middle Sacaton phases (circa AD 800–1050).

In addition to lifeforms, curvilinear designs such as scrolls, spirals, circles, and pinwheels on buffware pottery are often considered loosely diagnostic of Preclassic iconography (Haury 1976). The Hohokam pecked similar designs into rock faces and boulders in the South Mountains and elsewhere (e.g., Figure 5.8). Indeed, nearly 27 percent of the South Mountains petroglyph sample (n = 814) falls within the circle, concentric circle, curvilinear scroll, and miscellaneous curvilinear petroglyph design classes (Table 4.1). If we couple these curvilinear designs with the frequent occurrence of lifeforms and rarer instances of keys, crenulations, and designs in the Small Element Groups A and E, then we can consider about 75 percent (n = 2,267) of the analyzed Hohokam petroglyphs in the South Mountains kindred to ceramic designs diagnostic of Preclassic iconography. The residual 25 percent of the South Mountains petroglyphs consist mostly of difficult-to-classify miscellaneous and linear designs not found in pottery designs (Table 4.1).

The cross-media design comparison points toward a predominant, if not exclusive, Preclassic origin for the South Mountains petroglyphs. There are several interpretive conundrums to consider, however, before such a claim can be forwarded. One basic dilemma is that we really do not know what Classic period petroglyph

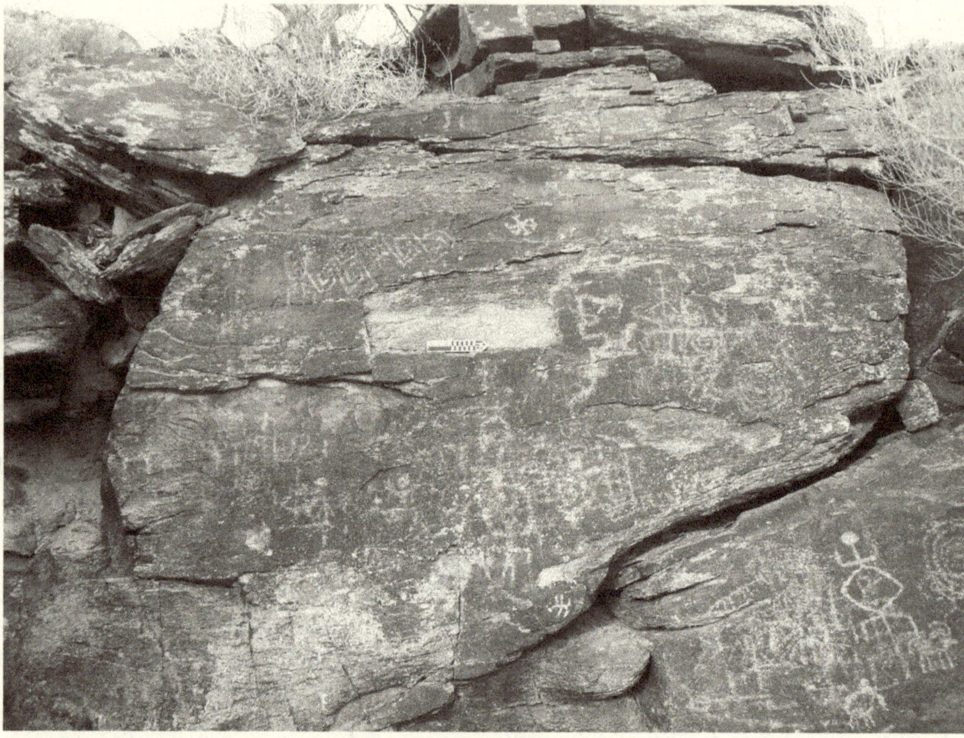

FIGURE 5.6. Complex panels dominated by lifeform petroglyphs. Several motifs in the bottom-center and right portions of the top panel are superimposed. Note the integration of the running connected-rectilinear scrolls with the anthropomorph at the top and the similar extent of patination (brightness) between these and the other motifs.

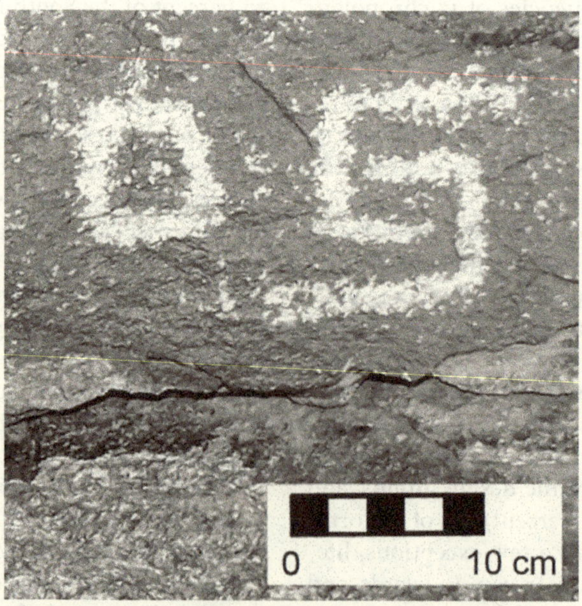

FIGURE 5.7. A pair of interlocked hooks and a square petroglyph. As depicted on Hohokam buffware pottery, interlocked hooks are a member of Wallace's (2004) Small Element Group C and date between the middle Sacaton and Soho phases.

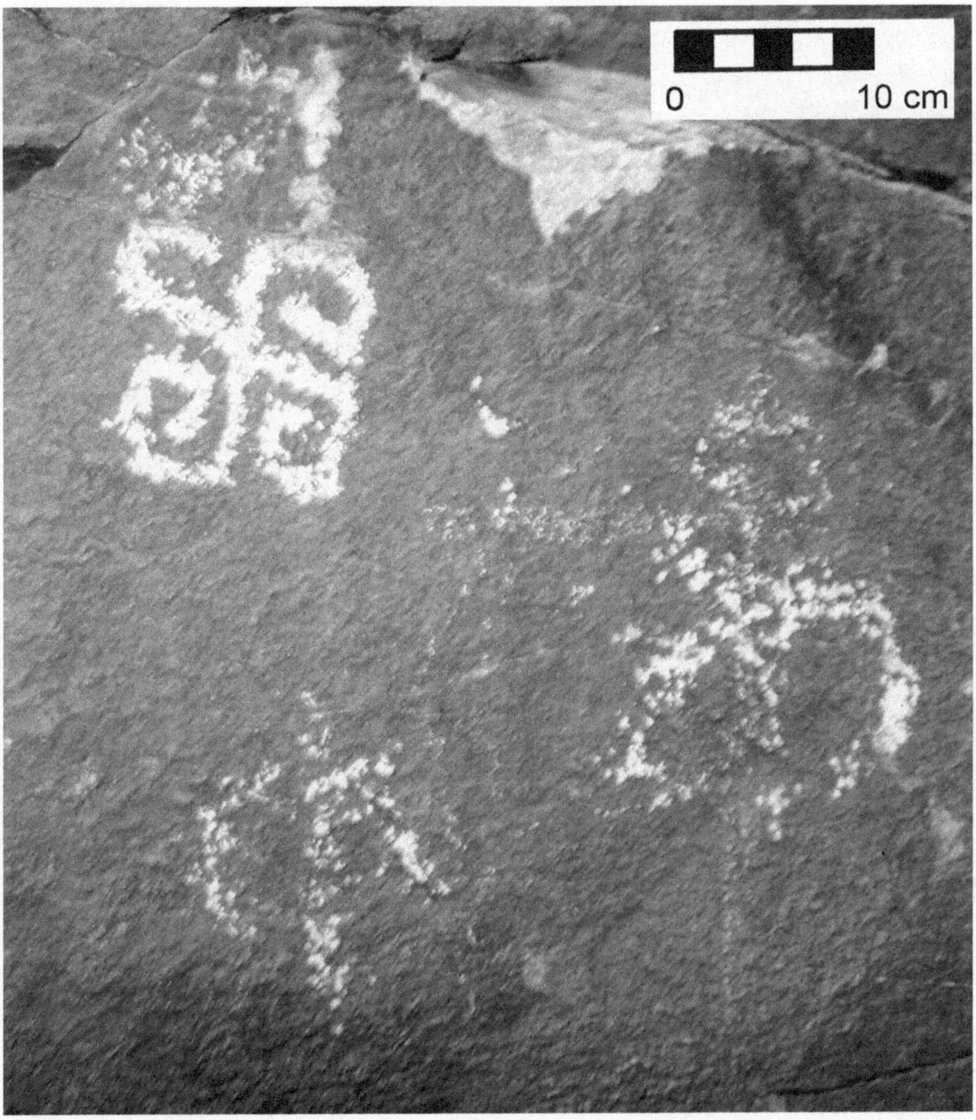

FIGURE 5.8. Pinwheel and unfinished anthropomorph petroglyphs. As depicted on Hohokam buffware pottery, pinwheels (or whorls) are a member of Wallace's (2004) Small Element Group A and date between the late Gila Butte and middle Sacaton phases.

designs would look like (see Chapter 3). The working hypothesis—that Classic period rock art consists of complex rectilinear designs—is based, rather shakily I should point out, on analogy to the Hohokam ceramic design sequence. Alongside a general paucity of circular designs, lifeforms, and other figurative elements, the unique qualities of Classic period ceramic designs include tight, rectilinear, basketry-like motifs and layouts, all of which are extremely rare among the South Mountains petroglyphs (e.g., Figure 5.9). If the analogy is roughly accurate, then it would appear that only a handful of petroglyphs, principally the rectilinear scrolls and a few other atypical designs, are of Classic period manufacture. Even these, however, may be Preclassic because rectilinear scrolls were often painted on Sacaton era buffware and show up as early,

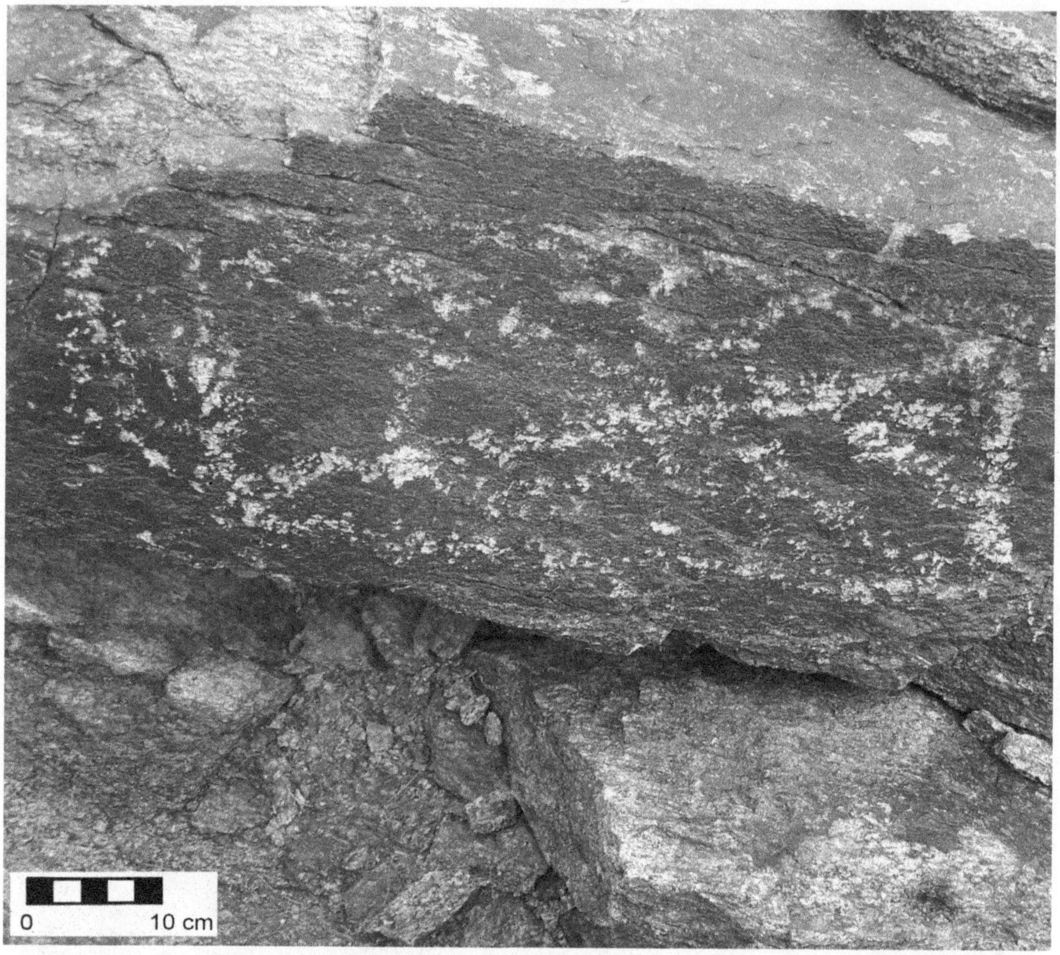

FIGURE 5.9. Rectangular, textile-like petroglyph.

albeit rarely, as the Colonial period. Their rare frequency as South Mountains petroglyph motifs, less than two-fifths of one percent of the analyzed sample, seems to approximate their rarity as Preclassic pottery designs.

Perhaps Salado iconography provides a more apt repertoire of symbols with which we should compare the South Mountains petroglyph motifs in order to look for Classic period designs among the rock art. This is a moot case, however, because only one petroglyph in the sample assemblage, an abstractly depicted bird (Figure 4.3, bottom center), can be likened to a Salado-esque motif, and that would be an extreme analogical stretch. Its juxtaposition in an integrated panel bearing lifeforms and other typical Hohokam glyphs, all with similar degrees of patination, argues against a late Classic manufacture. As I discussed in Chapter 3, we should not be surprised by the dearth of Salado polychrome style iconography, with its fluid and abstract motifs and layouts (Crown 1994), in Hohokam rock art because it is unclear if such vessels were manufactured in the Phoenix Basin.

Another question, related to the above conundrum, concerns the issue with which I prefaced this section: should we expect or have reason to assume that chronological changes in the South Mountains rock art corpus occurred in concert with design shifts on Hohokam pottery? It is reasonable to speculate that lifeform petroglyphs continued to be produced into the Classic period because portrayals of animal and human forms endured in media such as effigy vessels and shell jewelry, and even on the occasional ceramic. Even though the panel-level CA hints at a shift from a petroglyph assemblage dominated by curvilinear designs to one mixed with lifeform and rectilinear designs, and the cross-media design analysis shows that nearly all the designs shared by the two media are found almost exclusively on Preclassic pottery, our work is not finished. To this point, the chronology-in-the-making is based largely on analogy to the ceramic design sequence. We still need indicators internal to the petroglyph assemblage and other lines of associative evidence to confirm that this general shift in petroglyph iconography is due, at least in part, to time and that curvilinear and lifeform petroglyph designs were not produced during the Classic period. Results provided in the following two analyses—the first comparing the differing extents of rock repatination among petroglyph design classes and motif types and the second addressing the types of pottery associated with the South Mountains petroglyphs—round out the preliminary chronological picture drawn from the CA and the cross-media design analysis.

Desert Varnish

The dark, usually dull but sometimes glossy outer coating on the exposed surfaces of bedrock outcrops and boulders in arid climates is known as either rock varnish or desert varnish (hereafter I use "desert varnish" because it is more applicable to this book). Throughout western North America, desert varnish, which can take thousands of years to develop, is commonly found on mafic and felsic igneous landforms and boulders, though it is capable of forming on any rock type as long as the exposed surfaces remain stable (Dorn 1998, 2004, 2007). Given the smooth, sometimes polished appearance of some surfaces with a well-developed desert varnish, early researchers speculated that the varnish was due to aeolian erosion (e.g., Grant et al. 1968:43) or chemical alteration of the parent rock (e.g., Hobbs 1918). The formation of desert varnish is actually a complex, additive geochemical process whereby a manganese- and iron-rich layer "grows" over the surfaces of exposed rock. This outer layer is a type of rock coating, or a geochemical sediment that results from the accretional deposition of particles on the rock's surface (Dorn 1998; Dorn and Oberlander 1982; see also Thiagarajan and Lee 2004). This accretion usually begins after some degree of rock weathering—the chemical and mechanical processes that erode a rock's surface or alter its mineralogical structure, thus creating "weathering rinds"—has occurred. Desert varnish often grows over weathering rinds, a phenomenon that was instrumental in some early hypotheses explaining desert varnish formation. Georges Flamand (1921; see also Grant et al. 1968:44), for example, erroneously attributed varnish formation to capillary action in the rock. He argued that as water leaches into the rock, it dissolves and thus mobilizes certain elements, in effect creating a weathering rind. These mobile elements are then redeposited and concentrated as a film (i.e., varnish) on the rock's surface as it dries. Subsequent research has shown that the process is much more complex.

Desert varnish formation tends to initiate within moisture-retaining fissures and shallow depressions of the exposed rock face (Dorn 2007: 249; Villa et al. 1995). It then expands piecemeal across the rock's surface, somewhat like plaque on a tooth but at a much slower pace. The varnish is typically between 1 and 100 nm thick (Dorn 2004:251), and while the pace of its formation is conditioned by a number of parameters, it is usually somewhere in the range of several microns per millennium (Dorn 1998; Liu 2003; Liu and Broecker 2000, 2007). In cross-section and at high magnification, desert varnish appears as bands of alternating colors—often dark red-brown layers intermixed with those of lighter, orange-brown colors (Dorn and Oberlander 1982; Krinsley 1998; Krinsley et al. 1995)—known as varnish microlaminations (VMLs). The differences in color, which give desert varnish a banded and stratified appearance in cross-section, are due to fluctuations in a range of chemical, biological, and environmental factors, as discussed below.

Desert varnish is made up chiefly of particulates of aeolian dust that have fallen out and settled on the rock's face. Most of this dust is silica- and aluminum-rich clay particles (Engel and Sharp 1958), which have been cemented to the rock through a series of chemical and biological processes (Dorn 2004, 2007; Dorn and Oberlander 1982; Krinsley 1998; Potter and Rossman 1977). Other major contributors include manganese and iron oxides (in varying ratios, totaling approximately 20–30 percent)—which lend desert varnish its metallic, reddish brown-to-black color—and these are followed by trace amounts of other materials. It is the ratio between manganese and iron that accounts largely for the hues and chromas of the VMLs, with those richer in manganese having darker casts. The enhancement of manganese in desert varnish, where it is found in quantities 50 to 300 times greater than in the dust that falls on the rocks (Engel and Sharp 1958), remains one of the great "mysteries" of desert varnish research (Dorn 2004:253). The debate, detailed more fully by Ronald Dorn (1998, 2007:259–267), centers on whether the concentration of manganese in desert varnish is due to biotic or abiotic processes. David Krinsley (1998) has shown that it is not an either-or scenario, but that both processes are at play in a polygenetic model of varnish formation (Dorn 1998).

The polygenetic model of desert varnish is tied to the life cycles of lithobionts, several genera of bacteria that live on rock surfaces. Most geoscientists agree that these saxicolous microorganisms enhance manganese and iron over surrounding geological sources (Dorn and Oberlander 1981, 1982).[3] Since the concentration of manganese within desert varnish is likely correlated with the amount of manganese-enhancing bacteria present on the rock—and since, as organisms, these bacteria are sensitive to environmental and climatic factors—differentially colored VMLs signal significant and prolonged fluctuations in regional paleoclimatic regimes (e.g., Cremaschi 1996; Dorn 1990; Jones 1991; Lee and Bland 2003; Liu 2003; Liu and Broecker 2000, 2007, 2008a, 2008b; Liu and Dorn 1996; Liu et al. 2000; Zhou et al. 2000; see Hunt [1954] for an early correlation between desert varnish and precipitation rates). Therefore, the darker VMLs, which result from greater amounts of manganese-enhancing bacteria, correspond with relatively wet eras whereas the lighter, orange-brown layers correspond with drier climes. Researchers have since focused on correlating VMLs with known climatic intervals, such as the Little Ice Age, as a way to establish dates for varnish-covered archaeological features (e.g., Liu and Broecker 2007, 2008b).

VML analysis, although in its infancy, will doubtless prove informative on the chronologies of petroglyphs across the world. The chronological resolution it provides is nonetheless a limiting factor in its applicability since the VMLs, when calibrated, encapsulate between 500 and 1,800 years of varnish accumulation each (Liu and Broecker 2007:Table 5). There are surely circumstances where this degree of chronological precision will provide new insights (e.g., Whitley and Dorn 2010). As for the North American Desert West, including the Great Basin and the Greater Southwest, VML dating should, over time, help us get a better temporal grasp on the 8,000-year-long Western Archaic Tradition. In many cases, however, the resolution afforded by VML analysis is equal to or less than that available through other dating techniques. Most Gila (Hohokam) style petroglyphs, for example, likely date between AD 450 and 1450, when the Hohokam farmed the river valleys in southern Arizona, yet only two VMLs date to this millennium (see Liu and Broecker 2007:Table 5). The chronological break between these two VMLs is approximately AD 900, which is close to the Colonial-Sedentary period transition in the Hohokam cultural sequence. I believe we can obtain this degree of chronological resolution through other, less invasive methods. Combined with VML analysis's cost and labor investment (requiring thin-section analysis), the limited number of VML samples one could reasonably obtain and analyze, and the technique's permanent effect on the petroglyphs (requiring removal of a portion of the petroglyph), VML analysis is not, at this time, a viable option for developing a comprehensive chronological sequence for the thousands of South Mountains petroglyphs. Nonetheless, differential varnish accumulation, as a rough proxy for relative antiquity among a body of petroglyphs, remains a potential albeit far from foolproof aid for sequencing the South Mountains petroglyphs. In the following I therefore rely on less technical and less precise but noninvasive and cost-friendlier analyses and comparisons of the visual and measurable darkness of desert varnish over petroglyphs.

For ease of discussion, I refer to the combination of rock weathering and desert varnish accumulation as "patination." Repatination of a rock surface may occur after an event has caused the removal of an existing patina (varnish and/or weathering rind) and resulted in an exposure of virgin host rock. In a sense, making a petroglyph resets the rock's "patination clock" if it cut through the original overlying patina. The extent to which the newly exposed host rock is patinated, after a petroglyph removed the existing patina, provides a relative measure of how long the petroglyph has been exposed to weathering forces. Early researchers were not aware of the actual chemical, mechanical, and biological processes that produce weathering rinds and rock varnish, yet they understood that rock surfaces tend to become darker through time and that darker petroglyphs must therefore be older than lighter ones (e.g., Basedow 1914; Belzoni 1820:360–361). Indeed, repatination was instrumental in the development of some of the earliest stylistic classifications of petroglyphs in the Desert West (e.g., Grant et al. 1968; Heizer and Baumhoff 1962; Schaafsma 1980; Steward 1929; Turner 1963).

A number of factors affect the rate at which rock surfaces patinate (Dorn 1998:Table 10.7), however, and such variation can introduce confusion and difficulty in repatination studies. This quandary has become a classic problem for rock art studies. As early as the 1920s, Julian Steward (1929:72–73, 1937:417–418) cautioned researchers to consider geology and aspects of exposure in assessments of differential weathering of petroglyphs. Warren Moorehead, in his early examination of some South Mountains petroglyphs, must have been aware of these issues too when he observed that "in the Southwest [petroglyphs] may or may not weather, or at least only slightly; depending upon the conditions whether it is buried, or lies upon the surface or in a depression, or rests upon a knoll" (Moorehead 1906:91–92). Other influential parameters include lithology, microenvironmental conditions, and the erosional forces that act on existing desert varnish (Dorn 1998, 2004, 2007).

The factors are so complex that it is practically impossible to accurately assess a petroglyph's antiquity by virtue of the extent of its patination alone (e.g., Dorn 2005). Any such age assessment must be relative to the patination of other glyphs and grounded to some sort of calibration when possible. Perhaps the most straightforward way to control for sources of variation is to limit comparisons of relative patination to petroglyphs on the same rock face, since these, for the most part, are subject to the same weathering conditions, share an underlying mineralogy, and have similar aspects and orientations of exposure. Ideally, in such settings, where the weathering conditions are largely uniform, patination rates should be similar among observations. Since the pace of patination is known to vary across the same rock face (Dorn 2007:249), assessments of patina color and darkness are macroscopic averages of microscopic nuances in patination across a petroglyph's surface. Nevertheless, broad statistical patterns, afforded through large samples, should outweigh case-by-case discrepancies.

As I emphasize in this chapter, no single dating method is foolproof, and results from one method should be tested by and correlated with those of other techniques. Accordingly, I consider repatination, while notoriously troublesome, to be one piece of a chronological puzzle, and one that is capable of providing some reliable insights. In this vein, I use the following two sections to explore the utility of repatination as a tool for investigating temporal changes in petroglyph iconography in the South Mountains.

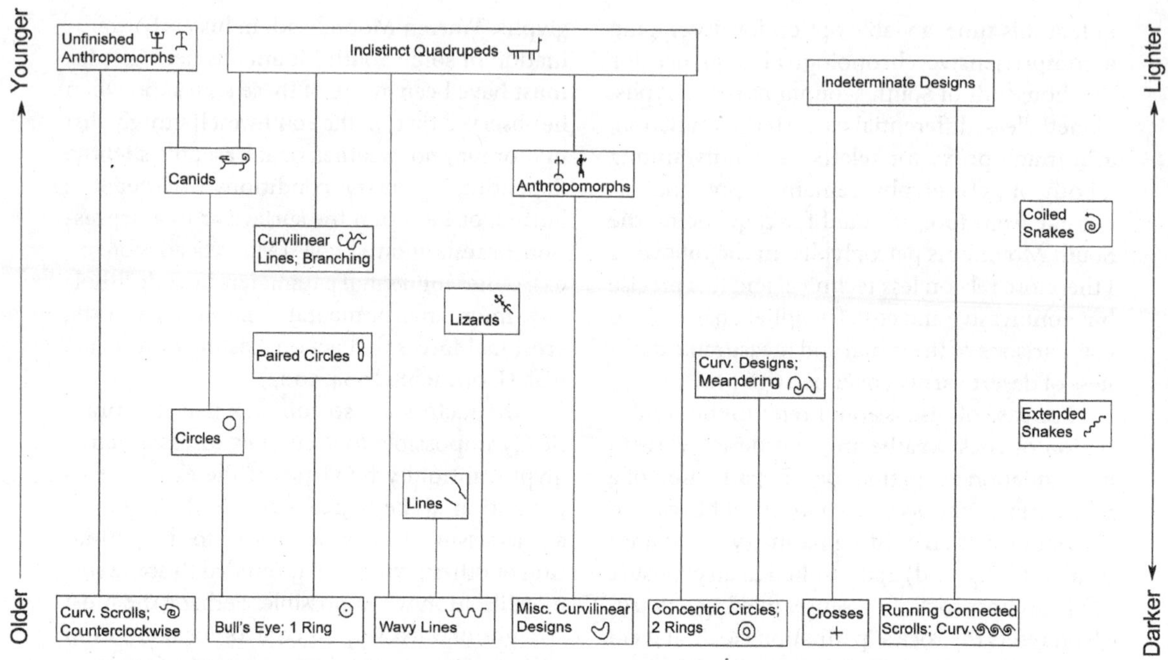

FIGURE 5.10. Relational matrix of petroglyph motifs with significant rank differences in patina darkness. Distances between motifs are not to scale, and only those connected via lines meet the significance threshold.

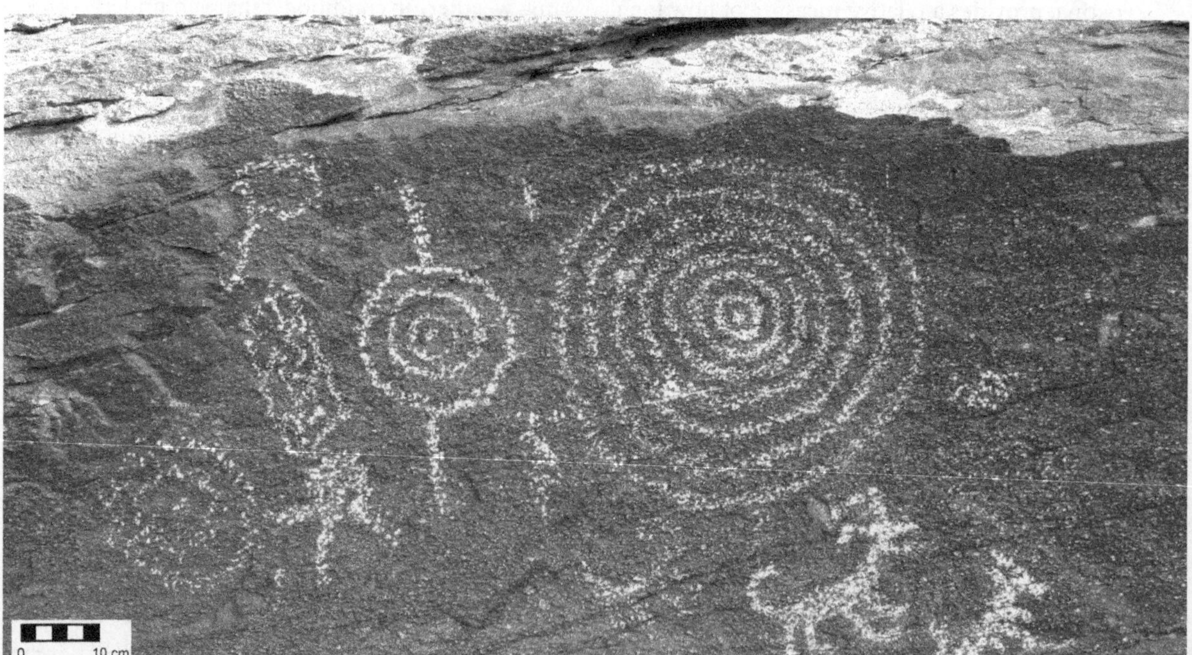

FIGURE 5.11. Panel with various bull's-eye and lifeform petroglyphs near a spring.

Patina Rank

During field recording I ranked the darkness of each petroglyph's patina relative to that of other petroglyphs on the same panel. The ranking began at a level of 1, the darkest petroglyphs on the panel, and proceeded to 2, 3, and so on, with increasing degrees of brightness. In instances where I could not detect any differences in patina darkness with my naked eye, which was often the case, I assigned the petroglyphs the same patina rank. Wallace and Holmlund (1986) and Bernardini (2009) performed similar, though not identical, patina rank comparisons at other settings in Arizona. In those studies the authors developed a series of rank-ordered patina classes, from no patina to very dark, to which they assigned each petroglyph. Their patina classes were thus predetermined, and the petroglyphs were ranked regardless of their darkness in relation to other petroglyphs on the same panel. In this way, variable degrees of darkness among petroglyphs on the same panel were subsumed under higher-order patina classes, which may have aggregated and thus obfuscated finer degrees of patina darkness among the petroglyphs. Nonetheless, Wes Bernardini's study at the Ancestral Pueblo site of Tutuveni, in northeastern Arizona, revealed a horizontally stratified petroglyph assemblage differentiated by patina darkness (Bernardini 2009:Figure 1.5), which I interpret as evidence of a broad temporal translocation in preferred sites of rock art production across that landform.[4]

Henry Wallace and James Holmlund's (1986) patination study of Archaic and Hohokam petroglyphs in the Picacho Mountains involved petroglyphs on different lithologies, in different topographic settings, and exposed to different microenvironmental nuances. Cautious of the vagaries inherent to patina development, they considered the lithologies to be similar enough to not have significantly affected repatination rates between rock types (Wallace and Holmlund 1986:77). They also monitored the petroglyphs' microenvironmental settings and observed that "other than in limited microenvironments... in no case were the differences between two such panels for glyph repatination great enough to modify [their] coding" (Wallace and Holmlund 1986:77). The Hohokam petroglyphs in the Picacho Mountains exhibit two ranks of patina darkness, which the investigators believe correspond to the Preclassic and Classic periods (Wallace and Holmlund 1986:103–104).[5]

The encouraging results from the Picacho Mountains and Tutuveni guided my methodology; however, I surmised that predetermined patina classes obfuscate finer-grained variability in patination among petroglyphs. To tease out any such finer detail, I instead ranked the petroglyphs' patinas only in relation to those of other petroglyphs on the same panel. This intrapanel ranking also served to control for the unique microenvironments and contexts that may have led to differing rates of patination among panels. The potential effect of differing lithologies on patination rates was not an issue here since all the petroglyphs in the SMRAP study areas were pecked, scratched, or abraded into outcroppings and boulders of metamorphosed granodiorite with nearly identical mineralogies.[6]

I used Mann-Whitney's U statistic for comparing patina ranks between petroglyph motif types in order to determine whether or not certain ones are recurrently brighter or darker than others when they co-occur on the same panels.[7] Statistically significant differences in patina ranks among petroglyph motifs betray an interesting pattern (Figure 5.10).[8] Curvilinear motif types, dominating the lower (older) end of the relational matrix in Figure 5.10, tend to have darker patinas than the various lifeforms that cluster in the upper (younger) tier. Thus, curvilinear motif forms are often older than many of the lifeform designs when they are found on the same panels. This chronological trend, however, is not clear-cut because there are ample instances where these various designs are not darker or brighter than the others when they co-occur (e.g., Figure 5.11). These distinctions in visible patina darkness among petroglyph motif types should thus be considered *tendencies*, not sharp turns or deviations in petroglyph iconography through time. Nevertheless, the metamorphosis of a petroglyph iconographic repertoire dominated by curvilinear designs to one later infused with lifeforms corresponds well with what we know about the evolution of Hohokam pottery designs and symbolism.

Petroglyph Reflectance

With the patina rank analysis, I qualitatively measured the degrees of patination by visually comparing the relative darkness of petroglyphs on the same panels. While the results are inspiring, the technique was useful for only a handful of motif types. This is because many of the motif types do not co-occur frequently enough for consistent differences in patina darkness to be identified among them, and under field conditions I was often unable to discern any visual differences in patina darkness. Not trusting my own eyes, I therefore also measured the petroglyphs' patina darknesses with a light meter, which is capable of detecting variations in a surface's brightness and color too slight to catch with the naked eye. Light meters, tools common to photography and the film industry, can quantify the amount of light petroglyphs reflect, a measure I refer to as "petroglyph reflectance" (*R*), and therefore offer a more objective though still imperfect means of measuring patina darkness.[9] While the accuracy of reflectance, as an aid for chronology building, is constrained by the same microenvironmental and geological parameters that condition patina rank differences noted above, the method's utility lies in its greater analytical objectivity and the generation of ratio-scale data for statistical investigations.[10]

I used a commercial handheld light meter to measure *R* values of 1,896 petroglyphs in the South Mountains.[11] These data express differences in relative degrees of petroglyph patination that complement the trend revealed by the prior patina rank analysis (Figure 5.12). There is a tendency for curvilinear designs (i.e., concentric circles and scrolls) to be darker (older) than other designs, whereas rectilinear scrolls tend to be brighter (younger) than all other prehistoric glyphs. Within these extremes along the reflectance spectrum, there is a slight shift from a design repertoire composed predominantly of geometric designs to one with a greater prevalence of lifeforms near the center of the distribution, but again these are broad tendencies.[12]

Petroglyph reflectance, a ratio-scale variable, is potentially suitable for calculating a calibrated rate of patination when the dates of the rock surfaces' initial exposure to patina-forming processes are known. Historic petroglyphs containing calendrical dates are ideal for calibrating such relative chronological orderings because they allow us to generate a ratio of patination relative to the timeframe between the petroglyphs' dates, and that rate could in theory be projected back in time to estimate the ages of much older petroglyphs (e.g., Figure 5.13). In fact, Robert Bednarik (2009) recently attempted this in an experimental colorimetric analysis of historic and archaeological petroglyphs, with rather inspiring results.

There are many historic petroglyphs in the South Mountains—I recorded 278 in the study area alone—but unfortunately I was unable to develop a meaningful patination rate calibrated to dated historic glyphs since there are only 19 glyphs with historic/modern dates in the SMRAP sample (Table 4.2). Euro-American and Hispanic residents of the Phoenix area, who likely made most of the historic petroglyphs during the twentieth century, preferred to remain anonymous and keep us guessing by simply leaving their initials most of the time (e.g., Figure 5.14). Furthermore, I could measure reflectance on less than half the historically dated petroglyphs, as most either did not fully penetrate the panel's existing patinas or were made through light or ephemeral etching/scratching. As a result, their line widths were too thin to be measured with the light meter because its spot finder targets a circular area with a diameter of about 1 cm.

Although calibrating a patination rate with historically dated rock surfaces is currently not an option, calculating a patination rate, albeit imprecisely and with added layers of assumption, is still possible based on the extent of patination between the darkest (oldest) petroglyphs and the historic ones. If we assume that the darkest glyphs date to the Pioneer period—the era to which the earliest ceramics in the South Mountains date and when the nearby villages were founded—then the petroglyph assemblage spans approximately 1,300 years, from about AD 650 to 1950. By taking the central tendencies, either the means or medians, in reflectance values for each design class as rough chronological

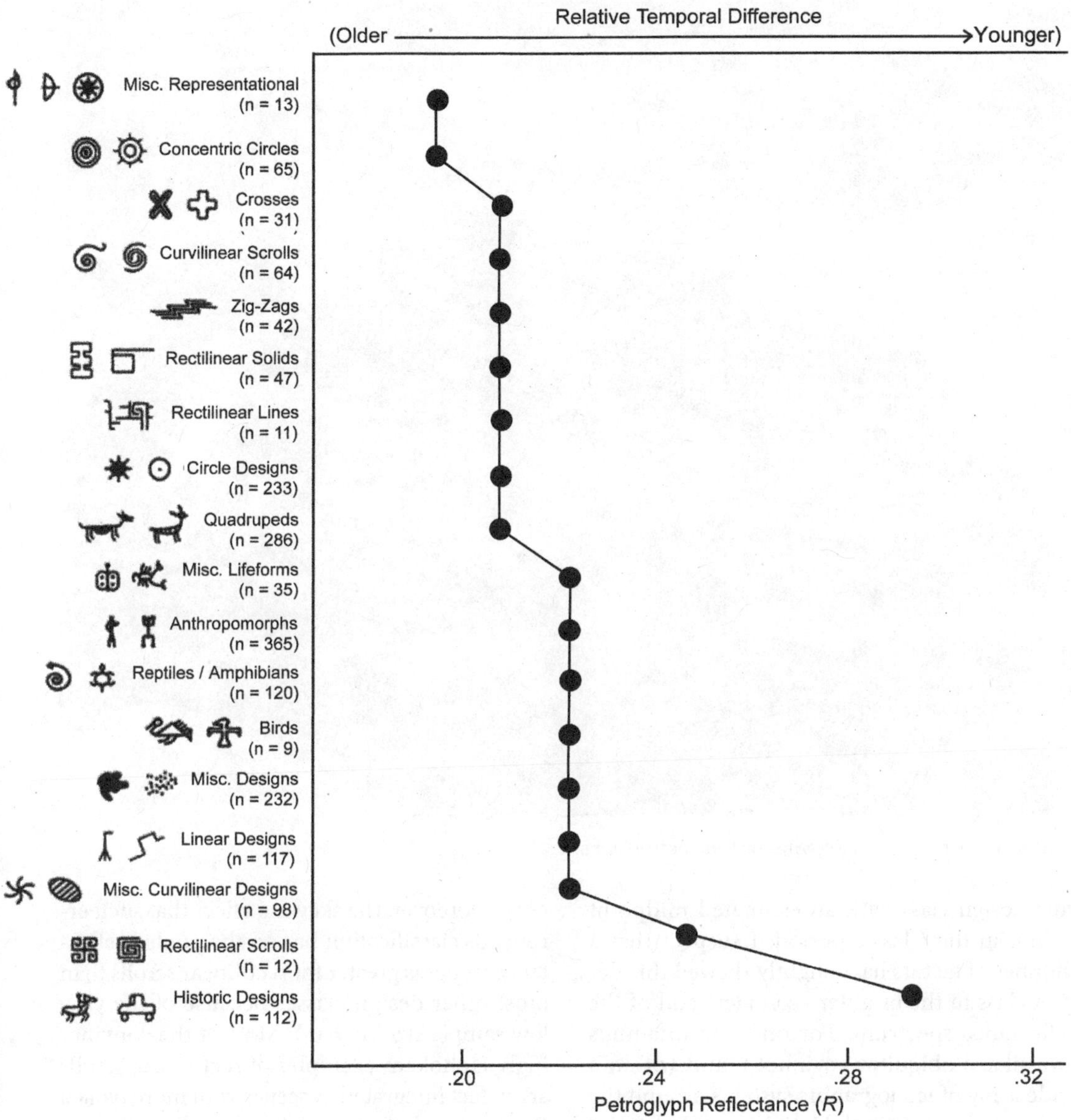

FIGURE 5.12. Medians in petroglyph reflectance by design class.

proxies for the midpoints in those designs' production spans, we can calculate a patination rate calibrated to the beginning and end of this 1,300-year period. The differences in mean and median reflectance between the miscellaneous representational designs, the darkest petroglyph design class on average, and the historic designs are 9 and 10 percent, respectively (Table 5.2). This difference in reflectance, relative to the 1,300 years of ongoing patination and desert varnish accumulation, therefore yields an estimated change of 1 percent in petroglyph reflectance every 130 (based on median values) to 150 (based on mean values) years.

Table 5.2 lists the retrodicted age estimates of the production-span midpoints for the design classes, most of which are concentrated in the Preclassic era. Rectilinear scrolls are the

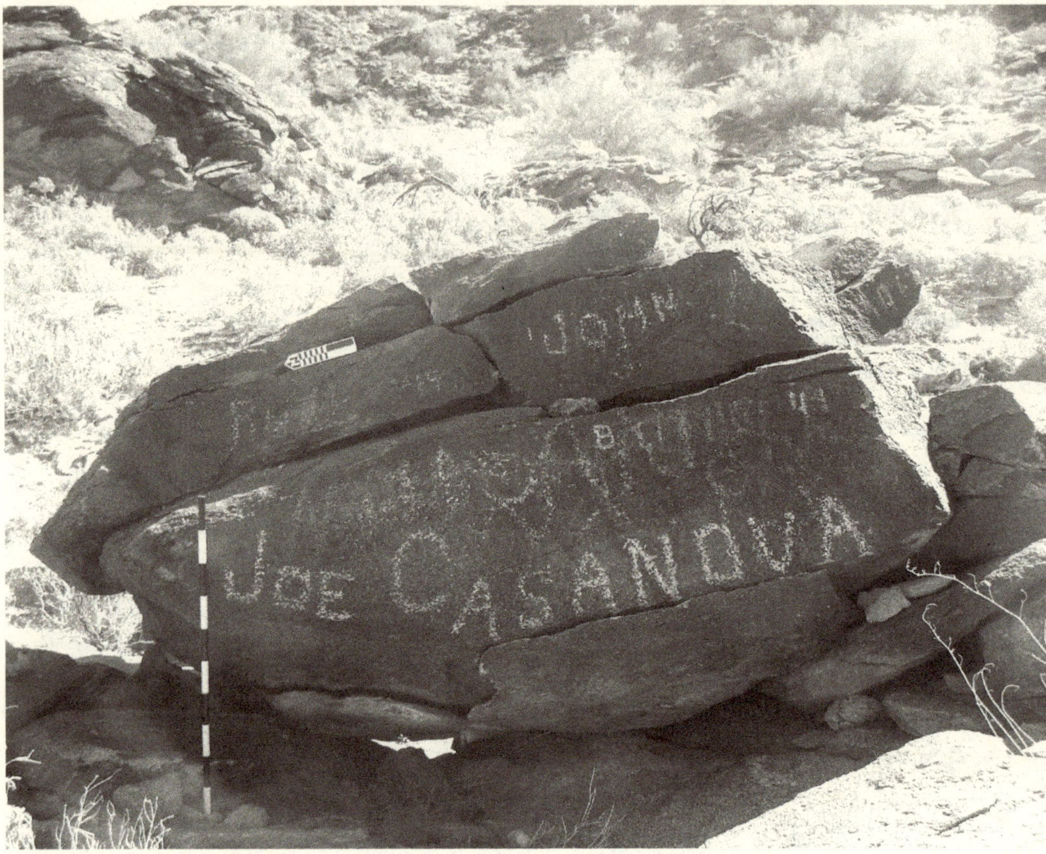

FIGURE 5.13. Group of panels with historic petroglyphs.

sole design class with an estimated midpoint falling in the Classic period. I suspect that a number of factors have slightly skewed this design class to the brighter (younger) end of the reflectance spectrum. For one, the infamous swastika, a ubiquitous symbol found within a wide array of iconographic systems around the globe, shows up in both Hohokam and historic/modern petroglyph iconography. When I found these in isolation from other historic glyphs, I erred on the side of caution and recorded them as Hohokam glyphs in the rectilinear scroll design class. While this potential error could apply to any solitary petroglyph regardless of motif type, several swastikas stick out as likely historic glyphs misclassified as Hohokam ones because they are more finely and deeply pecked into the panels, hinting at an indirect percussion manufacturing technique with metal tools (e.g., Figure 5.15). Moreover, the skewing effect that such erroneous classification has on the pooled reflectance values is greater for rectilinear scrolls than most other design classes because of the very low sample size (n = 12). Most of the convincingly Hohokam examples of rectilinear scrolls are in fact integrated in scenes with more typical Preclassic motifs, such as lifeforms (e.g., Figures 5.5 and 5.6, top left), suggesting that most date to this earlier era, although rare Classic occurrences cannot be fully ruled out.

Patination Summary

Results of the patina rank and petroglyph reflectance analyses are quite compatible with and support a broad though robust chronological pattern in Hohokam petroglyph iconography. In the South Mountains there is a penchant for curvilinear designs, primarily variations of curvilin-

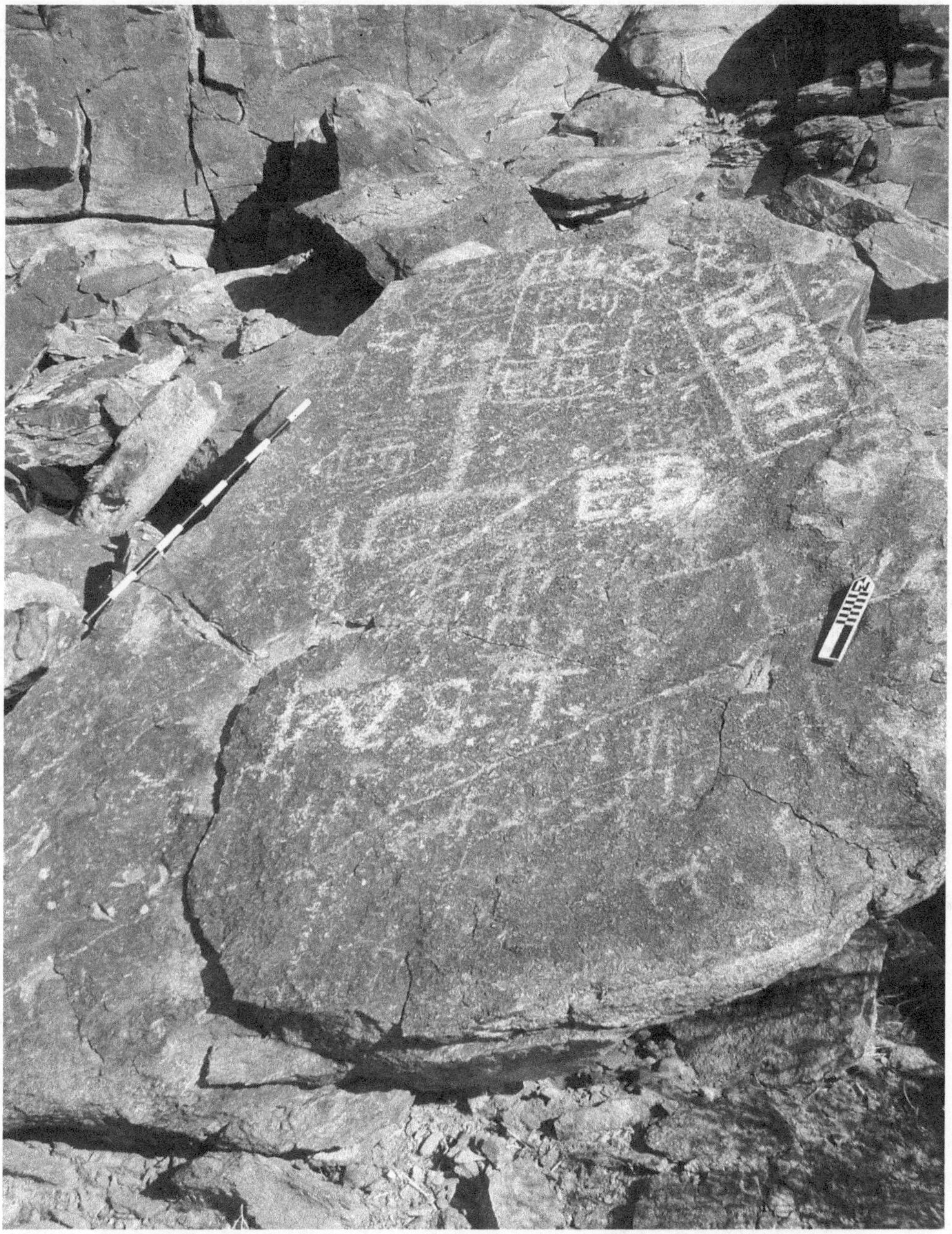

FIGURE 5.14. Panel with historic and modern initials pecked into a complex scene of Hohokam petroglyphs.

ear scrolls and concentric circles, to be darker (older) than most other petroglyphs when they are present on the same panel as well as across the landscape. From the other end, rectilinear scroll designs tend to be brighter (younger) than other Hohokam designs. Within these extremes there appears to have been a shift in emphasis toward figurative designs such as animal and human forms over time. The patination analyses also highlight the fact that a notable number of instances deviate from this general trend. Whereas the preponderance, popularity,

TABLE 5.2. Measures of Petroglyph Reflectance by Design Class.

Design Class	Reflectance Measures				Estimated Midpoint in Production Span[a]
	Count	Median	Mean	Stan. Dev.	
Miscellaneous Representational	13	0.19	0.21	0.05	AD 600–650
Concentric Circles	65	0.19	0.21	0.04	AD 600–650
Crosses	31	0.21	0.21	0.06	AD 860–910
Curvilinear Scrolls	64	0.21	0.21	0.04	AD 860–910
Zig-Zags	42	0.21	0.21	0.05	AD 860–910
Rectilinear Solids	47	0.21	0.22	0.07	AD 860–910
Rectilinear Lines	11	0.21	0.22	0.07	AD 860–910
Circle Designs	233	0.21	0.22	0.05	AD 860–910
Quadrupeds	286	0.21	0.23	0.06	AD 860–910
Miscellaneous Lifeforms	35	0.21	0.23	0.05	AD 860–910
Anthropomorphs	365	0.22	0.23	0.06	AD 990–1040
Reptiles/Amphibians	120	0.22	0.23	0.06	AD 990–1040
Birds	9	0.22	0.23	0.07	AD 990–1040
Miscellaneous Designs	232	0.22	0.23	0.07	AD 990–1040
Linear Designs	117	0.22	0.23	0.07	AD 990–1040
Miscellaneous Curv. Designs	98	0.22	0.23	0.05	AD 990–1040
Rectilinear Scrolls	12	0.25	0.25	0.04	AD 1380–1430
Historic Designs	112	0.29	0.30	0.08	AD 1900–1950

[a] Based on a projected 1 percent increase in reflectance every 130 years.

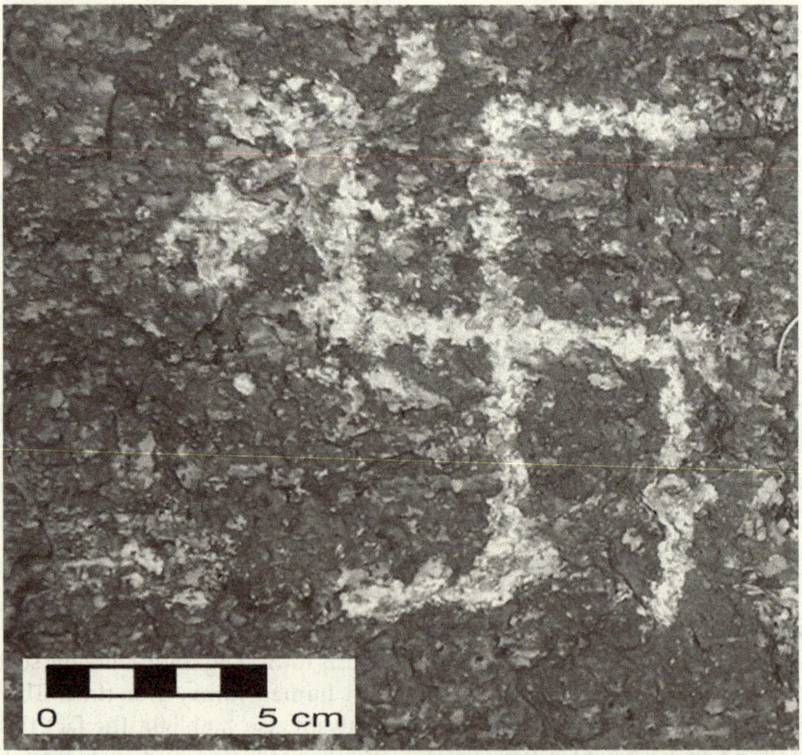

FIGURE 5.15. Historic or modern swastika petroglyph. The fine, deep execution of this specimen indicates that it was most likely crafted through incision or indirect percussion with a metal tool such as a nail.

and relevance of different motifs probably varied through time, considerable overlap in reflectance values among design classes, attested to by the relatively large standard deviations about their means (Table 5.2), suggests that most designs were made throughout the sequence. I should also point out that the patina-based chronology remains almost entirely relative, and the estimated midpoints in production span are highly speculative. It is the compatibility of this relative chronology with the results of other dating techniques that gives it credence.

I draw two implications from these analyses of patina darkness. First, while there seems to have been a general shift in petroglyph design choice through time, there is no indication here that early designs were dropped from the motif repertoire at any point in the sequence. Seemingly late designs, principally rectilinear scrolls, likewise are not exclusively brighter (younger) than other petroglyphs. The pattern is thus a temporal trend, not evidence of an outright transformation in petroglyph iconography. The other implication is that the inferential potential of analyses such as these is relatively weak for small sample sizes, such as panel- and site-level assemblages. Rather, to dampen the analytical noise introduced by the nuances, vagaries, and intricacies at work in desert varnish development and other patination processes, we should use fairly large datasets to garner relative chronologies that draw on comparative assessments of patina formation.

Results of three relative dating techniques—CA, cross-media design analysis, and repatination—harmonize well and therefore reinforce one another. This synergism underscores robust chronological patterns in the types of petroglyph designs produced in the South Mountains, with the emergent sequence approximating better-known changes in buffware pottery designs. The chronicle thus far is that there was an emphasis on curvilinear designs early in the sequence followed by an increased prevalence in lifeform symbolism. The rarity of rectilinear scrolls, occurring as frequently in rock art as they do on Preclassic decorated pottery, cautions against concluding that these petroglyphs were made only during the Classic period. The CA instead shows that they tend to be found on the same panels as quadrupeds, reptiles/amphibians, and other miscellaneous lifeforms (Figure 5.3), which on pottery are Colonial and early Sedentary period motifs.

In all, the series of relative dating techniques I employed support a general correspondence in the sequence of iconographic preferences between pottery and rock art, with the petroglyph chronicle ending around the late Sedentary turn to Style 3 in other media (Figure 3.4). It remains to be shown, however, whether the shared changes were synchronous; because the relative petroglyph chronology is only weakly calibrated to the Hohokam cultural trajectory, one could argue fairly that it borders on wishful thinking without further calibration. In the following and final analysis I use spatially associated ceramic artifacts to tether the petroglyph sequence to the broader archaeological record.

Associated Artifacts

When using temporally diagnostic artifacts to date spatially associated rock art, one assumes either that those artifacts had some relevance to the manufacture of the rock art or that the nearby activities evidenced by such artifacts were roughly contemporaneous with the practices surrounding the rock art's production. This assumption, which seems reasonable, in fact rests on a very questionable foundation. Since we are dealing with surface deposits, principles of stratigraphic association do not apply, and the presence of artifacts near rock art, while a spatial relationship, cannot be considered a priori to have a temporal basis. It is very possible that artifacts were deposited before or after the rock art's production, especially when such places were visited repeatedly over considerable spans of time. Indeed, more accessible or culturally important locations likely witnessed a range of activities unrelated, at least directly, to the rock art, and interpretations of contemporaneity drawn from nearby artifacts are thus more prone to fallacy. Independent evidence that a corpus of rock art accumulated through many years, centuries, or even millennia exacerbates the problem (Wallace and Holmlund 1986:71). I nonetheless contend that artifact associations serve as another heuristic that can be used in conjunction with the previous analyses to paint a coherent picture of temporal change in Hohokam rock art.

Reliance on associated artifacts as chronological indicators for nearby rock art is not uncommon, yet interpretations are often post hoc, qualitative, and supported by single-case scenarios. Rarely are data systematically generated and quantified in a manner to elucidate strong regional patterns of association. Christy Turner's (1963) pioneering work in Glen Canyon along the Colorado River is a notable exception. Turner drew on a number of contextual factors to distinguish five regional styles, then tallied the number of diagnostic surface sherds associated with each style. This enabled him to seriate the rock art styles and calibrate the sequence to the tree-ring-dated ceramic chronology.

The only example of a concerted effort to date Hohokam rock art by quantifying nearby artifacts is Wallace's seminal work in the Picacho Mountains (Wallace and Holmlund 1986). In that study Wallace leaned on artifacts "directly associated" with petroglyph sites to aid in developing a rock art chronology for the Picachos. Unfortunately, that survey turned up only twelve diagnostic ceramics and five projectile points associated with the petroglyphs (Wallace and Holmlund 1986:Table 5.1). Combined, those artifacts span approximately 8,000 years, and considering their limited frequency, they provide scant support for dating the thousands of nearby petroglyphs.

Wallace and Holmlund's study highlights several empirical hindrances to relying on artifacts to date nearby rock art. First, what warrants a direct association—specifically, how far is too far? Should artifacts falling within the boundaries of sites, à la Wallace's and Turner's approaches, be considered "associated," and what about those artifacts found 10, 50, or 1,000 m away from a petroglyph? This is a theoretical and methodological issue for which there is no correct answer. I aim to control for this by establishing a criterion of distance between artifact and petroglyph for them to be considered associated (see below). Second, landscapes that have witnessed thousands of years of continuous engagement and use by nearby communities are complicated geographical palimpsests whose archaeological residues are difficult to untangle when we are dealing solely with surface finds. Though there is no foolproof solution to this conundrum, a criterion of distance to define associations among artifacts, rock art, and other archaeological manifestations can again help us weave through the fray.

South Mountains Artifacts

The empirical problems I just described are less of an issue for the South Mountains, where by far the greater part of the archaeological cultural landscape, at least the dimensions evidenced materially through artifacts, is attributable to the Hohokam (see Chapter 4). While the ceramic data color a strong Preclassic tint to the South Mountains, finer-scale temporal resolution may be afforded by looking at more localized contexts. In the following, I focus on the artifacts found in close proximity to rock art panels.

As the CAs at the onset of this chapter reveal (Figures 5.2 and 5.3), chronologically relevant spatial patterns may not be clear at the site level but could be evident within sites. Such issues of scale require us to address spatial relationships freed from the notion of "sites." My goal is to determine whether certain petroglyph designs, within the larger site areas, are recurrently associated with particular types of ceramic wares, which could establish synchronicity between them. If rock art continued to be produced into the Classic period while other modes of engagement with the landscape subsided, I expect more diagnostic Classic period wares—principally Casa Grande Buffware, Redwares, and Salado Polychromes—to be found around panels relative to other settings. Moreover, different frequencies of diagnostic ceramics scattered around particular designs may betray associational redundancies—for example, consistent co-occurrences of zoomorphic designs with Colonial buffware or rectilinear designs with Sedentary or Classic wares—that further evidence tendencies in petroglyph design preference through time.

TABLE 5.3. Minimum Number of Vessels (MNV) Associated and Unassociated with Petroglyph Panels.

	Wares[a]			Forms			
	Plainware	Preclassic[b]	Classic[c]	Bowls	Jars	Indet.	Other
Near Panels	147	72	8	12	84	108	—
Away from Panels	482	265	40	57	344	419	1[d]
Total	629	337	48	69	428	527	1[d]

Note: Protohistoric vessels not included.

[a] Does not include indeterminate classifications.

[b] Includes Sacaton Redware and diagnostic Sedentary period plainwares.

[c] Includes two polychrome vessels, one Casa Grande Red-on-buff, and one Classic period plainware.

[d] Specimen is the rim of either a double jar form (e.g., Haury 1976:Figure 12.26.i') or anthropomorphic vessel (Haury 1976:Figure 11.10).

I established 10-m buffer zones around each petroglyph panel to explore for such within-site spatial relationships. This is a balanced approach, as the zones are large enough to encompass artifacts close to the rock art yet discrete enough to pick up on any potential differences in ceramic ware–petroglyph design associations across the site areas. In this way, artifacts may reside within the buffer of more than one rock art panel, so the associations are assessed as one-to-many relationships between the artifacts and the designs on the rock art panels.

Table 5.3 provides the MNVs for each ceramic ware associated with rock art panels and those found outside the buffers. As the total sample in Table 5.3 shows, there are approximately seven Preclassic pots for each Classic vessel in the South Mountains (337:48), a ratio mirrored in the sherd data (Table 4.3) and one supporting the prevailing Preclassic complexion of the archaeological landscape. This ratio is somewhat misleading, however, since the era represented by the Preclassic wares (circa AD 600–1125) is nearly twice as long as that of the Classic wares (circa AD 1125–1400). If we control for this disparity in durational representation by weighing the number of Classic vessels by a multiplier of two, the ratio of Preclassic to Classic pots is reduced to 3.5:1 but is nevertheless still skewed strongly toward Preclassic predominance.

If practices concerning rock art carried on while other means of engaging the South Mountains subsided, we should expect more Classic period artifacts (i.e., redware and polychrome vessels) to be found around petroglyphs than in other locales. Conversely, if rock art crafting and consumption came to a standstill while other practices persisted into the Classic, more Preclassic artifacts (i.e., buffwares) should be found around petroglyph panels. While Figure 5.16 shows that the proportions of different ware types around petroglyphs are quite similar to those in other contexts, there is a suggestive and perhaps meaningful difference. Based on the data in Table 5.3, the ratio of Preclassic to Classic pots around petroglyphs (9:1, or 4.4:1, when the Classic wares are weighted) is slightly higher than in other settings (6.6:1, or 3.3:1 when the Classic wares are weighted). Though the lack of a statistically significant difference in the types of wares around and away from petroglyphs suggests that practices relating to the crafting and consumption of rock art were roughly contemporaneous with the broader archaeological landscape (Figure 5.16), the slightly greater number of Preclassic pots relative to Classic ones around petroglyphs hints that petroglyph-related practices, as a whole, may lean toward an earlier stage of Hohokam engagement with the South Mountains. Regardless, the chronological picture is a clear one with a strong Preclassic tint to the practices undertaken throughout the SMRAP project areas irrespective of context and in spite of close proximity to several large Classic period platform-mound villages.

Though Preclassic ceramics abound near petroglyphs and overshadow the trace of Classic period wares, a closer look at the ceramic data may offer finer detail in pottery-petroglyph associations. For instance, certain pottery types,

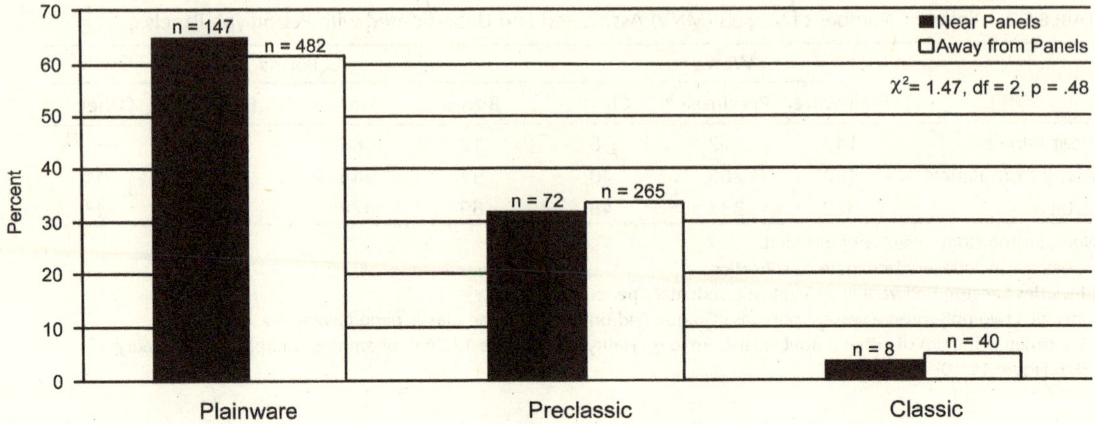

FIGURE 5.16. Comparison of ceramic wares found near and away from petroglyph panels.

such as Pioneer or Colonial red-on-buff, might cluster around particular petroglyph designs, thus permitting a closer age approximation for the associated petroglyphs within the larger Preclassic era. To investigate this, Table 5.4 enumerates the counts and percentages of ceramic types within 10 m of each petroglyph design class. Plainware is by far the dominant pottery type around petroglyphs, and there appears to be little to no tendency for Classic period pottery to cluster around any particular petroglyph design class.

A CA of the petroglyph design classes and diagnostic pottery presents these spatial associations in a reduced visual format, with the first two dimensions accounting for 40 percent of the variation in the dataset (Figure 5.17).[13] The strongest dimension, Factor 1, registers a notable split between Pioneer buffware and zig-zag petroglyphs with lesser influence on the other variables clustered in the plot's center. What is driving this profound difference in inertia between the two variables is unclear, but it is not based on any lack of association since the relative frequency of Pioneer sherds around zig-zag petroglyphs is similar to that of other petroglyph design classes (Table 5.4). These two variables also load strongly along the negative reach of Factor 2, which further differentiates these variables from the others in the plot's center. Like Factor 1, what is driving this separation is puzzling since Pioneer buffware is found around many of the other design classes in the center of the plot, albeit in low but comparable frequencies, and the relative frequencies of Colonial, Sedentary, and Indeterminate buffware around zig-zags are not much different than those around other design classes.

Whereas Pioneer buffware and zig-zag petroglyphs occupy the far corners of the lower two quadrants in the CA plot, less noticeable yet more intelligible and perhaps more relevant distinctions are discernible near the matrix's center (Figure 5.18). While tightly clustered, these variables are stretched vertically along Factor 2, a dimension with nearly as much explanatory strength as Factor 1. Examination of how all the ceramic and petroglyph design variables load along Factor 2 leads me to suggest that this dimension is capturing a temporal signature in the spatial correspondence among diagnostic ceramics and petroglyph designs. This is apparent in how the ceramics load along this axis: Pioneer buffware, the earliest pottery, loads in the bottom reaches; younger Colonial and Sedentary ceramics and Indeterminate buffwares (most of which are likely Colonial and Sedentary varieties) load positively and cluster in the upper-left quadrant; and Classic pottery falls at the upper end of the dimension. Factor 2 clearly organizes the pottery chronologically, from older (negatively loaded) to younger (positively loaded).

TABLE 5.4. Counts and Percentages of Ceramic Types near Petroglyph Design Classes.

		Preclassic					
Design Class	**Plainware**	**Pioneer Buffware**	**Colonial Buffware**	**Sedentary Pottery[a]**	**Indeterminate Buffware[b]**	**Classic[c]**	**Total**
Anthropomorphs	885	22	5	14	128	14	1,068
	82.9%	2.1%	0.5%	1.3%	12.0%	1.3%	
Birds	13	—	—	—	8	—	21
	61.9%				38.1%		
Circle Designs	1,061	8	4	3	165	29	1,270
	83.5%	0.6%	0.3%	0.2%	13.0%	2.3%	
Concentric Circles	197	10	2	—	41	1	251
	78.5%	4.0%	0.8%		16.3%	0.4%	
Crosses	162	—	—	—	24	—	186
	87.1%				12.9%		
Curv. Scrolls	379	1	—	2	44	10	436
	86.9%	0.2%		0.5%	10.1%	2.3%	
Linear Designs	217	4	—	7	78	—	306
	70.9%	1.3%		2.3%	25.5%		
Misc. Curvilinear	527	1	3	2	55	—	588
	89.6%	0.2%	0.5%	0.3%	9.4%		
Misc. Designs	2,208	11	12	18	138	6	2,393
	92.3%	0.5%	0.5%	0.8%	5.8%	0.3%	
Misc. Lifeforms	162	—	—	3	13	1	179
	90.5%			1.7%	7.3%	0.6%	
Misc. Representational	10	—	1	—	3	—	14
	71.4%		7.1%		21.4%		
Quadrupeds	465	4	8	19	73	16	585
	79.5%	0.7%	1.4%	3.2%	12.5%	2.7%	
Rectilinear Lines	40	—	—	—	3	—	43
	93.0%				7.0%		
Rectilinear Scrolls	8	3	2	—	5	—	18
	44.4%	16.7%	11.1%		27.8%		
Rectilinear Solids	67	1	—	1	23	—	92
	72.8%	1.1%		1.1%	25.0%		
Reptiles/Amphibians	305	—	—	10	45	2	362
	84.3%			2.8%	12.4%	0.6%	
Zig-Zags	254	5	2	1	16	—	278
	91.4%	1.8%	0.7%	0.4%	5.8%		
Total	6,960	70	39	80	862	79	8,090
	86.0%	0.9%	0.5%	1.0%	10.7%	1.0 %	

Note: Counts are minimum numbers of vessels (MNV), and they are linked to petroglyphs in a one-to-many relationship. Total counts are thus not the total number of MNV in the project area.

[a] Includes Sacaton Red-on-buff and Redware and diagnostic Sedentary period plainwares.

[b] May contain trace amounts of unidentifiable Casa Grande Red-on-buff.

[c] Includes Gila, Salt, and Wingfield Redwares; two polychrome vessels; one Casa Grande Red-on-buff; and one Classic period plainware.

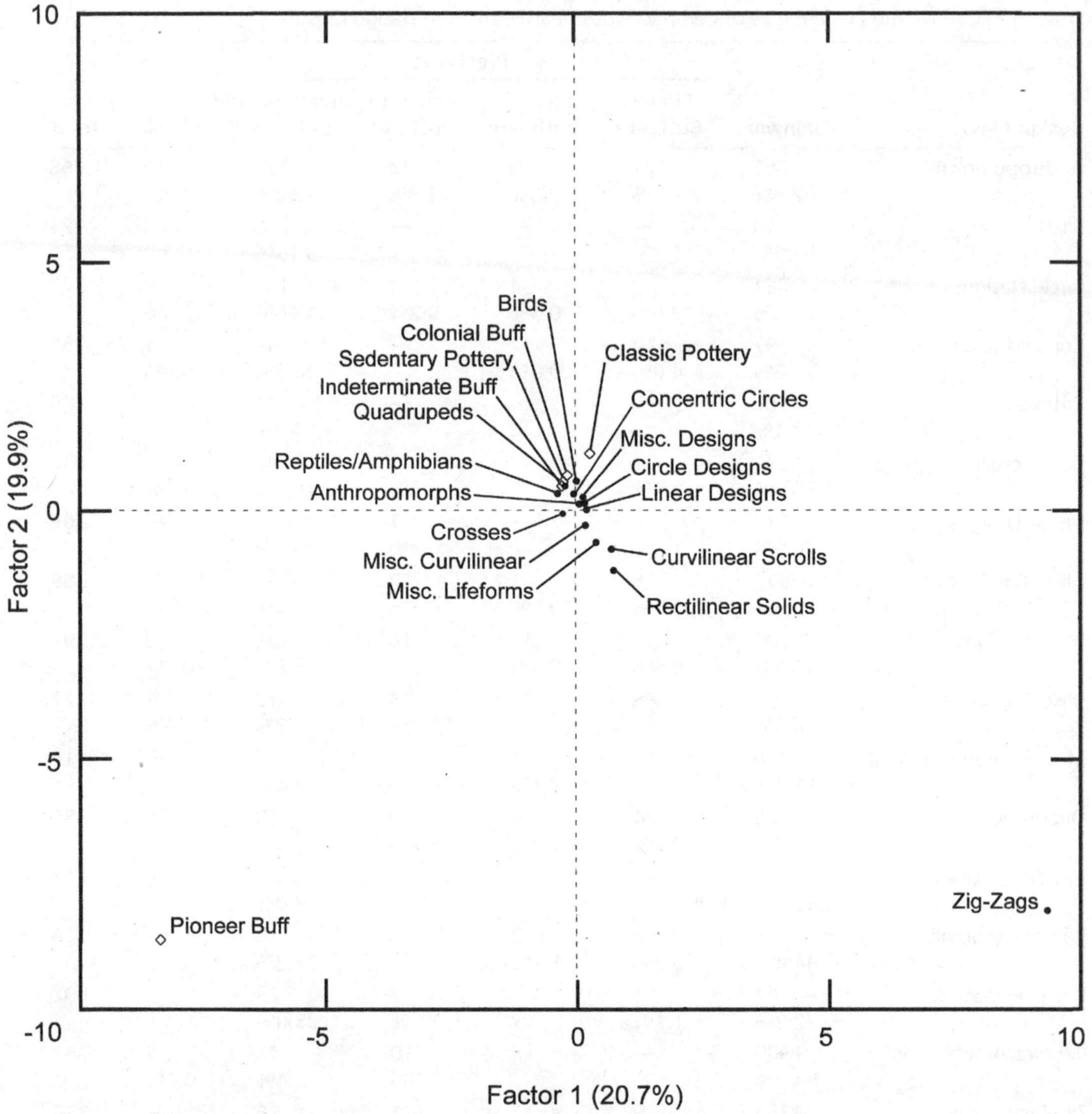

FIGURE 5.17. Correspondence analysis plot of petroglyph design classes and associated diagnostic pottery (individual cases not shown).

The chronological dispersion of pottery along Factor 2 in the CA serves as a sort of control and calibration for the potential chronological arrangement of petroglyph design classes. Along with Pioneer buffware, the cross, miscellaneous curvilinear, curvilinear scroll, rectilinear solid, zig-zag, and miscellaneous lifeform design classes load negatively. This suggests that the weight of the correspondence among these petroglyph designs with early ceramics is greater than that of the other design classes. The other design classes cluster around the center of the plot but nevertheless load positively on Factor 2, along with the younger Preclassic ceramics. Classic pottery is off by itself, seemingly isolated from the central cluster. Factor 2 appears to conveniently arrange the petroglyphs between early Preclassic (Pioneer) associations in the lower half and later Preclassic (Colonial and Sedentary) ones in the upper half. A number of petro-

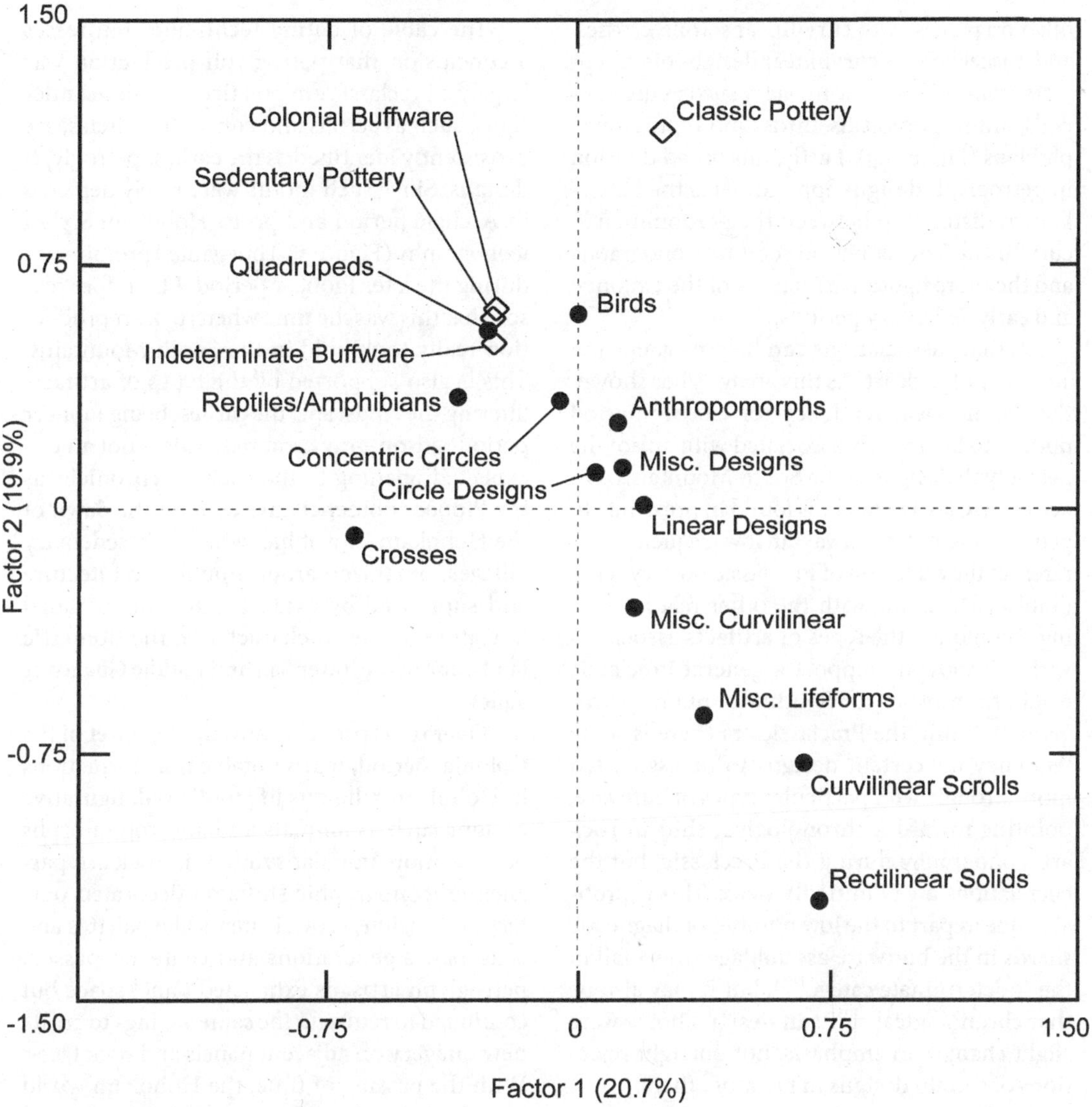

FIGURE 5.18. Magnified center of correspondence analysis plot of petroglyph design classes and associated diagnostic pottery (individual cases not shown).

glyph design classes have Classic pottery around them (Table 5.4), but as the CA plot shows, the associations are weak compared with other ware types.

In addition to how the pottery aligns along Factor 2, the chronological explanation for the general pattern of dispersion of petroglyph design classes along this dimension gains support through comparison with the other relative dating techniques. With the exception of miscellaneous lifeforms, the designs in the lower half of the CA plot are the same as those in the darker (older) spectrum of relative patination, as the patina rank (Figure 5.10) and petroglyph reflectance (Figure 5.12) analyses demonstrate. Likewise, the designs in the upper half of the CA plot compare favorably with those in the brighter (younger) spectrum of relative patination. This probable temporal division is also mirrored in how the design classes correspond with each other on panels, with curvilinear scrolls, crosses, and miscellaneous curvilinear designs often separate from zoomorphic imagery such as quadrupeds, anthropomorphs, birds, and reptiles/amphibians (Figure 5.3). Lastly, this broad division in petroglyph designs approximates the better-known distinction between the predominantly curvilinear Pioneer period ceramic iconography and the more figurative imagery of the Colonial and early Sedentary periods.

Artifact associations can help us gauge the antiquity of rock art. As this analysis has shown, there is no clear tendency for Classic period pottery to be strongly associated with any of the petroglyph designs in the South Mountains. On occasion, Classic pottery is found in proximity to petroglyphs, but it is always in low frequency and rarely at the exclusion of Preclassic pottery types (Table 5.4). In line with the other relative dating techniques, the types of artifacts associated with petroglyphs support a general Preclassic origin for most of the South Mountains petroglyphs. Within the Preclassic era there is some tendency for certain designs to be associated more strongly with particular types of buffware, pointing toward a chronological shift in rock art iconography during the Preclassic, but the correlations are admittedly weak. This is probably due in part to the low number of diagnostic sherds in the buffware assemblage (most fall in the Indeterminate category), but it may also be that chronological shifts in design choice were slight changes in emphasis, not outright rejections of certain designs in favor of others.

The Larger Temporal Picture

I have drawn on an amalgam of relative dating techniques to offer a fuller and more resolute ken of the antiquity of rock art in the South Mountains. Each technique is a weak and insufficient method when used alone, fraught with assumptions and limited temporal resolution. The insights afforded by each are, however, quite harmonious—indeed, they offer different angles on an underlying temporal trend—and when gleaned the results frame a synergistically robust chronicle of Hohokam rock art production in the South Mountains.

The cable of dating techniques buttresses a conclusion that petroglyph production was largely a Preclassic era practice. Curvilinear designs, such as scrolls and concentric circles, are consistently identified as the earliest petroglyph designs. Since such motifs were rarely depicted in Archaic period and proto-Hohokam Style 1 iconography (Figure 3.4) but gained prominence during the later Pioneer period, I therefore reason that this was the time when rock art production really took hold in the South Mountains. This is also supported by the types of artifacts littering the landscape, the earliest being Pioneer period red-on-gray ceramics. This is not an unexpected opening to the rock art chronicle, as the Pioneer nomenclature denotes the dawn of the Hohokam way of life, when fully sedentary villages, organized around public architecture and supported by extensive systems of canal irrigation, came to characterize the domestic landscape of the lower Salt and middle Gila River valleys.

Over time, probably around the onset of the Colonial period, when notable transformations in Hohokam religious life took hold, figurative designs such as animals and anthropomorphs became more popular symbols in rock art, paralleling iconographic shifts on decorated pottery and various esoteric items like palettes and censers. As generations and centuries passed, petroglyph artisans exhausted panel space but continued to return to the same settings to create new imagery on adjacent panels and rock faces. With the passing of time, the Hohokam world morphed along social, economic, and religious lines, yet petroglyph artisans were compelled to tie the new imagery, and perhaps new practices attendant to the rock art, to the old. In this way, the artisans and their rock art referenced the past through both place and placement among older, more abstract imagery.

The rock art chronicle ends with a predominance of lifeforms and rectilinear designs and a concomitant decline in curvilinear designs such as concentric circles and curvilinear scrolls. Rectilinear designs are commonly associated with Classic period iconography, which could easily and understandably lead one to construe that rock art production persisted throughout the Hohokam millennium. Rectilinear scrolls in rock art are nonetheless fairly uncommon (Table 4.1), and their frequency in the South Mountains, less than 1 percent of the petroglyph assemblage, approximates their frequency on Preclassic decorated pottery (Wallace 2001:Table 10.13). Likewise, unequivocal evidence that any of the rectilinear petroglyphs in the South Mountains are Classic period creations is lacking—redware does not cluster around them, they often occur on the same panels as more typical Preclassic designs such as lifeforms, and when they do they tend to express similar degrees of patination as the other petroglyphs. It seems that instead of Classic period petroglyphs, the few rectilinear scrolls more likely date to the Sedentary, a time when complex rectilinear designs came to dominate the ceramic design iconography but before the Hohokam all but jettisoned lively figurative motifs from their visual arts repertoire.

None of the dating techniques applied in this book can identify the antiquity of rock art bereft of allusions to and comparisons with other phenomena. This is an inherent limitation of relative dating techniques and a persistent challenge for this mode of material culture. Such methods can, however, help us discern broad patterns of chronological relevance. The results of each analysis, when interlaced, frame a portrait in which rock art production was primarily a Preclassic practice. A cessation in petroglyph making amid the sea of coeval social changes, all of which we summarily characterize as the onset of the Classic period, is corroborated by the kinds of ceramics sprinkled across the larger landscape and next to rock art panels. Sedentary period buffware dominates the datable decorated pottery assemblage (Table 4.4), whereas very few Classic period buffwares, redwares, or polychromes are found around petroglyphs, and only sparingly so throughout the mountains (Table 5.3). The chronological picture is also one in which shifts in rock art iconography were seemingly gradual and ever so slight. There were apparent trends in design frequency, or tendencies in preference, but not outright transmutations in the repertoire. This compares favorably with what we know of Preclassic iconography on ceramics, but as I bring to light in the following chapter, there was fundamental and meaningful iconographic dissidence between these two visual arts.

Given the limitations of dating individual specimens of rock art through relative techniques, some of the South Mountains petroglyphs may have been crafted during the Classic period, but the Preclassic emphasis is readily apparent. This was an important and heretofore unrecognized turn in social practice—indeed, it was an apostasy of tradition in how the Hohokam engaged the South Mountains landscape and coincided with major transformations in Hohokam society, particularly how religious knowledge and ritual space were accessed and controlled. As I show in the following chapters, Hohokam rock art production constituted ritual practices that mediated the communication of religious knowledge among people and between themselves and other-than-human agents. As both symbol and practice, it was a ligature in the relationship between the Hohokam and their cosmos. Ultimately, the control of this knowledge became the purview of a select few individuals and social groups, who interceded and took dominion over this more-than-material affinity that Hohokam communities had once nurtured and maintained with their sacred geography and the (super)natural world.

CHAPTER 6

Ritualization of Hohokam Rock Art

Religious practices... exist outside the human mind, in the relations between objects, elements, substances, bodies, buildings, and places. They can be experienced, cited by others, and reinterpreted. They are open to ambiguity, accommodation, contestation, and change. (Pauketat 2012:224)

My aim for this chapter is to peer through the cultural lattice the Hohokam plaited, strand over strand, across the South Mountains. Rock art is the tie that binds this larger, reflexive fabric of landscape experience and engagement, and it cannot be understood in isolation of the other threads, thrums, and knots to which it is woven. Other seemingly disparate activities, such as farming, harvesting plants and minerals, movement, and worship (see Chapter 4), simultaneously referenced and inspired the manufacture and (re)interpretation of rock art through copresence. The rock art was thus multivalent, having a place and purpose in a multitude of settings and contexts. We all too often miss such interconnectedness by approaching rock art as a unique class of "artifact." We do this when we relegate it to its own scholarly journals and circles, subject it to focus groups, and style it as an area of specialization and expertise.

Rock art is too enmeshed with the natural and cultural landscape to be divorced from the broader social world, and it is so multifarious that it defies any monolithic explanation or interpretation (e.g., McCall 2007, 2010; Whitley 1987). Rock art reaches far beyond the static logic of artifacts and symbols; it simultaneously materializes past action and intention while provoking future (re)action and (re)invention. In the following I am concerned largely with this active aspect, in particular how the South Mountains petroglyphs were instrumental in all-too-often overlooked ritual practices performed outside the Hohokam village. The ritualized nature of rock art, however, is not self-evident, so I rely on models espoused by two ritual theorists, Catherine Bell (1997) and Roy Rappaport (1999), to draw out the ritualized features evident in the structure and contexts of Hohokam petroglyphs.

Models of the ritual form enumerate the features shared by all ritual practices (see Chapter 2) and as such provide a means for assessing the degree to which Hohokam petroglyph production was ritualized. The elements fundamental to all ritual structure and performance acknowledged by different ritual theorists are quite similar (e.g., Figure 2.1), and from this broad agreement we can devise guidelines and systematic approaches for investigating ritual, in both the present and the past. The ritual model's utility extends beyond the basic identification of ritual practice; each element or feature yields a unique view of the ritual form, all of which contribute to a richer and fuller picture of the dialectic between ritual practice and structure.

My advocacy for a checklist-like method for investigating the ritual nature of rock art is neither novel nor unprecedented. David Lewis-Williams (1994, 1995) and June Ross and Iain Davidson (2006), for example, have isolated qualities of ancestral San and Australian Aborigine rock art, respectively, that they argue are consistent with ritual activity. Whereas Lewis-Williams developed a compelling argument founded almost entirely on ethnographic parallels, Ross and Davidson, who drew explicitly from Rappaport's ritual model, focused entirely on the spatial and stylistic structures of the rock art. Finding inspiration in these previous case studies, in the following I hybridize Rappaport's and Bell's models into a cohesive framework of ritual practice applicable not only to rock art but to archaeology in general. Rappaport's model is structure-centric, in that it concerns ritual's universal form and structure, or the "relations among the *perceptible* [as opposed to symbolic] features by which ritual is recognize as such" (Rappaport 1999:31; emphasis in original). Bell's model, on the other hand, is agency-centric, encapsulating the process of ritualization, or the strategy by which people differentiate modes of action, establish themselves in relation to the "sacred" and "profane," and define their identities in comparison to other agents involved in or observant of ritual performances. A blending of these models offers a balanced framework to address the socially constituted and religiously ordained forms of ritual practice, at the same time populating these structures with agents who are potentially knowledgeable, conscious, and aware of their actions and the social conditions within which they act.

I start with a review of the "five features of the ritual form" as outlined by Rappaport (1999). It is not that each feature is unique to ritual practice per se; rather, rituals are a unique mode of action because they exhibit all of them simultaneously. I then integrate Bell's (1997) "six characteristics of ritual-like activities" within this overarching structure (Figure 2.1). This model is designed not only to reveal patterns in artifact form, use, and deposition, a common means of circumstantiating ritual practices in archaeology (e.g., Marcus 2007), but also to bring out some of the textual qualities and embodied virtues of those rituals.

Five Features of the Ritual Form

Rappaport's (1999) contention that the uniqueness of ritual is afforded by the presence of five features—performance, encoded tradition, formalism, invariance, and occult efficacy—is slightly different from Bell's (1997) formula. Bell attends to a less finite and rigid structure for ritual activities, seeing the presence and absence of these features within a spectrum of action as relevant to understanding the degree of a ritual-like activity's social importance (Bell 1997:138–139). In turn, the identification of these five features, coupled with spatial and historical nuances in how people express them, yields an amalgamated, holistic perspective on the "structure" and "agency" at work in ritual practice.

Performance

Following Rappaport, "it may seem unnecessary if not downright absurd to emphasize what seems not only to be an obvious aspect of ritual, but intrinsic to its very conception" (1999:37). As inherent as performance may be to a definition or conception of ritual, it is an essential feature that differentiates action from "myth," "belief," and "religion." Ritual and myth may encode similar messages, and in many cases the former is dictated, justified, and ordained by the latter, yet ritual performance contains information not entirely encoded in myth and thus serves as a unique medium through which such information is communicated. "*The ritual form, to say the least, adds something to the substance of ritual, something that the symbolically encoded substance by itself cannot express*" (Rappaport 1999:31; emphasis in original). Indeed, ritual is one face within an "ideology of communication" and thus need not convey messages in the same way as other linguistic modes (Robbins 2001). Ritual's uniqueness, and perhaps effectiveness, is provided by the "special relationship between the liturgical order performed and the act of performing it" (Rappaport 1999:38). The elicitation of bodily experience through the performance of rituals is the "structural apprenticeship which leads to the em-bodying of the structures of the world" (Bourdieu 1977:89), or perhaps from Bell's (Bell 1992:98–101) perspective, the creation of a "ritualized body environment" (see also Bell 1990).

Ritual, as a mode of symbolic communication, is often likened to theatre or drama, in which performers broadcast social information to and elicit emotional responses from an audience. Much archaeological research has therefore focused, understandably so, on the tangibly overt and grandiose components of ritual practice, such as flashy vestments and public architecture, which undoubtedly had a ritualized orientation. Not all rituals involve groups of performers or necessitate a human audience (vision quests come to mind). This may seem to contradict communication's importance to ritual performance, yet solitary rituals operate to auto- or allo-communicate information to the self (e.g., Laughlin 1990; McCauley and Lawson 2007), and in the case of religious ritual an other-than-human—what we sometimes refer to as godly, supernatural, metaphysical, spiritual, and the like—audience is often witness to the performance (Rappaport 1999:51). We should therefore expect variable audience sizes across the spectrum of ritual practices, from a lone performer crouched in a small crevice on the side of a mountain to elaborate communal performances on elevated platforms where flamboyant and grandiose dress, oration, gestures, and caricatures play to the attention of large groups of onlookers and participants.

Rock art, as a visual remnant of actions, alone is proof of performance. In archaeology, a concern for performance seems redundant because we study the material residues of actions—objects, places, or the relations among them. The performance feature of the ritual form stipulates that since we are dealing with the self-evident, we should concentrate on the details and qualities of the performance. These aspects may betray the "framing" of ritual action, the intentional distinction of the ritual performance as something unique (Bell 1997:160). The strategy of framing involves designating specific activities, times, people, places, and objects for the ritual, which shifts our attention to the "who," "what," "when," and "where" of the ritual's performance.

Encoded Tradition

Tradition lies at the heart of ritual. Encoded tradition of the ritual form implies that some of the performances and utterances that constitute ritual practices were established by persons (though not necessarily humans) other than the performers. This characteristic of ritual is paradoxical because rituals change, and are invented, and in such instances they seem to defy tradition. Effective ritual change, or the ritualization of new or existing practices, however, involves rearranging, refashioning, and tinkering with existing elements of the ritual form (Bell 1997: 149–150; Kertzer 1988; Myerhoff 1977; Rappaport 1999:32). One's capacity, or agency, to "traditionalize" (Bell 1997) practices determines whether new or modified rituals are adopted by performers and accepted as legitimate ways of doing by the attendant audiences. The sanctification of ritual change often necessitates ascription of the new form by other-than-human agents or through cosmic transcendence (Rappaport 1999: 33; see also Wallace 1966).

Tradition entails allusions to a past state of being or events, hence the perpetual invocation of ancestors, the wielding of heirlooms and antiquities, the donning of outmoded garb, utterances in archaic speech, and similar sorts of legacies conjured and reconfigured during both established and newly developed rituals. The legitimacy of religious rituals, and the social relationships they instill, nurture, and reinforce, hinges on the "consciousness of sacred history" (Hause 1992), or the degree to which other-than-human agents and essences are invoked. Allusions to history are "appeal[s] to the authority of the past that subordinates the present" (Bell 1997:150). This ethos of historicity, then, is the basis for the sometimes passive and unquestioned acceptance of a rite's structure; the relations of power coalesced, showcased, and rejuvenated through performance; and the perpetuation of the status quo—the "we do it this way because that is the way it has always been done." Tradition naturalizes the ritualized activity, and in turn, ritual practices naturalize themselves as "appropriate *responses* to that environment" (Bell 1997:168; emphasis in original). In a sense, encoded tradition can be understood as "history turned into nature," or the *habitus* of ritual (Bourdieu 1977:78).

Formalism

Ritual practice is a consciously structured way of acting, and the maintenance of and adherence to established ritual forms are fundamental to our conception of ritual and underscore its perceived metaphysical efficacy. Formality pertains to a structured and "restricted code" of communication (Douglas 1973:44) as opposed to spontaneity and whimsical action. Indeed, rituals are governed by the socially accepted rules of their performance (Bell 1997:153–155). These rules "define the outer limits of what is acceptable, or they may orchestrate every step. In either case, they hold individuals to communally approved patterns of behavior, they testify to the legitimacy and power of that form of communal authority, and perhaps they also encourage human interactions by constraining the possible outcomes" (Bell 1997:155).

Formalism draws attention not to ritual's content or function but to the "form" in its performance. Formality conscribes rituals to places, times, persons, and situations. The concept subsumes "decorousness, punctiliousness, conformity to form, repetitiveness, regularity, and stylization" (Rappaport 1999:46). As archaeologists, we cannot observe firsthand the actual enactment of ritual actions, but we are adept at ascertaining some formal qualities of past doings and happenings. Patterns in spatial arrangement, association, and periodicity can attest to a practice's formality. Ritual practice, however, does not always necessitate strict adherence to form. There is a continuum between highly choreographed performance and spontaneous conduct within a spectrum of action we could consider ritualized (Bell 1997:139; Rappaport 1999:34–35). We should thus acknowledge, indeed expect, variable degrees of formalism in ritual practices in order to engender past performers with ritual competence and choice for compliance to the ritual form.

Invariance

Rappaport considers invariance, or the adherence to formality, an essential balance to formalism. Invariance implies an explicit intent, perhaps even struggle, for formality while acknowledging the occasions and circumstances when the elements of a ritual cannot or should not be maintained. There are instances when innovation will be required for the successful completion of the ritual act, or when rituals may encourage a degree of variation as part of their form. Invariance also accommodates changes in the contexts, characters, and accoutrements of performance, which inevitably must adapt to new circumstances through time.

Invariance in ritual practice, however, is not the passive routinization of action; it demands the "precise repetition and physical control" of action (Bell 1997:150). Invariance is the *conscious* and *disciplined* attempt to adhere to structure and scripture. I emphasize the consciousness and discipline of invariance to highlight the performers' awareness of their and others' motivations and actions during ritual performances. Invariance and formalism are why ritual practices are sometimes, perhaps more often than not, intentionally economically inefficient, thus out of place in and defiant of functionalist, rationalist, and evolutionary paradigms. Indeed, a "wastely" way of acting can be fundamental to a ritual's performance and its efficacy; such costly and irrational choices and actions are often responsible for the tangible traces—the esoteric objects, lavishly adorned artwork and vestments, and monuments and public edifices—through which archaeologists traditionally "find" ritual in the past (see Chapter 2).

Occult Efficacy

I am concerned with religious ritual as a meaningful and transformative form of social practice, and accordingly I invoke ritual's connection to religion as definitive of its existence. This is clearly a point of contention since ritual practices subsume a range of ritual-like actions that do not necessarily express allusions to the metaphysical and immaterial (e.g., Rappaport 1999:38–46). As touched on in Chapter 2, definitions of ritual are a matter of debate, one centering largely on the relation between religion and ritual, or the necessity of the former to substantiate the latter, and vice versa. Most scholars nonetheless contend that what we commonly acknowledge as ritual draws some of its essence, perhaps implicitly, from a religious orientation. This is because our notion of ritual, as a European, post-Enlightenment analytical construct, arose from the nineteenth-century social evolutionary debates on the origin of religion (Bell 1997:3). I focus on religious ritual, as a specific realm of ritual practice, because my questions and arguments concern the materialization of religious knowledge through action.

Religion is a term I use to encompass the many concepts that have come to bear on the metaphysical structure and explanation of material existence, such as cosmology, ideology, holy, sacred, myth, numinous, supernatural, and occult. Acts of religion, such as rituals and prayers, are accepted as effective even when they do not render an observable, tangible, or measurable outcome. This effect, or rather lack thereof, is essential to our consideration of what religious ritual is: "irrational" action concerned with the evocation of feeling, sense of being, and layers of identity in relation to place, others, and the religious structures and traditions in which actors maneuver. Occult efficacy, then, refers to the fact that ritual lacks an *immediate* material response. This is because performers see ritual acts as metaphysically efficacious, in that ritual performance causes an outcome that is abstracted or unattached to the physical state of its performance. "If ritual (in contrast to technique) does anything at all it doesn't do it by operating with matter and energy on matter and energy in accordance with physical laws of cause and effect, but by focusing agencies or forces of another sort upon whatever is to be affected" (Rappaport 1999:48). To performers, religious rituals are efficacious because they draw on a mystical means (i.e., magic, prayer, vision quests) to cause an effect. To analysts, religious rituals are efficacious because, for example, they help regulate the cultural system (e.g., Durkheim 1961; Rappaport 1971), ease the psychological state of performers (e.g., Freud 1913), and facilitate the "psychic discharge of guilt" (Merkur 1991).

Entreaties for occult efficacy are physically and therefore archaeologically evanescent for the simple reason that they have no material effect, and thus their "presence or absence [is] not always obvious" (Rappaport 1999:471n10). The archaeologist's "junk-bin drawer" of ritual items, those colorful yet costly and functionless items, can help us in this regard. They do not necessarily pinpoint what the occult is but instead shed light on the actions aimed to elicit occult efficacy. To this pool we can add symbols—the effigies, drawings, paintings, sculpture, and so on—that in all likelihood bear resemblance to religious personae and entities, metaphorize religious themes and undercurrents, or express collective experiences and goals that entertain the metaphysical. Bell (1997:155–159) sees sacral symbolism as a feature of ritualized practice, so in her paradigm rituals necessitate symbols. While this is somewhat circular (since rituals are themselves symbols), sacral symbols, or objects and images that evoke and express "values and attitudes associated with larger, more abstract, and relatively transcendent ideas" (Bell 1997:157), are common elements of ritual performance and can therefore evidence and inform on ritual practice.

Aspects of Ritual Action

Religious ritual practice is a structured manner in which people assume roles, perform acts, encode messages, and embody religion. As reviewed in Chapter 2, rituals, as structured patterns of "more or less invariant sequences of formal acts" (Rappaport 1999:24), should leave material traces, and thus some past ritual performances, as repetitive ways of acting, can be studied indirectly long after their enactment. We need not know a ritual's symbolic content, or its immaterial essence, to recognize it because rituals are identifiable by their perceptible features (Rappaport 1999:30–31). Accordingly, to effectively demonstrate the ritualized nature of past actions, we need to situate those practices in the ritual form.

At a recent symposium on the archaeology of ritual, the organizer noted that the repetitive, patterned quality of ritual performance lends it an "advantage" of recognition over other modes of practice because it has a "more physical and traceable effect" (Kyriakidis 2007:9). Archaeologies of ritual nonetheless entail more than identifying repetition in artifact use and deposition, for the obvious fact that not all repetitive patterns in practice ascribe to the ritual form. Pattern, in and of itself, is demonstrative only of repetition of action. Many daily practices

TABLE 6.1. Material Indicia for Rock Art as Religious Ritual Practice.

Aspect of Action	Associated Features of Ritual Form	Material Indicia of Ritual Form
Redundancy	• Formalism • Encoded Tradition • Invariance	• Spatial clusters • Limited design repertoire • Conformity in production technique • Specialized times • Symbols
Repetition	• Formalism • Encoded Tradition • Invariance	• Spatial density • Limited design repertoire • Specialized times • Symbols
Framing	• Performance • Encoded Tradition • Formalism	• Specialized places • Specialized times • Landscape modifications • Symbols
Symbolic Communication	• Performance • Formalism • Occult Efficacy	• Symbols • Accessibility for an audience
Functional Defiance	• Formalism • Encoded Tradition • Occult Efficacy	• Association with other ritualized activities • Offerings and esoterica
Allusion to Other-than-Human Agents and Essences	• Encoded Tradition • Occult Efficacy	• Symbols • Topographic locations • Offerings and esoterica • Association with other ritualized activities

are cyclical or repetitive (e.g., eating, sleeping), generate redundant and sometimes prominent compositions in artifact deposition (e.g., trash mounds), or derive from behavioral consistencies (e.g., trails), but we would be hard-pressed to argue convincingly that these are the residues of ritual practice. They are rather relics of a structured, customary, and routinized way of thinking, moving, and acting, what we might better think of as habitual "living."

An archaeology of ritual demands greater rigor than simply identifying patterns. It necessitates a coherent model that captures the essence of what we consider ritual practice to be. This is the value of the five features of the ritual form. Not only do they guide the kinds of middle-range questions to ask, they also establish a framework for distinguishing ritual from other patterned practices. Some features of the ritual form are nonetheless more nebulous and harder to discern than others, and incarnations of each feature are not identical across stages and situations. Moreover, we cannot observe ritual actions, only their materiality through objects and images and their long-term ramifications for space and place. We must therefore take a bottom-up approach and identify the ritual form indirectly by virtue of the actions that affected the objects, images, and places left for us to study.

Table 6.1 presents six aspects of action—redundancy, repetition, framing, symbolic communication, functional defiance, and allusion to other-than-human agents and essences—that evidence the five features of the religious ritual form. These qualities of action and performance encourage us to think about how ritual practices may leave perceptible traces of their form. I argue that past practices were ritualized when relics and the contexts of their creation, use, and disposal evidence each aspect of action that is consistent with the five features of the ritual form. Although I focus on rock art, this working taxonomy is robust and versatile enough to accommodate a wide array of archaeological subject matter and is useful for exploring a variable range of past ritual forms.

The Ritual Forms of South Mountains Petroglyphs

If rock art evidences ritual practice, six aspects of ritual action should be witnessed by the structure of the rock art assemblage and the contexts of its production and use. Rock art's ritualized qualities can be gleaned through a variety of material indicia, as enumerated in Table 6.1. In the remainder of this chapter I rely on these indicia to explore how the South Mountains petroglyphs evidence aspects of ritual action, and thus the ritual form. To do so, I expand on the initial observations of the rock art assemblage offered in Chapter 4, draw on contexts afforded by the larger archaeological landscape, and organize the investigation around the following six themes: space, stage, audience, time, performance, and symbolism.

Space

Rituals "take place" (sensu Smith 1987), in that they often necessitate specific locations and settings for their enactment (Rappaport 1999:209–215). How rituals are organized across space can evidence the formalism, invariance, encoded tradition, and in some instances occult efficacy of the ritual form (Table 6.1). Rituals order space and instill how places are used, perceived, and experienced within society. As Rappaport notes, "consideration of the liturgical ordering of mundane space lead[s] to consideration of the liturgical ordering of the social dynamics of that space" (1999:214). Liturgical ordering, in this sense, involves the rituals and sequences of rituals (Rappaport 1999:169), or the cycle of the ritual system. Ritualized places are essentially symbols because "the distinctive landscape, interiors, or the events that transpired there serve to imbue the site with a significance that can evoke emotional associations for those who visit there" (Bell 1997:157). The site of practice is thus inherent to the ritual's form, and it is demonstrative of how communities organized themselves in relation to religiously inspired places and landscapes. Spatial qualities also reveal how and the extent to which access to religiously important places was controlled.

If Hohokam rock art production constitutes what we consider ritual practice, or if the imagery was implicated in associated ritual performances, it may be witnessed in how petroglyphs are arranged across the landscape. Spatial clusters of rock art at a multiplicity of scales (e.g., Troncoso Melendez 2008), the density of petroglyphs in those clusters, and consistencies of association with characteristics of the natural and cultural environments evidence aspects of redundancy, repetition, framing, and allusions to other-than-human agents and essences inherent to religious ritual action.

Others have already shown that the Hohokam tended to place petroglyphs on the landforms closest to rivers (Hamann 1988; Hamann and Hedges 1986); indeed, as distance from rivers increases, the density of petroglyphs decreases (Nelson 1998). This should come as no surprise since the river floodplains hosted most Hohokam villages and were the lifeline of their extensive agricultural systems. As one moves outward from the rivers, they become increasingly distant from the domestic landscape, and we should therefore anticipate a general fall-off in extra-village activities, including rock art production, as a result.

The South Mountains, at just over 5 km south of the Salt River, are one of the principal landscape features of the Phoenix Basin and are literally in the backyard of several large Hohokam villages (Figure 3.2). This central position within the most densely inhabited region of the Ancient Southwest, coupled with the fact that the mountains' lithology, with a contrasting dark patina over a lighter host rock, is an ideal canvas for petroglyphs, is undoubtedly why the South Mountains house one of the densest agglomerations of Hohokam petroglyphs.[1] In this regard, the South Mountains petroglyphs make up one giant cluster of rock art. However, the petroglyphs are unevenly distributed across the landscape, clustering along the northeastern and eastern portions of the range (Snyder 1966:Figure 1; Wright 2011:Figure 19), those regions closest to the villages. The three project areas in this study provide a third and finer scale of spatial resolution, where we can address how the Hohokam strategically situated petroglyphs in those mountainous settings just beyond their villages' edges.

As Figures 4.4 and 4.5 show, rock art clusters, measured by both the clumping of panels and the density of petroglyphs, are most pronounced along the lower slopes of the mountains, adjacent to and just upslope of the bajada, and the degree of clumping and density tends to lessen in concordance with increased elevation. This is easily explainable by the mere fact that these lower-elevation settings are closest to the villages and required less effort to reach than places set deeper within the rugged and craggy mountains. But there is more to it than ease of access. Petroglyph density varies within this bajada setting, being highly concentrated in certain areas and more diffusely scattered and patchy between these petroglyph nodes, or hotspots. Further, the Hohokam created some extremely dense petroglyph clusters within the mountains' inner reaches, so proximity to village or field cannot fully account for locational choices in petroglyph manufacture. While the dense petroglyph clusters immediately catch our attention, the trickle of petroglyphs between them and in the high stretches of the mountains should not be overlooked. Although they lack density in terms of petroglyph counts, many of these lightly scattered panels constitute linear clusters contouring trails and canyon floors, which were natural corridors that guided and aided movement into and through the mountains.

Within the canvas of rock art draped over the South Mountains, and within each project area, a careful eye can discern four general tiers of petroglyph density and clustering (see Figures 4.4–4.6). The most substantial clusters appear as highly dense nodes in the blanket of petroglyphs covering the landscape and are found in fairly discrete locations, most of which are centered on rainfall-dependent, artesian springs. Moderately dense points along the ridgelines, at the mouths of certain canyons, and sometimes along the canyon floors near springs present a less substantial, second tier of petroglyph density. A third tier consists of a diffuse but fairly continuous spread of petroglyphs across the bajada, best expressed in the eastern portion of the central project area (Figure 4.5). A fourth tier, the most diffuse and least dense, is made up of those panels situated along various routes of movement, the trails that parallel ridgetops, contour slopes, and skirt canyon floors.

These four tiers evidence different scales of repetition, redundancy, and framing in practices involving rock art manufacture and viewing. In fact, they demonstrate variability in the "ritual depth" of certain places (Díaz-Andreu 2001, 2003), or the degree of religious importance ascribed to sections and features of the landscape. This aspect concerns the allusion to other-than-human agents and essences that are instrumental in religious ritual practices, a critical detail I expound on in Chapter 7. The redundancy and repetition of petroglyphs in specific places and their repeated associations with certain landscape settings evidence the invariance, encoded tradition, formalism, and performance features of the ritual form. Variations in petroglyph density and panel clustering potentially correspond to different ritual forms, implying that rock art was manufactured and manipulated during multiple types of and times for ritual practice. In the following I expand on these four tiers to address the second theme in rock art ritualism: stage.

Stage

Rituals may seem overly emotive, histrionic, and rigidly scripted, so much so that it is easy to liken them to theatre and drama (e.g., Turner 1974, 1982; see also Inomata and Coben 2006). Some rituals are indeed quite theatrical, perhaps even melodramatic, but ritual, theatre, and drama are not the same social acts. Moreover, theatre and drama, and even some sporting events, undoubtedly share qualities with ritual (Bell 1997:160–161; Rappaport 1999:38–39), yet ritual provides more than entertainment or instruction—it offers metaphysical efficacy. This is captured well by Rappaport: "The ritual act, this is to say, 'does something,' it is an action that is meant to affect the world and it is likely to do so. To act in a drama, in contrast, is not to take an action affecting the world, but only to imitate doing so" (1999:136). I nevertheless invoke "stage" as an essential component of ritual practice and evidence of the ritual form. A stage, though, does not necessarily imply a formal structure for hosting performances but simply denotes a socially recognized place for ritual practice.

Stages evidence several aspects of ritual action—framing, repetition, redundancy, and communication—and attention to nuance and detail can help us narrow down the identities of performers and audiences. The stage concept also reiterates the vital connection between performance and place but emphasizes the particular qualities of the setting that are integral to the performance. Again, to approach this in rock art, we may look for spatial clusters and density, the shapes of such clusters, and the associated topographic, environmental, and cultural contexts. In the following I outline seven settings, or stage types, in which the Hohokam engaged in crafting and viewing rock art, which foregrounds a consideration of the audiences that bore witness to the creation, manipulation, and interpretation of the petroglyphs.

As pointed out above, there are four broad tiers in clustering and density of rock art in the South Mountains that evidence the redundancy, repetition, and encoded tradition of the ritual form. The densest petroglyph clusters recur in two unique topographic settings, around springs and on elevated spaces, with the latter usually located on ridgetops towering over springs in the canyon floors. In fact, nearly 18, 50, and 60 percent of the petroglyphs are situated respectively within 10, 50, and 100 m of a spring, meaning that more than half the petroglyphs are hung on rocks near, and arguably in association with, springs (see Figures 4.4–4.6). These springs are found where the contact between brecciated and unbrecciated granodiorite is exposed at the mouths of the canyons, on the canyon floors, and rarely along ridgelines and slopes (see Wright 2011:116–127). Concentrations of Hohokam rock art around springs occur in other mountain ranges as well. For example, a large, well-known petroglyph cluster in Hieroglyphic Canyon in the Superstition Mountains, along the eastern rim of the Phoenix Basin, was also centered on a sizable spring (Weaver 1985). Weaver and Rosenburg (1978) reported on similar phenomena in the Sierra Estrella, just west of the South Mountains and across the Gila River, where petroglyphs cluster along the ridgetops near canyon mouths and around spring-like water tanks. Such consistencies in topographic association evidence a broad and recurrent relationship between springs and petroglyphs in the Phoenix Basin, one that was probably shared throughout the Hohokam world.

These earlier studies explained the petroglyph-spring affinity in economic terms because water is a vital resource for desert dwellers, especially when traveling or on extended forays away from the canal-irrigated villages. In such a materialist framework, rock art production was either passively and leisurely undertaken at watering holes during more "functional" pursuits, or, potentially, it served to signal ownership or authority over such valuable locales. While this may be true, the relationship among springs, hilltops, and rock art is also emblematic of the religious importance and ritualized connotation of these landscape features (e.g., Russell et al. 2009). In fact, since they are entirely rainfall dependent, the springs in the South Mountains were probably of limited economic use to the Hohokam.[2] Several lines of evidence actually argue against a strictly utilitarian and economic importance for the South Mountains springs. For one, since they are fed by precipitation, the springs flow for only a few days (at most) after rains, and the volume of their flow can be very limited—often a trickle at best and simply a dampness at worst.[3] The villages home to most of the people who roved and toiled in the South Mountains were rather close, within an hour's walk, and villagers could have brought water with them (hence the preponderance of jars in the ceramic assemblage; Table 4.3), returned home, or gathered water from an even closer canal branch.

If high rock art density and clustering around springs is due simply to more frequent visits for water while other activities were carried out, one would expect artifacts, especially broken water jars, to cluster in these locations as

TABLE 6.2. Counts of Petroglyphs and Artifacts Near and Away from Springs.

	Petroglyphs	Ceramics	Lithics
Near Springs	1,545	154	105
Away from Springs	1,510	871	563
Total	3,055	1,025	668

Note: An arbitrary 50-m buffer around springs was used to distinguish groups.

well. Such a scenario, however, is not found in the South Mountains. The data actually reveal a converse relationship: the number of artifacts around petroglyph-adorned springs, as presented in Table 6.2, is considerably less than in other contexts ($\chi^2 = 4{,}748.0$, df = 2, $p < .000$, $V^2 = 0.50$). There is also a dearth of other cultural features around these springs, the exceptions being three large, walled-in rockshelters that, as detailed in Chapter 4, were probably shrines. Instead of serving simply as way stations and watering holes, the springs somehow elicited the ritualized production of rock art. Tina Carpenter (2007:131–132, 137–138) described several of these special places as "destination sites" at the termini of pilgrimages. It is difficult to convincingly identify pilgrimages based solely on rock art (although ethnography can help; see Colton and Colton 1931; Lymer 2004), yet the springs clearly drew people to these locations for reasons other than the water that is (rarely) found there. Indeed, rock art and springs were complementary facies of the landscape; seeing and making petroglyphs were integral to the visual experience and use of these springs whereas the springs were cynosures for performances involving rock art. Springs were thus one stage for petroglyph-related ritual practices.

In addition to springs, the Hohokam sited dense clusters of rock art on level ridgetops and in saddles between hillocks along ridgelines. In some instances these are vicinal to springs in the canyon floors, suggesting a connection. Such cases evidence a second stage for rock art ritualism, one that involved the coupling of springs with elevated places affording expansive vistas across the lower Salt River valley. Not all elevated petroglyph clusters are proximate to springs or water tanks, however, and these places differ accordingly in several important respects. For instance, rock art is considerably less dense here than around springs, usually consisting of a handful of panels on an outcropping of boulders—the exception being the large agricultural complex at the northeastern edge of the mountains (Figure 4.6), a different stage type considered below. Ancillary archaeological features, principally small clearings, also tend to be found adjacent to these elevated clusters.

The small, elevated ridgetop petroglyph clusters are usually tied to other, similar settings via small footpaths, the Type II trails described in Chapter 4. Often these relatively level and anthropogenically cleared areas embedded in the craggy landscape are nodes within the webbed trail network, where multiple footpaths meet, merge, and resplinter. Given the limited extent of the level areas, the clearings' relatively diminutive sizes, and the overall remoteness, most of the elevated petroglyph clusters could accommodate only limited, small-group activities. Such activities were not exclusively concerned with the production of rock art. These clusters tend to have small assemblages of ceramic and stone artifacts, typically expedient flake and core tools, scattered around the cleared and level areas, most of which seem inconsequential to the manufacture of rock art.

Based on the types of artifacts and features associated with petroglyph clusters in saddles and along ridgetops, these settings constitute a third type of stage, central places for individual and small-group activities, likely focused on gathering and processing wild plants. In this sense, periodic excursions in pursuit of useful plants, and perhaps in some instances toolstone, were social, behavioral, and calendrical backdrops for petroglyph production. Rock art, however, was not manufactured during idle times of the workday, nor is there any indication that the Hohokam used it to demarcate ownership or address territorial concerns regarding the location of nearby resources. In these settings petroglyph clusters occur on outcrops in the center of the stage, with clearings and artifacts peripheral to and radiating out from the petroglyphs. The

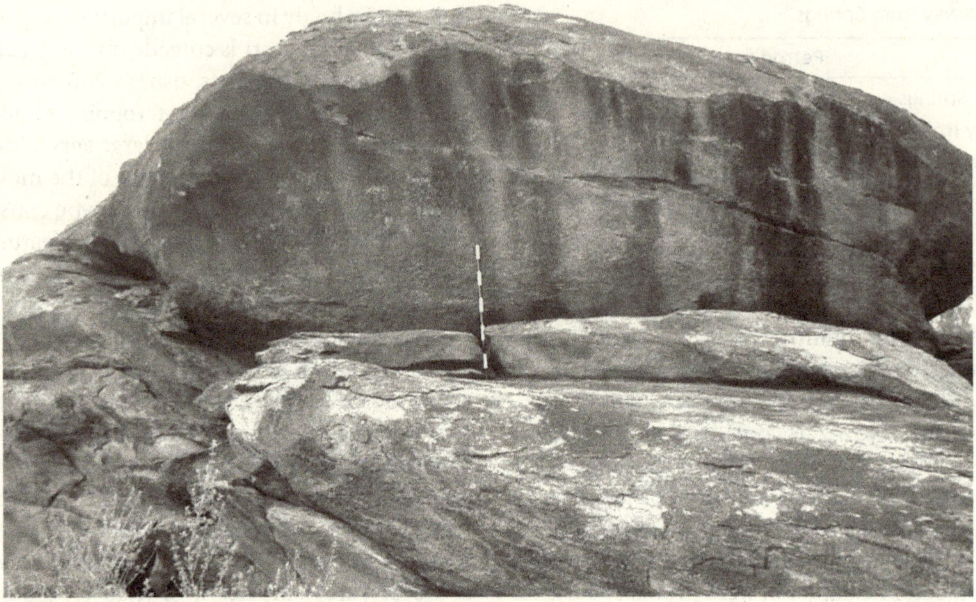

FIGURE 6.1. Overview of a large, towering set of panels along the bajada (facing south). The petroglyphs consist of a series of faint quadrupeds at the far left.

layouts of these stages suggest that, while not the sole focus, petroglyphs were the nuclei of activities carried out there.

The South Mountains' bajada was a fourth type of stage for ritual practices involving the crafting, viewing, and referencing of rock art. Figure 4.5 shows a fairly continuous spread of rock art along the mountains' lower margins, where the granodiorite boulders and outcrops meet weathered sand and gravel. Petroglyph density on this stage, however, fluctuates and appears correlated with proximity to agricultural terraces. A handful of spring-oriented stages occur within this low-level petroglyph concentration, but they stand out markedly in density. An elongated zone of bajada activities is evidenced by a diffuse scatter of lithic and ceramic artifacts whose density also varies in concordance with proximity to agricultural works. This lower reach of the mountains witnessed the husbandry, cultivation, and processing of crops, including agave and perhaps corn (Chapter 4), but the occurrence of artifacts, especially stone tools, away from agricultural features shows that the Hohokam sought, collected, and processed noncultivar, wild plants along the bajada as well. Trails contouring the bajada tie these various settings—petroglyphs on isolated panels, in small clusters, and in dense concentrations around springs—together into a cohesive, interactive system of practice and engagement with the South Mountains landscape.

The petroglyph cluster along the South Mountains' bajada, a transitional zone between the mountains' uplifted outcrops and the valley's sunken sandy soils, shows that seeing, creating, and being around rock art were experiences blended with other endeavors of mostly economic, or "mundane," concern, a polychotonous performative context similar to saddle and ridgetop stages. Again, however, the enstoned symbols are not relics or insignia of doodlers during workday lulls. Rather, Hohokam artisans strategically positioned petroglyphs to be seen by people as they interacted with and moved through this relatively high-traffic section of the mountains (see below). Most of the rock art is indeed quite visible, sometimes placed on prominent or towering "canvases" along the outcrops (e.g., Figure 6.1), so the manufacture and viewing of rock art were undoubtedly integral to the farming and other practices happening along these slopes.

Summit trails are a fifth type of stage for the production of rock art and ancillary ritual practices. In fact, these stages are more elaborate and formal versions of the other two spring-focused stage types reviewed above. Summit trails, as straight, built pathways (Figures 4.16 and 4.17), tie the fields and springs to the overhead summits, whose level and patchily cleared surfaces are adorned with a spattering of petroglyphs and topped with several shrine-like features and an occasional shrine stone (Figure 4.14). On these stages petroglyphs are concentrated at each end of the trails, with the densest areas at the basal entrees where ritual participants began their ascents and ended their descents (Figure 4.19 and 4.20). Atop the summits, the crafting and viewing of rock art were coupled with shrine-related ritualism and the offering of esoteric items, an amalgam of physically and metaphorically elevated practices afforded with expansive views across the valley's domestic and agricultural landscape. On summit trail stages, rock art was elemental to a ritual system prescribing direct and linear ritualized processions between springs and summits.

As noted above, the Hohokam sited a rock art cluster in a low saddle above the large agricultural complex in the easternmost project area (Figure 4.6), but the extremely high petroglyph density here is atypical of other saddle and ridgetop stages. Also unique to this setting are the presence of two circular shrines amid the rock art cluster and the large agricultural terraces just downslope (Figure 4.12). Although it bears topographic affinities to some other ridgetop stages, this one-of-a-kind agricultural complex–rock art cluster, what I call a "saddle shrine," is a sixth type of stage for rock art ritualism.[4]

There are many instances in the South Mountains where isolated petroglyphs adorn the trails people navigated as they passed through canyons and along the ridges. Often overlooked, these lone panels are an important thread in the cultural fabric the Hohokam wove over this greasy-sheened, craggy landscape, and the settings hosting these isolated panels and trail segments should be regarded as a seventh type of stage for the crafting and viewing of rock art. On these stages petroglyphs are not clustered in any sense of density (e.g., Figure 6.2), though their presence distinguishes the boulders, outcrops, and trails from other places on the landscape. Discernible in Figures 4.4–4.6, where panels are shown but lack petroglyph contours around them, these isolated and sometimes remote stages usually exhibit one to three petroglyphs that are often visible only as one immediately passes by on the trail (e.g., Figures 6.2 and 6.3). Unlike on the other stages, these petroglyphs are not tied to places within the landscape per se, such as springs, hilltops, or clearings, but rather are entangled with the experiences of corporeal movement and enlined transience (Ingold 2000, 2007a, 2011). Petroglyphs in such settings are commonly referred to as trail markers, but this interpretation seems unwarranted for the South Mountains because there are few points in this landscape where one's orientation becomes limited to the extent that a marker is necessary. It is actually difficult to get lost as one moves through these lower reaches of the mountains because the viewsheds and proximity to now-dilapidated Hohokam villages offer numerous points of reference and direction along the trails and in remote reaches of the canyon floors.

Several contextual factors indicate that these trail-centric petroglyphs were not simply navigational aids. For one, since the glyphs tend to be small, solitary motifs, they are indiscernible and sometimes practically invisible from any considerable distance, and therefore seem ineffective at broadcasting important information about the immediate environment, as we might expect from trail markers. Moreover, they are not positioned exclusively in any apparently significant settings, such as near toolstone outcrops, at forks in paths, or amid patches of useful flora, but rather seem stochastically and opportunistically placed along trails. The saddle and ridgetop stages, as nodes in the trail network, have more to do with trail forks and resource patches than do these isolated panels along trails. These contextual factors intimate that most trail-adorning

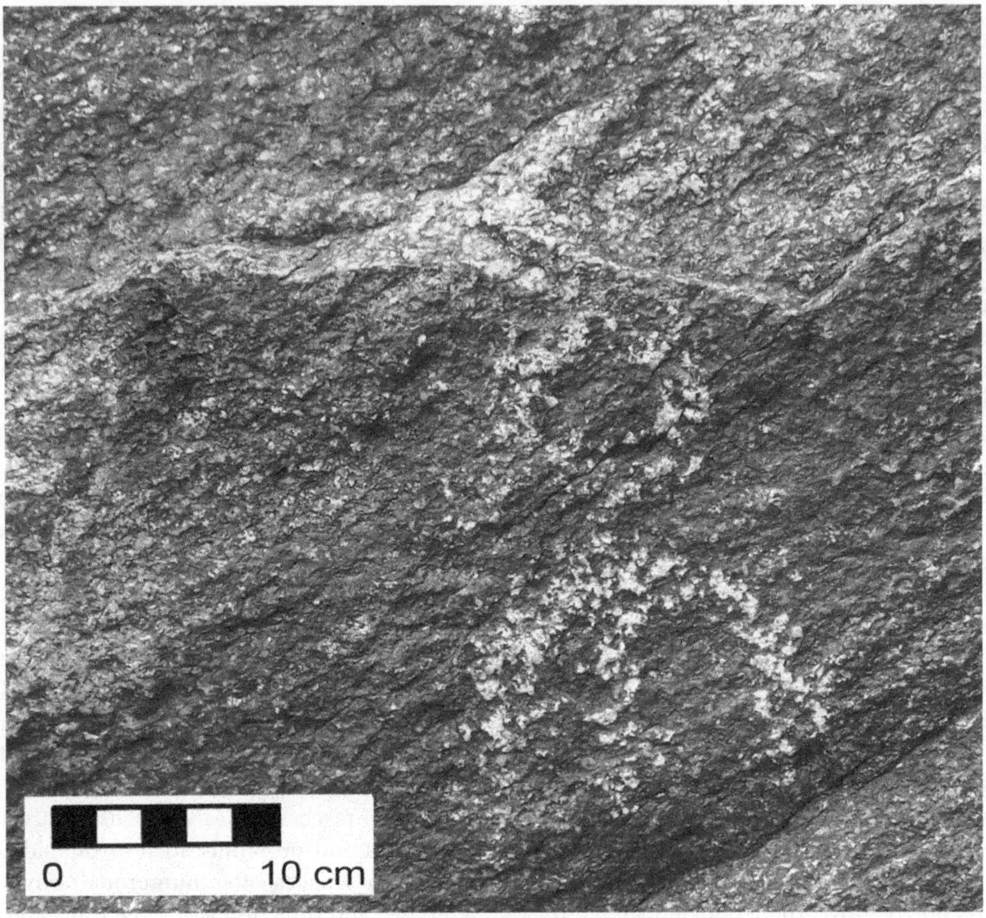

FIGURE 6.2. A small, inconspicuous anthropomorph petroglyph along a trail.

petroglyphs did not serve "functional" needs, in a positivistic sense of purpose, but instead relate to the phenomenology of movement through this polysemous landscape. Perhaps they encode revelations, reference hierophanies, historicize personal experiences, or are simply inscriptions of social identities onto (or into) the landscape. While the intentions remain speculative, the recurrence of isolated trail petroglyphs nonetheless betrays qualities of the ritual form, and as such constitutes a seventh type of stage for ritual practice. The lack of any sense of petroglyph density or spatial clustering suggests that these stages had less ritual depth than the others, or that the practices concerning rock art were less ritualized in these settings than elsewhere.

Contextual factors and spatial variability in petroglyph density differentiate the types of stages that hosted rock art ritualism in the South Mountains (Table 6.3). While each stage, and indeed each petroglyph, is a unique relic of ritual performance, the seven stage types—springs, hilltop springs, summit trails, the saddle shrine, saddles and ridgetops, the bajada, and trails—reveal topographic and presumably symbolic commonalities and differences among locations of petroglyph ritualism. Petroglyph clustering, which evidences the redundancy and repetition of the ritual form, hierarchically organizes the stages according to scalar density. In this way, the seven stage types correspond with degrees of ritualization in rock art performance, or the ritual depth of certain places, from sporadic occurrences along trails to highly concentrated and

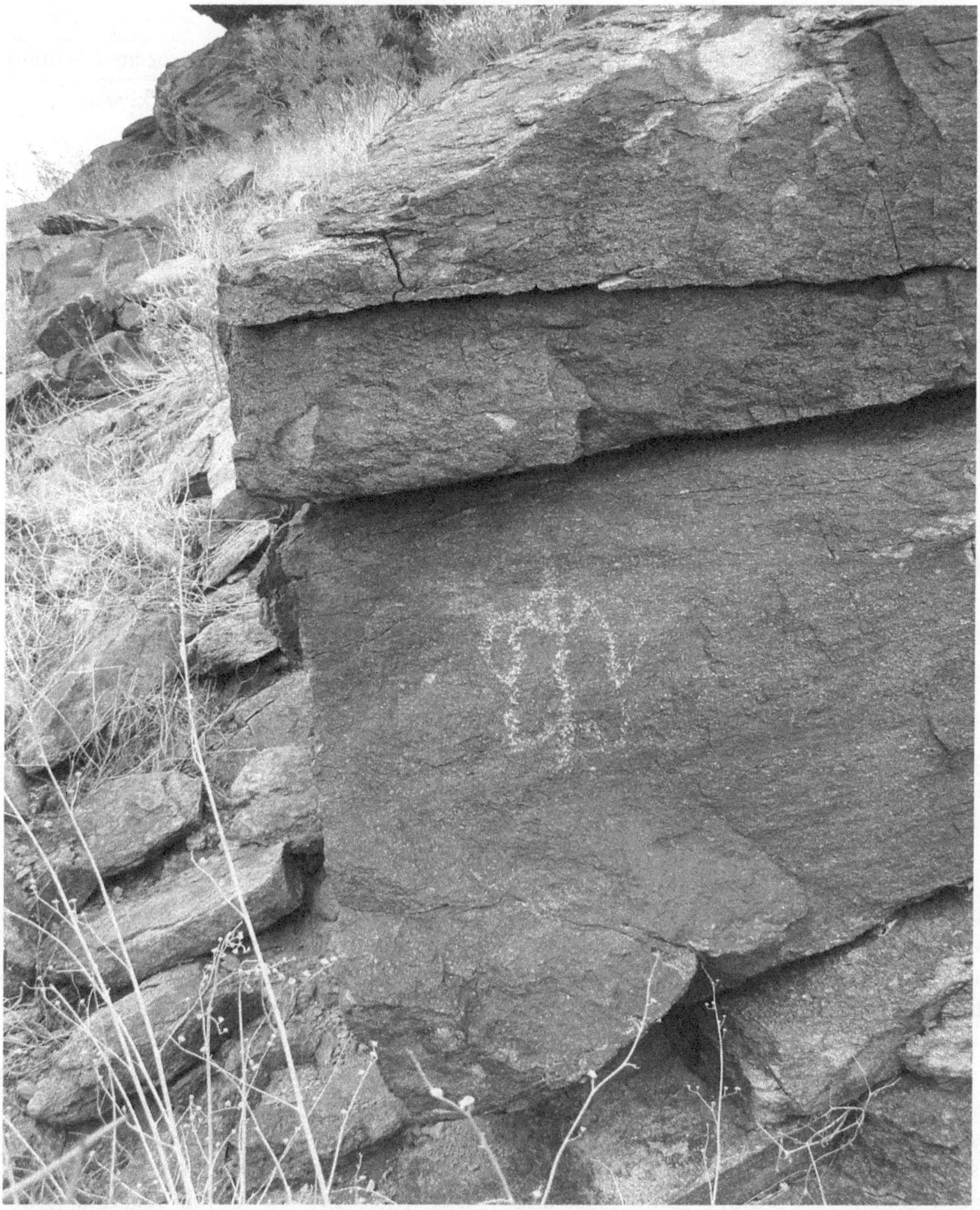

FIGURE 6.3. Panel with an uncategorizable lifeform petroglyph along a trail (facing northeast). Glyph is 31 cm tall.

very dense places around springs. Together the different stages form a network of mountain-oriented ritualism involving rock art. In the following I populate these stages with actors and audiences through consideration of the stages' proxemic qualities (Hall 1966, 1968; see also Mills 2007; Munson 2011:78–80).

Audience

Observation of performance is fundamental to our contention that ritual practice is a unique mode of social action, but as noted at the beginning of this chapter, audiences of ritual need not be large or even be people other than the performers. Accordingly, we should expect audience

TABLE 6.3. Seven Stages for the Performance of Rock Art.

Stage	Audience Size	Petroglyph Density	Artifact Density	Associated Features
Springs	Low to Moderate	Moderate to High	Low	• Rockshelters • Trails
Hilltop Springs	Moderate	High	Moderate	• Clearings • Trails • Rockshelters
Summit Trails	Moderate to High	High	Moderate	• Shrines • Cairns • Clearings • Trails • Agricultural Terraces • Roasting Pits
Saddle Shrines	Moderate to High	High	High	• Shrines • Trails • Clearings • Agricultural Terraces
Saddles and Ridgetops	Low to Moderate	Moderate to Low	Moderate	• Clearings • Trails
Bajada	Moderate	Moderate to Low	High	• Agricultural Terraces • Roasting Pits • Clearings • Rockshelters
Trails	Low	Low	Low	

size and identity to shift across stages. Peopling places, however, involves a heightened degree of abstraction when we are dealing with the framing of ritual performances. One way to approach an audience, albeit indirectly, is to consider the visibility and accessibility of the stages the rock art adorns (Bradley 2009). With artifacts and architecture, we can gauge their visibility through size, quantity, and contrast to surrounding settings (Carr 1995; see also Wobst 1977). In rock art studies, characteristics of the intended audience can be evidenced by a motif's size and thoroughness of its execution; the rock art's figurativeness, familiarity, or "intelligibility"; and the extent to which the stages or the glyphs are "public" or "private" settings (e.g., Bradley 2002; Bruder 1983; Loubser 2002; Munson 2002, 2012; Olsen 2004; Potter 2004; Robinson 2010; Wallace and Holmlund 1986; Whitley 1987). Additionally, rock art's connection to other activities can shed light on the identities of an audience. In this section I address the visibility of rock art ritualism by comparing attributes of the South Mountains petroglyph assemblage with the visibility and accessibility of the panels. I then consider the contexts and characteristics of the different stages in order to home in on the social compositions, identities, and sizes of the audiences.

Panel visibility, or how noticeable the rock art is within the landscape, is an experiential variable conditioned by a number of geomorphological factors, including aspect, orientation, and height above the surrounding terrain. Unfortunately, these measures, while quantifiable, do not accurately or effectively describe a panel's visibility as one actually moves through the mountains. Likewise, visibility can be a rather subjective and relative variable, something numerical data are ill-equipped to capture and incapable of reproducing, so I relied on qualitative appraisals to classify each panel and its corresponding rock art as either highly visible, moderately visible, or hidden. I took panel orientation (horizontal, vertical, overhead), aspect (e.g., facing a trail), and

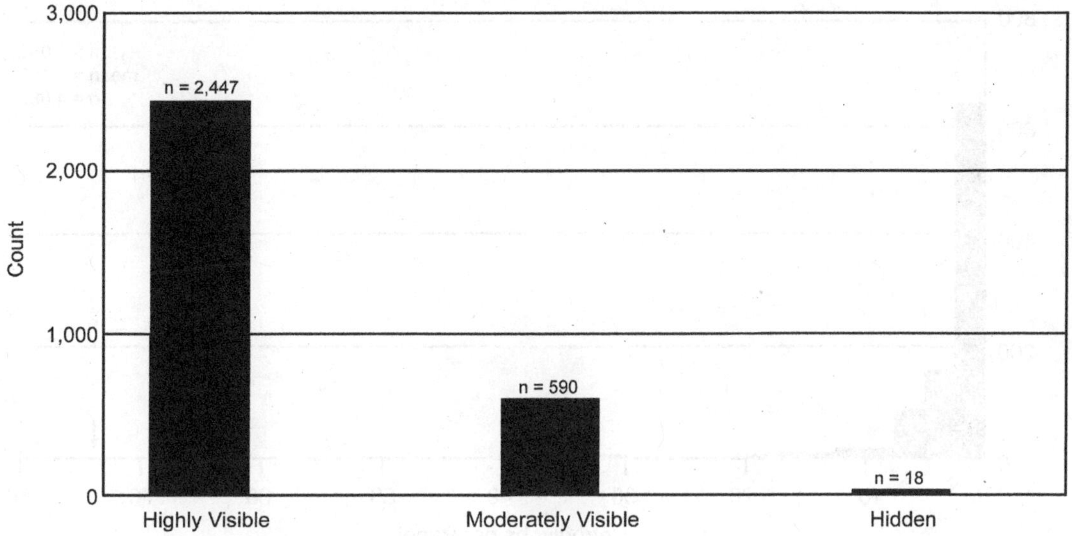

FIGURE 6.4. Degrees of visibility of South Mountains petroglyphs.

topographic position (e.g., perched on a high cliff face or tucked under a slight overhang) into consideration, but I ultimately scored the rock art's visibility while actually visiting and walking around the site areas and analyzing the panels in their environmental settings. The three degrees of visibility reduce a great deal of variability into three general categories, but they provide a means to distinguish broadly between private and public settings for the rock art.

As Figure 6.4 shows, most of the South Mountains petroglyphs, over 80 percent, are on highly visible panels. This category includes petroglyphs that seem to have been deliberately positioned to be noticed from afar (e.g., Figure 6.1) as well as those that are readily visible as one passes near them (e.g., Figure 6.3). High visibility thus denotes either intentionality for visibility or an absolute disregard for privacy. A much smaller number of petroglyphs, just below 20 percent, are on moderately visible panels. Moderately visible panels are those that can be seen only when one is immediately next to them; they are usually positioned on horizontal or oddly situated rock surfaces (e.g., Figure 6.2), which implies a lack of intent on the part of the artisan for the imagery to be readily noticed by others but no apparent concern for privacy. In contrast to more visible rock art, hidden panels and petroglyphs are very rare in the South Mountains. Of the sample assemblage considered here, only 18 petroglyphs, about one-half of one percent, are found on what I consider five hidden panels. Three of these panels, including the one bearing the impaled bighorn sheep inside a walled-in rockshelter (Figure 4.10), are positioned around one of the spring stages (see also Figure 5.5). The two other hidden panels include one exhibiting a very small and extremely faint lizard-like petroglyph inside an alcove and another difficult-to-see panel amid a cluster of petroglyphs at the base of a summit trail. Hidden panels do not necessarily imply that an artisan sought privacy or secrecy, but like moderately visible panels may simply indicate a general disregard for visibility.

With few exceptions, Hohokam artisans in the South Mountains placed petroglyphs in open and visible niches of the landscape with apparently little concern for privacy or control over access. Hidden rock art exists, but its rarity and fixity among other, more visible panels, sometimes in high-traffic areas such as around summit trails, suggest that privacy, secrecy, and concealment were not primary motivators for pecking those few images in secluded or hard-to-reach settings. This high degree of visibility shows a clear concern for audiences to witness rock art ritualism as well as intentionality in

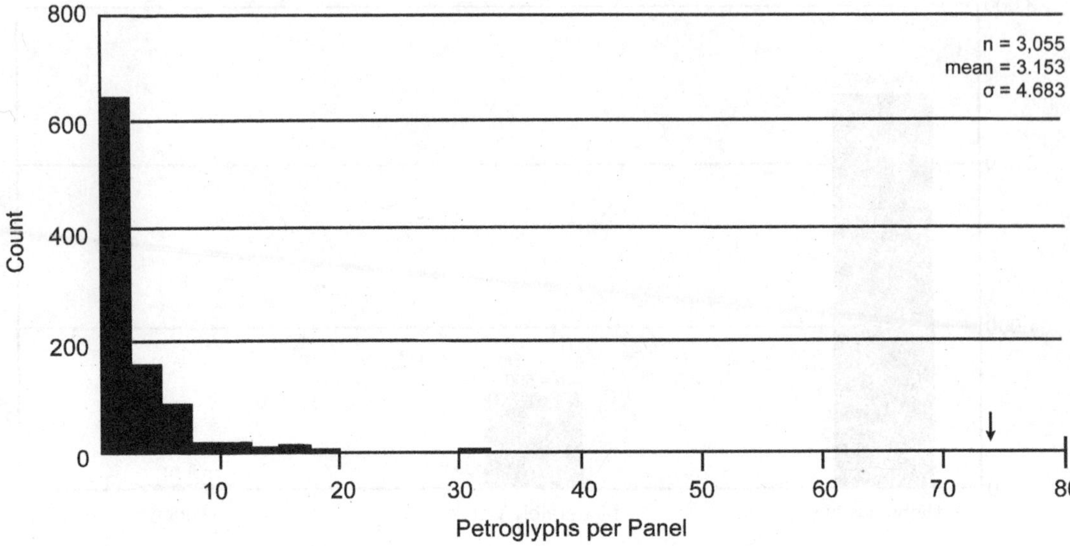

FIGURE 6.5. Number of petroglyphs per panel. The arrow denotes an extreme outlier (see Figure 6.6).

petroglyph placement, or the framing of the stages, by petroglyph artisans. But how calculated and deliberate were the choices in rock art placement? Is it that highly visible settings and large, noticeable rock faces simply enticed artisans to peck glyphs on those panels? It is possible to explore this by comparing the noticeability of the rock art with the general visibility of the panels within the landscape. I measured the rock art's noticeability through five quantitative variables: the number of petroglyphs on a panel, the percentage of a panel's surface area covered by rock art, petroglyph size, petroglyph height relative to the ground surface immediately below it, and the degree of execution involved in a petroglyph's production. I evaluate each of these below.

The number of petroglyphs on a panel not only attests to the density of rock art within the landscape, or the ritual depth of places, but also influences the panel's visual prominence and possibly even the allure of the overall stage; the greater number of petroglyphs catches the eye from a farther distance or stands out from other panels or backdrops. In the South Mountains, however, most panels exhibit relatively few petroglyphs (Figure 6.5). Some panels are fairly densely covered (e.g., Figures 5.6 and 6.6), but nearly half (48 percent) exhibit only 1 petroglyph, 85 percent show 5 or fewer, and nearly all (94 percent) portray 10 or fewer petroglyphs. Topography and landscape setting seem to have influenced a panel's attractiveness as a canvas, but the strength of the relationship between a panel's visibility and the number of petroglyphs on it, while statistically significant, is negligible (Table 6.4). This shows that even though most petroglyphs can be easily seen when one is near them (Figure 6.4), a panel's visibility had relatively little sway over the number of petroglyphs placed on it.

Another measure pertaining to the rock art's relative noticeability worth considering is the percentage of panel space, or surface area, covered by petroglyphs. A logical assumption would be that the number of petroglyphs is highly correlated with the percentage of a panel's surface area covered in rock art, but this is not the case ($R^2 = 0.063$, $p < .001$). The percentage of panel space covered by petroglyphs is therefore a similar yet independent proxy of the noticeability of rock art while one moves through the landscape. However, just as with the number of petroglyphs per panel (Figure 6.5), the percentage of a panel's surface area covered in rock art is relatively low (Figure 6.7). Most panels have less than one-

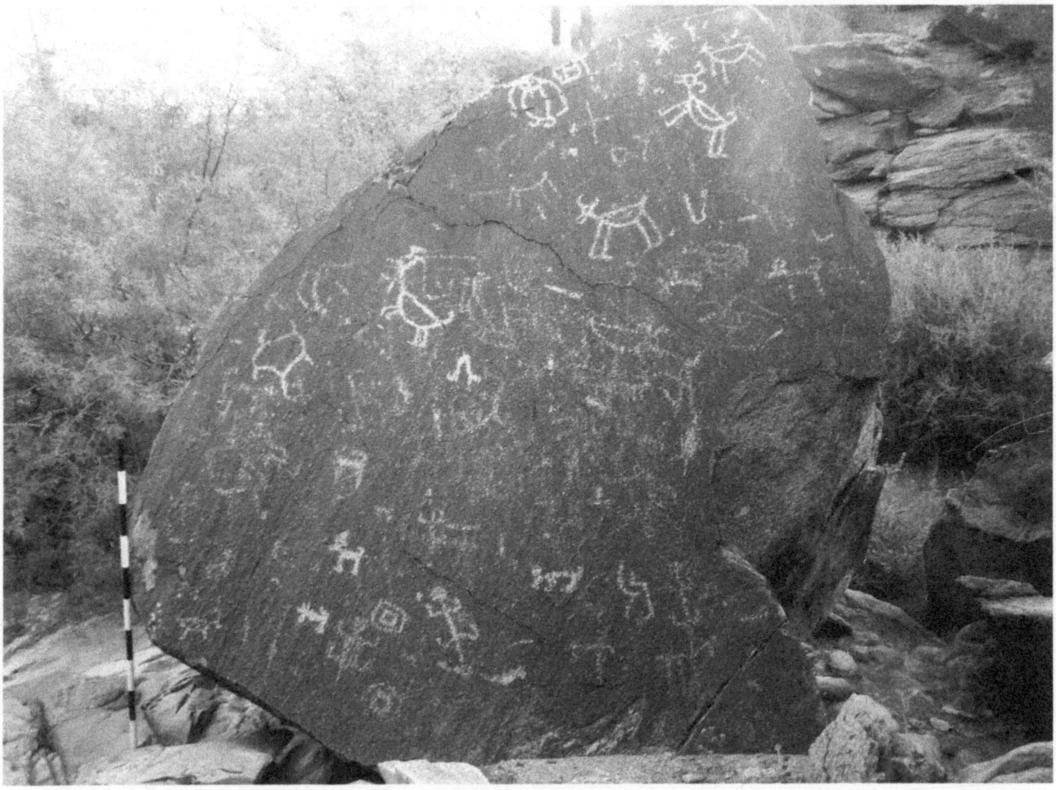

FIGURE 6.6. A densely covered petroglyph panel near a spring (facing northwest). With more than 75 petroglyphs, this is one of the densest petroglyph panels in the South Mountains.

TABLE 6.4. Correlations of Petroglyph and Panel Attributes with Aspects of Panel Size and Visibility.

Dependent Variable	Independent Variable	No. of Cases	Spearman's Coefficient (r_s)	*p*-value
Number of Petroglyphs	Panel Visibility	3,055	0.135	< .001
Petroglyph Size	Panel Visibility	3,055	-0.025	= .167
Degree of Execution	Panel Visibility	3,055	0.071	< .001
% of Panel Space Used	Panel Visibility	964	0.119	< .001

Dependent Variable	Independent Variable	No. of Cases	Pearson's Coefficient (R^2)	*p*-value
Number of Petroglyphs	Panel Size	3,055	0.055	< .001
Petroglyph Size	Height above Ground	3,055	0.005	< .001
% of Panel Space Used	Panel Size	964	0.051	< .001

fourth of their surfaces draped in petroglyphs, and many far less than that sparing amount.

In Figure 6.8 I compare the percentage of panel space covered by petroglyphs among the three degrees of panel visibility; while the figure hints that the area covered in rock art increases slightly with greater degree of visibility, careful examination suggests that this visual illusion is a product of sample size. A Spearman's measure of rank correlation shows that the percentage of panel space used is only weakly correlated with the panel's visibility (Table 6.4). Moreover, hidden panels, albeit poorly represented in this sample, have on average the greatest percentage

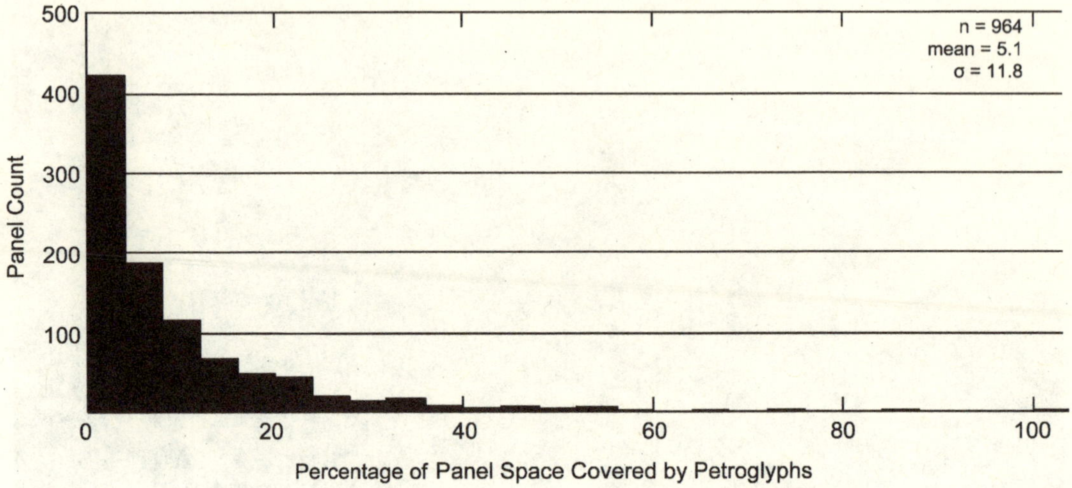

FIGURE 6.7. Number of panels by percentage of surface area covered by petroglyphs.

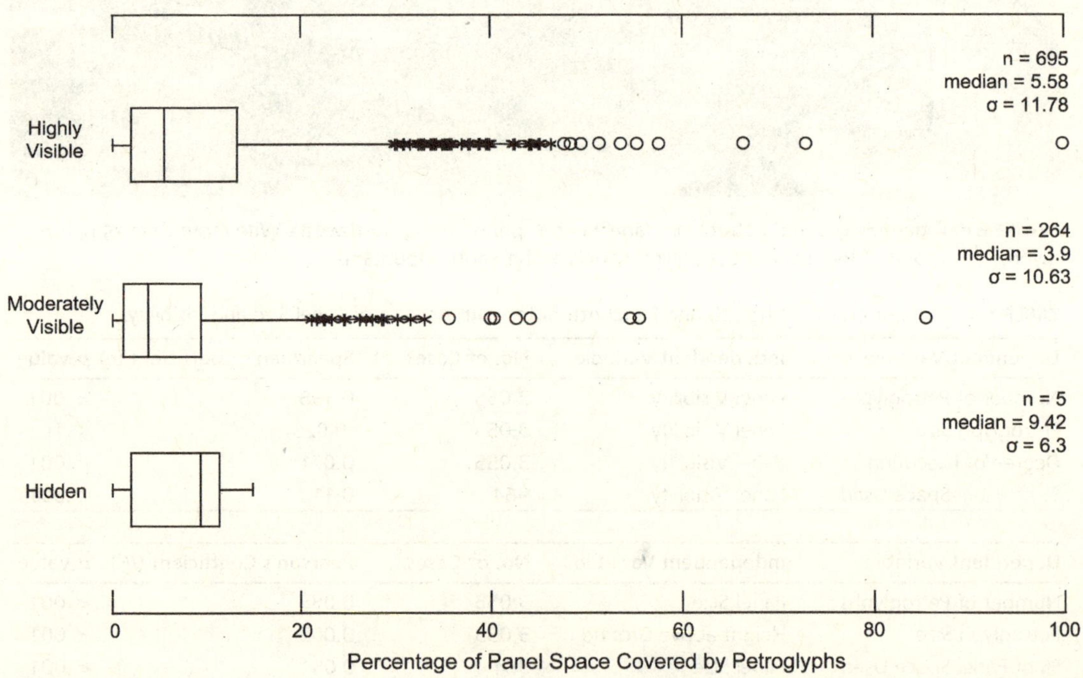

FIGURE 6.8. Box-and-whisker plots of the percentage of surface area covered by petroglyphs by panel visibility.

of surface area covered in petroglyphs, which is counterintuitive to a contention that more visible panels should exhibit more and larger rock art. The percentage of panel space covered by petroglyphs is likewise negligibly dependent on the panel's size (Table 6.4). Combined, these measures show that, any way we view it, panel visibility and size had little to do with how much rock art, weighed in terms of the number of petroglyphs and the surface area they cover, that Hohokam artisans placed on particular panels. Like the clustering of petroglyphs within the

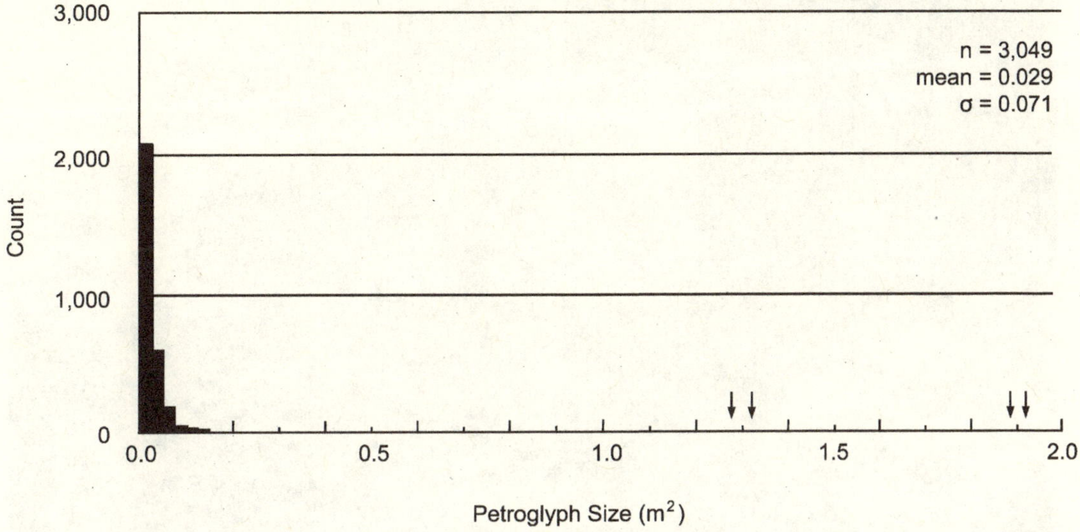

FIGURE 6.9. Size of South Mountains petroglyphs. The arrows denote extreme outliers, such as the two large anthropomorphs obfuscated under superimposing historic glyphs in Figure 5.14.

larger landscape, these measures underscore the nonrandom, intentional, and choreographed placement of rock art on and around the stages.

Petroglyph size also affects the overall noticeability of the imagery, but the vast majority of South Mountains petroglyphs are tiny (Figure 6.9). Nearly half the petroglyphs, 48 percent, are less than the size of one's hand (0.015 m^2), and nearly all, 91 percent, are smaller than a sheet of notebook paper (0.063 m^2). There are four notable outliers in Figure 6.9, but three are not convincingly oversized because they are not really "motifs," or discrete images or symbols, but instead consist of random pecking across a panel (e.g., Figure 6.10) and the dint framing of a natural quartz vein (Figure 6.11). The quartz vein is quite noticeable, and in some way likely inspired the crafting of rock art on that stage, but the dint frame outlining it is rather inconspicuous. The fourth exceptionally large glyph is a "rake" (Figure 6.12), but its topographic position, low to the ground and positioned along a trail in a somewhat narrow passage between bedrock outcrops, suggests that its size had little to do with drawing attention from afar.

Most of the South Mountains petroglyphs are situated at or below the eye level of an average adult (Figure 6.13). A small number of petroglyphs are located above eye level, some at considerable heights (e.g., Figure 6.1), which increases their ability to catch the eye from greater distances, but most were placed to draw one's attention while walking around the immediate stage area. If the size of a petroglyph is indicative of how noticeable the artisan wanted the imagery to be, we might expect larger petroglyphs to be positioned at higher elevations and their size to correspond with the panel's visibility. Strong correlations between petroglyph size and height above the ground or panel visibility do not occur in this dataset (Table 6.4), however, indicating that most often a petroglyph's size was conditioned by something other than an overt and vested interest in its being seen from afar. The relatively small sizes of South Mountains petroglyphs, and the tendency for them to be found at or below eye level, indicate that most were intended to be sensed and experienced close by with little concern for signaling to a more distant audience.

Along with their size and height above the ground, the intensity of execution—by pecking, abrading, and/or scratching—conditions a petroglyph's noticeability through contrast with the enframing rock face and adjacent petroglyphs. I presume that the degree of execution, measured

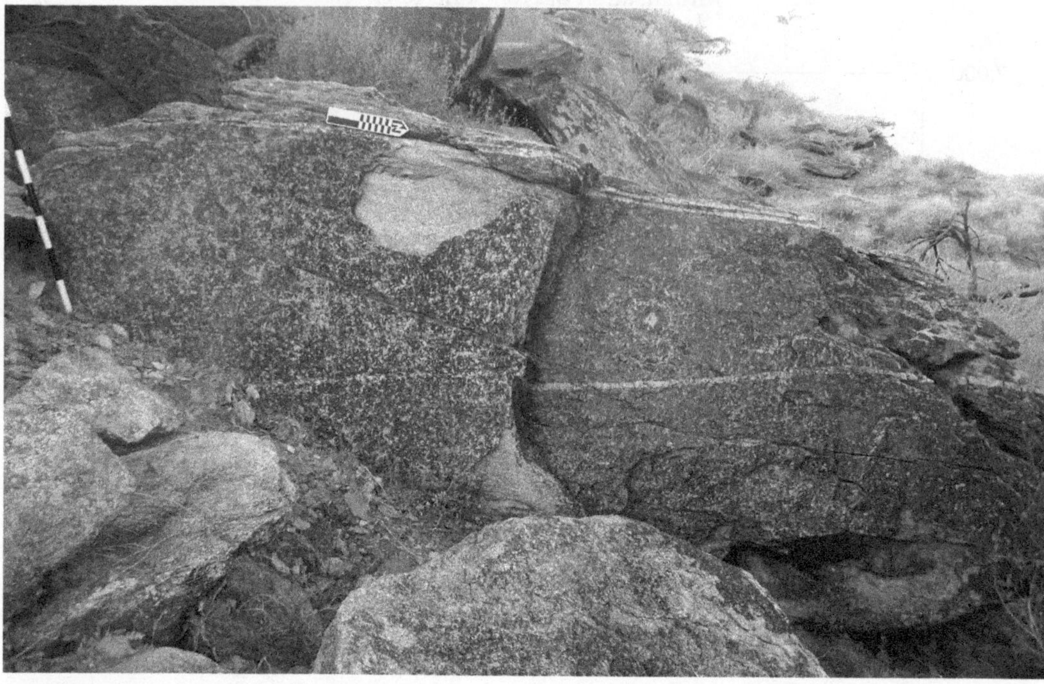

FIGURE 6.10. Panels with random pecking across most of their surfaces. A row of four lightly executed and faintly visible bull's-eyes are located near the center of the panels.

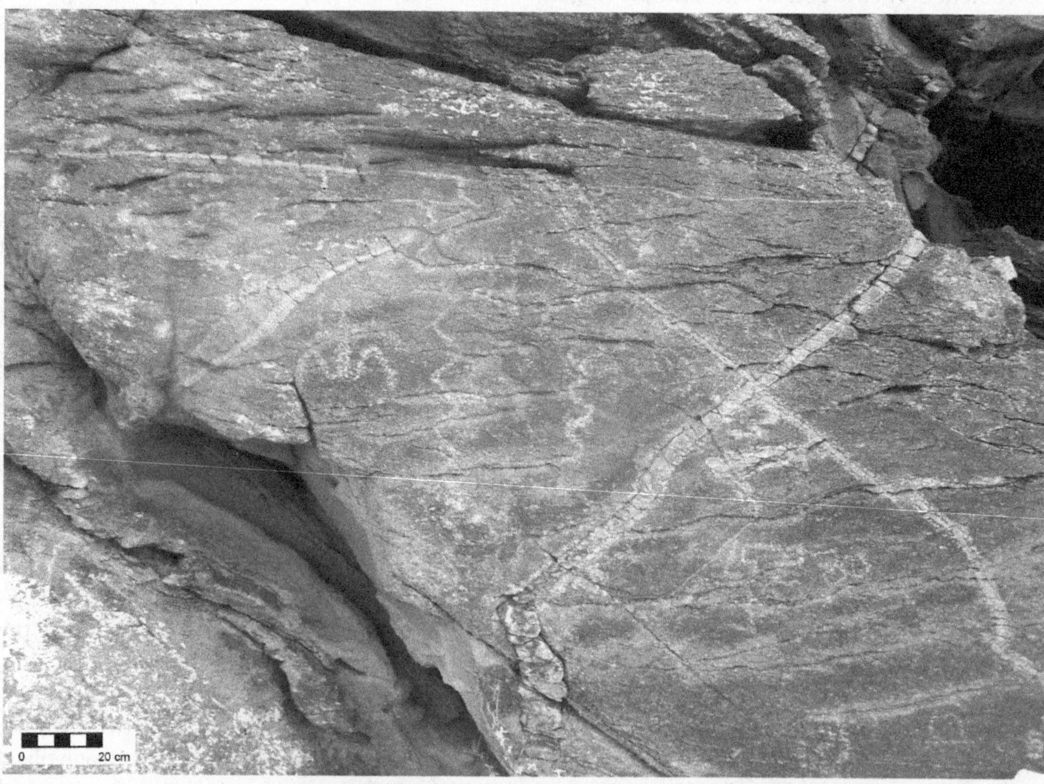

FIGURE 6.11. Panel with a large, X-shaped quartz vein and various lifeform petroglyphs. The quartz vein is outlined by a frame of petroglyph dints. Petroglyphs include an anthropomorph with legs spread open (*far left*) and two extended snakes and other faint glyphs to the right.

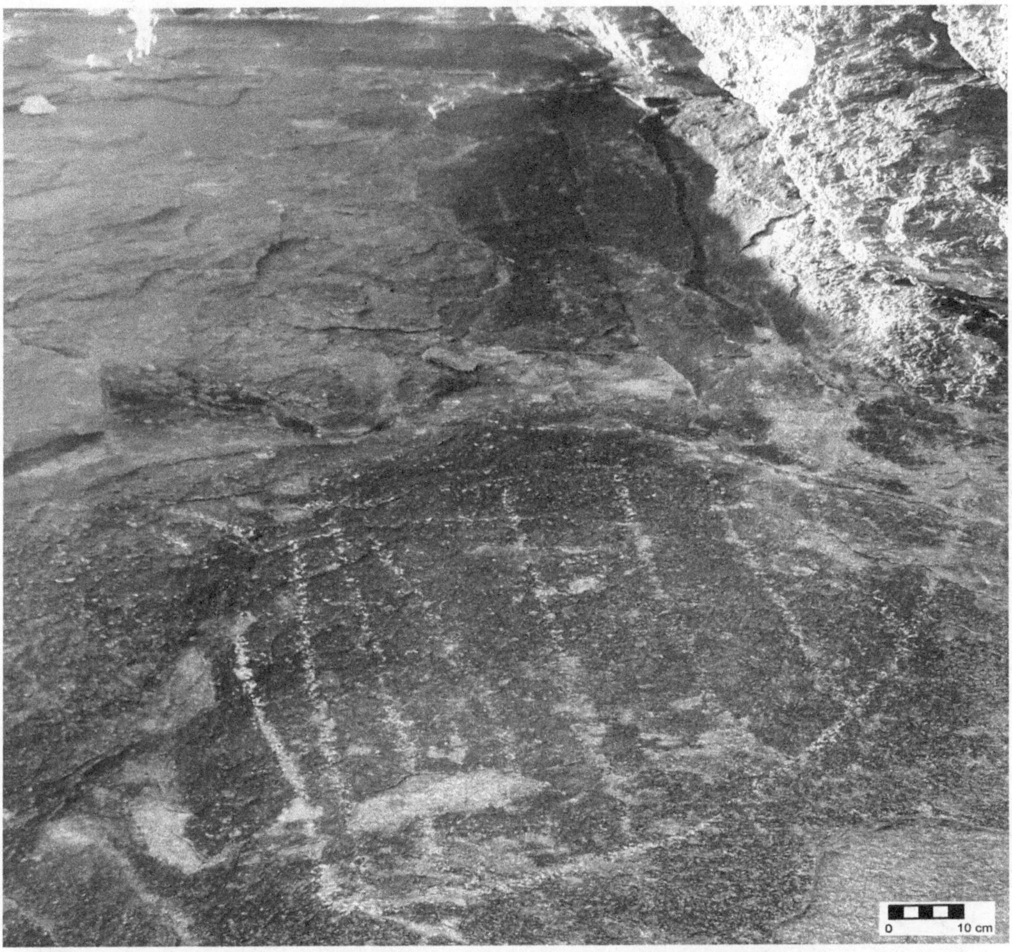

FIGURE 6.12. Panel with a large rake petroglyph.

FIGURE 6.13. Petroglyph height above ground surface. The arrow denotes an extreme outlier.

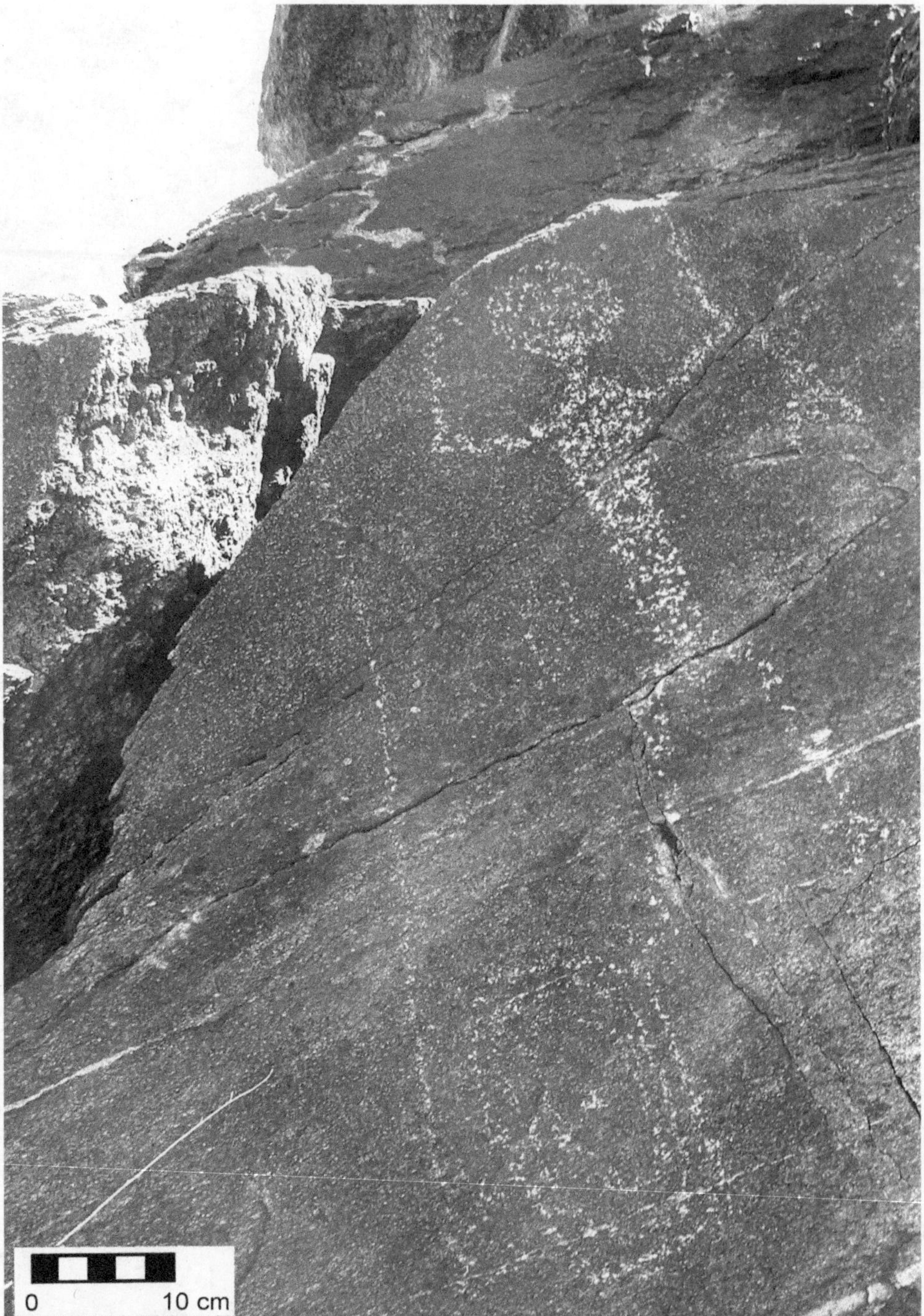

FIGURE 6.14. A pair of moderately executed petroglyphs.

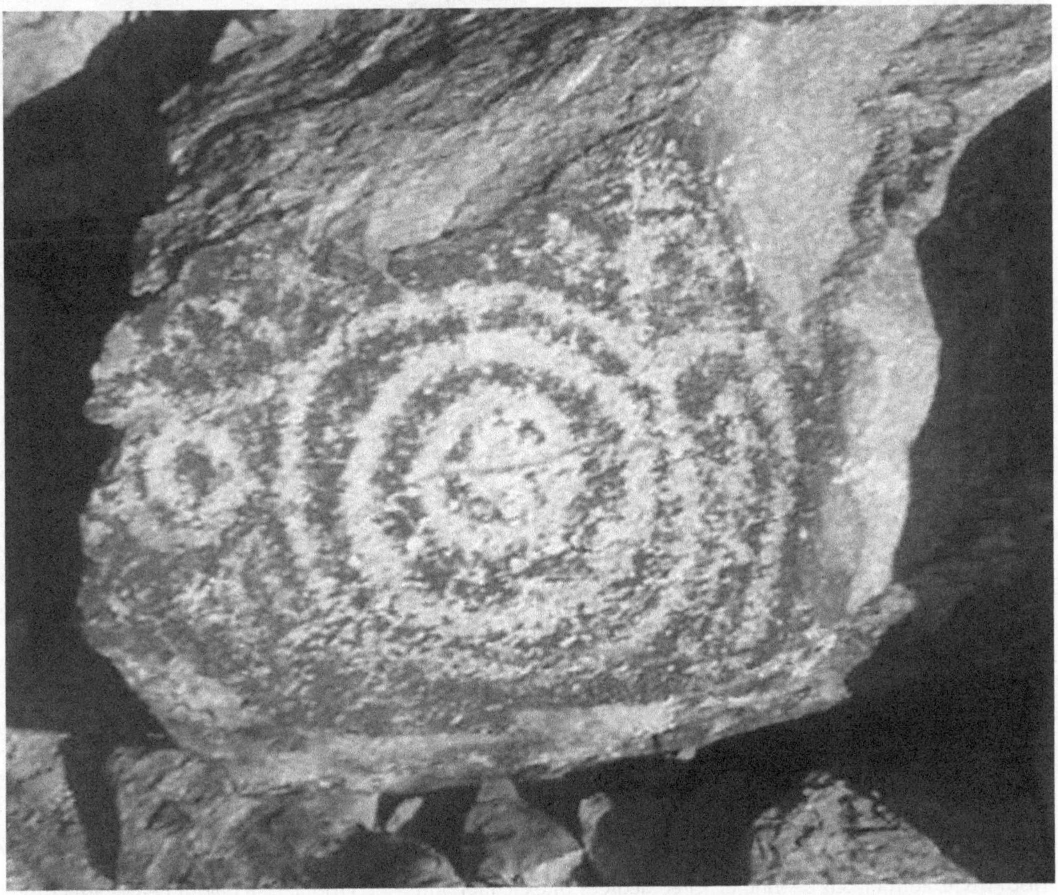

FIGURE 6.15. Panel with a heavily executed and repecked bull's-eye petroglyph at the saddle shrine. The glyph is 24 cm tall.

by petroglyph depth, thoroughness of pecking, and completion of the design, is due in most part to the artisan's desire for visibility and permanence. As noted in Chapter 4, I grouped the South Mountains petroglyphs into three classes of execution intensity (light, moderate, and heavy). Figures 6.14–6.17 provide examples of these three classes of intensity: lightly executed petroglyphs are often difficult to see under natural lighting, moderate execution offers enough contrast for the imagery to be seen from a reasonable distance, and heavy execution increases the contrast and draws immediate attention to that petroglyph relative to others. Nearly all the petroglyphs (~97 percent) exhibit light-to-moderate degrees of execution intensity (Figure 4.7), which is indicative of an expedient production technique. Heavily executed imagery, on the other hand, is very rare. If greater intensity of execution was due to a concern for noticeability by a larger audience, we might expect execution intensity to correlate positively with the visibility of the panel. But again, as Table 6.4 shows, such a relationship is meager at best. By and large, intensity of execution had little to do with broadcasting information to an audience beyond the immediate panel area. Perhaps the artisans perceived a "diminished return on investment" once a petroglyph was pecked to the point where the image was discernible and visible from around the stage's periphery.

Many of the South Mountains petroglyphs exhibit very light degrees of execution intensity. This is most evident in the few solely abraded

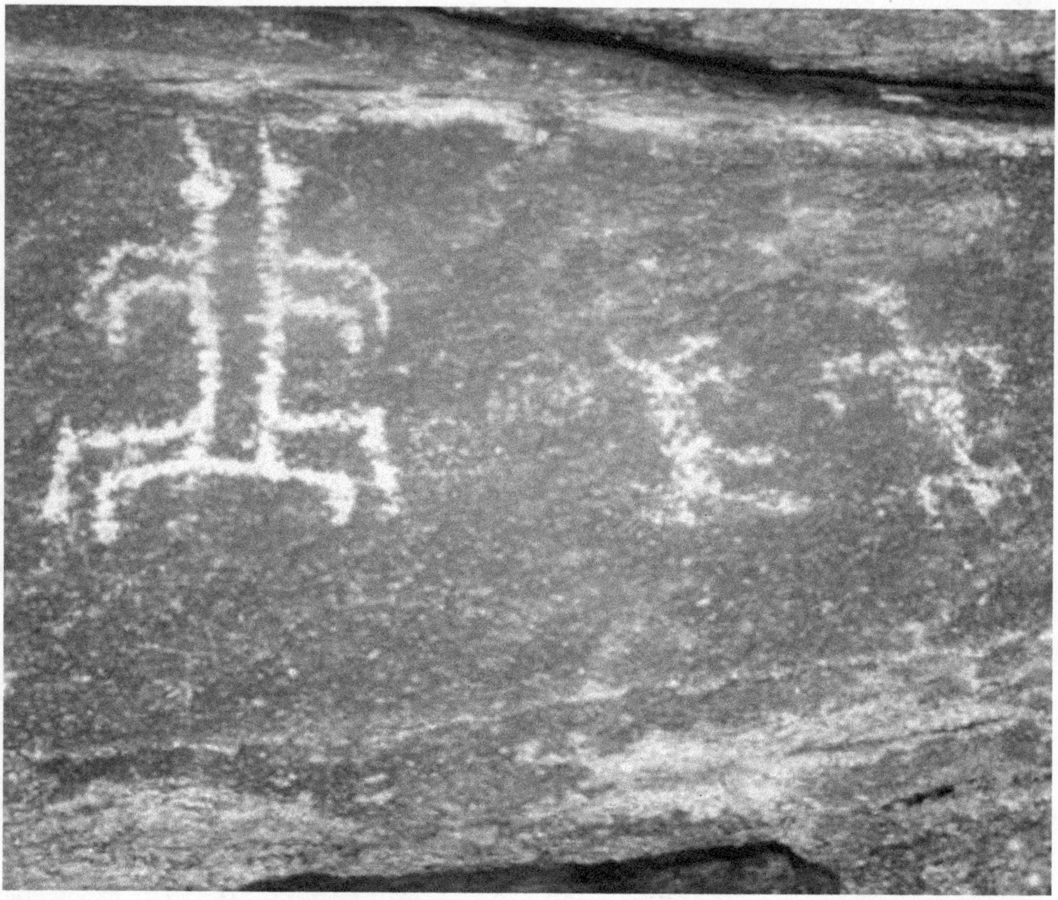

FIGURE 6.16. Petroglyphs bearing all three degrees of execution intensity. *From left:* a pair of heavily executed anthropomorphs with topknots and connected at the legs (twins?), a lightly executed pair of connected curvilinear scrolls, and a moderately executed canid and triangle-bodied anthropomorph. The connected pair of anthropomorphs are 39 cm tall.

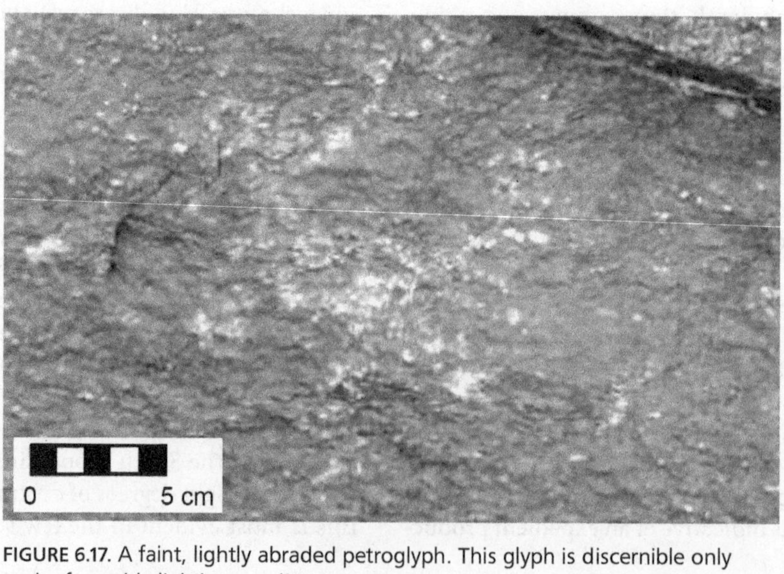

FIGURE 6.17. A faint, lightly abraded petroglyph. This glyph is discernible only under favorable lighting conditions.

petroglyphs, which are recognizable only by faint scratches and ghostly abrasions and visible only under certain lighting conditions (e.g., Figure 6.17). This makes finding such glyphs very difficult, and discerning the designs next to impossible. I surmise that when these ephemeral glyphs were created, the abrasion of a hammerstone across the panel made a fairly noticeable white chalk-like image until wind and rain washed away the loose, pulverized rock dust. Lightly pecked petroglyphs, too, probably provided an initial visual contrast of white rock powder on a dark, reddish-brown rock face, images whose only vestiges are a few shallow and sparse dint marks (e.g., Figure 6.16, center). Several scenarios may explain why the Hohokam rendered such lightly executed petroglyphs. For one, a faint or sparsely pecked petroglyph could have provided an outline, or "general idea," of an image that was never completed. Alternatively, perhaps the artisan was not concerned with the design's permanence or did not comprehend the effect of execution intensity on petroglyph noticeability and perpetuity (an unlikely scenario). Lightly executed glyphs may have served an immediate and expedient purpose with little consideration for an indelible impression. It may even be that the ephemerality or impermanence of such designs was intentional and integral to the ritual practices surrounding their production.

The overall visibility of South Mountains rock art bears on the sizes of the audiences attendant to rock art ritualism. Based on landscape context, most panels were intended to be seen and engaged as people moved about the stages on which the glyphs were placed whereas relatively few were positioned to draw attention from farther afield. This reveals a concern for communicating symbolic information and religious knowledge with others, a point I return to later. The petroglyphs nonetheless tend to be found at or below eye level, are relatively small, and are often lightly to moderately executed, all of which demonstrate that the noticeability and intelligibility of the imagery often required close proximity to the canvases. There are some obvious exceptions, but the majority of South Mountains petroglyphs were meant to be seen by a relatively small, close, and perhaps intimate audience at any one time. Audience capacity was also conditioned by the topographies and layouts of the stages on which rock art ritualism was carried out. Below I explore the topologies and assemblages of natural and cultural features for the seven stage types to approximate audience sizes and shed light on the potential identities of audience members.

As natural daises along the heavily trodden bajada, the elevated loges of the summit trail and saddle shrine stages could have accommodated the largest audiences of all the stage types. This may be why they supported a more diverse array of ritual practices accompanying rock art performances, as evidenced by such features as shrines, cairns, and clearings. Although performative gestures and orations could be seen and heard from afar, as detailed above the actual petroglyphs would not be discernible or intelligible from any considerable distance. Visually deciphering the rock art necessitated close proximity to the actual panels. Since the elevated sections of the stages are relatively small, 30 or less is a reasonable estimate of the number of people who could comfortably observe the rock art at any time. This suggests that some of the practices on these stages, including making rock art, may have been group performances, possibly involving more participants or participant-observers, than on other, smaller stages. This is attested to by the incredibly dense petroglyph clusters on these stages (e.g., Figures 4.19 and 4.20). The identities of the audience members may have been more diverse than in other contexts, too, because these stages could accommodate larger groups of spectators and participants and hosted wider arrays of ritual forms. On these largest stages the practices carried out may have drawn participants and audiences from multiple villages. Spectacles on these stages, however, were not witnessed by hundreds of people at a time, as were some community-wide ritual performances in the villages' plazas and ballcourts. The incorporation of agricultural facilities into these stages' choreographic structures instead implies that the crafting and viewing of rock art were related to farming in some way, and thus the audiences were most likely those individuals who toiled in the soil and stone along the adjacent terraces and participated in harvesting and processing the crops around nearby roasting pits.

Spring and composite spring-hilltop stages, while sometimes elevated above the bajada and canyon floors, have topographical structures that obstruct visibility from any great distance. The hilltops near springs can accommodate moderately large audiences, ranging from possibly 20 to 50 people at any one time, but this is an upper limit defined by the area of the stage and the sloping precipices along their peripheries. The topography immediately around most springs, nestled in secluded and sometimes constricted chambers of the canyon floors, restricts potential audience size to a much greater extent, and the paucity of archaeological features and artifacts on these stages (Table 6.2) undermines our ability to inquire into the identities of spectators and congregants. While their social identities elude us, the audience members' roles, as either actors or onlookers, during the ritual performances may have been more narrow, or "specialized," since these practices were apparently concentrated on the springs. Indeed, rituals in these focused and sheltered places possibly altered participants' and witnesses' identities; such social metamorphosis could have come through temporary role reversals during performances (e.g., male to female, farmer to mystic, descendant to ancestor, body to spirit), a social process akin to Victor Turner's (1966) notion of *communitas*, or through more permanent rites of passage (e.g., child to adult, apprentice to practitioner, life to death).

Like the spring and spring-hilltop stages, the bajada's topographic structure limits the audiences to moderately sized or relatively small groups. Large crowds can mass along the bajada because there are few physical barriers or visual impediments, but the topology of the rock art—at or below eye level, small, and scattered—indicates that seeing most of it required close proximity. Unlike the spring-centric stages' special audiences, rock art–related practices on the bajada were probably performed and observed by small groups of people farming the scattered terrace networks and engaging in ancillary subsistence-oriented forays because the petroglyphs sporadically dot boulders in, around, and between the field areas. Since bajada petroglyphs are not really raised over the surrounding stage, even seeing and hearing accompanying performances warranted relative closeness to the panels and thus limited potential audience sizes to those small groups working in the immediate area.

The topography of saddle and ridgetop stages, as mostly small, level perches within the rocky and rugged landscape, places narrower curbs on the ritual gatherings' sizes than the layouts of the other five stage types outlined above. The admixture of rock art with other cultural features and artifacts in these settings nonetheless makes it difficult to ascertain the social composition of the audiences. On ridgetops and in saddles the viewing and perhaps crafting of petroglyphs was tied to the acquisition of floral resources by small task groups or individuals, so audiences and performers likely consisted of individuals targeting certain areas and pursuing specific plants or mineral sources. In this way, the congregants were specialized and focused, but unlike the case of the spring-centric performances, the performers' and audiences' attention was directed less toward the rock art and more toward collecting food from the stage areas.

Of the seven stage types, petroglyphs along trails had the smallest audiences. The trails are, in effect, corridors between the bajada and saddle and ridgetop stages, so the audiences for trail petroglyphs were probably members of the same task groups moving through the landscape. These footpaths are simple and thin, usually less than 50 cm wide, which implies that the audiences passing by were small and choreographed in linear arrangements. The rock art on these stages is often obfuscated by topographic barriers, situated along slopes, and tucked in narrow passes atop ridges (e.g., Figures 6.2 and 6.3). Trail petroglyphs are therefore hard to see from any considerable distance; indeed, immediate proximity is required for both noticing the glyphs and comprehending the symbolism.

Each of the seven stage types accommodated a unique audience in terms of size, social composition, and emphasis and investment in rock art ritualism. The topographic structures of the different stages defined the number of people who could have congregated and participated in ritual practices engaging petroglyphs—from individuals along trails to dozens of people atop summits—but it is important to regard these simply as thresholds. Performances on the large, open stages may still have entailed small gatherings, perhaps even solitary practitioners. Even so, and while some of the stages within the mountains' inner stretches are somewhat secluded or difficult to access, none evidence intentional restrictions or obstacles to seeing, reaching, or touching the rock art. In fact, the wide distribution of petroglyphs, as well as their generally open visibility and high densities in certain locations, indicates that most of the rock art was meant to be viewed and tied to a range of other practices and was thus integral to fully experiencing this landscape. These factors underscore the performative nature of Hohokam rock art, as it was crafted, viewed, and (re)interpreted in a multiplicity of contexts, witnessed by variably sized groups, and accompanied by a miscellany of activities. Along with petroglyph density and choreographic structure, audience size and identity attest to different degrees of ritual depth and focus across stages. The rock art frames each stage in a nuanced way, and each stage contextualizes the rock art in a unique manner. The rock art's broad accessibility and relevance to an assortment of other activities suggest that the practices involving its production and consumption crossed social identities, or perhaps even temporarily erased social differences, within Hohokam communities.

Time

Rappaport (1999:169–215) gives considerable weight to the role of time in the structure (or structuring) of ritual. Rituals are not performed as happenstance but rather are culturally regimented into periods and sequences of social importance and religious providence. Ritual timing may be calendrically ordained, for example, by the movements of celestial bodies and turning of the seasons. It may also be socially decreed; an occasion, event, or desire may determine the time and type of ritual to be performed—rituals may indeed be reactions to situations. Pierre Smith (1982) draws a similar distinction between what he defines as "periodic" and "occasional" rituals. Periodic rituals are scheduled by the physical, or "natural," order of the world and cosmos, such as astronomical and biological rhythms. Examples include performances tied to important days of the year (e.g., solstices) and specific times in one's life cycle (e.g., birthdays and puberty). Occasional rituals, on the other hand, are timed according to other events of social or cultural significance that are not necessarily calendrically determined (e.g., war rituals).

Time is a factor in the repetition, redundancy, and framing of ritual practices, and it therefore bears on the performance, encoded tradition, formalism, and invariance of the ritual form (Table 6.1; see also Figure 2.1). With regard to archaeological applications of the ritual model, it behooves us to investigate whether the suspected ritual practices followed a temporal rhythm and, if possible, to ascertain the rhythm's tempo and meter. Our ability to probe the periodicity of past performances is dependent, in large part, on the layers of context that enwrap the materials we study. For example, the timing of a mortuary rite, as we might infer from a careful and deliberate inhumation or cremation burial, is self-evident—the ritual was performed after the individual's death (one hopes). Unfortunately, such signs of the times of ritual performance are often less clear.

Researchers occasionally assume or indirectly allude to the periodicity of rock art production and related ritualism through interpretations of the imagery. For instance, the literature is replete with astronomical explanations for rock art, which either tie rock art to cyclical celestial phenomena (e.g., solar calendars) or record unusual events such as supernovae or solar flares. Some rock art is argued to have been created during puberty rituals, as was done in the recent past (Hays-Gilpin 2004:107–146; Whitley 2006), so this mode of ritualism is understood as following a biological rhythm. Even the shamanistic, or neuropsychological, model explains the production of rock art as a sort of occasional ritual in response to individuals experiencing altered states of consciousness. In lieu of an appropriate ethnographic analogue for the Hohokam, I approach the timing of rock art ritualism in the South Mountains through landscape and archaeological contexts, principally the features of the stages adorned with the petroglyphs.

Activities around spring and spring-hilltop stages were limited largely to practices involving the crafting and viewing of rock art. There is little archaeological evidence for other activities on these stages, and the relatively small amount of artifacts in these places (Table 6.2) further evidences a performative focus on the springs. Consequently, the rock art around these stages was most likely tied to practices concerned directly with the springs, but in a more than economic manner, as discussed previously. These springs are not perennial water sources but are instead precipitation-fed and flow only after rains. For this reason, they are most active during the winter (November–March) and summer (August–October) rainy seasons. The ritual practices involving rock art on these stages were probably timed according to spring flows and therefore followed a seasonal rhythm. The question remains, however, whether the rock art ritualism was salutatory (i.e., gratitude for water) or supplicatory (i.e., prayer for water) in nature.

Summit trails, the saddle shrine, and portions of the bajada are three more types of stages for rock art ritualism. As with the two stage types just considered, the summit trails share an emphasis on springs, and some, if not all, of the attendant ritual practices were likely scheduled by the seasonal periodicity of spring flow as well. Unlike the spring stages, though, summit trails share an important contextual feature with the saddle shrine and bajada stages: the choreographed arrangement of agricultural terraces around the rock art. Several lines of evidence show that the Hohokam grew agave and possibly corn on these terraces and may have also used them to encourage useful native plants (see Chapter 4). The terraces fringe dense clusters of petroglyphs at the summits' feet, implying a symbolic symbiosis among hilltops (the sky), springs (water), farming (sustenance and fertility), and ritual participants who pecked the imagery and ascended the trails.

One of the advantages to farming agave is that, once planted, it requires minimal attention and little investment in watering (Gasser and Kwiatkowski 1991:427), so the attention given to farming and cultivating it in the South Mountains was probably concentrated around the times of initial planting and harvesting. Like rock art ritualism on the spring-oriented stages, though, it remains to be shown whether the production of rock art and other ritual activities on stages featuring farming facilities coincided with the spring-season ripening and harvesting of agave, possibly as a sort of community festival like those among the descendant O'odham (e.g., Lumholtz 1912:92–98; Mason 1920), or during intervals between harvests, perhaps as entreaties for its successful and bountiful maturation. Nonetheless, the timing of some ritual practices involving rock art on these three stages undoubtedly flowed with the seasonally conditioned biological rhythms of agave and possibly other important cultivars.

Ridgetops and saddles, as a sixth type of stage for rock art production and viewing, were also loci of activities concerning the gathering of economically useful flora. This is evidenced by the cleared, level areas in these settings, the presence of expedient stone tools and broken pottery, and the merging of Type II trails, the small footpaths used during short-term, relatively local forays targeting specific resources (see Darling and Eiselt 2009). In these settings artisans tended to position petroglyphs on boulders and outcrops near the stages' midpoints, symbolically central to all other practices carried out there. This suggests that performers and audiences scheduled the making, seeing, and engaging of rock art according to the timing of resource-gathering excursions. It is difficult to determine which plants the artisans sought, but the seasons of flowering and fruiting are the likely periods when saddles and ridgetops staged rock art ritualism.

Wallace (1983) has made a convincing case that the crafting of some rock art in the Tucson Basin occurred during the summertime, when mesquite pods ripen, because petroglyphs cluster around bedrock grindstones used for processing the pods into meal. Petroglyphs on the ridgetop and saddle stages in the South Mountains were probably similarly pecked in concert with the seasonal fruiting of edible or economically useful plants. Associated stone tools exhibit use-wear consistent with cutting, scraping, and chopping soft and fibrous materials, probably the processing of stems, twigs, and branches of various plants. The occasional presence of broken jars, most of which have highly constricted orifices, hints at the gathering of seeds, fruits, and flowers. A dearth of processing facilities, such as grinding slicks and mortars, however, hinders our ability to convincingly deduce which plants were sought and therefore the seasons they were targeted.

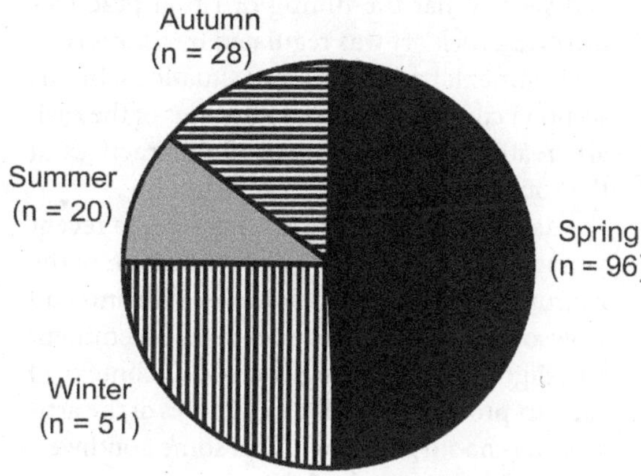

FIGURE 6.18. Ethnographically important flowering and fruiting plants by season of ripening (figure by Will Russell).

Spring is when most of the ethnographically documented important plants in the South Mountains flower and fruit, followed by winter, then autumn, and lastly summer (Figure 6.18; see also Wright 2011:Appendix A). This could indicate that spring was when most plant-gathering excursions, and associated rock art ritualism too, took place. Spring and winter, with cooler temperatures than other times of the year, just so happen to also be the most comfortable seasons for being in and moving around the South Mountains. Useful and edible wild plants bloom and fruit throughout the year, but the two often considered the most important—the saguaro cactus, for its succulent fruits, and the mesquite tree, for its highly nutritious, nutty-flavored legumes—ripen during summer. At present, narrowing down the exact season(s) Hohokam villagers visited saddle and ridgetop stages in pursuit of wild plants and, through associative reasoning, presumably engaged in related rock art ritualism remains challenging without further lines of evidence and additional research. It is quite plausible that each season witnessed the gathering of particular plants that flower and bloom at those times, so people may have created and engaged petroglyphs at various times throughout the year.

The production and consumption of rock art on the seventh stage type, trails, probably flowed with the seasonal fruiting of edible, useful, and desirable plants as well. This is because the petroglyph-adorned paths pass between ridgetops and saddles, bearing clear evidence for plant procurement. However, the relative infrequency of petroglyphs along trails, coupled with (1) their generally isolated nature as usually small, single glyphs on mostly solitary panels away from more heavily visited settings and (2) their seemingly haphazard placement in awkward and inconspicuous places, indicates that they were the least frequently performed and observed mode of rock art ritualism in the mountains. This suggests that their manufacture was more personal, or auto-allocative, than on other stages, perhaps regulated solely by one's interest in marking the land as one passed through it. Indeed, an absence of petroglyph clustering on trails shows that they held the least ritual depth of all stage types, and this may bear on why the ritual practices performed there adhered to less rigid structures and schedules.

Performance

To this point I have described seven types of stage on which Hohokam artisans crafted petroglyphs, contextualized these settings through the types of activities carried out there in addition to rock art ritualism, populated the stages with audiences of various sizes and identities, and shown that the timing of ritual practices involving rock art was regulated by a variety of environmental cues and social situations. In this section I consider the social identities of the rock art creators as performers of ritual practices in the South Mountains.

As touched on briefly in Chapter 1, in recent years shamanism, as a specific invocation of the neuropsychological model (Lewis-Williams and Dowson 1988, 1993), has become a preeminent paradigm for explaining the social context of rock art production and the identities of the artisans. It is no surprise, then, that some Southwest scholarship has invoked shamanism to explain elements of Hohokam rock art (e.g., Bostwick and Krocek 2002; Carpenter 2007; Empie 1999; Hedges 1994b; Loendorf and Loendorf 1995; Schoonover and Virden 1999). Shamanism is certainly an attractive explanation because it is easy to recognize that ancestral rock art is often found in places of religious importance to descendant communities. Moreover, the neuropsychological model's contention that the entoptic forms seen during altered states of consciousness are biologically determined and therefore culturally universal can account for why some geometric and abstract rock art designs akin to entoptic forms or phosphenes occur throughout the world yet manifest unique qualities we might consider local "styles." Ethnographic sources, albeit scant, tend to describe rock art, too, in mystical terms, often as tools, products, or signatures of "medicine men," spirits, dream helpers, and the like (Whitley 2000b). Shamanism is understandably an alluring inference, and it sits well with Americanist archaeology's historically positivistic bent since the underlying theory and patois borrow from scientific disciplines like biology and neurology and therefore bestow an aura of nomotheticism (e.g., Winkelman 2008).

There is little doubt that some rock art in the *longue durée* of human sociality was carved out and painted by shamans, some during altered states of consciousness and some afterward, possibly even as visual records of visionary experiences. It is also true that rock art was often made in shamanistic societies, because shamanism, in the broadest sense, encapsulates a wide range of religious practices and organizational structures of religious knowledge that characterized much of the human past. Nonetheless, when such explanations fail to implicate rock art in historical social processes, our identification, or rather revelation, of shamanism does little more than craft culture histories (see Chapter 2).

Did Hohokam shamans peck the petroglyphs in the South Mountains or elsewhere throughout the Hohokam world? Possibly, but as alluded to in Chapter 1, relying simply on the portrayal of what may be interpreted as phosphenes, or construals thereof, in rock art to prove that it records visions experienced under altered states of consciousness—the predominant manner in which scholars employ the neuropsychological model to rock art and other visual media—is a bit misleading and borderline tautologous. This is because, as the model was originally presented, far too many designs could be interpreted as deriving from phosphenes, or entoptic forms, since these rudimentary shapes (grids, parallel lines, circles, zig-zags, arcs, and branching meanders) are the building blocks of nearly all designs. Compounding the problem is that according to the model, trancers morph these basic forms into increasingly figurative and recognizable shapes and scenes as they transcend into deeper states of altered consciousness. Nearly any visual design, from a dot to Leonardo da Vinci's *Last Supper*, could thus be a construal of phosphenes or entoptic forms.

This inherent fallacy of the neuropsychological model, what Jeremy Dronfield (1996) calls the "ubiquitous-shapes argument," was voiced immediately by several scholars in commentary published alongside the original article by Lewis-Williams and Dowson (1988), and the issue has since become a revolving point of debate. Dronfield (1996) has shown that while certain motifs and design elements may potentially be "diagnostic" of altered states of consciousness based solely on their likeness to "endogenous" imagery seen during altered states of consciousness, those presented in the original model are not. Indeed, Dronfield's research reveals that although the neuropsychological model has potential, the mere presence of entoptic-like designs in visual arts is far from evincive of the designs' derivation from visions seen during trance experiences or other modes of hallucinatory altered states of consciousness. For this reason and others, Lewis-Williams, who popularized the neuropsychological model and its application in rock art research, has since clarified that a shamanic origin for rock art is a credible interpretation only when each of the three trance stages—as gauged by three degrees of contortion to the entoptic forms—are portrayed in the same rock art scene (Lewis-Williams 2001).

Turning to the South Mountains, we find that there is little in the rock art's contexts or imagery to suggest that much, if any, of it was created during altered states of consciousness, or that it records trance-induced visionary experiences. For one, most panels bear fewer than three petroglyphs (Figure 6.5), too few to convincingly show all three stages of entoptic-form contortion as called for by Lewis-Williams's (2001) revision to the neuropsychological model. Originally, Lewis-Williams and Dowson (1988:205–206) considered the presence of all six basic entoptic forms in a culturally delimited rock art assemblage to be strong support for a trance-induced neuropsychological origin of the imagery. While there are potential analogues among the South Mountains petroglyphs for each entoptic form, they are notably rare (Figure 6.19). In fact, based on the very liberal, inclusive tally, glyphs resembling entoptic forms account for just over 25 percent of the South Mountains rock art assemblage, and most are familiar circular designs, symbols ubiquitous in indigenous Southwestern visual arts with no ethnographic basis to suggest that they derive from hallucinatory visions. According to Whitley, "although there is no firm guideline for accepting or rejecting a shamanistic interpretation using this comparative process, generally, the [neuropsychological] model should account for a substantial portion of a rock art corpus, and it should certainly accommodate more than it excludes if the corpus is, in fact, shamanistic in origin" (2011:142). Quantitatively speaking, the number of petroglyphs in the South Mountains bearing gross affinities to entoptic forms falls far short of a "substantial portion" of the assemblage and definitely excludes more than it accommodates. This does not prove that shamans or others undergoing trance experiences did not create any of the rock art, but simply shows that in this case the neuropsychological model fails to support a shamanistic origin for the larger petroglyph corpus and related ritual practices.

Complementing the neuropsychological model, particular themes read into rock art imagery and other media are sometimes taken as evidence for their shamanistic origin (Halifax 1982; VanPool 2009; VanPool and VanPool 2007). These may include depictions of therianthropes (hybridized lifeforms) (e.g., Burkitt 1921; Jolly 2002; Schaafsma 1994; Whitley 2000a; see also VanPool 2003), trance-inducing or hallucinogenic substances such as datura and mushrooms (e.g., Kaplan 1975), and portrayals of shamanic transcendence of the cosmos (e.g., Boyd 1996, 2003). Though datura effigy pots are known, unambiguous portrayals of hallucinogenic plants in Hohokam rock art does not exist in the South Mountains or elsewhere, at least based on published studies. Unequivocal depictions of therianthropes (e.g., Figure 6.20) or scenes of shamanic transcendence are also too infrequent (nonexistent?) in Hohokam rock art to suggest that much of the imagery was made or inspired by shamans. Some pipette petroglyphs (e.g., Figure 6.21), albeit extremely rare (Russell and Wright 2008), look as though anthropomorphic and animalistic characters are moving through or into them (e.g., Figure 6.22), possibly relating narratives of cosmic transcendence along an *axis mundi* (Wright and Russell 2011). Yet if these enigmatic scenes portray transcendence, it remains to be determined whether the figures are shamans since other social actors can transcend the cosmos through, for example, rites of passage (van Gennep 1960), and such religious rituals do not always entail trance experiences or altered states of consciousness.

Landscape settings also point to an other-than-shamanic origin and use for most of the South Mountains petroglyphs. As detailed above, the majority of South Mountains petroglyphs are situated in readily visible and easily accessible

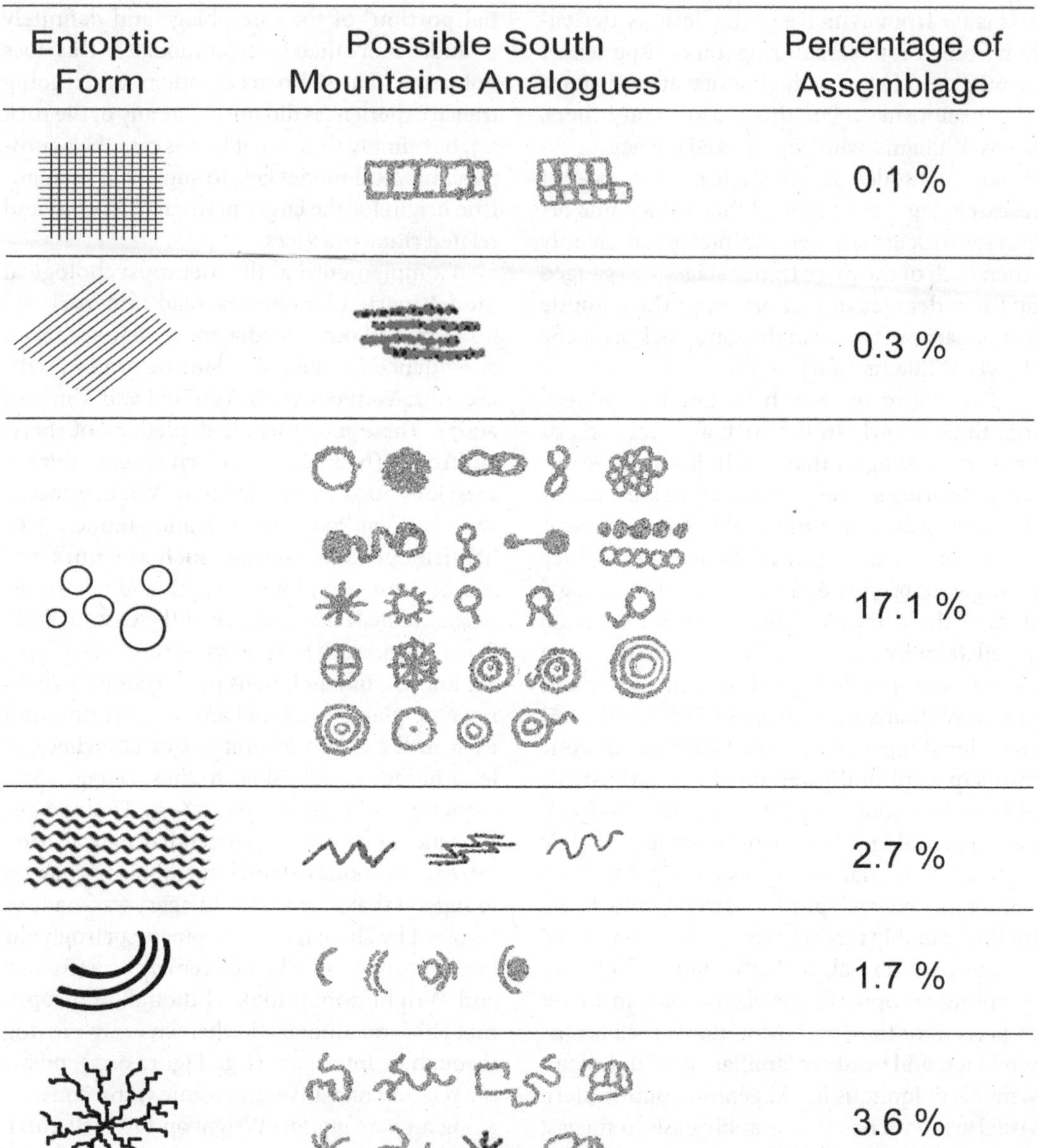

FIGURE 6.19. Entoptic forms and possible South Mountains analogues. The entoptic forms follow Lewis-Williams and Dowson (1988:Figure 1) and are based on research by Siegel (1977).

portions of the mountains, in dense concentrations along the bajada and at the mouths of canyons. Aside from those centered on springs, the choreographic structures of the stages suggest that the rock art was associated with farming and other subsistence-oriented activities that seem far removed from shamanism or trance experiences. Further, very few petroglyphs were placed in alcoves, rockshelters, or caves, hidden and secluded settings often equated with shamanistic rock art traditions in western North America (e.g., Patterson 1998; Sutton 1982; Whitley 1992,

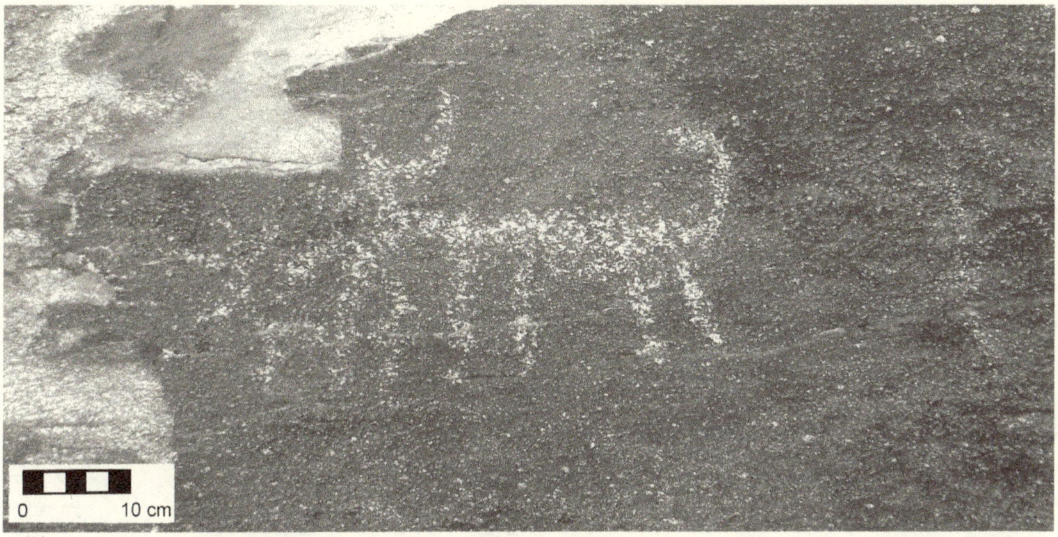

FIGURE 6.20. A pair of superimposed antlered-quadruped petroglyphs. Bostwick and Krocek (2002:Figure 277) interpret this scene as a human (shaman) transforming into a quadruped.

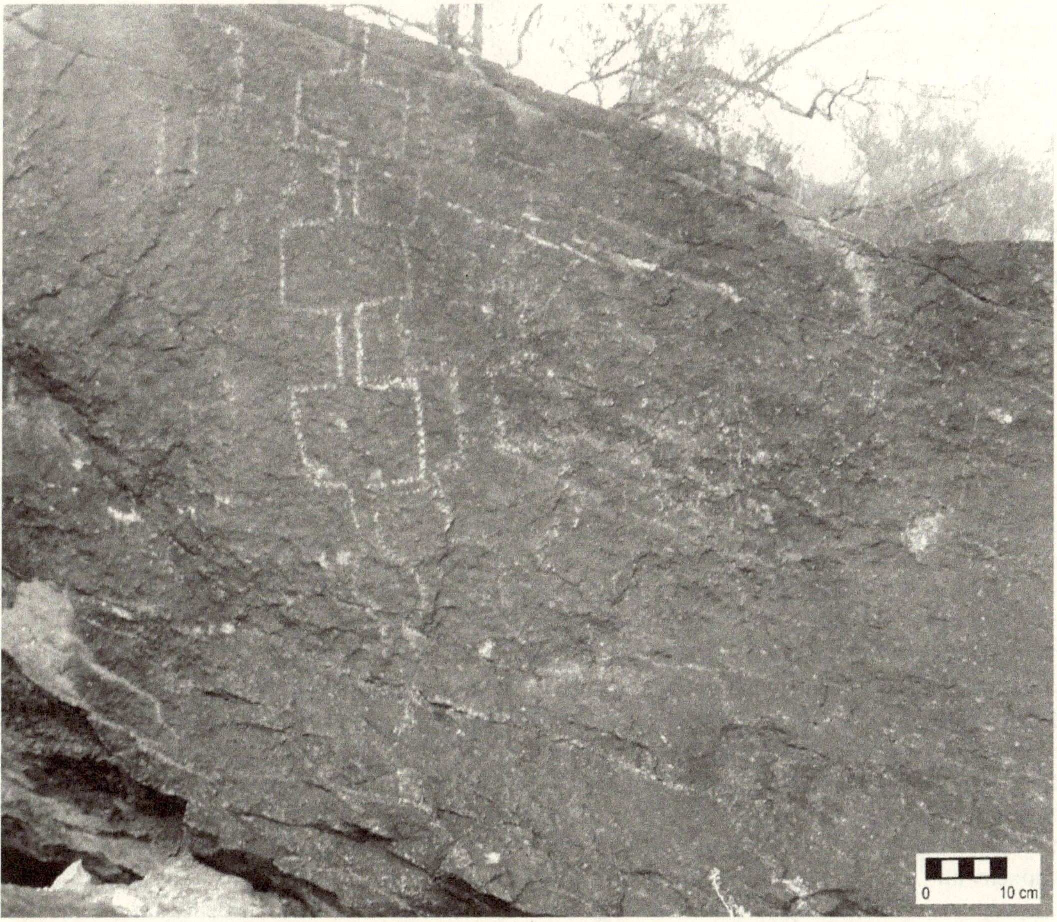

FIGURE 6.21. Panel with three variations of pipette petroglyphs (facing south). *From top left:* a lightly executed one-box example, a moderately executed four-box example with one circular and three rectangular compartments, and a lightly executed three-box example.

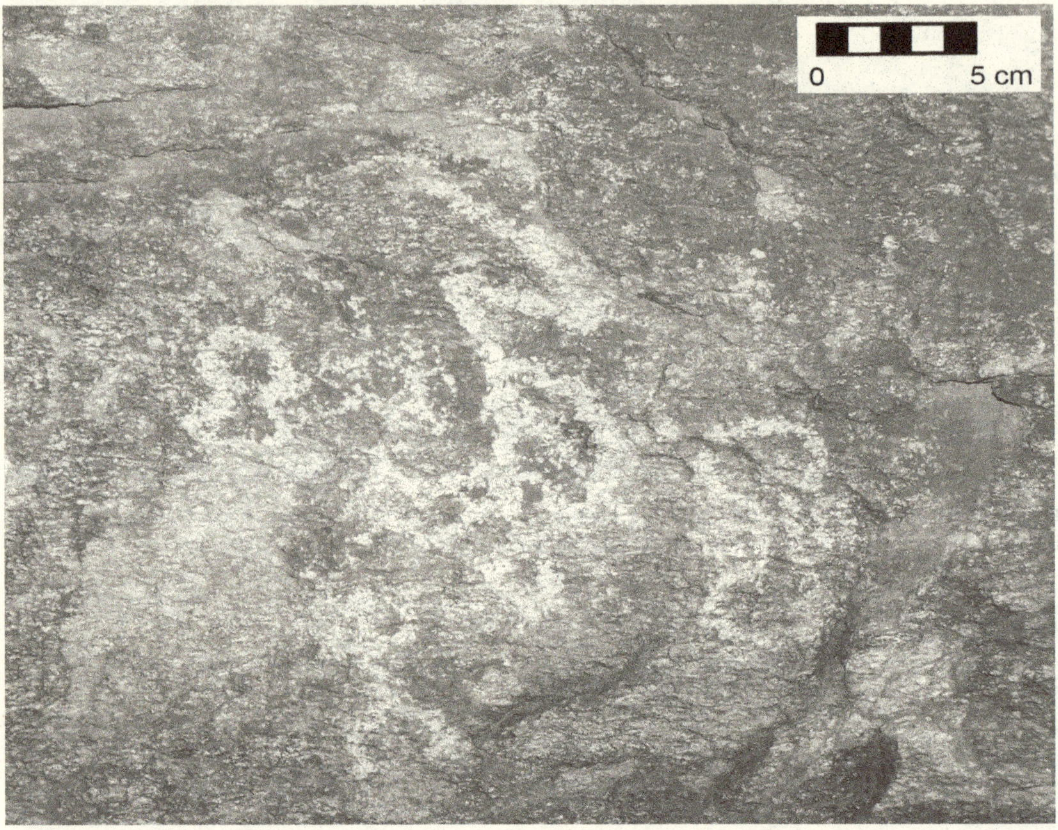

FIGURE 6.22. Panel with two pipettes, an anthropomorph, and a waterbird petroglyph. This panel is adjacent to the entrance of a walled-in rockshelter near a spring, which has Preclassic buffware and plainware eroding out of it.

1994, 2000a; Whitley, Dorn et al. 1999; Whitley, Simon, and Dorn 1999).

Based on the forms and themes portrayed, the relatively participatory, open, and integrative layouts of the stages, and a dearth of ethnographic accounts by descendants of the Hohokam and other agricultural communities in the Southwest that tie rock art to shamans, shamanistic rites, or altered states of consciousness, most, if not all, of the South Mountains petroglyphs cannot be cogently attributed to a shamanistic origin. Shamans or others desiring to record trance experiences and visions may have crafted some of the rock art, but it is clear they were not the only social personae with the capacity and authority to do so. This, however, does not mean the petroglyphs lacked religious import. It shows rather that just as there are variations in stage types and accoutrements, audience sizes and identities, and periodicities of performance, a cast of different social actors was responsible for the network of ritual performances involving South Mountains rock art. If not shamans, who held the religious knowledge and authority to wield it in the ritual practices surrounding rock art?

One way to glean the identities of those responsible for crafting the South Mountains petroglyphs is to consider the ancillary activities carried out on and around the stages. A consideration of the forms and presumed functions of artifacts placed, broken, or dropped around petroglyphs can aid us in this regard. If unique social actors—or people separate, independent, or disjoined from those carrying out other activities such as farming and plant collecting in the surrounding landscape—were the ones engaged in rock art ritualism, it is reasonable to suspect that such distinctions in practice may be evident in the types of artifacts found near and away from the panels. In the previous chapter I compared the types of ceramic wares found vicinal to different petroglyph designs as a way to date the rock art, and contrasted those wares with the aggregate ceramic assemblage from other settings. I take that analysis a step further with the following comparison of ceramic vessel forms and stone tool types the Hohokam left in the environs of the petroglyphs and in other places.

Chapter 4 presents data showing a drastic underrepresentation of bowls in the South Mountains ceramic assemblage compared with village contexts. In villages the ratio of jars to bowls was approximately one to one (Table 4.5), but in the South Mountains it was over six to one (Table 4.3). This dominance of jars is likely due to a more narrow, focused, and logistical set of concerns and tasks undertaken in the mountains, such as the need for carrying water, harvested crops, toolstone, and perhaps minerals between the villages and the mountains' slopes. Along these lines, if the activities surrounding rock art differed from this general taskscape, we could expect a higher ratio of bowls to jars around petroglyphs, perhaps as evidence for ritual practices involving feasting, oblations, or mixing paints. This, however, is not the case; just as there is only negligible difference in the proportions of different ceramic wares proximate to and away from petroglyphs, the types of and ratios among vessel forms are practically the same (Table 5.3; $\chi^2 < 0.00$, df = 1, $p > .90$). As in the other settings, jars, when present, predominate around petroglyph panels, showing that practices near and away from rock art panels utilized similar ceramic wares *and* forms.

In addition to the thousands of ceramic sherds scattered about the mountains, stone artifacts can evidence the types of activities carried out near petroglyphs, presumably in conjunction with the pecking and viewing of petroglyphs. As reviewed in Chapter 4, nearly all the hundreds of stone artifacts are of nonlocal origin, mostly cores and primary flakes of rounded, hard igneous and metamorphic river cobbles brought into the mountains from the nearby villages. The only artifacts of local stone are cores and flakes found at a handful of quarries centered on felsite dikes and rarer instances of minimally worked quartz nodules. Although the Hohokam collected tabular slabs of South Mountains granodiorite and fashioned them into architectural stones and possibly groundstone implements for use in nearby villages (e.g., Bustoz et al. 2009:141), we found no evidence of granodiorite quarrying or groundstone manufacture in the mountains. The granodiorite was not fashioned into flaked stone tools because, unlike the felsite, it does not fracture conchoidally, and it was not used to peck petroglyphs because it is too friable to effectively penetrate and remove desert varnish from other boulders and outcrops.

TABLE 6.5. Counts of Use-Wear Patterns on Stone Artifacts.

Performance	Near Panels	Away from Panels	Total
Percussion	13	48	61
Tool Production	42	143	185
Chopping	3	20	23
Scraping/Planing	21	106	127
Cutting	9	67	76
Pulping	3	18	21
Miscellaneous Grinding	13	50	63
Manuports	6	10	16
Other	2	21	23
Total	112	483	595

Note: Table includes only collected and analyzed artifacts. An arbitrary 10-m buffer was used to distinguish between "near" and "away."

The South Mountains stone artifact assemblage has two unique aspects: (1) there is a very low proportion of debitage, or flake waste, associated with tool production and (2) many of the tools, while expedient and informal, either had multiple purposes or, once brought from the villages to the mountains, were used in different manners. Many of the artifacts exhibit use-wear consistent with distinct and perhaps unrelated activities. Table 6.5 tabulates instances of use-wear on stone artifacts found proximate to and

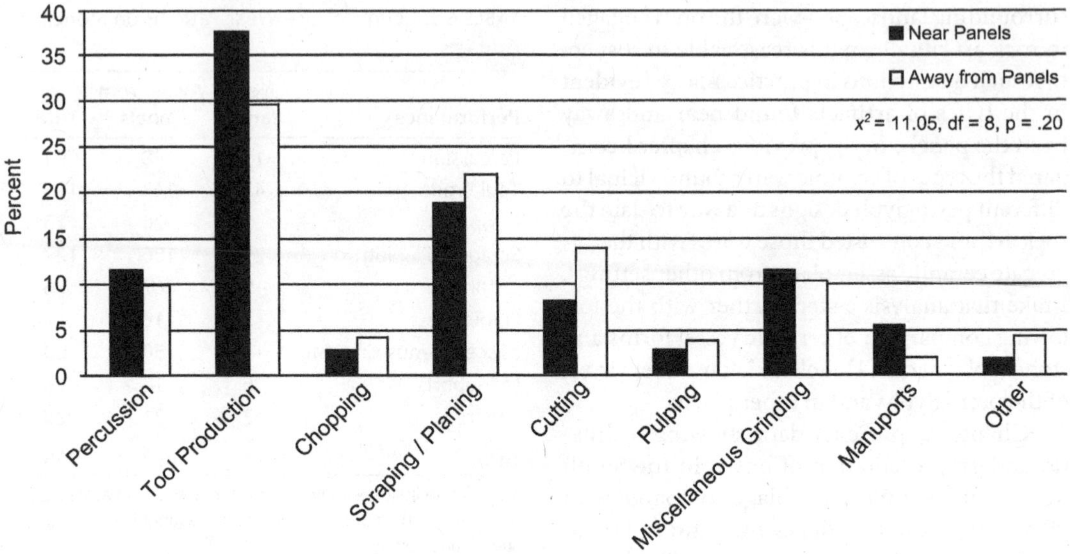

FIGURE 6.23. Use-wear on stone artifacts near and away from petroglyph panels.

away from petroglyph panels. The table reports the number of cases of use-wear (n = 595) on tools collected and analyzed from the project areas (n = 503), not the total number of tools observed. Some tools are therefore included in more than one performance category.

As brought to light in Chapter 4, evidence for flaked tool production and lithic reduction (i.e., cores and debitage) is scant outside the quarry areas, yet Table 6.5 shows a considerable number of artifacts consistent with tool manufacture. Most are cores that were not worked and reduced in the immediate areas where they were found but instead had secondary uses as choppers, pulpers, planers, hammers, and so on. These tools quite likely served as cores in the villages, or elsewhere, and were brought to the mountains to be used for other purposes. What the data in Table 6.5 suggest is that Hohokam villagers brought already-reduced cores to the mountains and employed them in a range of activities, including but not limited to processing crops and wild plants and manufacturing petroglyphs.

Looking at the distribution of stone tools across the landscape, we see only minor discrepancies between the types and proportions of use-wear patterns on tools found around petroglyphs and in other settings (Figure 6.23). Although the proportions of tools bearing indications of percussion, tool production, and grinding are higher around petroglyphs, the differences are too slight to suggest, with a reasonable degree of confidence, that stone tools were used differently around rock art panels than elsewhere in the mountains ($\chi^2 = 11.05$, df = 8, $p = .20$). With the exception of spring stages, which show a paucity of archaeological features aside from petroglyphs, consistency in the types, forms, and presumably functions of stone and ceramic artifacts between areas that bear rock art and those that do not adds support to the notion that most petroglyphs were neither hidden nor sequestered from other pursuits. It also suggests that the rock art and the stages it adorns were not revered to the point that carrying out other, perhaps less ritualized, or "mundane," activities around them was taboo. Instead, the artifact data, along with the choreographic structures of the stages, indicate that rock art was integrated with the experiences of people of various social identities as they engaged in a range of other pursuits in and around the South Mountains. For this reason, the people performing ritual practices involving the crafting and viewing of petroglyphs were probably the same as those farming the nearby terraces, gathering toolstone, seeking and har-

TABLE 6.6. Rates of Hohokam Petroglyph Production by Person and Year.

		Annual Rate of Production		Annual Rate of Production per Person per Year		
	Count	Preclassic Only (500 Years)	Full Spectrum (900 Years)	Low Population Estimate[a] (300 people/village)	High Population Estimate[a] (1,000 people/village)	Comments
Current Project	3,055	6.1/year	3.4/year	0.004–0.007/ person/year	0.001–0.002/ person/year	Nearby villages: Pueblo Viejo, Las Canopas, Los Hornos
Adjusted[b]	3,819	7.6/year	4.2/year	0.005–0.008/ person/year	0.001–0.003/ person/year	
South Mountains	8,000	16.0/year	8.9/year	0.005–0.009/ person/year	0.001–0.003/ person/year	Nearby villages: Villa Buena, Pueblo Viejo, Las Canopas, Los Hornos, Los Guanacos, Las Estufas
Adjusted[b]	10,000	20.0/year	11.1/year	0.006–0.011/ person/year	0.002–0.003/ person/year	

[a] Rough estimates based on demographic work at Grewe/Casa Grande by Craig (2004).
[b] A 125 percent adjustment to account for eroded, damaged, and stolen panels (see Golio and Snyder 1993; Hedges 1994a).

vesting wild plants, and walking the webbed trails woven throughout the landscape.

In all, an assortment of contextual factors and artifact data argue that rock art ritualism in the South Mountains was (1) performed on an array of different stage types; (2) performed by people, other than shamans or similar figures experiencing altered states of consciousness, from nearby villages; (3) witnessed by variably sized audiences with sundry social identities; and (4) probably scheduled and cued to the timing of both environmental and social factors. The actual production of rock art, however, was far from a common, daily practice; whereas this study concerns more than 3,000 petroglyphs from the northeastern slopes, and we know, based on Bostwick and Krocek's (2002) work, that more than 7,000 exist in the South Mountains landscape, such large numbers are, in fact, far too few to indicate that many people were making petroglyphs at any point in time. To better understand the identities of the producers, we should scale the frequency of petroglyph manufacture to the populations of the communities responsible for it. There are three factors to weigh in this regard: the number of people in a specified region who could have crafted the rock art; the number of petroglyphs in that same region; and the time elapsed between the oldest and youngest rock art (Wallace 2008:226). With such data we can estimate the number of petroglyphs made as well as the rate of their production for a given period of time.

Table 6.6 provides a rudimentary model for the rates of Hohokam petroglyph production in the South Mountains. This model considers and contrasts two production spans, one limited to the Preclassic era only (Snaketown through middle Sacaton, ~500 years), when it appears most of the petroglyphs were made (see Chapter 5), and the other inclusive of the full historical spectrum of Hohokam residence in the lower Salt River valley (Snaketown through Civano, ~900 years). It also takes into account the sizes of adjacent villages, whose residents were likely the people engaged in petroglyph-related activities in the South Mountains (Chapter 4), by scaling momentary population at both low (~300 people/village) and high (~1,000 people/village) estimates. The table models production rates for the current project areas in the northeast stretch of the mountains as well as for the entire South Mountains landscape, based on an estimate of 8,000 petroglyphs. There are obviously many caveats not considered here: for example, production rates were not uniform among artisans, community size fluctuated through time and varied between villages, and on occasion people probably produced more than one petroglyph, all of which would influence the estimated production rate to some degree. While imperfect and far from exact, the model offers a baseline for thinking about, in gross quantitative terms, how often Hohokam villagers engaged in ritual practices that entailed crafting petroglyphs.

The data presented in Table 6.6 yield estimated production rates of approximately 3 to 6 petroglyphs per year in this study's project areas, depending on whether we rely on the Preclassic-only or full-spectrum version of the reconstruction. This calculation is curiously close to Wallace's (2008:227) estimate for Archaic petroglyphs in the Picacho Mountains of southern Arizona and Whitley's (1982:280–284) for the Coso Range in eastern California. If we scale these figures to momentary population estimates, the model suggests that in the areas reported on in this book, somewhere between 1 and 7 petroglyphs, or 1 and 8 if we adjust the tally for probably defaced/stolen/eroded/undiscovered examples, were pecked each year for every 1,000 potential artisans from nearby villages. With regard to the larger South Mountains landscape, the estimated rate of production was similarly between 1 and 9 glyphs, or 2 and 11 when adjusted for missing cases, per 1,000 villagers annually. Clearly, any way we do the math—low vs. high village population levels, 500- vs. 900-year production spans, or project areas vs. the entire mountain range—few Hohokam villagers ever added to the South Mountains rock art corpus, and those instances in which they did were seemingly few and far between. This is possibly one reason anthropologists in the American Southwest and elsewhere have historically had difficulty gleaning from informants consistent interpretations of the imagery and determining who exactly crafted the rock art (Wallace 2008:227–228; see also Whitley 2000b).

The estimates in Table 6.6 seem too low to even suggest that rock art production ever amounted to a significant cultural practice among the Hohokam. However, if we consider how many people were actually visiting and traipsing across the South Mountains in any given year, the rate comes closer to what we might consider uncommon but frequent enough that rock art cannot be easily dismissed as social minutiae, religiously irrelevant, or culturally frivolous. Fragments of at least 1,000 broken pottery vessels are sprinkled across the same areas where Hohokam artisans pecked 3,055 petroglyphs (Table 4.3). This scales the estimated production rate to about three petroglyphs for each broken pot. If, for instance, someone dropped and broke a pot once every three times he or she trudged up and into the mountains, we can approximate, at least quantitatively, that that individual accounts for one petroglyph on each of his or her visits. What we are dealing with, then, is a long history of relatively light though tactically arranged and symbolically important jaunts and sojourns to the South Mountains, attested to by the spatially clustered nature of a relatively small number of redundant artifact and feature types in a repetitive series of settings. A production rate implying that a handful of glyphs were made by a few individuals in any given year compares favorably with this murmurous rhythm and slow tempo of landscape engagement.

Another roundabout way to reveal the identities of petroglyph producers is to consider the technologies employed in crafting the rock art. Hohokam artisans combined three execution techniques into seven technological styles of petroglyph manufacture: pecking, scratching, abrading, pecking-abrading, pecking-scratching, abrading-scratching, and pecking-abrading-scratching (Figure 6.24). Certain techniques were undoubtedly more efficient or effective at removing patinas than others, which may have weighed on the artisan's choice of technique. These data nonetheless illustrate variance and personal choice in the performance of petroglyph manufacture, though it is obvious that direct percussion pecking was the preferred mode of craftsmanship. Such prevalence of a single technological style over a range of suitable

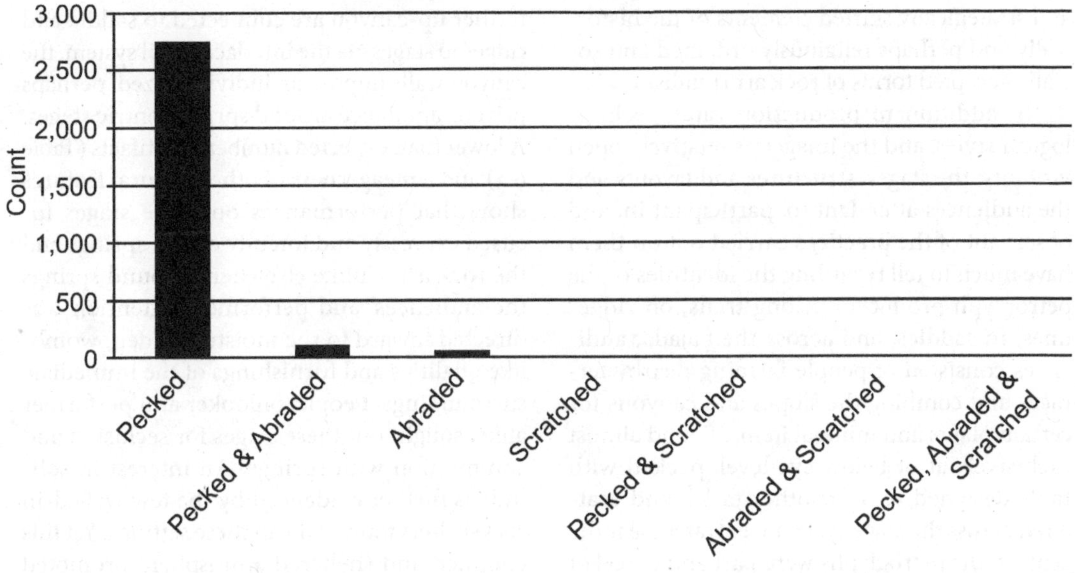

FIGURE 6.24. Execution techniques of South Mountains petroglyphs.

though perhaps less effective techniques could imply that few people ever made petroglyphs, as suggested above, and that they continued to use their preferred technique, and possibly tools as well (see Chapter 4), time after time.

It may be that the rhythmic sounds and echoes from hammering the rocks, as opposed to scratching or abrading, were integral to the ritual practice of making petroglyphs (Ouzman 2001; Rainbird 2002; Whiting 2008). Alternatively, from a more materialistic perspective, pecking may have simply been the most efficient and therefore favored means of creating a permanent petroglyph. If abraded and scratched petroglyphs were "trial and error" efforts, since they are seemingly the least effective and most time-consuming techniques for leaving a lasting visual impression on the rocks, such rare instances (Figure 6.24) show that there was not much of a learning curve to executing Hohokam petroglyphs. Since many performances concerning rock art were open, accessible, and seemingly public and social events, it is very possible that artisans learned their technique through either observation or participation in the performance (Wright and Bostwick 2009). Such learning, whether from examining the petroglyphs or actually watching and/or assisting others make them, corroborates that pecking, as the choice technological style, was actually part of the encoded tradition of petroglyph ritualism.

The strong tendency toward formalism in petroglyph craftsmanship is a prime example of the ritualization process in action. Hammering out a petroglyph is no easy task; it requires the appropriate stone implements, which must have been lugged several kilometers from the villages, a search for a suitable canvas, and at least 15 minutes of constant, concentrated, careful hammering to craft a small, average-sized glyph. By and large, instances of petroglyph manufacture were conscious, planned, vigorous, and sensory-rich exertions of one's body and mind. That the vast majority of petroglyphs in the South Mountains are products of a single technological style, pecking, shows that artisans followed a particular mode of craftsmanship across stages, actors, and generations, that is, they maintained formalism in performance. Provided that the adherence to form was cognizant and intentional, attested to by the necessary focus and preparation, it also underscores the invariance of the ritual form, the consciousness and discipline entailed in obeying liturgical rules and ritual forms. Petroglyphs that depart from this normative mode of production were instances in which the performance called for innovation or deviation, performers lacked requisite ritual competence, or actors knowingly and strategically skirted elements of the historically and perhaps religiously ordained and socially accepted forms of rock art ritualism.

In addition to production rates, technological styles, and the imagery's relatively open visibility, the stages' structures and layouts and the audiences attendant to, participant in, and observant of the practices carried out on them have much to tell regarding the identities of the petroglyph producers. Along trails, on ridgelines, in saddles, and across the bajada, audiences consisted of people farming nearby terraces and combing the slopes and canyons for certain plants and mineral items. Found almost exclusively at or below eye level, pecked with tools designed also for other tasks, and scattered across the stages yet concentrated near the centers, the petroglyphs were part and parcel of the audiences' other routines. Indeed, on these stages the audiences and performers were probably one and the same.

A scenario in which petroglyph artisans shared social identities with an audience of farmers, plant collectors, and daytrippers to the South Mountains likely carried over to the summit trails and saddle shrine because these elevated stages are spatially bound and symbolically enlined with agricultural works at their feet. As specialized architectural features, however, the footpaths and pseudo-causeways stretching between the fields and the summits betray a greater degree of formalism on these stages than elsewhere. The ritual performances and processions played out on natural daises, at heights above and apart from activities around them. This elevated distinction may have translated to the personae engaged in rock art ritualism as they rose above their surroundings and peers by ascending the summits during performances. Such heightened states of being and status were nevertheless temporary and fleeting because the performers ultimately descended the summits and found themselves back again among the masses.

Audiences and performers on spring and spring-hilltop stages differed from all the others in several significant respects. While several are nestled in canyon mouths between agricultural works along the bajadas, and others located farther up-canyon are connected to saddle and ridgetop stages via the interlaced trail system, the canyon walls impose an individualized, perhaps private, ambiance around spring-centric stages. A lower than expected number of artifacts (Table 6.2) and a meagerness of other cultural features show that performances on these stages focused expressly and intently on the springs and the rock art. Unlike elsewhere, around springs the audiences' and performers' attention was directed inward to the moisture-laden, womblike qualities and furnishings of the immediate surroundings. People, onlooker and performer alike, sought out these stages for seclusion and communion with springs. An interest in solitude is further evidenced by the few walled-in rockshelters found only in these settings. Yet this confined and sheltered atmosphere promoted intimacy over secrecy and restriction because the stages are quite accessible, the petroglyphs are prominent and inviting, and the imagery is highly figurative and seemingly intelligible. Audiences, which must have been relatively small at any one time, and performers were corporeally acquainted, sensually synchronized, and symbolically kindred during performances in these introspective settings.

The spring-oriented stages' uniqueness implies that the attendant ritual practices and the identities of both witnesses and participants were more focused and distinctive relative to those at other stages. If shamans, or others engaged in transcendental practices or experiencing altered states of consciousness, favored any of the South Mountains stages, it would probably have been these more secluded and religiously charged settings. However, since these places are nestled in and around other, less focused stages, some in very close proximity with nothing more than canyon walls serving as barriers, they were not cordoned off from the eyes, ears, and reach of nonperformers engaged in other pursuits. Moreover, the rock art around springs is just as figurative, noticeable, and "complete," that is, similarly sized and thoroughly pecked, as that on other stages, with the one key difference being considerably greater density around springs than elsewhere (Figures 4.4 and 4.5). For these reasons, performers and audiences on spring stages, whether shamans or not, shared elements of social identity with individuals offstage. For people engaged in rock art ritualism around springs, it was a temporary respite from the routine toils of farming the surrounding landscape and the daily travails of village life.

While it appears that many of the crafters of the South Mountains petroglyphs were what we may consider common, everyday people, we should not forget the social institutions to which they possibly belonged but of which we have limited knowledge, and how such identities may be inscribed in the choice and placement of certain motifs. Pueblo peoples of the Four Corners region, for instance, organize themselves into exogamous matrilineal descent groups of clans and phratries with totemic names and referential symbols (Eggan 1950; Stephen 1936; Titiev 1944). The Akimel O'odham follow a less complex, more loosely structured, and poorly understood (to anthropologists, that is) totemic clan-based system of social organization composed of what Frank Russell (1908) labeled sibs. It is well known that some late precontact and protohistoric rock art around the Hopi Mesas are proto-Hopi clan symbols placed at important stations along pilgrimage routes (Bernardini 2005, 2009; Colton and Colton 1931). Since both the Hopi and O'odham have ancestral ties to the Hohokam (Teague 1993), perhaps the Hohokam organized themselves into similar clans and phratries and encoded those identities through petroglyph symbolism in the South Mountains. While possible, any such clan symbolism is not distinct in style or form from the broad suite of motifs found throughout the northern Sonoran Desert nor do the motifs pattern in clusters of related clans and phratries as they do at proto-Hopi sites such as Tutuveni (Russell and Wright 2009). Indeed, the presence and nature of clans or a similar mode of descent group identity and social organization among the Hohokam remains a nagging enigma in Southwestern archaeology.

Indigenous Southwest peoples also organize themselves into ceremonial societies, such as religious sodalities, priesthoods, and moieties, which along with the totemic descent groups diffuse power, integrate communities, facilitate migrations, and define personhood. This mode of social organization has considerable antiquity, dating back several centuries, perhaps even millennia. Ancestral Pueblo people, for example, may have formulated sodalities to organize their communities and the ritual calendar as far back as the founding of Chaco's earliest villages, if not earlier (Ware 2002; Ware and Blinman 2000). Based on the layout of Snaketown and notable dualisms in ritual materials, such as architecture (mound vs. ballcourt), colors (red vs. blue/aqua), and iconography (bird vs. reptile/amphibian), Wilcox has suggested that the Hohokam formed ceremonial societies, possibly a moiety, at least by the Sedentary period and probably earlier (Wilcox et al. 1981, 2008). In a similar vein, Wallace's (2014; Wallace and Lindeman 2003, 2012, 2013) notion of a Hohokam Revitalization Movement at the onset of the Colonial period premises that ritual authority within and among villages was linked together through a religious sodality, what he refers to as a Ballcourt Society. And over the years, Hohokam research has witnessed countless anecdotal claims that certain conspicuous or esoteric grave accompaniments or mortuary offerings, such as shell pendants, bracelets, and trumpets, and censers, palettes, hairpins, and wands, were badges of office or insignia of membership in religious societies.

As with talismans, medallions, and tokens, certain iconographic symbols in rock art may have been emblems of identity tied to particular sodalities, but without an appropriate ethnographic parallel from communities that share history with the Hohokam (such as the Hopi clan symbols), how are we ever to allot a sense of surety to such speculation? Too little theorizing and research has been directed toward whether certain symbols or motifs in Hohokam iconography reference either clan or sodality membership. One way to approach this would be to examine if and how potential symbolic markers are patterned along preexisting social divisions within and among communities at differing scales of inclusiveness, such as between canal systems, villages, house clusters, houses,

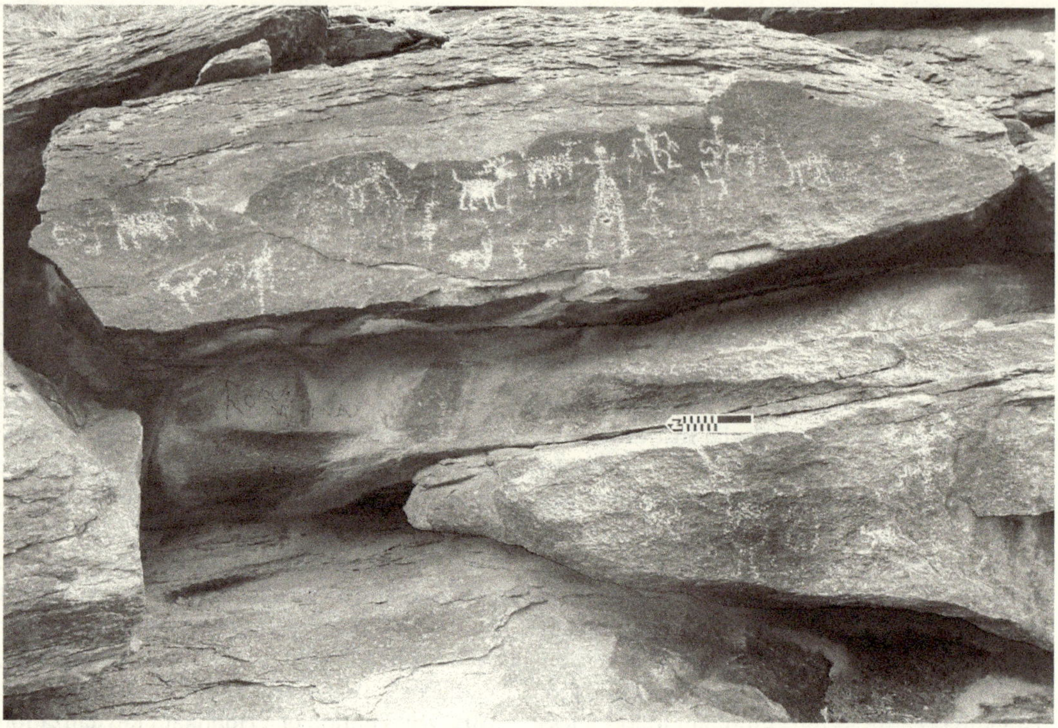

FIGURE 6.25. Panel with a feminine-themed scene of petroglyphs above a spring (see Russell et al. 2009). The hole at the center, straddled by an anthropomorph, is a natural vug with a reddish, iron-rich film streaking out of it.

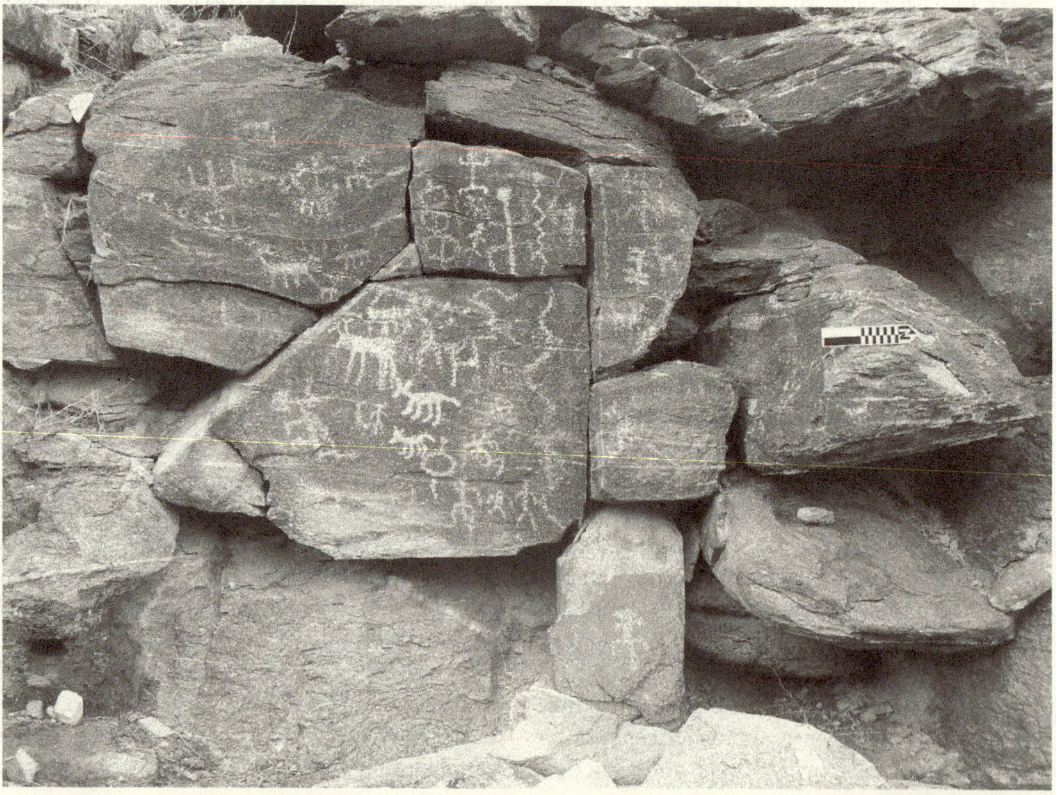

FIGURE 6.26. Panel with a potentially masculine-themed scene of petroglyphs above a spring (see Russell et al. 2009). This set of panels is counterpoised by the feminine-themed scene on the east side of the spring (see Figure 6.25).

cemeteries, and graves. And while recent research has taken this on (e.g., Czarzasty and Rice 2009), the breadth of the question is so large and the project areas and datasets we usually study so narrow that such worthwhile efforts have so far offered only cursory and unsurprisingly inconclusive results. It is infamously difficult to reconcile modes of social organization with traditional archaeological methods and classification schemes, and without ethnographic insights or clearer lines of archaeological evidence from villages tying particular symbols to certain institutions of social organization, assertions that any of the South Mountains petroglyphs are similar icons of identity or membership remain conjectural and potentially off-target about how the Hohokam organized themselves within and outside their communities.

Though there is at present no indication that any of the South Mountains petroglyphs were markers of membership in religious societies or descent groups, if particular motifs cluster together on stages or along trails it could intimate that they reference some sort of social group's presence, management, or authority over places. My preliminary explorations into spatial patterning in South Mountains rock art, however, showed that for the most part different motif types do not cluster on any particular stage or among different stage types, nor are they neatly enlined on panels like the proto-Hopi clan symbols along pilgrimage routes. There is nonetheless some potential dualism apparent in the structure of South Mountains petroglyphs. For instance, on one spring stage the rock art seems to be split between what has been interpreted as feminine-themed motifs on an eastern panel (Figure 6.25) and masculine-themed motifs on a western series of integrated panels above the spring (Figure 6.26), so Hohokam gender divisions and unions may have been written into the landscape (Russell et al. 2009; see also Hernbrode and Boyle 2013). With regard to sodalities, some stages, especially the spring-oriented examples, the summit trails, and the saddle shrine, have not one but two dense clusters of petroglyphs (Figures 4.4–4.6), a spatial division that may reference a duality in Hohokam social organization, religious authority, and ritual practice, that is, a moiety structure that organized the ritual network and its calendar.[5] Such interpretations remain hypothetical, however, and further well-designed and thoroughly theorized structural analyses are clearly in order and might have much to reveal pertaining to the identities of the rock art artisans.

As summarized above, the crafters of much of the South Mountains rock art were also the audiences. Indeed, in rock art ritualism the performer and the engaged audience constituted a congregation—"the defining relationship of the members of a congregation to the event at which they are present is *participation*" (Rappaport 1999:39; emphasis in original). Multiple lines of indirect evidence suggest that these congregations were farmers, sojourners, and the like from nearby villages who came to the mountains for a number of reasons, one of which happened to be rock art–related ritual practices. Indirect evidence has its limits, so more specific aspects of the crafters' identities, such as age, gender, and status, remain cloudy. The point here, though, is that there were multiple petroglyph makers with different social identities within Hohokam communities whose performances were scheduled in unique ways, attended by different audiences of various sizes, and carried out across a multiplicity of stages. Considerable diversity in stages and audiences reveals that since multiple social actors were responsible for the petroglyphs, allied ritual practices were not necessarily restricted to specific personae such as shamans but were instead connected to the social situations and relations in which people aligned themselves. Below I approach this apparent fluidity of ritual practice and availability of religious knowledge through the symbolism engraved in Hohokam rock art.

Symbolism

Symbols are a manifest feature of ritual practice for the mere fact that rituals are, in and of themselves, symbolic acts. Indeed, the religious principles enacted and embodied through rituals make up a system of symbols for the natural order. For our purposes, symbolic communication is an aspect of ritual action that betokens the performance, formalism, and occult efficacy features of the ritual form (Table 6.1). This is because one's performance, at minimum, strategically communicates one's presence and position in relation to others through religious canons. Some modes of symbolic discourse, such as verbal language and choreographed movements, leave little for archaeologists to find and (re) interpret after the act. Iconographic symbols, especially those with a sacral aura, nevertheless offer us a way to approach unpacking past ritual practices.

With rock art, symbolism is a self-evident feature of the ritual form, but it is worthwhile to explore the nature of such symbolism to better understand qualities of the ritual performance. The types of symbols employed, and the meshing of symbols from different media, add depth to our acumen of ancient ritual practice. In this book I place emphasis on the production of and engagement with symbols instead of the information they referenced and conveyed. This is intentional because, as brought out in Chapters 1 and 2, the time is ripe—arguably overdue—to push the "archaeology of symbols" (Robb 1998) beyond the structuralist and symbolist realms of interpretation and thick description and engender people with the strategies and situations with which they opted to create and wield symbols. Setting symbolic meanings and citations aside for the time being, the qualities, features, and contextual textures of the media and iconography allow us to understand those situations where people found the employment of symbols useful or necessary. Here I compare the South Mountains petroglyph assemblage to the iconography found on Hohokam pottery. While shedding added light on the petroglyph producers' identities, it also spotlights dissimilarities between the iconography which, I suggest, expose the sacral nature of some of the rock art. A much-needed examination of iconography across media, however, is not currently possible since there are few published tabulations of designs on pottery or other visual arts. The following is consequently brief and asks more than it answers, yet the insights are nonetheless revelatory.

In Chapter 5 I relied on the presence of certain temporally diagnostic motifs on pottery as a chronological proxy for similar designs in rock art. That analysis intimated that motif frequencies are quite different between media (Table 5.1), but this schism in Hohokam visual arts has long been realized. In fact, Turney (1929) saw little commonality between designs in petroglyphs and on ancient pottery in the lower Salt River valley and therefore argued that each was the work of a different cultural group. Many points of accordance between the two media have since come to light, some too compelling to consider dubious. These include triangle-bodied waterbirds (Bostwick 1998), canids with upturned and curled tails, and humans with hourglass torsos (Bostwick 1999), to name just a few. Some of these, such as hourglass figures (e.g., Jernigan 1992), were not proprietary to the Hohokam, but their portrayal as petroglyphs around Hohokam villages and in the design fields on red-on-buff pottery of the Colonial and Sedentary periods betrays a cultural and chronological affinity between media. One thing to keep in mind when considering cross-media design comparisons is that quality of design execution is conditioned in large part by the materials used in each medium. Pecking an image into a granitic boulder with a large, heavy hammerstone will not yield the detail and intricacy afforded by brush strokes on a pot, so we should expect differences in quality and perhaps even an absence of certain stylistic nuances in the more cumbersome petroglyphs.[6]

The chronologically sensitive motifs depicted in both media are reviewed in Chapter 5, but the body of shared symbols is far more inclusive. Wallace (2001, 2004) has provided tallies of red-on-buff motifs, but unfortunately those reports include counts only of the temporally diagnostic motifs and he subsumed most of the figurative designs under a general category of lifeforms. Although of great utility for chronological studies, at present those tallies are of little help for quantitatively contrasting iconography between media, so I turn to earlier and less comprehensive motif inventories. Years ago, Haury (1976:Figures 12.73, 12.86, 12.87, and 12.99) published a tabulation of pottery motifs from

TABLE 6.7. Lifeforms on Preclassic Hohokam Pottery and in South Mountains Petroglyphs.

Lifeforms	Snaketown Sherds[a]	Whole Buffware Vessels[b]	South Mountains	Total
Birds	385	72	13	470
Reptiles	341	24	169	534
Humans	308	12	542	862
Quadrupeds	146	22	445	613
Other Lifeforms	69	6	41	116
Total	1,249	136	1,210	2,595

[a] Data from Haury (1976:Tables 12.73, 12.86, and 12.87).
[b] Data from Smith (2000:Tables 1 and 5) on whole vessels from Snaketown, Grewe, and the Gila Bend region.

Snaketown, though we should exercise caution when considering his counts for geometric designs because the typology and tabulations were "representative, though not exhaustive, of this aspect of Hohokam painting" (Haury 1976:245). More recently, Alexa Smith (2000) published data on the frequencies of different lifeforms on a small sample of whole Preclassic buffware vessels from Snaketown, Grewe, and the Gila Bend region, which complements Haury's work by providing a broader representation of pottery designs from multiple communities.[7] Although limited to lifeforms, Smith's and Haury's pottery design data coupled with the South Mountains petroglyphs present the first opportunity since Turney's efforts nearly a century ago to quantitatively compare Hohokam iconography between ceramic and parietal stone media.

Table 6.7 lists count data pertaining to five types of lifeform as depicted on Preclassic pottery, tabulated from samples of both sherds (Haury 1976) and whole vessels (Smith 2000), and in South Mountains rock art. What we notice first, as Figure 6.27 shows well, are the statistically significant differences in the ratios of lifeforms between Haury's and Smith's pottery motif tabulations ($\chi^2 = 38.15$, df = 4, $p < .000$, $V^2 = 0.03$). There are a number of sampling factors that are probably driving this, including Smith's broader representation of vessels from villages across the Hohokam world, disparate depositional contexts, and as Cramer's measure of association (V^2) suggests, differences in sample size.[8] Regardless of the discrepancies between the two pottery samples, the ratios of lifeforms in the South Mountains petroglyph assemblage differ significantly from those on pottery ($\chi^2 = 724.28$, df = 8, $p < .000$, $V^2 = 0.14$); birds predominate on pottery whereas anthropomorphs and quadrupeds superabound in rock art (Figure 6.27). Likewise, some lifeform motifs found on pottery were rarely depicted in rock art, if at all. Fish, for example, make up just over 1.5 percent of the lifeform motifs on pottery sherds from Snaketown (Haury 1976) and 1.5 percent of those on whole vessels in Smith's (2000) sample, but there have yet to be any reports of fish motifs in Hohokam rock art.[9] With the exception of a single example at Quail Point along the lower Gila River (Hedges and Hamann 1995)—which could easily be attributed to a Patayan cultural tradition—quail, too, are absent from Hohokam rock art iconography, yet they make up 10.3 and 12.1 percent of Smith's (2000) and Haury's (1976) red-on-buff lifeform tallies, respectively. Rabbits, as a final example, are lacking from the lexicons of both pottery iconography and rock art, presenting a curious symbolic co-absence from Hohokam visual art at large.

It is not as though rabbits, quail, and fish were unknown or of little importance to the Hohokam. These common animals populated fields and perennial rivers such as the Salt and Gila and were, in fact, popular food sources for ancient communities throughout the Phoenix Basin. At the large village of Pueblo Grande, for instance, faunal refuse was composed of 34 percent rabbits and 27.5 percent fish (James 1994b:Table 7.2).

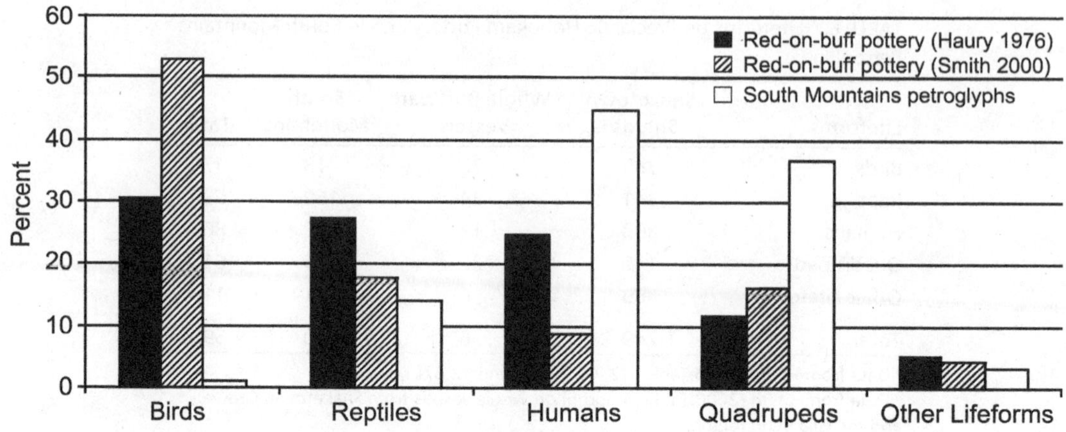

FIGURE 6.27. Ratios between lifeform motifs on Preclassic buffware pottery and in South Mountains rock art.

Of lesser note, quail bones constituted just one-third of one percent of the Pueblo Grande faunal assemblage and have been recovered in similarly low frequencies from many other villages, so while uncommon they were nevertheless a ubiquitous food source across much of the Hohokam world (Dean 2003). Could it be that the Hohokam held some sort of taboo regarding which animals to depict, call on, or reference through rock art, or does this relate in some other way to how they conceptualized and valued such everyday creatures? Speculation aside, that Hohokam artisans simply replicated in their arts what they saw from their everyday experiences cannot explain the selective employment of symbols in different media. There was clearly something social and meaningful going on.

The simple cross-media analysis of design motifs above raises three important points to consider regarding symbolism in Hohokam visual arts: (1) Hohokam artisans depicted considerably more lifeforms in rock art than on Preclassic decorated pottery (46.0 percent of motifs in rock art versus 1.1 percent on decorated pottery; see Table 5.1); (2) the ratios of the types of lifeforms they portrayed in each media differ significantly; and (3) artisans seemingly favored or restricted certain motifs, both figurative lifeforms and abstract geometrics, for specific media. This simple contrast goes to show that there were strong, centuries-long social customs and religious mores pertaining to the appropriate modes, contexts, and situations for symbolic expression and communication which Hohokam artisans abided by and in so doing perpetuated. We can couch the disjunctive iconography among Hohokam visual arts in structural terms. Through ethnological research, Warren DeBoer (1991) developed a useful distinction between "pervasive" and "partitive" systems of decorative organization, which offers a valuable way to think about symbolism archaeologically. Pervasive systems are those in which design structures and iconography cross media. Such modes of organization are more fluid and open to transformation in toto because innovations in one art medium trigger or follow change in others. Partitive systems, on the other hand, lack organizational integration and may even support and encourage different styles, structures, and lexicons among media. In partitive systems, design evolution in one medium is more likely to occur independent from and irrespective of the conservatism of others. Like many things cultural, most decorative systems fall along a continuum of organizational integration and structural cohesion between fully partitive and pervasive archetypes.

At the heart of decorative systems lie the social underpinnings—the institutions and relational webs in which agents maneuver—that influence which styles and symbols people depict and how they organize them. People may conceptualize or value media differently, which could differentially guide the type and arrangement of iconography they use, the flexibility of the overall design structure, and the rate, direction, and acceptance of innovation in each medium and at different points in time (e.g., Kohler et al. 2004). Indeed, the effects of such social processes on art and craft have long been observed among indigenous Southwest communities (e.g., Bunzel 1929). Partitions in Southwest visual arts include distinctions in styles and iconography between genders (e.g., Hays 1992; Hays-Gilpin 2004:102–105) and between religious and domestic contexts of production and use (e.g., Bunzel 1929:84–85; Hays-Gilpin 2000:95). In this way, decorative organization follows both personal and institutional pathways. Personal organization entertains issues of identity, choice, and social position whereas institutional organization pertains to structural conditions, hegemonies, and opportunities relevant to the use of symbolism within a community. Accordingly, archaeological styles, designs, and other aspects of symbolism evidence the knowledgeability, choices, and actions of bygone individuals (agency), their histories, relationships, and social situations in which they opted to use symbolism (structure), and whether those choices ultimately transformed the overall decorative organization within and across media (power) (e.g., Hegmon and Kulow 2005; Van Keuren 2012).

The extent of design pervasion in Hohokam visual arts offers glimpses of the artisans' identities and, simultaneously, the structural conditions bearing on their choices. The Preclassic Hohokam school of design resides somewhere along the continuum between pervasive and partitive systems of organization because while there was considerable intermedium sharing of iconography, ceramic designs and rock art are far from mirror reflections of each other. As the cursory analysis above revealed, artisans maintained preferences and restrictions on which symbols to depict in each medium. Organizational layouts of motifs and design fields, too, are markedly different between petroglyph panels and ceramic vessels. While sloppy, messy, and rough are common descriptors for their execution, and though their layouts have been called "unschooled" (Amsden 1936:44), buffware pottery designs are in fact complexly structured and highly patterned (e.g., Zaslow 1981; Zaslow and Dittert 1977), perhaps evidenced best by the tightly knit Style 3 layouts on Sacaton and Casa Grande Buffware pottery (Figure 3.4). Rock art is (dis)organized in a completely different way. In fact, Hohokam rock art gives an immediate impression of a haphazard, random, and unintegrated arrangement of crudely pecked motifs, compositions one may deem to be lacking planning and structure (e.g., Figures 4.3, 5.6, 5.14, and 6.6). Such a criticism would be premature and demonstrative only of our (i.e., Modernist, colonialist, industrialist, etc.) sensibilities and tastes, an aesthetic probably not shared by the original artisans and their audiences. Design organization in Hohokam rock art is sorely understudied, and although it differs considerably from pottery layouts, we cannot simply dismiss it as unrefined and defiant of any structure. Dissimilarity in decorative organization and symbolism is emblematic of differences in the producers, audiences, technologies, and social conditions encircling the manufacture, display, interpretation, and jurisdiction of each medium rather than superiorities and inferiorities in skill, intent, and aestheticism.

Some of the partitiveness in Hohokam decorative organization may be due to gender differences between communities of craftspeople. Wallace (1983), for example, has suggested that Hohokam petroglyphs around stationary mesquite grinding facilities in the Tucson Basin were pecked by women because gathering and processing mesquite pods were predominantly feminine tasks among descendant Tohono O'odham peoples. More recently, Munson (2002:215–219), in addressing rock art and social aspects of its execution on the Pajarito Plateau in New Mexico, concluded that incongruity between pottery designs and rock art reveals a partitive system of design organization among Ancestral Pueblo communities along the Rio Grande. She surmised that these media were the purview of different social groups of craftspeople defined possibly along gender lines, an assessment based on ethnographic analogy with descendant Pueblo peoples and supported by cross-cultural regularities among preindustrial, noncapitalist economies (Munson 2002:215–219). It is well known that women were the principal potters among the historic Pueblos (e.g., Mills and Crown 1995; Tanner 1976), and cross-culturally, women tend to focus on crafting soft materials, such as textiles and pottery, whereas men often work with harder substances such as stone and wood (Munson 2011:50). It is reasonable to assume that Ancestral Pueblo peoples followed similar gender divisions in craftwork.

Practices concerning the crafting, engagement, and interpretation of many of the South Mountains petroglyphs were tethered spatially, sensationally, and practically to agricultural endeavors and similar subsistence-related pursuits, and gender may account for some of the partitiveness in Hohokam decorative organization—men as providers and petroglyph makers, women as stay-at-home pottery painters. Hohokam men may have been the farmers and tenders of irrigated agricultural plots along the canals, which was the case among descendant O'odham communities (Castetter and Bell 1942), and were thus the artisans of petroglyphs on stages that hosted agricultural facilities and the like. Such a characterization, though, is rather simplistic and reductionist and arises dangerously and possibly offensively from Western colonialist notions of gender roles. Farming niches and wild plants in the South Mountains could very well have been the domain of women seeking to complement domestic agricultural surpluses, like the cadres of Tohono O'odham women who gather mesquite pods, or possibly even to compete economically with men. In such a way, Hohokam women may have empowered themselves through a strategic relationship with the South Mountains landscape. We cannot say with any surety that women were not involved in farming and other subsistence-oriented activities in the mountains, so we cannot rule them out as crafters of petroglyphs in and around agricultural fields either.

The contention that men had little to do with Hohokam pottery manufacture is also suspect. While possibly true of Ancestral Pueblo potters, any assumption that Hohokam buffware was decorated solely or primarily by female hands, thus yielding a decorative organization to ceramics distinct from a seemingly male-oriented one for petroglyphs, actually has little archaeological support. Utilitarian plainware and higher-valued redware vessels were made at multiple villages in the lower Salt River valley, and some of the communities along the northeast reach of the South Mountains specialized in certain forms, particularly large plainware jars in the Preclassic and polished redware bowls and jars later, and exchanged them throughout the valley (Abbott 2000, 2003a, 2009). However, the overwhelming majority of decorated buffware pottery was manufactured at a select few villages along the middle Gila River (Abbott et al. 2001; Kelly 2013). For this reason, women living at villages in the lower Salt River valley, where the petroglyph artisans resided (see Chapter 4), did not participate to any large extent in making or painting Hohokam buffware vessels. Indeed, crafters of plainware and redware pots in the vicinity of the South Mountains quite likely included men and women: at Las Canopas, for instance, two of the three people interred with implements consistent with pottery manufacture were male (Rice et al. 2009:332). It is only reasonable to deduce that men were involved in crafting buffware vessels at villages along the middle Gila, too. Attributing partitiveness in decorative organization between rock art and ceramics to gender differences in craftwork based on quaint and quasi-chauvinistic notions of men as farmers and women as potters just does not meet muster for the Hohokam scenario. Something else must account for the iconographic schism between media.

Efforts on the part of the artisans to control the use of symbols, or the messages they broadcast, may also affect the types and complexity of designs in certain media and therefore render partitions in systems of decorative organization. Esoteric knowledge, a potentially potent source of social power, may have been coveted, owned, or secreted by certain members of a community (e.g., Brandt 1980, 1994; Potter and Perry 2000), which conditioned what was communicated through symbols and how. Perhaps shamans or other religious figures were keepers and wielders of such knowledge and controlled how it was symbolized in rock art. They may have purposely created abstract, ambiguous, and unfamiliar designs as a way to exercise and demonstrate their access to and possession of arcane knowledge, or even to conceal it from competitors or more dominant hegemonies (e.g., Mobley-Tanaka 2002). This could explain why Hohokam rock art compositions are seemingly less structured, or disorganized, in comparison to the more intricate designs and layouts on buffware pottery. However, there is little evidence to show that shamans or others experiencing altered states of consciousness crafted any, and certainly not all, of the South Mountains petroglyphs. Though they are often geometric and sometimes ambiguous, it would be a stretch to consider the petroglyphs to be examples of abstract symbolism. Many of the motifs, over 36 percent, are of recognizable lifeforms, all of which also adorned decorated pottery used prolifically in domestic and "mundane" contexts—albeit in much lower frequencies and different proportions. Some of the geometric rock art motifs turn up in buffware pottery designs too (e.g., Figure 5.7), and none of the abstract, geometric rock-art-only designs are terribly labyrinthine, at least not to the extent to suggest convincingly that the artisans equated design complexity with mastery over religious knowledge and esoteric skills or authority over sacral symbols.

As detailed above, artisans stationed rock art in open, visible settings with apparently little hindrance to or restriction on who could witness its creation or access it later. In fact, some petroglyph arrangements appear to have been choreographed to draw attention to them and the immediate area. Rock art symbolism and its manufacture, meaning, and interpretation were not the discipline or domain of a particular gender identity or institutionalized personage; rather, the ritualized creation of rock art and related practices, as well as access to and control over the relevant knowledge and symbolism, were fluid performances open to onlookers. Even in the shade and seclusion around springs, rock art is highly figurative and situated predominantly on vertical panels at eye level, usually in inviting though sometimes seemingly imposing arrangements (e.g., Figures 5.11, 6.1, 6.6, 6.25, and 6.26), which suggests that it was meant to be seen and probably understood by others on the stage.

Though the focus so far has been on decorative partitiveness, congruity in the types of motifs wielded by Hohokam potters and rock art artisans shows that some of the knowledge encoded in the symbolism was shared, to a degree, among community members and between contexts. This suggests that the South Mountains petroglyphs were made by denizens from the local villages who did not necessarily have socially recognized differences in identity, status, or religious authority from other villagers. They were instead the farmers, gatherers, and other characters and actors who ventured into and engaged the South Mountains for a number of reasons and in a variety of settings and scenarios. A sense of openness to sharing both religious knowledge and the ability to showcase it through symbolism is attested to by consistency in the intensity of execution (Figure 4.7) and a general uniformity in the size (Figure 6.9) of petroglyphs, especially when they occupy the same and adjacent panels. This, along with a paucity of superimpositioning in the petroglyph assemblage, intimates that there was little competition between artisans across stages or when using the same canvases. While there are rare instances in which it seems people erased or obfuscated existing designs by pecking or abrading over them (e.g., Figures 4.3 and 5.6), reinterpreted or revitalized symbols by repecking particular glyphs (e.g., Figure 6.15), or redirected narratives by modifying existing motifs (e.g., Figure 6.28) or adding to panels, for the most part there was an air of respect, perhaps even reverence, among artisans for previously pecked imagery. Indeed, there may have been an ethos of cooperation at work in Hohokam rock art ritualism. There are nonetheless notable differences in the structure, organization, and motif choices between Hohokam rock art and pottery designs, but they are best understood as demonstrative of variation among the audiences and spectators, the type of

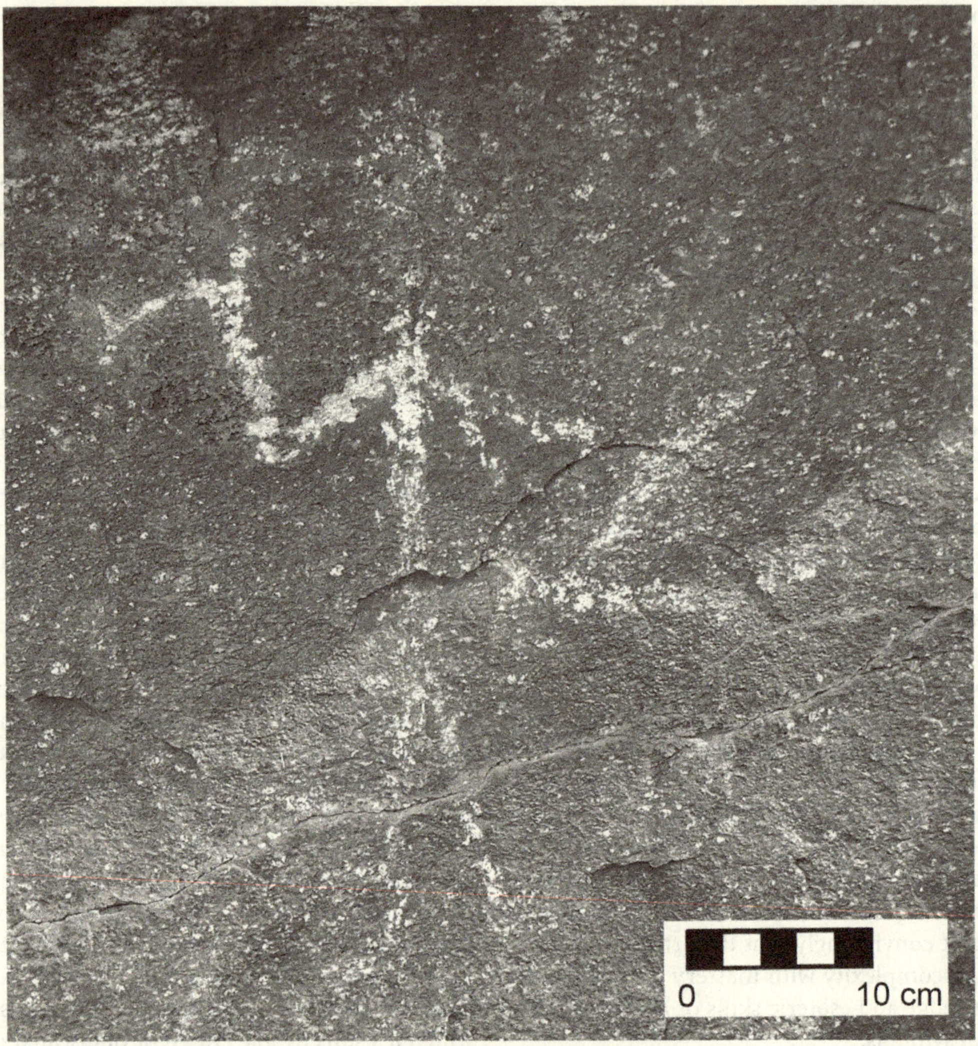

FIGURE 6.28. A zig-zag petroglyph refashioned into an anthropomorph.

knowledge conveyed through symbolism, and the intentions and strategies of artisans working in each medium.

I now return to the main question posed in this chapter: whether the practices surrounding the manufacture and viewing of Hohokam rock art were ritualized. Symbols can reveal the redundancy, repetition, framing, symbolic communication, and allusions to other-than-human agents and entities inherent to ritual action. These, in turn, constitute Rappaport's (1999) five features of the ritual form: formalism, encoded tradition, invariance, performance, and occult efficacy (Table 6.1). Symbolic communication is teleologically evident, but the designs in the South Mountains rock art assemblage are also quite redundant and repetitious. I classified the assemblage into 103 different motif types, yet more than half the petroglyphs, excluding the indeterminate designs, fall within only 10 motif categories (Table 4.2). Evidently, much of the information conveyed through rock art was encapsulated in a handful of symbols, and as the site-level CA in Chapter 5 shows (Figure 5.2), Hohokam artisans recreated this limited suite of symbols over and over in various settings across the landscape. These enstoned symbols also framed places on the landscape: springs, summits, ridges, agricultural fields, trails, and activity areas. In all, the South Mountains petroglyphs, as symbols, manifest four aspects of action—repetition, redundancy, symbolic communication, and framing—characteristic of the ritual form. As considered at length in the following chapter, the rock art corpus also evidences allusions to other-than-human agents and essences, a fifth aspect of ritual action and one that moves petroglyph ritualism out of the secular and squarely into the realm of religious experience.

Summary

This chapter cast a thick description of the ways in which the Phoenix Basin Hohokam incorporated rock art in ritual practices in the South Mountains. Petroglyphs were crafted and viewed on at least seven different types of stage by a variety of social actors. Congregations of performers and their audiences engaged in repetitive and redundant practices that called on figurative and abstract symbolism, and they timed these ritualized practices according to calendrical, occasional, and possibly biological rhythms. These qualities of performance evince four definitive features of the universal ritual form: formalism, encoded tradition, invariance, and performance. The nuances and vagaries among stages, performers, schedules, and audiences nevertheless testify to the different degrees of ritualization across performances. Indeed, the stages vary in ritual depth, and the petroglyphs, artifacts, and other relics evidence this hierarchy within the ritual system—from the occasional solitary trail petroglyph to the formalized summit trails and dense petroglyph concentrations around springs.

The manufacture, viewing, and interpretation of Hohokam rock art, as open, participatory engagements, were practices instrumental to the ways people conceptualized, experienced, and related with the South Mountains landscape. That is as true for today's visitors as it was for villagers centuries ago during the Hohokam millennium. The capacity, or agency, to participate in these ancient ritual performances was not restricted to a few social personae, and the performances were not sheltered from the gaze of others. In fact, the figurative, simple, and familiar symbolism of most of the rock art, its patterned distribution across the landscape, its generally easy and open accessibility, and its relatively high visibility suggest that many, if not most, of these ritual practices were inviting and that audiences were fundamental to some of the performances. The crafting of new petroglyphs was undoubtedly rare, but this is, in part, a product of how infrequently Hohokam villagers ventured into the South Mountains and how small their overall footprint was. Considering the ratio of three petroglyphs for each broken vessel in the project areas—which contain some of the densest concentrations of rock art in the whole range—it is quite possible that only a few people were farming, traipsing over, and engaging this landscape at any time. And when they did, they made only a few glyphs, if any, while in the company of relatively small audiences.

Qualities, properties, and inherences of the petroglyphs and the stages they adorn point toward the ritualism embedded in their manufacture and use, but this chapter only skirted the religious quintessence of Hohokam rock art, or the fifth feature of the ritual form: occult efficacy. In the following chapter I look at the way ritual practices surrounding the creation, witnessing, and interpretation of rock art were enmeshed in a religious structure and how participation in these practices empowered everyday people by positioning them in relationship with other-than-human agents and essences. After several centuries Hohokam communities eventually transformed the way they managed the religious knowledge once embodied and displayed in symbolism and ritual practices, such as petroglyph manufacture. This transformation in religious structure and the relationship communities held with sacred places in the landscape was tied to, perhaps even used to justify, many of the social changes that spread through the Hohokam world in the late AD 1000s and 1100s.

CHAPTER 7

Hohokam Rock Art as Religious Knowledge

It has been said before, these mountains will not listen if we simply speak words to them. They will only hear us if we come with melody, rhythm, pitch, and harmony. To these circling mountains we must speak with voices in songs, rhythmic speeches, orations, and prayers. We must be prepared with repetition, a singular, undisturbed beat. That is the way of mountains. This is what they want to hear. (Zepeda 2013)

In the previous chapter I laid bare the ritualization inherent in Hohokam rock art by pinpointing how the practices surrounding its production and use were consistent with four defining features of the universal ritual form: encoded tradition, formalism, performance, and invariance. I reserved discussion on the fifth feature—occult efficacy—for this chapter because the topic bears pertinently on understanding rock art's relation to Hohokam social transformations and therefore deserves its own treatment. As I detail below, to understand the occult efficacy once elicited through the petroglyphs, we must realize and acknowledge that the stages on which rock art ritualism was performed held deep religious significance—they were, in fact, sacred ground to the Hohokam. These places grounded communities to the cosmos and aligned ritual participants with unseen though omnipresent, other-than-human forces, entities, and agencies. Hohokam rock art was a means of communicating, engaging, and relating with this spiritual, metaphysical, immaterial dimension of a not-entirely-tangible world, which attests to the occult efficacy feature of the ritual form.

To make this case, in the following I reconsider the "archaeologist's perspective" (sensu Wilcox 1991b) on Hohokam religion through a particularistic structural framework that, via induction, draws into focus the religious foundation of the different stages on which Hohokam villagers carried out rock art–related practices. With this foundation in place, I then attend to a deficiency in archaeology's traditional, hypermaterialistic impression of the relationship the Hohokam nurtured with their desert environment. To best understand the South Mountains landscape and the rock art spread across and woven throughout it, we must engender our concepts of Hohokam religion and ritual practice with an animistic ontology. By doing so, we can appreciate that crafting, viewing, and interpreting rock art entailed much more than communicating information to a human audience or recording visionary experiences. It instead facilitated a relationship people maintained with the religious structures and metaphysical principles that conditioned experiences and gave meaning to life, all the while materializing that relationship for others to witness and judge.

Reconsidering Hohokam Religion

As we saw in Chapter 3, Wilcox's (1987a) Mesoamerican Cosmological Metastructure (MCM) currently provides the best archaeological model of Hohokam religion. This is because the MCM does not rest on a definitive, top-down interpretation of symbolic meaning and religious knowledge, but offers rather a historically grounded religious structure in which diverse modes of practice, variable forms of architecture, and a suite of symbols can be aptly fixed. It nonetheless has interpretive value because it delineates a realm of plausible ancient metaphysical themes inherited by and embedded within the shared currents of indigenous Southwestern and Mesoamerican religions; this allows us to contextualize, to some extent, ancestral Hohokam ritual practices and interpolate the impetuses and desired outcomes for certain actions. Indeed, the resilience of indigenous religions to the destabilizing, acculturative forces that accompanied the social upheavals wrought by centuries of oppressive and sometimes violent colonialism is one of the marvels in Southwestern/Mesoamerican anthropology. This is seen most clearly in the persistence of mythic narratives, actors (heroes and deities), contexts (places and worlds), premises (structures), and themes, what Alfredo López Austin (2002:36–45) refers to as the "nuclear elements of ancient religion" passed down to and perpetuated by Colonial Mexican Indians.[1] "It is interesting to show how indigenous [Mexican] societies maintained many of the thematic threads in their myths in the face of evangelization and how there is a notable likeness among the modern indigenous myths in spite of differences in ethnic background, linguistic affiliation, and development under the colonial regime" (López Austin 2002:45). A brief, incomplete list of such thematic threads as they pertain to the Hohokam includes ancestor veneration, a tiered cosmos with astronomically derived directional symbolism, intoxication, fire as a transformative force, smoke, color symbolism, fertility, rain and water as evocable entities, and the ritual importance of animals.

The MCM is comprehensive and has long served as a suitable model of Hohokam religion, yet regional archaeologists' traditional emphasis on excavating villages and mapping hydraulic systems has neglected a fundamental religious principle—the sacredness of landscape. Borrowing concepts from the Mayan sacred landscape, Wilcox (1987a:149) posited that the MCM shrines at certain "natural" places—mountains, caves and holes, rocks, trees, and the like—were the sites of an *axis mundi* that aligned and connected the tiered cosmos, and that such places afforded a means of communicating with supernatural beings. Most attention, however, has been given to how the Hohokam brought forth religious structures and principles through ritual practices and architecture *within* villages. For a fuller appreciation of Hohokam religious life, we need a better grasp of what the Hohokam were doing, or could have been doing, while beyond the village gaze. We would be well advised to reorient our approach to the Hohokam landscape away from simple dualistic notions of "cultural" vs. "natural," or "village" vs. "wilderness," and toward a unified cultural surface with variable depths (e.g., Zedeño 1997).

My first objective, then, is to better explicate the positions certain extra-village places probably held in relation to Hohokam religious premises and practices. Specifically, I look to ethnographic accounts on O'odham, Puebloan, and Mesoamerican religions, as branches on a spiritual pedigree reaching back millennia, to show that indigenous Southwestern and Mesoamerican peoples imbue mountains and springs with similar types of metaphysical connotations, mythic histories, and occult agencies. This suggests that underlying themes of religious potency and spiritual vibrancy attributed to such places are germs of an ancient religious structure, or cosmovision, akin to Wilcox's MCM. In all likelihood, mountains and springs figured in the sacred landscapes of ancestral peoples such as the Hohokam in a similar way as they do among more recent, descendant communities for which ethnographic insight is available. Commonalities among Mesoamerican and Southwestern religions are well known and widely accepted, and establish interpretive parameters useful for limning ancient Southwest religious structures (e.g., Bahr 2004; Boyd 2003; Brew 1943; Crown 1994; DiPeso 1974; Ellis and Hammack 1968; Fewkes 1893, 1900; Gladwin et al. 1937; Haury 1976; Hays-Gilpin and Hill 1999, 2000; Hays-Gilpin and Schaafsma 2010; Hedrick et al. 1974; Hill 1992; James 2000; Mathiowetz 2011; McGuire 2012; Parsons 1933; Riley 1963; Schaafsma 1999; Schaafsma and Taube 2006; Sutherland 1998; Taube 2001; Underhill 1948; Wallace 2014; Wallace and Lindeman 2013; Whittlesey 2004, 2007; Wilcox 1987a, 1991a, 1991b; Wilcox and Sternberg

1981; Wright and Russell 2011; Young 1989, 1994). More particular to the case at hand, some Hohokam cultural legacies, including elements of ritual and religion, undoubtedly endure among the O'odham (e.g., Darling and Lewis 2007; Ferguson and Colwell-Chanthaphonh 2006; Wells 2006) and some Pueblo communities (e.g., Dongoske et al. 1997; Ferguson and Lamaomvaya 1999; Teague 1988, 1993). The Zuni and O'odham languages, which belong to completely different linguistic families, even share words for the title of some religious offices, such as the *shiwanna* (Shaul and Hill 1998), pointing to a shared genealogy of religious institutions and actors with roots among the Hohokam. Elements of mutual histories, such as shared language, material culture, ancestry, and social memory, establish Mesoamerican, Pueblo, and O'odham religious principles and structures as relevant and appropriate, though not analogous, ethnographic sources for glimpses into Hohokam religion.

Mountains

The sacredness of certain hills and mountains figures into the religious lives of countless communities throughout the world, so the fact that Mesoamerican, Pueblo, and O'odham peoples revere such places comes as no surprise. What makes the Southwestern/Mesoamerican manifestation of this nearly universal religious premise more than interesting is the degree of similitude in mythologies about mountains as well as the ritual practices performed and the ceremonial architecture erected in such places. López Austin (2002:51–53), for instance, sees among the indigenous religions of Mexico and the American Southwest a unifying theme of a "great cosmic mountain" that he takes as a creation myth explaining how gods came to live under the earth and in the mountains. The cosmic mountain is replicated by each indigenous group, which ascribes patron deities to local landforms, thus conceptualizing the mythic personae as "hearts of the mountains." Historic and contemporary expressions of this mythic premise include, to name just a few examples, Tlaloc's abode in mountains around Tenochtitlán, the Puebloan kachinas who reside in mountains (such as at Zuni Heaven), Puebloan mythic figures like Spiderwoman who inhabit local landforms, and the O'odham's Elder Brother, I'itoi, who took up residence in the South Mountains. Mountains were also home to the much older Mayan rain god Chaak, a belief still held by contemporary descendants in Guatemala (Thompson 1970). Given the antiquity and geographic breadth of the nexus between mountains and mythic figures, principally fertility-oriented rain deities, across Mesoamerica and into the American Southwest, it is reasonable to presume that the Hohokam regarded particular rises and mountains, perhaps even the South Mountains, in similar mythic vein.

Though interpretation of ancient mythology and pantheons, however believable, remains uncomfortably conjectural to many, more concrete, tangible, and thus demonstrable indicators of the religious significance of mountains within the MCM are manifested by parallels in mountain-oriented ritual practices and architectural complexes among indigenous Southwestern and Mesoamerican peoples. Indeed, there is a pervasive dualistic thread of rain-focused spring-mountain ritualism woven into the multihued indigenous religious fabric. In Mesoamerica, spring-mountain ritualism arose at least by the Early Formative (circa 1200–800 BC), possibly as early as 1500 BC, at El Manatí near the Olmec village of San Lorenzo in Mexico's southern Gulf Coast lowlands. El Manatí is a prominent hill with springs around its base where early Olmec ritual performances included offerings of carved stone figures and wooden sculptures, rubber balls used in the ritual ballgame, and the bones of children (perhaps sacrificial victims) in the springs (Ortíz and Rodríguez 2000). Remarkably similar vestiges of this millennia-old mode of ritualism were perpetuated by more recent Mesoamerican communities. For example, Aztec ritualists performed rain rituals, some entailing human sacrifices to Tlaloc, at shrines atop various hills and mountains. A temple on Mount Tlaloc and a dynastic retreat literally cut into the nearby Hill of Tetzcotzingo, both in the Valley of Mexico, are two exemplars of such ritual constructs (Townsend 1982, 1992, 2000:140–152).

As the highest peak in the mountains lining the eastern rim of the Valley of Mexico, Mount Tlaloc towers over this center of the Aztec world as well as the densely inhabited Valley of Puebla farther east. The temple, whose attendant ritual performances were recorded from Aztec oral histories by the sixteenth-century friar Diego Durán (1971), consists of a dry-laid masonry quadrangle whose walls once rose to about 3 m in height. Entrance to the temple, from the west, is afforded by a long, strictly linear processional way enclosed by masonry walls of a similar height and construction. A large, deep rectangular shaft, presumably a symbolic earth navel (omphalos) like a Pueblo sipapu, was cut into the temple's floor on its eastern side. A simple makeshift structure of perishable materials was once located inside the temple's walls, as were a sculpture of Tlaloc, since lost to time or vandals, and several basalt boulders. Like the Tlaloc sculpture, the large stones, named after surrounding peaks, were effigies of deities assigned to other peaks visible on the horizon. The temple's walls and its stone effigies have orientations along cardinal and intercardinal directions that point to sun-horizon positions at 20-day intervals and have other sunrise alignments with surrounding peaks on days when similar ritual performances were held (Iwaniszewski 1994). The temple is essentially a miniaturized replica of the Aztec sacred landscape and ritual calendar. The primary ritual at the Mount Tlaloc temple was an annual springtime pilgrimage by the allied rulers of the nearby cities, who, as priestly leaders, were vested with calling forth the mountain's rains and moving the world from the dry to the wet season. With offerings of blood and food to the effigies, Townsend (2000:144) sees this ritual performance, or "mythic happening," as a symbolic act of fertilization of an earthen womb (the temple and its omphalos) on the part of Aztec priestly leaders.

Not far from Mount Tlaloc is the much lower conically shaped Hill of Tetzcotzingo, a ritualized summit redesigned by Netzahualcoyotl, ruler of Tetzcoco (a city-state that, with Tenochtitlán and Tlacopán, formed the legendary Aztec Triple Alliance), into a dynastic retreat around AD 1460 (Townsend 1982). Royal gardens for exotic plants and then a large system of agricultural terraces stretched outward from the hill's base. Cut into and circumambulating the hill were a formal path and an adjoining aqueduct that was fed from springs on Mount Tlaloc to the east; the path and the aqueduct separate this lower agricultural zone from a network of shrines on the hill's upper region. The shrines, consisting of effigies of various deities and commemorative monuments to Netzahualcoyotl, follow the natural east-west axis of the hill's ridge, which, as Townsend (2000:148) points out, parallels the path of the sun. Four water receptacles for ritual bathing cut into bedrock and fed by the aqueduct were sited near cardinal points along the circumambulation path. Atop the hill are the remains of a temple and a large Tlaloc mask petroglyph. Also cut into the slope are two linear trails that ascend the summit, linking the zone of agricultural works to the various shrines and the dilapidated temple complex above. The Hill of Tetzcotzingo served as an administrative facility where Netzahualcoyotl held ceremonies and gave orations regarding the allocation of water and land rights to the various communities under his jurisdiction.

At both the Mount Tlaloc temple and the Hill of Tetzcotzingo, Aztec priestly leaders undertook elaborate rainmaking rituals in which they personified deities and led ritualized processions to the summits. The ritual facilities at both include constructed linear paths and shrines oriented to cardinal directions and aligned with positions on the horizon where the sun rises and sets on days of heightened significance to the ritual calendar. Similar ritual facilities atop hills and mountains are found throughout the Greater Southwest, including the South Mountains. Indeed, the summit trail complex around Goodman Hilltop (Figure 4.15) bears an uncanny likeness to the Hill of Tetzcotzingo: a circumambulation path (not shown in Figure 4.15) around the hill's base separating the agricultural terraces from the upper zone of petroglyphs and shrines; a spring (instead of spring-fed baths) along this path; summit trails cut into the hillside that served as corridors between the agricultural terraces and petroglyph clusters at the hill's base and the shrines and petroglyphs on its summit; and the cardinal orientation of the layout of cairns and bedrock outcrops at the hill's apex.

Much closer to the Hohokam world, Pueblo peoples continue to perform mountaintop rain rituals similar to those among the Aztec. A well-known case in point concerns the four mountains defining the Tewa sacred landscape (Ortiz 1969): the northern Tse Shu Pin ("Hazy Mountain," or Conjilon Peak), the southern Oku Pin ("Turtle Mountain," or Sandia Mountain), the eastern Ku Sehn Pin ("Stone Man Mountain," or Truchas Peak), and the western Tsikomo ("Obsidian-Covered Mountain"). Each peak is allied with a lake or pond that is home to the "Dry Food Who Never Did Become," the Tewa counterpart to the kachinas of the Western Pueblos. Each peak also bears an earth navel, in the form of a keyhole-shaped dry-laid masonry shrine oriented to a particular village. These shrines, as communicative gateways to the upper and lower worlds, serve to collect blessings from otherworldly beings and direct them toward the villages. They are likewise places of mythic emergence, and thus home of the Towa é, kachina-like beings who accompanied the Tewa on their journey out of the underworld.

The Tewa make pilgrimages to the crests of these four mountains to perform both private and communal rituals. The western Tsikomo, in the direction from which moisture-laden clouds arrive, is the destination of annual rain retreats by the village leaders, who travel to its introitus-like shrine offering gifts as prayers for rain. Positioned between the sacred mountains and the villages are four flat-topped sacred hills with caves or tunnels within them: the northern Tema Yoh, the southern Tun Yoh, the eastern Tsi Mayoh, and the southwestern Toma Yoh. The Towa é watch over the Tewa villages from these hills, whereas Tsave Yoh, masked supernatural whippers, live within the caves (Ortiz 1969:18–19, 24, 140–141nn5, 6). Tewa cosmology maintains metaphoric conceptions and symbolic associations of the landscape akin to those of Mesoamerica: sources of water, caves and other earth navels, shrines, rain deities, ancestors, pilgrimages, and village leadership are bundled together in the sacred mountains and hills that not only define the boundary of the Tewa world but also bind and center it in relation to the cardinal directions and the tiered cosmos.

The ritual features of the Tewa's Tsikomo, sacred mountain of the west, are the best known of the four peaks among scholars (e.g., Curtis 1926; Douglass 1917; Parsons 1929; see also Ortman 2009, 2012:92). Six "rain roads," rock-lined linear trails that bring to mind the Aztec temple atop Mount Tlaloc, converge at a circular stone shrine atop the mountain. These ritualized trails are concentrated along the eastern half of the mountain, and each is oriented toward a particular Tewa village. Two of the rain roads are 30 to 45 cm deep, presumably dug into the hillside. Within the shrine is a small depression symbolic of water, and Tewa pilgrims place prayer feathers and sticks just to the west of it. Again, there are clear parallels between these formal stages and the summit trail complexes in the South Mountains: excavated and rock-lined linear trails concentrated on the eastern side of the summit that coalesce at a shrine on the top of the summit (Figure 4.15).

The Akimel O'odham and Pee Posh conceptualize mountains in and around the Phoenix Basin as mythic abodes of other-than-human agents and essences of various sorts (Bahr et al. 1973:232; Spier 1933:252–253). This is more than superstition or a "big idea" about the land; it is a relationship with a sacred, animated landscape that they foster through ritualized engagement with their surroundings. The O'odham materialize this relationship by erecting and visiting shrines and caching esoterica and ritual paraphernalia in nearby mountains and hills (Russell 1908:254–256; see also Bahr et al. 1985; Clark 1967; Haury 1945). As for the Pee Posh, they once sought out caves within mountains for vision quests (Spier 1933:244–245), one of which was the Double Butte cave in Tempe (Haury 1945: 193–203), just over 3 km from the northeastern end of the South Mountains. In particular, the South Mountains, as a stage for a series of dramatic mythic events (Bahr et al. 1994) as well as one of the houses of I'itoi, the Elder Brother culture hero (Russell 1908:206–230), are integral to O'odham mythology, religion, and cultural identity.

This brief survey of the spiritual and ritual significance of mountains to Southwestern and Mesoamerican indigenes provides a baseline for understanding how the South Mountains likely figured into a Hohokam religious structure. As these accounts demonstrate, and as the distribution of petroglyphs and shrines across the South Mountains landscape shows (see Chapter 4), ritual depth varies among mountains and within them. Entire landforms are conceptually important, but ritual practices are centered on particular places within them too, with greater attention given to caves and summits. In this way, we can approach the occult efficacy of rock art ritualism via the general presence of petroglyphs within the South Mountains as well as by examining their strategic positioning at certain places, faces, and niches within the landscape. Interpretation of the symbolism is not necessary to establish the rock art's connection to practices geared toward eliciting occult efficacy. Often, features of the stage, in this case summits, rockshelters, and water sources within mountains, alone are evidence of the occult efficacy inherent to the ritual form.

Springs

Like mountains, springs are imbued with considerable religious importance within Mesoamerican and Southwestern cultural traditions. Springs are literally places where water bleeds out of the ground, a phenomenon layered in metaphors and one likely to conjure amazement and deep reverence, especially for communities in extremely arid environments like the Sonoran Desert. In fact, the Tohono O'odham maintain two sacred springs as ritual centers, one near Santa Rosa, Arizona, and another at the center of several villages in Sonora, Mexico (Davis 1920; Lumholtz 1912:103–106). Lakes and springs figure prominently in Pueblo religions as liminal places between the present living surface and a watery underworld from where, according to the Western Pueblo cosmology, kachinas emerge (Ellis and Hammack 1968:31; Parsons 1939:213; see also Ellis 1994:109–110). Nearly all springs in Hopi country, whether flowing or extinct, can be considered shrines since they are home to rain beings and are often adorned with prayer offerings (Fewkes 1906:370–373). For the Zuni and Hopi, spring water is an essential ingredient in a ritualized paint recipe that infuses prayer sticks with potent color and directional symbolism (Bunzel 1932a:860; Stevenson 1904:96). These prayer sticks, typically fashioned for use in rainmaking rituals, are commonly placed as offerings near springs. The Hopi also place other types of offerings in or near springs, such as bowls of food (Beaglehole 1937:30), and use spring water for various rituals performed within villages and around agricultural fields (Parsons 1939:164, 376–377, 481–482).

Springs and lakes stage a number of other Pueblo ritual performances in addition to prayers and offerings. For example, initiates of the K'osa society at Nambe Pueblo undergo ritual submersion in the waters of a mountain lake as a rite of passage (Hill 1982:298). Some Pueblo rituals require pilgrimages to springs for water to be brought back to the villages and used later in the ceremony. These pilgrimages are often undertaken only by village elders, clan leaders, or priests, the "Made People" in Tewa cosmology (Ortiz 1969), who control and disperse the water among the community. At Acoma the Kachina Ceremony of the Corn Clan entails a pilgrimage of seven kachina impersonators (all chosen by the Corn Clan), the head of the Corn Clan, and some other elders to a spring west of the pueblo where they pray and collect water. On returning to the pueblo, and after dancing, bathing, and feasting, the clan head gives the water to the War Chief, who makes a round of the village, offering a few drops to each household (Parsons 1939: 764–766). Additional ritual pilgrimages by War Chiefs and other ritual leaders seeking spring water on behalf of the community are performed at Acoma (Parsons 1939:593), among the Hopi (Fewkes 1906:348), and at Zia Pueblo (White 1962:234).

As part of various Hopi rituals, participants place offerings of serpent effigies at designated springs (e.g., Fewkes 1891, 1906:355; Geertz and

Lomatuway'ma 1987:178–179; Stephen 1936:319–322; Titiev 1944:122–123). After the Snake Dance at Oraibi, live serpents are placed at four Snake shrines, each positioned at the base of Third Mesa and aligned to the pueblo along cardinal directions, several of which bear serpentine petroglyphs (Fewkes 1906:361–362). Contact and communion with the mythical plumed serpent, which lives within the watery underworld, is afforded through springs (Lomatuway'ma et al. 1993:18), primarily at Tawapa, Walpi's Sun Shrine, and Moñwiba, Hano's Sun Shrine (Fewkes 1906:355, 372). Like the Hopi, Tewa-speaking residents of the Eastern Pueblos consider springs and other natural bodies of water home to the water serpent, or *awanyu* (Harrington 1916:201; Parsons 1929:184, 230). And as with the Hopi Snake Dance, Tewa-speaking ritual pilgrims from Jemez Pueblo, bearing effigies of the water serpent, embark on choreographed processions to local springs (Parsons 1939:202). For Laguna Pueblo, an extinct hot spring known as the Snake Pit doubles as the community's Sun Shrine, Osách Kámuh. According to legend, the two-headed water serpent once lived in a lake near the main pueblo but later swam eastward, finally submerging into the underworld via this aqueous portal (Ellis and Hammack 1968:32).

At Zuni, springs and lakes are openings to a system of waterways that connect with oceans (Bunzel 1932b:487) and are guarded by the horned serpent (Dutton 1963:49). A. W. Whipple, citing the nineteenth-century Zuni governor Pedro Pino, provides an early account of a Zuni conception of springs:

> In the valley of Zuni there is a singular spring, surrounded by high walls of earth, upon the top of which are many earthern [*sic*] jars fixed in an inverted position.... Pedro Pino, governor of this frontier pueblo, visited our camp, and was questioned regarding this fountain. He replied: "We live in a country without acequias, and, for the growth of our crops, depend upon rain. To obtain this blessing from the Great Spirit, it is necessary for us to perform the rites and observe the ceremonies of our ancestors. This spring has ever been held sacred to the rain god. No animal may drink of its waters. It must be annually cleansed with ancient vases, which, having been transmitted from generation to generation by the caciques, are then placed upon the walls, never to be removed. The frog, the tortoise, and the rattlesnake, represented upon them, are sacred to Montezuma, the patron of the place, who would consume by lightning any sacrilegious hand that should dare to take these relics away." (Whipple et al. 1855:39–40)

The Zuni collect water, plants, mud, and clay from in and around springs and use them in various rituals within the pueblo (Parsons 1939:352). In Zuni mythology, springs were important stops during the initial migration once the Zuni emerged into this world, and many remain sites of shrines and pilgrimages (Ferguson 2007:399–400). Bathing in waters of one of the first springs encountered along this primordial migration transformed Zuni ancestors from a semi-aquatic physical state to their present human condition (Benedict 1935; Ferguson 2007; Ferguson and Hart 1985; Parsons 1923; Stevenson 1904:28).

Some Pueblo communities mimic or replicate natural bodies of water such as springs and lakes within villages. Snead (2006), for example, suggests that some rain-fed reservoirs, or catchment basins, at Ancestral Pueblo villages were actually of limited utilitarian value because any runoff water retained would be stagnant and polluted with domestic refuse. He instead takes them as metaphors for lakes and springs (Snead 2006:215); such religiously vibrant limnetic places are integral to the conceptual centering of villages in relation to the four cardinal directions among the Tewa (Harrington 1916:310; Ortiz 1969).[2] Indeed, the lake at Laguna Pueblo is an anthropogenically created pool, a pseudoform of public architecture integral to community identity and instrumental in village ritual life. Just as communities may sight, position, and align themselves and their villages in relation to a sacred geography, in some instances they also map that sacred geography onto, into, and according to the village's layout and in so doing internalize and domesticate features of the spiritual landscape. Given the arrangement of Snaketown's buildings and edifices in reference to cardinal and intercardinal directions, and the tripartite assemblage of ritual architecture emblematic of a tiered cosmos (ballcourt = underworld, plaza = middleworld, mound = upperworld), as Wilcox and colleagues (1981) brought to our attention, perhaps the subterranean feature described as a "well" in the plaza, at the heart and center of the community, was part of a Hohokam sacred geography bundled and brought inward like the pools and lakes at various Pueblo villages.

Summary

As for exact details of the religious significance and perhaps the mythic histories the Hohokam attributed to springs and mountains, we likely will never know with absolute conviction or have complete faith in our interpretations. Yet as Pauketat (2013) has shown for contemporaneous Cahokian communities of the American Bottom, there probably never was a single, top-down Hohokam religion to which all ascribed, but rather numerous, individualized, and community-centered religions built from the ground up that drew from a shared understanding of cosmic order. We see this today in the similar though not identical mythologies and ritual practices at work among the various Pueblos, for instance. This review of a few Pueblo, O'odham, and Mesoamerican religious principles and premises, albeit cursory, nevertheless illuminates broad, robust, and deeply historical mythic and religious themes with branches stretching throughout Mesoamerica and the American Southwest, and probably farther, and with millennia-long roots penetrating as far back as Mesoamerica's early Formative and the southern Southwest's Early Agricultural periods, if not deeper. Hohokam religion(s) undoubtedly belonged to this spiritual genealogy.

Indigenous myths about and rituals performed at springs and mountains differ at multiple scales across Mesoamerica and the American Southwest, but a religious orientation for each of these spiritually laden places is clearly ubiquitous. Mountains are stairways to an upperworld, places where people can literally touch the sky, clouds, and astral bodies. Springs are portals to an aqueous underworld, places of primordial emergence and links to a mythic past. Both are stages for hierophanies and cosmic transcendence, sites of offering and prayer, and home to deities, ancestral beings, and mythic persons. In all likelihood, the synergistic co-presence of springs and lakes in mountains is and has long been symbolically important and presents some of the most religiously revered and spiritually significant places in the sacred landscape. This is exemplified by the Aztecan *altepetls*, or "watery mountains," and the mountain-spring homes of Pueblo kachinas (Parsons 1939), both of which fuse connotations of springs and mountains into a single geographical taxon, unite the tiered cosmos, and serve as extremely important and powerful ritual stages. This structural element of particular Southwestern and Mesoamerican religious traditions provides strong support that the Hohokam held these places in similar regard. Elsewhere, Greenwood and White (1970) have shown that by at least the ninth century springs and hilltops figured into the Mogollon sacred landscape too, underscoring the extent to which such elements of the MCM were shared across the Greater Southwest and most of Mesoamerica centuries if not millennia before the rise of the Aztec empire.

That the Hohokam sought occult efficacy through rock art ritualism is evidenced by the petroglyphs' placement within the South Mountains, and more specifically by their intentional and redundant production in certain settings, particularly around springs and on hilltops above springs (Chapter 6). Indeed, as Bell writes: "What makes activities around certain symbols seem ritual-like is really twofold: the way they differentiate some places from others by means of distinctive acts and responses and the way they evoke experiences of a greater, higher, or more universalized reality—the group, the nation, humankind, the power of God, or the balance of the cosmos" (1997:159). For now, we can only speculate what intentions the Hohokam had that would have necessitated such supernatural succor. It is reasonable to infer that the ritual performances concerned rain or fertility, given metaphorical relationships of mountains with rain and clouds, and springs with water, femininity, and emergence. Perhaps this, too, is why some of the densest concentrations of rock art as well as ritual facilities such as summit trails and shrines are found near and perched above runoff-irrigated agricultural features. There are, however, at least seven types of stage on which rock art ritualism was acted out, so the intentions requesting or drawing on occult efficacy probably varied among performances, stages, and participants.

A spatial and performative correlation of rock art with springs and hilltops in the South Mountains is not a new insight in Southwestern archaeology. As a matter of fact, some of the earliest anthropological research in the region acknowledged the intentional and religiously inspired association of rock art with springs (e.g., Fewkes 1906; Hough 1906). What the South Mountains case reveals is that Hohokam rock art is not a collection of doodles or decorations scattered about the landscape or signs of warning, ownership, or territoriality, but rather was crafted, experienced, and interpreted during ritual practices held at sacred places. Rock art was enmeshed in a relational field between people and their sacred landscape as well as the other-than-human agents and essences dwelling within and upon it. Indeed, Hohokam artisans used petroglyphs for communing, engaging, and relating with these other-than-humans. The mountains and springs, and perhaps even the rock art panels, were "animated," but not in the classical sense that the Hohokam viewed them as "alive" or vested them with "spirits" and "souls." As I elaborate below, animism is instead about relativity among subjects, not beliefs about things; it is both ecology and ontology—a way of being in and knowing the world—not simply a religion. Religions operate within ontologies and are embodied in ritual practice.

Animism

Edward Tylor (1871) fathered the classical concept of animism to explain what he observed to be a deep-seated, cross-cultural belief in spirits and souls (see also Stocking 1971). Such universality pointed to a neuropsychological explanation for spiritual beliefs, so animism was argued to have roots reaching deep into our species' evolutionary past. Tylor theorized that since animism was the primogenitor of all religions, its origin was tied to early human dream activity. Perception and understanding of such immaterial experiences begat a primal belief in spirits which early humans attributed to ancestors as well as nonhuman beings and objects. At the time, Tylor's theory of animism fit comfortably within the nineteenth-century heyday of social evolutionism. Animism provided an explanation for why European religions, considered to be the most refined but holding to lingering animistic survivals, shared elements with indigenous, tribal, non-Western belief systems—those still attributing life and souls to things, whether living, dead, or inorganic—that had yet to "evolve" into more rational and objective understandings of the world. Consequently, animism was often equated with a childish way of thinking and taken to be demonstrative of an underdeveloped psyche characteristic of non-European peoples (e.g., Piaget 1929). Indeed, it quickly became an overtly racist measure of indigenous peoples' mental capacity and perceptive acumen, with the Caucasian mindset surely and not surprisingly serving as the baseline (e.g., Dennis 1940, 1943; Dennis and Russell 1940; Russell 1940; Russell and Dennis 1939; see also Madsen 1982). Though instrumental in early anthropological and psychological research on religion, the study of animism and indigenous ontologies in general took a rear seat in the discipline's theoretical trajectory. As Philippe Descola (1992:114) notes, with the early twentieth century's turn toward ecological studies and cultural materialism, animism became a taboo subject in anthropological discourse because it drew unwanted attention to what many believed to be an irrational manner of life among indigenous cultures. It simply did not fit well with then-popular functionalist and objectivist paradigms.

In recent years, socially minded anthropologists have recast animism in a new mold (e.g., Bird-David 1990, 1999; Descola and Pálsson 1996; Fausto 2007; Harvey 2002, 2006; Helander-Renvall 2009; Ingold 2000, 2006, 2007b, 2011;

Nadasdy 2007; Pederson 2001; Stringer 1999; Viveiros de Castro 1998, 2004; Willerslev 2004, 2007). These reflections on animism have in fact ushered in a new post-Western (sensu Haber 2009) paradigm radically different from Tylor's framework. Tylor subscribed to a positivist view of culture and social institutions, and his approach was founded in a dualistic Cartesian ontology of object-subject relations (Bird-David 1999; Harvey 2006; see also Hornborg 2006). This is understandable because, as the quintessential armchair anthropologist, Tylor had little interaction with or firsthand accounts of the communities he was studying other than European Spiritualists of the late nineteenth century (Bird-David 1999; Harvey 2006; Stocking 1971). He was also working in an era of Colonialism when social and political agendas sought theoretical justification for racial subjugation (D'Andrade 1995; see also McCann 2003). Nurit Bird-David captures this sentiment best: "Positivistic ideas about the meaning of 'nature,' 'life,' and 'personhood' misdirected these previous attempts to understand the local concepts. Classical theoreticians (it is argued) attributed their own modernist ideas of self to 'primitive peoples' while asserting that the 'primitive peoples' read their idea of self into others!" (1999:S68).

Anthropological paradigms have shifted, or what may be punned as "evolved," since Tylor's day. We are now less emphatic about positivist explanations for cultural practices and universalist propositions for behaviors—though these remain strong contributions to anthropological knowledge. Greater weight is now given to studying, understanding, and ultimately appreciating social practices, processes, and structures from alternative points of view. Accordingly, we can no longer isolate what has been regarded as peoples' irrational beliefs from their practical, adaptive, rational acts; rather, we must acknowledge that our perceptions of others' irrationality derive, in part, from our Cartesian underpinnings (see Chapter 2), and we should regard such irrational acts as, more often than not, quite logical and cogent within the communities we research (e.g., Brück 1999).

This post-positivist turn has brought about a proverbial reinvention of the wheel regarding animism—though perhaps of a less square and more circular form. Post-Tylorian theorists do not consider animism a religion per se; it is not about believing in souls or assigning life to inert material objects; nor is it solely a way of *thinking about* animals and items (e.g., Lévi-Strauss 1963, 1966). Animism instead concerns a reflexive relationship between people, their environment, and other-than-human agents and essences with whom they share it. It is a way of *thinking with*, *relating with*, and *being with* other subjects, not objects. Animism contra Objectivism poses "subject-subject relatedness" versus "subject-object relatedness" (Bird-David 1993). In this sense, it is about crafting personhood, in that people define themselves and broadcast their identities—that is, actively create their own persons—in relation to dynamic socio-physico-religio-geographies (e.g., Ingold 2000, 2011; Latour 2005; Thomas 2001). Animistic ways of knowing, personifying, and deifying the environment through enmeshment in complex fields and multinoded networks of active and reactive agents are part of the universal human condition (Malafouris 2004, 2007) and are probably innately tied to the deep evolution of "perception/response systems" (Helveston and Hodgson 2010:61). Indeed, as one psychiatrist has said, animism is the "natural" state of human reasoning and perception whereas "learned" objectivity "overwrites" inherent subjective and relativistic modes of knowing and being (Charlton 2007).

Tylor may have been right about animism's cognitive basis and archaic origin, but his insistence that it is an inferior, childish, and false way of seeing the world and reading the environment shrouds such pioneering insights in antiquated, racist, and quasi-fascist colonial notions of socio-evolutionary advancement. Though the intersection of non-Western relational ontologies with Cartesian, dualistic, and Objectivist ones seemingly plants the seeds for an epistemological crisis, they may be more profitably considered two equally valuable and mutually correct ways of understanding (Porr and Bell 2012). Instead of crossing, these two lines of reasoning may in fact run parallel because relativistic perceptions and practices all too often permeate even the most objective paradigms (a scientist's good-luck charm comes to mind). This is, in fact, the essence of Bruno Latour's (1993) enlightening contention that "we have never been modern."

Archaeologies of Animism

Investigations of neo-animism have begun to surface in various strands of archaeological scholarship (e.g., Alberti and Bray 2009; Brown and Walker 2008; Creese 2011; Herva 2005, 2006a, 2006b; Herva and Ylimaunu 2009; Kamash 2008; Losey 2010; Reynolds 2009; VanPool and Newsome 2012). The reason for this is straightforward: animism explains why we, as a collective humanity, revere certain "things," both now and in the past, to the point where we practically afford them biographies and agentic properties in social processes (e.g., Gell 1998; Gosden 2005; Groleau 2009; Mills 2004; Mills and Ferguson 2008; Zedeño 2008, 2009), and why we have a tendency to imbue "natural" spaces with histories and metaphysical ambience (e.g., Brown and Emery 2008; Insoll 2007; Scarre 2008). Neo-animism is one field within a growing body of relational archaeologies (Watts 2013), whose lineage can be traced through previous relativist theoretical movements concerning human-environment relations, such as affordances (Gibson 1979), artifact biographies (Kopytoff 1986), monumentality (Thomas 1993), landscape phenomenology (Tilley 1994), object agency (Gell 1998), materiality (DeMarrais et al. 2004), and memory work (Mills and Walker 2008). These ever-developing subjective paradigms have gained considerable favor in light of the "contradictions and inconsistencies in dealing with the variety and complexity of human life" which decades of ecological and strictly evolutionary archaeologies have left in their wake (Porr and Bell 2012:171).

Entangled in a reflexive, mutually conditioning give-and-take with our environments, we seek out, husband, and nurture relationships with our surroundings, be they objects, animals, or places, because they give culturally embedded meaning to life. Through an animistic perspective, we can better approach our and others' perceived irrational ritual practices—that is, "offerings" of esoterica, the ritual framing of place, and the "killing" and mortuary interment of objects, animals, and buildings—as we now ken them as intrinsic to the kinship people foster with other-than-human beings who populate material and immaterial worlds. These practices are logical, practical, and rational because they are both bodily and mental engagements with places and things, and through these *relations* people recreate their identities and renew the layered worlds in which they exist. Since animism is not religion, but rather an ontology within which religions are anchored and operate, we can address animistically reasoned actions without knowing the beliefs and symbolic meanings, or the religious beings and myths, underscoring those choices and practices.

Art and Animism

At times, relational archaeologies draw on forms of and depictions in works of art to evidence animistic ontologies (e.g., Herva 2006a; Ingold 2000; Kamash 2008). Accordingly, researchers theorize that animistic practices can be witnessed through symbol choice, design structure, object form, and spatial configuration (e.g., Ingold 2000; see also Bird-David 2006) or interpreted from figures and scenes portrayed in imagery (e.g., Creese 2011; Dowson 2009; Herva 2006a). This is because "art invites people to explore and engage with the surrounding world through the perceptual system" (Herva 2006b:233). Studies emphasizing artistic forms and imagery, while often insightful and useful for probing the depth and diversity of animistic practices, construct a paradox by implicitly positioning the artwork as an object or representation. This exposes an underlying disjunction in Western, Modernist, non-indigenous understandings of relational ontologies. As Porr and Bell (2012) lament, even though archaeologists are more interested in and adept at engendering the past with strains of animism and other relational ontologies, our methods, discourse, and indeed the discipline as a whole are born of a Cartesian tradition and Objectivist worldview. Consequently, our many theories of human sociality and the manners in which we currently practice archaeology disassociate ourselves and the larger academy of Western scholarship from our research subjects through essentialist distinctions and illusory dichotomies between familiar and alien ways of thinking and being, or between "correct," scientific, and educated reasoning and the perceived falsities of ancient and non-Western epistemologies. Instead of denigrating other ways of experiencing and knowing, as was customary in prior genera of anthropological research, we now tend to fetishize them, and in so doing we continue to perpetuate colonialist notions of "otherness." Given the complexity of this epistemological impasse, the research at hand admittedly struggles with reconciling multiple ways of knowing and perceiving art and falls short of balancing Objectivist and Relativist points of view. My goal, however, is to take a few steps in that direction by reprojecting Hohokam rock art as something other than a constellation of passive, two-dimensional reflections of life experiences, objects, or environments.

In relational ontologies, works of "art" may not constitute representations of the world or emotional expressions but could instead be interactive instruments for relating, engaging, and communicating with other-than-human agents and essences. Though as archaeologists we often fixate on the roles of objects and materials in social relations, practices, and the reproduction of social structures (i.e., object "agency"), such other-than-human agents need not be the symbols in the art. The art or object may actually be a "window" through which material and immaterial agents communicate or engage in other modes of symbolic intercourse. Indeed, "images have long been used by religious peoples around the world to communicate with the unseen, mysterious, and potentially uncontrollable forces that are understood to govern life" (Morgan 2005:59). Diné (Navajo) drypaintings provide a fine example of a religious artistic practice grounded in such a relational perspective (Bahti and Baatsoslanii Joe 2009). Drypaintings conform well to Western sensibilities of "art"—their colors evoke emotion and sentiment, their symbols "represent" certain themes, they follow particular design structures and grammars, they are formally prepared as canvases with borders, and their manufacture involves training and apprenticeship. However, aside from commercialized examples manufactured for the tourist industry (Parezo 1983), drypaintings are neither permanent nor decorative works meant for display to a human audience. They are rather complexly arranged juxtapositions of emotionally charged symbols intended solely for communicating with immaterial, spiritual agents (Kluckhohn and Leighton 1946), and their impermanence is actually imperative to their metaphysical efficacy. It is my contention that, sans the exigency of impermanence, the Hohokam implicated rock art in a similar sacred dialogue with animate, agentic elements of their environment.

Talking with Rocks

Though it is fraught with the same Western cultural bias and Cartesian (mis)perception of subject-object relatedness with which we wrestle, I nevertheless use the term "art" repeatedly throughout this book for the mere reason that it is an easily understandable and recognizable concept. As brushed on above, however, I do not consider non-Western imagery and craftwork to be art in a romanticized, European, museological sense, and I argue that our ideas of what art is or "does" within animistic ontologies should not fall solely into a Modernist paradigm of art-represents-reality. By eschewing aesthetic judgments and hiding objectifying eyes, we can better frame art as a strategy for exchanging and relating information of various sorts and origins because, as a semiotic system, that is something it does regardless of the artisans' original intentions. Ecological and evolutionary flavors of anthropological theory have long cast rock art as an adaptive mechanism for sharing vital clues about environmental resources or one's reproductive fitness, which would in theory subject the practice and the symbols chosen to social and environmental selective pressures (e.g., Barton et al. 1994). Rock art's communicative quality is well founded, but within animistic ontologies the artisans' aims may not be so reductionist. The artwork actually facilitates a network of social relations by relaying messages, intentions, and emotions among the self, other humans, and other-than-humans. In some instances, rock art artisans were not concerned with a human audience, but as religious ritual practice the rock art's manufacture was a nonverbal, embodied, spiritual conversation between performers and other-than-human subjects through symbols, gestures, schedules, and places of performance. This dialogue was part and parcel of a relationship people developed and perpetually negotiated with a sacred geography mapped onto their physical environment.

As a growing body of case studies shows (e.g., Creese 2011; Dowson 2009; Janik 2007; Wallis 2009), animistic and similar relational perspectives have great promise for rock art research because they account for why some rock art was placed in highly secluded settings and in regions distant from settlements—places where people other than the performer were clearly not the intended audience (Munson 2011:92–93). Robert Wallis (2009), for example, has made the case that ancient rock art in and around Great Britain was an active and intentional means of communicating with other-than-human persons. His perspective encapsulates the rock art, its producers, and the landscape on which it is found in "rhizomic" networks of relationality. Wallis shows that in animistic worldviews landscapes are not conceptualized as passive receptacles for symbolism and exertion of human will, but instead are equally engaged in a reflexive dialectic between humans and other-than-humans through rock art symbols where both humans and places are both consumers and producers of the messages. This approach "animates" landscapes and places them in a position of reciprocity with humans (Thomas 2001), as well as with other other-than-human subjects. Wallis's example of rhizomic personhood offers a much-needed critical shift in thinking about rock art, landscapes, and religion in a more holistic, less Cartesian sense than is often forwarded. I take a very similar perspective with regard to the South Mountains petroglyphs.

As discussed above, the South Mountains, as a prominently elevated, darkly colored, and craggily textured landmass, likely held layers of religious significance for the Hohokam residing around them. Springs within the mountains, too, were more than water fountains for thirsty sojourners and farmers; they were sacred places that figured metaphorically in Hohokam religion and ritual practice. In Chapter 6 I showed that petroglyphs tend to cluster in various ways around springs, on hilltops, and on hilltops above springs. The Hohokam imbued these stages with religious significance and mythological histories and therefore understood them as the wellsprings of occult efficacy sought through rock art ritualism. We do not need to know the exact nature of such metaphysical, immaterial, occult agencies—gods, spirits, and so on—to appreciate that certain places are favored as frames for religious ritual practices because they are the dwelling sites or bosoms of powerful, transcendental, other-than-human persons. Petroglyphs are one means of relating, engaging, and communicating with animated places and the beings accessible there. In this sense, South Mountains rock art was a channel in the "geopiety" (Tuan 1976:11) between the Hohokam and places of sacral importance that animated their landscape. I expand on this conversation below.

Ritual Communication

Rock art is both a set of graphic, information-laden symbols and the material product of ritual practices. Though the messages may be arcane and unintelligible, few scholars deny that ritual, considered broadly, is a choreographed composition of symbols, so it is easy to understand why it is often analyzed through linguistic, semiotic, and semantic lenses (see Bell [1997:61–76] for a review). Indeed, one of ritual's fundamental qualities is the unique way in which it communicates (Rappaport 1999; Robbins 2001; Tambiah 1968). Rituals air overt and subtle, explicit and implicit, dogmatic and subversive, and doxic and agentic messages simultaneously and harmoniously through unified performances. This capacity for broadcasting diverse, and sometimes opposed or contradictory, messages is best articulated in Rappaport's (1979, 1999) distinction between self-referential and canonical messages. Self-referential messages convey a performer's state of being and status vis-à-vis the web of social relations, institutions, and situations in which the performer is currently enmeshed. As participants in rituals, performers communicate a multiplicity of self-referential messages to themselves and others, including (1) knowledge of and willingness to act in accordance with socially recognized and acceptable modes of religious practice; (2) submission to the historical authority of the ritualized social structures in which they place themselves; and (3) having the socially and religiously legitimated clout, capital, and permission to engage in sacred discourse through ritual performance. We should keep in mind, however, that performance does not imply a straightforward acceptance of, submission to, or belief in dogma but is instead a public and strategic act of social and religious conformance (Rappaport 1999:119–124).

In contrast to self-referential messages, canonical messages are formally encoded in ritual performances and are thus less susceptible to nuance and misinterpretation. Canonical messages are those we associate with the ritual form, liturgy, and religious principles embodied in the performance. They are the dogmatic messages embedded in scripts, symbols, and sequences of acts, and their numinous quality and occult origin transcend performers' personal aims. Nevertheless, whereas rituals offer a religiously ordained milieu for the broadcasting of self-referential information, canonical messages serve as powerful, spiritually derived conveyances to which actors can strategically align themselves and affix their interests. Indeed, during rituals "variant self-referential messages are sanctified, which is to say certified, through their association with the highly invariant canonical stream" (Rappaport 1999:329). Through ritual practice, performers blend canonical and self-referential information into a unified, polyreferential message in which personal identities and positions are intermixed among and legitimated through cultural and religious values and principles. Ritual, then, is "*a very complex form in which the two classes of messages are dependent upon each other*" (Rappaport 1999:58; emphasis in original).

The dual nature of ritual communication presents a microcosm of the structure and agency dialectic at work in social reproduction. Canonical messages, like the ritual form, are structures within which people act. Self-referential messaging, therefore, is a strategy for people working within these structures to align themselves with an extra-human aura of authority, history, and explanation. Rituals not only allow actors to wrap and shield themselves in the sanctifying shadow of religious principles but also afford them opportunities to potentially transmute knowledge and manipulate ritual and religious structures. This is the substantiating process of ritualization. In Chapter 2 I described ritual mastery as a social theatre in which performers vie for access to, possession of, and control over religious knowledge. Ritual participation implicates performers in a sacred dialogue with the "ultimate sources of power" (Bell 1992:141) while temporarily enmeshing them and other agents, including other-than-humans, in a web of power relations regarding the generation and administration of authoritative resources (Giddens 1984)—in this case, religious knowledge.

South Mountains Rock Art and Religious Knowledge

As an element of religious ritual practice, rock art manufacture in the South Mountains involved canonical and self-referential messaging among a congregation of human and other-than-human performers and witnesses. We cannot decipher the canonical messages with any assuredness, but judging by broadly shared themes in mountain- and spring-centered ritualism, some of the information quite likely pertained to issues regarding rain and fertility. However, while it is natural to ask and tempting to speculate, this book is not explicitly concerned with interpreting canonical messages, such as what the petroglyphs may "mean" or "symbolize." Doing so would risk sidetracking the equally important headway made toward understanding the active role of rock art in social processes. In fact, I have admittedly downplayed symbolic interpretation in order to transcend traditional analytic modes and reframe rock art as meaningful social practice guided by history and cultural mores yet also instrumental in the reproduction and transformation of such structural conditions. The key feature of the canonical messages I wish to draw attention to instead is the connection to knowledge.

As brought to light in Chapter 6, Hohokam rock art is characterized by redundancy and repetition of symbols, production techniques, and stages of performance. These factors, which indicate the formalism, encoded tradition, and invariance of the ritual form, also underscore the canonical virtues of the rock art. South Mountains rock art embedded canonized messages in symbol (motif), performance (manufacture), and place (stage), and was therefore a vehicle for the transmission of religious knowledge. More precisely, religious knowledge informed and structured the iconography as well as the ritual form of petroglyph production. In addition to broadcasting existing bodies of knowledge, rock art ritualism may have validated them or even promoted the generation of new threads of knowledge—ascertained through dreams, visions, omens, or another sort—via communion with other-than-human agents at religiously important places. In this way, both the message (information) and performance (means to obtain information and put it to use) constitute the authoritative resource of religious knowledge.

Through ritual practice, performers air self-referential information, such as status, allegiance, devotion, and competence, and they leverage it in a socially dynamic struggle over religious knowledge encoded in the ritual's canonical messages. "Formalized activities can communicate complex sociocultural messages very economically, particularly messages about social classification, hierarchical relationships, and the negotiation of identity and position in the social nexus" (Bell 1997:141). As actors participate in religious rituals, they simultaneously convey their relationship to religious dogma and metaphysical agencies and legitimate their access to, possession of, and mastery over the requisite religious knowledge to human and other-than-human witnesses. Performers do not simply display their identities through rituals; they actively craft and define elements of personhood via a negotiatory relationship with the organic and superorganic congregation as well as the broader community of adherents to those religious principles.

To comprehend the self-referential messages in the ritualized manufacture and viewing of rock art, we need to consider the size and identity of the audience(s) and the stages of performance. The audience for Hohokam rock art varied across stages, yet on each there was probably little permanent or institutionalized social distance between audience and performer(s). Human audiences were composed of people interacting with the various mise-en-scènes where rock art ritualism and related practices were carried out. Most audiences were small, consisting usually of individuals or task groups in the course of plant-gathering forays, whereas on elevated stages like the saddle shrine and summit trails they *could* have been more substantial, perhaps upward of a hundred witnesses at any one time. Even on these more open stages most petroglyphs are not visible from any considerable distance or advantaged viewpoint, suggesting that the audience for the imagery was smaller than what the stages could accommodate. Some stages exhibit heightened degrees of formality through either architectural features such as shrines and summit trails or an intimate focus on an unusual environmental setting like springs. The attendant ritual practices were likewise formal engagements and may have been the purview of a specialized class of performers or a select few individuals, perhaps socially recognized personae such as religious leaders, initiates, or others seeking to establish or revitalize relationships with other-than-human agents and essences. During such performances the ritual actors strategically positioned themselves in a religiously sanctioned negotiation over social power by demonstrating, convincing, and justifying to an audience their authority over religious knowledge and affiliation with a divine agency.

On other, less formalized stages, such as around agricultural terraces and along trails, rock art ritualism was accompanied by ancillary practices not solely or directly concerned with communing with other-than-human subjects. Some of the canonized religious information was nevertheless similar to what was relayed on the more formal stages because there is little to no difference in petroglyph symbolism across stages (Figure 5.2). However, because features of the stages are also sacral symbols infused with mythic ambience, religious meaning, and spiritual potency, the information embedded in canonical messages certainly differed to some extent among stages and performances. What is interesting, then, is that while the content in the individualized, self-referential, and some of the canonical messages varied by performance, they all drew on the same narrow set of relatively uniformly dimensioned (Figure 6.9), standardly crafted (Figure 6.24) petroglyph symbols. This points to shared aims and interests among performers as well as widely held religious themes underlying the broader network of mountain-oriented ritualism. It seems that on each stage and probably during each performance the rock art evidences a ritually based elicitation of occult efficacy founded on religious principles that wove other-than-human agencies into the South Mountains. In effect, each stage attests to a different socio-environmental scenario in which ritual actors engaged and communed with numinous forces animating a sacred landscape, a spiritual relationship and religious alignment enacted and legitimated before the critical eyes of accompanying audiences.

Summary

Religious ritual is a field of highly sensuous action where performance *showcases* the repetitive embodiment of religious knowledge. When performers crafted rock art, they were communicating canonical information through sacral symbolism in multiple media (petroglyphs, performances, and places) to themselves and a more-than-human congregation. To these sacred, transcendental messages performers tied self-referential information that signaled to that same audience their alignment with the underlying religious premises and principles and relationship with mythic, deific, celestial subjects. As Pauketat comments, "a petroglyph was powerful because of its place as a point of articulation in a complex and historically contingent field wherein people, places, spirit beings, and rocks, among other things, connect" (2012:230). Hohokam glyphmakers demonstrated through ritual practice that they held the requisite religious know-how—the symbolic capital embodied in the ritual's performance and encoded in the symbolism—as well as the ability, legitimacy, duty, and courage to commune with mythic beings, sacred places, and other other-than-human agents.

Hohokam rock art in the South Mountains exhibits all the trappings of an established mode of ritual practice—performance, invariance, formalism, encoded tradition, and occult efficacy. Much of the petroglyph symbolism, however, was not restricted to this field of ritual communication and engagement with an animated, sacred landscape. While Hohokam glyphmakers and potters clearly favored different motif assemblages and followed different design structures, there are considerable iconographic similarities among these visual art systems (Chapter 6) as well as with other craft industries of ritual paraphernalia, such as figurines, palettes, and censers. In addition to the shared suite of geometric and figurative designs, iconographic shifts in rock art, on pottery, and among lesser-studied but equally important visual arts were broadly synchronous (Chapter 5; see also Figure 3.4). This degree of symbolic pervasiveness across religious and domestic media and through history points to the embeddedness and fluidity of religious knowledge within the Preclassic Hohokam world, whereas iconographic dissimilarities and nuances pertain to differential contexts of production and use, social configurations of audiences, and dispositions of artisans for each artistic medium.

Like the open, visible settings for most of the petroglyphs, the commonness of rock art motifs in other media shows that the symbolism (though not necessarily the encoded messages) was neither esoteric nor arcane. This pervasiveness and accessibility in religiously charged symbolism compares favorably with the participatory nature of Preclassic Hohokam ritual life—plaza-centered ceremonies like feasting and vivid mortuary rites; ballgames whose courts could accommodate large audiences, perhaps even whole villages; public orations atop low, capped mounds; and the wide sharing of identity-crafting tokens (e.g., shell bracelets, red-on-buff pottery, palettes) of membership in or alignment with a religious movement that blended a southern exoticism with an archaic familiarity (Chapter 3). Nevertheless, this fluidity of religious knowledge, sharing of sacral symbolism, and emphasis on open-access ritualism did not persist over the course of the Hohokam millennium. The turn toward the Classic period brought about a history-changing shift in the social dynamics surrounding the struggle over religious knowledge and the way communities practiced and lived their religion. Concomitant with that transformation was a rejection of rock art and related mountain-centered rituals as appropriate means for communing and relating with other-than-human essences and occult forces animating the landscape. As I discuss in the following chapter, this jettison of ritual communalism coincided with an usurpation of religious knowledge and sacred ground by emerging politico-religious leaders. The new ritual masters naturalized their religious authority by capitalizing on connections to platform mounds, new public ritual edifices that replicated and domesticated elements of the sacred geography and brought them under the auspices of village leaders.

CHAPTER 8

Rock Art and Transformation of the Hohokam Social World

"Human worlds." Each human society develops a unique culture, which is also to say that it constructs a unique world that includes not only a special understanding of the trees and rocks and water surrounding it, but of the things, many unseen, as real as those trees and animals and rocks. It is in terms of their existence, no less than in terms of the existence of physical things, that people operate and transform not only their social systems but the ecosystems surrounding them. (Rappaport 1999:8)

The study of ancient religion has traditionally fallen within broader and somewhat vaguer research on "ideology," a strategy by which aggressive actors vie for social power through manipulation of beliefs, symbols, worldviews, morality, and cultural perceptions (e.g., DeMarrais et al. 1996; McGuire 1992b). Ideology is a Marxist construct, and archaeological scholarship in its shadow commonly pits elite ideologies versus commoner or communal forms, and frames them in class-like structures of domination (e.g., Demarest and Conrad 1992; McGuire 1992a; McGuire and Saitta 1996; Miller et al. 1989; Saitta 1994). I do not cast Hohokam religion a priori in such a domineering and top-heavy light; I contend it is more fruitful to consider it both a structuring principle (an explanation of the world and body of metaphysically ordained, historically transcendent social rules and customs) and an authoritative resource (an avenue for transformative social action). Religious knowledge is a form of immaterial capital, or intellectual property, and one's access, possession, or control of it can serve as a vital and potent source of social power (see Chapter 2). In this sense, the *social organization* of religious knowledge can be likened to an ideology, but religion in and of itself is not so antagonistic.

In the following I summarize and compare current conceptions of the social organization of religious knowledge among the Hohokam during the Preclassic and Classic eras. Chapter 3 offers a more detailed overview of Hohokam religion, and similar, complementary, and parallel syntheses have been forwarded by Wilcox (1987a; Wilcox and Sternberg 1983; Wilcox et al. 1981) and more recently Wallace (2014; Wallace and Lindeman 2003, 2012, 2013). After this synopsis I show how rock art ritualism proxied the organization of religious knowledge within Hohokam communities. Inevitably, the distribution of this authoritative resource, as a relationship of power among community members, transformed in concert with a number of other changes in social organization, demography, and cultural practice. I suggest that a rearrangement of politico-religious authority was made by new or existing ritual leaders who, seeking to expand their influence in the late Sedentary and Classic periods, took position as the custodians of religious knowledge and sanctioned themselves as the intermediaries between the community and the cosmos. Whether this was due to a willing divestment of religious knowledge and ritual position on the part of community members or a strategic arrest of these resources and privileges by politically minded or power-driven actors remains in question. The rock art evidence, however, suggests that this forfeiture, or circumscription, met little to no resistance by the communities at large, at least at first.

Religious Knowledge in the Preclassic Era

The social organization of religious knowledge during the Preclassic may be characterized aptly as "communal" (Bayman 2002:77), in the sense that the forms of ritual architecture and the distribution of ritual paraphernalia evidence an inclusive, participatory ritual system (McGuire 1992b; Preucel 1996; Wallace et al. 1995). Indeed, a high degree of public participation was elementary to Hohokam religious life and ritual practice from the earliest days of the Pioneer period. Sensory-rich religious rituals were enacted at an assortment of places—starting with performances in plazas and moving to small capped mounds and ballcourts, symbolic architectural facilities engineered to accommodate audiences. Over time, communities embedded religious principles such as directionality, a tiered cosmos, and metaphors of a sacred geography in village layouts (Wilcox 1987a; Wilcox and Sternberg 1983). Perhaps the earliest and longest-lived signs of this public and participatory ritual system and its tie to the domestic landscape are early Pioneer cremation burials in village plazas (Wallace and Lindeman 2003). This transformative mortuary ritual bundled fire and flesh, smoke and earth, life and death. The inferno's light, heat, and smell ensured that the rite of passage, performed in the heart of the village, was experienced by all in attendance, possibly entire communities. The interment of cremated remains in plazas provided villagers unimpeded, ready, and daily access to the dead. Veneration of ancestors was also afforded by the figurine complex that seems to have been integral to the domestic lives of many households by at least the Pioneer period (Aragon 2013; Stinson 2004, 2010; Thomas and King 1985; Wilcox and Sternberg 1983).

Wallace (2008, 2014; Wallace and Lindeman 2003) has suggested that the organization of religious knowledge in formative Hohokam communities likely followed a shamanistic model, in which certain individuals held socially recognized roles responsible for accessing and controlling esoteric knowledge for the betterment of the community. This was probably a perpetuation of the organizational scheme of earlier, incipient agricultural communities across the Greater Southwest (Underhill 1948). However, an experimentation with Mesoamerican-inspired concepts and ritual practices in the Snaketown phase gained momentum and led to an outright transformation of the Hohokam ritual system, a cultural metamorphosis recognized as the Colonial period (Doyel 1991a; Wallace 2014; Wallace and Lindeman 2013; Wallace et al. 1995; Wilcox 1987a, 1991b). This was when most of the archaeological culture traits considered emblematic of the Hohokam (red-on-buff pottery, ballcourts, shell jewelry, etc.) exploded across the desert regions of what is now southern and central Arizona, from the San Pedro River to the Mogollon Rim, and from the Great Bend of the Gila River to the headwaters of the Salt River (Figure 3.1). Many of the new tokens of Hohokamness—palettes, censers, pyrite mirrors, and so on—held ritual significance. The origins of the Hohokam are therefore intertwined with a horizontal religious transformation that melded age-old indigenous practices and beliefs with new cosmic concepts, metaphysical principles, and mythic understandings of a Mesoamerican derivation.

The rapid and far-reaching metanoia across the Hohokam world at the onset of the Colonial period, as seen in esoterica, architecture, and symbolism, was presaged and may have been instigated by a series of environmental and cosmic calamities. According to Wallace (2014; Wallace and Lindeman 2003, 2013; Wallace et al. 1995), the AD 700s was an unstable and rather agriculturally unfavorable time to be living in southern Arizona. During that century a number of deleterious perturbations in rainfall and streamflow wracked the Phoenix Basin, and as a result local farmers experienced some of the worst droughts and floods they would ever face (Graybill et al. 2006). To make matters worse, two total solar eclipses in the same century (Masse and Espenak 2006; Masse and Soklow 2005) possibly inspired the Hohokam to reevaluate their position in relation to the cosmic order, the effectiveness of the existing ritual system, and the authority and legitimacy of their religious leaders.

In light of such detrimental and unprecedented events, either Hohokam religious leaders or charismatic people outside the then-current politico-religious power structure seeking to revitalize their position and authority ventured south into Mesoamerica or its hinterlands to acquire novel and exotic religious knowledge and trinkets of their sojourns. This Hohokam Revitalization Movement planted the seeds for an intervillage, socio-political experiment that united community leaders through membership in a religious sodality, what Wallace (2014) refers to as the "Ballcourt Society." This new corporate formation of ritual leaders brought about a reorganization in how religious knowledge was shared across and between communities. The popularity and success of the Ballcourt Society, the renewed religious order, and a revitalized ritual system created demand for certain symbols associated with this exciting social movement, such as shell jewelry, middle Gila buffware pottery, and Style 2 iconography (Figure 3.4). Calendrically regulated, sodality-sponsored ballgames at court-equipped villages facilitated the rapid dissemination of religious know-how and the regular exchange of ritual goods far and wide. Average villagers' participation was integral to the execution and operation of this religious revival.

After the revitalization movement's initial thrust, and once the Ballcourt Society became a common denominator for village politico-religious guidance and leadership, slight differences in mortuary treatment and the types and quantities of burial accoutrements among individuals suggest that socially recognized status differentials started taking root (Craig 2000). The cremation ritual nonetheless erased such differences upon death (McGuire 1992b). Ritual practices surrounding figurines branched out from household contexts to include mortuary ones too, showing that the custom of ancestor veneration remained important if not more so. The religious revitalization and the cultural florescence that followed must have been successful and rewarding since the Ballcourt Society and all that it stood for persisted for generations. Something about it, however, was not sustainable because by the middle Sedentary its unifying tethers were fraying as nuances of the pan-Hohokam religious identity and ritual structure arose to meet local interests and needs.

Eventually, and perhaps just as quickly as the revitalization movement blazed across the Hohokam world, villagers rejected the Ballcourt Society as a suitable scheme for organizing religious knowledge and ritual practice. This entailed the withering and demise of the ballcourt network and a concomitant contraction in the trade and exchange of buffware pottery, a once ubiquitous hallmark of Hohokam identity. Much of the formerly vital and distinctive suite of Hohokam esoterica and ritual paraphernalia likewise became obsolete and was laid to rest in rubbish heaps, in crematory fires, and on dilapidated house floors. What exactly fomented this turn from what had been a thriving and voguish style of living and practicing a Hohokam religion remains a vexing question in Southwest anthropology (though water scarcity continues to be a championed explanation; see below), but it set in motion an outright circumscription of religious knowledge by particular social segments or personages in the communities.

The Classic Period Circumscription of Religious Knowledge

The social transformation to the Classic period encompassed much more than an eschewal of the Ballcourt Society and a reworking of the ritual system, but research from various camps and of differing theoretical persuasions agrees that what happened had a religious underpinning nonetheless (e.g., Bayman 2001, 2002; Downum and Bostwick 2003; Doyel 1991a, 2000a, 2007; Fish and Fish 2000; Gregory 1991; Howard 2006; Neitzel 1991; Preucel 1996; Wilcox 1987a, 1991b, 1991c). The unraveling of the ballcourt network and the rise of moundtop ceremonialism ushered in a fundamental reconfiguration of the Hohokam religious structure, including a refashioned ritual system and reorganization in the

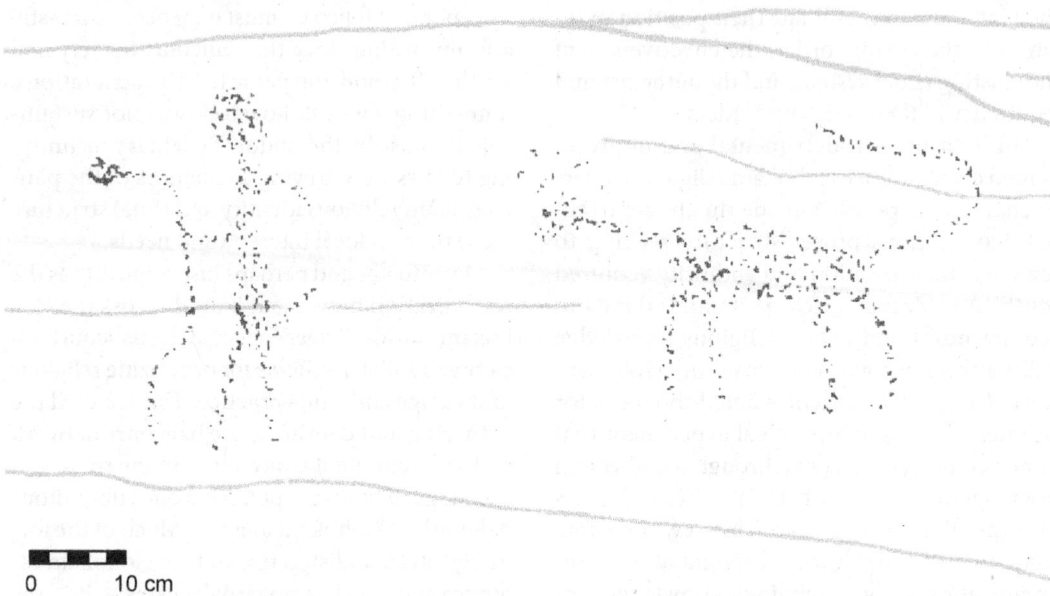

FIGURE 8.1. Panel with a staff-wielding anthropomorph and an unusual quadruped petroglyph. Quadrupeds with sinuous tails such as this are sometimes interpreted as mountain lions.

distribution of religious knowledge. The schism from the old ways was so profound that it left footprints in the well-documented demographic upheaval at the Sedentary/Classic transition. For example, many—though not all—ballcourt villages, as ritual centers for peripheral villages and hamlets, ceased to host residential communities (Doyel 1980, 2000a; Wilcox et al. 1981; Woodson 2010; see also Hill et al. 2004). Villagers even walked away from Snaketown, which Wallace (2014; Wallace and Lindeman 2013) hypothesizes was the central seat of the Ballcourt Society. Within newly established villages and those that weathered the storm, the Hohokam also cast aside many ritual practices and symbols that once united their society. As outlined in Chapter 3, several lines of evidence show that social groups tied to the platform mounds eventually co-opted much of the surviving and new ritual paraphernalia, sequestered ritual practices, and consequently circumscribed the religious knowledge bound to and embodied in such items and performances, separating it from the broader community. This is best witnessed through shifts in iconography, the stages for ritual performances, and the spatial distribution of esoterica.

A canon of the Hohokam Revitalization Movement in the Colonial period was a rapidly and widely adopted suite of amazingly uniform and standardized figurative and geometric motifs, some with undeniable but hard-to-explain Mesoamerican antecedents, in multiple media. This set of new design elements and the ways they were arranged in increasingly patterned layouts are defining qualities of what Wallace (1995b, 2001, 2004; Wallace et al. 1995) classifies as Style 2 in Hohokam visual arts (see Figure 3.4). Usually associated with the red paintings on widely traded, specialist-crafted buffware pottery originating predominantly from villages along the middle Gila River (Abbott 2009; Kelly 2013; Lack 2013), both the geometric and lifeform motifs in Style 2 appear on arguably more ritualized objects such as palettes and censers, and in rock art (Figures 8.1, 8.2, 8.3, and 8.4; see also Figures 5.5, 5.7, 5.8, 6.6, 6.22, 6.25, and 6.26), but in seemingly different proportions (see Chapter 6). The reason this design repertoire spread like wildfire across the Hohokam world and spanned domestic and public, secular and religious contexts is that it materialized the religious order and some of the mythic premises packaged up with the new system of ballcourt ritualism (Lack

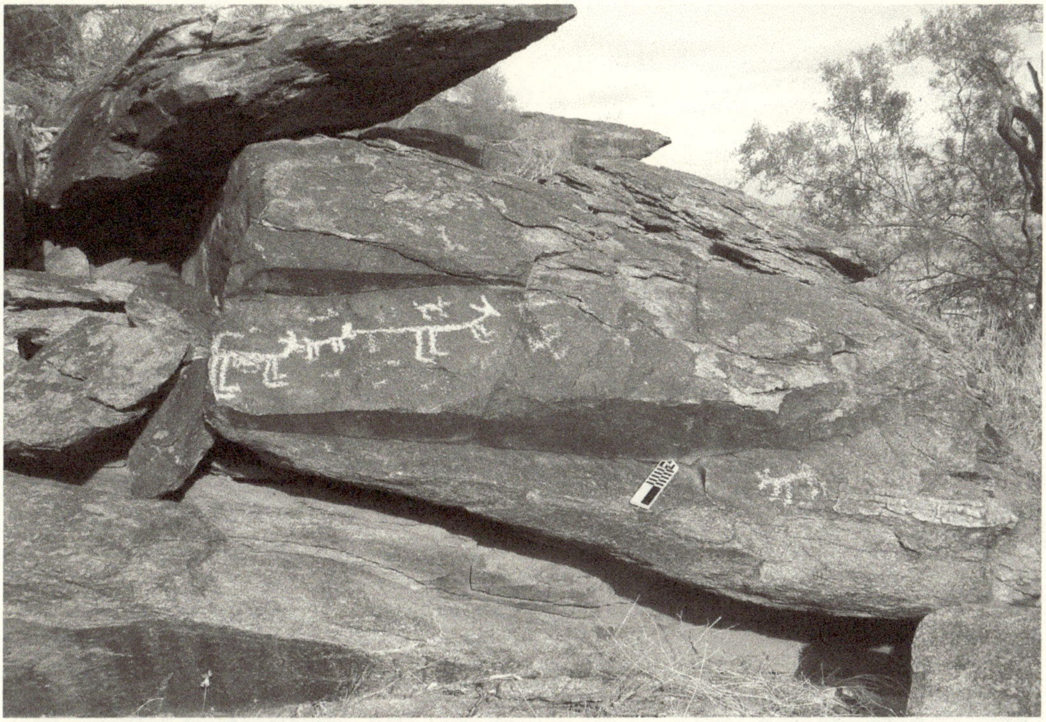

FIGURE 8.2. Overview of panels with various canid petroglyphs.

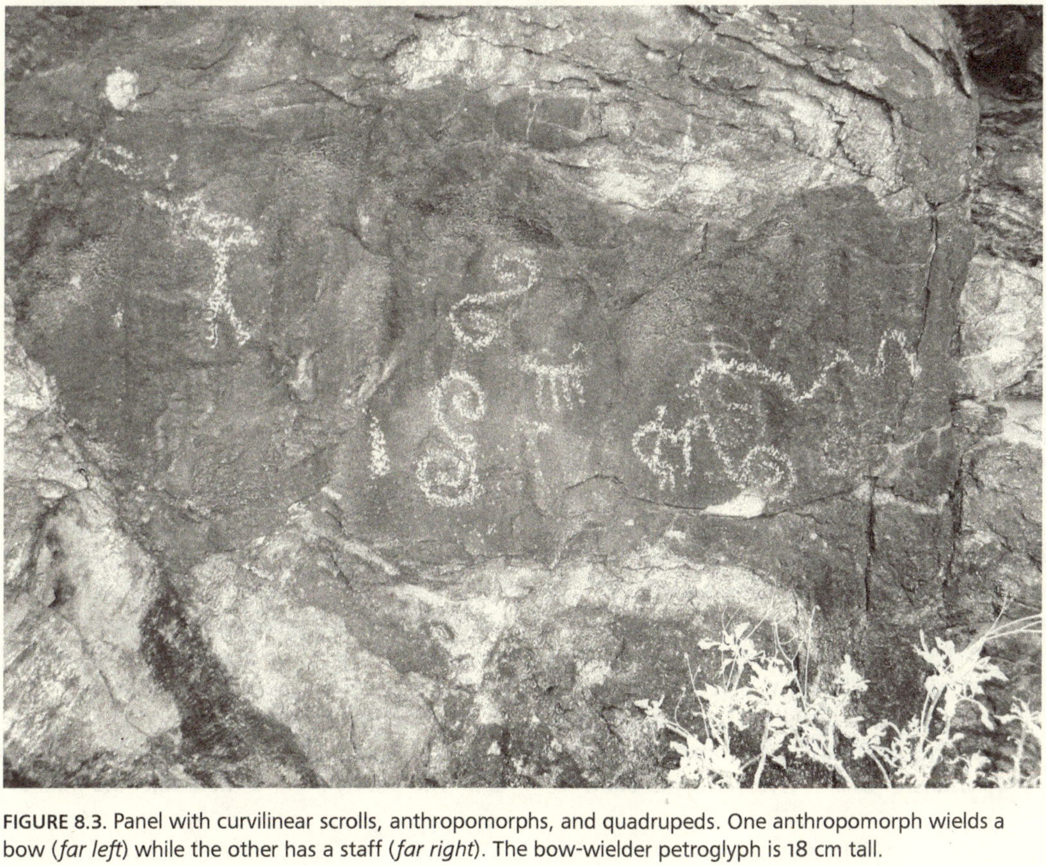

FIGURE 8.3. Panel with curvilinear scrolls, anthropomorphs, and quadrupeds. One anthropomorph wields a bow (*far left*) while the other has a staff (*far right*). The bow-wielder petroglyph is 18 cm tall.

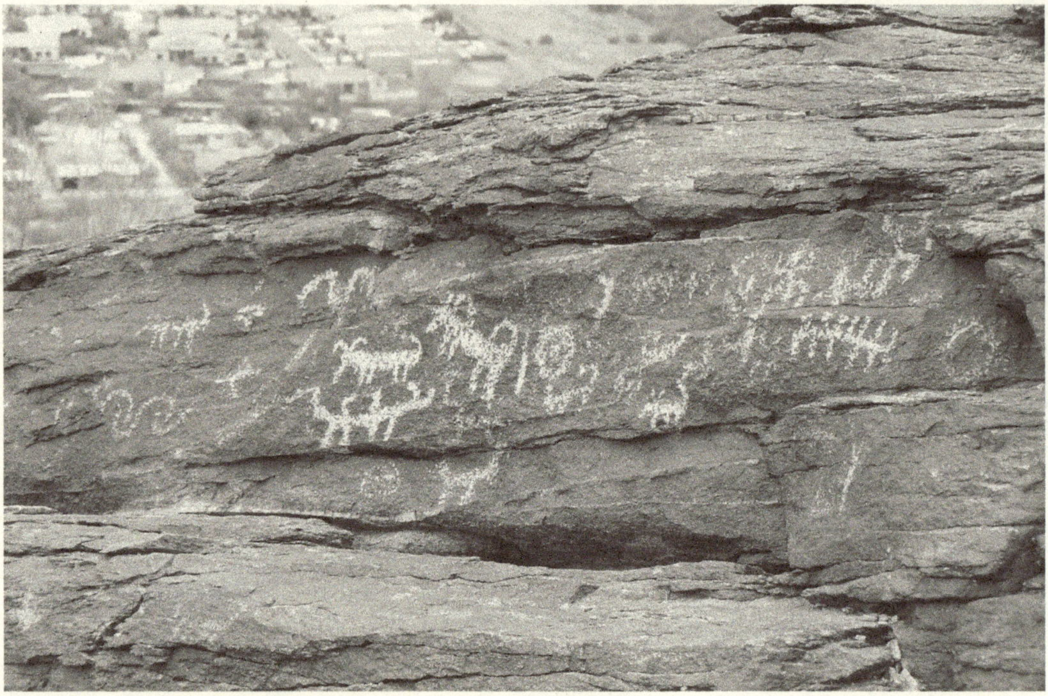

FIGURE 8.4. Overview of a densely covered panel with an assortment of curvilinear geometric and lifeform petroglyphs (facing northeast). The circle petroglyph at far right is 9 cm tall.

2013; Wallace 2014; Wallace and Lindeman 2012, 2013; Wallace et al. 1995; Wilcox 1991b).

Some familiar motifs, particularly animals, humans, and other lifeforms, were dropped from the Hohokam iconographic lexicon during the late Sedentary and early Classic. Hohokam ceramic designs consequently turned from a relatively inviting, lively, and intelligible juxtaposition of naturalistic and simple geometric elements to a more complex arrangement of predominantly linear and rectilinear designs and patterns largely devoid of recognizable icons and narrative scenes. Though their symbolic meanings and any metaphysical or occult properties or virtues attributed to them elude us, animals figured strongly in Preclassic Hohokam religion and ritualism (Wallace 2008; Wilcox 1991b; Wilcox et al. 2008). As Haury understood it:

> The animal additions to palettes and indeed the effigy palettes, the snakes, lizards, birds, and other animals drawn from the desert environment which so richly decorate stone receptacles, seem to qualify as esoterica rather than commonly possessed items. Beliefs in the power of animals as the cause of illnesses and that effigies of them can effect cures are not unknown among existing desert tribes. That art played a dual role among the Hohokam, to please and to protect, to erase drabness, and to be iconographic, seems certain. (1976:356–357)

Since animal and human depictions persisted in less abundant sculptural forms such as effigies and carvings, they did not disappear entirely from Hohokam visual arts after the curtains fell on ballcourt ritualism and communities underwent an associated social transformation. Their near absence on late Sedentary and early Classic period pottery and ritual paraphernalia, together with the lapse in rock art in which animals and anthropomorphs were favored subjects, nevertheless shows that public access to religiously inspired imagery—from the individuals who painted and owned buffware pots or pecked glyphs into rocks to those whose bodies were burned and interred with Style 2–adorned objects and offerings—was fettered. Animal themes resurfaced on pottery in the late Classic with the introduction of Salado polychromes, but the new and foreign designs emphasized snakes and birds, which are more abstract and quite different from earlier naturalistic depictions (Crown 1994).

The turn to the Classic period also saw the stages for community ritualism and the storehouses of ritual paraphernalia move from the open settings of plazas and ballcourts to the more confined and restricted platform mounds and their surrounding precincts in the villages' centers. This cramp in ritual practice and alignment of religious authority to and around platform mounds followed a centuries-long evolutionary trajectory. As loci of community-oriented rituals, Colonial period capped mounds and the primogenitor platform mounds of the Sedentary may have actually encouraged viewership by elevating performances above the surrounding landscape. By the end of the Sedentary, however, newly erected palisades around and large pithouses atop some mounds began to immure the performances enacted on them. Ritual leaders cemented the seclusion and secrecy of moundtop ritualism during the late Classic with the erection of adobe and masonry walls and restrictive architectural arrangements around and atop these ritual pillars of the community (Gregory 1991; Howard 1992). This served to separate the religious knowledge encoded in ritual performances from the community at large and institutionalized it within both the villages' central precincts and the social groups or personages vested with their custodianship.

The circumscription of religious knowledge in Classic period Hohokam society is also evident in how objects of ritual importance are patterned throughout villages, across social groups, and among individuals. During the Preclassic, ritual objects abounded and were dispersed among community members and contexts. The wide use of anthropomorphic figurines in household rituals is just one example. The village of La Ciudad, where nearly every Preclassic household had either a censer or a palette (Rice 1987b:178–185), offers another case of the ubiquitous occurrence of ritualized materials throughout communities. However, as the transformative social processes at the dawn of the Classic unfolded, the Hohokam swapped old forms of ritual paraphernalia for new ones, left some types of esoterica by the wayside, and seemingly reconsidered who could possess which types of ritual objects, how many they could have, and where they should be kept. Items of ritual significance were increasingly concentrated in fewer places and controlled by fewer people. For instance, most of the ritual paraphernalia at Pueblo Grande was stored or discarded on and around the platform mound (Downum and Bostwick 2003:194). Unlike earlier examples usually found in male burials, Classic era shell trumpets, instrumental in ritual performances (Mills and Ferguson 2008) and quite possibly insignia of ritual authority or leadership offices (Bayman 2002), are typically recovered from platform mounds and their precincts to the near exclusion of other settings.

The gradual culmination in mound architecture from low rises of refuse to engineered platforms reached its apex in the late Classic with the erection of compounds and multistory buildings atop them. What actually transpired on the mounds in terms of social organization and leadership remains a debated topic in Hohokam research (Elson and Abbott 2000). Were they sites of communal ritual, temples, or elite residences? The uncertainty comes from the very real possibility they served each of these purposes and more at different times and in different places (Doelle et al. 1995). Communities adopted and adapted the platform mound concept to suit local needs, interests, and modes of social organization. The generally accepted scenario for Phoenix Basin mound communities is that the earliest forms in the late Sedentary and early Classic continued to serve as loci for community ritualism, perhaps as mini-temples (Gregory 1987; Downum and Bostwick 2003; Doyel 1991a, 2000b). With the raising of retaining walls and compound architecture atop the mounds in the late Classic, certain social groups or individuals co-opted these important community spaces. While they likely remained the nuclei of community ritualism, a sort of custodianship of moundtop ceremonialism took hold among certain privileged social groups. With that new responsibility came greater control over religious knowledge and an intensification in ritual mastery.

By the late Classic, most moundtops were fully enclosed and cordoned by layers of compound walls and precinct roomblocks. The coordinated placement of such enshrouding structures atop and around the villages' central ritual stages finally materialized what had been a growing division between the moundtops' stewards and other community members. According to Fish and Fish, the rise of Hohokam platform mounds implies that "ritual became more centralized, with performers and observers of communal events becoming a more exclusive subset of the population" (2000:162). With the co-optation of moundtop space by compound architecture, what had served as edifices supporting village ritualism and celebrating community identity and descent became institutionalized seats of power and authority, and as the concentrations of ritual paraphernalia show, that authority had a religious draw.

The archaeology of Classic period platform mounds reveals that individuals and/or corporate groups aligned with the mounds wielded a nexus of religious and political authority, vital sources of social power that were increasingly sequestered from other villagers. As Douglas Mitchell (2003; Mitchell and Brunson-Hadley 2001) suggests, newly established vertical (hierarchical) social distinctions were juxtaposed among existing horizontal (heterarchical) status differences in Classic period Hohokam society. Such status contrasts are most evident in the late Classic, when obvious economic differences indicative of elites began to appear in the distribution of the types and amounts of grave goods among burials (e.g., Mitchell 2003; Loendorf 2001), of which the most ostentatious were the pair of sarcophagi burials at Los Muertos and Casa Grande (Mitchell and Brunson-Hadley 2001). As social hierarchies expand—what appears to have occurred among the Hohokam—avenues for participation in ritual practices constrict (Kertzer 1988:52). By the end, most Hohokam villagers were left out in the cold as they forfeited their roles in village ritualism and stations in religious life to those who took responsibility for the community's spiritual well-being by surmounting the village's ritual center.

The ill-fated social experiment in Hohokam politico-religious leadership tied to platform mounds had a short and swift tenure, however, as community after community turned its back and gave up on a mound-centric way of life. In a sound case of archaeological and oral historical common ground, the unprecedented ascendancy of Hohokam politico-religious authority and its demise is marked and mythologized in narratives from descendant communities describing mass unrest, insurrection, and the eventual overthrow and execution of debaucherous and tyrannical "lords" at platform mound villages (e.g., Bahr et al. 1994; Russell 1908; Teague 1988, 1993).[1] To bring this historical trajectory back to the matter at hand, what relevance did the South Mountains rock art and related ritual practices have to the Classic period transformation of the Hohokam social world?

Rock Art through the Transformation

In the Preclassic Hohokam world, people lived religion at their own volition. Low-level religious leaders of some sort—evinced by the occasional lavish or richly endowed burial, the presence of Big Houses, and the hierarchy in building size around plazas—were mainstays of village life, but they were not the sole actors visiting sacred places and practicing rituals focused on maintaining relationships with the metaphysical. The institutionalized openness wrought by the Ballcourt Society, its attendant ritual system, and the prestige-neutralizing cremation ritual kept such leaders in check and prevented aggrandizement of religious knowledge and the usurpation of ritual mastery by religious overachievers. Ritual and religion were thus relatively level playing fields.

The structure of the South Mountains rock art assemblage mirrors the fluidity of religious knowledge and openness of ritual practice characteristic of the Preclassic. Petroglyphs are spread across the landscape, found on multiple and diverse stages, visually inviting and topographically accessible, and associated with an array of ritualized and subsistence-related practices; they depict designs similar to those found on pottery and were crafted by people of various social positions and with differing aims (see Chapter 6). Petroglyph manufacture, albeit an infrequent practice, and the larger system of mountain ritualism of which it was a part, therefore pierced nascent social hierarchies and spanned disparate social identities within communities. Just as for today's modern urban populace, the South Mountains were an uplifted sanctuary where denizens from nearby communities escaped the troubles and toils of daily life. For the Preclassic Hohokam, however, the mountains offered a series of stages where people—religious leaders and less exalted villagers alike—engaged in ritual practices concerned with relating and communing with mythic, metaphysical, cosmological, other-than-human subjects (see Chapter 7).

Something about the social transformation during the terminal Sedentary and early Classic nonetheless led Hohokam communities to rewrite the rules and reconfigure the playing field for their ritual system. A shying away from ancestral ways in favor of a reworked ritual system and new venues for ritual mastery is attested to by, as elaborated above, an ebbing in buffware manufacture and exchange, subsidence in figurative iconography on decorated pottery, disappearance of once-essential items from ritual toolkits, reorganization of the ballcourt network into a structure of platform-mound ceremonialism, and depopulation of centuries-old ritual centers. Villagers complemented this religious move with a dismissal of petroglyph ritualism in the South Mountains and quite possibly elsewhere (see Chapter 5), but was this due to shifts in the organization of religious knowledge or to some other rearrangement in social dynamics within villages?

It may be that by the Classic period the landscape beyond the village edge became too hostile for people to risk life or limb venturing into the South Mountains to continue a long tradition of Hohokam rock art ritualism. Wilcox and others (Wilcox 2005; Wilcox and Holmlund 2007; Wilcox et al. 2001a, 2001b, 2007; see also Rice 2001) have detailed in depth the formation of large buffer zones around the lower Salt River valley and the defensive posturing of settlements in the Classic period, which they take as strong evidence for an interregional concern for and pattern of organized raiding and warfare between the Salt River communities and a Verde Confederacy to the north. There are several reasons, however, why this scenario fails to account for the late Sedentary/early Classic waning in rock art ritualism in the South Mountains. For one, the timing does not line up; though settlements in the northern periphery had defensive characteristics as early as AD 1100, in Wilcox's warfare model the landscape did not turn overly deadly until around AD 1275, well into the Classic period. Analyses of associated diagnostic artifacts and iconography suggest that the end of South Mountains rock art ritualism occurred sometime during or slightly after the transitional phase between the Sedentary and Classic periods (Chapter 5), predating any supposed defensive organization of Salt River communities (as suggested by population massing and compound architecture) and military campaigning implied by a hypothesized Verde Confederacy by at least a century, maybe two.

Another reason why late Classic interregional tensions cannot account for the cessation in South Mountains rock art ritualism is that this small mountain range is nowhere near a buffer zone, nor is it situated between two hypothetically warring factions. Indeed, the most visited and utilized areas of the mountains are within 3 km of a major ballcourt or platform mound village (Figure 3.2), and most villagers engaging in rock art ritual practices were from just two canal systems, Canal System 1 along the mountains' eastern edge and Canal 7 paralleling the northern bajada. While each ballcourt and platform mound village probably held some degree of political autonomy from other centers or village clusters along the same canal (e.g., Crown 1987; Doyel 1981; Fish and Fish 1991, 2000; Gregory

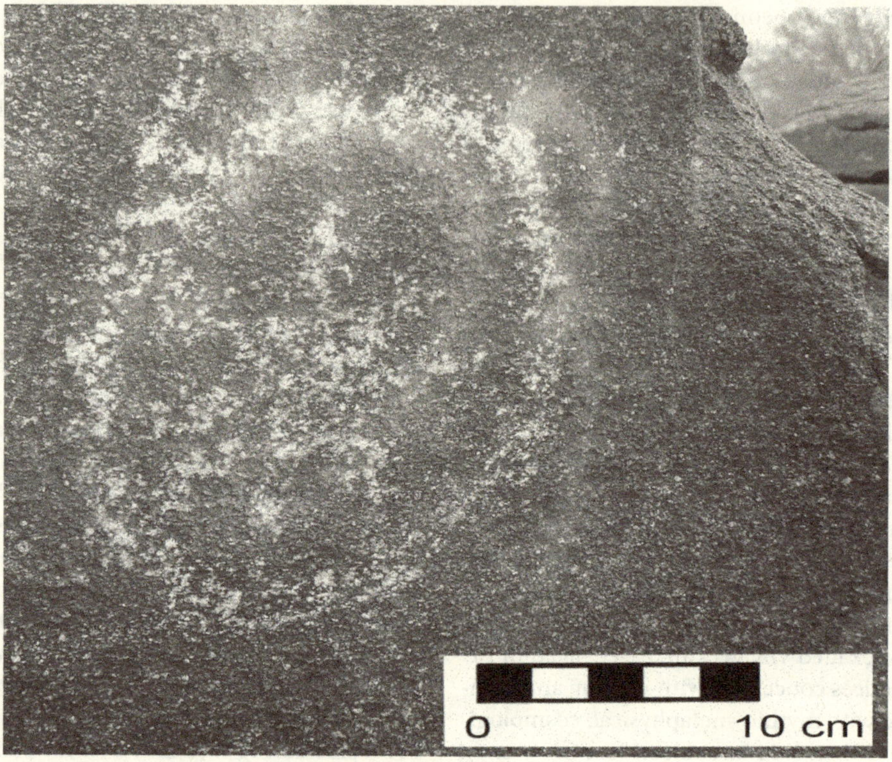

FIGURE 8.5. A possible shield petroglyph. Panel is located above a spring. The hazy texture at the top of the petroglyph is spray-paint graffiti.

1991; Howard 2006; Wilcox 1991c), the irrigation network's maintenance and managerial needs (e.g., Howard 1993; Hunt et al. 2005; Nichols and Neitzel 1984), along with exchange relationships (e.g., Abbott et al. 2006) and possible residential migration along the canals (e.g., Rice et al. 2009:343–347), emphasized and promoted cooperation over conflict. Intervillage grievances along and between canals surely arose, but the competing and quarreling factions all shared the same water source and it was in their interest to band together in response to any external threats (Rice 1998).

Lastly, the iconography portrayed in South Mountains rock art lacks any unambiguous reference or likeness to scenes of conflict, violence, or warfare, as we might expect if some of it dated to a time when such social turmoil and unrest were persistent and stressing aspects of daily life, ritual concern, or social identity—the way Wilcox's warfare model characterizes the Classic period Hohokam world. Motifs and scenes of warriors, shields, trophy heads, and similar metaphors for warfare and violence in rock art are well known from late Pueblo contexts on the Colorado Plateau and in the northern Rio Grande valley (e.g., Crotty 2001; Schaafsma 2000), which was contemporaneous with what was transpiring among the late Classic Hohokam. However, of the more than 3,000 South Mountains petroglyphs analyzed for this study, only two bear any faint reference to warfare or conflict (Figures 8.5 and 8.6). Both glyphs are simple circular designs that *may* symbolize shields; these alone are admittedly unconvincing examples of warfare symbolism in Hohokam rock art. This means that either (1) warfare never reached the level of severity that it did in the Pueblo world or that is implied by the Verde Confederacy scenario or (2) South Mountains rock art ritualism ended before Hohokam warfare turned endemic. The second scenario fits the chronological picture best.

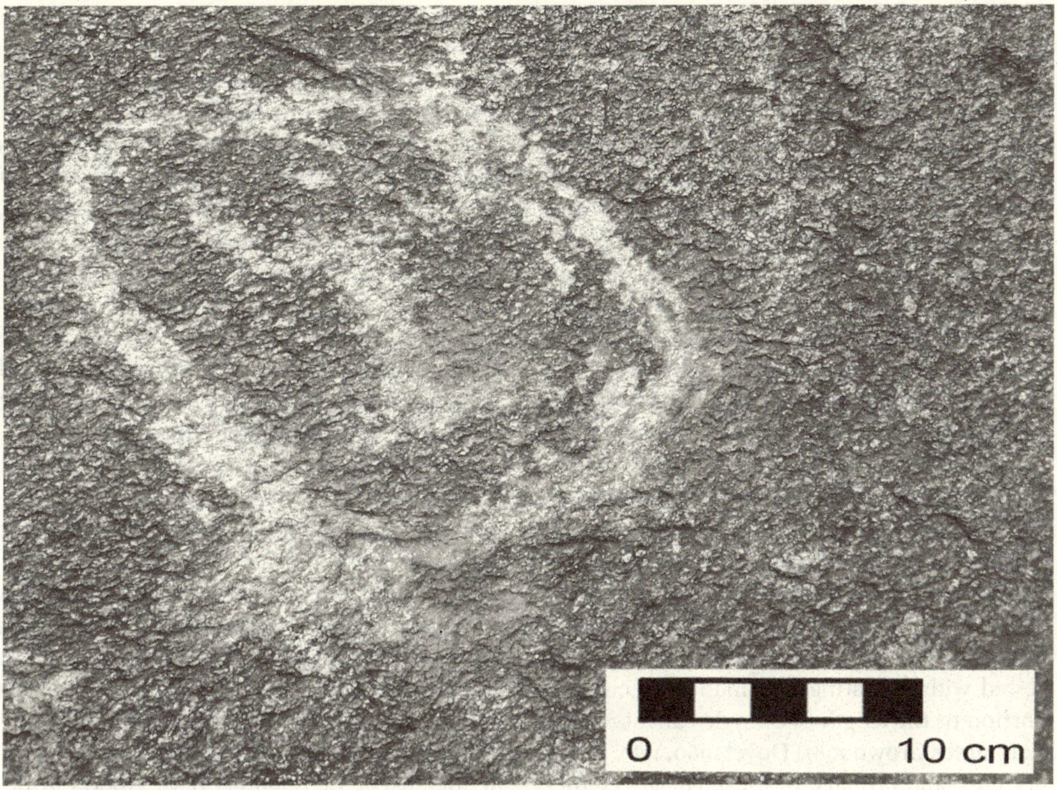

FIGURE 8.6. A possible shield petroglyph. Panel is located above a spring.

The Politics of Ritual Practice

Since external threats cannot fully explain why rock art ritualism in the South Mountains came to a close in the late Sedentary and early Classic, the answer must lie in the social dynamics internal to the Hohokam world. The reason, however, is not simply a by-product of a depopulated or forsaken landscape as communities responded to many social, environmental, and hydrological pushes and pulls. The continued residence of thousands of Hohokam villagers around the South Mountains' periphery during the Classic period, at sizable platform-mound villages such as Pueblo Viejo, Las Canopas, and Los Muertos, discredits any notion that population shuffling throughout the region simply left the mountains a remote and unattended landscape after the Preclassic. The closure of rock art ritualism was rather a notable and substantial turn in cultural practice and had to do with the reorganization of religious knowledge occurring in Hohokam communities. We must therefore peer into the socio-political structure of Hohokam communities to better grasp why villagers around the South Mountains opted out of a centuries-old tradition of crafting rock art and perpetuating the larger ritual system of which it was a part.

As an irrigation-based agricultural society, Hohokam political organization has long found itself under the microscope of neo-evolutionary models of political evolution and the formation of states (e.g., Wittfogel 1957). The underlying assumption has been that demands for labor and coordination for managing the irrigation network necessitated increased levels of political integration, and through feedback mechanisms this process ultimately led to centralized seats of power and political authority. However, instead of a textbook scenario in which an irrigation society *had* to develop a centralized political organization, the Hohokam never put a state-level political apparatus into practice. As one of a number of exceptions to the rule, Hohokam research has since had a healthy, heaping dose of inquiry into why this never came about, how exactly and to what extent Hohokam communities were integrated, and how management of the irrigation network was coordinated and accomplished among the many canal systems and their attendant but seemingly somewhat politically autonomous villages, all of which relied on a single large, though not limitless, water source.

At a minimum, villages sharing a canal had to interact and cooperate on occasion and at least on a semi-regular basis in order to effectively manage, maintain, and operate the irrigation network, so research into Hohokam social organization has tended to either conflate or fail to differentiate between modes and institutions of political and irrigation organization. As Woodson (2010) has shown, archaeologists thus often discuss Hohokam socio-political organization in terms of irrigation communities (cooperatives vested with operating and managing either a portion or the length of a single canal or canal system; see Crown 1987; Doyel 1980, 1981; Gregory 1991) and primary, or focal, villages (settlement complexes consisting of population centers with public architecture surrounded by smaller, dependent, satellite-like villages and hamlets; see Abbott et al. 2006; Fish and Fish 2000; Rice 2000). Given their larger size, the presence of public architecture, and sometimes a greater longevity than other settlements and habitation types, focal villages are often assumed to have been loci of some form of organizational leadership, presumably a type of political authority. The debate has centered largely on how focal villages, which often shared a canal or canal system with other focal villages (see Figure 3.2), worked together to operate the irrigation network.

One reason archaeologists have struggled to differentiate between Hohokam modes of political and irrigation organization is that the Hohokam settlement pattern was apparently conditioned by both factors. Most focal villages and village clusters, as presumed political units or segments (Rice 2000), were usually settled along canals at approximately 5-km intervals (Crown 1987; Fish and Fish 1991, 2000; Gregory 1991; Gregory and Nials 1985; Wilcox 1991c). It is very plausible that this regular spacing had much to do with the administrative needs for efficiently operating the irrigation infrastructure and field systems. For one, as Chisholm's (1979) research demonstrated, distances between settlements and fields greater than 3 to 4 km commonly call for modifications to the settlement pattern (i.e., an intermediate settlement or facility, such as a fieldhouse). Moreover, as a recurrent structural factor of Hohokam settlement organization along canals, this regular spacing carried through nearly the entire Hohokam cultural sequence—the arrangement of both ballcourt and later platform-mound villages adhered to this 5-km protocol—and was thus somewhat independent of the widely contended socio-political transformation between the Preclassic and Classic.

Regularly spaced along canals (i.e., irrigation organization) with relatively larger populations (i.e., political organization) and ritualized public architecture (i.e., religious organization), focal villages were probably seats for multiple forms of leadership, whether political, economic, hydraulic, defensive, or religious (e.g., Abbott 2000, 2003b; Elson 1998; Elson and Abbott 2000). For this reason, it is easy to see why researchers have had difficulty teasing apart different dimensions of Hohokam social organization. However, as Hunt and colleagues (2005) have emphasized, and as both Howard (2006) and Woodson (2010) have convincingly portrayed for the Phoenix Basin Hohokam, irrigation organization did not have to be nor was it always isomorphic with political organization. They were, in fact, two different spheres of social organization and sources of authority, which at different times and in different places coincided but at others did not.

Just as with the case of irrigation organization, the nexus between systems of ritual and political organization among Hohokam communities varied through space and time. Focal villages, with their public architecture, undoubtedly served as ritual centers throughout the Preclassic and Classic, but how and to what degree ritual authority was bound to other institutions of social organization (i.e., politics and irrigation) is not so obvious. One way to investigate this is to analyze how religious knowledge was distributed among the communities, since knowledge, as a form of symbolic capital, underscores all relationships of power and paves the pathways to authority (see Chapter 2). As I suggested above, though Preclassic Hohokam communities had low-level religious specialists, some of whom probably wore several leadership hats from both civic and religious institutions (e.g., Watkins and Rice 2009), they did not monopolize religious knowledge and ritual authority. Items of ritual importance circulated widely among common villagers who participated in an array of publicly visible or open ritual performances in plazas, ballcourts, and nonvillage settings like the South Mountains. Since most community members were either participants in or observers of the community's ritual practices and wielded their own ritual toolkits of figurines, palettes, censers, and the like, religious knowledge and ritual power were diffused throughout the community. Religion was a relatively level playing field where villagers were directly involved in the rhythm of the ritual cycle.

The open nature of Hohokam ritual participation began disappearing by the early Classic period, when ritual paraphernalia was noticeably concentrated on and around platform mounds, the new ritual stages, which over time became progressively cordoned from the community. This was not just a shift in the sites and accoutrements of ritual performance, as ballcourts were retired, mountain-oriented ritualism ebbed, and circular capped mounds were buried under larger, walled-in rectangular edifices. The fact that certain individuals or social segments aligned themselves exclusively with the platform mounds, at first placing pithouses on them, followed by compound architectural blocks, and finally erecting larger multistoried buildings atop a select few, shows that the authoritative resource of religious knowledge was controlled by a much smaller and perhaps better-organized group of people. With the rise of platform-mound ceremonialism, either existing ritual leaders, who had outlasted the dissolution of the Ballcourt Society, or a new batch of religious aspirants persuaded members of their respective communities to trade in or hand over their keys to the community's ritual system. What happened was that Hohokam ritual leaders, in effect, swapped strategies of ritual mastery, or the way religious knowledge was controlled, administered, and manipulated within and among communities. In the process, religious knowledge became a more potent source of social power—because fewer people were privy to it—and as a result wielders of this incorporeal property were able to exert their influence to greater effect and into other spheres of social life. The issue then revolves around how and why this reorganization in the distribution of religious knowledge came about.

Corporate versus Network

In response to the failure of neo-evolutionary models to explain ancient Southwestern forms of socio-political organization, socially minded archaeologists started looking to alternative forms of leadership for answers (e.g., Mills 2000). One model that has provoked considerable interest, especially in regard to the Hohokam scenario, is dual-processual theory (Blanton et al. 1996; see also Bayman 2002; Elson and Abbott 2000; Rice 2000). Dual processualism conceptualizes growth in organizational complexity and political leadership as following two strategies: networks in which individuals couple capital and charisma to accumulate status and social power, and corporate formations in which power is spread across members, personal prestige is downplayed or obfuscated, and authority tends to derive from knowledge rather than wealth or clout. For archaeologists, a corporate group is a catchall for a range of cooperative social arrangements such as families, lineages, clans, phratries, and sodalities, whereas people associated with lots of "stuff" and "status," usually gauged through burial goods, are often interpreted as successful networkers.

For the Hohokam, James Bayman (2002) contends that the Preclassic mode of socio-political organization followed a networking strategy because many social valuables, including ritual paraphernalia, are found tied to people and households and not necessarily concentrated in particular quarters of the villages or clustered around public works. For the Classic period, however, Bayman sees Hohokam socio-political leadership conforming more to a corporate strategy because many items believed to have once circulated among villagers in a prestige-goods economy (e.g., shell and obsidian) became cloistered in platform-mound villages. Imbued with "ideological" significance, such desirable objects transitioned from glorifying individuals and their achievements to legitimating corporate groups affiliated with platform mounds. Additional lines of evidence further suggest that platform mounds were emblematic of a corporate form of village leadership. For one, rather than elite residences, room layouts in compounds atop some of the mounds are arguably more consistent with what an arrangement of council chambers, presumably for representatives of the corporate groups, would look like (e.g., Downum and Bostwick 2003; Jacobs and Rice 1998; Rice 1995, 2000; however, see Fish and Fish 2000; Fish et al. 1992). Equally telling, Elson's (1998; Elson and Abbott 2000) cross-cultural research showed that platform mound-building societies almost always view the mounds as symbols of community identity and use them to honor or memorialize particular social groups or lineages.

This characterization of Hohokam socio-political organizational strategies is not universally agreed on. For example, while Glen Rice (2000; Rice et al. 2009) concurs with the notion that a predominantly corporate strategy was at work in the Classic period—he argues expressly that a cabal of ritual specialists, as delegates for each corporate group responsible for building and maintaining the platform mounds, resided on the mounds—he does not see evidence for a Preclassic organizational strategy emphasizing networks the way Bayman (2002) does. Instead, Rice's position is that, as a segmentary society, Hohokam leadership followed "a corporate strategy…[which] persisted from the Pioneer through Classic periods, and was accompanied by an increase in the size of the segments [i.e., corporate groups] and a continued process of segment amalgamation into progressively larger entities" (Rice et al. 2009:342–343). For Rice, the Preclassic/Classic transition did not involve an organizational shift from networkers to corporate groups as people shuffled among villages, settlements grew, and canals consolidated.

As with many topics in archaeology, socio-political organization is not an easily discernible, either-or situation, in this case a simplistic contrast between network and corporate strategies. Dual-processual theory positions organizational forms along a continuum from entirely network to entirely corporate strategies (Blanton et al. 1996). That is, within societies employing predominantly corporate strategies we will almost always find some number of variably successful networkers, and vice versa. To complicate the matter further, each strategy may also be favored simultaneously but in different spheres of the community's social dynamics; for example, there may be a mode of ritual or religious leadership based strongly on a networking strategy (e.g., shamans) operating alongside a system where civic authority rests in the hands of a corporate entity (e.g., a council of household leaders).

As Hunt et al. (2005), Howard (2006), and Woodson (2010), among others, argue, Hohokam socio-political organization was, at times, split among multiple forms of leadership in different dimensions of social life. The complexity inherent to the interconnected workings of different yet synchronous strategies of socio-political organization ensures that there is no simple way to characterize a community's style of leadership and governance, and the vagueness in how archaeologists deal with it shows that there is no easy and all-encompassing means for studying it. Looking at ritual practices, specifically how the distribution of ritual tools and religious knowledge was organized, will not answer all questions, but it offers a glimpse into the strategies employed in one dimension of socio-political organization—religion—which invariably complemented or conflicted with strategies operating in other spheres. Rock art, as a relic of ritual practice, can thus help us understand the nature of Hohokam religious authority and the strategies used to organize and contest it.

Networking through Rock Art

Like forms of ritual practice in the villages, Hohokam rock art in the South Mountains was a venue for relating, through the body, senses, and mind, with other-than-human essences accessible at designated stages and at certain prescribed times. More subtly but equally important, rock art is the material trace and symbolic legacy of rituals that stationed people with different social identities and of variable status in relations of power to each other as well as metaphysical agents. This field of power relations concerned the authority to perform and observe religious rituals, which were important avenues for displaying, and possibly acquiring, religious knowledge. The manufacture and use of Hohokam rock art were therefore components of a larger Preclassic ritual system that encouraged participation and empowered community members, commoner and leader alike, through a connection to religious places, principles, and knowledge.

The organization of ritual authority in Preclassic villages bears telltale signs of a networking strategy in that religious knowledge, though widely shared, was personally amassed, owned, and controlled by individuals. While villagers banded together as corporate entities during communal rituals at ballcourt events, around small mounds, and in plazas, they also engaged in more independent styles of ritual practice such as the crafting and use of figurines in domiciles and rock art in the mountains. They owned and wielded ritual objects and religious symbols that other villagers understood and could probably acquire themselves. In this mode of organization, people vied for social acceptance, status, and power by networking with other actors, including congregants at community ritual performances as well as metaphysical entities during both communal and individual ritual practices. Individual and small-group sojourns into the South Mountains, which on occasion involved ritual practices seeking engagement with other-than-human agents, some of which were marked and memorialized by rock art, was a vital component of this networking strategy. This characterization of the social organization of religious knowledge echoes Bayman's (2002) description of the Preclassic leadership strategy more generally, but as Rice (2000) argues, there very well may have been a corporate strategy at play as well. For instance, coordination and promotion of intervillage ritual gatherings tethered to the ballcourt network likely necessitated a corporate formation among religious leaders from different communities (i.e., a sodality). Indeed, such a mode of ritual integration and leadership is quite close to how Wallace (2014; Wallace and Lindeman 2012, 2013) envisions the Ballcourt Society.

For the Preclassic Hohokam, the organization of religious knowledge and ritual authority paired networking strategies *within* villages with a corporate group strategy *between* villages. Given the emphasis on communal ritualism, the Ballcourt Society may have even encouraged a degree of networking among villagers, possibly to obfuscate or divert attention from their own authority. Regardless, while slight differences in material wealth were not unprecedented, and even though some people appear to have had a little more ritual property than others, the fact that overtly successful ritual leaders who accumulated vastly more religious capital, in terms of ritual objects and knowledge, have yet to surface after more than a century of research suggests that individual aggrandizement among ritual practitioners was discouraged. Perhaps the institution(s) of corporate ritual leadership set restrictions on or raised impediments to the success of networkers. The cremation ritual, which became more elaborate during the age of the Ballcourt Society, may have been just such a check. As McGuire (1992b) put it, the ritual masked social inequalities by symbolically eradicating the person and his or her possessions on the funeral pyre.

With the unraveling of the Ballcourt Society and the turn to the Classic period, the Hohokam ritual system, and in consequence the network of power relations that simultaneously constituted but was also conditioned by it, transformed. The ballcourts fell into disrepair as platform mounds took center stage in village religious life. Ritual paraphernalia, which witnessed its own transformations (see Chapter 3), became attached to places rather than people, and those places were predominantly on and around the mounds. In consonance with profound changes in the types and configuration of ritual architecture, the apportionment of esoterica and ritual tools, and the distribution of religious knowledge within communities, the frequency of rock art manufacture and related mountain ritualism diminished considerably, if it did not cease altogether. The social transformation under way within villages clearly reverberated throughout the Hohokam landscape, from village to village, valley to valley, and practically everywhere in between.

So how did Hohokam religious leadership and ritual authority respond to the fracturing of the ballcourt network and the social cohesion it promoted and fostered? Speaking from the corporate perspective, Rice (2000) suggests that as settlements grew and canals merged into more complex hydrological works, existing corporate groups expanded to accommodate new members. According to this portrayal, the Preclassic corporate mode of socio-political organization did not necessarily witness a change in strategies, just scale, as villagers shed old ways in favor of new symbols of community identity. As a proponent of Preclassic networkers, Bayman (2002) sees it differently, positing a strengthening of corporate group power and a waning of networking strategies in the Classic. As I suggested above, these two interpretations are not mutually exclusive, at least in how ritual leadership and religious authority were organized. While there was a subsidence in networking strategies, it was accompanied by a reformation in corporate group leadership. In particular, the Ballcourt Society—the corporate glue that ensured the cyclical harmony of the seasons and the propagation of plants and animals, and ultimately united villages far and wide—disbanded. In its place a more insular or localized mode of corporate leadership may have risen to prominence, and to make their point, the leaders laid claim to the villages' mounds. The absence of clear archaeological signatures for a strong Preclassic corporate leadership structure within villages, like that inferred from the new arrangement of architecture on and around platform mounds, suggests that this Classic period form of corporate leadership was a new style of ritual authority flavored with a new taste in the social organization of religious knowledge. Part of this power grab was a new intolerance for villagers who interacted with the cosmos on their own behalf, as this responsibility became the purview of ritual leaders who directed the communities' religious lives from the mounds.

From Mountain to Village

The new religious and ritual leadership structure that coalesced around the platform mounds in the late Sedentary and early Classic empowered itself by wresting from villagers, or somehow persuading them to divest themselves of, some long-held ritual obligations, sacred privileges, and stores of religious knowledge. How did this usurpation of religious knowledge and co-optation of sacred space come about? Explaining what exactly happened to Hohokam socio-political organization requires much more insight than what rock art can afford, but the South Mountains scenario helps fill in the picture.

As touched on in Chapters 2 and 6, a successful and accepted transformation of a ritual system, as well as the restructuring of the power relations inherent to it, requires a perpetuation of some elements, qualities, and sentiments of the earlier system through the transformation. For the Hohokam, one way this was accomplished was through a reconceptualization of the sacred landscape, specifically the position of mountains relative to villages and ritual leaders. In the Preclassic Hohokam landscape, mountainous settings were mise-en-scènes for a batch of ritual practices, some of which sought communion or elicited occult efficacy from other-than-human subjects through shrines, offerings, and rock art. Indeed, the mountains provided a nested set of stages—hilltops, springs, curious outcrops, trails, and agricultural plots—that villagers visited in order to entertain and connect with mythic, metaphysical agents and understandings. Preclassic religious life thus tempered a ritual network of individualized and communal obligations and performances in the villages' familiar environs with a range of ritual practices that called for undomesticated stages removed from daily life. This ritual network bridged an internal world populated by fellow villagers with an external world loaded with mythic history, sited with sacred spaces, home to other-than-human essences, and beyond the full control and guardianship of any religious authority figures.

As Hohokam communities adjusted to the fractured ritual system and broken social scene of the late Sedentary/early Classic transformation, they traded ballcourts for platform mounds as the appropriate stages for communal ritualism and metaphysical engagement. Platform mounds, however, were not simply neutral venues devoid of any symbolic reference or sacred significance. As public monuments they were layered with multiple dimensions of meaning and metaphor. At one level these edifices commemorated the community and perhaps glorified particular lineages or corporate groups (Elson 1998; Elson and Abbott 2000). At another level the platform mounds were monumental metaphors for mountains (Bostwick 1992; Preucel 1996; Whittlesey 2009).

For the Hohokam and many other North American indigenous communities, mountains were and still are parcels of sacred geography and thus are polysemous symbols with mythical, historical, cultural, and moral meaning (see Chapter 7). They have been sites for innumerable ritual practices, from vision quests to pilgrimages, from prayers to puberty rites. The South Mountains and other uplifted masses rimming the Phoenix Basin and dotting the desert floor were powerful religious symbols for Hohokam communities as a whole but beyond the oversight, helm, or ownership of any one person or village. As community after community raised mounds within their domestic zone, they effigied elements of this sacred geography in miniaturized mountains. Villagers did not just idly watch these history-making happenings unfold. Whether or not this transference of sacred space from the outside in was organized or directed by special individuals or social segments of the community, everyone who contributed to the mounds' erection was complicit in the process. With each basket of dirt hauled and poured onto mound-forming piles, average villagers played a part in a choreographed communal performance of cosmic construction.

The point in the Hohokam historical trajectory at which mounds assumed the symbolism of mountains we may never know with assurance. As detailed in Chapter 3, the earliest mounds of the Pioneer period were simply rubbish pits that had breached their capacity. Sometime in the early Colonial period, and possibly as part of the Hohokam Revitalization Movement, people began to intentionally raise and level them by adding sterile dirt, and then capped and colored them with hardened white caliche, the same substance used to pave ballcourts. At that point, mounds were no longer simply "functional" features but instead took on a level of symbolic significance as circular, low-lying community monuments. Over time the number of these monuments multiplied and their sizes grew after continued construction episodes and recappings. In the Sedentary, villagers began encircling some with palisades, and around the time villagers quit building new ballcourts they began remodeling the circular capped mounds into rectangular platforms. This materialized the move from ballcourt ritualism to moundtop ceremonialism as the core of Hohokam religious life and community identity. With new shapes and contours, late Sedentary platform mounds were still sites of communal ritualism, but visual and physical access to the elevated stages was notably different than that of ballcourts. Large pithouses atop these early platform mounds were storehouses for ritual tools and costumes, shrines, proto-council chambers, temporary or permanent residences for ritual leaders, or something else altogether. Whatever their use, as permanent architectural fixtures they set the foundation for larger and more substantial moundtop compounds and courtyards in the middle and late Classic.

Mounds possibly took on mountain symbolism when they were first capped with white caliche (snowcapped peaks?), but the occurrence of multiple mounds within a village suggests that such symbolism was not vested in a single monument. Mounds may have been the responsibility of different segments of the communities and their ritual leaders, each with a mountain effigy to call its own. At Snaketown, villagers eventually raised and aligned eight mounds around the central precinct and its plaza (Haury 1976; Wilcox et al. 1981), perhaps centering and balancing the village within the cosmos similar to the way Tewa-speaking Pueblo communities situate themselves in relation to the four sacred mountains (Ortiz 1969). If mounds were ritual facilities and religious symbols for different social groups, plazas and ballcourts brought them together as one community and united them with other ballcourt communities through periodic intervillage festivals, markets, and ceremonies tied to the ballgame. When the ritual ballcourt network fell out of operation with the breakup of the Ballcourt Society, for whatever reason, communities needed something new with which to identify, and mounds filled that void. Different social segments and ritual leaders pooled their efforts, attention, and resources, both allocative and authoritative, into a single mound—a mountain effigy for the whole community.

Mounds underwent a continual process of metamorphosis throughout the Hohokam historical trajectory, but as religious metaphors they maintained their mountainous connotation through the turbulent social ups and downs between the Colonial and late Classic periods. Communities molded the mounds' symbolism to meet new ritual and political needs as they arose. When villagers redirected their focus from a conglomerate of several small mounds and a ballcourt or two to a centrally located mound, a single monument to the community, and began enclosing it with palisades and later walls, it signaled a profound reorganization of religious leadership within and between villages. Sacred symbolism and ritual authority were no longer diffused among smaller monuments and presumably the ritual leaders and social segments responsible for them. The concentration of ritual objects and sacred space to the platform mounds implies that the reformulated mode of Hohokam ritual organization and leadership co-opted the communities' bodies of religious knowledge. In so doing, they empowered themselves and increased their presence and influence in other spheres of social life. With greater power and responsibility, religious leaders essentially took on stronger roles in village politics.

Coincident with the religious reorganization in ritual practice and authority occurring in late Sedentary and early Classic villages, mountain ritualism at springs, shrines, peaks, and rock art sites in the South Mountains, if it did not cease entirely, subsided dramatically. Moundtops—as metaphoric mountains brought down in scale—took the place of real mountains as the appropriate stages for engaging other-than-human essences, and the new organization of religious leaders that took custodianship of the mounds propped themselves up as the intermediaries between the villagers and the cosmos. Mounds did not necessarily take on new symbolism when smaller capped mounds were traded in for larger rectangular versions, but rather ritual leaders repackaged that symbolism with a wrapping of community identity and investment that masked their growing authority. They persuaded community members to drop certain ritual practices (i.e., rock art) and translocate others from the mountains outside the villages and beyond the leaders' watchful gaze to the mounds under their care and control; shrines moved from rock piles, caves, and springs in the mountains to moundtop compound rooms filled with esoteric items and ritual offerings, and religious iconography moved from rock faces and the outsides of pots to the interior walls of compounds and multistory buildings.

An additional though little-studied and somewhat controversial sign of this sequestering of ritual practice from mountains to mounds comes from practices of Hohokam celestial observance. There are some architectural indicators that an indigenous astronomy figured into Preclassic Hohokam religious life. For instance, the directionality and apparent cardinal layout of some villages, such as Snaketown (Wilcox 1987a; Wilcox et al. 1981), probably relied to some extent on line-of-sight relations to the sun's annual path. More to this issue, the tendency for ballcourts to conform to roughly north-south and especially east-west alignments suggests further that seasonality and the solar cycle figured into the scheduling and symbolism of the ritual ballgame (Wilcox 1991a). There is also reasonable evidence that celestial observances were undertaken outside villages at places like hillocks and caves (e.g., Mixon and White 1991). Though poorly understood and not fully investigated in the present study, some Hohokam rock art sites (e.g., Bostwick and Plum 2005), including a few in the South Mountains (Bostwick and Krocek 2002:191–203; Holden 2008), were possibly visited or designed for solar or calendrical observances based on line-of-sight alignments to the horizon and light-and-shadow interactions with certain panels and glyphs on solstices and equinoxes.

Since rock art and other styles of mountain ritualism in the South Mountains and maybe elsewhere were phased out of Hohokam religious life in tandem with the turn from ballcourts to platform-mound ceremonialism, any astronomy-related practices involving the crafting of petroglyphs likely ceased as well. Once villagers capitulated to the idea of building compounds and courtyards atop mounds in the mid to late Classic, architectural features designed for watching and charting the movement of heavenly bodies were built into compound rooms on a number of platform mounds (e.g., Downum and Bostwick 2003; Howard 1995; Jacobs 1992). Indeed, the best-known example of a Hohokam astronomical facility comes from the upper floor of the four-story Casa Grande (e.g., Evans and Hillman 1981; Opperman 1979, 1980), whose lower level is actually an enclosed platform mound (Wilcox and Shenk 1977; Wilcox and Sternberg 1981).

As local O'odham villagers told Fray Pedro Font in the eighteenth century, about 300 years after the dissolution of Hohokam platform-mound villages in the terminal Classic/Polvorón, a princely "bitter man" at the Casa Grande watched and "saluted" the sun as it rose and set (see Teggart's [1913:23] translation in Chapter 3). This characterization of a rancorous ruler with ritual authority and religious duties corresponds well with descriptions from more contemporary O'odham accounts of a revolt against villainous despots, one living specifically at Casa Grande and others at large late Classic villages such as Pueblo Grande (Bahr et al. 1994; Teague 1988, 1993). With mountains brought to the center of villages, perhaps Hohokam skywatchers and celestial observers, possibly even "sun priests" like those known among historic and contemporary Pueblo peoples, no longer had to venture into the hills to perform their auspicious civic duties for scheduling agricultural and ritual pursuits. By the late Classic, they could offer and execute their services comfortably and surreptitiously from adobe rooms elevated toward the sky and aligned to the horizon and orbits of celestial bodies.

Coincidentally or not, the mountain-to-village transference of religious symbolism, ritual practice, and sacred space that accompanied the Preclassic-to-Classic social transformation across the Hohokam world is uncannily similar to how Andrea Stone (e.g., 1992), among others, describes the building of the Aztecan urban ritual landscape several centuries later. Recognizing a long Mesoamerican tradition of "folk" ritualism performed at topographic shrines such as mountains, caves, and springs, Stone makes a compelling case that an emerging, corporately organized elite class brought the folk religion under its control by mimicking shrines from the natural landscape in forms and arrangements of temples and causeways (see also Townsend 2000:152–163). Though influenced in some ways by events and people far to the south, the Hohokam never formed a state-like political apparatus akin to that of the Aztecs, Toltecs, Maya, or other complex Mesoamerican societies (Crown 1991a; Fish and Fish 2000). Nevertheless, as with a broadly shared religious structure, mythic history, and sacred geography, it seems their ritual leaders manipulated long-held, unquestioned religious tenets in a similar fashion, and by doing so they usurped the connections common people sought and nurtured with sacred, animated "natural" places in a resemblant guise. To augment their positions and influence, organizationally reformed politico-religious leaders at Hohokam platform-mound villages brought ritual and religious knowledge under their dominion by renovating the communities' monuments and aligning them to their interests. In order to accomplish this, and to save face after the downfall of the Ballcourt Society, they had to somehow persuade their communities to keep faith, and they did so by maintaining the mounds' metaphoric allusions to mountains.

A Mystical Means of Production

What was it about the late Sedentary Hohokam social landscape that encouraged communities to dismantle the ritual ballcourt network, turn aside from centuries-long intervalley exchange relationships, walk away from family farms and ancestral lands, establish new settlements or move into increasingly crowded villages, and shed once-vibrant ritual skins for a new religious life focused on platform-mound ceremonialism? Strife and conflict? Hunger or disease? Failure of existing leaders or the allure of new political contenders? Odds are there were a number of catalysts for this social transformation, each a compelling "push" or "pull" that, when combined with the others, cascaded into a tidal force that altered worldviews, refashioned social identities, and washed away deep historical connections among villages and valleys. Causality in Hohokam culture change leaves ample room for speculation and modeling, but in traditional processual fashion, explanations often look to population-resource imbalances as primary stimuli. To expand on this fully is beyond the aim and capability of this case study in rock art and ritual practice, especially since our attention has been directed at just one facet of this transformation—religion. The religious and ritual transfiguration of the late Sedentary and early Classic, however, was not insulated from the demographic and social events and processes unfolding at that time. In fact, they may all share the same provocateur: water. As elaborated below, Hohokam ritual and irrigation practices had similar goals.

Hohokam religion bundled together a range of themes and premises shared with other Southwestern and Mesoamerican people (see Chapters 3 and 7), one of which was a very ancient concern for agricultural fertility and its connection to weather events and solar cycles (Schaafsma and Taube 2006; Taube 2000). As recognized in Doyel's (1992, 2000a) posited Rainbow Way, the mythic significance and control of water figured strongly in Preclassic Hohokam ritual practice and religious observance. Many ritual objects materialized metaphors for water in reflective and opalescent properties—mica schist as pottery temper, phyllite palettes, pyrite mirrors, obsidian, and marine shell. The ritual ballgame's schedule may have been planned according to seasonal and agricultural cycles (Wilcox 1987a, 1991b), and possibly enacted choreographed missives to the cosmos for rain. The preponderance of ballcourts at regularly spaced focal villages along canals suggests further that the ballgame had some role, though a still-unclear one, in the organization of irrigation, possibly as a religious and public means for regulating events and labor responsibilities and mitigating disagreements over water allocation. Along these lines, the occult efficacy sought through ritualism in the South Mountains, including rock art around springs, rock pile shrines, hilltops, summit trails, and rainfall-dependent agricultural fields, each with the occasional offering of one or two river-rounded shrine stones—what Cushing (1890:169) called "water tamers"—probably also concerned water and fertility.

In the Preclassic, and especially during the era of the Hohokam Revitalization Movement, villagers prayed for and rejoiced at the arrival of rain, abundant streamflows, and agricultural bounty through communal and individual ritual practices within and outside the villages. Responsibility for bringing the rain and ensuring agricultural success through such mystical means was shared among common villagers and not fully vested in the authority of religious leaders. This blend of corporately organized and networking ritual practitioners was a winning strategy and reproductively rewarding religious lifestyle. For instance, Ingram (2008:150) finds the highest population growth rates for Canal System 2 in the lower Salt River valley during the Colonial period (see also Dean et al. 1994:Figure 4.11), coincident with the arrival and florescence of the ballcourt network.[2] Population growth in the middle Gila River valley at that time was not so pronounced but was "well within the range of growth rates typically expected from natural increases in birth over death rates in absence of substantial migration" (Woodson 2010:240).

The good times brought by the ballcourt network, however, could only go so far. Due to a combination of reduced streamflows for the Gila and Salt Rivers (Graybill et al. 2006) and greater demand for irrigated water to support a growing population, both Howard (2006) and Woodson (2010) contend that water scarcity became a real problem for irrigation communities throughout the Phoenix Basin during the Sedentary period. In prior centuries communities along individual canals could effectively manage the irrigation systems and allocate water to meet the demands of most users at most times. However, in classic systemic terms, a positive, self-disturbing feedback of growing demand from a larger pool of farmers facing dwindling water supplies in the late Sedentary and continuing through the Classic necessitated a series of social, demographic, and hydraulic responses. As others have detailed (e.g., Abbott and Foster 2003; Hill et al. 2004; Howard 1993, 2006; Wilcox et al. 1981; Woodson 2010), some of the more noticeable changes included (1) growth in the organizational complexity of irrigation through the consolidation of canals into longer canals or more complex canal systems; (2) migration out of tail-end villages and into ones farther up-canal; (3) migration from downriver canals to ones farther upriver; (4) the construction of new irrigation infrastructure, such as the Scottsdale System, upriver from other long-established canals in the lower Salt River valley; and (5) a relatively high rate of migration out of the middle Gila River valley and into villages and irrigation communities supported by canals fed from the Salt River's waters.

In step with the late Sedentary and early Classic demographic and social waves rippling through the Phoenix Basin, presumably in response to problems with and conflict over water, Hohokam villagers shied away from the ritual system that brought water from the sky and mountains and ensured the annual propagation of the plants and animals on which they relied. They did not, however, lose their religion. This is evident in the perpetuation of some religious symbols, such as water metaphors in the reflective properties of obsidian objects and mica schist and phyllite tempers in new types of buffware and redware, mountain metaphors encoded in mounds, and the continued though altered use of some ritual tools such as shell trumpets, effigy vessels, and shrine stones. Moreover, of those ballcourt villages that remained inhabited into the Classic, many raised platform mounds near the older ritual edifices, as though referencing these potent, ancestral religious symbols to legitimate the new order. With the compliance and assistance of the community, village leaders laid this new religious order of platform-mound ceremonialism over the skeleton of the ballcourt network. Taken together, it appears Hohokam villagers considered some elements of the Preclassic ritual system and religious lifestyle worth keeping, but no longer found the Ballcourt Society and its ritual game an effective way to organize religious knowledge, allocate ritual authority, build village cohesion and community identity, mediate conflicts, and secure life-giving water.

Dissatisfaction with the operation and efficacy of the ritual ballcourt network left a vacuum in the religious lives of the communities in the late Sedentary. Village leaders saw an opportunity to step in and craft something new and monumental out of the familiar and comfortable, cloak it in an aura of communalism, ancestry, and village identity, and in the process augment their power and widen their grasp over material and incorporeal resources. Focal villages, as ritual centers, irrigation hubs, bases of craft production and exchange, and nuclei for surrounding hamlets and fields, housed multiple seats of authority, in areas of religion, economics, and politics, and at times village leaders probably dabbled in different strains of this authority. For instance, ritual leaders could have feasibly held positions on an irrigation committee, and master craftspeople may have moonlighted as village council members. However, as Woodson (2010) shows for the middle Gila communities and Hunt et al. (2005) suggest for those in the lower Salt River valley, authority over irrigation matters above the village level did not always reside in the hands of village leaders. This heterotypic base of social power was the most likely scenario in which multiple focal villages, village clusters, and ritual centers were settled along the same canals. These more substantial settlements were usually spaced approximately 5 km apart and positioned around important distribution nodes in the irrigation infrastructure, such as the heads, tails, and branches of the main canals (e.g., Howard 1993, 2006). In such instances, which was quite often the case in the lower Salt River valley after the Pioneer period, the organization of irrigation at the level of the entire canal or canal system required cooperation and coordination among the different focal villages.

At times, village leaders, whether of economic, political, or religious stature, may have had their hands in or held control over irrigation and agricultural affairs for those fields and canal sections within their reach and under their jurisdiction. However, due to the organizational requirements for segmented (i.e., multiple focal villages) irrigation communities, "political leaders at ballcourt and platform mound villages did not necessarily have direct control over the means of agricultural production at the level of the canal system" (Woodson 2010:288, emphasis omitted). The segmentation of the Hohokam settlement pattern into multiple focal villages along canals in the Preclassic and Classic set thresholds on the amount of wealth and power that potential aggrandizers could amass, with the limits congruent to the fields tended, crafts produced, and canals managed and operated by denizens of the focal villages and their surrounds. Since the pathways to power and authority were truncated at the village level, leaders desiring greater control or prestige would have had to diversify their affairs and expand their web of relations into other social spheres. According to Woodson (2010:288), "aspiring elites seeking to control irrigated land or produce as an economic source of power probably had to achieve it through means other than direct control."

In the increasingly crowded and complex social landscape of the Sedentary period, and with irrigated water a scarcer commodity than ever before, village leaders may have reached the limit of their control over the actual means of production, or that control may have been threatened or loosened, and religious leaders aligned with the Ballcourt Society had a harder time convincing villagers that things would turn around. As their legitimacy to organize the communities' religious lives waned, the ballgame and other modes of ritual practice, such as rock art, lost their mystique. Hohokam farmers and crafters wanted and needed something new and began defecting from their communities. With such social and religious unrest, village leaders or entrepreneurial contenders—either of whom could have already held a nascent ritual authority—saw an opportunity to increase their clout and broaden their power. Instead of expanding their dominion over the actual means of production (i.e., labor, irrigation, fields, crop surpluses and other goods), they tapped another, immaterial source of capital by refashioning the enfeebled ritual system and thus reining in the "mystical means" (sensu Granero 1986:657) of production. This body of incorporeal property and authoritative resources included the religious knowledge materialized in ritual tools, encoded in symbols, and embodied in performances, as well as the relationship communities held with metaphysical, other-than-human agents and essences in their sacred geography.

Final Insights

Finding it harder to get water and left with a defunct system of intervillage ritual integration in the late Sedentary, Hohokam communities sought a new way to live and another means for communing with the cosmos. The need must have been dire because villagers handed over much of their role in the ritual network; they quit playing the ballgame, stopped making rock art and soliciting mountain shrines, and relinquished their ritual paraphernalia. The late Sedentary and early Classic usurpation of religious knowledge and ritual privilege by a reorganized village leadership aligned with the platform mounds was apparently successful and popular, at least for a while, since it occurred in village after village throughout much of the Hohokam world. Each community nevertheless mediated the transformation on its own terms and adopted the new order at its own pace, hence the fuzzy, patchy, and discombobulated archaeological mosaic of Hohokam cultural development that Gladwin and colleagues (1937) originally framed as the Santan phase of the Classic period (see also Doyel 2000a). Some communities, particularly those in the Agua Fria (e.g., Wilcox and Holmlund 2007), Verde (e.g., Whittlesey et al. 1997), and New River (e.g., Doyel and Elson 1985) watersheds along the Phoenix Basin's northern periphery (see also Lerner 1984; McGuire 1991), gave up allegiance to a Hohokam lifestyle. As for those villages closer to the Hohokam core region unwilling or unable to make the transition, their residents packed up and left for communities that had a better handle on the situation (Abbott and Foster 2003; Hill et al. 2004; Woodson 2010), most of which identified with platform mounds. These new monuments clearly drew a lot of attention and probably a lot of migrants, too.

The rock art in the South Mountains provides a unique lens into this late Sedentary/early Classic social transformation. The nexus of a rising ritual authority with the erection of platform mounds, edifices central to village structure and at the heart of the residents' identities, many of whom moved heaven (figuratively) and earth (literally) in order to build them, reveals that community leaders had a longer reach and stronger presence in village politics and religious matters than their ballcourt-era predecessors. However, it is unlikely that the new organization of politico-religious leadership, the nature of which continues to evade the prying eyes of archaeologists, had direct control over how individuals conducted themselves beyond the village gaze. Had villagers or competing, heterodoxic ritual leaders wanted to resist or contest the authority of the new platform-mound leadership, we might expect rock art ritualism—perhaps as an enactment of a "folk" religion—to have persisted, or even intensified, within the mountains and outside the leaders' oversight. In the South Mountains at least, and possibly elsewhere, villagers nonetheless shucked long-held elements, both private and public, of their ritual tradition, suggesting that communities welcomed the transfigured religious order and the evolution of an increasingly rigid and orthodox structure of domination centered on and around platform mounds. It is possible that the vestiges of a Classic period presence in the South Mountains—the light scatter of broken redwares and the rare polychrome sherd, and maybe even a few petroglyphs—are indicative of such a contravention, but if so it was neither long-lived nor successful.

The hand-in-handedness of shifting ritual practices, including the reconfiguring of stages, performers, accoutrements, liturgy, and above all venues, both within and outside villages in the late Sedentary and early Classic, evidences a broad-scale and largely unchallenged constriction of the Hohokam ritual system and a circumscription in the access to, distribution of, and control over religious knowledge. As Howard sees it, Hohokam leaders faced with growing demand for a shrinking water supply and seeing more and more farmers uprooting their lives and moving to villages with better prospects and more secure water rights, minted a "new ideology linked to platform mound ceremonialism [that] established new social and political relationships" (Howard 2006:289). What these ancient desert farmers developed or adopted was not a new religion per se, but rather a new way to organize the allocation of religious knowledge and ritual privilege among the community, which left those aligned with the platform mounds holding much larger shares. It was an ideological shift in which leaders naturalized their expanding authority by retaining certain elements, premises, and symbols of the older order. They successfully sold and obfuscated this usurpation by masking their interests in a facade of monumental communalism—group labor for irrigation maintenance and mound construction events, public orations and rituals atop them, and a unified, ancestor-based village identity codified in the mounds. They also made this transition palatable by refraining from taking residence atop the mounds, at least at first.

In the middle and late Classic, a century or two after communities swapped the ballcourt network for the new religious order, village leaders replaced the large pithouses and supplanted the illusion of communal space atop the platform mounds with restrictive architectural blocks and retaining walls. As Bell reminds us, "The greater the social distance experienced or desired between persons, the more their actions abide by those conventions that acknowledge social distance" (1997:143). The move from an open, not-yet-residential layout atop Hohokam platform mounds to one supporting enclosed quarters privy to a select privileged few solidified and materialized the social distance that had been accumulating between politico-religious leaders and the rest of the communities, an overt status distinction that may have carried over into the afterlife, as a few richly endowed burials suggest (e.g., Loendorf 2001; Mitchell 2003; Mitchell and Brunson-Hadley 2001).

What instigated this next step in the ascendency of moundtop leaders and elites is not fully known, but Howard (2006) and Woodson (2010) propose that a reorganization of the irrigation networks may be the culprit. According to their scenario, as communities responded to increasing demand for water by consolidating canals and rearranging the irrigation network's infrastructure, they likely developed a higher level of irrigation organization than what had been the norm for centuries. Although there is no indication of a valley-wide administration for irrigation matters, or for any other affairs, along the lower Salt River, in the Classic period once-independent irrigation communities had to cooperate to a greater extent in order to effectively and efficiently operate the more integrated and complex hydraulic systems. In essence, a higher tier of corporate organization—a sort of "irrigation consortium" (Hunt et al. 2005; Woodson 2010)—developed along some of the canals and canal systems from the amalgamation of irrigation communities and their increasingly aggregated platform-mound villages. In fact, Hunt et al. (2005) suggest that a corporate body of this sort may have managed the operation of Canal System 2 in the late Classic. A new organizational body such as this, which probably enlisted representatives from multiple focal villages along different stretches of the canals, opened new doors for village leaders, aspiring elites, and other aggressive networkers to once again expand their grasp over the means of agricultural production, this time beyond the limit of the village (Woodson 2010:281–282).

The overt status distinctions enshrined in moundtop architecture and symbolized in lavish grave lot assemblages in the late Classic may not have derived entirely from an economic basis. Religious knowledge continued to be a potent and valuable currency that village politico-religious leaders could convert into other authoritative and allocative resources and cash in to legitimize their move atop the mounds and justify an expanded reach over irrigated land and agricultural surpluses. However, since ritualism in the South Mountains petered out sometime during the late Sedentary and early Classic, the petroglyphs, mountain shrines, and other ritual stages do not offer much insight into what transpired once the leaders aligned with the platform mounds had effectively arrested the communities' stakes in ritual practice and religious knowledge and stepped up as intermediaries to the cosmos. Nevertheless, at about the same time communities in the Phoenix Basin capitulated to the presence of compounds atop their monuments, they found themselves enmeshed in a network of exchange and possibly production of Salado polychromes (Doyel 2000b; though see Abbott and Schaller 1992), a hybridized ceramic ware full of mystical metaphors and laden with a new flavor of Mesoamerican-inspired symbolism of serpents, macaws, flowers, butterflies, and the like (Searcy 2010).

Crown (1994) understands Salado vessels as tokens of participation in a panregional "Southwestern Cult," but the level of involvement the Phoenix Basin Hohokam had in this religious movement is debatable. If the existing or emerging elite tied to late Classic platform mounds in the Phoenix Basin had or sought control over a prestige goods economy, perhaps they capitalized on the exchange of these nonlocal wares adorned with exotic symbols in order to associate themselves with distant religious movements and esoteric knowledge, much like their Colonial period ancestors, who brought about the Hohokam Revitalization Movement. Perhaps this is why most Salado polychromes in the Phoenix Basin were traded in from surrounding regions (Abbott and Schaller 1992; Doyel 2000b), and why several large caches, some of which may have been storerooms of locally produced Salado knockoffs (Neuzil and Lyons 2006), have been unearthed at a handful of large platform-mound villages (e.g., Haury 1945). In any event, the arrival of Salado in the Phoenix Basin was a mediated admixture of refreshingly foreign concepts and symbols with the existing religious order centered on platform mounds. It was not an entirely new religion because, from a strictly material perspective, platform mounds remained standing in the same spots, the suite of ritual paraphernalia persisted relatively unchanged, redwares speckled with reflective mica schist and phyllite temper continued to be crafted and traded, and to top it all off rock art remained a derelict ritual practice. Rather than selling a new body of mythic premises, or reorganizing the distribution of religious knowledge while naturalizing a new ritual system, similar to what happened during the late Sedentary/early Classic social transformation, it appears as though late Classic politico-religious leaders infused an existing liturgy and choreography with mystical and tonic symbolism.

Even though the data and research presented in this book cannot speak to the late Classic scenario with any more surety or clarity than what is already available, it is worthwhile to put the Civano era religious reconfiguration, the token of which is Salado polychrome, into a historic context by contrasting it with the earlier rise of platform-mound ceremonialism. In the late Sedentary and early Classic, Hohokam communities faced demographic uncertainty, mounting concern over a waning water supply, and a discontent with the religious and ritual status quo. Village leaders, whose arms into the communities' economic lives had reached their shoulders, took a chance to empower themselves by assuming greater responsibility for mediating between the cosmos and the communities, a duty villagers were apparently willing to give up. In the early Classic this usurpation of the mystical means of production granted ritual leaders a more political assignment, in which they could leverage their ritual mastery and religious authority into other social fields.

Several generations later, after communities finished rearranging the valley's waterworks to meet new operational goals and efficiency standards, necessary for satisfying the higher demands stemming from reduced streamflow and increased village aggregation, Hohokam politico-religious leaders saw another occasion to amplify their power base. The reorganized irrigation networks opened doors for them to broaden their dominion over the actual means of production, and they legitimized this maneuver by rekindling their command over exotic, esoteric symbolism and knowledge, this time originating from the emerging Salado phenomenon to the east. This late precontact fusion of expanded religious and economic authority enabled leaders to amass enough clout to move their headquarters atop the platform mounds and above the masses. If villagers challenged this move, they did not do it through a revival in rock art ritualism in the South Mountains.

After about a century or two, however, the social distance crystallized by moundtop architecture and later multistory buildings reached a cleavage, and the Hohokam walked away from densely populated villages, complex irrigation networks, public works projects to build and remodel mounds, and the organizational strategies and leadership roles that oversaw it all. It is an epic tale best told by the O'odham, whose historical narratives describe a class-like struggle and eventual insurrection between themselves, heirs to the Hohokam legacy, and despotic and possibly foreign chiefs and priestly rulers seated atop platform mounds. Although the South Mountains petroglyphs are silent on these events, since by then making rock art had largely become an ancestral ritual practice, rock art ritualism remained an ever-present religious tradition. Indeed, O'odham observers continue to visit, give homage to, and engage with these numinous symbols pecked, ground, and etched on rocks around ancient shrines in their sacred desert landscape.

CHAPTER 9

Conclusion

As a case study in the social analysis of rock art, this book endeavored to demonstrate how there is much we can learn about Hohokam ritual practice and social transformation by looking at what was going on away from the bustle, din, and meddling of the village environs. Rock art in particular, and landscapes more broadly, offer insights that complement, and sometimes contradict, what we glean and interpret from domestic and residential settings. When brought together, intra- and extra-village perspectives provide a fuller understanding of the daily lives and experiences of ancient peoples, as well as how they structured and transformed their communities and identities, than what is available through either perspective alone. To this effect, I took an explicitly social stance regarding Hohokam rock art; instead of looking solely at the imagery through functionalist, semiotic, or aesthetic panes, I handled the rock art's crafting, viewing, and (re)interpretation as important and meaningful practices embedded in a more inclusive socio-religious lifestyle and manner of landscape engagement that did not dissipate at the village edge. I accomplished this by drawing on topographic, environmental, and archaeological data to examine the rock art's physical, historical, behavioral, temporal, and social contexts, which enabled me to tie the rock art to the communities responsible for it.

This integrative, contextual analysis revealed that the South Mountains were much more than a canvas for Hohokam petroglyphs. They hosted an array of subsistence-oriented and religion-inspired practices. Indeed, our notions of sacred and profane, of religious and mundane, are blurred in the South Mountains, and are probably altogether misleading constructs for understanding the Hohokam and many other indigenous, non-Western peoples. Since rock art was hung on surfaces outside villages, it may seem as though it was removed from the heart of daily experience and of little relevance to Hohokam life, but this is a terribly narrow, short-sighted vision of a rich Hohokam legacy. Layered in strata of metaphors, the South Mountains held considerable prominence in the lives of people residing around, moving through, and engaging with them, and through their rock art, as a bundle of religious monuments, villagers both materialized and perpetually renegotiated the distribution of religious knowledge within their communities. Hohokam religion was put into landforms and built into edifices, and it thus permeated life and was experienced and practiced both within and beyond the village. The South Mountains, and undoubtedly other "natural" places, figured prominently in Hohokam religion because they shelter sites of sacred geography, such as peaks and springs, which are imbued with mythic histories and house other-than-human agents and essences.

One reason people were drawn into the South Mountains was to continue a long tradition of visiting sanctuaries, reliquaries, and shrines in order to relate to and commune with cosmic bodies and metaphysical agencies. Rock art, crafted and strategically arranged around various stages, was part of this dialectical system of ritual communication and performance.

Stages varied in formality and ritual depth; some, such as springs and summit trails, likely were solely destinations for ritual performers whereas others, such as trails and agricultural terraces, hosted other, less ritualized practices as well. Thus rock art manufacture, albeit rare, was not the purview of a select few social actors nor was it restricted to a few secluded places. Rock art was undertaken in association with a range of other pursuits and was appreciated in different contexts and scenarios, evidencing variable degrees of its ritualization. In this way rock art was more than a constellation of symbols and pictorial reflections; it was a ritual practice nested within a larger ritual system that breached village borders and social identities. Performance and image, the symbols in rock art ritualism, broadcast canonical information and religious knowledge that served to align the congregation—the performers and their audience—with cosmic concepts and position them in relation to mythic premises and other-than-human agents. As wielders of such potent symbols, rock art artisans allied self-referential information to the canonical messages and in so doing renegotiated their position in a network of power relations with the rest of their human and other-than-human community.

The South Mountains rock art, which I argue was predominantly, if not exclusively, a Preclassic practice, shows that this strand of religious knowledge was tapped, possessed, and used by a variety of social actors in a range of settings and scenarios. The fluidity of ritual performance in the mountains mirrored the institutionalized openness of ceremony and ritual in Preclassic villages. As with pottery designs, over time rock art iconography incorporated a more figurative and representative suite of motifs, but artisans tended to hang it around the same stages and often on the same panels as much earlier works. Through this continuance of tradition and upkeep and renewal of sites of ritual performance, petroglyph artisans reinterpreted the past to meet their current religious needs. In this respect, the cessation of rock art and other modes of ritualism in the South Mountains between AD 1050 and 1150, during that archaeologically nebulous transition from the Sedentary to the Classic period, was an abrupt and profound break from a ritual history and social legacy etched in stone. It was not an isolated and irrelevant phenomenon because it coincided with broad structural changes in village religious life—attested to by shifts in public architecture, iconography, and ritual paraphernalia—all of which point toward a circumscription in the social organization of religious knowledge among community members. This came about through a usurpation of religious knowledge and ritual privilege by emerging or reinvigorated politico-religious leaders, a social transformation that communities accepted because it kept certain symbols and maintained some existing religious premises, such as mound-mountain metaphors. The rising politico-religious leaders, who cloaked their hegemonic maneuvers in an aura of community identity, a spirit of communal investment in public works, and a semblance of economic equality, used this new religious order to establish themselves in more domineering positions within an evolving power structure.

What instigated the Preclassic/Classic social transformation remains an area of concerted attention and focused research. Many point the finger at imbalances in population-environment systematics, principally the impact of mounting water scarcity due to reduced streamflows compounded by population growth. As a collective of irrigation-based subsistence farmers, the Hohokam were undoubtedly primarily concerned with water availability, and it may very well have had a role in the series of social changes that took place. The general direction of where people moved—up-canal, upriver, and to irrigation communities in the better-watered lower Salt River valley—and the major reworking of the irrigation systems in the late Preclassic show that access to water was a significant pull for marginal or disenfranchised farmers and their families. It is important to consider, however, that environmental stressors are mediated through social responses. This demographic and climatic instability presented the Hohokam with a crisis (sensu Giddens 1984) within and among communities over control of the actual means of production (water, corn surpluses, craft goods, and so on) as well as the mystical means of production (religious knowledge, symbols, and ritual authority).

In this cascade of social and ecological pressures, relationships of power over allocative and authoritative resources in Hohokam communities were clearly strained. Disturbances in the flow of power within social fields and across "cleavages" (Foucault 1978:96) between them create such "sites of struggle" (Stewart 2001:7), and through these sites empowered actors find avenues to implement transformative changes to the social status quo. Perhaps villagers lost faith in their organizational structures and governing bodies or became disenchanted with their ritual system, including ballgames, rock art, and the palette-and-censer crematory rite. Alternatively, village leaders or aspiring social entrepreneurs may have realized and capitalized on an opportunity to seize the reins of the communities' ritual system and steer it toward their own interests. Either way, the Preclassic/Classic social transformation entailed swapping an inclusive and vibrant religious lifestyle in which everyone participated for one increasingly cloistered and controlled by individuals or social groups allied with the platform mounds. The Classic period ritual system, centered mostly inside walls atop mounds, was over the heads, beyond the reach, and out of sight of the larger community. A lack of shared participation evidences an active and conscious construction of social distance between religious leaders and community members. This usurpation of religious knowledge and social distancing were apparently met with little resistance, since the turn toward platform-mound identity and ceremonialism was adopted by most communities across much of the area once tethered together through the Ballcourt Society.

Insights into religion and ritual practice drawn from the South Mountains petroglyphs add a novel, outside-looking-in perspective on Hohokam social transformations. Trends in rock art ritualism and related practices within this craggy, darkly varnished landscape paralleled those in the more familiar confines of the villages, evidencing a widely experienced religious lifestyle and a broadly felt series of ritual perturbations. What was witnessed in the South Mountains, however, particularly the abrupt end of rock art ritualism, may not be an accurate portrayal of how the turn to platform-mound ceremonialism influenced mountain ritualism in other reaches of the Hohokam world. In fact, petrographic data from the thousands of sherds scattered about the South Mountains show that it was mostly residents of the surrounding villages who were responsible for the landscape's archaeological legacy, so the rock art scenario reported on in this book may be only a local interpretation of the late Sedentary/early Classic social transformation. Further research should bear this out.

We know that the Preclassic/Classic transition and the attendant rise of platform-mound ceremonialism was not a neatly arranged, uniform social process across the Hohokam world because communities adopted the suite of changes at their own pace and in nuanced ways (Doelle et al. 1995; Doyel 2000a). Accordingly, this begs the question whether rock art and related flavors of mountain ritualism within and outside the Phoenix Basin had a similar structure and parallel trajectory. Wallace and Holmlund (1986) noted the possible presence of Classic period rock art in the Picacho Mountains, and recent surveys on and around Perry Mesa revealed clusters of Hohokam-like petroglyphs around Pueblo III (contemporaneous with the Hohokam early Classic) villages (e.g., Huang 2010; Simon et al. 2014), so rock art ritualism may very well have followed different historical paths throughout the Hohokam world. A clearer view of the nature and tempo of rock art ritualism in other regions, both near and far, will afford a better picture of how villages responded to the fracturing of the ballcourt network, negotiated their roles in a reformulated ritual system, and ultimately brought about the transformation of their social world.

APPENDIX

Petroglyph Typology

The typology used to inventory the South Mountains petroglyphs is a modified version of a long-used classification scheme for rock art designs in western North America, a scheme that has roots in early surveys (Cressman 1937; Steward 1929) and was subsequently standardized by Heizer and Baumhoff (1962). Similar typologies were followed in the first Hohokam petroglyph studies by White (1965), Snyder (1966), and Ferg (1979), of which Wallace has since published a number of expansions and revisions (Wallace 1983:83–89, 1997, 2000:Appendix D, 2008:Figure B.2; Wallace and Holmlund 1986:64–67, Figure D.3).

The typological procedure entails classifying petroglyphs (and pictographs) based on visual similarities to design archetypes and grouping them according to assumed thematic content. With a series of slight modifications and additions, detailed fully in the original study (Wright 2011:Appendix C), the following typology closely follows Wallace's classification system for Hohokam-style rock art elements. It is important to note that these are subjective groupings that probably differ in certain respects from those of the petroglyph producers (Wallace and Holmlund 1986:64; see also Ford 1954).

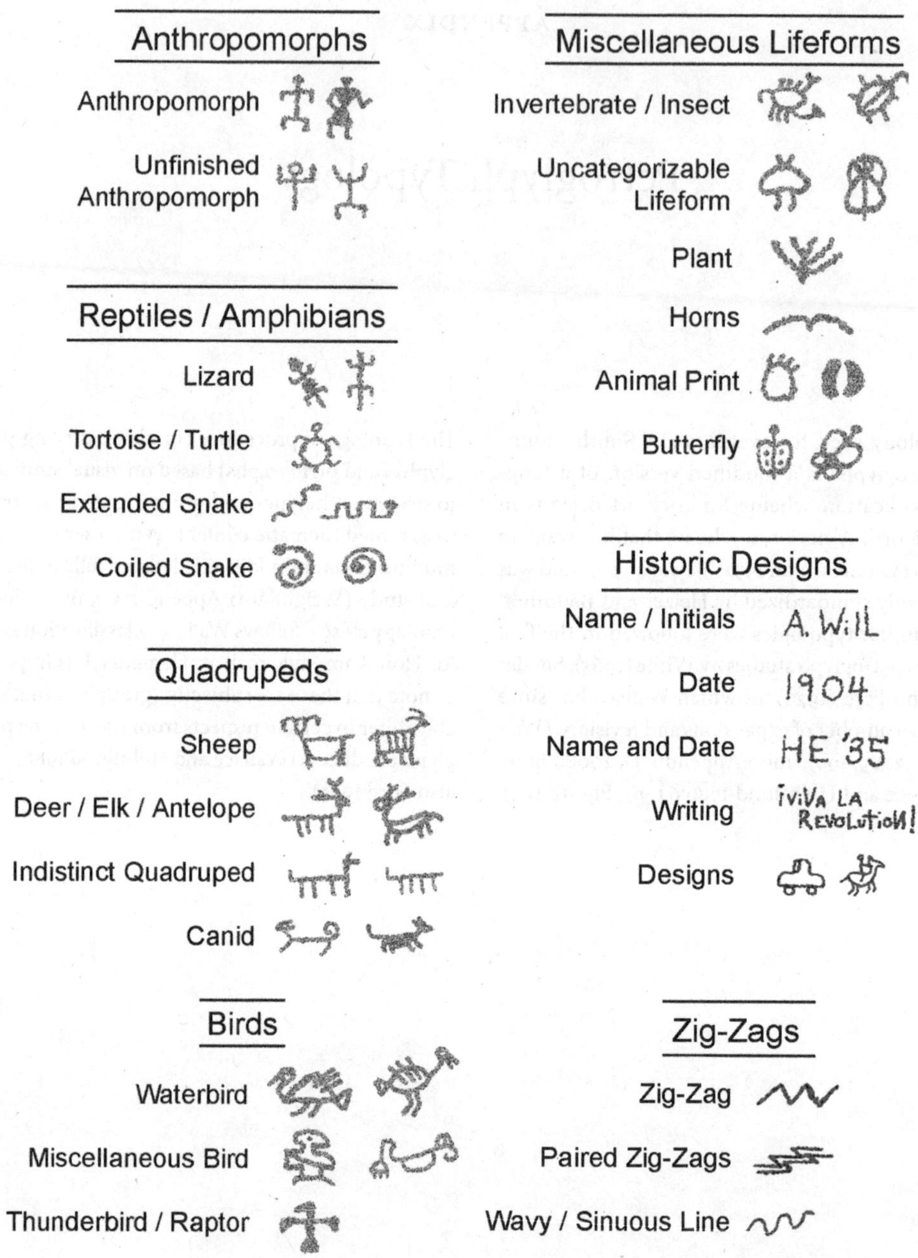
Anthropomorphs
Anthropomorph
Unfinished Anthropomorph
Reptiles / Amphibians
Lizard
Tortoise / Turtle
Extended Snake
Coiled Snake
Quadrupeds
Sheep
Deer / Elk / Antelope
Indistinct Quadruped
Canid
Birds
Waterbird
Miscellaneous Bird
Thunderbird / Raptor
Miscellaneous Lifeforms
Invertebrate / Insect
Uncategorizable Lifeform
Plant
Horns
Animal Print
Butterfly
Historic Designs
Name / Initials
A. WiL
Date
1904
Name and Date
HE '35
Writing
¡ViVA LA REVOLutioN!
Designs
Zig-Zags
Zig-Zag
Paired Zig-Zags
Wavy / Sinuous Line

Petroglyph Typology

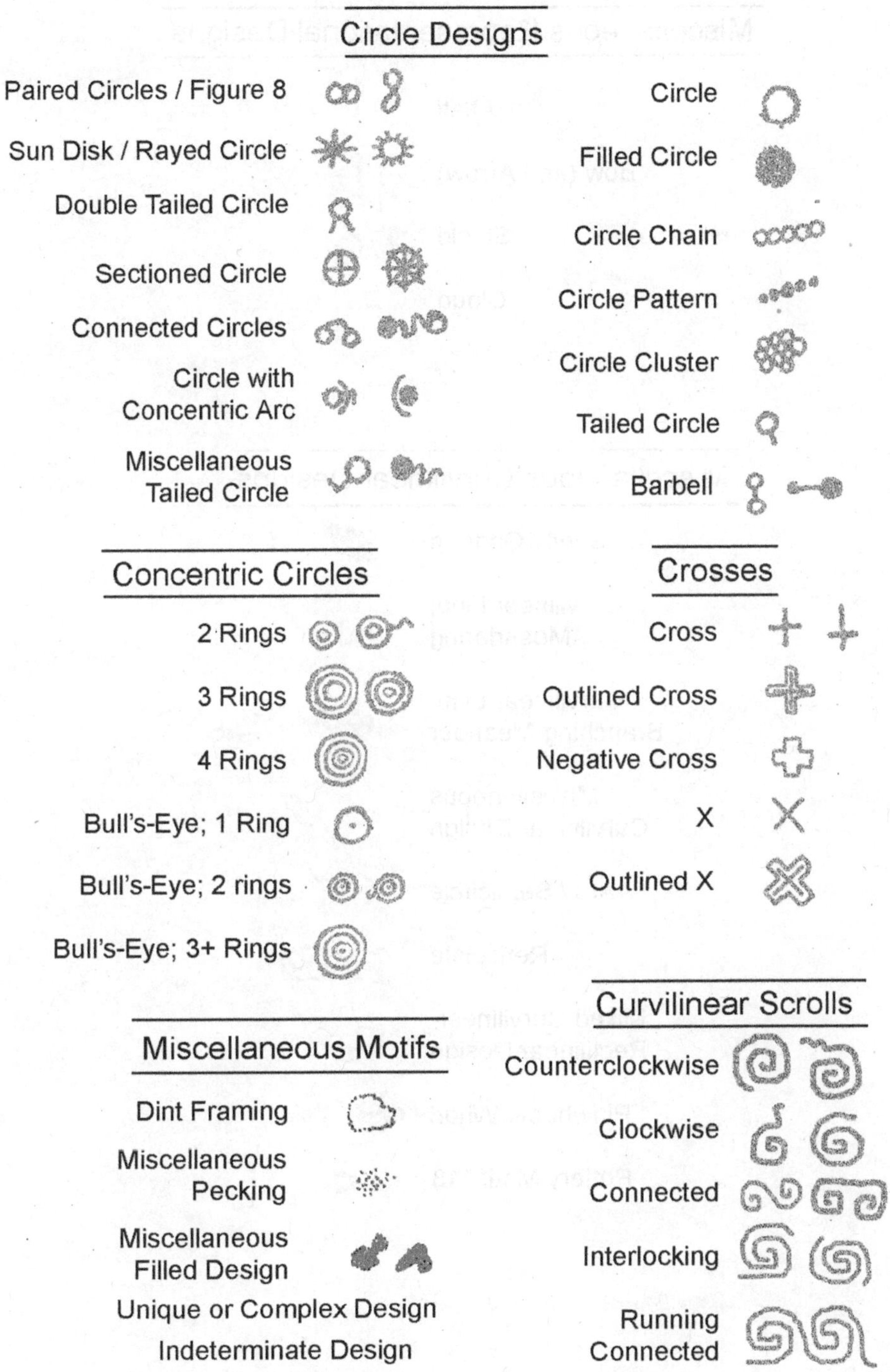

Miscellaneous Representational Designs

Atlatl 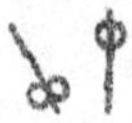

Bow (and Arrow) 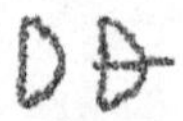

Shield 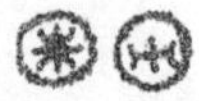

Cloud 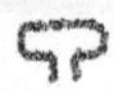

Miscellaneous Curvilinear Designs

Shell / Gridiron 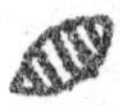

Curvilinear Line; Meandering 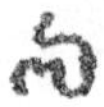

Curvilinear Line; Branching Meander 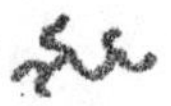

Miscellaneous Curvilinear Design 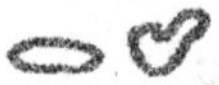

Arc / Semicircle 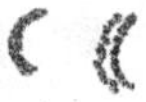

Reticulate 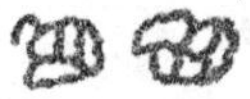

Mixed Curvilinear-Rectilinear Design 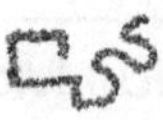

Pinwheel / Whorl 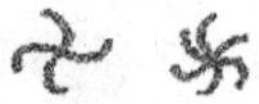

Pottery Motif 113 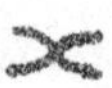

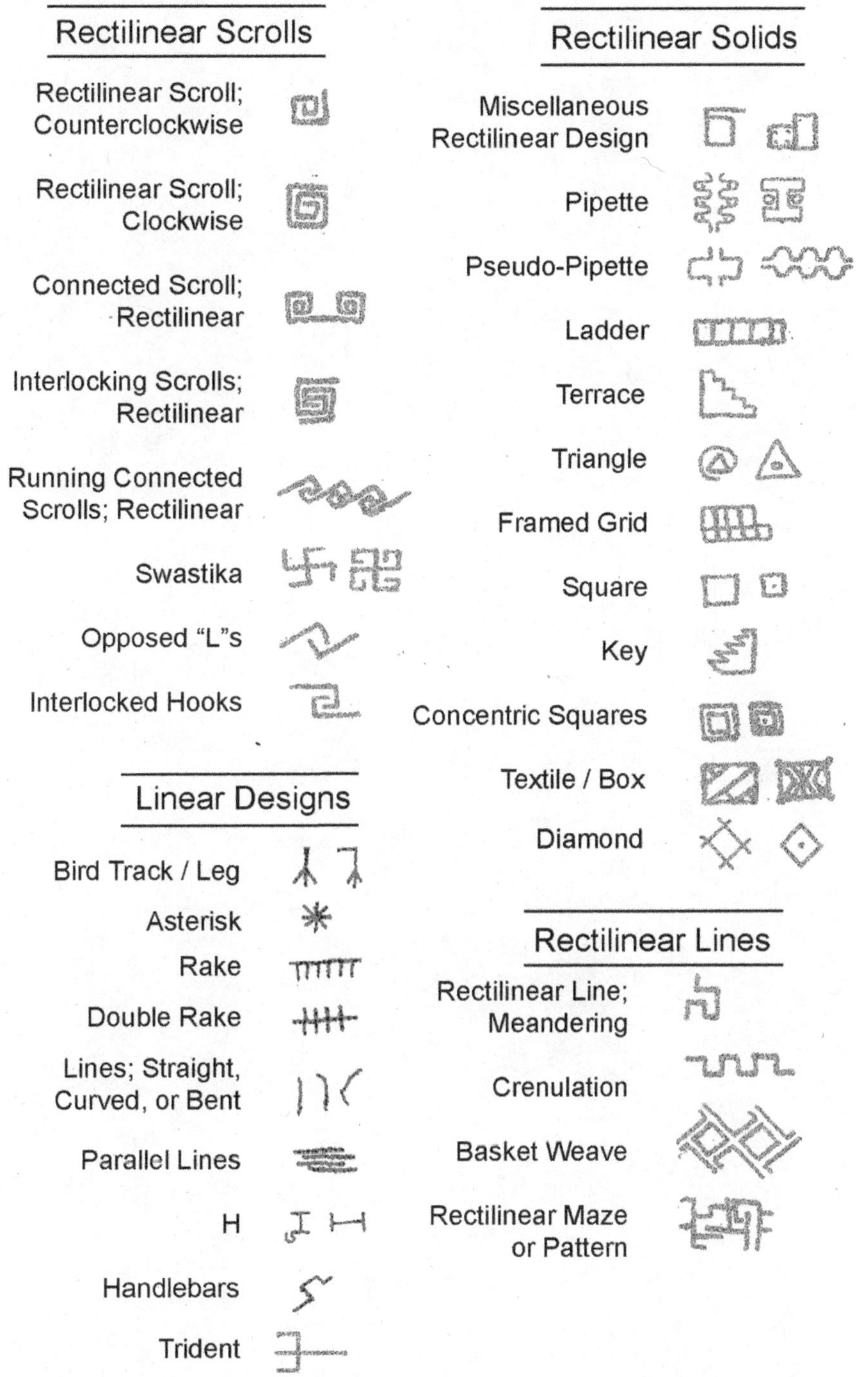
Rectilinear Scrolls
Rectilinear Scroll; Counterclockwise
Rectilinear Scroll; Clockwise
Connected Scroll; Rectilinear
Interlocking Scrolls; Rectilinear
Running Connected Scrolls; Rectilinear
Swastika
Opposed "L"s
Interlocked Hooks
Linear Designs
Bird Track / Leg
Asterisk
Rake
Double Rake
Lines; Straight, Curved, or Bent
Parallel Lines
H
Handlebars
Trident
Rectilinear Solids
Miscellaneous Rectilinear Design
Pipette
Pseudo-Pipette
Ladder
Terrace
Triangle
Framed Grid
Square
Key
Concentric Squares
Textile / Box
Diamond
Rectilinear Lines
Rectilinear Line; Meandering
Crenulation
Basket Weave
Rectilinear Maze or Pattern

Notes

Chapter 1

1. These and similar paintings are commonly called "piasa" pictographs, a reference to the mythological entities they possibly portray. Diaz-Granados and Duncan (2004:xxi) note that Marquette's discovery and account of this pictograph in his journal is one of the earliest recordings of rock art in the United States, if not the very first.
2. Mallery's main goal, however, was not to determine the evolutionary stage of Native Americans; he was instead interested primarily in the functions and meanings of the symbols and provided a range of possible explanations for their use (Mallery 1893:223–258).

Chapter 2

1. Howey and O'Shea's objective remains idealistic, however, because their study of the Midewiwin ceremony, albeit well developed, simply served to "establish [the] time depth" of this ritual and add to the "contexts of societies in the past" (Howey and O'Shea 2006:279). Contrary to their proposition, such attempts to "find" ritual and religion in the past still fail to operationalize these concepts in processes of social reproduction. They rather hold fast to the symbolist and structuralist schools and perpetuate the traditional isolation of ritual and religion from other domains of social reproduction.
2. Not only is this haphazard typological distinction between functional and nonfunctional items conceptually flawed (Brück 1999), the outright dismissal of ritual items perpetuates the traditional defeatist attitude toward ritual and religion (Merrifield 1987:2). Such practice oversimplifies not only the archaeological record but also how we are to interpret the past; it denigrates the depth, complexity, and value of indigenous beliefs and practices, and it improperly imposes Euro-American sentiments and structures on non-Western actors and communities.
3. I find fault with Renfrew's model because (1) it presupposes a deistic religion and (2) liminality implies that the ritual performer is a believer of the ritual's effectiveness, yet I present it to demonstrate how archaeologists have generally approached the topic. I find Bell's and Rappaport's models more holistic and adaptable to non-Western contexts.

Chapter 3

1. The earliest published use of "Hohokam" as an archaeological label that I am aware of was by Jesse Walter Fewkes (1912:117). The O'odham refer to themselves and their ancestors as *Huhugam*, but I retain the Hohokam colloquialism for farmers living in south-central Arizona between AD 1 and 1450. I nevertheless acknowledge that this is a simplistic culture-historical construct and that distinct social identities at intra- and intercommunity scales likely existed within the Hohokam world and persisted into the historic era.
2. The original period-and-phase sequence developed by Harold Gladwin and others (1937) considered the Santan to be the early part of the Classic period rather than the end of the Sedentary. Most Hohokam researchers no longer apply the Santan concept because the painted ceramic assemblage is dominated by Sacaton Red-on-buff. It is therefore now common practice to lump what was once considered Santan, and thus the beginnings of the Classic, with the terminus of the Sacaton phase of the Sedentary period. However, a sound argument can be made for keeping this nebulous era as part of the Classic period

because late Sacaton decorated buffwares have new elements and design layouts that continued into the Casa Grande Red-on-buff design lexicon of the Classic period. Likewise, an unburnished, micaceous, and thick-slipped redware (i.e., Santan Red), a forebear of the Classic period's Gila, Salt, and Wingfield Redwares, was originally considered a diagnostic attribute of the Santan phase but is now typically considered part of the late Sacaton pottery assemblage.

The epoch once encapsulated by the Santan phase, circa AD 1050–1150, and now referred to as the late Sacaton, was truly a transformative period and does not fit comfortably with either the Sedentary or the Classic. However, to keep this book's terminology and framework compatible with most other contemporaneous research in the Phoenix Basin, I consider this transitional era the late Sacaton of the Preclassic rather than the Santan of the early Classic period.

3. There is some controversy over whether or not the ballgame carried over into the Classic period. Ballcourts clearly continued to be present because few, if any, were ever leveled or obliterated (and several still exist). It is their continued use *as* ballcourts that is the question. Nevertheless, at large villages that span the Sedentary/Classic transition, ballcourts coexisted with platform mounds at seemingly choreographed spatial opposition in the village centers. That the ballcourts were not leveled or built over by later works is an important element of their symbolic relevance (Lekson 2008:169). As a side note, similar versions of this opposed dualism between Hohokam circular (ballcourts) and rectangular earthworks (platform mounds) show up in layouts of roughly contemporaneous circular and rectangular post-Chaco Great Houses in the Cibola area (Kintigh et al. 2004) and Hopewell earthworks along the Ohio River watershed in eastern North America (Bernardini 2004).
4. Particularistic structural models for New World indigenous religions are scalar with regard to the degree of shared history as well as similarities in ritual practices, mythologies, dogma, and so on—what I refer to here as themes, premises, and undercurrents. Indeed, given that current genetic and bioanthropological perspectives hold that most, if not all, Amerind peoples descend from a series of migration waves from the northeastern reaches of Eurasia (Meltzer 2009), a thread of shared religious principles among Amerind peoples with antecedents stretching to Paleolithic Siberia and its surrounds (e.g., Hulkrantz 1981; Underhill 1948; Whitley 2008) can be considered a very broad-scale particularistic structural model. Needless to say, much of the "particular" that makes such models useful is lost as the religious structures are broadened and pushed further back in time (see second half of Chapter 2). For this reason, I narrow my analysis to the commonalities among Pueblo, O'odham, and Mesoamerican religious structures because these cultural groups are spatially close and historically related and therefore have the most relevance for understanding religious structures and ritual practices in the Ancient Southwest.
5. Ferdon (1967) questioned Haury's interpretation and offered the idea that ballcourts were dance plazas. Wilcox and Sternberg (1983), however, have provided a compelling argument that these ovals were ballcourts, but I am of the opinion that they served a variety of public gathering and performance-related ritual activities in addition to ballgames (see also Wilcox et al. 2008:1n).
6. During his initial survey of Southwest ruins, Bandelier (1884) first noted the presence of platform mounds in the Tonto and Phoenix Basins as distinctive architectural features that differentiated these settlements from Ancestral Pueblo villages on the Colorado Plateau.
7. Nineteen of these, intentionally broken and burned, and possibly produced by a single individual, were unearthed in a Sedentary period cache with an assortment of other esoteric items at Snaketown (Haury 1976:177). Another 15 in a similar context were found at Los Guanacos (Haury 1945:174–175), hence the village's name.
8. A ritual association for medicine stones and the like may be presumptuous because they are most often found on house floors and in trash (Henry Wallace, personal communication 2010), and similar items have been used as gourd stoppers historically (Jenny Adams, personal communication 2010). On the other hand, Pioneer period figurines, which undoubtedly had a ritualized use, are also most often found on house floors and in refuse piles.
9. O'odham pilgrims and travelers are known to carry similar stones from villages and place them at trail shrines (Russell 1908:254).
10. Doyel (2000b:311) suggested that some Phoenix-area polychromes may have been locally manufactured as a possible "corona effect," or local emulation of exotic places and things. He cedes,

however, that the vast majority of Salado vessels at Hohokam villages in the Phoenix Basin appear to be trade items. If so, it remains to be determined what relationship this iconography had with its Hohokam consumers.

Chapter 4

1. Historically, the South Mountains have been referred to as both the Salt River Mountains (Turney 1929:Map) and the Maricopa Mountains (Hodge 1893:326). Today the Maricopa Mountains denote a range located farther west, approximately 30 km east of Gila Bend (Bahr et al. 1985).
2. A fuller description of the survey methodology and recorded variables as well as sample forms can be found in Wright (2011:128–149, Appendix B); comprehensive data tables for each petroglyph and petroglyph panel are available in Wright (2011:Appendices F, G, and H); and illustrations of each panel are provided in Wright (2011:Appendix E).
3. Al Aprad and I replicated 20 Gila style petroglyphs using cobble hammerstones on South Mountains granodiorite. The average-sized petroglyph (~15 cm × 15 cm) executed at a medium intensity took about 20 minutes. This is comparable to Busby's (Bard and Busby 1974; Busby et al. 1978) replications of Great Basin petroglyphs when controlling for differences in petroglyph size and pecking depth. Thus most of the Hohokam petroglyphs would have required less than 30 minutes to manufacture, and some considerably less.
4. Lundin (2001) documented a site just north of this quarry, and outside our project area, that consists largely of lithic materials in early stages of reduction. I presume this was a location for the continued reduction of this felsic toolstone.
5. Hieroglyphic Canyon is a private inholding owned by the Heard Boy Scout Ranch, so it was not included in the SMRAP project areas. However, many of the more visually appealing and unique motifs and panels adorning those canyon walls were illustrated and discussed by Bostwick and Krocek (2002).
6. Many of these trails have been traveled into historic and modern times, and numerous animals continue to use them, which makes identifying archaeological components difficult. The best way to identify ancient trails is through associated artifacts and connections to other archaeological features. It is quite likely that some of the trails bridge and blur historic, precontact, and faunal use because, once formed, they provide an infrastructure to facilitate passage across the rugged terrain—traversing the most energy-efficient routes by paralleling canyon floors and ridgetops and contouring slopes.
7. As a possible historic example, a cleared, linear trail once started at the cathedral in the Yaqui village of Guadalupe, just south of Tempe, Arizona, and ended at the summit of a hill at the east end of the South Mountains. A shrine, which site records at the Arizona State Museum show was still in use as late as the 1960s, was recorded on this hill. The trail guided and directed pilgrimages in a ritualized, linear fashion between the shrine and the village center.
8. These summit trails are undoubtedly of great antiquity: they lack historic trash in or around them, evidence of modern or historic land disturbance is absent, and several have fully grown trees and saguaro cacti growing in them. Indeed, the summit trails' archaeological contexts demonstrate their Hohokam origination; they are not only adjacent to other features and have diagnostic buffware sherds scattered about, but actually integrate petroglyphs, agricultural terraces, shrines, hilltops, and springs.
9. In excavated assemblages, MNVs are usually calculated from rim sherds. Given the nature of the South Mountains assemblage, comprising many small and fractured sherds, rims are uncommon and definitely not representative of the number of vessels found in the landscape. We thus calculated MNVs through two phases of collection and analysis. We made initial typological distinctions in the field, usually at the ware level, and subsequent distinctions based on vessel form and temper petrography in the laboratory. These groupings are conservative because we did not discriminate sherds unless there was clear evidence that they represented different vessels based on ware, form, or temper. In this sense, vessel representation is likely to be underestimated where surface densities of the same ware, form, or temper types are high or found in disturbed contexts. This is most relevant in the case of South Mountains granodiorite-tempered plainwares, which are ubiquitous in the South Mountains and elsewhere in the Salt River valley (Van Keuren et al. 1997).
10. While there are significant differences among the South Mountains ceramic sample recorded by the SMRAP and those reported by Bostwick

and Krocek (2002:Table 1) and Watts and Lack (2008:Table 5.1), the differences are meager and statistically weak ($\chi^2 = 36.77$, df = 4, $p < .000$, $V^2 = 0.01$). The SMRAP assemblage has a slightly inflated proportion of redware compared with the other samples, but it is still very low. This minor discrepancy may be attributable to different collection strategies and contexts of recovery across studies. The SMRAP sample likely represents a greater variety of depositional contexts because Bostwick focused heavily on rock art settings whereas Watts and Lack's analysis was limited in spatial representation and entailed a small assemblage associated primarily with farming, plant processing, and pit roasting.

11. Since small mammals, reptiles, and birds often inhabit agricultural fields, these pebbles could be sling stones or bola weights (Will Russell, personal communication 2007). This is possible, but in view of their inconsistencies in size and weight, and since their shapes are usually oblong and not spherical, they compare more favorably with shrine stones found in village contexts.

Chapter 5

1. This counters Snyder's (1966:707) more subjective assessment that a change in subject matter can be found between lower and higher sites, with the "more sophisticated ones (deer, human, quadruped, sun disc)" prevailing at higher elevations.
2. It is unclear if Turney's (1929) sample of decorated pottery was limited to buffware or included intrusive types and Salado polychromes, and whether his sample of "rock pictures" refers to the number of panels or individual motifs. Confusingly, Turney found only 22 cases where the pottery portrayed motifs that were also present in his sample of petroglyphs. These consist of six anthropomorphs, eight birds, and eight miscellaneous animals in the pottery designs. He also made the following puzzling observations: (1) anthropomorphic and bird designs are depicted differently in rock art than on pottery; (2) turtles appear on pottery but not as petroglyphs; (3) left-bent swastikas occur as petroglyphs but not as pottery motifs; (4) simple scrolls and coiled snakes also occur as petroglyphs but not as pottery motifs; and (5) petroglyphs on portable stone are rarely found in village contexts. These points, of which the first four can now be refuted, led Turney to suggest that the "pictographers" and "Canal Builders" (Hohokam) were not the same people but that the pictographers postdated the Canal Builders by about 1,000 years. Interestingly, Turney also noted the outlined cross's presence in both media, but since the other lines of evidence argued against a cultural connection between pottery and petroglyphs, he tautologically concluded that the pictographers must have copied the designs they saw on the Hohokam sherds scattered across the valley.
3. Dorn (1998, 2004:253, 2007:268–270) suggests there are four major steps in desert varnish formation: (1) budding bacteria on rock surfaces concentrate and therefore enhance manganese and iron over surrounding sources (Dorn and Oberlander 1982; see also Francis [1920] and Laudermilk [1931] for earlier allusions to this phenomenon); (2) "sheaths" made up of the casings of desiccated bacteria are then broken down by chemical dissolution, releasing manganese and iron minerals; (3) these now-mobile minerals are subsequently transported into the clay minerals that have settled on the rock's surface; and (4) the manganese and iron unite with oxygen inside the clay minerals, forming oxides that cement the clay minerals together and to the rock's surface.
4. Although Bernardini (2009) did not control for microenvironmental nuances, I do not believe they would significantly alter repatination rates across Tutuveni since all petroglyphs are located on a single rock type (sandstone), within a relatively small area (approximately 12.8 km^2), and in a fairly uniform topographic context. Studies across different landforms and geologies would be problematic due to greater variability in repatination rates.
5. Interestingly, the hypothesized chronological break between Wallace and Holmlund's (1986) patina ranks, around the Preclassic/Classic transition (circa AD 1100), is close to the AD 900 divide between two varnish microlaminations (WH2 and WH3 in Liu and Broecker 2007: Table 5). Wallace and Holmlund did not explain why they believe that the light patina class in the Picacho Mountains corresponds with the Classic period, but it may be due to two reasons. For one, they seem to have assumed that rock art continued to be crafted into the Classic, possibly because there are several small platform-mound villages in the immediate area. Also, the patina over rectilinear designs, principally a rectilinear scroll, long considered a diagnostic Classic period motif, was of the lighter class. Wallace's (2001, 2004) later work with ceramic iconogra-

phy has clearly shown that rectilinear scrolls and similar motifs were painted, albeit rarely, on pottery as early as the Pioneer period (see also Chapter 3). If the two discernible patina classes in the Picachos correspond with two varnish microlaminations, placing the patina class dividing line around AD 900 instead of around AD 1100, perhaps the petroglyphs with lighter patinas in the Picachos date to the Sedentary period rather than the Classic.

6. The South Mountains are composed of four major lithologies: Precambrian Estrella gneiss and Komatke granite in the western half that was intruded on by a single middle Tertiary pluton of Telegraph Pass granite and South Mountains granodiorite in the eastern half (Reynolds 1985). Petroglyphs are found on each of these host rocks, but all the glyphs considered in this book are on granodiorite in the northeastern stretch of the mountains. South Mountains granodiorite is predominantly composed of plagioclase and quartz with lesser amounts of potassium feldspar and biotite with accessory minerals of magnetite, apatite, zircon, and sphene. This composition gives the granodiorite a characteristic salt-and-pepper complexion.

   The granodiorite is increasingly metamorphosed toward the east, which has stretched and deformed the rock's fabric. The only significant mineralogical change brought about through the metamorphosis, however, was replacement and recrystallization of biotite. Since the unmetamorphosed granodiorite has a modal biotite composition of just 5 percent (Reynolds 1985:15), I consider the slight mineralogical differences within the structurally variable granodiorite negligible for my purposes here.

7. Patina ranks, as ordinal scale values, can be compared statistically via nonparametric tests of the median values since such tests do not assume that the parameters of the populations (petroglyph motif types) conform to a normal distribution (Corder and Forman 2009). I chose the nonparametric Mann-Whitney *U* test since sample sizes between motif types vary considerably. The Mann-Whitney test ranks ordinal scale values (patina rank is an ordinal variable of petroglyph darkness) and then sums the ranks between the populations, yielding a *U* statistic. The test determines with a degree of significance (*p*) whether differences between the populations' medians are coincidental due to sampling. I should note that the rank-order comparison of patinas includes only those motifs found on the same panel more than twice, since at least three observations are required for rank-order analysis. A large portion of the petroglyph sample, unfortunately, does not meet this standard, and some potentially chronologically sensitive motifs were consequently omitted from the analysis.

8. I define statistical significance as the probability of less than or equal to 5 percent ($p \leq .05$) that the *U* statistic incorrectly leads to a rejection of the null hypothesis (i.e., a Type I error). The null hypothesis here is that there is no difference in median patina ranks among petroglyph motif types. The *U* statistics and corresponding *p* values for pairwise comparisons are available in the original study (Wright 2011:Table 17).

9. Two other studies in the Desert West region of North America employed light meters to seriate petroglyph assemblages by comparing the amount of light that different motif types reflect relative to the amount of light falling on their surfaces (Brazeau 2007; Whitley 1982; Whitley et al. 1984). Whereas Brazeau (2007) found photometric analysis of reflected light useful for differentiating historic and prehistoric petroglyphs in southern Colorado, Whitley's (1982; Whitley et al. 1984) comparison of atlatls and bows in the Coso Range of southeastern California yielded ambiguous results. I have reassessed Whitley's original Coso Range data and shown that while the difference in reflected light is slight, it is statistically significant and suggests that atlatl petroglyphs tend to be darker (older) than bow petroglyphs (Wright 2011:271–281), as should be expected since bows largely replaced atlatls as the preferred hunting technology in the Great Basin (Bettinger and Eerkens 1999; Mesoudi and O'Brien 2008).

10. After I collected and analyzed the reflectance data for South Mountains petroglyphs, Bednarik published the exciting results of an experimental technique that dates petroglyphs through colorimetric analysis of their patinas (Bednarik 2009). He argues that colorimetric analyses are superior to photometric ones that employ light meters or similar instruments, as I have done here. Colorimetry and photometry of patinas on archaeological rock surfaces rely on the same underlying assumptions concerning patina age and development, lithology, and environment as well as how light waves interact with the patinated rock surfaces. Both techniques are

experimental, and further case studies of each and comparative studies of their effectiveness and accuracy are in order.

11. Methodology, data, descriptive statistics, and exploratory analyses are available in the original study (Wright 2011:142–145, 281–296).
12. Since the distributions of petroglyph reflectance for most of the design classes do not conform to a normal distribution (Wright 2011:Table 20), these data are not amenable to parametric statistical analyses. However, while a ratio-scale variable, petroglyph reflectance is also an ordinal-scale measure of patina darkness (lower *R* values register darker patinas). I therefore conducted a rank-order analysis of petroglyph reflectance using Mann-Whitney's *U* statistic, similar to the analysis of patina ranks though not restricted to same-panel provenance. This yielded significant differences in rank orders among the design classes that support the general shift from a design repertoire dominated by curvilinear and geometric classes to one with a greater emphasis on lifeforms. Likewise, rectilinear scrolls and historic designs ranked brighter (younger) than all the other design classes (Wright 2011: Table 23).
13. This analysis included 843 petroglyphs on 262 panels; I excluded rectilinear scrolls, rectilinear lines, and miscellaneous representational designs because I consider counts for these too low (n = 3, 3, and 4, respectively). Chi-square, which is the basis of CA, is unreliable with small sample sizes such as these, especially when counts are below five.

Chapter 6

1. Bostwick and Krocek (2002) identified more than 7,000 petroglyphs throughout the range, and there are likely more since their survey was, in effect, an unsystematic reconnaissance of Snyder's (1966) earlier though nonexhaustive survey. More than 3,000 Hohokam petroglyphs have been found in this study's three research areas, which accounts for just over 2 percent of the South Mountains landscape.
2. Elsewhere I provide considerable detail regarding the origin and geohydrology of springs in the South Mountains (Wright 2011:Chapter 3).
3. If it is raining, one need not visit a spring to get water because the countless tinajas scattered throughout the South Mountains serve as immediate water catchments. Springs provide a more delayed water supply, flowing for a short period after rains, but as animals had shown on my many visits, it is just as easy to dig into the sandy canyon floors to find water.
4. While this sixth stage type is unique, it may be an example of a summit trail because there is a deeply worn, fairly straight path littered with ceramics that extends from the western edge of the agricultural terraces to the saddle (Figure 4.6). A more convincing summit trail connecting the farming terraces to the rock art cluster may have existed but could have been obliterated by an old dirt road running from a parking lot in the center of the terraces to the saddle (this road is not shown in Figure 4.6). Early roads and park trails were often predicated on ancient trails.
5. I credit and thank David Wilcox for pointing out this dualism in the density of petroglyphs on certain stages and the potential link to a hypothesized moiety-like structure at work in rock art ritualism.
6. For example, this may be why it is difficult in many cases to distinguish phallic anthropomorphic figures from lizards in Hohokam rock art (Hays-Gilpin 2004:25–26).
7. Smith's (2000) work, though narrowly focused on one dimension of iconography, was pioneering for Hohokam research in two regards. First, it drew on O'odham ethnographic accounts to interpret some of the symbolism. Second, it was a rare instance of explicit comparison in design frequencies between pottery and rock art. Smith's research identified a higher proportion of bird motifs and a lower frequency of quadruped motifs on pottery than in petroglyphs in the Picacho Mountains. She also observed a greater prevalence of bighorn sheep motifs in rock art than on pottery. This latter point is somewhat perplexing because the Hohokam portrayed bighorn sheep in rock art only rarely. Sheep make up just over 1 percent of the petroglyphs in the Picachos (Wallace and Holmlund 1986:Table C-1), and less than 0.5 percent at Painted Rocks (Wallace 1989:Table D-2) and in the South Mountains (Table 4.2). Sheep motifs are virtually absent from the decorated buffware lexicon, so while they may be slightly more numerous in petroglyphs, they are far from "common in rock art" (Smith 2000:241).
8. Smith's (2000) data may misrepresent buffware designs and motif frequencies because her sample of whole vessels derives from private collections. Collectors may have preferentially acquired vessels with particular design attri-

butes or deliberately omitted others. Also, whole vessels are relatively uncommon from domestic contexts such as house floors and middens but are more prevalent in mortuary settings. If burials are overrepresented in Smith's sample, motif representations may be skewed if Hohokam mourners favored vessels with certain designs as grave goods.

9. Bostwick and Krocek (2002:Figure 12) report on a single fish petroglyph near Pima Canyon in the South Mountains but suggest it is not old enough to be of Hohokam manufacture.

Chapter 7

1. López Austin (2002) divides Colonial Mexican Indian religions into prehispanic and Christian molds. He further subdivides the prehispanic religions into Mesoamerican, Aridamerican (hunter-gatherer groups throughout what are now the southernmost reaches of New Mexico and Texas, the Baja Peninsula, and northern mainland Mexico), and Oasisamerican (agricultural communities along perennial rivers in otherwise uncultivable, xeric climes through the American Southwest and northwest Mexico, principally the Sonoran Desert). López Austin considers Hohokam, Mogollon, and Patayan to be Oasisamerican but interestingly and inexplicably omits Ancestral Pueblo from this taxonomy.
2. The natural sandstone tinajas in the mesa-top village of Acoma, at least one of which has been anthropogenically enhanced, may have similar metaphorical meaning and religious significance (Andrew Duff, personal communication 2010).

Chapter 8

1. Steve Lekson (2008:203–207) speculates that these new rulers were foreigners from regions on the Colorado Plateau to the north who brought elite forms of leadership with them as they depopulated the Four Corners region and migrated south. Even though Haury (1976) came to accept immigration as a catalyst for social change among the Preclassic Hohokam, most Hohokam archaeologists since the 1970s have been strongly reluctant to entertain migrationist (and diffusionist) models. This is probably due to the heavy strains of cultural ecological and adaptationist paradigms under which many practicing Hohokam researchers were trained, but it is widely accepted that Ancestral Pueblo peoples filtered into the valleys and mountains around the Phoenix and Tucson Basins (e.g., on Perry Mesa, in the Tonto Basin, along the Mogollon Rim, and in the San Pedro valley) in the late thirteenth and early fourteenth centuries. This corresponds to the Civano phase of the Hohokam cultural sequence, when many cultural practices and items with Puebloan antecedents (e.g., coursed-stone and adobe architecture, sherd-tempered pottery, polychromes, inhumations, and certain sources of obsidian) show up in much higher frequencies throughout the Phoenix Basin. For Lekson, all roads lead to Chaco. However, *if* the new Hohokam leaders were Pueblo migrants, or descendants of Pueblo migrants, there are much closer regions from where they could have originated (e.g., the Cibola, Kayenta, and Reserve regions, and the Little Colorado River valley).
2. It is important to consider that demographic fluctuations along Canal System 2 may not be representative for the lower Salt River valley as a whole. Interestingly, Smith and Rice (2009:250–253) use different metrics to reconstruct relative trends in population from a pooled sample of villages on Canal System 2 and Canal 7. Contrary to Ingram's (2008) calculations, they find a much lower population growth rate for the Colonial period and the highest growth occurring during the Sacaton. This discrepancy may be due to different datasets or population modeling techniques. Alternatively, the addition of Canal 7 to the equation may be altering the reconstructed growth rates. If so, Canal 7 possibly witnessed lower growth in the Colonial and higher growth in the Sacaton than Canal System 2. Nevertheless, in both reconstructions population growth during both the Colonial and Sedentary—the era of the Ballcourt Society—was higher than in the preceding Pioneer period.

References

Abbott, David R.

1993 The Pueblo Viejo Ceramics. In *Pueblo Viejo: Archaeological Excavations at a Classic Period Cemetery in El Reposo Park, Phoenix, Arizona*, edited by Mark Zyniecki, pp. 69–107. Archaeological Report No. 92–75. SWCA, Flagstaff, Arizona.

1994a Rough-Sort Analysis. In *The Pueblo Grande Project, Vol. 3: Ceramics and the Production and Exchange of Pottery in the Central Phoenix Basin, Part 1*, edited by David R. Abbott, pp. 7–13. Publications in Archaeology No. 20. Soil Systems, Phoenix.

1994b Detailed Analysis of Sherds. In *The Pueblo Grande Project, Vol. 3: Ceramics and the Production and Exchange of Pottery in the Central Phoenix Basin, Part 1*, edited by David R. Abbott, pp. 261–370. Publications in Archaeology No. 20. Soil Systems, Phoenix.

1995a Sherd Assemblage. In *The Pueblo Grande Museum Expansion Data Recovery Project*, edited by Michael S. Foster, pp. 33–45. Technical Report No. 95-17. Soil Systems, Phoenix.

1995b Rough Sort Ceramic Analysis. In *Archaeology at the Head of the Scottsdale Canal System, Vol. 2: Studies of Artifacts and Biological Remains*, edited by T. Kathleen Henderson and David R. Abbott, pp. 1–14. Anthropological Papers No. 95-1. Northland Research, Flagstaff, Arizona.

1995c Detailed Ceramic Analysis (with a contribution by Mark A. Williams). In *Archaeology at the Head of the Scottsdale Canal System, Vol. 2: Studies of Artifacts and Biological Remains*, edited by T. Kathleen Henderson and David R. Abbott, pp. 57–115. Anthropological Papers No. 95-1. Northland Research, Flagstaff, Arizona.

1997 Ceramics. In *Archaeological and Archival Investigations of Las Canopas: The Esteban Park Project*, edited by Mark R. Hackbarth, pp. 87–104. Anthropological Papers No. 6. Pueblo Grande Museum, Phoenix.

2000 *Ceramics and Community Organization among the Hohokam*. University of Arizona Press, Tucson.

2001 Detailed Sherd Analysis. In *The Grewe Archaeological Research Report, Vol. 2: Material Culture, Part 1: Ceramic Studies*, edited by David R. Abbott, pp. 76–106. Anthropological Papers No. 99-1. Northland Research, Flagstaff, Arizona.

2003a Ceramics, Communities, and Irrigation Management. In *Centuries of Decline during the Hohokam Classic Period at Pueblo Grande*, edited by David R. Abbott, pp. 148–165. University of Arizona Press, Tucson.

2003b The Politics of Decline in Canal System 2. In *Centuries of Decline during the Hohokam Classic Period at Pueblo Grande*, edited by David R. Abbott, pp. 201–227. University of Arizona Press, Tucson.

2009 Extensive and Long-Term Specialization: Hohokam Ceramic Production in the Phoenix Basin, Arizona. *American Antiquity* 74:531–557.

Abbott, David R. (editor)

2003 *Centuries of Decline during the Hohokam Classic Period at Pueblo Grande*. University of Arizona Press, Tucson.

Abbott, David R., Cory Dale Breternitz, and Christine K. Robinson

2003 Challenging Conventional Conceptions. In *Centuries of Decline during the Hohokam Classic Period at Pueblo Grande*, edited by David R. Abbott, pp. 3–23. University of Arizona Press, Tucson.

Abbott, David R., and Michael S. Foster
2003 Site Structure, Chronology, and Population. In *Centuries of Decline during the Hohokam Classic Period at Pueblo Grande*, edited by David R. Abbott, pp. 24–47. University of Arizona Press, Tucson.

Abbott, David R., and T. Kathleen Henderson
2001 Appendix A: Ceramic Rough-Sort Counts. In *The Grewe Archaeological Research Report, Vol. 2: Material Culture, Part 1: Ceramic Studies*, edited by David R. Abbott, pp. 273–306. Anthropological Papers No. 99-1. Northland Research, Flagstaff, Arizona.

Abbott, David R., Scott E. Ingram, and Brent G. Kober
2006 Hohokam Exchange and Early Classic Period Organization in Central Arizona: Focal Villages or Linear Communities? *Journal of Field Archaeology* 31:285–305.

Abbott, David R., Douglas R. Mitchell, and Josephine A. Merewether
1994 Chronology. In *The Pueblo Grande Project, Vol. 2: Feature Descriptions, Chronology, and Site Structure*, edited by Douglas R. Mitchell, pp. 157–254. Publications in Archaeology No. 20. Soil Systems, Phoenix.

Abbott, David R., and David M. Schaller
1992 Exploring the Production and Social Significance of Salado Polychrome at Central Phoenix Basin Hohokam Sites. In *Proceedings of the Second Salado Conference, Globe, Arizona, 1992*, edited by Richard C. Lange and Stephen Germick, pp. 248–257. Occasional Paper. Arizona Archaeological Society, Phoenix.

Abbott, David R., Alexa M. Smith, and Emiliano Gallaga
2007 Ballcourts and Ceramics: The Case for Hohokam Marketplaces in the Arizona Desert. *American Antiquity* 72:461–484.

Abbott, David R., Susan L. Stinson, and Scott Van Keuren
2001 The Economic Implications of Hohokam Buff Ware Exchange during the Early Sedentary Period. *Kiva* 67(1):7–28.

Adams, E. Charles
1991 *The Origin and Development of the Pueblo Katsina Cult.* University of Arizona Press, Tucson.

Adams, E. Charles, and Andrew I. Duff (editors)
2004 *The Protohistoric Pueblo World, A.D. 1275–1600.* University of Arizona Press, Tucson.

Adams, Jenny L.
2003 Analyzed Ground Stone Artifacts. In *Archaeological Excavations at Valencia Vieja: Appendices and Supplemental Data*, edited by Henry D. Wallace and Michael W. Lindeman, pp. 79–90. Technical Report No. 2001-11. Desert Archaeology, Tucson, Arizona.

Alberti, Benjamin, and Tamara L. Bray (editors)
2009 Special Section: "Animating Archaeology: Of Subjects, Objects, and Alternative Ontologies." *Cambridge Archaeological Journal* 19(3).

Aldenderfer, Mark S.
1993 Ritual, Hierarchy, and Change in Foraging Societies. *Journal of Anthropological Archaeology* 12:1–40.

Amsden, Charles
1936 *An Analysis of Hohokam Pottery Designs.* Medallion Papers No. 23. Gila Pueblo, Globe, Arizona.

Anderies, John M.
2006 Robustness, Institutions, and Large-Scale Change in Social-Ecological Systems: The Hohokam of the Phoenix Basin. *Journal of Institutional Economics* 2:133–155.

Anschuetz, Kurt F., Richard H. Wilshusen, and Cherie L. Scheick
2001 An Archaeology of Landscapes: Perspectives and Directions. *Journal of Archaeological Research* 9:157–211.

Aragon, Leslie D.
2013 Figuring Out Figurines: An Ontological Approach to Hohokam Anthropomorphic Figurines from the Phoenix Basin. Unpublished Master's thesis, Department of Anthropology, University of Arizona, Tucson.

Arizona Republic
1959 Predecessors to the Ho Ho Kam? June 3, pp. 14–15. Phoenix.

Arnold, Bettina
2001 The Limits of Agency in the Analysis of Elite Iron Age Celtic Burials. *Journal of Social Archaeology* 1:210–224.

Arnold, Dean E.
1985 *Ceramic Theory and Cultural Processes.* Cambridge University Press, New York.

Ashmore, Wendy, and Bernard Knapp (editors)
1999 *Archaeologies of Landscape: Contemporary Perspectives.* Blackwell, Oxford.

Aune, Michael B., and Valerie DeMarinis
1996 Introduction. In *Religious and Social Ritual: Interdisciplinary Explorations*, edited by

Michael B. Aune and Valerie DeMarinis, pp. 1–16. State University of New York Press, Albany.

Aune, Michael B., and Valerie DeMarinis (editors)
1996 *Religious and Social Ritual: Interdisciplinary Explorations*. State University of New York Press, Albany.

Bahr, Donald M.
1971 Who Were the Hohokam? The Evidence from Pima-Papago Myths. *Ethnohistory* 18: 245–266.
1986 Pima Swallow Songs. *Cultural Anthropology* 1:171–187.
2001 *O'odham Creation and Related Events, as Told to Ruth Benedict in 1927 in Prose, Oratory, and Song*. University of Arizona Press, Tucson.
2004 Temptation and Glory in One Pima and Two Aztec Mythologies. *Journal of the Southwest* 46:705–761.

Bahr, Donald M., Ricardo Baptista, Kris Butler, Edward Dora, Gretchen Fletcher, Vincent Joseph, John Lewis, Sally Pablo, and Emmett White
1985 *The Meaning of the Maricopa Mountains to the Indians Living Nearest to Them*. Report No. 72b. Office of Cultural Resource Management, Arizona State University, Tempe.

Bahr, Donald M., Joseph Giff, and Manuel Havier
1979 Piman Songs on Hunting. *Ethnomusicology* 23:245–296.

Bahr, Donald M., Juan Gregorio, David Lopez, and Albert Alvarez
1973 *Piman Shamanism and Staying Sickness* (Ka:cim Mumkidag). University of Arizona Press, Tucson.

Bahr, Donald M., and J. Richard Haefer
1978 Song in Piman Curing. *Ethnomusicology* 22: 89–122.

Bahr, Donald M., Juan Smith, William Smith Allison, and Julian Hayden
1994 *The Short, Swift Time of Gods on Earth: The Hohokam Chronicles*. University of California Press, Berkeley.

Bahti, Mark
1970 A Cache at Huerfano Butte. *Kiva* 36(2):17–22.

Bahti, Mark, and Eugene Baatsoslanii Joe
2009 *Navajo Sandpaintings*. Rio Nuevo Press, Tucson, Arizona.

Bandelier, Adolf F.
1884 Appendix. Report of A. F. Bandelier on His Investigations in New Mexico during the Years 1883–1884. In *Annual Report of the Archaeological Institute of America* 5:55–98. University Press, Cambridge, Massachusetts.
1892 *Final Report of Investigations among the Indians of the Southwestern United States, Carried on Mainly in the Years from 1880 to 1885, Part 2*. Papers of the Archaeological Institute of America, American Series No. 4. University Press, Cambridge, Massachusetts.

Bard, James C., and Colin I. Busby
1974 The Manufacture of a Petroglyph: A Replicative Experiment. *Contributions of the University of California Archaeological Research Facility* 20:83–102. Berkeley.

Barrett, John C.
1991 Toward an Archaeology of Ritual. In *Sacred and Profane: Proceedings of a Conference on Archaeology, Ritual and Religion; Oxford, 1989*, edited by Paul Garwood, David Jennings, Robin Skeates, and Judith Toms, pp. 1–9. Monograph No. 32. Oxford University Committee for Archaeology, Institute of Archaeology, Oxford.
2001 Agency, the Duality of Structure, and the Problem of the Archaeological Record. In *Archaeological Theory Today*, edited by Ian Hodder, pp. 141–164. Polity Press, London.

Barth, Frederick
1975 *Ritual and Knowledge among the Baktaman of New Guinea*. Universitetsforlaget, Oslo.
1987 *Cosmologies in the Making: A Generative Approach to Cultural Variation in Inner New Guinea*. Cambridge University Press, Cambridge.

Bartlett, John Russell
1854 *Personal Narrative of Explorations and Incidents in Texas, New Mexico, California, Sonora and Chihuahua, Connected with the United States and Mexican Boundary Commission, during the Years 1850, '51, '52, and '53*. Vol. 2. D. Appleton, New York.

Barton, Michael C., Geoffrey A. Clark, and Allison E. Cohen
1994 Art as Information: Explaining Upper Palaeolithic Art in Western Europe. *World Archaeology* 26:185–206.

Basedow, Herbert
1914 Aboriginal Rock Carvings of Great Antiquity in South Australia. *Journal of the Royal Anthropological Institute* 44:195–211.

Baxter, Michael J.
1994 *Exploratory Multivariate Analysis in Archaeology.* Edinburgh University Press, Edinburgh.
2003 *Statistics in Archaeology.* Oxford University Press, Oxford.

Bayman, James M.
1996 Shell Ornament Consumption in a Classic Hohokam Platform Mound Community Center. *Journal of Field Archaeology* 23: 403–418.
2001 The Hohokam of Southwest North America. *Journal of World Prehistory* 15:257–311.
2002 Hohokam Craft Economies and the Materialization of Power. *Journal of Archaeological Method and Theory* 19:69–95.

Bayman, James M., Richard H. Hevly, Boma Johnson, Karl J. Reinhard, and Richard Ryan
1996 Analytical Perspectives on a Protohistoric Cache of Ceramic Jars from the Lower Colorado Desert. *Journal of California and Great Basin Anthropology* 18:131–154.

Beaglehole, Ernest
1937 *Notes on Hopi Economic Life.* Publications in Anthropology No. 15. Yale University, New Haven, Connecticut.

Beck, Margaret E.
2002 The Ball-on-Three-Ball Test for Tensile Strength: Refined Methodology and Results for Three Hohokam Ceramic Types. *American Antiquity* 67:558–569.

Bednarik, Robert G.
1996 Only Time Will Tell: A Review of the Methodology of Direct Rock Art Dating. *Archaeometry* 38:1–13.
2002 The Dating of Rock Art: A Critique. *Journal of Archaeological Science* 29:1213–1233.
2009 Experimental Colorimetric Analysis of Petroglyphs. *Rock Art Research* 26:55–64.

Bégouën, Count Henri
1929 The Magic Origin of Prehistoric Art. *Antiquity* 3:5–19.

Bell, Catherine
1990 The Ritual Body and the Dynamics of Ritual Power. *Journal of Ritual Studies* 4:299–313.
1992 *Ritual Theory, Ritual Practice.* Oxford University Press, Oxford.
1997 *Ritual: Perspectives and Dimensions.* Oxford University Press, Oxford.
2007 Response: Defining the Need for a Definition. In *The Archaeology of Ritual,* edited by Evangelos Kyriakidis, pp. 277–288. Advanced Seminar No. 3. Cotsen Institute of Archaeology, University of California, Los Angeles.

Bellavia, Cara, Adrienne Tremblay, and Douglas R. Mitchell
2007 *An Archaeological Survey of the 110-Acre Carver Mountain II Development in Phoenix, Maricopa County, Arizona.* Cultural Resource Report No. 06-584. SWCA, Phoenix.

Belzoni, Giovanni
1820 *Narrative of the Operations and Recent Discoveries within the Pyramids, Temples, Tombs and Excavations in Egypt and Nubia; and of a Journey to the Coast of the Red Sea, in Search of the Ancient Berenice; and Another to the Oasis of Jupiter Ammon.* Vol. 1. J. Murray, London.

Bender, Barbara (editor)
1993 *Landscape: Politics and Perspectives.* Berg, Oxford.

Benedict, Ruth
1935 *Zuni Mythology.* 2 vols. Columbia University Press, New York.

Berggren, Karin
2000 The Knowledge-*able* Agent? On the Paradoxes of Power. In *Philosophy and Archaeological Practice: Perspectives for the 21st Century,* edited by Cornelius Holtorf and Hakan Karlsson, pp. 39–52. Bricoleur Press, Lindome, Sweden.

Bernardini, Wesley
2004 Hopewell Geometric Earthworks: A Case Study in the Referential and Experiential Meaning of Monuments. *Journal of Anthropological Archaeology* 23:331–356.
2005 *Hopi Oral Tradition and the Archaeology of Identity.* University of Arizona Press, Tucson.
2009 *Hopi History in Stone: The Tutuveni Petroglyph Site.* Archaeological Series No. 200. Arizona State Museum, University of Arizona, Tucson.

Berrocal, María Cruz, and Juan Vincent García
2007 Rock Art as an Archaeological and Social Indicator: The Neolithisation of the Iberian Peninsula. *Journal of Anthropological Archaeology* 26:676–697.

Bettinger, Robert L., and Jelmer Eerkens
1999 Point Typologies, Cultural Transmission, and the Spread of Bow-and-Arrow Technology in the Prehistoric Great Basin. *American Antiquity* 64:231–242.

Binford, Lewis R.
1962 Archaeology as Anthropology. *American Antiquity* 28:217–225.

References

Bird-David, Nurit

1990 The Giving Environment: Another Perspective on the Economic System of Gatherer-Hunters. *Current Anthropology* 31:183–96.

1993 Tribal Metaphorization of Human-Nature Relatedness. In *Environmentalism: The View from Anthropology*, edited by Kay Milton, pp. 112–125. Routledge, London.

1999 Animism Revisited: Personhood, Environment, and Relational Epistemology. *Current Anthropology* 40:S67–S91.

2006 Animistic Epistemology: Why Do Some Hunter-Gatherers Not Depict Animals? *Ethnos* 71:33–50.

Blanton, Richard E., Gary M. Feinman, Stephen A. Kowalewski, and Peter N. Peregrine

1996 A Dual-Processual Theory for the Evolution of Mesoamerican Civilization. *Current Anthropology* 37:1–14.

Bleige Bird, Rebecca, and Eric Alden Smith

2005 Signaling Theory, Strategic Interaction, and Symbolic Capital. *Current Anthropology* 46: 221–248.

Bloch, Maurice

1975 Property and the End of Affinity. In *Marxist Analyses and Social Anthropology*, edited by Maurice Bloch, pp. 203–222. Malaby Press, London.

1977 The Past and the Present in the Present. *Man* 18:391–404.

1986 *From Blessing to Violence: History and Ideology in the Circumcision Ritual of the Merina of Madagascar.* Cambridge University Press, Cambridge.

Boekelman, Henry J.

1936 Shell Trumpet from Arizona. *American Antiquity* 2:27–31.

Boivin, Nicole

2009 Grasping the Elusive and Unknowable: Material Culture in Ritual Practice. *Material Religion* 5(3):266–287.

Bølviken, Erik, Ericka Helskog, Knut Helskog, Inger Marie Holm-Olsen, Leiv Solheim, and Reidar Bertelsen

1982 Correspondence Analysis: An Alternative to Principal Components. *World Archaeology* 14:41–60.

Bostwick, Todd W.

1992 Platform Mound Ceremonialism in Southern Arizona: Possible Symbolic Meanings of Hohokam and Salado Platform Mounds. In *Proceedings of the Second Salado Conference, Globe, Arizona, 1992*, edited by Richard C. Lange and Stephen Germick, pp. 78–85. Occasional Paper. Arizona Archaeological Society, Phoenix.

1998 Songs of the Waterbird: Hohokam Petroglyph Bird Designs in the South Mountains, Phoenix, Arizona. In *American Indian Rock Art*, Vol. 22, edited by Steven M. Freers, pp. 119–128. American Rock Art Research Association, Tucson, Arizona.

1999 Hourglass Anthropomorph Petroglyphs in the South Mountains, Arizona. In *American Indian Rock Art*, Vol. 23, edited by Steven M. Freers, pp. 121–132. American Rock Art Research Association, Tucson, Arizona.

2008a *Beneath the Runways: Archaeology of Sky Harbor International Airport.* City of Phoenix Parks and Recreation Department and Aviation Department, Phoenix.

2008b The South Mountain Rock Art Project: A Collaborative Effort in Recording Rock Art as Archaeology in a City Park. In *Set in Stone: A Binational Workshop on Petroglyph Management in the United States and Mexico*, compiled by Joseph P. Sánchez, Angelica Sánchez-Clark, and Edwina L. Abreu, pp. 82–97. Petroglyph National Monument, National Park Service, Albuquerque, New Mexico.

Bostwick, Todd W., and Peter Krocek

2002 *Landscape of the Spirits: Hohokam Rock Art at South Mountain Park.* University of Arizona Press, Tucson.

Bostwick, Todd W., and Stan Plum

2005 The Shaw Butte Hilltop Site: A Prehistoric Hohokam Observatory. In *Current Studies in Archaeoastronomy: Conversations across Space and Time*, edited by John W. Fountain and Rolf M. Sinclair, pp. 151–160. Carolina Academic Press, Durham, North Carolina.

Bostwick, Todd W., Stephanie M. Whittlesey, and Douglas R. Craig

2009 Reconstructing the Sacred in Hohokam Archaeology: Cosmology, Mythology, and Ritual. Paper presented at the Arizona Archaeological Council Fall Conference, October 28, Pueblo Grande Museum, Phoenix.

Bourdieu, Pierre

1977 *Outline of a Theory of Practice.* Translated by Richard Nices. Cambridge University Press, Cambridge.

1985 The Social Space and Genesis of Groups. *Theory and Society* 14(6):723–744.

1986 The Forms of Capital. In *Handbook of Theory and Research for the Sociology of Education*,

edited by John G. Richardson, pp. 241–258. Greenwood Press, New York.
1990 *The Logic of Practice.* Translated by Richard Nices. Stanford University Press, Stanford, California.

Bowie, Fiona
2000 *The Anthropology of Religion.* Blackwell, Oxford.

Boyd, Caroline E.
1996 Shamanic Journeys into the Otherworld of the Archaic Chichimec. *Latin American Antiquity* 7:152–164.
2003 *Rock Art of the Lower Pecos.* Texas A&M University Press, College Station.

Bradley, Richard
1991 Rock Art and Perceptions of the Landscape. *Cambridge Archaeological Journal* 1:77–101.
1997 *Rock Art and the Prehistory of Atlantic Europe: Signing the Land.* Routledge, London.
2000 *An Archaeology of Natural Places.* Routledge, London.
2002 Access, Style, and Imagery: The Audience for Prehistoric Rock Art in Atlantic Spain and Portugal, 4000–2000 BC. *Oxford Journal of Archaeology* 21:231–247.
2005 *Ritual and Domestic Life in Prehistoric Europe.* Routledge, London.
2009 *Image and Audience: Rethinking Prehistoric Art.* Oxford University Press, Oxford.

Bradley, Ronna Jane Earthman
1996 *The Role of Casas Grandes in the Prehistoric Shell Exchange Networks within the Southwest.* Ph.D. dissertation, Department of Anthropology, Arizona State University, Tempe. University Microfilms, Ann Arbor, Michigan.

Brandt, Elizabeth
1980 On Secrecy and the Control of Knowledge: Taos Pueblo. In *Secrecy: A Cross-Cultural Perspective*, edited by Stanton K. Tefft, pp. 123–146. Human Sciences Press, New York.
1994 Egalitarianism, Hierarchy, and Centralization in the Pueblos. In *The Ancient Southwestern Community*, edited by Wirt H. Wills and Robert D. Leonard, pp. 9–23. University of New Mexico Press, Albuquerque.

Brazeau, Craig
2007 Chronologically Dating Rock Art and Elements and Its Importance in the Symbolic Interpretation of Cultural Identity. Unpublished Master's thesis, Department of Anthropology, University of Colorado, Boulder.

Breuil, Abbé Henri
1933 *Les peintures ruprestres schématiques de la peninsule Ibérique.* Singer-Polignac, Lagny, France.

Brew, John Otis
1943 On the Pueblo IV and on the Katchina-Tlaloc Relations. In *El norte de México y el sur de los Estados Unidos: Tercera Reunión de Mesa Redonda sobre Problemas Antropológicos de México y Centro América*, pp. 241–245. Sociedad Mexicana de Antropología, Mexico City.
1946 *Archaeology of Alkali Ridge, Southeastern Utah, with a Review of the Prehistory of the Mesa Verde Division of the San Juan and Some Observations on Archaeological Systematics.* Papers of the Peabody Museum of American Archaeology and Ethnology No. 21. Harvard University, Cambridge, Massachusetts.

Broda, Johanna
1991 The Sacred Landscape of Aztec Calendar Festival: Myth, Nature and Society. In *To Change Place: Aztec Ceremonial Landscapes*, edited by David Carrasco, pp. 74–120. University Press of Colorado, Niwot.

Brown, Emily J.
2005 Instruments of Power: Musical Performance in the Rituals of Ancestral Puebloans of the Southwest. Unpublished Ph.D. dissertation, Department of Anthropology, Columbia University, New York.

Brown, Herbert
1906 A Pima-Maricopa Ceremony. *American Anthropologist* 8:688–690.

Brown, Linda A., and Kitty F. Emery
2008 Negotiations with the Animate Forest: Hunting Shrines in the Guatemalan Highlands. *Journal of Archaeological Method and Theory* 15:300–337.

Brown, Linda A., and William H. Walker (editors)
2008 Special Issue: "Archaeology, Animism, and Non-human Agents." *Journal of Archaeological Method and Theory* 15(3).

Brück, Joanna
1999 Ritual and Rationality: Some Problems of Interpretation in European Archaeology. *Journal of European Archaeology* 2:313–344.

Bruder, J. Simon
1983 *Archaeological Investigations at the Hedgepeth Hills Petroglyph Site.* Research Paper No. 28. Museum of Northern Arizona, Flagstaff.

Brunson, Judy Lynn
1990 *The Social Organization of the Los Muertos Hohokam: A Reanalysis of Cushing's Hemenway Expedition Data.* 2 vols. Ph.D. dissertation, Department of Anthropology, Arizona State University, Tempe. University Microfilms, Ann Arbor, Michigan.

Bunzel, Ruth
1929 *The Pueblo Potter: A Study of Creative Imagination in Primitive Art.* Columbia University Press, New York.
1932a Zuñi Katcinas. *Annual Report of the Bureau of American Ethnology* 47:837–1086. U.S. Government Printing Office, Washington, D.C.
1932b Introduction to Zuñi Ceremonialism. *Annual Report of the Bureau of American Ethnology* 47:467–544. U.S. Government Printing Office, Washington, D.C.

Burkitt, Miles C.
1921 A New Find in Palaeolithic Cave Art. *Man* 21:183–185.

Burton, Jeffrey F.
1988 Hunters and the Hunted: The Prehistoric Art of Tom Ketchum Cave. *Kiva* 53(4):335–356.

Busby, Colin I., Robert Fleming, Robert Hayes, and Karen Nissen
1978 The Manufacture of Petroglyphs: Additional Replicative Experiments from the Western Great Basin. In *Four Rock Art Studies*, edited by C. William Clewlow Jr., pp. 89–103. Publications on North American Rock Art No. 1. Ballena Press, Socorro, New Mexico.

Bustoz, David, Glen E. Rice, and Charles Matthew Thomas
2009 Analysis of Special Artifacts, Flaked Stone, Groundstone, and Iconography at Las Canopas. In *Excavations at Las Canopas: A Hohokam Village in the Phoenix Basin*, edited by John L. Czarzasty and Glen E. Rice, pp. 117–169. Anthropological Papers No. 17. Pueblo Grande Museum, Phoenix.

Cable, John S., and Wilma Allen
1982 Artifact Description and Analysis. In *City of Phoenix: Archaeology of the Original Townsite, Blocks 1 and 2, Part I.* Publications in Archaeology No. 1. Soil Systems, Phoenix.

Cable, John S., and David E. Doyel
1987 Pioneer Period Village Structure and Settlement Pattern in the Phoenix Basin. In *The Hohokam Village: Site Structure and Organization*, edited by David E. Doyel, pp. 21–71. Southwestern and Rocky Mountain Division of the American Association for the Advancement of Science, Glenwood Springs, Colorado.

Cable, John S., Kathleen S. Hoffman, David E. Doyel, and Frank Ritz (editors)
1985 *City of Phoenix: Archaeology of the Original Townsite: Block 24 East.* Publications in Archaeology No. 8. Soil Systems, Phoenix.

Carot, Patricia
2001 *Le site de Loma Alta, Lac de Zacapu, Michoacan, Mexique.* Monographs in American Archaeology No. 9. BAR International Series No. 920. Archaeopress, Oxford.

Carpenter, Tina
2007 Hohokam Rock Art in Two Canyons in the South Mountains, Phoenix, Arizona. Unpublished Master's thesis, Department of Anthropology, Northern Arizona University, Flagstaff.

Carr, Christopher
1995 A Unified Middle-Range Theory of Artifact Design. In *Style, Society, and Person*, edited by Christopher Carr and Jill E. Neitzel, pp. 171–258. Plenum Press, New York.

Cartailhac, Émile
1902 Les cavernes ornées de dessins, la Grottoe d'Altamira, Espagne: "Mea culpa d'un sceptique." *L'Anthropologie* 13:348–354.

Carter, Alan
1989 *The Philosophical Foundations of Property Rights.* Harvester Wheatsheaf, New York.

Castetter, Edward F., and Willis H. Bell
1942 *Pima and Papago Indian Agriculture.* Inter-Americana Studies No. 1. University of New Mexico Press, Albuquerque.

Chamberlin, Matthew
2012 Plazas, Performance, and Symbolic Power in Ancestral Pueblo Religion. In *Religious Transformation in the Late Pre-Hispanic Pueblo World*, edited by Donna M. Glowacki and Scott Van Keuren, pp. 130–152. University of Arizona Press, Tucson.

Charlton, Bruce G.
2007 Alienation, Recovered Animism and Altered States of Consciousness. *Medical Hypotheses* 68:727–731.

Chenault, Mark L.
1996 *The Polvorón Phase and the Hohokam Collapse.* Ph.D. dissertation, Department of Anthropology, University of Colorado, Boulder. University Microfilms, Ann Arbor, Michigan.
2000 In Defense of the Polvorón Phase. In *The Hohokam Village Revisited*, edited by

David E. Doyel, Suzanne K. Fish, and Paul R. Fish, pp. 277–286. Southwestern and Rocky Mountain Division of the American Association for the Advancement of Science, Fort Collins, Colorado.

Chenault, Mark L., and John M. Lindly

2006 Guanacos, Symbolism, and Religion during the Hohokam Pre-Classic. In *Religion in the Prehispanic Southwest*, edited by Christine S. VanPool, Todd L. VanPool, and David A. Phillips Jr., pp. 115–134. Archaeology of Religion No. 5. AltaMira Press, Lanham, Maryland.

Chippindale, Christopher

2001 Studying Ancient Pictures as Pictures. In *Handbook of Rock Art Research*, edited by David S. Whitley, pp. 247–272. AltaMira Press, Walnut Creek, California.

2004 From Millimetre Up to Kilometre: A Framework of Space and Scale for Reporting and Studying Rock-Art in Its Landscape. In *The Figured Landscapes of Rock-Art: Looking at Pictures in Place*, edited by Christopher Chippindale and George Nash, pp. 102–117. Cambridge University Press, Cambridge.

Chippindale, Christopher, and George Nash (editors)

2004 *The Figured Landscapes of Rock-Art: Looking at Pictures in Place*. Cambridge University Press, Cambridge.

Chippindale, Christopher, and Paul S. C. Taçon

1998 The Many Ways of Dating Arnhem Land Rock-Art, North Australia. In *The Archaeology of Rock-Art*, edited by Christopher Chippindale and Paul S. C. Taçon, pp. 90–111. Cambridge University Press, Cambridge.

Chisholm, Michael

1979 *Rural Settlement and Land Use: An Essay on Location*. 3rd ed. Hutchinson University Library, London.

Chouin, Gérard

2002 Sacred Groves as Historical and Archaeological Markers in Southern Ghana. *Ghana Studies* 5:177–196.

Clark, Geoffrey A.

1967 A Cache of Papago Miniature Pottery from Kitt Peak, South-Central Arizona. *Kiva* 32(4):128–142.

Clark, Jeffery J.

2001 *Tracking Prehistoric Migrations: Pueblo Settlers among the Tonto Basin Hohokam*. Anthropological Papers No. 65. University of Arizona Press, Tucson.

Clouse, Robert Alan

2004 Pattern and Function at the Jeffers Petroglyphs, Minnesota. In *The Rock-Art of Eastern North America: Capturing Images and Insights*, edited by Carol Diaz-Granados and James R. Duncan, pp. 110–125. University of Alabama Press, Tuscaloosa.

Cohodas, Marvin

1975 The Symbolism and Ritual Function of the Middle Classic Ball Game in Mesoamerica. *American Indian Quarterly* 2:99–130.

Colton, Mary Russel F., and Harold S. Colton

1931 Petroglyphs: The Record of a Great Adventure. *American Anthropologist* 33:32–37.

Conkey, Margaret W.

2001 Structural and Semiotic Approaches. In *Handbook of Rock Art Research*, edited by David S. Whitley, pp. 273–310. AltaMira Press, Walnut Creek, California.

Corder, Gregory W. and Dale I. Forman

2009 *Nonparametric Statistics for Non-statisticians: A Step-by-Step Approach*. John Wiley and Sons, Hoboken, New Jersey.

Cosgrove, Cornelius B.

1947 *Caves of the Upper Gila and Hueco Areas in New Mexico and Texas*. Papers of the Peabody Museum of Archaeology and Ethnology Vol. 24, No. 2. Harvard University, Cambridge, Massachusetts.

Coulam, Nancy J., and Alan R. Schroedl

2004 Late Archaic Totemism in the Greater American Southwest. *American Antiquity* 69:41–52.

Cowgill, George

1968 Archaeological Applications of Factor, Cluster and Proximity Analysis. *American Antiquity* 33:367–375.

1972 Models, Methods, and Techniques for Seriation. In *Models in Archaeology*, edited by David L. Clarke, pp. 381–424. Methuen, London.

Craig, Douglas B.

1988 Archaeological Investigations at AA:16:49 (ASM), the Dakota Wash Mitigation. Anthropology Series, Archaeological Report No. 14. Manuscript on file, Pima Community College, Tucson.

2000 The Demographic Implications of Architectural Change at the Grewe Site. In *The Hohokam Village Revisited*, edited by David E. Doyel, Suzanne K. Fish, and Paul R. Fish, pp. 139–166. Southwestern and Rocky Mountain Division of the American Associ-

ation for the Advancement of Science, Fort Collins, Colorado.
2001 *The Grewe Archaeological Research Project, Vol. 3: Synthesis*. Anthropological Papers No. 99-1. Northland Research, Tempe, Arizona.
2004 *Beyond Snaketown: Household Inequality and Political Power in Early Hohokam Society*. Ph.D. dissertation, Department of Anthropology, University of Arizona, Tucson. University Microfilms, Ann Arbor, Michigan.

Creese, John L.
2011 Algonquian Rock Art and the Landscape of Power. *Journal of Social Archaeology* 11:3–20.

Cremaschi, Mauro
1996 The Desert Varnish in the Messak Sattafet (Fezzan, Libyan Sahara), Age, Archaeological Context and Paleo-Environmental Implication. *Geoarchaeology: An International Journal* 11:393–421.

Cressman, Luther S.
1937 *Petroglyphs of Oregon*. Studies in Anthropology No. 1. University of Oregon, Eugene.

Crotty, Helen K.
2001 Shields, Shield Bearers, and Warfare Imagery in Anasazi Art, 1200–1500. In *Deadly Landscapes: Case Studies in Prehistoric Southwestern Warfare*, edited by Glen E. Rice and Steven A. LeBlanc, pp. 65–83. University of Utah Press, Salt Lake City.

Crown, Patricia L.
1981 Analysis of the Las Colinas Ceramics. In *The 1968 Excavations at Mound 8, Las Colinas Ruins Group, Phoenix, Arizona*, edited by Laurens C. Hammack and Alan P. Sullivan, pp. 87–169. Archaeological Series No. 154. Arizona State Museum, University of Arizona, Tucson.
1984 Adaptation through Diversity: An Examination of Population Pressure and Agricultural Technology in the Salt-Gila Basin. In *Prehistoric Agricultural Strategies in the Southwest*, edited by Suzanne K. Fish and Paul R. Fish, pp. 5–25. Anthropological Research Papers No. 33. Arizona State University, Tempe.
1987 Classic Period Hohokam Settlement and Land Use in the Casa Grande Ruins Area, Arizona. *Journal of Field Archaeology* 14: 147–162.
1990 The Hohokam of the American Southwest. *Journal of World Prehistory* 4:223–255.
1991a The Hohokam: Current Views of Prehistory and the Regional System. In *Chaco and Hohokam: Prehistoric Regional Systems in the American Southwest*, edited by Patricia L. Crown and W. James Judge, pp. 135–157. School of American Research Press, Santa Fe, New Mexico.
1991b The Role of Exchange and Interaction in Salt-Gila Basin Hohokam Prehistory. In *Exploring the Hohokam: Prehistoric Desert Peoples of the American Southwest*, edited by George J. Gumerman, pp. 383–416. Amerind Foundation New World Series No. 1. University of New Mexico Press, Albuquerque.
1994 *Ceramics and Ideology: Salado Polychrome Pottery*. University of New Mexico Press, Albuquerque.

Crown, Patricia L., and Suzanne K. Fish
1996 Gender and Status in the Hohokam Pre-Classic to Classic Transition. *American Anthropologist* 98:803–817.

Crown, Patricia L., and W. J. Hurst
2009 Evidence of Cacao Use in the Prehispanic American Southwest. *Proceedings of the National Academy of Sciences* 106:2110–2113.

Curtis, Edward S.
1926 *The Tewa; The Zuni*. The North American Indian Vol. 17. Plimpton Press, Norwood, Massachusetts.

Cushing, Frank Hamilton
1890 Preliminary Notes on the Origin, Working Hypothesis and Primary Researches of the Hemenway Southwestern Archaeological Expedition. In *Compte-rendu du Congrès International des Américanistes de la Septième Session, Berlin, 1888*, pp. 151–194. Librairie W. H. Kühl, Berlin.
1892 Manual Concepts: A Study of the Influence of Hand Usage on Culture Growth. *American Anthropologist* 5:289–317.

Czarzasty, John L., and David Bustoz
2012 A Hohokam Kiln at Las Canopas. *Kiva* 77(4): 383–393.

Czarzasty, John L., and Glen E. Rice (editors)
2009 *Excavations at Las Canopas: A Hohokam Village in the Phoenix Basin*. Anthropological Papers No. 17. Pueblo Grande Museum, Phoenix.

D'Andrade, Roy
1995 Moral Models in Anthropology. *Current Anthropology* 36:399–408.

Darling, J. Andrew
2006 Pima Song and the Archaeology of Space. Draft report submitted to the Cultural

Resource Management Program, Gila River Indian Community, Sacaton, Arizona.

Darling, J. Andrew, and B. Sunday Eiselt

2009 Trail Research in the Gila Bend Area. In *Trails, Rock Features, and Homesteading in the Gila Bend Area: A Report on the State Route 85 Gila Bend to Buckeye Archaeological Project*, edited by John L. Czarzasty, Kathleen Peterson, Glen E. Rice, and J. Andrew Darling, pp. 199–228. Anthropological Field Studies No. 43. Arizona State University, Tempe. Anthropological Research Papers No. 4. Gila River Indian Community, Sacaton, Arizona.

Darling, J. Andrew, and Barnaby V. Lewis

2007 Songscapes and Calendar Sticks. In *The Hohokam Millennium*, edited by Suzanne K. Fish and Paul R. Fish, pp. 130–139. School for Advanced Research Press, Santa Fe, New Mexico.

Dart, Allen

1995 Ground Stone Artifacts. In *Archaeological Investigations at Los Morteros, a Prehistoric Settlement in the Northern Tucson Basin*, Part 2, edited by Henry D. Wallace, pp. 503–566. Anthropological Papers No. 17. Center for Desert Archaeology, Tucson, Arizona.

David, Bruno, and Meredith Wilson (editors)

2002 *Inscribed Landscapes: Marking and Making Place.* University of Hawaii Press, Honolulu.

Davis, Edward J.

1920 The Papago Ceremony of Vikita. *Indian Notes and Monographs* 3(4):159–177. Museum of the American Indian, New York.

Davis, John

1809 An Attempt to Explain the Inscription on the Dighton Rock; In a Letter to the Rev. Samuel Webber, D.D. *Memoirs of the American Academy of Arts and Sciences* 3(1):197–205. Cambridge, Massachusetts.

Dean, Jeffrey S.

1991 Thoughts on Hohokam Chronology. In *Exploring the Hohokam: Prehistoric Desert Peoples of the American Southwest*, edited by George J. Gumerman, pp. 61–149. Amerind Foundation New World Series No. 1. University of New Mexico Press, Albuquerque.

Dean, Jeffrey S. (editor)

2000 *Salado.* Amerind Foundation New World Studies Series No. 4. University of New Mexico Press, Albuquerque.

Dean, Jeffrey S., William H. Doelle, and Janet D. Orcutt

1994 Adaptive Stress, Environment, and Demography. In *Themes in Southwest Prehistory*, edited by George J. Gumerman, pp. 53–86. School of American Research Press, Santa Fe, New Mexico.

Dean, Rebecca Marie

2003 *People, Pests, and Prey: The Emergence of Agricultural Economies in the Desert Southwest.* Ph.D. dissertation, Department of Anthropology, University of Arizona, Tucson. University Microfilms, Ann Arbor, Michigan.

DeBoer, Warren

1991 The Decorative Burden: Design, Medium, and Change. In *Ceramic Ethnoarchaeology*, edited by William Longacre, pp. 144–161. University of Arizona Press, Tucson.

Demarest, Arthur A., and Geoffrey W. Conrad

1992 *Ideology and Pre-Columbian Civilizations.* School of American Research Press, Santa Fe, New Mexico.

DeMarrais, Elizabeth, Luis Jaime Castillo, and Timothy Earle

1996 Ideology, Materialization, and Power Strategies. *Current Anthropology* 37:15–31.

DeMarrais, Elizabeth, Chris Gosden, and Colin Renfrew (editors)

2004 *Rethinking Materiality: The Engagement of Mind with the Material World.* McDonald Institute for Archaeological Research, Cambridge.

Dennis, Wayne

1940 *The Hopi Child.* D. Appleton-Century, New York.

1943 Animism and Related Tendencies in Hopi Children. *Journal of Abnormal and Social Psychology* 38:21–35.

Dennis, Wayne, and Roger Russell

1940 Piaget's Questions Applied to Zuni Children. *Child Development* 11:181–187.

Descola, Philippe

1992 Societies of Nature and the Nature of Society. In *Conceptualizing Society*, edited by Adam Kuper, pp. 107–126. Routledge, London.

Descola, Philippe, and Gisli Pálsson (editors)

1996 *Nature and Society: Anthropological Perspectives.* Routledge, London.

Díaz-Andreu, Margarita

2001 Marking the Landscape: Iberian Post-Palaeolithic Art, Identities, and the Sacred.

In *European Landscapes of Rock-Art*, edited by George H. Nash and Christopher Chippindale, pp. 158–175. Routledge, London.
2003 Rock Art and Ritual Landscape in Central Spain: The Rock Carvings of La Hinojosa (Cuenca). *Oxford Journal of Archaeology* 22:35–51.

Diaz-Granados, Carol, and James R. Duncan
2004 Preface. In *The Rock-Art of Eastern North America: Capturing Images and Insights*, edited by Carol Diaz-Granados and James R. Duncan, pp. xxi–xxii. University of Alabama Press, Tuscaloosa.

DiPeso, Charles C.
1974 *Casas Grandes: A Fallen Trading Center of the Gran Chichimeca, Vol. 2: Medio Period.* Northland Press, Flagstaff, Arizona.

Dirks, Nicholas B.
1992 Ritual and Resistance: Subversion as a Social Fact. In *Contesting Power: Resistance and Everyday Social Relations in South Asia*, edited by Douglas Haynes and Gyan Prakash, pp. 483–503. University of California Press, Berkeley.

Dixon, Keith A.
1965 A Petroglyph-Decorated Metate from the Bradshaw Mountains, Arizona. *Kiva* 31(1): 55–56.

Dobres, Marcia Anne
2000 *Technology and Social Agency: Outlining an Anthropological Framework for Archaeology.* Blackwell, Oxford.

Dobres, Marcia Anne, and John E. Robb (editors)
2000 *Agency in Archaeology.* Routledge, London.

Doelle, William H., David A. Gregory, and Henry D. Wallace
1995 Classic Period Platform Mound Systems in Southern Arizona. In *The Roosevelt Community Development Study: New Perspectives on Tonto Basin Prehistory*, edited by Mark D. Elson, Mariam T. Stark, and David A. Gregory, pp. 385–440. Anthropological Papers No. 15. Center for Desert Archaeology, Tucson, Arizona.

Doelle, William H., and Henry D. Wallace
1991 The Changing Role of the Tucson Basin in the Hohokam Regional System. In *Exploring the Hohokam: Prehistoric Desert Peoples of the American Southwest*, edited by George J. Gumerman, pp. 279–345. Amerind Foundation New World Series No. 1. University of New Mexico Press, Albuquerque.

Domenech, Emmanuel M.
1860 *Seven Years' Residence in the Great Deserts of North America.* Vol. 1. Longman, Green, Longman, and Roberts, London.

Dongoske, Kurt E., Michael Yeatts, Roger Anyon, and T. J. Ferguson
1997 Archaeological Cultures and Cultural Affiliation: Hopi and Zuni Perspectives in the American Southwest. *American Antiquity* 62:600–608.

Doolittle, William E., and James A. Neely (editors)
2004 *The Safford Valley Grids: Prehistoric Cultivation in the Southern Arizona Desert.* Anthropological Papers No. 70. University of Arizona Press, Tucson.

Doran, James E., and Frank R. Hodson
1975 *Mathematics and Computers in Archaeology.* Harvard University Press, Cambridge, Massachusetts.

Dorn, Ronald I.
1990 Quaternary Alkalinity Fluctuations Recorded in Rock Varnish Microlaminations on Western U.S.A. Volcanics. *Palaeogeography, Palaeoclimatology, Palaeoecology* 76:291–310.
1998 *Rock Coatings.* Elsevier, Amsterdam.
2001 Chronometric Techniques: Engravings. In *Handbook of Rock Art Research*, edited by David S. Whitley, pp. 167–189. AltaMira Press, Walnut Creek, California.
2004 Desert Varnish. In *Encyclopedia of Geomorphology*, edited by Andrew S. Goudie, pp. 251–254. Routledge, London.
2005 Why Testify for the Defense? *La Pintura* 31(2):8–12.
2007 Rock Varnish. In *Geochemical Sediments and Landscapes*, edited by David J. Nash and Sue J. McLaren, pp. 246–297. Blackwell, London.

Dorn, Ronald I., and Theodore M. Oberlander
1981 Microbial Origin of Desert Varnish. *Science* 213(4513):1245–1247.
1982 Rock Varnish. *Progress in Physical Geography* 6:317–367.

Douglas, Mary
1973 *Natural Symbols: Explorations in Cosmology.* Random House, New York.

Douglass, William B.
1917 Notes on the Shrines of the Tewas and Other Pueblo Indians. In *Proceedings of the Nineteenth International Congress of Americanists*, edited by Frank W. Hodge, pp. 344–378. Washington, D.C.

Downum, Christian E., and Todd W. Bostwick

2003 The Platform Mound. In *Centuries of Decline during the Hohokam Classic Period at Pueblo Grande*, edited by David R. Abbott, pp. 166–200. University of Arizona Press, Tucson.

Dowson, Thomas A.

2001 Queer Theory and Feminist Theory: Towards a Sociology of Sexual Politics in Rock Art Research. In *Theoretical Perspectives in Rock Art Research*, edited by Knut Helskog, pp. 312–329. Institute for Comparative Research in Human Culture, Oslo.

2009 Re-animating Hunter-Gatherer Rock-Art Research. *Cambridge Archaeological Journal* 19:378–387.

Doyel, David E.

1974 *Excavations in the Escalante Ruin Group, Southern Arizona*. Archaeological Series No. 37. Arizona State Museum, University of Arizona, Tucson.

1980 Hohokam Social Organization and the Sedentary to Classic Transition. In *Current Issues in Hohokam Prehistory*, edited by David E. Doyel and Fred Plog, pp. 23–40. Anthropological Research Papers No. 23. Arizona State University, Tempe.

1981 *Late Hohokam Prehistory in Southern Arizona*. Contributions to Archaeology No. 2. Gila Press, Scottsdale, Arizona.

1984 Sedentary Period Hohokam Paleo-economy in the New River Drainage, Central Arizona. In *Prehistoric Agricultural Strategies in the Southwest*, edited by Suzanne K. Fish and Paul R. Fish, pp. 35–52. Anthropological Research Papers No. 33. Arizona State University, Tempe.

1991a Hohokam Cultural Evolution in the Phoenix Basin. In *Exploring the Hohokam: Prehistoric Desert Peoples of the American Southwest*, edited by George J. Gumerman, pp. 231–278. Amerind Foundation New World Series No. 1. University of New Mexico Press, Albuquerque.

1991b Hohokam Exchange and Interaction. In *Chaco and Hohokam: Prehistoric Regional Systems in the American Southwest*, edited by Patricia L. Crown and W. James Judge, pp. 231–278. School of American Research Press, Santa Fe, New Mexico.

1992 On Models and Methods: Comments on the History of Archaeological Research in the Southern Southwest. In *Proceedings of the Second Salado Conference, Globe, Arizona, 1992*, edited by Richard C. Lange and Stephen Germick, pp. 345–351. Occasional Paper. Arizona Archaeological Society, Phoenix.

1993 On Rivers and Boundaries in the Phoenix Basin, Arizona. *Kiva* 58(4):455–474.

1996 Resource Mobilization and Hohokam Society: Analysis of Obsidian Artifacts from the Gatlin Site. *Kiva* 62(1):45–60.

2000a The Santan Phase in the Phoenix Basin. In *The Hohokam Village Revisited*, edited by David E. Doyel, Suzanne K. Fish, and Paul R. Fish, pp. 221–244. Southwestern and Rocky Mountain Division of the American Association for the Advancement of Science, Glenwood Springs, Colorado.

2000b In Pursuit of the Salado in the Sonoran Desert. In *Salado*, edited by Jeffrey S. Dean, pp. 295–314. Amerind Foundation New World Series No. 4. University of New Mexico Press, Albuquerque.

2007 Irrigation, Production, and Power in Phoenix Basin Hohokam Society. In *The Hohokam Millennium*, edited by Suzanne K. Fish and Paul R. Fish, pp. 83–89. School for Advanced Research Press, Santa Fe, New Mexico.

Doyel, David E., and Mark D. Elson (editors)

1985 *Hohokam Settlement and Economic Systems in the Central New River Drainage, Arizona*. Publications in Archaeology No. 4. Soil Systems, Phoenix.

Doyel, David E., and Emil W. Haury

1976 Summary of Conference Session. *Kiva* 42(1): 127–134.

Dronfield, Jeremy

1996 The Vision Thing: Diagnosis of Endogenous Derivation in Abstract Arts. *Current Anthropology* 37:373–391.

Duff, Andrew I.

1996 Ceramic Micro-seriation: Types or Attributes? *American Antiquity* 61:89–101.

Dunne, Peter Masten (translator)

1955 *Jacobo Sedelmayr, Missionary, Frontiersman, Explorer, in Arizona and Sonora: Four Original Manuscript Narratives, 1744–1751*. Arizona Pioneers' Historical Society, Tucson.

Dunnell, Robert C.

2008 Archaeological Things: Languages of Observation. In *Time's River: Archaeological Syntheses from the Lower Mississippi River Valley*, edited by Janet Rafferty and Evan

Peacock, pp. 45–68. University of Alabama Press, Tuscaloosa.

Dunnell, Robert C., and William S. Dancey

1983 The Siteless Survey: A Regional Scale Data Collection Strategy. In *Advances in Archaeological Method and Theory*, Vol. 6, edited by Michael B. Schiffer, pp. 267–287. Academic Press, New York.

Durán, Fray Diego

1971 *Book of the Gods and Rites and the Ancient Calendar*. Translated by Doris Heyden and Fernando Horcasitas. University of Oklahoma Press, Norman.

Durkheim, Emile

1961 *The Elementary Forms of Religious Life*. Translated by John W. Swain. Free Press, New York.

Dutton, Bertha P.

1963 *Sun Father's Way: The Kiva Murals of Kuaua*. University of New Mexico Press, Albuquerque.

Eggan, Fred

1950 *Social Organization of the Western Pueblo*. University of Chicago Press, Chicago.

Eliade, Mircea

1964 *Shamanism: Archaic Techniques of Ecstasy*. Translated by Willard Trask. Princeton University Press, Princeton, New Jersey.

Ellis, Florence Hawley

1994 Pueblo Religious Patterns, Especially Types of Shrines and Areas for Collecting Herbs and Other Religious Necessities. In *Artifacts, Shrines, and Pueblos: Papers in Honor of Gordon Page*, edited by Meliha S. Duran and David T. Kirkpatrick, pp. 101–112. Papers No. 20. Archaeological Society of New Mexico, Albuquerque.

Ellis, Florence Hawley, and Laurens Hammack

1968 The Inner Sanctum of Feather Cave, a Mogollon Sun and Earth Shrine Linking Mexico and the Southwest. *American Antiquity* 33:25–44.

Elson, Mark D.

1998 *Expanding the View of Hohokam Platform Mounds: An Ethnographic Perspective*. Anthropological Papers No. 63. University of Arizona Press, Tucson.

2007 Into the Earth and Up to the Sky: Hohokam Ritual Architecture. In *The Hohokam Millennium*, edited by Suzanne K. Fish and Paul R. Fish, pp. 49–55. School for Advanced Research Press, Santa Fe, New Mexico.

Elson, Mark D., and David R. Abbott

2000 Organizational Variability in Platform Mound-Building Groups in the American Southwest. In *Alternative Leadership Strategies in the Prehispanic Southwest*, edited by Barbara J. Mills, pp. 117–135. University of Arizona Press, Tucson.

Emerson, Thomas E., and Timothy R. Pauketat

2008 Historical-Processual Archaeology and Culture Making: Unpacking the Southern Cult and Mississippian Religion. In *Belief in the Past: Theoretical Approaches to an Archaeology of Religion*, edited by David S. Whitley and Kelley A. Hays-Gilpin, pp. 167–188. Left Coast Press, Walnut Creek, California.

Emory, William Hemsley

1848 *Notes of a Military Reconnaissance, from Fort Leavenworth, in Missouri, to San Diego, in California, Including Parts of the Arkansas, del Norte, and Gila Rivers* (with contributions by James William Abert, Albert Gallatin, Joseph C. Hubbard, and John Torrey). U.S. War Department, Washington, D.C.

Empie, Sunnie

1999 The Empie Petroglyph Site, AZ U:1:165(ASM), in North Scottsdale, Arizona. In *McDowell Mountains Archaeological Symposium*, edited by K. J. Schroeder, pp. 251–259. Publications in Anthropology No. 10. Roadrunner Archaeology, Tempe, Arizona.

Engel, Celeste G., and Robert P. Sharp

1958 Chemical Data on Desert Varnish. *Geological Society of America Bulletin* 69:487–518.

Evans, John H., and Harry Hillman

1981 *Documentations of Some Lunar and Solar Events at Casa Grande, Arizona*. Anthropological Papers No. 22. Ballena Press, Ramona, California.

Fairén-Jiménez, Sara

2007 Rock Art and Social Life: Revisiting the Neolithic Transition in Mediterranean Iberia. *Journal of Social Archaeology* 7:123–143.

Fausto, Carlos

2007 Feasting on People: Eating Animals and Humans in Amazonia. *Current Anthropology* 48:497–530.

Feinman, Gary M.

1991 Hohokam Archaeology in the Eighties: An Outside View. In *Exploring the Hohokam: Prehistoric Desert Peoples of the American Southwest*, edited by George J. Gumerman, pp. 461–483. Amerind Foundation New World Series No. 1. University of New Mexico Press, Albuquerque.

Ferdon, Edwin N., Jr.
1967 The Hohokam "Ballcourt": An Alternative View of Its Function. *Kiva* 33(1):1–14.

Ferg, Alan
1979 The Petroglyphs of Tumamoc Hill. *Kiva* 45(1–2):95–118.
1988 Appendix E: Exotic Artifacts and Shrines. In *Erich F. Schmidt's Investigations of Salado Sites in Central Arizona*, by John Hohmann and Linda B. Kelley, pp. 205–218. Bulletin No. 56. Museum of Northern Arizona, Flagstaff.

Ferg, Alan, and Jim I. Mead
1993 *Red Cave: A Prehistoric Cave Shrine in Southeastern Arizona*. Arizona Archaeologist No. 26. Arizona Archaeological Society, Phoenix.

Ferguson, T. J.
2007 Zuni Traditional History and Cultural Geography. In *Zuni Origins: Toward a New Synthesis of Southwestern Archaeology*, edited by David A. Gregory and David R. Wilcox, pp. 377–403. University of Arizona Press, Tucson.

Ferguson, T. J., and Chip Colwell-Chanthaphonh
2006 *History Is in the Land: Multivocal Tribal Traditions in Arizona's San Pedro Valley*. University of Arizona Press, Tucson.

Ferguson, T. J., and E. Richard Hart
1985 *A Zuni Atlas*. University of Oklahoma Press, Norman.

Ferguson, T. J., and M. Lamaomvaya
1999 *Hoopoq'yaqam niqw Wukoskyavi (Those Who Went to the Northeast and Tonto Basin): Hopi-Salado Cultural Affiliation Study*. Heritage Resources Management Consultants, Tucson, Arizona.

Fewkes, Jesse Walter
1891 A Suggestion as to the Meaning of the Moki Snake Dance. *Journal of American Folk-Lore* 4:129–138.
1892a A Few Tusayan Pictographs. *American Anthropologist* 5:9–26.
1892b A Report on the Present Condition of a Ruin in Arizona Called Casa Grande. *Journal of American Ethnology and Archaeology* 2:177–193.
1893 A Central American Ceremony which Suggests the Snake Dance of the Tusayan. *American Anthropologist* 6:285–306.
1897 Tusayan Totemic Signatures. *American Anthropologist* 10:1–11.
1898a Archaeological Expedition into Arizona in 1895. *Annual Report of the Bureau of American Ethnology* 17:519–744. U.S. Government Printing Office, Washington, D.C.
1898b An Ancient Human Effigy Vase from Arizona. *American Anthropologist* 11:165–170.
1900 Tusayan Flute and Snake Ceremonies. *Annual Report of the Bureau of American Ethnology* 19:957–1011. U.S. Government Printing Office, Washington, D.C.
1906 Hopi Shrines near the East Mesa, Arizona. *American Anthropologist* 8:346–375.
1912 Casa Grande, Arizona. *Annual Report of the Bureau of American Ethnology* 28:25–223. U.S. Government Printing Office, Washington, D.C.

Fish, Paul R., and Suzanne K. Fish
1991 Hohokam Political and Social Organization. In *Exploring the Hohokam: Prehistoric Desert Peoples of the American Southwest*, edited by George J. Gumerman, pp. 151–175. Amerind Foundation New World Series No. 1. University of New Mexico Press, Albuquerque.

Fish, Suzanne K., and Paul R. Fish
2000 Civic-Territorial Organization and the Roots of Hohokam Complexity. In *The Hohokam Village Revisited*, edited by David E. Doyel, Suzanne K. Fish, and Paul R. Fish, pp. 373–390. Southwestern and Rocky Mountain Division of the American Association for the Advancement of Science, Fort Collins, Colorado.

Fish, Suzanne K., and Paul R. Fish (editors)
2007 *The Hohokam Millennium*. School for Advanced Research Press, Santa Fe, New Mexico.

Fish, Suzanne K., Paul R. Fish, and John H. Madsen (editors)
1992 *The Marana Community in the Hohokam World*. Anthropological Papers No. 56. University of Arizona Press, Tucson.

Flamand, Georges Barthélemy Médéric
1921 *Les pierres écrites (Hadjrat-Mektoubat): Gravures et inscriptions rupestres du Nord-Africain*. Masson, Paris.

Fogelin, Lars
2007 The Archaeology of Religious Ritual. *Annual Review of Anthropology* 36:55–71.

Fogelin, Lars (editor)
2008 *Religion, Archaeology, and the Material World*. Occasional Paper No. 36. Center for Archaeological Investigations, Southern Illinois University, Carbondale.

Ford, James A.
1954 On the Concept of Types. *American Anthropologist* 56:42–54.
Foster, Michael S.
1994 Intrusive Ceramics. In *The Pueblo Grande Project, Vol. 4: Material Culture*, edited by Michael S. Foster, pp. 119–165. Publications in Archaeology No. 20. Soil Systems, Phoenix.
Foster, Michael S., and Steven R. James
2004 Dogs, Deer, or Guanacos: Zoomorphic Figurines from Pueblo Grande, Central Arizona. *Journal of Field Archaeology* 29:165–176.
Foucault, Michel
1978 *The History of Sexuality, Vol. 1: An Introduction*. Translated by Robert Hurley. Pantheon, New York.
1980 *Power/Knowledge: Selected Interviews and Other Writings, 1972–1977*. Edited by Colin Gordon. Pantheon, New York.
Fowler, Chris
2004 *The Archaeology of Personhood*. Routledge, London.
Fowles, Severin M.
2010 The Southwest School of Landscape Archaeology. *Annual Review of Anthropology* 39: 453–468.
2012 *An Archaeology of Doings: Secularism and the Study of Pueblo Religion*. School for Advanced Research Press, Santa Fe, New Mexico.
Francis, Julie E.
2001 Style and Classification. In *Handbook of Rock Art Research*, edited by David S. Whitley, pp. 221–244. AltaMira Press, Walnut Creek, California.
Francis, William D.
1920 The Origin of Black Coatings of Iron and Manganese Oxides on Rocks. *Proceedings of the Royal Society of Queensland* 32:110–116.
Freud, Sigmund
1913 *Totem und Tabu: Einige Übereinstimmungen im Seelenleben der Wilden und der Neurotiker*. H. Heller, Leipzig.
Fulton, William Shirley
1941 *A Ceremonial Cave in the Winchester Mountains, Arizona*. Amerind Foundation Series No. 2. Amerind Foundation, Dragoon, Arizona.
Gallardo, Francisco, and Patricio De Souza
2008 Rock Art, Modes of Production, and Social Identities during the Early Formative Period in the Atacama Desert (Northern Chile). In *Archaeologies of Art: Time, Place, Identity*, edited by Inés Domingo Sanz, Dánae Fiore, and Sally K. Mays, pp. 79–97. One World Archaeology No. 55. Left Coast Press, Walnut Creek, California.
Garfinkel, Alan P.
2006 Paradigm Shifts, Rock Art Studies, and the "Coso Sheep Cult" of Eastern California. *North American Archaeologist* 27:203–244.
Garwood, Paul, David Jennings, Robin Skeates, and Judith Toms (editors)
1991 *Sacred and Profane: Proceedings of a Conference on Archaeology, Ritual and Religion, Oxford, 1989*. Monograph No. 32. Oxford University Committee for Archaeology, Institute of Archaeology, Oxford.
Gasser, Robert E., and Scott W. Kwiatkowski
1991 Food for Thought: Recognizing Patterns in Hohokam Subsistence. In *Exploring the Hohokam: Prehistoric Desert Peoples of the American Southwest*, edited by George J. Gumerman, pp. 417–459. Amerind Foundation New World Series No. 1. University of New Mexico Press, Albuquerque.
Geertz, Armin W., and Michael Lomatuway'ma
1987 *Children of Cottonwood: Piety and Ceremonialism in Hopi Indian Puppetry*. University of Nebraska Press, Lincoln.
Geertz, Clifford
1973 *The Interpretation of Cultures*. Basic Books, New York.
Gell, Alfred
1998 *Art and Agency: An Anthropological Theory*. Clarendon Press, Oxford.
Gibson, James John
1979 *The Ecological Approach to Visual Perception*. Houghton Mifflin, Boston.
Giddens, Anthony
1979 *Central Problems in Social Theory: Action, Structure and Contradiction in Social Analysis*. University of California Press, Berkeley.
1984 *The Constitution of Society: Outline of a Theory of Structuration*. Polity Press, Cambridge.
Gillespie, William B.
1995 Vertebrate Remains from Los Morteros. In *Archaeological Investigations at Los Morteros, a Prehistoric Settlement in the Northern Tucson Basin*, Part 2, edited by Henry D. Wallace, pp. 673–719. Anthropological Papers No. 17. Center for Desert Archaeology, Tucson, Arizona.

Gladwin, Harold S.
1928 *Excavations at Casa Grande, Arizona.* Medallion Papers No. 2. Gila Pueblo, Globe, Arizona.
1942 *Excavations at Snaketown III: Revisions.* Medallion Papers No. 30. Gila Pueblo, Globe, Arizona.

Gladwin, Harold S., Emil W. Haury, Edwin B. Sayles, and Nora Gladwin
1937 *Excavations at Snaketown I: Material Culture.* Medallion Papers No. 25. Gila Pueblo, Globe, Arizona.

Gladwin, Winifred, and Harold S. Gladwin
1929a *The Red-on-Buff Culture of the Gila Basin.* Medallion Papers No. 3. Gila Pueblo, Globe, Arizona.
1929b *The Red-on-Buff Culture of the Papaguería.* Medallion Papers No. 4. Gila Pueblo, Globe, Arizona.
1930 *The Western Range of the Red-on-Buff Culture.* Medallion Papers No. 5. Gila Pueblo, Globe, Arizona.
1935 *The Eastern Range of the Red-on-Buff Culture.* Medallion Papers No. 16. Gila Pueblo, Globe, Arizona.
1948 *Excavations at Snaketown IV: Review and Conclusions.* Medallion Papers No. 38. Gila Pueblo, Globe, Arizona.

Glowacki, Donna M., and Scott Van Keuren (editors)
2012 *Religious Transformation in the Late Pre-Hispanic Pueblo World.* University of Arizona Press, Tucson.

Gluckman, Max
1963 *Order and Rebellion in Tribal Africa.* Free Press, Glencoe, Illinois.
1965 *Politics, Law and Ritual in Tribal Society.* Aldine, Chicago.

Golio, J. J., Susie Bradshaw, Ernest Snyder, and Mike Golio
1995 An Analysis of the Pipette Element in Hohokam Rock Art. In *Rock Art Papers,* Vol. 12, edited by Ken Hedges, pp. 95–106. Papers No. 33. Museum of Man, San Diego, California.

Golio, J. J., and Mike Golio
2004 Hohokam Bola Petroglyphs in the South Mountains of Phoenix. In *American Indian Rock Art,* Vol. 30, edited by Joseph T. O'Connor, pp. 111–118. American Rock Art Research Association, Tucson, Arizona.
2005 Hohokam Hunting Petroglyphs in the South Mountains of Phoenix. In *Rock Art Papers,* Vol. 17, edited by Ken Hedges, pp. 109–115. Papers No. 43. Museum of Man, San Diego, California.

Golio, J. J., and Ernest Snyder
1993 Petroglyph Surveys of South Mountain, 1991/1964. In *Rock Art Papers,* Vol. 10, edited by Ken Hedges, pp. 1–6. Papers No. 20. Museum of Man, San Diego, California.

Gosden, Christopher
2005 What Do Objects Want? *Journal of Archaeological Method and Theory* 12:193–211.

Granero, Fernando Santos
1986 Power, Ideology and the Ritual of Production in Lowland South America. *Man* 21: 657–679.

Grant, Campbell, James W. Baird, and J. Kenneth Pringle
1968 *Rock Drawings of the Coso Range, Inyo County, California.* Manturango Museum Publication No. 4. China Lake, California.

Graybill, Donald A., David A. Gregory, Gary S. Funkhouser, and Fred L. Nials
2006 Long-Term Streamflow Reconstructions, River Channel Morphology, and Aboriginal Irrigation Systems along the Salt and Gila Rivers. In *Environmental Change and Human Adaptation in the Ancient Southwest,* edited by David E. Doyel and Jeffrey S. Dean, pp. 69–123. University of Utah Press, Salt Lake City.

Grebinger, Paul F.
1976 Salado Perspectives from the Middle Santa Cruz Valley. *Kiva* 42(1):39–46.

Greenacre, Michael
1994 Correspondence Analysis and Its Interpretation. In *Correspondence Analysis in the Social Sciences: Recent Developments and Applications,* edited by Michael Greenacre and Jörg Blasius, pp. 3–22. Academic Press, New York.

Greenacre, Michael, and Jörg Blasius (editors)
1994 *Correspondence Analysis in the Social Sciences: Recent Developments and Applications.* Academic Press, New York.

Greenwald, David H., Dawn M. Greenwald, Gregory Seymour, Pat H. Stein, and Mary-Ellen Walsh-Anduze
1996 Archaeological Testing at Pueblo Salado, Areas 15 and 16: Methods and Results. In *Life on the Floodplain: Further Investigations at Pueblo Salado for Phoenix Sky Harbor International Airport, Vol. 1: Preliminary Investigations and Research Design,* edited by David

H. Greenwald, Jean H. Ballagh, and Mark Zyniecki, pp. 57–81. Anthropological Papers No. 4. Pueblo Grande Museum, Phoenix.

Greenwald, David H., Mary-Ellen Walsh-Anduze, Mark Zyniecki, and Jean H. Ballagh

1996 Archaeological Testing at Pueblo Salado, Area 6: Methods and Results. In *Life on the Floodplain: Further Investigations at Pueblo Salado for Phoenix Sky Harbor International Airport, Vol. 1: Preliminary Investigations and Research Design*, edited by David H. Greenwald, Jean H. Ballagh, and Mark Zyniecki, pp. 17–55. Anthropological Papers No. 4. Pueblo Grande Museum, Phoenix.

Greenwood, Ned H., and C. W. White

1970 Mogollon Ritual: A Spatial Configuration of a Non-Village Pattern. *Archaeology* 23: 298–301.

Gregory, David A.

1987 The Morphology of Platform Mounds and the Structure of Classic Period Hohokam Sites. In *The Hohokam Village: Site Structure and Organization*, edited by David E. Doyel, pp. 183–210. Southwestern and Rocky Mountain Division of the American Association for the Advancement of Science, Glenwood Springs, Colorado.

1988 The Architectural Development of Hohokam Platform Mounds. In *The 1982–1984 Excavations at Las Colinas, Vol. 2: The Site and Its Features*, by David A. Gregory, William L. Deaver, Suzanne K. Fish, Ronald Gardiner, Robert W. Layhe, Fred L. Nials, and Lynn S. Teague, pp. 319–32. Archaeological Series No. 162. Arizona State Museum, University of Arizona, Tucson.

1991 Form and Variation in Hohokam Settlement Patterns. In *Chaco and Hohokam: Prehistoric Regional Systems in the American Southwest*, edited by Patricia L. Crown and W. James Judge, pp. 159–194. School of American Research Press, Santa Fe, New Mexico.

Gregory, David A. (editor)

2001 *Excavations in the Santa Cruz River Floodplain: The Early Agricultural Period Component at Los Pozos.* Anthropological Papers No. 21. Center for Desert Archaeology, Tucson, Arizona.

Gregory, David A., David R. Abbott, Deni J. Seymour, and Nancy M. Bannister

1988 *The 1982–1984 Excavations at Las Colinas, Vol. 3: The Mound 8 Precinct.* Archaeological Series No. 162. Arizona State Museum, University of Arizona, Tucson.

Gregory, David A., and Fred L. Nials

1985 Observations Concerning the Distribution of Classic Period Hohokam Platform Mounds. In *Proceedings of the 1983 Hohokam Symposium*, edited by Alfred E. Dittert and Donald E. Dove, pp. 378–388. Occasional Paper No. 2. Arizona Archaeological Society, Phoenix.

Gregory, David A., Michelle N. Stevens, Fred L. Nials, Mark R. Schurr, and Michael W. Diehl

2007 *Excavations in the Santa Cruz Floodplain: Further Investigations at Los Pozos.* Anthropological Papers No. 27. Center for Desert Archaeology, Tucson, Arizona.

Groleau, Amy B.

2009 Special Finds: Locating Animism in the Archaeological Record. *Cambridge Archaeological Journal* 19:398–406.

Haber, A. F.

2009 Animism, Relatedness, Life: Post-Western Perspectives. *Cambridge Archaeological Journal* 19:418–430.

Hackbarth, Mark R.

1992 *Prehistoric and Historic Occupation of the Lower Verde River Valley: The State Route 87 Verde Bridge Project.* Arizona Department of Transpiration Contract No. 89–28. Northland Research, Flagstaff, Arizona.

1997a *Excavations at Las Acequias, AZ U:9:44 (ASU), Mesa, Arizona.* Technical Report No. 96-4. Northland Research, Flagstaff, Arizona.

1997b Archival Investigations. In *Archaeological and Archival Investigations of Las Canopas: The Esteban Park Project*, edited by Mark R. Hackbarth, pp. 17–56. Anthropological Papers No. 6. Pueblo Grande Museum, Phoenix.

1999 The Last Ditch Site: Archaeology along Mayo Boulevard, Scottsdale, Arizona. In *McDowell Mountains Archaeological Symposium*, edited by K. J. Schroeder, pp. 49–70. Publications in Anthropology No. 10. Roadrunner Archaeology, Tempe, Arizona.

Halifax, Joan

1982 *Shaman: The Wounded Healer.* Crossroad, New York.

Hall, Edward T.

1966 *The Hidden Dimension.* Doubleday, Garden City, New York.

1968 Proxemics. *Current Anthropology* 9(2–3):83–95.

Hall, Robert L.
1997 *An Archaeology of the Soul: North American Indian Belief and Ritual.* University of Illinois Press, Urbana.

Hamann, Diane L.
1988 A Regional View of Hohokam Rock Art. Unpublished Master's thesis, Department of Anthropology, Arizona State University, Tempe.

Hamann, Diane L., and Ken Hedges
1986 Topographical Distribution of Hohokam Petroglyph Sites. In *Rock Art Papers*, Vol. 4, edited by Ken Hedges, pp. 77–86. Papers No. 21. Museum of Man, San Diego, California.

Hammond, George P., and Edward H. Howes (editors)
1950 *Overland to California on the Southwestern Trail, 1849: Diary of Robert Eccleston.* University of California Press, Berkeley.

Harrington, John P.
1916 *The Ethnogeography of the Tewa Indians.* Annual Report of the Bureau of American Ethnology, Vol. 29. U.S. Government Printing Office, Washington, D.C.

Harrison, Simon
1992 Ritual as Intellectual Property. *Man* 27:225–244.

Hartley, Ralph J.
1991 Rockshelters and Rock Art: An Assessment of Site Use. In *Proceedings of the Anasazi Symposium 1991*, edited by Art Hutchinson and Jack E. Smith, pp. 165–190. Mesa Verde Museum Association, Mesa Verde National Monument, Colorado.
1992 *Rock Art of the Northern Colorado Plateau.* Worldwide Archaeology Series No. 1. Aldershot, Avebury, U.K.

Hartley, Ralph J., and Anne M. Wolley Vawser
1997 Wayfinding in the Desert: Evaluating the Role of Rock Art through GIS. In *Rock Art as Visual Ecology*, edited by Paul Faulstich, pp. 55–76. Proceedings of the International Rock Art Congress No. 1. American Rock Art Research Association, Tucson, Arizona.
1998 Spatial Behaviour and Learning in the Prehistoric Environment of the Colorado River Drainage (South-Eastern Utah), Western North America. In *The Archaeology of Rock-Art*, edited by Christopher Chippindale and Paul S. C. Taçon, pp. 185–211. Cambridge University Press, Cambridge.

Harvey, Graham
2000 Introduction. In *Indigenous Religions: A Companion*, edited by Graham Harvey, pp. 1–19. Cassell, London.
2006 *Animism: Respecting the Living World.* Columbia University Press, New York.

Harvey, Graham (editor)
2002 *Readings in Indigenous Religions.* Continuum, London.

Haury, Emil W.
1937 A Pre-Spanish Rubber Ball from Arizona. *American Antiquity* 2:282–288.
1945 *The Excavation of Los Muertos and Neighboring Ruins in the Salt River Valley, Southern Arizona.* Papers of the Peabody Museum of American Archaeology and Ethnology Vol. 24, No. 1. Harvard University, Cambridge, Massachusetts.
1947 A Large Pre-Columbian Copper Bell from the Southwest. *American Antiquity* 13: 80–82.
1976 *The Hohokam: Desert Farmers and Craftsmen, Snaketown, 1964–1965.* University of Arizona Press, Tucson.

Haury, Emil W., Kirk Bryan, Edwin H. Colbert, Norman E. Gabel, Clara Lee Tanner, and Theo F. Buehrer
1950 *The Stratigraphy and Archaeology of Ventana Cave, Arizona.* University of Arizona Press, Tucson.

Haury, Emil W., and Carol A. Gifford
1959 A Thirteenth Century "Strongbox." *Kiva* 24(4):1–11.

Haury, Emil W., and Lisa W. Huckell (editors)
1993 A Prehistoric Cotton Cache from the Pinaleño Mountains, Arizona. *Kiva* 59(2)95–147.

Hause, Melissa Thorson
1992 A Place in Sacred History: Coronation Ritual and Architecture in Ottonian Mainz. *Journal of Ritual Studies* 6:134–157.

Hawkes, Christopher F.
1954 Archaeological Theory and Method: Some Suggestions from the Old World. *American Anthropologist* 56:155–168.

Hawley, Florence G.
1937 Chemical Investigation of the Incrustation on Pottery Vessels and Palettes from Snaketown. In *Excavations at Snaketown I: Material Culture*, by Harold S. Gladwin, Emil W. Haury, Edwin B. Sayles, and Nora Gladwin, pp. 282–289. Medallion Papers No. 25. Gila Pueblo, Globe, Arizona.
1942 The Use of Lead Mineral by the Hohokam

in Cremation Ceremonials. *Southwestern Journal of Anthropology* 3:69–77.

Hayden, Brian

1987 Alliances and Ritual Ecstasy: Human Responses to Resource Stress. *Journal of the Scientific Study of Religion* 26:81–91.

1995 Pathways to Power: Principles for Creating Economic Inequalities. In *Foundations of Social Inequality*, edited by T. Douglas Price and Gary M. Feinman, pp. 15–86. Plenum Press, New York.

Hayden, Julian D.

1957 *Excavations, 1940, at University Indian Ruin.* Southwestern Monuments Association Technical Series No. 5. Gila Pueblo, Globe, Arizona.

1967 A Summary Prehistory and History of the Sierra Pinacate, Sonora. *American Antiquity* 32:335–344.

1972 Hohokam Petroglyphs of the Sierra Pinacate, Sonora, and the Hohokam Shell Expeditions. *Kiva* 37(2):74–83.

1977 Wihom-ki. *Kiva* 43(1):31–35.

Hays, Kelley A.

1992 *Anasazi Ceramics as Text and Tool: Toward a Theory of Ceramic Design "Messaging."* Ph.D. dissertation, Department of Anthropology, University of Arizona, Tucson. University Microfilms, Ann Arbor, Michigan.

Hays-Gilpin, Kelley A.

2000 Gender Ideology and Ritual Activities. In *Women and Men in the Prehispanic Southwest: Labor, Power, and Prestige*, edited by Patricia L. Crown, pp. 91–135. School of American Research Press, Santa Fe, New Mexico.

2004 *Ambiguous Images: Gender and Rock Art.* AltaMira Press, Walnut Creek, California.

Hays-Gilpin, Kelley A., and Jane H. Hill

1999 The Flower World in Material Culture: An Iconographic Complex in the Southwest and Mesoamerica. *Journal of Anthropological Research* 55:1–37.

2000 The Flower World in Prehistoric Southwest Material Culture. In *The Archaeology of Regional Interaction: Warfare and Exchange across the American Southwest and Beyond*, edited by Michelle Hegmon, pp. 411–428. University of Colorado Press, Boulder.

Hays-Gilpin, Kelley A., and Polly Schaafsma (editors)

2010 *Painting and the Cosmos: Metaphor and Worldview in Images from the Southwest and Mesoamerica.* Bulletin No. 67. Museum of Northern Arizona, Flagstaff.

Hedges, Ken

1976 Southern California Rock Art as Shamanic Art. In *American Indian Rock Art*, Vol. 2, edited by Kay Sutherland, pp. 126–138. American Rock Art Research Association, Tucson, Arizona.

1982 Great Basin Rock Art Styles: A Revisionist View. In *American Indian Rock Art*, Vols. 7–8, edited by Frank G. Bock, pp. 205–211. American Rock Art Research Association, Tucson, Arizona.

1992 Shamanistic Aspects of California Rock Art. In *California Indian Shamanism*, edited by Lowell John Bean, pp. 67–88. Ballena Press, Menlo Park, California.

1994a The Case of the Missing Petroglyphs: Large-Scale Vandalism at Sierra Estrella. In *Rock Art Papers*, Vol. 11, edited by Ken Hedges, pp. 93–94. Papers No. 31. Museum of Man, San Diego, California.

1994b Pipette Dreams and the Primordial Snake-Canoe: Analysis of a Hallucinatory Form Constant. In *Shamanism and Rock Art in North America*, edited by Solveig A. Turpin, pp. 103–124. Special Publication No. 1. Rock Art Foundation, San Antonio, Texas.

Hedges, Ken, and Diane Hamann

1992 Look to the Mountaintop: Rock Art at Texas Hill. In *American Indian Rock Art*, Vol. 17, edited by Donald E. Weaver, pp. 45–55. American Rock Art Research Association, Tucson, Arizona.

1995 Petroglyphs at Quail Point, Southwestern Arizona. In *Rock Art Papers*, Vol. 12, edited by Ken Hedges, pp. 89–94. Papers No. 33. Museum of Man, San Diego, California.

Hedrick, Basil C., J. Charles Kelley, and Carroll L. Riley (editors)

1974 *The Mesoamerican Southwest.* Southern Illinois University Press, Carbondale.

Hegmon, Michelle, and Stephanie Kulow

2005 Painting as Agency, Style as Structure: Innovations in Mimbres Pottery Designs from Southwest New Mexico. *Journal of Archaeological Method and Theory* 12:313–334.

Hegmon, Michelle, Matthew A. Peeples, Ann P. Kinzig, Stephanie Kulow, Cathryn M. Meegan, and Margaret C. Nelson

2008 Social Transformation and Its Human Costs in the Prehispanic U.S. Southwest. *American Anthropologist* 110:312–324.

Heidke, James M.
1999 Cienega Phase Incipient Plain Ware from Southeastern Arizona. *Kiva* 64(3):311–338.

Heizer, Robert F., and Martin A. Baumhoff
1962 *Prehistoric Rock Art of Nevada and Eastern California*. University of California Press, Berkeley.

Helander-Renvall, Elina
2009 Animism, Personhood and the Nature of Reality: Sami Perspectives. *Polar Record* 46:44–56.

Helvenston, Patricia A., and Paul G. Bahn
2003 Testing the "Three Stages of Trance" Model; with Comments by John L. Bradshaw and Christopher Chippindale. *Cambridge Archaeological Journal* 13:213–224.
2005 *Waking the Trance Fixed*. Wasteland Press, Louisville, Kentucky.

Helvenston, Patricia A., and Derek Hodgson
2010 The Neuropsychology of "Animism": Implications for Understanding Rock Art. *Rock Art Research* 27:61–94.

Henderson, T. Kathleen
1987 *Structure and Organization at La Ciudad*. Anthropological Field Studies No. 18. Arizona State University, Tempe.
1995 *The Prehistoric Archaeology of Heritage Square*. Anthropological Papers No. 3. Pueblo Grande Museum, Phoenix.
2003 Ceramic Analysis and Feature Chronology. In *Hohokam Farming on the Salt River Floodplain: Excavations at the Sky Harbor Airport North Runway*, edited by T. Kathleen Henderson, pp. 139–172. Anthropological Papers No. 9. Pueblo Grande Museum, Phoenix. Anthropological Papers No. 42. Center for Desert Archaeology, Tucson, Arizona.

Henderson, T. Kathleen (editor)
1989 *Prehistoric Agricultural Activities on the Lehi-Mesa Terrace: Excavations at La Cuenca del Sedimento*. Arizona Department of Transportation Contract No. 86–102. Northland Research, Flagstaff, Arizona.

Henderson, T. Kathleen, and Tiffany C. Clark
2004 Changing Perspectives: Considerations of Past Agricultural Use of the Salt River Floodplain. In *Hohokam Farming on the Salt River Floodplain: Refining Models and Analytical Methods*, edited by T. Kathleen Henderson, pp. 167–186. Anthropological Papers No. 10. Pueblo Grande Museum, Phoenix. Anthropological Papers No. 43. Center for Desert Archaeology, Tucson, Arizona.

Henderson, T. Kathleen, and Mark R. Hackbarth
1995 Project Setting and Research Design. In *Archaeology at the Head of the Scottsdale Canal System, Vol. 1: Project Background and Site Descriptions*, edited by Mark R. Hackbarth, Douglas B. Craig, and T. Kathleen Henderson, pp. 9–30. Anthropological Papers No. 95-1. Northland Research, Flagstaff, Arizona.
2000 What Is Going on at the Hohokam Village? A Fourteenth and Fifteenth Century Perspective. In *The Hohokam Village Revisited*, edited by David E. Doyel, Suzanne K. Fish, and Paul R. Fish, pp. 287–316. Southwestern and Rocky Mountain Division of the American Association for the Advancement of Science, Fort Collins, Colorado.

Hernbrode, Janine, and Peter Boyle
2013 Gender in Hohokam Imagery and Landscape: Sutherland Wash Rock Art District, Coronado National Forest, Arizona. In *American Indian Rock Art*, Vol. 39, edited by Bill Hyder, pp. 43–54. American Rock Art Research Association, Tucson, Arizona.

Herva, Vessa-Pekka
2005 The Life of Buildings: Minoan Building Deposits in an Ecological Perspective. *Oxford Journal of Archaeology* 24:215–227.
2006a Flower Lovers, after All? Rethinking Religion and Human-Environment Relations in Minoan Crete. *World Archaeology* 38:586–598.
2006b Marvels of the System: Art, Perception and Engagement with the Environment in Minoan Crete. *Archaeological Dialogues* 13:221–240.

Herva, Vessa-Pekka, and Tilmo Ylimaunu
2009 Folk Beliefs, Special Deposits, and Engagement with the Environment in Early Modern Northern Finland. *Journal of Anthropological Archaeology* 28:234–243.

Hill, J. Brett, Jeffery J. Clark, and William H. Doelle
2010 Depopulation of the Northern Southwest: A Macroregional Perspective. In *Leaving Mesa Verde: Peril and Change in the Thirteenth-Century Southwest*, edited by Timothy A. Kohler, Mark D. Varien, and Aaron M. Wright, pp. 34–52. University of Arizona Press, Tucson.

Hill, J. Brett, Jeffery J. Clark, William H. Doelle, and Patrick D. Lyons
2004 Prehistoric Demography in the Southwest: Migration, Coalescence, and Hohokam Population Decline. *American Antiquity* 69:689–716.

Hill, Jane H.
1992 The Flower World of Old Uto-Aztecan. *Journal of Anthropological Research* 48:117–44.

Hill, Mark O.
1974 Correspondence Analysis: A Neglected Multivariate Method. *Applied Statistics* 23:346–354.

Hill, Willard W.
1982 *An Ethnography of Santa Clara Pueblo.* University of New Mexico Press, Albuquerque.

Hobbs, William H.
1918 The Peculiar Weathering Processes of Desert Regions with Illustrations from Egypt and the Soudan. *Michigan Academy of Sciences Annual Report* 20:93–98.

Hodder, Ian
1982 *The Present Past.* B. T. Batsford, London.
1988 *Reading the Past.* Cambridge University Press, Cambridge.

Hodder, Ian (editor)
1982 *Symbolic and Structural Archaeology.* Cambridge University Press, Cambridge.

Hodge, Frederick Webb
1893 Prehistoric Irrigation in Arizona. *American Anthropologist* 6:323–330.

Hodgson, Derek
2000 Shamanism, Phosphenes, and Early Art: An Alternative Synthesis. *Current Anthropology* 41:866–873.
2006 Altered States of Consciousness and Palaeoart: An Alternative Neurovisual Explanation. *Cambridge Archaeological Journal* 16: 27–37.

Hoffman, Charles Marshall
1997 *Alliance Formation and Social Interaction during the Sedentary Period: A Stylistic Analysis of Hohokam Arrowpoints.* Ph.D. dissertation, Department of Anthropology, Arizona State University, Tempe. University Microfilms, Ann Arbor, Michigan.

Holden, Wes
1980 Rock Writing of South Mountain, Phoenix, Arizona. *Artifact* 18(1):43–51.
2008 The Sun-Struck Site, South Mountain Park—Phoenix, Arizona: A Four-Year Solar Alignment Study. Manuscript on file, Department of Parks and Recreation, Pueblo Grande Museum, Phoenix.

Homans, George C.
1941 Anxiety and Ritual: The Theories of Malinowski and Radcliffe-Brown. *American Anthropologist* 43:164–172.

Hornborg, Alf
2006 Animism, Fetishism, and Objectivism as Strategies of Knowing (or Not Knowing) the World. *Ethnos* 71:21–32.

Hough, Walter
1906 Sacred Springs in the Southwest. *Records of the Past* 5(6):163–169.

Howard, Ann Valdo, and Richard W. Effland Jr.
1990 Artifact Assemblages from Structures. In *Archaeological Investigations at La Ciudad de Los Hornos: Lassen Substation Parcel,* edited by Richard W. Effland Jr., pp. 87–130. Arizona Archaeologist No. 24. Arizona Archaeological Society, Phoenix. Cultural Resource Report No. 52. Archaeological Consulting Services, Tempe, Arizona.

Howard, Jerry B.
1985 Courtyard Groups and Domestic Cycling: A Hypothetical Model of Growth. In *Proceedings of the 1983 Hohokam Symposium,* edited by Alfred E. Dittert and Donald E. Dove, pp. 311–326. Occasional Paper No. 2. Arizona Archaeological Society, Phoenix.
1990 Los Hornos: Site Structure and Community Patterning at a Large Hohokam Village. In *One Hundred Years of Archaeology at La Ciudad de Los Hornos,* edited by David R. Wilcox, Jerry B. Howard, and Rueben H. Nelson, pp. 73–110. Publications in Archaeology No. 16. Soil Systems, Phoenix.
1991 System Reconstruction: The Evolution of an Irrigation System. In *The Operation and Evolution of an Irrigation System: The East Papago Canal Study,* edited by Jerry B. Howard and Gary A. Huckleberry, pp. 5.1–5.33. Publications in Archaeology No. 18. Soil Systems, Phoenix.
1992 Architecture and Ideology: An Approach to the Functional Analysis of Platform Mounds. In *Proceedings of the Second Salado Conference, Globe, Arizona, 1992,* edited by Richard C. Lange and Stephen Germick, pp. 69–77. Occasional Paper. Arizona Archaeological Society, Phoenix.
1993 A Paleohydraulic Approach to Examining Agricultural Intensification in Hohokam Irrigation Systems. *Research in Economic Anthropology* 7:261–322.
1995 Preserving Temples of Clay: A Stabilization Plan for the Mesa Grande. Manuscript on file, Mesa Southwest Museum, Mesa, Arizona.
2006 Hohokam Irrigation Communities: A Study of Internal Structure, External Relationships, and Sociopolitical Complexity. Unpublished Ph.D. dissertation, School of

Human Evolution and Social Change, Arizona State University, Tempe.
Howard, Jerry B., and Gary A. Huckleberry (editors)
1991 *The Operation and Evolution of an Irrigation System: The East Papago Canal Study.* Publications in Archaeology No. 18. Soil Systems, Phoenix.
Howey, Meghan C. L., and John M. O'Shea
2006 Bear's Journey and the Study of Ritual in Archaeology. *American Antiquity* 71:261–282.
Huang, Jennifer K. K.
2005 Recording the Rock Art of Baby Canyon Pueblo, Agua Fria National Monument: Phases I–II. In *Rock Art Papers*, Vol. 17, edited by Ken Hedges, pp. 101–115. Papers No. 43. Museum of Man, San Diego, California.
2010 *Petroglyphs of Baby Canyon Pueblo, Agua Fria National Monument, Arizona: Final Report* (with contributions by Tammy Stone and Peter Welsh). Office of Cultural Resource Management Report No. 98. Archaeological Research Institute, Arizona State University, Tempe.
Huckell, Bruce B.
1996 The Archaic Prehistory of the American Southwest. *Journal of World Prehistory* 10:305–373.
Hulkrantz, Åke
1966 An Ecological Approach to Religion. *Ethnos* 31:131–150.
1967 Historical Approaches in American Ethnology. *Ethnologia Europaea* 1:96–116.
1978 Ecological and Phenomenological Aspects of Shamanism. In *Shamanism in Siberia*, edited by Vilmos Diószegi and Mihaly Hoppál, pp. 27–58. Akadémiai Kiadó, Budapest.
1979 Ecology of Religion: Its Scope and Methodology. In *Science of Religion: Studies in Methodology*, edited by Lauri Honko, pp. 221–236. Mouton, The Hague.
1981 *Belief and Worship in Native America.* Syracuse University Press, Syracuse, New York.
1986 Rock Drawings as Evidence of Religion: Some Principal Points of View. In *Words and Objects: Towards a Dialogue between Archaeology and History of Religion*, edited by Gro Steinsland, pp. 42–66. Institute for Comparative Research in Human Culture, Norwegian University Press, Oslo.
Humphrey, Caroline, and James Laidlaw
1994 *The Archetypal Actions of Ritual: A Theory of Ritual Illustrated by the Jain Rite of Worship.* Clarendon Press, Oxford.
Hunt, Charles B.
1954 Desert Varnish. *Science* 120(3109):183–184.
Hunt, Robert C., David Guillet, David R. Abbott, James M. Bayman, Paul R. Fish, Suzanne K. Fish, Keith Kintigh, and James A. Neely
2005 Plausible Ethnographic Analogies for the Social Organization of Hohokam Canal Irrigation. *American Antiquity* 70:433–456.
Hunter, Christi Assad
1995 Vertebrate Faunal Remains from the MTS Sites. In *Archaeology at the Head of the Scottsdale Canal System, Vol. 2: Studies of Artifacts and Biological Remains*, edited by T. Kathleen Henderson and David R. Abbott, pp. 201–246. Anthropological Papers No. 95-1. Northland Research, Flagstaff, Arizona.
Ingold, Timothy
2000 *The Perception of the Environment: Essays in Livelihood, Dwelling and Skill.* Routledge, London.
2006 Rethinking the Animate, Re-animating Thought. *Ethnos* 71:9–20.
2007a *Lines: A Brief History.* Routledge, London.
2007b Earth, Sky, Wind and Weather. *Journal of the Royal Anthropological Institute* 13(N.S.):S19–S38.
2011 *Being Alive: Essays on Movement, Knowledge, and Description.* Routledge, London.
Ingram, Scott E.
2008 Streamflow and Population Change in the Lower Salt River Valley of Central Arizona, ca. A.D. 775 to 1450. *American Antiquity* 73: 136–165.
Inomata, Takeshi, and Lawrence S. Coben (editors)
2006 *Theatres of Power and Community in Premodern Societies.* AltaMira Press, Walnut Creek, California.
Insoll, Timothy
2004 *Archaeology, Ritual, Religion.* Routledge, London.
2007 "Natural" or "Human" Spaces? Tallensi Sacred Groves and Shrines and Their Potential Implications for Aspects of Northern European Prehistory and Phenomenological Interpretation. *Norwegian Archaeological Review* 40:138–158.
Irwin, Donald C.
1993 Agave Specialization in the Northeastern Periphery: Tabular Tool Evidence from AZ U:9:83 (ASM). Unpublished Master's thesis,

Department of Anthropology, Arizona State University, Tempe.

Iwaniszewski, Stanislaw

1994 Archaeology and Archaeoastronomy of Mount Tlaloc, Mexico: A Reconsideration. *Latin American Antiquity* 5:158–176.

Jacobs, David

1992 Increasing Ceremonial Secrecy at a Salado Platform Mound. In *Developing Perspectives on Tonto Basin Prehistory*, edited by Charles L. Redman and Glen E. Rice, pp. 45–60. Roosevelt Monograph Series No. 2. Anthropological Field Studies No. 26. Office of Cultural Resource Management, Department of Anthropology, Arizona State University, Tempe.

Jacobs, David, and Glen E. Rice

1998 The Function of U:4:33/132, The Cline Terrace Mound. In *A Salado Platform Mound on Tonto Creek, Roosevelt Platform Study: Report on Cline Terrace Mound, Cline Terrace Complex*, edited by David Jacobs, pp. 577–586. Roosevelt Monograph Series No. 7. Anthropological Field Studies No. 36. Office of Cultural Resource Management, Department of Anthropology, Arizona State University, Tempe.

James, Steven R.

1994a Bone Artifacts. In *The Pueblo Grande Project, Vol. 4: Material Culture*, edited by Michael S. Foster, pp. 263–311. Publications in Archaeology No. 20. Soil Systems, Phoenix.

1994b Hohokam Hunting and Fishing Patterns at Pueblo Grande: Results of the Archaeofaunal Analysis. In *The Pueblo Grande Project, Vol. 5: Environment and Subsistence*, edited by Scott Kwiatkowski, pp. 250–318. Publications in Archaeology No. 20. Soil Systems, Phoenix.

2003 Hunting and Fishing Patterns Leading to Resource Depletion. In *Centuries of Decline during the Hohokam Classic Period at Pueblo Grande*, edited by David R. Abbott, pp. 70–81. University of Arizona Press, Tucson.

James, Susan E.

2000 Some Aspects of the Aztec Religion in the Hopi Kachina Cult. *Journal of the Southwest* 42:897–926.

Janik, Liliana

2007 Animism in the Rock Art and Material Culture of Prehistoric Siberia. In *Cult in Context: Reconsidering Ritual in Archaeology*, edited by D. A. Barrowclough and C. Malone, pp. 191–197. Oxbow Books, Oxford.

Jarman, Neil

1992 Troubled Images. *Critique of Anthropology* 12:144–165.

Jernigan, Wesley

1992 *Hour-Glass Rock Art Figures of Southeastern Arizona*. Publication No. 4. Museum of Anthropology, Eastern Arizona College, Thatcher.

Johnson, Ann Stofer

1958 Similarities in Hohokam and Chalchihuites Artifacts. *American Antiquity* 24:126–130.

Johnson, Matthew H.

1989 Conceptions of Agency in Archaeological Interpretation. *Journal of Anthropological Archaeology* 8:198–211.

2006 On the Nature of Theoretical Archaeology and Archaeological Theory. *Archaeological Dialogues* 13:117–132.

Johnston, Abraham Robinson

1848 *Journal of Captain A. R. Johnston, First Dragoons*. 30th Congress, 1st Session, Executive Document No. 41, pp. 565–614. Wendell and Benthuysen, Washington, D.C.

Jolly, Pieter

2002 Therianthropes in San Rock Art. *South African Archaeological Bulletin* 57:85–103.

Jones, Charles E.

1991 Characteristics and Origin of Rock Varnish from the Hyperarid Coastal Deserts of Northern Peru. *Quaternary Research* 35: 116–129.

Joyce, Arthur A., and Marcus Winter

1996 Ideology, Power, and Urban Society in Pre-Hispanic Oaxaca. *Current Anthropology* 38:33–47.

Joyce, Rosemary A., and Jeanne Lopiparo

2005 PostScript: Doing Agency in Archaeology. *Journal of Archaeological Method and Theory* 12:365–374.

Kamash, Zena

2008 What Lies Beneath? Perceptions of the Ontological Paradox of Water. *World Archaeology* 40:224–237.

Kaplan, Reid W.

1975 The Sacred Mushroom in Scandinavia. *Man* 10:72–79.

Kearns, Timothy M.

1975 Rock Art. In *An Archaeological Survey of the Orme Reservoir*, edited by Veletta Canouts, pp. 94–95, 313–331. Archaeological Series

No. 92. Arizona State Museum, University of Arizona, Tucson.

Kelly, Sophia

2013 *A Multi-factor Analysis of the Emergence of a Specialist-Based Economy among the Phoenix Basin Hohokam*. Ph.D. dissertation, School of Human Evolution and Social Change, Arizona State University, Tempe. University Microfilms, Ann Arbor, Michigan.

Kendall, Edward Augustus

1809 Account of the Writing-Rock in Taunton River; In a Letter to the Hon. John Davis, Esq., Record Secretary of the American Academy of Arts and Sciences. *Memoirs of the American Academy* 3(1):165–191. Cambridge, Massachusetts.

Kertzer, David I.

1988 *Ritual, Politics and Power*. Yale University Press, New Haven, Connecticut.

Keyser, James D.

1992 *Indian Rock Art of the Columbia Plateau*. University of Washington Press, Seattle.

2001 Relative Dating Methods. In *Handbook of Rock Art Research*, edited by David S. Whitley, pp. 116–138. AltaMira Press, Walnut Creek, California.

Keyser, James D., and Greer Rabiega

1999 Petroglyph Manufacture by Indirect Percussion: The Potential Occurrence of Tools and Debitage in Datable Context. *Journal of California and Great Basin Anthropology* 21(1):124–136.

Keyser, James D., and David S. Whitley

2006 Sympathetic Magic in Western North American Rock Art. *American Antiquity* 71:3–26.

Kidder, Alfred V., and Samuel J. Guernsey

1919 *Archaeological Explorations in Northeastern Arizona*. Bureau of American Ethnology Bulletin No. 65. U.S. Government Printing Office, Washington, D.C.

Kintigh, Keith W., Donna M. Glowacki, and Deborah L. Huntley

2004 Long-Term Settlement History and the Emergence of Towns in the Zuni Area. *American Antiquity* 69:432–456.

Kisselburg, JoAnn E.

1987 Specialization and Differentiation: Nonsubsistence Economic Pursuits in Courtyard Systems at La Ciudad. In *The Hohokam Village: Site Structure and Organization*, edited by David E. Doyel, pp. 159–170. Southwestern and Rocky Mountain Division of the American Association for the Advancement of Science, Glenwood Springs, Colorado.

Kluckhohn, Clyde, and Dorothy Leighton

1946 *The Navaho*. Harvard University Press, Cambridge, Massachusetts.

Knapp, A. Bernard, and Peter van Dommelen

2008 Past Practices: Rethinking Individuals and Agents in Archaeology. *Cambridge Archaeological Journal* 18:15–34.

Kohler, Timothy A., Stephanie VanBuskirk, and Samantha M. Ruscavage-Barz

2004 Vessels and Villages: Evidence for Conformist Transmission in Early Village Aggregations on the Pajarito Plateau, New Mexico. *Journal of Anthropological Archaeology* 23:100–118.

Kohler, Timothy A., Mark D. Varien, and Aaron M. Wright (editors)

2010 *Leaving Mesa Verde: Peril and Change in the Thirteenth-Century Southwest*. Amerind Studies in Archaeology No. 5. University of Arizona Press, Tucson.

Kopytoff, Igor

1986 The Cultural Biography of Things: Commoditization as Process. In *The Social Life of Things: Commodities in Cultural Perspective*, edited by A. Appadurai, pp. 64–91. Cambridge University Press, Cambridge.

Kowalewski, Stephen A.

2008 Regional Settlement Pattern Studies. *Journal of Archaeological Research* 16:225–285.

Kozak, David L., and David I. Lopez

1999 *Devil Sickness and Devil Songs*. Smithsonian Institution Press, Washington, D.C.

Krinsley, David H.

1998 Models of Rock Varnish Formation Constrained by High Resolution Transmission Electron Microscopy. *Sedimentology* 45:711–725.

Krinsley, David H., Ronald I. Dorn, and N. Keith Tovey

1995 Nanometer-Scale Layering in Rock Varnish: Implications for Genesis and Paleoenvironmental Interpretation. *Journal of Geology* 103:106–113.

Kruger, Kari Anna

1993 A Definitive Analysis of Hohokam Stone Palettes. Unpublished Master's thesis, Department of Anthropology, Northern Illinois University, DeKalb.

Kruse-Peeples, Melissa R.

2013 *The Ancient Agroecology of Perry Mesa: Integrating Runoff, Nutrients, and Climate*.

Ph.D. dissertation, School of Human Evolution and Social Change, Arizona State University, Tempe. University Microfilms, Ann Arbor, Michigan.

Kwiatkowski, Scott M.

2003 Evidence for Subsistence Problems. In *Centuries of Decline during the Hohokam Classic Period at Pueblo Grande*, edited by David R. Abbott, pp. 48–69. University of Arizona Press, Tucson.

Kyriakidis, Evangelos

2007 Finding Ritual: Calibrating the Evidence. In *The Archaeology of Ritual*, edited by Evangelos Kyriakidis, pp. 9–22. Advanced Seminar No. 3. Cotsen Institute of Archaeology, University of California, Los Angeles.

Kyriakidis, Evangelos (editor)

2007 *The Archaeology of Ritual*. Advanced Seminar No. 3. Cotsen Institute of Archaeology, University of California, Los Angeles.

Lack, Andrew D.

2007 Pueblo Poniente Ceramic Analysis. In *The Terrazona Archaeological Project: Investigations in a Portion of Pueblo Poniente, AZ T:11:164 (ASM), a Hohokam Site in Southwestern Phoenix, Maricopa County, Arizona*, edited by Thomas E. Wright, pp. 125–141. Occasional Papers No. 8. Pueblo Grande Museum, Phoenix. Report No. 2005:167. Archaeological Research Services, Tempe, Arizona.

2013 *Innovation in Context: The Process of Stylistic Change among Hohokam Potters in the Phoenix Basin*. Ph.D. dissertation, School of Human Evolution and Social Change, Arizona State University, Tempe. University Microfilms, Ann Arbor, Michigan.

Laming-Emperaire, Annette

1959 *Lascaux: Paintings and Engravings*. Pelican, Harmondsworth, U.K.

1962 *La signification de l'art rupestre paleolithique*. Editions A. & J. Picard, Paris.

Landon, George M.

1979 The Petroglyphs and Other Features at Jagow Well. In *American Indian Rock Art*, Vol. 5, edited by Frank G. Bock, Ken Hedges, Georgia Lee, and Helen Michaelis, pp. 99–114. American Rock Art Research Association, Tucson, Arizona.

Latour, Bruno

1993 *We Have Never Been Modern*. Harvard University Press, Cambridge, Massachusetts.

2005 *Reassembling the Social: An Introduction to Actor-Network Theory*. Oxford University Press, Oxford.

Laudermilk, John D.

1931 On the Origin of Desert Varnish. *American Journal of Science* 21(121):51–66.

Laughlin, Charles D.

1990 Ritual and the Symbolic Function: A Summary of Biogenetic Structural Theory. *Journal of Ritual Studies* 4:16–39.

Layton, Robert

2003 Art and Agency: A Reassessment. *Journal of the Royal Anthropological Institute* 9: 447–464.

Leach, Edmund R.

1976 *Culture and Communication*. Cambridge University Press, Cambridge.

LeBlanc, Steven A.

1999 *Prehistoric Warfare in the American Southwest*. University of Utah Press, Salt Lake City.

Lee, Martin R., and Phil A. Bland

2003 Dating Climatic Change in Hot Deserts Using Desert Varnish on Meteorite Finds. *Earth and Planetary Science Letters* 206: 187–198.

Lekson, Stephen H.

2008 *A History of the Ancient Southwest*. School for Advanced Research Press, Santa Fe, New Mexico.

Lerner, Shereen Ann

1984 *Modeling Spatial Organization in the Hohokam Periphery*. Ph.D. dissertation, Department of Anthropology, Arizona State University, Tempe. University Microfilms, Ann Arbor, Michigan.

Leroi-Gourhan, André

1958 Repartition et groupement des animaux dans l'arte pariétal paléolithique. *Bulletin de la Société Préhistorique Française* 55: 515–527.

1965 *Préhistoire de l'arte occidental*. Mazenod, Paris.

Lévi-Strauss, Claude

1958 *Anthropologie structurale*. Plon, Paris.

1963 *Totemism*. Translated by Rodney Needham. Beacon Press, Boston.

1966 *The Savage Mind*. Translated by George Weidenfeld and Nicolson, Ltd. University of Chicago Press, Chicago.

Lewis, Gilbert

1980 *Day of Shining Red: An Essay on Understanding Ritual*. Cambridge University Press, Cambridge.

Lewis-Williams, J. David

1972 The Syntax and Function of the Giant's Castle Rock Paintings. *South African Archaeological Bulletin* 27:49–65.

1977 Ezeljagdspoort Revisited: New Light on an Enigmatic Rock-Painting. *South African Archaeological Bulletin* 32:165–169.

1980 Ethnography and Iconography: Aspects of Southern San Thought and Art. *Man* 15:467–482.

1981 The Thin Red Line: Southern San Notions and Rock Paintings of Supernatural Potency. *South African Archaeological Bulletin* 36: 5–13.

1991 Wrestling with Analogy: A Methodological Dilemma in Upper Palaeolithic Art Research. *Proceedings of the Prehistoric Society* 57:149–162.

1994 Rock Art and Ritual: South Africa and Beyond. *Complutum* 5:277–289.

1995 Modelling the Production and Consumption of Rock Art. *South African Archaeological Bulletin* 50:143–154.

2001 Brainstorming Images: Neuropsychology and Rock Art Research. In *Handbook of Rock Art Research*, edited by David S. Whitley, pp. 332–357. AltaMira Press, Walnut Creek, California.

2002 *A Cosmos in Stone: Interpreting Religion and Society through Rock Art*. AltaMira Press, Walnut Creek, California.

2003 Putting the Record Straight: Rock Art and Shamanism. *Antiquity* 77:165–170.

2004 Neuropsychology and Upper Palaeolithic Art: Observations on the Progress of Altered States of Consciousness. *Cambridge Archaeological Journal* 14:107–111.

Lewis-Williams, J. David, and Thomas A. Dowson

1988 The Signs of All Times: Entoptic Phenomena in Upper Paleolithic Art. *Current Anthropology* 29:201–217.

1993 On Vision and Power in the Neolithic: Evidence from the Decorated Monuments. *Current Anthropology* 34:55–65.

Lindauer, Owen

2000 A Schoolhouse Point Mesa Perspective on Salado Community Development. In *Salado*, edited by Jeffrey S. Dean, pp. 219–240. Amerind Foundation New World Studies Series No. 4. University of New Mexico Press, Albuquerque.

Liu, Tanzhuo

2003 Blind Testing of Rock Varnish Microstratigraphy as a Chronometric Indicator: Results on Late Quaternary Lava Flows in the Mojave Desert, California. *Geomorphology* 53:209–234.

Liu, Tanzhuo, and Wallace S. Broecker

2000 How Fast Does Rock Varnish Grow? *Geology* 28:183–186.

2007 Holocene Rock Varnish Microstratigraphy and Its Chronometric Application in Drylands of Western USA. *Geomorphology* 84:1–21.

2008a Rock Varnish Evidence for Latest Pleistocene Millennial-Scale Wet Events in the Drylands of Western United States. *Geology* 36:403–406.

2008b Rock Varnish Microlamination Dating of Late Quaternary Features in the Drylands of Western USA. *Geomorphology* 93:501–523.

Liu, Tanzhuo, Wallace S. Broecker, John W. Bell, and Charles Mandeville

2000 Terminal Pleistocene Wet Event Recorded in Rock Varnish from the Las Vegas Valley, Southern Nevada. *Palaeogeography, Palaeoclimatology, Palaeoecology* 161:423–433.

Liu, Tanzhuo, and Ronald I. Dorn

1996 Understanding Spatial Variability in Environmental Changes in Drylands with Rock Varnish Microlaminations. *Annals of the Association of American Geographers* 86:187–212.

Loendorf, Christopher

2001 Salado Burial Practices. In *Ancient Burial Practices in the American Southwest: Archaeology, Physical Anthropology, and Native American Perspectives*, edited by Douglas R. Mitchell and Judy L. Brunson-Hadley, pp. 123–148. University of New Mexico Press, Albuquerque.

Loendorf, Lawrence L., and Christopher Loendorf

1995 *With Zig-Zag Lines I'm Painted: Hohokam Petroglyphs on Tempe Butte, Arizona*. Loendorf and Associates, Tempe, Arizona.

Lomatuway'ma, Michael, Lorena Lomatuway'ma, and Sidney Namingha Jr.

1993 *Hopi Ruin Legends*. Edited by Ekkehart Malotki. Northern Arizona University, Flagstaff.

López Austin, Alfredo

2002 Indigenous Mythology from Present-Day Mexico. In *Native Religions and Cultures of Central and South America: Anthropology of the Sacred*, edited by Lawrence E. Sullivan, pp. 33–66. Continuum, New York.

Losey, Robert
2010 Animism as a Means of Exploring Archaeological Fishing Structures on Willapa Bay, Washington, USA. *Cambridge Archaeological Journal* 20:17–32.

Loubser, Johannes H. N.
2002 *Tripping on the Snake, or On a Quest for Visions Forgotten: An Assessment of Selected Rock Art Sites in the Hell's Canyon National Recreation Area.* Technical Report No. 963. New South Associates, Stone Mountain, Georgia.

Lowell, Edith S.
1990 Paletas and Tabletas: Comparison of Hohokam Stone Palettes with Snuff Trays of South America. *Kiva* 55(4):321–355.

Lowie, Robert H.
1921 *Primitive Society.* Routledge and Kegan Paul, London.

Lucero, Lisa J.
2003 The Politics of Ritual: The Emergence of Classic Maya Rulers. *Current Anthropology* 44:523–558.

Lumholtz, Carl
1912 *New Trails in Mexico: An Account of One Year's Exploration in North-Western Sonora, Mexico, and South-Western Arizona, 1909–1910.* Charles Scribner's Sons, London.

Lundin, Deil
2001 *An Archaeological Survey of Approximately 17 Acres at the Southeast Intersection of 20th Street and Euclid Avenue, Phoenix, Maricopa County, Arizona.* Cultural Resources Report No. 01-419. SWCA, Phoenix.

Lymer, Kenneth
2004 Rags and Rock Art: The Landscapes of Holy Site Pilgrimage in the Republic of Kazakhstan. *World Archaeology* 36:158–172.

Lyons, Patrick D.
2003 *Ancestral Hopi Migrations.* Anthropological Papers No. 68. University of Arizona Press, Tucson.

Lyons, Patrick D., Elizabeth J. Miksa, Sergio F. Castro-Reino, and Carlos Lavayen
2005 Using Petrography to Demonstrate the Link between Roosevelt Red Ware and Ancient Immigrants. Paper presented at the 70th Annual Meeting of the Society for American Archaeology, Salt Lake City, Utah.

Mabry, Jonathan B.
2000 The Red Mountain Phase and the Origins of Hohokam Villages. In *The Hohokam Village Revisited,* edited by David E. Doyel, Suzanne K. Fish, and Paul R. Fish, pp. 1–28. Southwestern and Rocky Mountain Division of the American Association for the Advancement of Science, Fort Collins, Colorado.
2002 The Role of Irrigation in the Transition to Agriculture and Sedentism in the Southwest: A Risk Management Model. *In Traditions, Transitions, and Technologies: Themes in Southwestern Archaeology,* edited by Sarah H. Schlanger, pp. 178–199. University Press of Colorado, Boulder.
2005 Diversity in Early Southwestern Farming and Optimization Models of Transitions to Agriculture. In *Subsistence and Resource Use Strategies of Early Agricultural Communities in Southern Arizona,* edited by Michael W. Diehl, pp. 113–152. Anthropological Papers No. 34. Center for Desert Archaeology, Tucson, Arizona.

Mabry, Jonathan B. (editor)
1998 *Archaeological Investigations of Early Village Sites in the Middle Santa Cruz Valley: Analyses and Synthesis.* 2 parts. Anthropological Papers No. 19. Center for Desert Archaeology, Tucson, Arizona.
2008 *Las Capas: Early Irrigation and Sedentism in a Southwestern Floodplain.* Anthropological Papers No. 28. Center for Desert Archaeology, Tucson, Arizona.

Mabry, Jonathan B., Deborah L. Swartz, Helga Wöcherl, Jeffery J. Clark, Gavin H. Archer, and Michael Lindeman
1997 *Archaeological Investigations at Early Village Sites in the Middle Santa Cruz Valley: Site and Feature Descriptions.* Anthropological Papers No. 18. Center for Desert Archaeology, Tucson, Arizona.

Madsen, Millard C.
1982 Animism and Related Tendencies in Hopi Children: A Replication of Dennis. *Journal of Cross-Cultural Psychology* 13:117–124.

Madsen, Torsten
1989 Seriation and Multivariate Statistics. In *Computer Applications and Quantitative Methods in Archaeology, 1989,* edited by Sebastian Rahtz and Julie Richards, pp. 205–214. BAR International Series No. 548. Archaeopress, London.

Madsen, Torsten (editor)
1988 *Multivariate Statistics in Archaeology: Numerical Approaches in Scandinavian Archaeology.* Jutland Archaeological Society

Publication No. 21. Aarhus University Press, Aarhus, Denmark.

Magne, Martin P. R., and Michael A. Klassen

1991 A Multivariate Study of Rock Art Anthropomorphs at Writing-on-Stone, Southern Alberta. *American Antiquity* 56:389–418.

Malafouris, Lambros

2004 The Cognitive Basis of Material Engagement: Where Brain, Body, and Culture Conflate. In *Rethinking Materiality: The Engagement of Mind with the Material World*, edited by Elizabeth DeMarrais, Chris Gosden, and Colin Renfrew, pp. 53–62. McDonald Institute for Archaeological Research, Cambridge.

2007 The Sacred Engagement: Outline of a Hypothesis about the Origin of Human Religious Intelligence. In *Cult in Context: Reconsidering Ritual in Archaeology*, edited by D. A. Barrowclough and C. Malone, pp. 198–204. Oxbow Books, Oxford.

Malinowski, Bronislaw

1925 Magic, Science and Religion. In *Science, Religion and Reality*, edited by Joseph Needham, pp. 19–84. Macmillan, New York.

Mallery, Garrick

1886 *Pictographs of the North American Indians: A Preliminary Paper.* Annual Report of the Bureau of American Ethnology, Vol. 4. Smithsonian Institution, U.S. Government Printing Office, Washington, D.C.

1893 *Picture-Writing of the American Indians.* Annual Report of the Bureau of American Ethnology, Vol. 10. Smithsonian Institution, U.S. Government Printing Office, Washington, D.C.

Mann, Michael

1986 *The Sources of Social Power, Vol. 1: A History of Power from the Beginning to A.D. 1760.* Cambridge University Press, Cambridge.

Marcus, Joyce

2007 Rethinking Ritual. In *The Archaeology of Ritual*, edited by Evangelos Kyriakidis, pp. 43–76. Advanced Seminar No. 3. Cotsen Institute of Archaeology, University of California, Los Angeles.

Marquardt, William H.

1978 Advances in Archaeological Seriation. In *Advances in Archaeological Method and Theory*, Vol. 1, edited by Michael B. Schiffer, pp. 263–274. Academic Press, New York.

Marshall, John T.

2001 Ballcourt. In *The Grewe Archaeological Project, Vol. 1: Project Background and Feature Descriptions*, edited by Douglas B. Craig, pp. 109–124. Anthropological Papers No. 99-1. Northland Research, Tempe, Arizona.

Martineau, LaVan

1973 *The Rocks Begin to Speak.* K.C. Publications, Las Vegas, Nevada.

Martynec, Rick, and Sandy Martynec

1995 Did the Tohono O'odham Make Petroglyphs? In *Rock Art Papers*, Vol. 12, edited by Ken Hedges, pp. 81–87. Papers No. 33. Museum of Man, San Diego, California.

Mason, J. Alden

1920 The Papago Harvest Festival. *American Anthropologist* 22:13–25.

Mason, Ronald J.

2000 Archaeology and Native North American Oral Traditions. *American Antiquity* 65: 239–266.

Masse, W. Bruce

1991 The Quest for Subsistence Sufficiency and Civilization in the Sonoran Desert. In *Chaco and Hohokam: Prehistoric Regional Systems in the American Southwest*, edited by Patricia L. Crown and W. James Judge, pp. 195–224. School of American Research Press, Santa Fe, New Mexico.

Masse, W. Bruce, and Fred Espenak

2006 Sky as Environment: Solar Eclipses and Hohokam Sociopolitical Geography. In *Environmental Change and Human Adaptation in the Ancient Southwest*, edited by David E. Doyel and Jeffrey S. Dean, pp. 228–280. University of Utah Press, Salt Lake City.

Masse, W. Bruce, and Robert Soklow

2005 Black Suns and Dark Times: Cultural Responses to Solar Eclipses in the Ancient Puebloan Southwest. In *Current Studies in Archaeoastronomy: Conversations across Space and Time*, edited by John W. Fountain and Rolf M. Sinclair, pp. 47–67. Carolina Academic Press, Durham, North Carolina.

Mather, Cotton

1714 An Extract of Several Letters from Cotton Mather, D.D., to John Woodward, M.D., and Richard Waller, Esq; S. R. Sec. *Philosophical Transactions* 29(338):62–71.

Mathiowetz, Michael Dean

2011 *The Diurnal Path of the Sun: Ideology and Interregional Interaction in Ancient Northwest Mexico and the American Southwest.* Ph.D. dissertation, Department of Anthropology, University of California, Riverside. University Microfilms, Ann Arbor, Michigan.

McBrinn, Maxine
2005 *Social Identities among Archaic Mobile Hunters and Gatherers in the American Southwest.* Archaeological Series No. 197. Arizona State Museum, University of Arizona, Tucson.

McCall, Grant S.
2007 Add Shamans and Stir? A Critical Review of the Shamanism Model of Forager Rock Art Production. *Journal of Anthropological Archaeology* 26:224–233.
2010 Changing Views of Drakensberg San Rock Art: Examining Landscape Use, Ritual Activity, and Contact through Multivariate Content-Based Spatial Analysis. *American Antiquity* 75:773–791.

McCann, Andrew
2003 The Savage Metropolis: Animism, Aesthetics and the Pleasures of a Vanished Race. *Textual Practice* 17:317–333.

McCauley, Robert N., and Thomas Lawson
2007 Cognition, Religious Ritual, and Action. In *The Archaeology of Ritual*, edited by Evangelos Kyriakidis, pp. 209–254. Advanced Seminar No. 3. Cotsen Institute of Archaeology, University of California, Los Angeles.

McDonnell, Mac, David E. Doyel, and Elinor Large
1995 Plain Ware, Red Ware, and Other Ceramic Artifacts. In *Archaeological Excavations at Pueblo Blanco: The MCDOT Alma School Road Project, Vol. 1*, edited by David E. Doyel, Andrew T. Black, and Barbara S. Macnider, pp. 187–250. Cultural Resource Report No. 90. Archaeological Consulting Services, Tempe, Arizona.

McGregor, John C.
1943 Burial of an Early American Magician. *Proceedings of the American Philosophical Society* 86(2):270–298.

McGuire, Randall H.
1991 On the Outside Looking In: The Concept of Periphery in Hohokam Archaeology. In *Exploring the Hohokam: Prehistoric Desert Peoples of the American Southwest*, edited by George J. Gumerman, pp. 347–382. Amerind Foundation New World Series No. 1. University of New Mexico Press, Albuquerque.
1992a *A Marxist Archaeology.* Academic Press, San Diego, California.
1992b *Death, Society, and Ideology in a Hohokam Community.* Westview Press, Boulder, Colorado.
2012 Pueblo Religion and the Mesoamerican Connection. In *Religious Transformation in the Late Pre-Hispanic Pueblo World*, edited by Donna M. Glowacki and Scott Van Keuren, pp. 23–49. University of Arizona Press, Tucson.

McGuire, Randall H., and Ann Valdo Howard
1987 The Structure and Organization of Hohokam Shell Exchange. *Kiva* 52(2):113–146.

McGuire, Randall H., and Dean J. Saitta
1996 Although They Have Petty Captains, They Obey Them Badly: The Dialectics of Prehispanic Western Pueblo Social Organization. *American Antiquity* 61:197–216.

Meltzer, David J.
2009 *First Peoples in a New World: Colonizing Ice Age America.* University of California Press, Berkeley.

Merkur, Daniel
1991 The Discharge of Guilt: Psychoanalytic Theories of Ritual. *Journal of Ritual Studies* 5:15–32.

Merrifield, Ralph
1987 *The Archaeology of Ritual and Magic.* B. T. Batsford, London.

Mesoudi, Alex, and Michael J. O'Brien
2008 The Cultural Transmission of Great Basin Projectile-Point Technology I: Experimental Simulation. *American Antiquity* 73:3–28.

Midvale, Frank
1930s Original unpublished notes, maps, and photographs of early Phoenix archaeology. Documents on file, Arizona Collection, Hayden Library, Arizona State University, Tempe.

Miksicek, Charles H.
1982 Macro-botanical Remains. In *Hohokam Archaeology along the Salt-Gila Aqueduct Central Arizona Project, Vol. 1: Research Design*, by Lynn S. Teague and Patricia L. Crown, pp. 155–161. Archaeological Series No. 150. Arizona State Museum, University of Arizona, Tucson.

Miller, Daniel, M. Rowlands, and Christopher Tilley (editors)
1989 *Domination and Resistance.* Unwin Hyman, London.

Miller, Daniel, and Christopher Tilley (editors)
1984 *Ideology, Power and Prehistory.* Cambridge University Press, Cambridge.

Mills, Barbara J.
2004 The Establishment and Defeat of Hierarchy: Inalienable Possessions and the History of Collective Prestige Structures in the

Puebloan Southwest. *American Anthropologist* 106:238–251.
2007 Performing the Feast: Visual Display and Suprahousehold Commensalism in the Puebloan Southwest. *American Antiquity* 72(2):210–239.

Mills, Barbara J. (editor)
2000 *Alternative Leadership Strategies in the Prehispanic Southwest.* University of Arizona Press, Tucson.

Mills, Barbara J., and Patricia L. Crown
1995 Ceramic Production in the American Southwest: An Introduction. In *Ceramic Production in the American Southwest*, edited by Barbara J. Mills and Patricia L. Crown, pp. 1–29. University of Arizona Press, Tucson.

Mills, Barbara J., Mark D. Elson, Paul R. Fish, Glen E. Rice, and Henry D. Wallace
2013 Ritual Practice and Hohokam Trajectories. In *Hohokam Trajectories in World Perspective*, edited by Suzanne K. Fish and Paul R. Fish. University of Arizona Press, Tucson. In preparation.

Mills, Barbara J., and T. J. Ferguson
2008 Animate Objects: Shell Trumpets and Ritual Networks in the Greater Southwest. *Journal of Archaeological Method and Theory* 15:338–361.

Mills, Barbara J., and William H. Walker (editors)
2008 *Memory Work: Archaeologies of Material Practice.* School for Advanced Research Press, Santa Fe, New Mexico.

Mindeleff, Cosmos
1896 Casa Grande Ruin. *Annual Report of the Bureau of Ethnology* 13:289–319. U.S. Government Printing Office, Washington, D.C.
1897 The Repair of Casa Grande. *Annual Report of the Bureau of Ethnology* 15:321–349. U.S. Government Printing Office, Washington, D.C.

Mitchell, Douglas R.
2003 Burial and Society. In *Centuries of Decline during the Hohokam Classic Period at Pueblo Grande*, edited by David R. Abbott, pp. 107–127. University of Arizona Press, Tucson.

Mitchell, Douglas R., and Judy L. Brunson-Hadley
2001 An Evaluation of Classic Period Hohokam Burials and Society: Chiefs, Priests, or Acephalous Complexity. In *Ancient Burial Practices in the American Southwest: Archaeology, Physical Anthropology, and Native American Perspectives*, edited by Douglas R. Mitchell and Judy L. Brunson-Hadley, pp. 45–67. University of New Mexico Press, Albuquerque.

Mithen, Steven
1997 Cognitive Archaeology, Evolutionary Psychology and Cultural Transmission, with Particular Reference to Religious Ideas. In *Rediscovering Darwin: Evolutionary Theory and Archeological Explanation*, edited by C. Michael Barton and Geoffrey A. Clark, pp. 67–74. Archeological Papers No. 7. American Anthropological Association, Arlington, Virginia.

Mixon, Benjamin, and Raymond E. White
1991 Skywatchers of the Salt River Valley Hohokam. *Astronomy Quarterly* 8:245–259.

Mobley-Tanaka, Jeanette L.
2002 Crossed Cultures, Crossed Meanings: The Manipulation of Ritual Imagery in Early Historic Pueblo Resistance. In *Archaeologies of the Pueblo Revolt: Identity, Meaning, and Renewal in the Pueblo World*, edited by Robert W. Preucel, pp. 77–84. University of New Mexico Press, Albuquerque.

Moore, Jerry D.
1996 The Archaeology of Plazas and the Proxemics of Ritual: Three Andean Traditions. *American Anthropologist* 98:789–902.

Moorehead, Warren K.
1906 *A Narrative of Explorations in New Mexico, Arizona, Indiana, etc., Together with a Brief History of the Department.* Bulletin No. 3. Department of Archaeology, Phillips Academy, Andover, Massachusetts.

Moreno, Jerryll
2003 Petroglyphs of the Lake Pleasant Regional Park. *Kiva* 68(3):185–219.

Morgan, David
2005 *The Sacred Gaze: Religious Visual Culture in Theory and Practice.* University of California Press, Berkeley.

Morgan, Lewis Henry
1877 *Ancient Society, or, Researches in the Lines of Human Progress from Savagery through Barbarism to Civilization.* Henry Holt, New York.

Morris, Donald H.
1969 Red Mountain: An Early Pioneer Period Hohokam Site in the Salt River Valley. *American Antiquity* 34:40–53.

Morris, Donald H., and Mahhmoud El-Najjar
1971 An Unusual Classic Period Burial from Las Colinas, Salt River Valley, Central Arizona. *Kiva* 31(4):31–35.

Morss, Neil
1954 *Clay Figurines of the American Southwest.* Papers of the Peabody Museum of American Archaeology Vol. 49, No. 1. Harvard University, Cambridge, Massachusetts.

Morwood, Michael J.
1980 Time, Space and Prehistoric Art: A Principal Component Analysis. *Archaeology and Physical Anthropology in Oceania* 15(2):98–109.
2002 *Visions from the Past: The Archaeology of Australian Aboriginal Art.* Smithsonian Institution Press, Washington, D.C.

Motsinger, Thomas N.
1994 The Dutch Canal Ruin Ceramic Assemblage. In *Early Desert Farming and Irrigation Settlements: Archaeological Investigations in the Phoenix Sky Harbor Center, Vol. 2: Dutch Canal Ruin*, edited by David H. Greenwald, Mark Zyniecki, and Dawn M. Greenwald, pp. 207–228. Anthropological Research Paper No. 4. SWCA, Flagstaff, Arizona.
1995 Ceramic Analysis. In *Early Desert Farming and Irrigation Settlements: Archaeological Investigations in the Phoenix Sky Harbor Center, Vol. 3: Pueblo Salado*, edited by David H. Greenwald, Mark L. Chenault, and Dawn M. Greenwald, pp. 171–186. Anthropological Research Paper No. 4. SWCA, Flagstaff, Arizona.

Munson, Marit
2002 *On Boundaries and Beliefs: Rock Art and Identity on the Pajarito Plateau.* Ph.D. dissertation, Department of Anthropology, University of New Mexico, Albuquerque. University Microfilms, Ann Arbor, Michigan.
2011 *The Archaeology of Art in the American Southwest.* AltaMira Press, Lanham, Maryland.
2012 Iconography, Space, and Practice: Rio Grande Rock Art, A.D. 1150–1600. In *Religious Transformation in the Late Pre-Hispanic Pueblo World*, edited by Donna M. Glowacki and Scott Van Keuren, pp. 109–129. University of Arizona Press, Tucson.

Myerhoff, Barbara G.
1977 We Don't Wrap Herring in a Printed Page: Fictions and Continuity in Secular Ritual. In *Secular Ritual*, edited by Sally F. Moore and Barbara G. Myerhoff, pp. 199–223. Cornell University Press, Ithaca, New York.

Nadasdy, Paul
2007 The Gift in the Animal: The Ontology of Hunting and Human-Animal Sociality. *American Ethnologist* 34:25–43.

Nash, George H. (editor)
2000 *Place and Space: World Perspectives of Rock Art and Landscape.* BAR International Series No. 902. Archaeopress, Oxford.

Nash, George H., and Christopher Chippindale (editors)
2002 *European Landscapes of Rock-Art.* Routledge, London.

Neely, James A., and William E. Doolittle
2004 Answers and Questions. In *The Safford Valley Grids: Prehistoric Cultivation in the Southern Arizona Desert*, edited by William E. Doolittle and James A. Neely, pp. 125–141. Anthropological Papers No. 70. University of Arizona Press, Tucson.

Neitzel, Jill
1991 Hohokam Material Culture and Behavior: The Dimensions of Organizational Change. In *Exploring the Hohokam: Prehistoric Desert Peoples of the American Southwest*, edited by George J. Gumerman, pp. 177–230. Amerind Foundation New World Series No. 1. University of New Mexico Press, Albuquerque.

Nelson, Ben E., and Destiny Crider
2005 Posibles pasajes migratorios en el norte de México y el suroeste de los Estados Unidos durante el Epiclásico y el Postclásico. In *Reacomodos demográficos del Clásico al Postclásico en el centro de México*, edited by Linda Manzanilla, pp. 75–102. Instituto de Investigaciones Antropológicas, Universidad Nacional Autónoma de México, Mexico City.

Nelson, Leslie Margaret
1998 Why Here? Petroglyph Site Analysis Using Geographic Information Systems. Unpublished Master's thesis, Department of Anthropology, Arizona State University, Tempe.

Nelson, Richard S.
1981 *The Role of a Puchteca System in Hohokam Exchange.* Ph.D. dissertation, Department of Anthropology, New York University, New York. University Microfilms, Ann Arbor, Michigan.
1991 *Hohokam Marine Shell Exchange and Artifacts.* Archaeological Series No. 179. Arizona State Museum, University of Arizona, Tucson.

Neuzil, Anna A., and Patrick D. Lyons
2006 *An Analysis of Whole Vessels from the Mills Collection Curated at Eastern Arizona*

College, Thatcher, Arizona. Technical Report No. 2005-01. Center for Desert Archaeology, Tucson, Arizona.

Nicholay, Scott, and James E. Brady

2004 Footsteps in the Dark Zone: Ritual Cave Use in Southwest Prehistory. Paper presented at the 69th Annual Meeting of the Society for American Archaeology, Quebec.

Nichols, Linda M., and Gary M. Feinman

1989 A Regional Perspective on Hohokam Irrigation in the Lower Salt River Valley, Arizona. In *The Sociopolitical Structure of Prehistoric Southwestern Societies*, edited by Steadman Upham, Kent G. Lightfoot, and Roberta A. Jewett, pp. 199–235. Westview Press, Boulder, Colorado.

Nichols, Linda M., and Jill Neitzel

1984 Canal Irrigation and Sociopolitical Organization in the Lower Salt River Valley: A Diachronic Analysis. In *Prehistoric Agricultural Strategies in the Southwest*, edited by Suzanne K. Fish and Paul R. Fish, pp. 161–178. Anthropological Research Papers No. 38. Arizona State University, Tempe.

North, Chris, Michael S. Foster, John M. Lindly, and Douglas R. Mitchell

2005 A Newly Discovered Clovis Point from the Phoenix Basin and an Update on Arizona Clovis Point Attributes. *Kiva* 70(3):293–307.

Oliver, Theodore J.

2001 Warfare in Tonto Basin. In *Deadly Landscapes: Case Studies in Prehistoric Southwestern Warfare*, edited by Glen E. Rice and Steven A. LeBlanc, pp. 195–218. University of Utah Press, Salt Lake City.

Olsen, Nancy H.

2004 Pajarito Plateau Rock Art. In *Archaeology of Bandelier National Monument: Village Formation on the Pajarito Plateau, New Mexico*, edited by Timothy A. Kohler, pp. 265–291. University of New Mexico Press, Albuquerque.

Opperman, Renee G.

1979 Research at Casa Grande. *Archaeoastronomy* 2(3):12–14.

1980 *Astronomical Implications of the Architecture at Casa Grande, Arizona*. Occasional Publications in Anthropological Archaeology No. 9. University of Northern Colorado, Greeley.

Ortiz, Alfonso

1969 *The Tewa World: Space, Time, Being, and Becoming in a Pueblo Society*. University of Chicago Press, Chicago.

Ortíz, Panciano, and María del Carmen Rodríguez

2000 The Sacred Hill of El Manatí. In *Olmec Art and Archaeology in Mesoamerica*, edited by John E. Clark and Mary E. Pye, pp. 75–93. Yale University Press, New Haven, Connecticut.

Ortman, Scott G.

2009 Action, Place, and Space in the Castle Rock Community. In *The Social Construction of Communities: Agency, Structure, and Identity in the Prehispanic Southwest*, edited by Mark D. Varien and James M. Potter, pp. 125–154. AltaMira Press, Lanham, Maryland.

2012 Bowls to Gardens: A History of Tewa Community Metaphors. In *Religious Transformation in the Late Pre-Hispanic Pueblo World*, edited by Donna M. Glowacki and Scott Van Keuren, pp. 84–108. University of Arizona Press, Tucson.

Ortner, Sherry B.

2001 Practice, Power and the Past. *Journal of Social Archaeology* 1:271–278.

2006 *Anthropology and Social Theory: Culture, Power and the Acting Self*. Duke University Press, Durham, North Carolina.

Osborne, Carolyn

1965 The Preparation of Agave Fiber. *American Antiquity* 31:45–50.

Ouzman, Sven

2001 Seeing Is Deceiving: Rock Art and the Non-visual. *World Archaeology* 33(2):237–256.

Parezo, Nancy J.

1983 *Navajo Sandpainting: From Religious Act to Commercial Art*. University of Arizona Press, Tucson.

Parkman, Francis

1897 *La Salle and the Discovery of the Great West: France and England in North America, Part 3*. Vol. 1. The Works of Francis Parkman, Champlain Edition, Vol. 5. Little, Brown, Boston.

Parsons, Elsie Clews

1923 The Origin Myth of the Zuni. *Journal of American Folk-Lore* 36:135–162.

1929 *The Social Organization of the Tewa of New Mexico*. Memoir No. 36. American Anthropological Association, Menasha, Wisconsin.

1933 Some Aztec and Pueblo Parallels. *American Anthropologist* 35:611–631.

1939 *Pueblo Indian Religion*. 2 vols. University of Chicago Press, Chicago.

Patrick, Herbert R.

1903 *The Ancient Canal Systems and Pueblos of the Salt River Valley, Arizona*. Bulletin No. 1. Phoenix Free Press, Phoenix.

Patterson, Carol

1998 Seeking Power at Willow Creek Cave, Northern California. *Anthropology of Consciousness* 9:38–49.

Patterson-Rudolph, Carol

1997 *On the Trail of Spiderwoman: Petroglyphs, Pictographs, and Myths of the Southwest*. Ancient City Press, Santa Fe, New Mexico.

Pauketat, Timothy A.

2001 Practice and History in Archaeology: An Emerging Paradigm. *Archaeological Theory* 1:73–98.

2009 Interview. In *Annual Review of the School for Advanced Research on the Human Experience*, p. 12. School for Advanced Research, Santa Fe, New Mexico.

2012 Getting Religion: Lessons from Ancestral Pueblo History. In *Religious Transformation in the Late Pre-Hispanic Pueblo World*, edited by Donna M. Glowacki and Scott Van Keuren, pp. 221–238. University of Arizona Press, Tucson.

2013 *An Archaeology of the Cosmos: Rethinking Agency and Religion in Ancient America*. Routledge, New York.

Pederson, Morten A.

2001 Totemism, Animism, and North Asian Indigenous Ontologies. *Journal of the Royal Anthropological Institute* 7:411–427.

Phillips, Bruce G.

2008 Flotation Analysis. In *Data Recovery at Six Sites in the 66 Acre Desert Rose Development in South Phoenix, Arizona*, edited by Corey Dale Breternitz, Brandie M. Stork, and Christine K. Robinson, pp. 7.1–7.8. Occasional Papers No. 9. Pueblo Grande Museum, Phoenix. Technical Report No. 06-38. Soil Systems, Phoenix.

Phillips, David A., Jr., Christine S. VanPool, and Todd L. VanPool

2006 The Horned Serpent Tradition in the North American Southwest. In *Religion in the Prehispanic Southwest*, edited by Christine S. VanPool, Todd L. VanPool, and David A. Phillips Jr., pp. 17–29. Archaeology of Religion No. 5. AltaMira Press, Lanham, Maryland.

Piaget, Jean

1929 *The Child's Conception of the World*. Harcourt Brace Jovanovich, New York.

Porr, Martin, and Hannah Rachel Bell

2012 "Rock-Art," "Animism" and Two-Way Thinking: Toward a Complementary Epistemology in Understanding of Material Culture and "Rock-Art" of Hunting and Gathering People. *Journal of Archaeological Method and Theory* 19:161–205.

Potter, James M.

2004 The Creation of Person, the Creation of Place: Hunting Landscapes in the American Southwest. *American Antiquity* 69:322–338.

Potter, James M., and Elizabeth M. Perry

2000 Ritual as a Power Resource in the American Southwest. In *Alternative Leadership Strategies in the Prehistoric Southwest*, edited by Barbara J. Mills, pp. 60–78. University of Arizona Press, Tucson.

Potter, Russell M., and George R. Rossman

1977 Desert Varnish: The Importance of Clay Minerals. *Science* 196(4297):1446–1448.

Preucel, Robert W.

1996 Cooking Status: Hohokam Ideology, Power, and Social Reproduction. In *Interpreting Southwestern Diversity: Underlying Principles and Overarching Patterns*, edited by Paul R. Fish and J. Jefferson Reid, pp. 125–131. Anthropological Research Papers No. 48. Arizona State University, Tempe.

Quinlan, Angus R.

2000a The Ventriloquist's Dummy: A Critical Review of Shamanism and Rock Art in Far Western North America. *Journal of California and Great Basin Anthropology* 22:92–108.

2000b Reply to Whitley. *Journal of California and Great Basin Anthropology* 22:129–132.

Quinlan, Angus R., and Alanah Woody

2003 Marks of Distinction: Rock Art and Ethnic Identification in the Great Basin. *American Antiquity* 68:372–390.

Rafn, Charles Christian

1845 *Antiquitates Americanae*. Societas Regia Antiquariorum Septentrionalium, Copenhagen.

Rainbird, Paul

2002 Making Sense of Petroglyphs: The Sound of Rock Art. In *Inscribed Landscapes: Marking and Making Place*, edited by Bruno David and Meredith Wilson, pp. 93–103. University of Hawaii Press, Honolulu.

Rakita, Gordon F. M.
2009 *Ancestors and Elites: Emergent Complexity and Ritual Practices in the Casas Grandes Polity.* AltaMira Press, Walnut Creek, California.

Rakita, Gordon F. M., and Jane E. Buikstra (compilers)
2008 *An Archaeological Perspective on Ritual, Religion, and Ideology from* American Antiquity *and* Latin American Antiquity. SAA Press, Washington, D.C.

Ranger, Terence
2007 Living Ritual and Indigenous Archaeology: The Case of Zimbabwe. In *The Archaeology of Ritual*, edited by Evangelos Kyriakidis, pp. 123–153. Advanced Seminar No. 3. Cotsen Institute of Archaeology, University of California, Los Angeles.

Rappaport, Roy A.
1971 Ritual, Sanctity, and Cybernetics. *American Anthropologist* 73:59–76.
1979 *Ecology, Meaning and Religion.* North Atlantic Books, Richmond, California.
1999 *Ritual and Religion in the Making of Humanity.* Cambridge Studies in Social and Cultural Anthropology No. 110. Cambridge University Press, Cambridge.

Reagan, Albert B.
1933 Some Notes on the Snake Pictographs of Nine Mile Canyon, Utah. *American Anthropologist* 35:550–551.
1935 Petroglyphs Show that the Ancients of the Southwest Wore Masks. *American Anthropologist* 37:707–708.

Reff, Daniel T.
1991 Anthropological Analysis of Exploration Texts: Cultural Discourse and the Ethnological Import of Fray Marcos de Niza's Journey to Cibola. *American Anthropologist* 93:636–655.

Reinach, Solomon
1903 L'arte et la magie: A propos des peintures et des gravures de l'âge du renne. *L'Anthropologie* 14:257–266.

Renfrew, Colin
1985 *The Archaeology of Cult: The Sanctuary at Phylakopi.* Thames and Hudson, London.
1994 The Archaeology of Religion. In *The Ancient Mind*, edited by Colin Renfrew and Ezra B. W. Zubrow, pp. 47–54. New Directions in Archaeology No. 1. Cambridge University Press, Cambridge.

Reynolds, Ffion
2009 Regenerating Substances: Quartz as an Animistic Agent. *Time and Mind* 2:153–156.

Reynolds, Stephen J.
1985 *Geology of the South Mountains, Central Arizona.* Bulletin No. 195. Arizona Bureau of Geology and Mineral Technology, Geological Survey Branch, University of Arizona, Tucson.

Rice, Glen E.
1987a The Marana Community: A Twelfth Century Hohokam Chiefdom. In *Studies in the Hohokam Community of Marana*, edited by Glen E. Rice, pp. 249–253. Anthropological Field Studies No. 15. Arizona State University, Tempe.
1987b *A Spatial Analysis of the Hohokam Community of La Ciudad.* Anthropological Field Studies No. 16. Office of Cultural Resource Management, Department of Anthropology, Arizona State University, Tempe.
1990 Variability in the Development of Classic Period Elites. In *A Design for Salado Research*, edited by Glen E. Rice, pp. 31–40. Roosevelt Monograph Series No. 1. Anthropological Field Studies No. 22. Arizona State University, Tempe.
1992 Modeling the Development of Complexity in the Sonoran Desert of Arizona. In *Developing Perspectives on Tonto Basin Prehistory*, edited by Charles L. Redman, Glen E. Rice, and Kathryn E. Pedrick, pp. 11–26. Anthropological Field Studies No. 26. Arizona State University, Tempe.
1995 Special Artifacts and Evidence for the Differentiation of Residential and Ritual Rooms at Bass Point Mound. In *Where the Rivers Converge: Roosevelt Platform Mound Study; Report on the Rock Island Complex*, edited by Owen Lindauer, pp. 331–349. Roosevelt Monograph Series No. 4. Anthropological Field Studies No. 33. Arizona State University, Tempe.
1998 War and Water: An Ecological Perspective on Hohokam Irrigation. *Kiva* 63(3):263–301.
2000 Hohokam and Salado Segmentary Organization: The Evidence from the Roosevelt Platform Mound Study. In *Salado*, edited by Jeffrey S. Dean, pp. 143–166. University of New Mexico Press, Albuquerque.
2001 Warfare and Massing in the Salt and Gila Basins of Central Arizona. In *Deadly Land-*

scapes: Case Studies in Prehistoric Southwestern Warfare, edited by Glen E. Rice and Steven A. LeBlanc, pp. 289–330. University of Utah Press, Salt Lake City.

Rice, Glen E., John L. Czarzasty, Christopher Watkins, and Erik Steinbach
2009 Findings of the Las Canopas Data Recovery Project. In *Excavations at Las Canopas: A Hohokam Village in the Phoenix Basin*, edited by John L. Czarzasty and Glen E. Rice, pp. 325–347. Anthropological Papers No. 17. Pueblo Grande Museum, Phoenix.

Rice, Glen E., and Steven A. LeBlanc (editors)
2001 *Deadly Landscapes: Case Studies in Prehistoric Southwestern Warfare*. University of Utah Press, Salt Lake City.

Rice, Glen E., and Kathleen Peterson
2009 History of Hohokam Ceramic Production and Exchange on Canal Seven. In *Excavations at Las Canopas: A Hohokam Village in the Phoenix Basin*, edited by John L. Czarzasty and Glen E. Rice, pp. 63–93. Anthropological Papers No. 17. Pueblo Grande Museum, Phoenix.

Riel-Salvatore, Julien
2005 Limitations of Shamanistic Interpretive Models for Southern Africa and Upper Paleolithic Rock Art. In *Making Marks: Graduate Studies in Rock Art Research at the New Millennium*, edited by Jennifer K. K. Huang and Elizabeth V. Culley, pp. 93–100. Occasional Paper No. 5. American Rock Art Research Association, Tucson, Arizona.

Riley, Carroll L.
1963 Color-Direction Symbolism. An Example of Mexican-Southwestern Contacts. *América Indígena* 23(1):49–58.
1975 The Road to Hawikuh: Trade and Trade Routes to Cibola-Zuni during Late Prehistoric and Historic Times. *Kiva* 41(2):137–159.

Ringrose, Trevor J.
1992 Bootstrapping and Correspondence Analysis in Archaeology. *Journal of Archaeological Science* 19:615–629.

Robb, John E.
1998 The Archaeology of Symbols. *Annual Review of Anthropology* 27:329–346.

Robbins, Joel
2001 Ritual Communication and Linguistic Ideology: A Reading and Partial Reformulation of Rappaport's Theory of Ritual. *Current Anthropology* 42:591–605.

Robinson, David W.
2010 Land Use, Land Ideology: An Integrated Geographic Information Systems Analysis of Rock Art within South-Central California. *American Antiquity* 75:792–818.

Rodgers, James B.
1974 *An Archaeological Survey of the Cave Buttes Dam Alternative Site and Reservoir, Arizona*. Anthropological Research Papers No. 8. Arizona State University, Tempe.
1976 *An Archaeological Investigation of Buckeye Hills East, Maricopa County, Arizona*. Anthropological Research Papers No. 10. Arizona State University, Tempe.
1977 *An Archaeological Investigation of the Granite Reef Aqueduct, Cave Creek Archaeological District, Arizona*. Anthropological Research Papers No. 12. Arizona State University, Tempe.

Rogers, Adam C.
2008 Religious Place and Its Interaction with Urbanization in the Roman Era. *Journal of Social Archaeology* 8:37–62.

Rogers, Malcolm
1939 *Early Lithic Industries of the Colorado River and Adjacent Desert Areas*. Papers No. 3. Museum of Man, San Diego, California.
1966 *Ancient Hunters of the Far West*. Union-Tribune Publishing Co., San Diego, California.

Ross, June, and Iain Davidson
2006 Rock Art and Ritual: An Archaeological Analysis of Rock Art in Arid Central Australia. *Journal of Archaeological Method and Theory* 13:305–341.

Rowe, Marvin W.
2005 Dating Studies of Prehistoric Pictographs in North America. In *Discovering North American Rock Art*, edited by Lawrence L. Loendorf, Christopher Chippindale, and David S. Whitley, pp. 240–264. University of Arizona Press, Tucson.

Ruscavage-Barz, Samantha M.
1993 Los Guanacos Ceramics. In *Archaeological Investigations at Los Guanacos: Exploring Cultural Changes in Late Hohokam Society*, edited by Todd L. Howell, pp. 53–69. Northland Research, Flagstaff, Arizona.

Ruscavage-Barz, Samantha M., and Elizabeth A. Bagwell
2006 Gathering Spaces and Bounded Places: The Religious Significance of Plaza-Oriented

Communities in the Northern Rio Grande, New Mexico. In *Religion in the Prehispanic Southwest*, edited by Christine S. VanPool, Todd L. VanPool, and David A. Phillips Jr., pp. 81–101. Archaeology of Religion No. 5. AltaMira Press, Lanham, Maryland.

Rusling, James F.

1877 *The Great West and Pacific Coast; Or Fifteen Thousand Miles by Stage-Coach, Ambulance, Horseback, Railroad, and Steamer—Across the Continent and along the Pacific Slope—Through the Rocky Mountains, Down the Columbia River, Over the Sierra Nevadas—among Indians, Mormons, Miners and Mexicans*. Sheldon, New York.

Russell, Bertrand

1938 *Power: A New Social Analysis*. Allen and Unwin, London.

Russell, Frank

1908 The Pima Indians. *Annual Report of the Bureau of American Ethnology* 26:3–339. Smithsonian Institution, U.S. Government Printing Office, Washington, D.C.

Russell, Roger

1940 Studies in Animism: II. The Development of Animism. *Journal of Genetic Psychology* 56:353–366.

Russell, Roger, and Wayne Dennis

1939 Studies in Animism, I: A Standardized Procedure for the Investigation of Animism. *Journal of Genetic Psychology* 55:389–400.

Russell, William G.

2014 Keeping Track: Ceremonial Racetracks, Integration, and Change in Central Arizona. In *Alliance and Landscape on Perry Mesa in the Fourteenth Century*, edited by David R. Abbott and Katherine A. Spielmann, pp. 161–185. University of Utah Press, Salt Lake City.

Russell, William G., Hoski Schaafsma, and Katherine Spielmann

2011 Toward Common Ground: Racing as an Integrative Strategy in Prehistoric Central Arizona, A.D. 1000–1400. *Kiva* 76(4):377–411.

Russell, William G., and Aaron M. Wright

2008 How Far Is a Pipette? Iconographic Evidence for Inter-regional Connectivity in the Prehistoric Southwest and Beyond. *Artifact* 46: 19–45.

2009 Footprints to the South: The Search for Proto-Hopi Clan Symbols in the South Mountains of Phoenix, Arizona. In *American Indian Rock Art*, Vol. 35, edited by James D. Keyser, David Kaiser, George Poetschat, and Michael W. Taylor, pp. 43–60. American Rock Art Research Association, Tucson, Arizona.

Russell, William G., Aaron M. Wright, Tina Carpenter, and Caitlin Guthrie

2009 Stained Rocks and Storied Walls: Fertility, Sexuality, and Rock Art in the Hohokam Landscape. In *American Indian Rock Art*, Vol. 35, edited by James D. Keyser, David Kaiser, George Poetschat, and Michael W. Taylor, pp. 27–42. American Rock Art Research Association, Tucson, Arizona.

Saitta, Dean J.

1994 Class and Community in the Prehistoric Southwest. In *The Ancient Southwestern Community: Models and Methods for the Study of Prehistoric Social Organization*, edited by Wirt H. Wills and Robert D. Leonard, pp. 25–43. University of New Mexico Press, Albuquerque.

Salmon, Wesley

1973 *Logic*. 2nd ed. Prentice-Hall, Englewood Cliffs, New Jersey.

Saunders, Nicholas J.

1988 *Chatoyer*: Anthropological Reflections on Archaeological Mirrors. In *Recent Studies in Pre-Columbian Archaeology*, edited by Nicholas J. Saunders and Oliver de Montmollin, pp. 1–40. BAR International Series No. 42. Archaeopress, Oxford.

Savage, Steve, and Todd W. Bostwick

2001 The Pueblo Grande Museum Database. Electronic resource managed by Pueblo Grande Museum, Phoenix, accessed May 6, 2010.

Scarre, Christopher

2008 Shrines of the Land and Places of Power: Religion and the Transition to Farming in Western Europe. In *Belief in the Past: Theoretical Approaches to the Archaeology of Religion*, edited by David S. Whitley and Kelley A. Hays-Gilpin, pp. 209–226. Left Coast Press, Walnut Creek, California.

Schaafsma, Polly

1980 *Indian Rock Art of the Southwest*. University of New Mexico Press, Albuquerque.

1985 Form, Content, and Function: Theory and Method in North American Rock Art Studies. In *Advances in Archaeological Method and Theory*, Vol. 8, edited by Michael B. Schiffer, pp. 237–277. Academic Press, New York.

1994 Trance and Transformation in the Canyons:

Shamanism and Early Rock Art on the Colorado Plateau. In *Shamanism and Rock Art in North America*, edited by Solveig A. Turpin, pp. 45–72. Rock Art Foundation, San Antonio, Texas.
1999 Tlalocs, Kachinas, Sacred Bundles, and Related Symbolism in the Southwest and Mesoamerica. In *The Casas Grandes World*, edited by Curtis F. Schaafsma and Carroll L. Riley, pp. 164–192. University of Utah Press, Salt Lake City.
2000 *Warrior, Shield, and Star: Imagery and Ideology of Pueblo Warfare*. West Edge Press, Santa Fe, New Mexico.
2001 Quetzalcoatl and the Horned and Feathered Serpent of the Southwest. In *Road to Aztlan: Art from a Mythic Homeland*, edited by Virginia M. Fields and Victor Zamudio-Taylor, pp. 102–123. Los Angeles County Museum of Art, Los Angeles.

Schaafsma, Polly, and Karl A. Taube
2006 Bringing the Rain: An Ideology of Rain Making in the Pueblo Southwest and Mesoamerica. In *A Pre-Columbian World*, edited by Jeffrey Quilter and Mary Miller, pp. 231–286. Dumbarton Oaks Research Library and Collection, Washington, D.C.

Schachner, Gregson
2001 Ritual Control and Transformation in Middle-Range Societies: An Example from the American Southwest. *Journal of Anthropological Archaeology* 20:168–194.

Schmidt, Erich F.
1928 *Time-Relations of Prehistoric Pottery Types in Southern Arizona*. Anthropological Papers Vol. 30, Part 5. American Museum of Natural History, New York.

Schoonover, Grace, and Christine H. Virden
1999 Prehistoric Rock Art in the McDowell Mountains Region: A Preliminary Overview of Several Sites. In *McDowell Mountains Archaeological Symposium*, edited by K. J. Schroeder, pp. 231–250. Publications in Anthropology No. 10. Roadrunner Archaeology, Tempe, Arizona.

Schroeder, Albert Henry
1953 The Bearing of Architecture on the Developments in the Hohokam Classic Period. *Southwestern Journal of Anthropology* 9: 174–194.

Searcy, Michael T.
2010 *Symbols and Sociopolitical Organization: Mesoamerican Iconography in the U.S. Southwest/Northwest Mexico*. Ph.D. dissertation, Department of Anthropology, University of Oklahoma, Norman. University Microfilms, Ann Arbor, Michigan.

Shanks, Michael, and Christopher Tilley
1987 *Social Theory and Archaeology*. Polity Press, Cambridge.

Shaul, David Leedom, and John M. Andresen
1989 A Case for Yuman Participation in the Hohokam Regional System. *Kiva* 54(2):105–126.

Shaul, David Leedom, and Jane H. Hill
1998 Tepimans, Yumans, and Other Hohokam. *American Antiquity* 63:375–396.

Shennan, Stephen
1997 *Quantifying Archaeology*. 2nd ed. University of Iowa Press, Iowa City.

Sheridan, Alan
1980 *Michel Foucault: The Will to Truth*. Tavistock, London.

Sheridan, Susan Guise
2003 Childhood Health as an Indicator of Biological Stress. In *Centuries of Decline during the Hohokam Classic Period at Pueblo Grande*, edited by David R. Abbott, pp. 82–106. University of Arizona Press, Tucson.

Siegel, Ronald K.
1977 Hallucinations. *Scientific American* 237:132–140.

Simon, Arleyn W., Jennifer K. K. Huang, Tina C. Hart, and Will G. Russell
2014 Demarcation of Landscape: Rock Art Evidence for Alliance, Conflict, and Subsistence at Perry Mesa. In *Alliance and Landscape on Perry Mesa in the Fourteenth Century*, edited by David R. Abbott and Katherine A. Spielmann, pp. 104–130. University of Utah Press, Salt Lake City.

Simon, Arleyn W., Aaron M. Wright, Steve Swanson, and Todd W. Bostwick
2013 *Results of Archaeological Test Excavations at the Northeast Terraces, AZ U:9:280(ASM), a Preclassic Hohokam Agricultural and Ritual Complex near the South Mountains, Phoenix, Arizona* (with contributions by Glenn Stuart, Nathan Wilson, and Jessica Blaz). Office of Cultural Resource Management Report. Archaeological Research Institute, Arizona State University, Tempe. In preparation.

Simpson, Bob
1997 Possession, Dispossession and the Social Distribution of Knowledge among Sri Lankan Ritual Specialists. *Journal of the Royal Anthropological Institute* 3:43–59.

Smith, Alexa M.
2000 Zoomorphic Iconography on Preclassic Hohokam Red-on-Buff Pottery: A Whole Vessel Study from the Gila River Basin. *Kiva* 66(2):223–247.
2001 The GARP Whole Vessels. In *The Grewe Archaeological Research Report, Vol. 2: Material Culture, Part 1: Ceramic Studies*, edited by David R. Abbott, pp. 107–124. Anthropological Papers No. 99-1. Northland Research, Flagstaff, Arizona.

Smith, Claire
1992 The Articulation of Style and Social Structure in Australian Aboriginal Art. *Australian Aboriginal Studies* 1:28–34.

Smith, Jamie K., and Glen E. Rice
2009 Changes in Hohokam Demographic Patterns in the Phoenix Basin. In *Excavations at Las Canopas: A Hohokam Village in the Phoenix Basin*, edited by John L. Czarzasty and Glen E. Rice, pp. 249–266. Anthropological Papers No. 17. Pueblo Grande Museum, Phoenix.

Smith, Johnathan Z.
1987 *To Take Place: Toward Theory in Ritual*. University of Chicago Press, Chicago.

Smith, Pierre
1982 Aspects of the Organization of Rites. In *Between Belief and Transgression: Structuralist Essays in Religion, History and Myth*, edited by Michael Izard and Pierre Smith, pp. 103–128. University of Chicago Press, Chicago.

Snead, James E.
2006 Mirror of the Earth: Water, Landscape, and Meaning in the Precolumbian Southwest. In *Precolumbian Water Management: Ideology, Ritual, and Power*, edited by Lisa Lucero and Barbara Fash, pp. 205–220. University of Arizona Press, Tucson.
2008 *Ancestral Landscapes of the Pueblo World*. University of Arizona Press, Tucson.

Snyder, Ernest
1966 Petroglyphs of the South Mountains of Arizona. *American Antiquity* 31:705–709.
1975 Petroglyphs of the South Mountains of Arizona. In *American Indian Rock Art*, Vol. 1, edited by Shari T. Grove, pp. 105–109. American Rock Art Research Association, Tucson, Arizona.

Spaulding, Albert C.
1953 Statistical Techniques for the Discovery of Artifact Types. *American Antiquity* 18: 305–313.
1977 On Growth and Form in Archaeology: Multivariate Analysis. *Journal of Anthropological Research* 33:1–15.

Spencer, Walter Baldwin, and Francis James Gillen
1899 *The Native Tribes of Central Australia*. Macmillan, London.

Spier, Leslie
1933 *Yuman Tribes of the Gila River*. University of Chicago Press, Chicago.

Sprague, Roderick
1964 Inventory of Prehistoric Southwestern Copper Bells: Additions and Corrections I. *Kiva* 30(1):18–24.

Sprague, Roderick, and Aldo Signori
1963 Inventory of Prehistoric Southwestern Copper Bells. *Kiva* 28(4):1–20.

Steadman, Sharon R.
2009 *Archaeology of Religion: Cultures and Their Beliefs in Worldwide Context*. Left Coast Press, Walnut Creek, California.

Stein, John R., and Stephen H. Lekson
1992 Anasazi Ritual Landscapes. In *Anasazi Regional Organization and the Chaco System*, edited by David E. Doyel, pp. 87–100. Anthropological Papers No. 5. Maxwell Museum of Anthropology, University of New Mexico, Albuquerque.

Stein, Pat
1981 *The Palo Verde Archaeological Investigations: Part 1, Aboriginal Resources at the Palo Verde Plant Site*. Research Report No. 21. Museum of Northern Arizona Press, Flagstaff.

Stephen, Alexander M.
1936 *Hopi Journal of Alexander M. Stephen*. 2 vols. Edited by Elsie Clews Parsons. Contributions to Anthropology No. 23. Columbia University Press, New York.

Stevenson, Matilda Coxe
1904 *The Zuñi Indians*. Annual Report of the Bureau of American Ethnology, Vol. 23. U.S. Government Printing Office, Washington, D.C.

Steward, Julian H.
1929 Petroglyphs of California and Adjoining States. *University of California Publications in American Archaeology and Ethnology* 24:52–238. Los Angeles.
1936 The Economic and Social Basis of Primitive Bands. In *Essays in Honor of A. L. Kroeber*, edited by Robert H. Lowie, pp. 331–350. University of California Press, Berkeley.
1937 Petroglyphs of the United States. In *Annual Report of the Board of Regents of the Smithso-*

nian Institution Showing the Operations, Expenditures, and Condition of the Institution for the Year Ended June 30 1936*, compiled by Charles G. Abbott, pp. 391–426. Publication No. 3405. U.S. Government Printing Office, Washington, D.C.

1942 The Direct Historical Approach to Archaeology. *American Antiquity* 7:337–343.

1968 Foreword. In *Rock Drawings of the Coso Range, Inyo County, California*, by Campbell Grant, James W. Baird, and J. Kenneth Pringle, pp. vii–x. Manturango Museum Publication No. 4. China Lake, California.

Stewart, Angus

2001 *Theories of Power and Domination: The Politics of Empowerment in Late Modernity.* Sage Publications, London.

Stinson, Susan

2004 *Household Ritual, Gender, and Figurines in the Hohokam Regional System.* Ph.D. dissertation, Department of Anthropology, University of Arizona, Tucson. University Microfilms, Ann Arbor, Michigan.

2005 Remembering the Ancestors: Ceramic Figurines from Las Capas and Los Pozos. In *Material Cultures and Lifeways of Early Agricultural Sites in Southern Arizona*, edited by R. Jane Sliva, pp. 207–216. Anthropological Papers No. 35. Center for Desert Archaeology, Tucson, Arizona.

2010 Gender, Household Ritual, and Figurines in the Hohokam Ritual System. In *Engendering Households in the Prehistoric Southwest*, edited by Barbara J. Roth, pp. 116–135. University of Arizona Press, Tucson.

Stockett, Miranda K.

2007 Performing Power: Identity, Ritual, and Materiality in a Late Classic Southeast Mesoamerican Crafting Community. *Ancient Mesoamerica* 18:91–105.

Stocking, George W., Jr.

1971 Animism in Theory and Practice: E. B. Tylor's Unpublished Notes on "Spiritualism." *Man* 6:88–104.

Stone, Andrea

1992 From Ritual in the Landscape to Capture in the Urban Center: The Recreation of Ritual Environments in Mesoamerica. *Journal of Ritual Studies* 6:110–132.

Stone, Tammy

2003 Hohokam Exchange in Social Context. In *Centuries of Decline during the Hohokam Classic Period at Pueblo Grande*, edited by David R. Abbott, pp. 128–147. University of Arizona Press, Tucson.

Stone, Tammy, and Michael S. Foster

1994 Miscellaneous Artifacts. In *The Pueblo Grande Project, Vol. 4: Material Culture*, edited by Michael S. Foster, pp. 203–262. Publications in Archaeology No. 20. Soil Systems, Phoenix.

Stortz, Martha Ellen

1996 Ritual Power, Ritual Authority: Configurations and Reconfigurations in the Era of Manifestations. In *Religious and Social Ritual: Interdisciplinary Explorations*, edited by Michael B. Aune and Valerie DeMarinis, pp. 105–135. State University of New York Press, Albany.

Stringer, Martin D.

1999 Rethinking Animism: Thoughts from the Infancy of Our Discipline. *Journal of the Royal Anthropological Institute* 5:541–555.

Strong, William Duncan

1935 *An Introduction to Nebraska Archaeology.* Miscellaneous Collections Vol. 93, No. 10. Smithsonian Institution, Washington, D.C.

Stuart, Glenn S. L.

2013 Appendix: Paleoethnobotany of Prehistoric Agricultural Terraces, South Mountain Park, Phoenix, Arizona. In *Results of Archaeological Test Excavations at the Northeast Terraces, AZ U:9:280 (ASM), a Preclassic Hohokam Agricultural and Ritual Complex near the South Mountains, South-Central Arizona*, by Arleyn W. Simon, Aaron M. Wright, Steve Swanson, and Todd Bostwick. Office of Cultural Resource Management Report. Archaeological Research Institute, Arizona State University, Tempe. In preparation.

Stubing, Michael, and Douglas R. Mitchell

1999 The Fountain Hills Archaic: Archaeological Testing of Sites AZ U:5:182 (ASM) and AZ U:5:188 (ASM). In *McDowell Mountains Archaeological Symposium*, edited by K. J. Schroeder, pp. 15–26. Publications in Anthropology No. 10. Roadrunner Archaeology, Tempe, Arizona.

Sundstrom, Linea

1990 *Rock Art of the Southern Black Hills: A Contextual Approach.* Garland Publishing, New York.

2002 Prayers in Stone: Hoofprint-Vulva-Groove Rock Art in the Context of Northern Plains Religion. In *Rock Art and Culture Processes*, edited by Solveig Turpin, pp. 1–26. Special

Publication No. 3. Rock Art Foundation, San Antonio, Texas.

Sutherland, Kay

1998 Mesoamerican Ceremony among the Prehistoric Jornada Mogollon. In *Rock Art of the Chihuahuan Desert Borderlands*, edited by Sheron Smith-Savage and Robert J. Mallouf, pp. 61–87. Center for Big Bend Studies Occasional Papers No. 3. Sull Ross State University and Texas Parks and Wildlife Department, Alpine, Texas.

Sutton, Mark Q.

1982 Kawaiisu Mythology and Rock Art: One Example. *Journal of California and Great Basin Anthropology* 4:148–154.

Swanson, Steve, and Todd W. Bostwick

2007 South Mountain Rock Art Project Field Manual: Recording Rock Art as Archaeology in the South Mountains. Rev. ed. Manuscript on file, Pueblo Grande Museum, Phoenix.

Swartz, Benjamin K., Jr., and Thomas S. Hurlbutt

1994 Space, Place and Territory in Rock Art Interpretation. *Rock Art Research* 11:13–22.

Swartz, Benjamin K., Jr., and John K. Zancanella

1991 The Management and Recording Procedures in the Preservation of Petroglyph Resources. In *Rock Art and Posterity: Conserving, Managing, and Recording Rock Art*, edited by Colin Pearson and Benjamin K. Swartz Jr., pp. 115–116. Occasional Paper No. 4. Australian Rock Art Research Association, Melbourne.

Tambiah, Stanley J.

1968 The Magical Power of Words. *Man* 3:175–208.

1990 *Magic, Science, Religion, and the Scope of Rationality.* Cambridge University Press, Cambridge.

Tanner, Clara Lee

1976 *Prehistoric Southwestern Craft Arts.* University of Arizona Press, Tucson.

Taube, Karl A.

2000 Lightning Celts and Corn Fetishes: The Formative Olmec and the Development of Maize Symbolism in Mesoamerica and the American Southwest. In *Olmec Art and Archaeology: Social Complexity in the Formative Period*, edited by John E. Clark and Mary Pye, pp. 296–337. Studies in the History of Art No. 58. National Gallery of Art, Washington, D.C.

2001 The Breath of Life: The Symbolism of Wind in Mesoamerica and the American Southwest. In *The Road to Aztlan: Art from a Mythic Homeland*, edited by Virginia M. Fields and Victor Zamudio-Taylor, pp. 102–123. Los Angeles County Museum of Art, Los Angeles.

Teague, Lynn S.

1985 The Organization of Hohokam Exchange. In *Proceedings of the 1983 Hohokam Symposium*, edited by Alfred E. Dittert Jr. and Donald E. Dove, pp. 397–419. Occasional Paper No. 2. Arizona Archaeological Society, Phoenix.

1988 The Postclassic and the Fate of the Hohokam. In *The 1982–1984 Excavations at Las Colinas, Vol. 6: Synthesis and Conclusions*, by Lynn S. Teague and William L. Deaver, pp. 145–167. Archaeological Series No. 162. Arizona State Museum, University of Arizona, Tucson.

1993 Prehistory and the Traditions of the O'odham and Hopi. *Kiva* 58(4):435–454.

Teague, Lynn S., and William L. Deaver

1989 *The 1982–1984 Excavations at Las Colinas, Vol. 6: Synthesis and Conclusions.* Archaeological Series No. 162. Arizona State Museum, University of Arizona, Tucson.

Teggart, Frederick J.

1913 *The Anza Expedition of 1775–1776, Diary of Pedro Font.* Publications of the Academy of Pacific Coast History Vol. 3, No. 1. University of California, Berkeley.

Thiagarajan, Nivedita, and Cin-Ty A. Lee

2004 Trace-Element Evidence for the Origin of Desert Varnish by Direct Aqueous Atmospheric Deposition. *Earth and Planetary Science Letters* 224:131–141.

Thomas, Charles Matthew, and Jeffrey Howard King

1985 Hohokam Figurine Assemblages: A Suggested Ritual Context. In *Proceedings of the 1983 Hohokam Symposium, Part 2*, edited by Alfred E. Dittert Jr. and Donald E. Dove, pp. 687–732. Occasional Paper No. 2. Arizona Archaeological Society, Phoenix.

Thomas, David Hurst

1974 Nonsite Sampling in Archaeology: Up the Creek without a Site? In *Sampling in Archaeology*, edited by James W. Mueller, pp. 61–81. University of Arizona Press, Tucson.

Thomas, Julian

1993 The Hermeneutics of Megalithic Space. In *Interpretive Archaeology*, edited by Christopher Tilley, pp. 73–97. Berg, Oxford.

2001 Archaeologies of Place and Landscape. In *Archaeological Theory Today*, edited by Ian Hodder, pp. 165–186. Polity Press, Cambridge.
2004 *Archaeology and Modernity*. Routledge, London.

Thomas, Trudy
1983 Material Culture of Gatecliff Shelter: Incised Stones. In *The Archaeology of Monitor Valley 2: Gatecliff Shelter*, by David Hurst Thomas, pp. 246–278. Anthropological Papers Vol. 59, Part 1. Museum of Natural History, New York.

Thompson, J. Eric S.
1970 *Maya History and Religion*. University of Oklahoma Press, Norman.

Thwaites, Reuben Gold (editor and translator)
1900 *The Jesuit Relations and Allied Documents: Travels and Explorations of the Jesuit Missionaries in New France, 1610–1791*. Vol. 59. Imperial Press, Cleveland, Ohio.

Tilley, Christopher
1994 *A Phenomenology of Landscape: Places, Paths and Monuments*. Oxford University Press, Oxford.
2004 *The Materiality of Stone: Explorations in Landscape Phenomenology*. Berg, Oxford.

Titiev, Mischa
1937 A Hopi Salt Expedition. *American Anthropologist* 39:244–258.
1944 *Old Oraibi: A Study of the Hopi Indians of Third Mesa*. Papers of the Peabody Museum of American Archaeology and Ethnology Vol. 22, No. 1. Harvard University, Cambridge, Massachusetts.

Townsend, Richard F.
1982 Pyramid and Sacred Mountain. In *Archaeoastronomy and Ethnoastronomy in the American Tropics*, edited by Anthony Aveni and Gary Urton, pp. 37–62. Annals Vol. 385. New York Academy of Sciences, New York.
1992 The Renewal of Nature at the Temple of Tlaloc. In *The Ancient Americas: Art from Sacred Landscapes*, edited by Richard F. Townsend, pp. 171–186. Art Institute of Chicago, Chicago.
2000 *The Aztecs*. Rev. ed. Thames and Hudson, New York.

Trigger, Bruce G.
1989 *A History of Archaeological Thought*. Cambridge University Press, Cambridge.

Tripcevich, Nicholas
2004 Mobile GIS in Archaeological Survey. *SAA Archaeological Record* 4(3):17–22.

Troncoso Melendez, Andrés
2008 Spatial Syntax of Rock Art. *Rock Art Research* 25:3–11.

Tuan, Yi-Fu
1976 Geopiety: A Theme in Man's Attachment to Nature and to Place. In *Geographies of the Mind*, edited by David Lowenthal and Martyn J. Bowden, pp. 11–39. Oxford University Press, New York.

Turner, Christy G., II
1963 *Petrographs of the Glen Canyon Region*. Museum of Northern Arizona Bulletin No. 38, Glen Canyon Series No. 4. Northern Arizona Society of Science and Art, Flagstaff.

Turner, Victor
1966 *The Ritual Process: Structure and Anti-structure*. Aldine, Chicago.
1968 *The Drums of Affliction*. Oxford University Press, Oxford.
1974 *Dramas, Fields and Metaphors: Symbolic Action in Human Society*. Cornell University Press, Ithaca, New York.
1982 *From Ritual to Theatre: The Human Seriousness of Play*. Performing Arts Journal Publications, New York.

Turney, Omar A.
1924 *The Land of the Stone Hoe*. Arizona Republican Print Shop, Phoenix.
1928 Why Pictured Rocks? *Arizona, Old and New* 1(1):8–9, 24–27.
1929 *Prehistoric Irrigation in Arizona*. Arizona Historical Review 2(1–4). Arizona State Historian, Phoenix.

Turpin, Solveig A. (editor)
1994 *Shamanism and Rock Art in North America*. Special Publication No. 1. Rock Art Foundation, San Antonio, Texas.

Tylor, Edward Burnett
1871 *Primitive Culture: Researches into the Development of Mythology, Philosophy, Religion, Art, and Custom*. 2 vols. John Murray, London.

Ucko, Peter J., and Robert Layton (editors)
1999 *The Archaeology and Anthropology of Landscape: Shaping Your Landscape*. Routledge, New York.

Ucko, Peter J., and Andree Rosenfeld
1967 *Palaeolithic Cave Art*. McGraw-Hill, New York.

Underhill, Ruth M.
1938 *Singing for Power: The Song Magic of the Papago Indians of Arizona*. University of California Press, Berkeley.

1939 *Social Organization of the Papago Indians.* Columbia University Press, New York.

1946 *Papago Indian Religion.* Columbia University Press, New York.

1948 *Ceremonial Patterns in the Greater Southwest.* American Ethnological Society Monograph No. 13. J. J. Augustin, New York.

Underhill, Ruth M., Donald M. Bahr, Baptisto Lopez, Jose Pando, and David Lopez

1979 *Rainhouse and Ocean: Speeches for the Papago Year.* Museum of Northern Arizona Press, Flagstaff.

Upham, Steadman, and Glen E. Rice

1980 Up the Canal without a Paddle: Modeling Hohokam Interaction and Exchange. In *Current Issues in Hohokam Prehistory,* edited by David E. Doyel and Fred Plog, pp. 78–105. Anthropological Research Papers No. 2. Arizona State University, Tempe.

Van Dyke, Ruth M.

2007 *The Chaco Experience: Landscape and Ideology at the Center Place.* School for Advanced Research Press, Santa Fe, New Mexico.

van Gennep, Arnold

1960 *The Rites of Passage.* Translated by Monica B. Vizedom and Gabrielle L. Caffee. University of Chicago Press, Chicago.

1973 On the Method to Be Followed in the Study of Rites and Myths. In *Classical Approaches to the Study of Religion: Aims, Methods and Theories of Research,* Vol. 1, edited by Jacques Waardenburg, pp. 287–300. Mouton, The Hague.

Van Keuren, Scott

2012 The Materiality of Religious Belief in East-Central Arizona. In *Religious Transformation in the Late Pre-Hispanic Pueblo World,* edited by Donna M. Glowacki and Scott Van Keuren, pp. 175–195. University of Arizona Press, Tucson.

Van Keuren, Scott, Susan L. Stinson, and David R. Abbott

1997 Specialized Production of Hohokam Plain Ware Ceramics in the Lower Salt River Valley. *Kiva* 63(2):155–175.

VanPool, Christine S.

2003 The Shaman-Priests of the Casas Grandes Region, Chihuahua. *American Antiquity* 14:696–717.

2009 The Signs of the Sacred: Identifying Shamans Using Archaeological Evidence. *Journal of Anthropological Archaeology* 28:177–190.

VanPool, Christine S., and Elizabeth Newsome

2012 The Spirit in the Material: A Case Study of Animism in the American Southwest. *American Antiquity* 77:243–262.

VanPool, Christine S., and Todd L. VanPool

2007 *Signs of the Casas Grandes Shamans.* University of Utah Press, Salt Lake City.

VanPool, Christine S., Todd L. VanPool, and David A. Phillips Jr. (editors)

2006 *Religion in the Prehispanic Southwest.* Archaeology of Religion No. 5. AltaMira Press, Lanham, Maryland.

VanPool, Todd L., Christine S. VanPool, and David A. Phillips Jr.

2006 The Casas Grandes and Salado Phenomena: Evidence for a Religious Schism in the Greater Southwest. In *Religion in the Prehispanic Southwest,* edited by Christine S. VanPool, Todd L. VanPool, and David A. Phillips Jr., pp. 235–251. Archaeology of Religion No. 5. AltaMira Press, Lanham, Maryland.

Vargas, Victoria D.

1995 *Copper Bell Trade Patterns in the Prehispanic U.S. Southwest and Northwest Mexico.* Archaeological Series No. 187. Arizona State Museum, University of Arizona, Tucson.

2001 Mesoamerican Copper Bells in the Pre-Hispanic Southwestern United States and Northwestern Mexico. In *The Road to Aztlan: Art from a Mythic Homeland,* edited by Virginia M. Fields and Victor Zamudio-Taylor, pp. 196–211. Los Angeles County Museum of Art, Los Angeles.

Varien, Mark D.

1999 *Sedentism and Mobility in a Social Landscape.* University of Arizona Press, Tucson.

Varien, Mark D., and James M. Potter (editors)

2009 *The Social Construction of Communities: Agency, Structure, and Identity in the Prehispanic Southwest.* AltaMira Press, Lanham, Maryland.

Verhoeven, Marc

2002 Ritual and Ideology in the Pre-pottery Neolithic B of the Levant and Southern Anatolia. *Cambridge Archaeological Journal* 12:233–258.

Villa, Niccole, Ronald I. Dorn, and John Clark

1995 Fine Material in Rock Fractures: Aeolian Dust or Weathering? In *Desert Aeolian Processes,* edited by Vatche P. Tchakerian, pp. 219–231. Chapman and Hall, London.

Vinnicombe, Patricia

1967 Rock-Painting Analysis. *South African Archaeological Bulletin* 22:129–141.

1972 Myth, Motive, and Selection in Southern African Rock Art. *Africa* 42:192–204.

Viveiros de Castro, E.

1998 Cosmological Deixis and Amerindian Perspectivism. *Journal of the Royal Anthropological Institute* 4:469–488.

2004 Exchanging Perspectives: The Transformation of Objects into Subjects in Amerindian Ontologies. *Common Knowledge* 10:463–484.

Vivian, Gwinn R.

1965 An Archaeological Survey of the Lower Gila River, Arizona. *Kiva* 30(4):95–146.

1974 Conservation and Diversion: Water-Control Systems in the Anasazi Southwest. In *Irrigation's Impact on Society*, edited by Theodore E. Downing and McGuire Gibson, pp. 95–112. Anthropological Papers No. 25. University of Arizona Press, Tucson.

von Werlhof, Jay C.

1965 Rock Art of Owens Valley, California. *Reports of the University of California Archaeological Survey* 65:1–128. Berkeley.

Walker, William H.

1995 Ceremonial Trash? In *Expanding Archaeology*, edited by James M. Skibo, William H. Walker, and Axel Nielsen, pp. 67–79. University of Utah Press, Salt Lake City.

1996 Ritual Deposits: Another Perspective. In *River of Change: Prehistory of the Middle Little Colorado River*, edited by E. Charles Adams, pp. 75–91. University of Arizona Press, Tucson.

1999 Ritual, Life Histories, and the Afterlives of People and Things. *Journal of the Southwest* 41:383–405.

2002 Stratigraphy and Practical Reason. *American Anthropologist* 104:159–177.

2008 Practice and Nonhuman Social Actors: The Afterlife Histories of Witches and Dogs in the American Southwest. In *Memory Work: Archaeologies of Material Practice*, edited by Barbara J. Mills and William H. Walker, pp. 137–158. School for Advanced Research Press, Santa Fe, New Mexico.

Wallace, Anthony F. C.

1966 *Religion: An Anthropological Review*. Random House, New York.

Wallace, Henry D.

1983 The Mortars, Petroglyphs, and Trincheras on Rillito Peak. *Kiva* 48(3).

1989 *Archaeological Investigations at Petroglyph Sites in the Painted Rock Reservoir Area, Southwestern Arizona*. Technical Report No. 89-5. Institute for American Research, Tucson, Arizona.

1995a Miscellaneous Artifacts. In *Archaeological Investigations at Los Morteros, a Prehistoric Settlement in the Northern Tucson Basin*, Part 2, edited by Henry D. Wallace, pp. 605–659. Anthropological Papers No. 17. Center for Desert Archaeology, Tucson, Arizona.

1995b Decorated Buffware and Brownware Ceramics. In *The Roosevelt Community Development Study, Vol. 2: Ceramic Chronology, Technology, and Economics*, edited by James M. Heidke and Miriam T. Stark, pp. 19–84. Anthropological Papers No. 14. Center for Desert Archaeology, Tucson, Arizona.

1997 Petroglyphs in the Horseshoe Reservoir Area of the Lower Verde Valley, Central Arizona. In *Vanishing River: Landscapes and Lives of the Lower Verde Valley: The Lower Verde Archaeological Project* (on CD-ROM of supplemental data), edited by Stephanie M. Whittlesey, Richard Ciolek-Torrello, and Jeffrey H. Altschul. Statistical Research Press, Tucson, Arizona.

2000 Petroglyph Site Documentation in the Wild Burro and Ruelas Canyons of the Tortolita Mountains. In *Archaeological Testing at Sixteen Sites in the Southern Foothills of the Tortolita Mountains*, edited by James M. Vint, pp. 93–126. Technical Report No. 98-11. Desert Archaeology, Tucson, Arizona.

2001 Time Seriation and Typological Refinement of the Middle Gila Buffware Sequence: Snaketown through Soho Phase. In *Grewe Archaeological Project, Vol. 2: Material Culture, Part 1: Ceramic Studies*, edited by David R. Abbott, pp. 177–261. Anthropological Papers No. 99-1. Northland Research, Tempe, Arizona.

2004 Update to the Middle Gila Buffware Ceramic Sequence. In *Hohokam Farming on the Salt River Floodplain: Refining Models and Analytical Methods*, edited by T. Kathleen Henderson, pp. 45–124. Anthropological Papers No. 10. Pueblo Grande Museum, Phoenix. Anthropological Papers No. 43. Center for Desert Archaeology, Tucson, Arizona.

2008 The Petroglyphs of Atlatl Ridge, Tortolita Mountains, Pima County, Arizona. In *Life in the Foothills: Archaeological Investigations in the Tortolita Mountains of Southern Arizona*, edited by Deborah A. Swartz, pp. 159–231.

Anthropological Papers No. 46. Center for Desert Archaeology, Tucson, Arizona.
2009 Hohokam Multistory Architecture. *Archaeology Southwest* 23(4):13–14.
2014 Ritual Transformation and Cultural Revitalization: Explaining Hohokam in Pre-A.D. 1000 Southeastern Arizona. In *Between Mimbres and Hohokam: Exploring the Archaeology and History of Southeastern Arizona and Southwestern New Mexico*, edited by Henry D. Wallace, pp. 433–500. Archaeology Southwest, Tucson, Arizona.

Wallace, Henry D. (editor)
2003 *Roots of Sedentism: Archaeological Excavations at Valencia Vieja, a Founding Village in the Tucson Basin of Southern Arizona.* Anthropological Papers No. 29. Center for Desert Archaeology, Tucson, Arizona.

Wallace, Henry D., and William H. Doelle
2001 Classic Period Warfare in Southern Arizona. In *Deadly Landscapes: Case Studies in Prehistoric Southwestern Warfare*, edited by Glen E. Rice and Steven A. LeBlanc, pp. 239–288. University of Utah Press, Salt Lake City.

Wallace, Henry D., James M. Heidke, and William H. Doelle
1995 Hohokam Origins. *Kiva* 60(4):575–618.

Wallace, Henry D., and James P. Holmlund
1986 *Petroglyphs of the Picacho Mountains, South Central Arizona.* Anthropological Papers No. 6. Institute for American Research, Tucson, Arizona.

Wallace, Henry D., and Michael W. Lindeman
2003 Valencia Vieja and the Origins of Hohokam Culture. In *Roots of Sedentism: Archaeological Excavations at Valencia Vieja, a Founding Village in the Tucson Basin of Southern Arizona*, edited by Henry D. Wallace, pp. 371–406. Anthropological Papers No. 29. Center for Desert Archaeology, Tucson, Arizona.
2012 Hohokam Village Formation in the Phoenix and Tucson Basins. In *Southwestern Pithouse Communities, AD 200–900*, edited by Lisa C. Young and Sarah A. Herr, pp. 33–44. University of Arizona Press, Tucson.
2013 The Florescence of a Regional Center: Hohokam Cultural Development in the Tucson Basin, A.D. 700 to 1150. In *Hohokam Trajectories in World Perspective*, edited by Paul R. Fish and Suzanne K. Fish. University of Arizona Press, Tucson. In preparation.

Wallis, Robert J.
2009 Re-enchanting Rock Art Landscapes: Animic Ontologies, Nonhuman Agency and Rhizomic Personhood. *Time and Mind* 2:47–70.

Walsh-Anduze, Mary-Ellen
1993 Supplemental Ceramic Analysis. In *Pueblo Viejo: Archaeological Excavations at a Classic Period Cemetery in El Reposo Park, Phoenix, Arizona*, edited by Mark Zyniecki, pp. 69–107. Archaeological Report No. 229-232. SWCA, Flagstaff, Arizona.
1994 The Pueblo Grande Whole Vessel Study: An Examination of Production and Short-Distance Exchange. In *The Pueblo Grande Project, Vol. 3: Ceramics and the Production and Exchange of Pottery in the Central Phoenix Basin, Part 1*, edited by David R. Abbott, pp. 149–259. Publications in Archaeology No. 20. Soil Systems, Phoenix.
1996a Ceramic Temper Studies and Whole Vessel Analysis. In *Early Desert Farming and Irrigation Settlements: Archaeological Investigations in the Phoenix Sky Harbor Center, Vol. 4: Special Studies, Synthesis, and Conclusions*, edited by David H. Greenwald and Jean H. Ballagh, pp. 169–191. Anthropological Research Paper No. 4. SWCA, Flagstaff, Arizona.
1996b Ceramic Analysis, Areas 15 and 16: Functional, Spatial, and Temporal Associations. In *Life on the Floodplain: Further Investigations at Pueblo Salado for Phoenix Sky Harbor International Airport, Vol. 2: Data Recovery and Re-evaluation, Part 1: The Report*, edited by David H. Greenwald, Jean H. Ballagh, Douglas R. Mitchell, and Richard A. Anduze, pp. 85–95. Anthropological Papers No. 4. Pueblo Grande Museum, Phoenix.
1996c Changes in the Structure of Hohokam Ceramic Production: The Results of the Pueblo Salado Ceramic Study. In *Life on the Floodplain: Further Investigations at Pueblo Salado for Phoenix Sky Harbor International Airport, Vol. 2: Data Recovery and Re-evaluation, Part 1: The Report*, edited by David H. Greenwald, Jean H. Ballagh, Douglas R. Mitchell, and Richard A. Anduze, pp. 97–140. Anthropological Papers No. 4. Pueblo Grande Museum, Phoenix.

Ware, John A.
2002 Descent Group and Sodality: Alternative

Pueblo Social Histories. In *Traditions, Transitions, and Technologies: Themes in Southwestern Archaeology*, edited by Sarah H. Schlanger, pp. 94–112. University Press of Colorado, Boulder.

Ware, John A., and Eric Blinman
2000 Cultural Collapse and Reorganization: The Origin and Spread of Pueblo Ritual Sodalities. In *The Archaeology of Regional Interaction: Religion, Warfare, and Exchange across the American Southwest and Beyond*, edited by Michelle Hegmon, pp. 381–409. University Press of Colorado, Boulder.

Washburn, Dorothy K., William N. Washburn, and Petia A. Shipkova
2011 The Prehistoric Drug Trade: Widespread Consumption of Cacao in Ancestral Pueblo and Hohokam Communities in the American Southwest. *Journal of Archaeological Science* 38:1634–1640.

Wasley, William W.
1962 A Ceremonial Cave on Bonita Creek. *American Antiquity* 27:380–394.

Wasley, William W., and David E. Doyel
1980 Classic Period Hohokam. *Kiva* 45(4):337–352.

Watkins, Christopher, and Glen E. Rice
2009 Hohokam Funerary Ritual on Canal Seven. In *Excavations at Las Canopas: A Hohokam Village in the Phoenix Basin*, edited by John L. Czarzasty and Glen E. Rice, pp. 267–323. Anthropological Papers No. 17. Pueblo Grande Museum, Phoenix.

Watts, Christopher (editor)
2013 *Relational Archaeologies: Humans, Animals, Things*. Routledge, London.

Watts, Joshua, and Andrew D. Lack
2008 Ceramic Analysis. In *Data Recovery at Six Sites in the 66 Acre Desert Rose Development in South Phoenix, Arizona*, edited by Corey Dale Breternitz, Brandie M. Stork, and Christine K. Robinson, pp. 5.1–5.14. Occasional Papers No. 9. Pueblo Grande Museum, Phoenix. Technical Report No. 06-38. Soil Systems, Phoenix.

Weaver, Donald E., Jr.
1972 A Cultural-Ecological Model for the Classic Hohokam Period in the Lower Salt River Valley. *Kiva* 38(1):43–52.
1977 *Investigations Concerning the Hohokam Classic Period in the Lower Salt River Valley, Arizona*. Arizona Archaeologist No. 9. Arizona Archaeological Society, Phoenix.
1985 *Hieroglyphic Canyon*. Monograph No. 1. American Rock Art Research Association, Tucson, Arizona.

Weaver, Donald E., Jr., and Bettina H. Rosenburg
1978 Petroglyphs of the Southern Sierra Estrella: A Locational Interpretation. In *American Indian Rock Art*, Vol. 4, edited by Ernest Snyder, Alice J. Bock, and Frank G. Bock, pp. 108–123. American Rock Art Research Association, Tucson, Arizona.

Weeks, Rex
2001 Indirect Percussion: Fact or Fiction? In *American Indian Rock Art*, Vol. 27, edited by Steven Freers and Alanah Woody, pp. 117–121. American Rock Art Research Association, Tucson, Arizona.

Wellman, Klaus
1979 *A Survey of North American Indian Rock Art*. Akademische Drucke und Verlagsanstalt, Graz, Austria.

Wells, E. Christian
2006 *From Hohokam to O'odham: The Protohistoric Occupation of the Middle Gila River Valley, Central Arizona*. Anthropological Research Papers No. 3. Gila River Indian Community, Sacaton, Arizona.

Wells, E. Christian, Glen E. Rice, and John C. Ravesloot
2004 Peopling Landscapes between Villages in the Middle Gila River Valley of Central Arizona. *American Antiquity* 69:627–652.

Whipple, A. W., Thomas Ewbank, and William W. Turner
1855 *Report upon the Indian Tribes*. Explorations and Surveys for a Railroad Route from the Mississippi River to the Pacific Ocean, Part 3. U.S. War Department, Washington, D.C.

White, Cheryl Ann
1965 The Petroglyphs of Saguaro National Monument, Tucson, Arizona. Unpublished Senior Honors thesis, Department of Anthropology, University of Arizona, Tucson.

White, Devin Alan
2004 *Hohokam Palettes*. Archaeological Series No. 196. Arizona State Museum, University of Arizona, Tucson.
2007 *Transportation, Integration, and Facilitation: Prehistoric Trail Networks of the Western Papaguería*. Ph.D. dissertation, Department of Anthropology, University of Colorado, Boulder. University Microfilms, Ann Arbor, Michigan.

White, Leslie
1962 *The Pueblo of Sia, New Mexico.* Bureau of American Ethnology Bulletin No. 184. Smithsonian Institution, Washington, D.C.

Whitehouse, Ruth
1996 Ritual Objects: Archaeological Joke or Neglected Evidence? In *Approaches to the Study of Ritual: Italy and the Ancient Mediterranean*, edited by John B. Wilkins, pp. 9–30. Accordia Research Centre, London.

Whiting, Christopher
2008 Petroglyphs in the South Mountains: Some Experimental Archaeology. Manuscript on file, Archaeological Research Institute, Arizona State University, Tempe.

Whitley, David S.
1982 *The Study of North American Rock Art: A Case Study from South-Central California.* Ph.D. dissertation, Department of Anthropology, University of California, Los Angeles. University Microfilms, Ann Arbor, Michigan.
1987 Socioreligious Context and Rock Art in East-Central California. *Journal of Anthropological Archaeology* 6:159–188.
1992 Shamanism and Rock Art in Far Western North America. *Cambridge Archaeological Journal* 2:89–113.
1994 By the Hunter, for the Gatherer: Art, Social Relations and Subsistence Change in the Prehistoric Great Basin. *World Archaeology* 25:356–373.
1998 Finding Rain in the Desert: Landscape, Gender and Far Western North American Rock-Art. In *The Archaeology of Rock-Art*, edited by Christopher Chippindale and Paul S. C. Taçon, pp. 11–29. Cambridge University Press, Cambridge.
2000a *The Art of the Shaman: Rock Art of California.* University of Utah Press, Salt Lake City.
2000b Response to Quinlan. *Journal of California and Great Basin Anthropology* 22:108–129.
2006 Rock Art and Rites of Passage in Far Western North America. In *Talking with the Past: The Ethnography of Rock Art*, edited by James D. Keyser, George Poetschat, and Michael W. Taylor, pp. 295–325. Oregon Archaeological Society, Portland.
2008 Archaeological Evidence for Conceptual Metaphors as Enduring Knowledge Structures. *Time and Mind* 1:7–30.
2009 Comments on Howey and O'Shea's "Bear's Journey and the Study of Ritual in Archaeology." *American Antiquity* 74:183–188.
2011 *Introduction to Rock Art Research.* 2nd ed. Left Coast Press, Walnut Creek, California.

Whitley, David S. (editor)
1998 *Reader in Archaeological Theory: Postprocessual and Cognitive Approaches.* Routledge, London.

Whitley, David S., James Baird, Jean Bennett, and Robert G. Tuck Jr.
1984 The Use of Relative Repatination in Chronological Ordering of Petroglyph Assemblages. *Journal of New World Archaeology* 6(3): 19–25.

Whitley, David S., and Ronald I. Dorn
2010 The Coso Petroglyph Chronology. *Pacific Coast Archaeological Society Quarterly* 43:135–157.

Whitley, David S., Ronald I. Dorn, Joseph M. Simon, Robert Rechtman, and Tamara K. Whitley
1999 Sally's Rockshelter and the Archaeology of the Vision Quest. *Cambridge Archaeological Journal* 9:221–246.

Whitley, David S., and Kelley A. Hays-Gilpin (editors)
2008 *Belief in the Past: Theoretical Approaches to the Archaeology of Religion.* Left Coast Press, Walnut Creek, California.

Whitley, David S., and James D. Keyser
2003 Faith in the Past: Debating an Archaeology of Religion. *Antiquity* 77:385–393.

Whitley, David S., Joseph M. Simon, and Ronald I. Dorn
1999 The Vision Quest in the Coso Range. In *American Indian Rock Art*, Vol. 25, edited by Steven M. Freers, pp. 1–31. American Rock Art Research Association, Tucson, Arizona.

Whittaker, John C., Sarah Koeman, and Rachel Taylor
2000 Some Experiments in Petroglyph Technology. In *1999 International Rock Art Congress Proceedings, Vol. 1: Papers Presented at the Twelfth International Rock Art Congress, Ripon, Wisconsin, May 23–31, 1999*, edited by Peggy Whitehead and Lawrence Loendorf, pp. 155–167. American Rock Art Research Association, Tucson, Arizona.

Whittlesey, Charles
1878 Rock Inscriptions in the United States—Ancient Alphabets of Asia. *Tracts of the Western Reserve and Northern Ohio Historical Society* 2(42):41–55.

Whittlesey, Stephanie M.
1997 Rethinking the Core-Periphery Model of the Pre-Classic Period Hohokam. In *Vanishing River: Landscapes and Lives of the Lower Verde Valley; The Lower Verde Archaeological Project*, edited by Stephanie M. Whittlesey, Richard Ciolek-Torrello, and Jeffrey H. Altschul, pp. 597–628. Statistical Research Press, Tucson, Arizona.
2004 Mesoamerica, the Hohokam, and the Tucson Basin. In *Pots, Potters, and Models: Archaeological Investigations at the SRI Locus of the West Branch Site, Tucson, Arizona, Vol. 2: Synthesis and Interpretations*, edited by Stephanie M. Whittlesey, pp. 509–530. Technical Series No. 80. Statistical Research, Tucson, Arizona.
2007 Hohokam Ceramics, Hohokam Beliefs. In *The Hohokam Millennium*, edited by Suzanne K. Fish and Paul R. Fish, pp. 65–73. School for Advanced Research Press, Santa Fe, New Mexico.
2009 Mountains, Mounds and Meaning: Metaphor in the Hohokam Cultural Landscape. In *The Archaeology of Meaningful Places*, edited by Brenda J. Bowser and Maria Nieves Zedeño, pp. 73–89. University of Utah Press, Salt Lake City.

Whittlesey, Stephanie M., Richard Ciolek-Torrello, and Jeffrey H. Altschul (editors)
1997 *Vanishing River: Landscapes and Lives of the Lower Verde Valley: The Lower Verde Archaeological Project*. Statistical Research Press, Tucson, Arizona.

Wilcox, David R.
1979 The Hohokam Regional System. In *An Archaeological Test of the Sites in the Gila Butte–Santan Region, South-Central Arizona*, edited by Glen E. Rice, David R. Wilcox, Ken Rafferty, and James Schoenwetter, pp. 77–116. Anthropological Research Papers No. 18. Arizona State University, Tempe.
1980 The Current Status of the Hohokam Concept. In *Current Issues in Hohokam Prehistory*, edited by David E. Doyel and Fred Plog, pp. 236–242. Anthropological Research Papers No. 23. Arizona State University, Tempe.
1987a The Evolution of Hohokam Ceremonial Systems. In *Astronomy and Ceremony in the Prehistoric Southwest*, edited by John Carlson and W. James Judge, pp. 149–168. Papers No. 2. Maxwell Museum of Anthropology, Albuquerque, New Mexico.
1987b *Frank Midvale's Investigations of the Site of La Ciudad*. Anthropological Field Studies No. 19. Arizona State University, Tempe.
1988 The Regional Context of the Brady Wash and Picacho Peak Area Sites. In *Hohokam Settlements along the Slopes of the Picacho Mountains*, edited by Richard Ciolek-Torrello and David R. Wilcox, pp. 244–267. Research Paper No. 35(6). Museum of Northern Arizona, Flagstaff.
1991a The Mesoamerican Ballgame in the American Southwest. In *The Mesoamerican Ballgame*, edited by Vernon Scarborough and David R. Wilcox, pp. 101–125. University of Arizona Press, Tucson.
1991b Hohokam Religion: An Archaeologist's Perspective. In *The Hohokam: Ancient People of the Desert*, edited by David Grant Noble, pp. 47–61. School of American Research Press, Santa Fe, New Mexico.
1991c Hohokam Social Complexity. In *Chaco and Hohokam: Prehistoric Regional Systems in the American Southwest*, edited by Patricia L. Crown and W. James Judge, pp. 253–276. School of American Research Press, Santa Fe, New Mexico.
1993 Pueblo Grande in the Nineteenth Century. In *Archaeology of the Pueblo Grande Platform Mound and Surrounding Features, Vol. 1: Introduction to the Archival Project and History of Archaeological Research*, edited by Christian E. Downum and Todd W. Bostwick, pp. 43–72. Anthropological Papers No. 1. Pueblo Grande Museum, Phoenix.
1999 A Peregrine View of Macroregional Systems in the North American Southwest, A.D. 750–1250. In *Great Towns and Regional Polities in the Prehistoric American Southwest and Southeast*, edited by Jill E. Neitzel, pp. 115–142. University of New Mexico Press, Albuquerque.
2005 Big Issues: New Synthesis. *Plateau* 2(1):8–21.

Wilcox, David R., and James P. Holmlund
2007 *The Archaeology of Perry Mesa and Its World*. Occasional Paper No. 3. Ralph M. Bilby Research Center, Northern Arizona University, Flagstaff.

Wilcox, David R., and Jerry B. Howard
1990 La Ciudad de Los Hornos: A History of Research. In *One Hundred Years of Archaeology*

at La Ciudad de Los Hornos, edited by David R. Wilcox, Jerry B. Howard, and Rueben H. Nelson, pp. 21–72. Publications in Archaeology No. 16. Soil Systems, Phoenix.

Wilcox, David R., Thomas R. McGuire, and Charles Sternberg

1981 *Snaketown Revisited: A Partial Cultural Resource Survey, Analysis of Site Structure, and an Ethnohistoric Study of the Proposed Hohokam-Pima National Monument.* Archaeological Series No. 155. Arizona State Museum, University of Arizona, Tucson.

Wilcox, David R., Gerald Robertson Jr., and J. Scott Wood

2001a Organized for War: The Perry Mesa Settlement System and Its Central-Arizona Neighbors. In *Deadly Landscapes: Case Studies in Prehistoric Southwestern Warfare*, edited by Glen E. Rice and Steven A. LeBlanc, pp. 141–194. University of Utah Press, Salt Lake City.

2001b Antecedents to Perry Mesa: Early Pueblo III Defensive Refuge Systems in West-Central Arizona. In *Deadly Landscapes: Case Studies in Prehistoric Southwestern Warfare*, edited by Glen E. Rice and Steven A. LeBlanc, pp. 109–140. University of Utah Press, Salt Lake City.

Wilcox, David R., and Lynette O. Shenk

1977 *The Architecture of the Casa Grande and Its Interpretation.* Archaeological Series No. 115. Arizona State Museum, University of Arizona, Tucson.

Wilcox, David R., and Charles Sternberg

1981 *Additional Studies of the Architecture of the Casa Grande and Its Interpretation.* Archaeological Series No. 146. Arizona State Museum, University of Arizona, Tucson.

1983 *Hohokam Ballcourts and Their Interpretation.* Archaeological Series No. 160. Arizona State Museum, University of Arizona, Tucson.

Wilcox, David R., Judith Rowe Taylor, Joseph Vogel, and J. Scott Wood

2007 Delineating Hilltop Settlements in West-Central Arizona, AD 1100–1400. In *Enduring Borderland Traditions: Trincheras Sites in Time, Space, and Society*, edited by Suzanne K. Fish, Paul R. Fish, and Maria Elisa Villalpando, pp. 195–228. University of Arizona Press, Tucson.

Wilcox, David R., Phil C. Wiegand, J. Scott Wood, and Jerry B. Howard

2008 Ancient Cultural Interplay of the American Southwest in the Mexican Northwest. *Journal of the Southwest* 50:103–206.

Wilcox, Michael

2010 Marketing Conquest and the Vanishing Indian: An Indigenous Response to Jared Diamond's Archaeology of the Southwest. In *Questioning Collapse: Human Resilience, Ecological Vulnerability, and the Aftermath of Empire*, edited by Patricia A. McAnany and Norman Yoffee, pp. 113–141. Cambridge University Press, Cambridge.

Willerslev, Rane

2004 Not Animal, Not Not-Animal: Hunting, Imitation and Empathetic Knowledge among the Siberian Yukaghirs. *Journal of the Royal Anthropological Institute* 10:629–652.

2007 *Soul Hunters: Hunting, Animism, and Personhood among the Siberian Yukaghirs.* University of California Press, Berkeley.

Wilson, Meredith

1998 Pacific Rock-Art and Cultural Genesis: A Multivariate Exploration. In *The Archaeology of Rock-Art*, edited by Christopher Chippindale and Paul S. C. Taçon, pp. 163–184. Cambridge University Press, Cambridge.

Winkelman, Michael

2008 Cross-Cultural and Biogenetic Perspectives on the Origins of Shamanism. In *Belief in the Past: Theoretical Approaches to the Archaeology of Religion*, edited by David S. Whitley and Kelley A. Hays-Gilpin, pp. 43–66. Left Coast Press, Walnut Creek, California.

Wittfogel, Karl A.

1957 *Oriental Despotism: A Comparative Study of Total Power.* Yale University Press, New Haven, Connecticut.

Wobst, H. Martin

1977 Stylistic Behavior and Information Exchange. In *For the Director: Research Essays in Honor of James B. Griffin*, edited by Charles E. Cleland, pp. 317–342. Anthropological Papers No. 61. Museum of Anthropology, University of Michigan, Ann Arbor.

Woodbury, Richard B.

1961 *Prehistoric Agriculture at Point of Pines, Arizona.* Memoir No. 17. Society for American Archaeology, Washington, D.C.

Woodson, Michael Kyle

2010 *The Social Organization of Hohokam Irrigation in the Middle Gila River Valley, Arizona.* Ph.D. dissertation, School of Human Evolution and Social Change, Arizona State

University, Tempe. University Microfilms, Ann Arbor, Michigan.

Woodward, Arthur
1941 Hohokam Mosaic Mirrors. *Los Angeles County Museum Quarterly* 1(4):6–11.

Wright, Aaron M.
2011 *Hohokam Rock Art, Ritual Practice, and Social Transformation in the Phoenix Basin.* Ph.D. dissertation, Department of Anthropology, Washington State University, Pullman. University Microfilms, Ann Arbor, Michigan.

Wright, Aaron M., and Todd W. Bostwick
2009 The Technological Styles of Hohokam Rock Art Production in the South Mountains, South-Central Arizona. In *American Indian Rock Art*, Vol. 35, edited by James D. Keyser, David Kaiser, George Poetschat, and Michael W. Taylor, pp. 61–78. American Rock Art Research Association, Tucson, Arizona.

Wright, Aaron M., and William G. Russell
2011 The Pipette, the Tiered Cosmos, and the Materialization of Transcendence in the Rock Art of the North American Southwest. *Journal of Social Archaeology* 11(3):361–386.

Wright, Aaron M., Steve Swanson, and Todd W. Bostwick
2007 Rock Art and Landscape Archaeology in Arizona's South Mountains. *Archaeology Southwest* 21(4):18.

Wright, Thomas E.
1999 Brown's Ranch Rock Shelter: An Archaic, Hohokam, and Yavapai Encampment in the McDowell Mountains. In *McDowell Mountains Archaeological Symposium*, edited by K. J. Schroeder, pp. 95–110. Publications in Anthropology No. 10. Roadrunner Archaeology, Tempe, Arizona.

Wylie, Alison
1989 Archaeological Cables and Tacking: The Implications of Practice for Bernstein's "Options beyond Objectivism and Relativism." *Philosophy of the Social Sciences* 19:1–18.

Young, M. Jane
1989 The Southwest Connection: Similarities between Western Pueblo and Mesoamerican Cosmology. In *World Archaeoastronomy*, edited by Anthony Aveni, pp. 167–179. Cambridge University Press, Cambridge, Massachusetts.
1994 The Interaction between Western Pueblo and Mesoamerican Ideology/Cosmology. In *Kachinas in the Pueblo World*, edited by Polly Schaafsma, pp. 107–120. University of New Mexico Press, Albuquerque.

Zaslow, Bert
1981 *Pattern Dissemination in the Prehistoric Southwest and Mesoamerica.* Anthropological Research Papers No. 25. Arizona State University, Tempe.

Zaslow, Bert, and Alfred E. Dittert Jr.
1977 The Pattern Technology of the Hohokam. In *Pattern Mathematics and Archaeology*, edited by Bert Zaslow and Alfred E. Dittert Jr., pp. 1–28. Anthropological Research Papers No. 2. Arizona State University, Tempe.

Zedeño, María Nieves
1997 Landscapes, Land Use, and the History of Territory Formation: An Example from the Puebloan Southwest. *Journal of Archaeological Method and Theory* 4:67–103.
2008 Bundled Worlds: The Roles and Interactions of Complex Objects from the North American Plains. *Journal of Archaeological Method and Theory* 15:362–378.
2009 Animating by Association: Index Objects and Relational Taxonomies. *Cambridge Archaeological Journal* 19:407–414.

Zepeda, Ofelia
2013 Music Mountains. *Arizona Highways* 89(11):46.

Zhou, Bengang G., Tanzhuo Liu, and Yuming M. Zhang
2000 Rock Varnish Microlaminations from Northern Tianshan, Xinjiang, and Their Paleoclimatic Implications. *Chinese Science Bulletin* 45:372–379.

Index